Politics in Organizations

Theory and Research Considerations

Edited by

Gerald R. Ferris
Florida State University

Darren C. Treadway
State University of New York at Buffalo

Routledge
Taylor & Francis Group
New York   London

The Organizational Frontiers Series

SIOP Organizational Frontiers Series

Series Editor

Eduardo Salas
University of Central Florida

Ferris/Treadway: (2012) *Politics in Organizations: Theory and Research Considerations*
Jones: (2011) *Nepotism in Organizations*
Hofmann/Frese: (2011) *Error in Organizations*
Outtz: (2009) *Adverse Impact: Implications for Organizational Staffing and High Stakes Selection*
Kozlowski/Salas: (2009) *Learning, Training, and Development in Organizations*
Klein/Becker/Meyer: (2009) *Commitment in Organizations: Accumulated Wisdom and New Directions*
Salas/Goodwin/Burke: (2009) *Team Effectiveness in Complex Organizations*
Kanfer/Chen/Pritchard: (2008) *Work Motivation: Past, Present, and Future*
De Dreu/Gelfand: (2008) *The Psychology of Conflict and Conflict Management in Organizations*
Ostroff/Judge: (2007) *Perspectives on Organizational Fit*
Baum/Frese/Baron: (2007) *The Psychology of Entrepreneurship*
Weekley/Ployhart: (2006) *Situational Judgment Tests: Theory, Measurement, and Application*
Dipboye/Colella: (2005) *Discrimination at Work: The Psychological and Organizational Bases*
Griffin/O'Leary-Kelly: (2004) *The Dark Side of Organizational Behavior*
Hofmann/Tetrick: (2003) *Health and Safety in Organizations*
Jackson/Hitt/DeNisi: (2003) *Managing Knowledge for Sustained Competitive Knowledge*
Barrick/Ryan: (2003) *Personality and Work*
Lord/Klimoski/Kanfer: (2002) *Emotions in the Workplace*
Drasgow/Schmitt: (2002) *Measuring and Analyzing Behavior in Organizations*
Feldman: (2002) *Work Careers*
Zaccaro/Klimoski: (2001) *The Nature of Organizational Leadership*
Rynes/Gerhart: (2000) *Compensation in Organizations*
Klein/Kozlowski: (2000) *Multilevel Theory, Research, and Methods in Organizations*
Ilgen/Pulakos: (1999) *The Changing Nature of Performance*
Earley/Erez: (1997) *New Perspectives on International I-O Psychology*
Murphy: (1996) *Individual Differences and Behavior in Organizations*
Guzzo/Salas: (1995) *Team Effectiveness and Decision Making*
Howard: (1995) *The Changing Nature of Work*
Schmitt/Borman: (1993) *Personnel Selection in Organizations*
Zedeck: (1991) *Work, Families and Organizations*
Schneider: (1990) *Organizational Culture and Climate*
Goldstein: (1989) *Training and Development in Organizations*
Campbell/Campbell: (1988) *Productivity in Organizations*
Hall: (1987) *Career Development in Organizations*

Routledge
Taylor & Francis Group
711 Third Avenue
New York, NY 10017

Routledge
Taylor & Francis Group
27 Church Road
Hove, East Sussex BN3 2FA

© 2012 by Taylor & Francis Group, LLC
Routledge is an imprint of Taylor & Francis Group, an Informa business

Printed in the United States of America on acid-free paper
Version Date: 20111031

International Standard Book Number: 978-0-415-88213-2 (Hardback)

Library of Congress Cataloging-in-Publication Data

Politics in organizations : theory and research considerations / editors, Gerald R. Ferris, Darren C. Treadway.
    p. cm. -- (SIOP organizational frontiers series)
    Includes bibliographical references and index.
    ISBN 978-0-415-88213-2 (hardcover : alk. paper)
    1. Office politics. 2. Organizational behavior. 3. Corporate culture. I. Ferris, Gerald R. II. Treadway, Darren C.

HD58.7.P647 2012
302.3'5--dc23   2011044088

**Visit the Taylor & Francis Web site at
http://www.taylorandfrancis.com**

**and the Psychology Press Web site at
http://www.psypress.com**

To my lovely wife, Pam, and our wonderful children:

Ellie, Emily, Erin, Jennifer, Matthew, and Stephen.

Jerry

To Stacy, Dylan, Maya, Mom, and Dad.

Thank you for your love and support.

Darren

Contents

SECTION I Construct Specification, Theory Development, and Methodological Considerations

SECTION III Individual Differences in
Organizational Politics

Series Foreword

Politics is all around us. In any activity where there are humans interacting, there is some sort of politics. There is politics at schools, homes, and sports or social clubs and in government. And certainly there is politics at work—organizational politics. This is a topic we all talk about and believe we are all experts at, but it is really not well understood. It is a topic that fascinates us, and we love to discuss it at cocktail parties; however, we know little about its nature. It is a topic that generates emotions, passion, and (sometimes) irrational actions and feelings, but we don't know what triggers these behaviors. So this is a much welcomed (and refreshing) topic for us—organizational politics.

This volume covers a broad territory and gives us a rich and coherent set of ideas, thinking, theories, and approaches to begin to understand this phenomenon. It covers all the dimensions and features that may comprise the nature of organizational politics from cultural issues to leadership to personality to strategy. We get, from the authors, a wealth of insight into how to study and understand organizational politics. This is a one-of-a-kind volume for us on a topic that needs much science around it. We hope this volume motivates more research, more dialogue, and more debate on what comprises organizational politics.

On behalf of the Society for Industrial & Organizational Psychology (SIOP) Frontiers Book Series editorial board—thank you, Jerry and Darren, for giving us such a wonderful and provocative volume. You and your chapter collaborators have provided us with a scholarly and motivating volume on a great topic. Well done.

Eduardo Salas, PhD
SIOP Organizational Frontiers Series Editor
University of Central Florida

Preface

The rational perspective on organizations suggests that the most qualified person always gets hired or promoted, the highest performer gets the highest pay increase, and the most attractive job assignments go only to the most competent employees. This perspective is precisely what is conveyed through traditional rational views of organizations, which are, for example, reflected in most textbook treatments of this subject matter. That is all well and good as long as organizations really operate this way and such outcomes always come about this way.

Unfortunately, there always have been too many exceptions to such outcomes, where things do not work this way in organizations, to place too much confidence in the rational perspective exclusively. Instead, scholars and practitioners alike searched for alternative views and thus initiated interest in the political perspective on organizations as a way to accommodate exceptions to rationality and to explain a lot about how organizations (and the people in them) operate on a day-to-day basis. As this perspective gained credibility and acceptance in the field, *organizational politics* became an increasingly important area of scientific inquiry and has occupied the attention of scholars for decades and continues to do so.

Politics in Organizations: Theory and Research Considerations is the next volume in the Society for Industrial & Organizational Psychology (SIOP) Frontiers Book Series, and it represents a coordinated effort to shed new light on the nature of organizational politics. The objectives in developing this volume focused on going to top scholars in organizational politics for their ideas on important new issues and directions to pursue in the field to enhance understanding of this important area of inquiry. Additionally, renowned scholars in other areas of organizational research (e.g., justice, citizenship, abusive supervision, social networks) were approached and asked to think about how and why politics might resonate, and be effectively integrated, with their own individual area of expertise. The belief was that the outcomes of such scholarly discussions would enlighten the area of politics in ways not previously envisioned.

ORGANIZATION OF THE BOOK

The chapters in *Politics in Organizations: Theory and Research Considerations* are organized into three parts. Section I includes Chapters 1–4, which address a variety of key politics issues ranging from the historical evolution of the field to domain delineation and construct specification to theory development challenges to measurement and methodological considerations. In Chapter 1, we provide a historical sketch of organizational politics research, attempt to accurately characterize the construct domain, and propose a useful workable definition of politics in an effort to develop some construct consistency. Then, we discuss some important issues and directions for future research.

Many, if not most, characterizations of organizational politics over the years have cast the construct in a decidedly negative light. In Chapter 2, Wayne A. Hochwarter argues that such negative views of politics are not representative of the full construct domain and proposes the positive aspects of organizational politics and a future research agenda that investigates this new perspective. It is fair to classify the current status of theory in organizational politics as underdeveloped. Douglas A. Lepisto and Michael G. Pratt, in Chapter 3, review theory in organizational politics and propose needed direction for future work in this area. In Chapter 4, Lynn A. McFarland, Chad H. Van Iddekinge, and Robert E. Ployhart consider the many challenges and complexities of choosing or developing sound psychometric methods and measures of organizational politics. After a critical review of prior measurement techniques, they discuss methodological and analytical approaches that represent potentially productive new steps in organizational politics research.

Section II includes 10 chapters, each of which provides an integration of organizational politics with important organizational behavior constructs or areas of inquiry. Chapters 5–7 discuss some of the most complex and controversial relationships within the organizational politics literature: those that relate to the very nature of organizational politics as having functional versus dysfunctional consequences for the organization or individual. Maureen L. Ambrose discusses the interrelated nature of organizational politics and justice in Chapter 5. From her thorough investigation of the literature she advances an intriguing research agenda that addresses both the foundational and multilevel challenges of integrating politics and justice. In Chapter 6, Mark C. Bolino and William H. Turnley review research challenging the notion that organizational citizenship behaviors stem from, and result in, positive organizational experiences. Further, they discuss the implications of this for research on attributions, motivation, and organizational effectiveness. Chapter 7 extends that abusive supervision stems, at least partially, from strategic motivations. In positioning abusive behavior as strategic, Bennett J. Tepper, Michelle K. Duffy, and Denise M. Breaux-Soignet introduce a challenging new perspective into the discussion of why supervisors engage in abuse of their subordinates.

Chapters 8 and 9 focus on contextual conditions as they relate to organizational politics. Pamela L. Perrewé, Christopher C. Rosen, and Christina Maslach discuss the role of organizational politics as a contextual stressor in Chapter 8. They develop a process model of politics and stress that unifies the diverse literature and offers unique insights into how future research may benefit from this conceptualization. Similarly stressing the importance of context, Lawrence R. James and Rustin D. Meyer discuss how a leader's need for power and subsequent behavior affect the emergence of toxic or developmental organizational climates in Chapter 9.

Chapters 10–12 turn attention to the impact of relationships on organizational politics. In Chapter 10, Eran Vigoda-Gadot and Dana R. Vashdi review the literature on organizational politics within teams and articulate research directions that position future analysis at the level of the team. Francis J. Yammarino and Michael D. Mumford examine the critical relationship between organizational politics and leadership in Chapter 11. Their extensive multilevel model develops that politics and leadership intersect in the process of developing pragmatic deals between leader and subordinate. Expanding these dyadic relationships, Chapter 12 considers a social network explanation of organizational politics. Daniel J. Brass and David M. Krackhardt provide a perspective of power and politics that emphasizes the importance of social structure rather than individual characteristics. In doing so, this chapter highlights important considerations in the development of organizational politics theory.

The final set of chapters in Section II focuses on macro-considerations in organizational politics. In Chapter 13, Robert A. Baron, Sean Lux, Garry L. Adams, and Bruce T. Lamont explain the manner in which organizational politics, entrepreneurship, and strategic management interrelate. They note the importance of political skill in new venture development, strategy formulation, and implementation; they advance the intriguing suggestion that political skill may be an organizational-level construct that varies across companies to predict strategic success. Chapter 14 directs attention to the lack of cross-cultural consideration in construct specification and model development within the organizational politics literature. In this chapter, Lisa M. Leslie and Michele J. Gelfand offer a critical review of the literature that specifies the nature and expression of politics across cultures. They further discuss the implications of cross-cultural politics on expatriates and cross-national mergers.

Part III of the book includes four chapters that focus on individual differences and organizational politics. In Chapter 15 Atira C. Charles and Stella Nkomo examine the role of race in society and organizational politics. They introduce the concept of racialized organizational politics perceptions and develop a model that encourages researchers to reconsider the race in organizational politics. Gerald R. Ferris, Darren C. Treadway, Robyn L. Brouer, and Timothy P. Munyon review the rapidly expanding literature on political skill in Chapter 16. They analyze the most pressing issues in the development of this construct and present researchers with concepts for future consideration. Many of the chapters to this point have touched on the various motives that are at the core of political behavior, and in Chapter 17, Treadway offers a framework of political will that envisions the positive versus negative nature of organizational politics as an issue of the competing motivations residing in each individual actor. The role of personality in perceptions of and reactions to organizational politics is considered by L. A. Witt and Paul E. Spector in Chapter 18. The complexity inherent in their portrayal of the impact of personality dimensions and configurations on politics perceptions encourages future researchers to more deeply evaluate the nature of personality—politics relationships.

Gerald R. Ferris

Darren C. Treadway

Acknowledgments

An edited volume of original chapters, like this one, is reflective of the coordinated efforts of many, and we would like to acknowledge those who contributed meaningfully in helping this project to come about in a high-quality way. Initially, we extend our most sincere thanks and appreciation to the authors of the chapters, without whose individual and collective efforts this volume would not have been possible. Some were scholars familiar with organizational politics subject matter but were asked to stretch their knowledge, skills, and experience by suggesting substantial new directions we need to pursue to push ahead the study of organizational politics. Others were chosen to write chapters specifically because of their expertise, not on the topic of organizational politics, but in other areas that appear to have some natural, and not so obvious, links to organizational politics—and to forge those links in new and creative ways. Across all chapters, the ideas are fresh and insightful, and those interested in doing research on organizational politics should find a wealth of leads and new ideas to pursue.

Second, we must acknowledge the wonderful opportunity extended to us, and the great support provided by, the Society for Industrial & Organizational Psychology (SIOP), with particular reference to the SIOP Organizational Frontiers Series editorial board and series editor Eduardo Salas. The ideas, feedback on the initial prospectus, and strong support provided throughout the development of this volume have been greatly appreciated and contributed substantially to the quality of this volume.

Last, but certainly by no means least, we would be seriously remiss if we failed to express our most sincere gratitude to our publisher, Routledge/Taylor & Francis. In particular, senior editor Anne Duffy worked closely with us from the very beginning and gave us continued encouragement and support for the direction we were moving. Anne was a genuine pleasure with whom to work, and this book benefited considerably from her involvement, assistance, and advice based on her extensive experience and expertise in the publishing industry.

Gerald R. Ferris

Darren C. Treadway

Editors

Gerald R. Ferris is the Francis Eppes Professor of Management and professor of psychology at Florida State University. Ferris received a PhD in business administration from the University of Illinois at Urbana–Champaign. Ferris is a fellow of the American Psychological Association, the Society for Industrial and Organizational Psychology, and the American Psychological Society. He has research interests in the areas of social and political influence in organizations, the nature and consequences of personal reputation in organizations, the underlying dimensions and characterization of work relationships, and particularly how politics, reputation, and work relationships play key roles in human resources management practices. Ferris is the author of numerous articles published in such scholarly journals as the *Journal of Applied Psychology, Organizational Behavior and Human Decision Processes, Personnel Psychology, Academy of Management Journal*, and *Academy of Management Review*. He founded and served as editor of the annual series *Research in Personnel and Human Resources Management* from its origin in 1981 until 2003. He has authored or edited a number of books including *Political Skill at Work* (Davies-Black, 2005), *Handbook of Human Resource Management* (Blackwell, 1995), *Strategy and Human Resources Management* (South-Western, 1991), and *Method & Analysis in Organizational Research* (Reston Publishing, 1984). Ferris has been the recipient of a number of distinctions and honors, including the Heneman Career Achievement Award in 2001 and the Thomas A. Mahoney Mentoring Award in 2010, both from the Human Resources Division of the Academy of Management.

Darren C. Treadway is an associate professor of organization and human resources at the State University of New York (SUNY) at Buffalo. He received a PhD from Florida State University in 2003 and an MBA from Virginia Tech in 1996. Treadway's research interests include social influence processes in organizations, with particular reference to organizational politics, political skill, and leadership. His research has been published in leading journals such as the *Journal of Applied Psychology, Journal of Management, Leadership Quarterly, Journal of Organizational Behavior,* and *Human Relations*. His research has twice been awarded the Emerald Publishing Citation of Excellence. Prior to his employment with SUNY, Treadway was on the faculty at the University of Mississippi, where he was twice named the Researcher of the Year. His cumulative contributions earned him the 2009 SUNY at Buffalo Exceptional Scholar Award. Treadway currently serves on the editorial board of *Leadership Quarterly*.

Contributors

Garry L. Adams is an associate professor in strategic management at Auburn University. He received a PhD in management with a specialization in strategic management from Florida State University. Adams's research interests include corporate governance, power and politics in organizations, organizational learning and resource management, and merger and acquisition integration processes. His work has been published or is in press in outlets such as the *Journal of Applied Psychology, Academy of Management Review, Leadership Quarterly, Business Horizons, Journal of Knowledge Management, Journal of Business and Psychology, Journal of Leadership and Organizational Studies, Journal of Managerial Issues,* and the initial volume of *The Many Faces of Multi-Level Issues.* Adams is on the editorial board of the *Journal of Management* and has served as an ad hoc reviewer for the *Academy of Management Journal, Journal of Business Research, Knowledge Management Research and Practice* and *Journal of Applied Social Psychology.* He is a member of the Academy of Management, the Strategic Management Society, and the Southern Management Association and is a McKnight Fellow. Adams has prior work experience in the oil refining industry.

Maureen L. Ambrose is the Gordon J. Barnett Professor of Business Ethics in the College of Business at the University of Central Florida. She received her PhD in psychology in 1986 from the University of Illinois at Urbana–Champaign. Her research interests include organizational fairness, ethics, and workplace deviance. Her work has appeared in the *Academy of Management Journal, Academy of Management Review, Journal of Applied Psychology, Journal of Management, Organizational Behavior and Human Decision Processes,* and *Administrative Sciences Quarterly.* Ambrose is a fellow of the Academy of Management and the Society for Industrial and Organizational Psychology.

Robert A. Baron is the Spears Professor of Entrepreneurship at Oklahoma State University. Baron received his PhD from the University of Iowa in the field of social psychology. He has published papers in a wide range of journals such as the *Journal of Applied Psychology, Academy of Management Journal, Management Science, Academy of Management Review,* and *Journal of Personality and Social Psychology* and is the author of numerous books in both management and psychology. He is currently associate editor for the *Strategic Entrepreneurship Journal* and is a member of the editorial boards of *Academy of Management Journal* and *Journal of Business Venturing.* He holds three U.S. patents and was founder and chief executive officer of IEP, Inc. Baron's current interests focus on the role of cognitive and social factors in entrepreneurship.

Mark C. Bolino is an associate professor and the McCasland Foundation Professor of American Free Enterprise in the Price College of Business at the University of Oklahoma. He received his PhD from the University of South Carolina. Bolino's research interests include organizational citizenship behavior, impression management, global careers, and psychological contracts. His work has appeared in such journals as the *Academy of Management Review, Journal of Applied Psychology,* and *Personnel Psychology.* Bolino currently serves on the editorial boards of the *Journal of Applied Psychology, Journal of Organizational Behavior, Journal of Management,* and *Organizational Behavior and Human Decision Processes.*

Daniel J. Brass is the J. Henning Hilliard Professor of Innovation Management and director of LINKS—The International Center for the Study of Social Networks in Business (http://www.linkscenter.org) in the Gatton College of Business and Economics at the University of Kentucky. He received his PhD in business administration from the University of Illinois at Urbana–Champaign. His work has appeared in *Administrative Science Quarterly, Academy of Management Journal, Academy of Management Review, Journal of Applied Psychology, Organization Science, Organizational Behavior and Human Decision Processes,* and *Science.* Brass served as associate editor of *Administrative Science Quarterly* from 1995 to 2007. His research on the antecedents and consequences of social networks in organizations has been cited more than 5,000 times.

Denise M. Breaux-Soignet is an assistant professor of management in the Sam M. Walton College of Business at the University of Arkansas. She received a PhD in organizational behavior and human resources management from Florida State University. Her current research focuses on leader dysfunction and aggression with an emphasis on the relationships among abusive supervision, organizational justice, and emotions. She also studies organizational and individual reactions to natural disasters, organizational politics, and work stress. Her work has been published in *Organizational Behavior and Human Decision Processes, Journal of Management, Organizational Dynamics*, and *Journal of Leadership and Organizational Studies.* She serves on the editorial review board of the United States Air Force Academy's *Journal of Character and Leadership Integration* and reviews for numerous journals in management and organizational psychology.

Robyn L. Brouer is an assistant professor of organization and human resources in the School of Management at the State University of New York at Buffalo. She received her PhD from Florida State University with a specialization in organizational behavior and human resource management. Brouer has conducted research in the areas of leadership, leader–follower relationships, social influence and effectiveness, person–environment fit, and work stress. She has published articles in such journals as the *Journal of Management, Leadership Quarterly, Journal of Leadership & Organizational Studies, Journal of Organizational Behavior, Human Resource Management Review*, and *Journal of Managerial Psychology.*

Atira C. Charles is an assistant professor of management in the College of Business at Florida State University. She received her PhD in organizational behavior from Arizona State University. Charles's research has been published in many journals, such as the *Journal of Management Development, International Encyclopedia of Organization Studies, Human Resource Management, Organizational Dynamics,* and *Academy of Management Annals.* Her research revolves around racial and gender identity management in the workplace, organizational management of differences, communication and feedback processes, and mentoring within diverse organizations. Also, inspired by her teaching philosophy, Charles is working on research related to how individuals can motivate themselves to positive and productive action through self-reflection and introspection.

Michelle K. Duffy is a professor of organizational behavior and human resources and the Board of Overseers Professor in the Carlson School at the University of Minnesota. Duffy received her PhD in organizational behavior from the University of Arkansas. Her research explores antecedents and consequences of antisocial behavior, the role of affect and emotions in organizations, and employee well-being. Duffy's work has been published in such outlets as the *Journal of Applied Psychology, Organizational Behavior and Human Decision Processes, Academy of Management Journal,* and *Journal of Management.* She serves on numerous editorial boards and is incoming associate editor of the *Journal of Management.*

Michele J. Gelfand is a professor of psychology and distinguished university scholar teacher at the University of Maryland at College Park. Gelfand received her PhD in social/organizational psychology from the University of Illinois at Urbana–Champaign. Her work explores cultural influences on conflict, negotiation, justice, and revenge; workplace diversity and discrimination; and theory and methods in cross-cultural psychology and has been published in outlets including the *Journal of Applied Psychology,* the *Journal of Personality and Social Psychology, Organizational Behavior and Human Decision Processes, Academy of Management Review, Academy of Management Journal,* and *Annual Review of Psychology.* Gelfand is a founding coeditor of the Advances in Culture and Psychology series and Frontiers of Culture and Psychology series, serves on numerous editorial boards in social and organizational psychology, is past associate editor of *Applied Psychology: An International Review,* and is currently associate editor of *Social Psychological and Personality Science.*

Wayne A. Hochwarter is the Jim Moran Professor of Management at Florida State University. He received his PhD from Florida State University and has held faculty positions at Mississippi State University and the University of Alabama prior to his current appointment. His research focuses on a wide range of topics including influence behavior, stress, engagement, and supervisory behavior. In recent years, his studies have been published in *Administrative Science Quarterly, Organizational Behavior and Human Decision Processes, Journal of Applied Psychology, Journal of Vocational Behavior,* and *Journal of Management.*

Lawrence R. James is a professor of psychology and management at the Georgia Institute of Technology. He earned his PhD at the University of Utah in 1970, soon after which he was awarded a National Research Council postdoctorate. Following the postdoctorate, he joined the faculty in the Institute of Behavior Research at Texas Christian University, where he attained the rank of professor and headed the Organizational–Industrial Research Group. In 1980, James moved to the Georgia Institute of Technology, where he was professor of psychology and coordinator of the Industrial/Organizational Psychology Program. He moved to the University of Tennessee in 1988 as the Pilot Oil Chair of Excellence in Management. James is the author of numerous articles and papers and the lead author of three books. He is or has been a member of the editorial boards of the *Journal of Applied Psychology, Organizational Research Methods, Organizational Behavior and Human Decision Processes, Academy of Management Review, Human Performance, Human Resources Management,* and *Journal of Management.*

David M. Krackhardt is a professor of organizations in the Heinz School of Public Policy and Management and the Graduate School of Industrial Administration at Carnegie Mellon University. He received a PhD in business administration from the University of California at Irvine and a BS degree from the Massachusetts Institute of Technology. He has held prior appointments at Cornell University's Graduate School of Management, the University of Chicago's Graduate School of Business, INSEAD (France), and the Harvard Business School. Over the past 15 years, Krackhardt's research has focused on how the theoretical insights and methodological innovations of network analysis can enhance our understanding of how organizations function. His published works have appeared in a variety of journals in the fields of psychology, sociology, anthropology, and management, including the *Academy of Management Journal, Academy of Management Review, Administrative Science Quarterly, Journal of Applied Psychology, Journal of Personality and Social Psychology, Organizational Behavior and Human Decision Processes, Social Networks,* and *Strategic Management Journal.*

Bruce T. Lamont is the DeSantis Professor of Business Administration and associate dean of graduate programs in the College of Business at Florida State University. Lamont received his PhD in strategic management from the University of North Carolina at Chapel Hill. He has published numerous journal articles, appearing in such outlets as the *Academy of Management Journal, Academy of Management Review, Journal of International Business Studies, Journal of Management,* and *Strategic Management Journal.* Lamont currently serves on the editorial review board for the *Strategic Management Journal* and as a representative at large on the board of the Strategy Process Interest Group of the Strategic Management Society. He has also served on the editorial review boards of the *Academy of Management Journal* and *Journal of Management,* the executive and research committees of the Business Policy and Strategy Division of the Academy of Management, and the board of governors of the Southern Management Association. His current research addresses the effective management of acquisition integration processes, knowledge investments, and novel applications of organization theory.

Douglas A. Lepisto is a doctoral student in the Carroll School of Management at Boston College. He received an MA in social science from the University of Chicago in 2007 and a BA in psychology from Kalamazoo College in 2004. His research interests broadly examine the origins, varieties, and consequences of different meanings of work. Through his work he seeks to understand how people get their ideas of what makes work worth doing and what this means for subjective experience and action. He examines these issues with particular attention to meaning-making processes, identity, occupations, and culture.

Lisa M. Leslie is an assistant professor of human resources and industrial relations in the Carlson School of Management at the University of Minnesota. Leslie earned her PhD in organizational psychology from the University of Maryland in 2007. Her primary area of expertise is gender and diversity in organizations, and she has additional interests in cross-cultural organizational behavior and conflict management. Her current research interests include ethnic and gender diversity in workgroups and teams, attributions to discrimination, minimizing the stigmatizing effects of Affirmative Action plans, and the impact of flexible work practices on the careers of women and parents. Her research has appeared in a number of outlets, including the *Journal of Applied Psychology, Journal of Organizational Behavior, Organizational Behavior and Human Decision Processes,* and *Research in Organizational Behavior.*

Sean Lux is an assistant professor of entrepreneurship at the University of South Florida. He received a PhD in management with a specialization in strategic management from Florida State University. Lux's research focuses on how individual actors shape their environment to their advantage. He has studied this phenomenon in multiple settings and levels of analysis including how individuals shape their social networks, how politics shapes firm governance, and how firms shape the institutional environment. His work has been published in the *Journal of Management* and *Academy of Management Best Paper Proceedings*, and he has served as an ad hoc reviewer for the *Academy of Management Journal* and *Journal of Small Business Management*. He is a member of the Academy of Management, the Southern Management Association, and United States Association of Small Business and Entrepreneurship. Lux has served in leadership positions in the U.S. Army and startup ventures.

Christina Maslach is a professor of psychology at the University of California at Berkeley. She received her AB from Harvard College in 1967 and her PhD in psychology from Stanford University in 1971. She is best known as one of the pioneering researchers on job burnout and the author of the *Maslach Burnout Inventory* (MBI), the most widely used research measure in the burnout field. She has written numerous articles and five books on this topic, and these research contributions led her to be honored by the American Association for the Advancement of Science. In 2009, she received two awards from the *Journal of Organizational Behavior* for coauthoring two (of the eight) most influential articles in its 30-year history and was nationally recognized as Professor of the Year in 1997. At the University of California at Berkeley, she received the Berkeley Citation (the university's highest honor), the Distinguished Teaching Award, and the Berkeley Faculty Service Award.

Lynn A. McFarland is the president of Human Capital Solutions, Inc., a consulting firm specializing in the design and validation of selection procedures. She is also an adjunct faculty member in the psychology department at Clemson University. She earned her PhD at Michigan State University and continues to publish research on employee selection with an emphasis on impression management and influence tactic use as well as on noncognitive measurement, and diversity. Her work has appeared in the *Journal of Applied Psychology*, *Personnel Psychology*, and *Journal of Management*.

Rustin D. Meyer is an assistant professor of psychology at the Georgia Institute of Technology. He received his PhD from Purdue University. His research interests focus on better understanding the ways individual differences and situational characteristics interact to affect organizational behavior, with a particular emphasis on the concept of situational strength. His research has appeared in such journals as the *Journal of Organizational Behavior, Journal of Management,* and *Industrial-Organizational Psychology: Perspective on Science and Practice.*

Michael D. Mumford is the George Lynn Cross Distinguished Research Professor of Psychology at the University of Oklahoma, where he directs the Center for Applied Social Research. He received his doctoral degree from the University of Georgia in 1983 in the fields of industrial and organizational psychology and psychometrics. Mumford is a fellow of the American Psychological Association (Divisions 3, 5, 14), the Society for Industrial and Organizational Psychology, and the American Psychological Society. He has written more than 270 articles on creativity, innovation, planning, leadership, and ethics. He served as the senior editor of the *Leadership Quarterly* and is on the editorial boards of *Creativity Research Journal, Journal of Creative Behavior, IEEE Transactions on Engineering Management,* and *Journal of Business Ethics.* Mumford has served as principal investigator on grants totaling more than $30 million from the National Science Foundation, National Institutes of Health, Department of Defense, Department of Labor, and Department of State. He is a recipient of the Society for Industrial and Organizational Psychology's M. Scott Myers Award for Applied Research in the Workplace.

Timothy P. Munyon is an assistant professor of management in the College of Business and Economics at West Virginia University. He received a PhD in management from Florida State University. His research interests include the nature, process dynamics, and dimensions of dyadic work relationships; the design of work at executive and other job levels; the roles of organizational politics and political skill in organizational science research; and social context effects on important human resources practices and decisions. Munyon has published in outlets such as the *Journal of Management, Journal of Organizational Behavior, Research in Personnel and Human Resource Management, Organizational Dynamics, Business Horizons,* and *Human Resource Management Review.*

Stella M. Nkomo is a professor in the Department of Human Resource Management at the University of Pretoria in South Africa. She received her PhD in human resource management from the University of Massachusetts at Amherst. Her internationally recognized research on race and gender and diversity in organizations has been published in several journals including the *Academy of Management Review; Academy of Management Learning and Education Journal; Academy of Management Executive; Journal of Organization Behavior; Journal of Applied Behavioral Science; Organization: The Critical Journal of Organization, Theory and Society; Journal of Occupational and Organizational Psychology; Strategic Management Journal; Work and Occupations;* and *Sex Roles.* Nkomo is the coauthor of two books, *Our Separate Ways: Black and White Women and the Struggle for Professional Identity* (Harvard Business School Press) and *Courageous Conversations: A Collection of Interviews and Reflections on Responsible Leadership by South African Captains of Industry* (Van Schaik Publishers).

Pamela L. Perrewé is the Haywood and Betty Taylor Eminent Scholar of Business Administration and Distinguished Research Professor at Florida State University. She received her bachelor's in psychology from Purdue University and her master's and PhD in management from the University of Nebraska. Perrewé primarily teaches courses in organizational behavior and human resource management and has taught at the undergraduate, MBA, and PhD levels. Perrewé has focused her research interests in the areas of job stress, burnout, coping, mentoring, organizational politics, emotion, and personality. She has published several books and more than 20 book chapters and 100 journal articles in journals such as *Academy of Management Journal, Journal of Management, Journal of Applied Psychology,* and *Organizational Behavior and Human Decision Processes.* She is coeditor of an annual series titled *Research in Occupational Stress and Well Being* (Emerald Publishing) and is director for the Human Resource Management Center at Florida State University.

Robert E. Ployhart is a professor of management and Moore Research Fellow in the Darla Moore School of Business at the University of South Carolina. He received his PhD from Michigan State University. His primary research interests include staffing, recruitment, human capital, and advanced statistical methods. He has published over 50 articles in leading management and psychology journals and has served as associate editor for the *Journal of Applied Psychology* and *Organizational Behavior and Human Decision Processes* and as coeditor for a special issue of

Organizational Research Methods. Ployhart is a fellow of the Society for Industrial and Organizational Psychology.

Michael G. Pratt is a Winston Center Fellow and professor of organizational studies and, by courtesy, psychology at Boston College. He earned his PhD in organizational psychology from the University of Michigan. His research centers on how individuals relate to and connect with their work, occupations, professions, and organizations. He currently explores these connections primarily through the lenses of multiple identities, multiple emotions (ambivalence), sensemaking, and intuition. His work has appeared in various outlets, including the *Academy of Management Annual Review, Academy of Management Journal, Academy of Management Review, Organizational Research Methods*, and *Administrative Science Quarterly*. He also coedited a book (with Anat Rafaeli) titled *Artifacts and Organizations: Beyond Mere Symbolism* (Lawrence Erlbaum, 2006). He recently completed his tenure as the inaugural associate editor for qualitative research for the *Academy of Management Journal*.

Christopher C. Rosen is an assistant professor of management in the Sam M. Walton College of Business at the University of Arkansas. He received a PhD in industrial and organizational psychology from the University of Akron. Rosen has taught organizational behavior, statistics, and research methods courses at the undergraduate and PhD levels. His research interests include organizational politics, employee–organization exchange relationships, occupational health and well-being, and the measurement and modeling of personality. Rosen's research has been published in outlets such as *Academy of Management Journal, Journal of Applied Psychology, Journal of Management, Journal of Organizational Behavior, Organizational Behavior and Human Decision Processes,* and *Personnel Psychology*.

Paul E. Spector is the Distinguished University Professor of Industrial/ Organizational (I/O) Psychology and director of the I/O doctoral program at the University of South Florida. He is also director of the Sunshine Education and Research Center's Occupational Health Psychology doctoral program funded by the National Institute for Occupational Safety and Health (NIOSH). He is associate editor for the Point/Counterpoint section of the *Journal of Organizational Behavior* and associate editor for *Work & Stress* and is on the editorial boards of the *Journal of Applied Psychology,*

Organizational Research Methods, and *Human Resources Management Review*. His main research interests are in occupational health psychology, including injuries, stress and workplace aggression, and research methodology.

Bennett J. Tepper is a professor of managerial sciences in the J. Mack Robinson College of Business at Georgia State University. He received a PhD in organizational psychology from the University of Miami. His research on leadership, prosocial and antisocial work behavior, and well-being has been published in *Academy of Management Journal, Journal of Applied Psychology, Organizational Behavior and Human Decision Processes*, and *Personnel Psychology*, among others. Tepper is a fellow of the American Psychological Association, Society for Industrial and Organizational Psychology, and Southern Management Association. He has served on several editorial boards, and he currently serves as associate editor for the *Academy of Management Journal*.

William H. Turnley is a professor and the Forrer Chair of Business Ethics in the College of Business Administration at Kansas State University. He received his PhD from the University of South Carolina. His research interests include psychological contracts, organizational citizenship behavior, impression management, and business ethics. His research has appeared in such journals as the *Academy of Management Review, Journal of Applied Psychology*, and *Journal of Management*. He has served on the editorial boards of *Organizational Behavior and Human Decision Processes, Journal of Management, Journal of Organizational Behavior*, and *Human Relations*.

Chad H. Van Iddekinge is the Synovus Associate Professor of Management at Florida State University. He received his PhD in industrial and organizational psychology from Clemson University. His research focuses on how organizations make staffing decisions and the effects of those decisions on individual, team, and unit performance. Van Iddekinge's research has been published in journals such as the *Academy of Management, Human Performance, Journal of Applied Psychology, Journal of Management*, and *Personnel Psychology*. Currently, he is associate editor for *Personnel Psychology* and serves on the editorial board of the *Journal of Applied Psychology*.

Dana R. Vashdi is a lecturer in the Division of Public Administration and Policy in the School of Political Science at the University of Haifa in Israel. She received her PhD in industrial/organizational psychology from the Technion—The Israel Institute of Technology. Her research focuses on team work and team management, employee well-being, and public health policy and management. She has published articles in many journals including the *Academy of Management Journal, British Medical Journal, Human Resource Management,* and *European Union Politics.*

Eran Vigoda-Gadot is a professor of public administration and management in the School of Political Science at the University of Haifa in Israel. Currently, he is head of the school and of the Center for Public Management and Policy (CPMP). In addition, he is member of several consulting committees working closely with public institutions and local municipalities in Israel. He received his PhD from the University of Haifa in 1998 and spent time as a visiting professor in Britain, Ireland, Canada (McGill), and the United States (Harvard Kennedy School and University of Georgia). Vigoda-Gadot is author and coauthor of more than 150 articles and book chapters, 9 books and symposiums, as well as many other scholarly presentations and working papers. His work has been published in *Public Administration Review (PAR); Journal of Public Administration Research and Theory (JPART); American Review of Public Administration (ARPA); Human Relations, Administration & Society; Journal of Business Research Journal of Vocational Behavior; Journal of Organizational Behavior; Political Psychology,* and many others.

L. A. Witt is a professor of psychology and management and director of the industrial/organizational psychology PhD program at the University of Houston. He received a PhD in industrial/organizational psychology from Tulane University. His research interests include goal alignment, criterion development, customer service, adaptive performance, the configural nature of the Big Five personality traits, and social effectiveness. His research has been published in such journals as the *Journal of Applied Psychology, Personnel Psychology, Journal of Management, Journal of Organizational Behavior,* and *Journal of Vocational Behavior.*

Francis J. Yammarino is the State University of New York (SUNY) Distinguished Professor of Management and director of the Center for Leadership Studies at the State University of New York at Binghamton. He received his PhD in management from the State University of New York at Buffalo. He has served as editor of the *Leadership Quarterly* and *Research in Multi-Level Issues* and on the editorial review board of the *Academy of Management Journal, Journal of Applied Psychology, Leadership Quarterly, Journal of Organizational Behavior, Organizational Research Methods, Personnel Psychology, Group & Organization Management,* and *Journal of Leadership & Organization Studies*. He is a fellow of the Society for Industrial and Organizational Psychology and the Association for Psychological Sciences. Yammarino has published 14 books and about 150 journal articles and book chapters, has received several teaching and research awards, and is the recipient of nearly $3 million in research grants from various public and private organizations. He has been a consultant to numerous organizations including IBM, TRW, Medtronic, Lockheed Martin, the United Way, and the U.S. Army, Navy, Air Force, and Department of Education. He has served on many committees in the Academy of Management and Society for Industrial and Organizational Psychology and as an elected representative at large for the Organizational Behavior and Research Methods Divisions of the Academy of Management.

Section I

Construct Specification, Theory Development, and Methodological Considerations

1

Politics in Organizations: History, Construct Specification, and Research Directions

Gerald R. Ferris
Florida State University

Darren C. Treadway
State University of New York at Buffalo

Power, politics, and influence in organizations have remained inextricably intertwined constructs for decades. Generally speaking, power is regarded as the exercise of influence over others, and it represents one of the most interesting aspects of the organizational sciences and has for several decades. Pfeffer's (1981) position on the dynamics of these important constructs was that power reflects the exercise of influence, that politics encompasses the methods and techniques of influence, and that political skill provides the savvy and skill set to effectively leverage such tactics and resources and to transform them into power and influence over others. Indeed, "whereas Mintzberg tended to associate political skill explicitly with formal power, the political skill construct, as it is characterized today, fits better with the ideas of some scholars concerning the exercise of influence devoid of formal authority" (Perrewé, Zellars, Ferris, Rossi, Kacmar, & Ralston, 2004, p.142).

Research in organizational politics has strong roots in theory and research on social influence and has been developed and advanced largely through the contributions of scholars such as Erving Goffman, Edward Jones, James Tedeschi, Barry Schlenker, Mark Leary, and others over the past half-century (for reviews, see Ferris, Hochwarter, Douglas, Blass, Kolodinsky, & Treadway, 2002; Higgins, Judge, & Ferris, 2003; Jones, 1990). This body of work has articulated the precise nature of influence tactics and strategies and their predictors and outcomes, and extensive empirical research has been published to systematically examine these theoretical arguments.

Until recently, the style of delivery and execution of influence, which largely explained the success of influence efforts, was missing from this base of theory and research (Jones, 1990). This missing piece was provided by the political skill construct. Politically skilled individuals are able to accurately diagnose social contexts and then to situationally adapt their behavior such that they select the proper methods and tactics to influence others. Also, this set of competencies increases the effectiveness of social influence attempts through effective style and delivery (e.g., Ferris, Treadway, Perrewé, Brouer, Douglas, & Lux, 2007).

In its broadest sense, the area of organizational politics includes theory and research on power, influence, and politics, and the style of delivery and execution of influence, which has focused on political skill (see Chapter 16). Additionally, another largely parallel body of research has emerged over the past several decades in the area of organizational politics, and it has focused on perceptions of organizational politics (e.g., Ferris, Adams, Kolodinsky, Hochwarter, & Ammeter, 2002). This area focuses on individuals' subjective perceptions of their work environments as being characterized by more or less political activity, and it dates back to Gandz and Murray's (1980) initial investigation and to Ferris, Russ, and Fandt's (1989) conceptual model nearly a decade later.

Collectively, then, the conceptual net is cast somewhat widely when considering the term *organizational politics* theory and research, and that is the scope of this chapter. In this chapter, the stage is set for the remaining chapters in this volume by reviewing the history of organizational politics research, by characterizing the scope, nature, and characterization of the construct domain, as well as by proposing a workable definition. Then, some important issues are discussed that emerge in the study of organizational politics, and needed areas of research in the future are identified.

By no means is this chapter characterized as covering all of the issues, literature, and so forth in a field as large as organizational politics. Indeed, other much more comprehensive reviews of work in this area have been published in the past decade or so, to which the interested reader is referred (e.g., Ferris, Adams, et al., 2002; Ferris & Hochwarter, 2011; Ferris, Hochwarter, Douglas, Blass, Kolodinsky, & Treadway, 2002; Kacmar & Baron, 1999; Lux, Ferris, Brouer, Laird, & Summers, 2008; Silvester, 2008; Vigoda-Gadot & Drory, 2006).

HISTORICAL REVIEW AND EVOLUTION OF POLITICS CONSTRUCT

The study of power and politics in organizations covers writing across 5 centuries. Plato, Aristotle, and Machiavelli all discussed the effective use of power in organizations and society. Though it is beyond the scope of this chapter to review the totality of this vast literature, it is instructive to readers of this volume to chart the theoretical progression of thought within the organizational sciences. This progression encompasses 50 years of research and offers insight into the foundations from which, the mechanisms through which, and the quality of which political activity affects the behavior in and of organizations.

Macro-Organizations Research

While laypersons typically view political behavior as unseemly, dishonest, and self-serving, researchers at the macrolevel (i.e., organizational theory and organizational sociology scholars) have viewed politics as representing much less vicious phenomena. These scholars have characterized politics as necessary but not evil. For example, Bacharach and Lawler (1980, p. 2) suggested that "in describing the processes of organizations as political acts, we are not making a moral judgment; we simply are making an observation about a process." At the very least, it must be recognized that power can be exercised for positive as well as negative reasons (Pfeffer, 1992).

Rather than subverting the goals of organizations, macro-organizational researchers have viewed the internal conflict that exists between competing interest groups as vital for innovation and success. Indeed, individuals accomplish their objectives and goals through their ability to influence not only people but also, more importantly, coalitions of people. Cyert and March (1963) suggested that individual behavior in organizations was driven by coalitions, as were the establishment of goals and the implementation of strategy. Through the alignment of interest groups' resources, coalitions are able to gain relative power, and it is through this power that organizations as a whole are affected (Bacharach & Lawler, 1980). Indeed, conflict in organizations makes it more likely that the interests of the most powerful coalition will be served rather than the interests of other organizational members (Baldridge, 1971).

Inherent in these discussions of politics within and among coalitions is the prominence of interpersonal power. Weber (1954, p. 323) suggested that power was "the possibility of imposing one's own will upon the behavior of other persons." Congruently, power has been distinguished as potential influence or force (Emerson, 1962; Pfeffer, 1992), such that "the power of Actor A over actor B is the amount of resistance on the part of B which can be potentially overcome by A" (Emerson, 1962, p. 32). Most noteworthy among research on power in organizations has been the five bases of power established by French and Raven (1959): coercive, legitimate, expert, referent, and reward. It is from these bases that individuals are able to influence their interest groups and coalitions and thus to affect the structure and direction of their organizations.

More recently, researchers have begun to more comprehensively analyze the relationships depicted by Cyert, March, Bacharach, Lawler, and Pfeffer with the use of social network analysis. By analyzing patterns of social networks in organizations, researchers can identify not only the coalitions that have been formed but also the individuals who are critical to their formation. More powerful employees typically are more centrally located in social networks (Brass, 1984; Brass & Burkhardt, 1993) and have more friendship ties (Lee & Tiedens, 2001) than employees with less power.

Micro-Organizations Research

Serious scholarship on influence and politics perhaps can be credited to the interesting and innovative work of Erving Goffman in 1959. His theatrical performance metaphor creatively examined the nature of interpersonal influence in everyday interactions with others. This dramaturgical view laid the foundation for viewing organizational participants as actors who selectively choose the reality they disclose to the various audiences with whom they interact. To paraphrase Shakespeare, all the world's a stage, and in the organizational context the men and women are merely players.

Moving this view more deeply into the organizational sciences, Burns (1961) began to speculate on the presumed moral illegitimacy of political behavior in the organizational context. He argued that the organizationally cohesive forces of cooperation and competitiveness are both the product of, and the incubator for, political behavior. Furthermore, he suggested that these political behaviors represented a mechanism for the survival of the individual and could be seen as legitimate to the degree that one's interests aligned with those of the actor.

It is this perceptual aspect of political behavior that leads many to label political activity as being morally illegitimate rather than as simply a way organizations and individuals perpetuate their interests. Moving more closely to a value-free understanding of politics in organizations conveyed by macrolevel theorists, Burns rejected the notion that politics represented a separate system of organizing but viewed them as informal policies as they were integrated into the social fabric of organizations.

Despite the eloquence of Burns's (1961) arguments, Porter, Allen, and Angle (1981) noted that academics largely ignored the concept of political activity in organizations. The view of these scholars was less focused on the validation of the political perspective of organizations but more concerned with describing the behaviors through which political activity is initiated. Their seminal model of upward influence behavior is noteworthy in its prescience to capture the broad themes of future research in one integrative conceptualization. Specifically, these scholars recognized that the social norms surrounding any influence attempt would affect both the tactic's choice and the tactic's effectiveness. These themes have emerged in the subsequently dominant research thrusts relating to influence tactics, perceptions of organizational politics, and political skill.

Social Psychology Research

From these broader concerns of positioning politics as a valid organizational system, social psychologists began engaging in research programs that sought to identify the behaviors through which political influence was implemented in organizations. Whereas this research has moved forward under many monikers (e.g., political behavior, influence tactics, self-presentation, impression management, interpersonal influence), the present viewpoint is that the overlap between these constructs far exceeds the differences between them. Much of the specified distinctions between these concepts lies in either the goals toward which they are focused or the attributions others make to the motivation of the actors. It is suggested that these distinctions are far too fine-grained and are subject to manipulation and errors in attribution and thus that investigating these ideas simultaneously should best advance the field.

Initiating the stream of research on influence or political behaviors was Jones's (1964) extensive treatise on ingratiation. His work demonstrated the tremendous power that ingratiation, as a strategic form of flattery, could demonstrate on interpersonal interactions/relationships. This research further revealed that, while ultimately positive, the impact of ingratiation on any dyadic relationship was a product of the value of the message content and the power differentials between the parties involved.

The work of Jones (1964) can be viewed as a launching point for research that sought to increase both the breadth and precision of behaviors used to influence others in organizations. Within this vast literature, two frameworks have come to dominate the landscape. The first of these is Jones and Pittman's (1982) classification of impression management tactics. They defined impression management behaviors as "the conscious or unconscious attempt to control images that are projected in real or imagined social interactions" (Schlenker, 1980, p. 6). The Jones and Pittman framework outlined five impression management tactics: self-promotion, ingratiation, exemplification, intimidation, and supplication (Bolino & Turnley, 1999).

The second framework addressed the concept of influence tactics in organizations. Kipnis and his colleagues (Kipnis, Schmidt, & Wilkinson, 1980) pioneered this work with a simple and powerful question: What did you do to get your way? These scholars argued that early conceptualizations were plagued by their lack of distinctiveness between the categories of influence. To address this concern, their work defined eight dimensions of personal influence ranging from "soft" tactics such as ingratiation to assertive tactics that relied on intimidation and confrontation. Their research demonstrated that influence behavior is directed at subordinates, coworkers, and supervisors, but the tactics employed were different based on the audience they were attempting to influence.

While researchers were focusing on understanding the types of behaviors that individuals employed to advance their ideas and themselves in organizations, other scholars were sowing the seeds of what became the dominant area of investigation during the last 2 decades. Burns (1961) implied that although all organizations are in essence political, the degree to which individuals perceive others' behavior to be political may vary. Similarly, Porter et al. (1981) suggested that organizations have specific norms for the acceptable type and amount of political activity. Expanding these notions, Gandz and Murray (1980) suggested that organizational politics is a subjective rather than an objective phenomenon. They argued that although politics in organizations was pervasive and often functional, it was distinguished as being political by others' perceptions of the self-serving intent of the actors.

Expanding the concept of *perceptions of organizational politics*, Ferris et al. (1989) proposed a broad model of the contextual, interpersonal, and individual influences on the formation and outcomes of individuals' perceptions of politics in their work environments. This model has demonstrated considerable influence in the politics literature in the last 2 decades, with considerable heuristic value in producing a wide array of studies testing portions, or all, of the model. In contrast, research consistently has shown that employees who perceive they have promotion opportunities and more interaction with their supervisor are less likely to perceive politics in their workplace. Because perceptions of politics rely on a perception of others' behavior as being self-serving, it is not surprising that perceptions of politics have been shown to be a reliable predictor of increased job tension and decreased job satisfaction (see Ferris, Adams, et al., 2002 for full review of antecedents and consequences).

Most recently, the present authors have launched a program of research that recognizes power and politics as perceptual entities that are subject to manipulation and interpretation. Within this perceptual arena, individuals vary in their ability to influence and understand others. This ability is labeled *political skill,* and it is defined as "the ability to effectively understand others at work, and to use such knowledge to influence others to act in ways that enhance one's personal and/or organizational objectives" (Ferris, Treadway, et al., 2005, p. 127). The rapidly growing body of research investigating this concept has been overwhelmingly supportive of the basic premises that politically skilled employees are more effective in implementing political behaviors in organizations (e.g., Kolodinsky, Treadway, & Ferris, 2007; Treadway, Ferris, Duke, Adams, & Thatcher, 2007), in coping with stressful environments (Perrewé et al., 2004), and in effectively engaging others as leaders (Treadway et al., 2004).

Practitioner Literature

Casual perusal of the business section of most bookstores reveals just how much the general public is interested in organizational politics, because the shelves are loaded with how-to books on playing politics to get ahead. It is difficult to identify a particular time when such books became popular, but a very likely starting point was the surprising success of Dale Carnegie's (1936) *How to Win Friends and Influence People* (for its time—the publisher and author never expected the book to sell very well, and it has now sold well over 25 million copies). One might reasonably trace the interest in self-help influence books to Carnegie, whose courses offered and books sold still constitute a thriving business venture. Clearly, the tone and perspective of Carnegie's book are uniformly positive, characterizing interpersonal influence as a good thing, and not as manipulative, deceptive, and nasty like the way the dark issues of politics have been described in, for example, *The Prince* (Machiavelli, 1940).

Examination of some recent books in the practitioner literature appears to suggest that writers have continued the perpetuation of a favorable or positive view of politics and influence. The general message seems to be that politics are a fact of life and go on in all organizations, so one would be well advised to learn to play the game as well as possible while maintaining integrity and to turn it into career and personal effectiveness (e.g., DuBrin, 2009; McIntyre, 2005; Ranker, Gautrey, & Phipps, 2008; Reardon, 2000). After all these years, since Carnegie's (1936) first volume, politics still seems to be about dealing with people. Shell and Moussa (2007) referred to their notions of *strategic persuasion* as the *art of woo,* where woo means the ability to win people over to your way of thinking or doing things without applying coercive efforts.

Others have identified the set of qualities that lead to interpersonal influence effectiveness as *political skill* (Ferris, Davidson, & Perrewé, 2005), *political savvy* (DeLuca, 1999), or *political intelligence* (McIntyre, 2005; Reardon, 2005). Stengel (2000) published a very clever and creatively presented history of flattery, emphasizing just how important ingratiation is in interpersonal influence. Sanders's (2005) *likeability factor* has a very simple message: If you can just get people to like you, good things will happen (e.g., better jobs, higher pay). Further, he suggests that raising your likeability factor is accomplished by friendliness, relevance (i.e., connecting with others), empathy, and realness (i.e., integrity).

Construct Domain Space of Organizational Politics

Given the diverse perspectives applied to the study of organizational politics, it is not surprising that the domain has several separate conceptualizations of influence behavior. Thus, there is some need for clarity as to our perspective on the constructs within this field and how the limits of the construct domain space are set for the present perspective on organizational politics. The position proposed here is that theory and research developed under the labels of impression management, self-presentation, intraorganizational influence, influence tactics, power, and organizational politics tend to share more in common than they reflect differences. Much of the distinction among these various concepts rests on the perceived immoral or self-serving nature of behaviors labeled as political.

Although creating this distinction offers ample room for the development of new yet similar constructs, it falsely assumes that actors and observers are able to accurately perceive the intentions of others and of themselves. In the next sections, this position is explained by discussing areas of potential confusion within the domain of organizational politics. The similarity, or lack thereof, among various definitions of influence behavior in organizations is evaluated to arrive at an understanding of the domain of political behavior in organizations. Ultimately, organizational politics is assessed with respect to whether it is more of a functional or dysfunctional phenomenon in the workplace.

Political Behavior

Research has been plagued by the inability to consistently define political behavior in organizations (Drory & Romm, 1990). Traditional definitions of political behavior position this activity as self-serving and strategic. For example, Allen, Madison, Porter, Renwick, and Mayes (1979, p. 77) suggested that political behavior was defined by "intentional acts of influence to enhance or protect the self-interest of individuals or groups." Similarly, political activity has been defined as "those activities taken within an organization to acquire, develop, and use power and other resources to obtain one's preferred outcomes" (Pfeffer, 1981). Indeed, all traditional definitions of politics represent these influence attempts as being designed to protect or promote the actors' self-interest (Kacmar & Carlson, 1997).

Organizational politics serves as a context within which employees understand the inherent ambiguity in the workplace. Thus, it is not surprising that organizational politics is seen as flourishing within and fueling conflict in the workplace. Others have classified political behavior as unauthorized activity undertaken to secure outcomes not attainable via organizationally sanctioned means (Mayes & Allen, 1977) or a power struggle over workplace assets (Vigoda, 2003). Political behavior has been described as a social disease (Chanlat, 1997) in need of swift eradication (Buchanan, 2008; Voyer, 1994).

Perhaps because of the negative light in which political behavior has been viewed in organizations and society, researchers often have steered clear of labeling their constructs as political. Instead, they have developed research streams that do not explicitly acknowledge that the behavior of individuals is most always suited to pursue their own interests, causes, or objectives, whether that self-focus is evident to the actor. This sentiment is echoed in work on self-presentation that suggested power maintenance and acquisition is a central goal of self-presentation attempts (Jones & Pittman, 1982).

As a type of social influence, self-presentation behavior is enacted as a means of obtaining desired responses from others (Leary, 1995). The perspectives advanced by these scholars provide some support for under-standing the more subtle ways innocuous, everyday presentation behaviors ultimately are attempts to satiate one's need for power and image main-tenance. As such, these behaviors can be classified under the umbrella of political behavior.

The view adopted here is that eliminating the value-laden distinctions among definitions or characterizations of political behavior results in a set of characteristics that can be integrated into a single, yet largely rep-resentative, definition of the broad construct of organizational politics. Such an approach is believed to capture a less exclusively positive or nega-tive tone and more of a neutral and objective perspective. Therefore, the present perspective is in agreement with Sederberg (1984), who charac-terized organizational politics as attempts to "create, maintain, modify, or abandon shared meanings" (p. 7). Furthermore, "the objective is to manage the meaning of situations in such a way as to produce desired, self-serving responses or outcomes" (Ferris, Fedor, & King, 1994, p. 4). As shared meaning is managed through political processes, politics becomes an important aspect of achieving personal (Luthans, Rosenkrantz, & Hennessey, 1985) and organizational goals (Pfeffer, 1981). This view of politics tends to be more value free and functional, provides balance with early pejorative views of politics in organizations, and lays the foundation upon which this book is developed and theory and research are examined.

Conclusions on the Organizational Politics Construct

In examination of the historical background of organizational politics as an area of scientific inquiry, it appears that several observations and conclusions can be drawn. First, it seems fair to state that, overall, organizational politics has gotten a bad rap. The construct has been disproportionately characterized as negative in nature. Note, for example, how Ferris, Perrewé, Anthony, and Gilmore (2000, p. 25) start off their article: "Only in America do we use the word 'politics' to describe the process so well; 'poli' in Latin meaning 'many' and 'tics' meaning blood-sucking creatures!"

This stands in contrast to the realities that politics can be used for positive purposes and the more neutral characterizations by scholars such as Weick, Daft, Pondy, and Pfeffer, who implied that politics are neither inherently good nor bad but rather that they are essential for organizational survival. Indeed, the negative perspective on politics seems to have been promoted much more actively by the more micro-oriented scholars, who seemed to associate it with the seedier side of organizational life (e.g., characterized as the *dark side* by some). Extending this generally positive and necessary view of politics, Buchanan (2008) reported in an investigation of 250 British managers that political behavior appeared to be quite common and that most respondents perceived it as necessary and ethical in nature. Furthermore, responding managers attributed organizational change, effectiveness, and reputation to political tactics.

However, the contemporary zeitgeist regarding politics seems to favor a neutral to more positive view, and that is one promoted in this book (see Chapter 2 on the positive aspects of organizational politics). In so doing, the intention is to simply wish to balance out what has not been balanced treatment in the past by discussing the potentially positive sides of organizational politics. However, in so doing, the fact that politics can lead to negative outcomes is not ignored, and those areas are discussed as well.

DIRECTIONS FOR FUTURE RESEARCH

The area of organizational politics is one of the most intuitively appealing areas of study in the organizational sciences. Its importance is seen in the familiarity that employees have with political behavior and influence in their workplace. Despite its merits, organizational politics research has progressed slowly and is marked by a few dominant paradigms and models. Unlike previous books on organizational politics that sought to expand the understanding by asking politics researchers to push the boundaries of their own constructs, prolific scholars in other areas of inquiry have been brought together here to discuss how political perspectives can expand their research streams and, thus, the domain of organizational politics. The belief is that this approach will lead to more eclectic models of political activity that are more expansive in thought and conceptualization and that thus reflect the potential to take quantum leaps forward in theory, research, and practice.

Although diverse in their treatments of the topic, two themes are evident in the chapters that follow. First, these chapters focus on expanding the theory of politics through the use of cross-disciplinary viewpoints that stress the multilevel nature of the phenomena. Further, the cross-disciplinary perspective calls for both mixed-method and multistudy packages to advance the construct. Also, toward expanding such theory, organizational politics must be more accurately contextualized within organizations.

Theory Development in Politics Research

Organizations are inherently nested, and thus it should be no surprise that organizational politics is a similarly nested construct. Despite this reality, few scholars have proposed models of multilevel political activity in organizations (e.g., Ferris, Adams, et al., 2002; Johns, 1999; Treadway, Breland, Williams, Williams, & Yang, in press). Although noteworthy work has been published in the organizational sciences, which specifies levels within organizations, it is suggested that the traditional multilevel treatments of employees being nested in units, or teams being nested in organizations, are far too elementary and ignore the complexities of the workplace social fabric.

Cumulatively, the chapters that follow not only recognize the structural considerations that underlie politics but also extend the relational and temporal conditions that provide the context within which political behavior is engaged. Thus, the traditional structural framing of nesting is found to be incomplete, so these structures are discussed as constraints on the establishment of perspective and relationships in organizations. Most obviously, in areas such as leadership (Chapter 11), social networks

(Chapter 12), and teams (Chapter 10), it is seen that, at their core, organizations are relational entities.

Establishing stronger theory necessarily requires both increased rigor in, and expansion of, research designs. Thus, it is suggested that researchers should move beyond single-study packages, and focus on constructive replications to advance theory. As discussed by Lykken (1968), constructive replications include changes not only in subjects but also in the operationalizations of constructs, the procedures used, and the sources of ratings for the dependent variable. Beyond offering further confidence in the theoretical linkages of any particular model, these replications are particularly useful in that they allow for the development of theoretical extensions and for testing of multiple-linkage models (Tsui, 1999) and truly for the "interplay between theory and method" (Van Maanen, Sorensen, & Mitchell, 2007). Furthermore, the field's current enamor with meta-analysis is best served through the use of constructive replication in primary research, as it provides for better quality input for meta-analytic procedures (Eden, 2002).

Indeed, the multiple purposes of multistudy research packages (e.g., theory testing and validation, theory extensions) have stimulated a tremendous increase in such publications in the top organizational science journals in recent years. In an extensive 20-year review of eight organizational science journals—*Academy of Management Journal, Administrative Science Quarterly, Journal of Applied Psychology, Journal of Management, Organizational Behavior and Human Decision Processes, Organization Science, Personnel Psychology,* and *Strategic Management Journal*—Hochwarter, Ferris, and Hanes (2011) reported considerable increases in the publication of 457 multistudy packages across all eight journals in the period from 1990 to 1999 and 614 published collectively in the period from 2000 to 2010.

The use of constructive replication also allows for researchers to overcome one of the weaknesses of the organizational politics research area—that is, the lack of measure congruence and, in some cases, construct definition. As previously discussed, the areas of impression management, political behavior, influence tactics, and self-presentation have similar characteristics but typically have been independently investigated. Constructive replication would allow for researchers to demonstrate the similarities in these constructs while increasing the strength of their research.

Some research in the field of organizational politics already has begun to use constructive replication as a basis for testing research models. For example, Treadway, Ferris, Perrewé, Hochwarter, Witt, and Goodman (2005) used multiple operationalizations of performance and perceived politics across three samples to establish that the performance of older employees was less likely to be affected by perceptions of politics than was the performance of younger employees.

More expansively, Hochwarter, Ferris, Laird, Treadway, and Gallagher (2010) used five samples across three studies not only to constructively replicate their findings but also to assess a multilinkage model. Their first study established an inverted U-shaped relationship between organizational politics perceptions and job satisfaction. Their second study extended this inverted U-shaped relationship to job tension. In their final study, they were able to test whether personal resources acted as a buffer for perceptions of politics, thus reporting that the nonlinear relationship existed only for those with lower levels of resources.

Beyond the use of constructive replication and multistudy packages, future research will benefit from qualitative and mixed-method research. By its very nature, organizational politics represents the type of phenomena that would greatly benefit from sound qualitative investigation, yet little has been conducted and published to date. Smith, Plowman, Duchon, and Quinn (2009) conducted a qualitative investigation of what they called *high-reputation plant managers*, using political skill theory and research as a theoretical foundation. Their observations confirmed severable aspects of political skill theory and they offered some powerful propositions regarding the role of political skill in leadership. They found that political skill was related to leadership style, noting that politically skilled mangers were more likely to empower their subordinates and to engage in goal setting and management by objectives, with specific accountabilities built in for performance. They provided a theory of plant manager effectiveness "as a combination of political skill and the use of unobtrusive and systemic power to achieve both affective and substantive outcomes" (p. 428).

While in their entirety, the chapters in this book make a significant contribution to the expansion of politics theory, two chapters specifically address the role of theory building (Chapter 2 and Chapter 3) and one addresses measurement (Chapter 4) within this field. Another area of future theory and research emphasis in organizational politics relates to the nature of *context* and its importance in understanding organizational phenomena. Politics as context, and politics within particular contexts, seems to present quite fruitful areas for future work in developing a more informed understanding of organizational politics. Indeed, the contextualization of organizational politics essentially serves as an overarching framework for the chapters in Sections II and III of the book, as different sets of issues are examined with respect to politics that relate to context.

Politics and Context

Contemporary organizational science theory and research increasingly have emphasized the importance of considering contextual factors when attempting to explain organizational experiences (Johns, 2001, 2006). Mowday and Sutton (1993) described context as "stimuli and phenomena that surround and thus exist in the environment external to the individual, most often at a different level of analysis" (p. 198). Cappelli and Sherer (1991) suggested that context represents "the surroundings associated with phenomena which help to illuminate that [sic] phenomena, typically factors associated with units of analysis above those expressly under investigation" (p. 56).

Similarly, Rousseau and Fried (2001) noted that "contextualization entails linking observations to a set of relevant facts, events, or points, of view that make possible research and theory that form the part of the larger whole" (p. 1). Finally, Blalock (1984) noted that the "essential feature of all contextual-effects models is an allowance for macro processes that are presumed to have an impact on the individual actor above the effects of any individual-level variables that may be operating" (p. 354).

Context assists with the framing of phenomena in ways that influence perceptions and interpretations of them, which in turn affect the decisions made and actions taken about such phenomena. It is noteworthy to highlight the contextual implications of this research, because the relationships among persons, subunits, and organizations are investigated against a dynamic, yet often subtle, social context. Obviously, work outcomes such as work performance and well-being reflect ongoing social interactions in the workplace, which occur against a backdrop of organizational context, social norms, and so forth, all of which can affect the outcomes of such social processes, and imply that both indirect and direct social effects may be nested within one another (e.g., Ferris & Mitchell, 1987).

A concern with context addresses Scarr's (1985) argument that, as organizational scientists, there is a general tendency to overemphasize proximal and to underemphasize distal causes of social behavior. Recognition of the increased importance of context is reflective of a philosophy of science movement that highlights contextual psychology and the critical roles of temporality and context (e.g., Gergen, 1985; Packer, 1985). This perspective supports the notion that phenomena occurring within organizational contexts, at least to some extent, can be interpreted as socially constructed realities (e.g., Gergen, 1985).

Shore and colleagues (2004) described context as "the locus of obligations surrounding employee–organization relationships" (p. 324) and maintained that "context contains the terms and conditions of the relationship" (p. 325). Hence, they stressed that because supervisor–subordinate relationships are embedded within context, researchers should treat the role of context as more central. Shore et al. elaborated that context is inherently complex because there are always multiple contexts simultaneously influencing any one phenomenon. Furthermore, Johns (2001) guided researchers by stressing the advantage of considering both contextual constraints and opportunities for the particular phenomenon under consideration.

Role theory (Katz & Kahn, 1978) provides an excellent example of context and of meso theory in organizations because it describes how individual-level understandings and workplace behaviors derive from interpretations of social features. That is, cultural characteristics affect organizational structures and systems, which in turn affect subunit and group actions, which affect interpersonal relationships, which affect individual cognitions and behaviors. Katz and Kahn's discussion of role development confirms that "enactment does not occur in isolation; it is shaped by additional or contextual factors" (p. 195).

Meso-level conceptualizations, which inherently involve a focus on context, are needed to address the shortcomings that exist in the organizational sciences research literature. Indeed, it is evident to most observers that fully comprehending the context of politics is essential to gain insight into the phenomenon (Johns, 2001, 2006). Thus, context represents the features surrounding a phenomenon that exert influence on employee attitudes or behaviors (Strong, Jeanneret, McPhail, Blakley, & D'Egidio, 1999).

Organizational science scholars have appealed for increased sensitivity of contextual effects in organizational research (Griffin, 2007; Whetten, 2009), largely because of its in situ impact on role perceptions and interpretations of workplace dynamics (Ferris, Munyon, Basik, & Buckley, 2008). Context is an important feature of research on organizational politics because it is the context that frames political dynamics, and at the same time politics is the context that frames other organizational behavior. Therefore, this volume notes some research that has framed politics as context and suggests that future research continue in this area.

Political contexts were highlighted in qualitative examinations of myths and politics in organizational environments (Ferris, Fedor, Chachere, & Pondy, 1989) and in the influence of political cultures (Riley, 1983). Also, Rosen, Chang, Johnson, and Levy (2009) focused on how two prominent features of the organizational context (i.e., politics perceptions and procedural justice) shaped employee–organization exchange relationships, responding to appeals for such research by Shore et al. (2004). Treadway and his colleagues (Treadway, Adams, Ranft, & Ferris, 2009) also developed a meso-level model that discussed the interplay between the political skill of chief executive officer celebrities and the external and internal environments in organizations.

In a two-study investigation, Kapoutsis, Papalexandris, Nikolopoulos, Hochwarter, and Ferris (2011) examined perceptions of organizational politics as a contextual backdrop against which to better understand the prediction of job performance from political skill. Using resource theories to argue that high levels of political skill will demonstrate their strongest positive effects on job performance when politics perceptions are perceived as low, results demonstrated that, in settings characterized by lower politics, high levels of political skill predicted significant increases in job performance, whereas these effects were attenuated in high politics environments.

It has been suggested that political skill is critical in understanding the social context of organizations (Ferris, Treadway, et al., 2005). Perhaps because of the inherent overlap between justice and politics (Cropanzano & Kacmar, 1995), researchers have evaluated justice as a context within which politically skilled individuals make decisions regarding their contributions at work. Andrews, Kacmar, and Harris (2009) found that the relationship between political skill and work contribution (i.e., performance and citizenship behavior) was most pronounced in low justice contexts, suggesting perhaps that political environments might cause individuals to expend resources in some settings and allow for accumulation in others. These results confirm the importance of considering political features of the external environment when conducting substantive research. In recognition of the importance of justice, this volume provides critical analysis and discussion concerning the role of justice and politics in organizations (Chapter 6).

Related to the foregoing section focusing on politics as context, another area of research importance is the nature of social networks, which are contextual factors in their own right, and how politics play out within such contexts. At its core, organizational politics always has been about social networks and their use for the acquistion and maintenance of power. Indeed, Ferris, Treadway, et al. (2005, 2007) positioned networking ability as a critical competency of politically skilled individuals. Specifically, because political skill makes the interpretation of social networks more accurate and allows employees the behavioral flexibility to engage these networks, it is more likely that these highly skilled employees will be central in work-related social networks.

Some recent research has begun to explore theese relationships. Treadway, Breland, Williams, Yang, and Shaughnessy (2010) reported that political skill interacts with narcissim to predict social network positioing. Specifically, employees with high political skill and high narcissim were more strongly positioned in advice and performance networks, whereas their political skill deficient counterparts were not strongly positioned despite possessing high levels of narcissism. In another study, Treadway Breland, Williams, Cho, Yang, and Ferris (in press) investigated how politically skilled indivduals acquire advantageous positioning in interpersonal influence networks as a result of their past performance. They found that high performers who were high in political skill were capable of translating their previous accomplishments into greater influence over others, whereas those low in political skill were not.

In recognition of the relationship among organizational politics, political skill, and social networks, this book includes a chapter by accomplished social network scholars Brass and Krackhardt (Chapter 13). Furthermore, because much of the work on perceptions of organizational politics has been associated with political climates and cultures and the theoretical and empirical foundations of the work on climate are taken from early path-breaking work by James and his colleagues, Chapter 9 is included in this volume to address politics and climate in efforts to address those aspects of context.

CONCLUSION

Organizational politics is a phenomenon that has been with us—in mere observation, scholarly discussion, or systematic research—for three-quarters of a century. To state that very little is still known about politics not only would be an understatement but also would be a serious slight to all of the fine work that scholars in this area have contributed over time. However, it is quite fair to conclude that there is much more to learn about organizational politics. Furthermore, the remaining chapters in this book represent important issues that will meaningfully advance understanding of politics phenomena, will lay out agendas for important new theory and research, and represent important contributions to the literature in their own right. So, without further ado, these editors encourage thoughtful attention to and consideration of the important ideas presented in the chapters in this volume. Collectively, the fine and accomplished authors assembled here effectively have pushed back the frontiers of knowledge with respect to organizational politics, and their ideas will undoubtedly influence thinking in this area for years to come.

REFERENCES

Allen, R., Madison, D., Porter, L., Renwick, P., & Mayes, B. (1979). Organizational politics: Tactics and characteristics of its actors. *California Management Review, 22,* 77–83.

Andrews, M.C., & Kacmar, K.M. (2001). Discriminating among organizational politics, justice, and support. *Journal of Organizational Behavior, 22,* 347–366.

Andrews, M.C., Kacmar, K.M., & Harris, K.J. (2009). Got political skill? The impact of justice on the importance of political skill for job performance. *Journal of Applied Psychology, 94,* 1427–1437.

Bacharach, S.B., & Lawler, E.J. (1980). *Power and politics in organizations.* San Francisco: Jossey-Bass.

Baldridge, J.V. (1971). *Power and conflict in the university.* New York: Wiley.

Blalock, H.M. (1984). Contextual effects models: Theoretical and methodological issues. *Annual Review of Sociology, 10,* 353–372.

Bolino, M.C., & Turnley, W.H. (1991). Measuring impression management in organizations: A scale development based on the Jones and Pittman taxonomy. *Organizational Research Methods, 2,* 187–206.

Brass, D.J. (1984). Being in the right place: A structural analysis of individual influence in an organization. *Administrative Science Quarterly, 29,* 518–539.

Brass, D.J., & Burkhardt, M.E. (1993). Potential power and power use: An investigation of structure and behavior. *Academy of Management Journal, 36,* 441–470.

Buchanan, D. (2008). You stab my back, I'll stab yours: Management experience and perceptions of organizational political behavior. *British Journal of Management, 19*, 49–64.

Burns, T. (1961). Micropolitics: Mechanisms of institutional change. *Administrative Science Quarterly, 6*, 257–281.

Cappelli, P., & Scherer, P. (1991). The missing role of context in OB: The need for a meso-level approach. *Research in Organizational Behavior, 13*, 55–110.

Carnegie, D. (1936). *How to win friends and influence people.* New York: Simon & Schuster.

Chanlat, J. (1997). Conflict and politics. In A. Sorge & M. Warner (Eds.), *Handbook of organizational behavior* (pp. 472–480). London: International Thomson.

Cropanzano, R.S., & Kacman, K.M. (Eds.). (1995). *Organizational politics, justice, and support: Managing the social climate of the workplace.* Westport, CT: Quorum Books.

Cyert, R.M., & March, J.G. (1963). *A behavioral theory of the firm.* Englewood Cliffs, NJ: Prentice-Hall.

DeLuca, J.R. (1999). *Political savvy: Systematic approaches to leadership behind the scenes.* Berwyn, PA: Evergreen Business Group.

Drory, A., & Romm, T. (1990). The definition of organizational politics: A review. *Human Relations, 43*, 1133–1154.

DuBrin, A.J. (2009). *Political behavior in organizations.* Thousand Oaks, CA: Sage Publications.

Eden, D. (2002). From the editors. *Academy of Management Journal, 45*, 841–846.

Emerson, R. (1962). Power-dependence relations. *American Sociological Review, 27*, 31–41.

Ferris, G.R., Adams, G., Kolodinsky, R.W., Hochwarter, W.A., & Ammeter, A.P. (2002). Perceptions of organizational politics: Theory and research directions. In F. Yammarino & F. Dansereau (Eds.), *Research in multi-level issues, Volume 1: The many faces of multi-level issues* (pp. 179–254). Oxford, UK: JAI Press/Elsevier Science.

Ferris, G.R., Bowen, M.G., Treadway, D.C., Hochwarter, W.A., Hall, A.T., & Perrewé, P.L. (2006). The assumed linearity of organizational phenomena: Implications for occupational stress and well-being. In P. Perrewé & D. Ganster (Eds.), *Research in occupational stress and well-being* (pp. 205–232). Oxford, UK: Elsevier.

Ferris, G.R., Davidson, S.L., & Perrewé, P. L. (2005). *Political skill at work: Impact on work effectiveness.* Mountain View, CA: Davies-Black Publishing.

Ferris, G.R., Fedor, D.B., Chachere, J.G., & Pondy, L.R. (1989). Myths and politics in organizational contexts. *Group and Organization Studies, 14*, 83–103.

Ferris, G.R., Fedor, D.B., & King, T.R. (1994). A political conceptualization of managerial behavior. *Human Resource Management Review, 4*, 1–34.

Ferris, G.R., & Hochwarter, W.A. (2011). Organizational politics. In S. Zedeck (Ed.), *APA handbook of industrial and organizational psychology* (Vol. 3, pp. 435–459). Washington, DC: American Psychological Association.

Ferris, G.R., Hochwarter, W.A., Douglas, C., Blass, F.R., Kolodinsky, R.W., & Treadway, D.C. (2002). Social influence processes in organizations and human resources systems. In G.R. Ferris & J.J. Martocchio (Eds.), *Research in personnel and human resources management* (pp. 65–127). Oxford, UK: JAI Press/Elsevier Science.

Ferris, G.R., King, T.R., Judge, T.A., & Kacmar, K.M. (1991). The management of shared meaning: Opportunism in the reflection of attitudes, beliefs, and values. In R.A. Giacalone & P. Rosenfeld (Eds.), *Applied impression management: How image making affects managerial decisions* (pp. 41–64). Newbury Park, CA: Sage Publications.

Ferris, G.R., & Mitchell, T.R. (1987). The components of social influence and their importance for human resources research. In K.M. Rowland & G.R. Ferris (Eds.), *Research in personnel and human resources management* (Vol. 5, pp. 103–128). Greenwich, CT: JAI Press.

Ferris, G.R., Munyon, T.P., Basik, K.J., & Buckley, M.R. (2008). The performance evaluation context: Social, emotional, cognitive, political, and relationship components. *Human Resource Management Review, 18,* 146–163.

Ferris, G.R., Perrewé, P.L., Anthony, W.P., & Gilmore, D.C. (2000). Political skill at work. *Organizational Dynamics, 28,* 25–37.

Ferris, G.R., Russ, G.S., & Fandt, P.M. (1989). Politics in organizations. In R. Giacalone & P. Rosenfeld (Eds.), *Impression management in the organization* (pp. 143–170). Hillsdale, NJ: Lawrence Erlbaum.

Ferris, G.R., Treadway, D.C., Kolodinsky, R.W., Hochwarter, W.A., Kacmar, C.J., Douglas, C., et al. (2005). Development and validation of the political skill inventory. *Journal of Management, 31,* 126–152.

Ferris, G.R., Treadway, D.C., Perrewé, P.L., Brouer, R.L., Douglas, C., & Lux, S. (2007). Political skill in organizations. *Journal of Management, 33,* 290–320.

French, J.R.P., & Raven, B. (1959). The bases of social power. In D. Cartwright & A. Zander (Eds.), *Group dynamics* (pp. 150–167). New York: Harper and Row.

Gandz, J., & Murray, V. (1980). The experience of workplace politics. *Academy of Management Journal, 23,* 237–251.

Gergen, K.J. (1985). The social constructionist movement in modern psychology. *American Psychologist, 40,* 266–275.

Goffman, E. (1959). *The presentation of self in everyday life.* New York: Doubleday Anchor Books.

Griffin, M. (2007). Specifying organizational contexts: Systematic links between contexts and processes in organizational behavior. *Journal of Organizational Behavior, 28,* 859–863.

Higgins, C.A., Judge, T.A., & Ferris, G.R. (2003). Influence tactics and work outcomes: A meta-analysis. *Journal of Organizational Behavior, 24,* 89–106.

Hochwarter, W.A., Ferris, G.R., & Hanes, T.J. (2011). Multi-study packages in organizational science research. In D.J. Ketchen Jr. & D.D. Bergh (Eds.), *Research methodology in strategy and management* (Vol. 6). Bingley, UK: Emerald Group Publishing Limited.

Hochwarter, W.A., Ferris, G.R., Laird, M.D., Treadway, D.C., & Gallagher, V.C. (2010). Nonlinear politics perceptions—work outcomes relationships: A three-study, five-sample investigation. *Journal of Management, 36,* 740–763.

Hochwarter, W.A., Kacmar, C.J., Perrewé, P.L., & Johnson, D. (2003). Perceived organizational support as a mediator of the relationship between politics perceptions and work outcomes. *Journal of Vocational Behavior, 63,* 438–465.

Johns, G. (1999). A multi-level theory of self-serving behavior in and by organizations. In R.I. Sutton & B.M. Staw (Eds.), *Research in organizational behavior* (Vol. 21, pp 1–38). Stamford, CT: JAI Press.

Johns, G. (2001). In praise of context. *Journal of Organizational Behavior, 22,* 31–42.

Johns, G. (2006). The essential impact of context on organizational behavior. *Academy of Management Review, 31,* 385–408.

Jones, E. (1990). *Interpersonal perception.* New York: Freeman.

Jones, E.E. (1964). *Ingratiation: A social psychological analysis.* New York: Appleton-Century-Crofts.

Jones, E.E., & Pittman, T.S. (1982). Toward a general theory of strategic self-presentation. In J. Suls (Ed.), *Psychological perspectives on the self* (pp. 231–261). Hillsdale, NJ: Lawrence Erlbaum.

Kacmar, K., & Baron, R. (1999). Organizational politics: The state of the field, links to related processes, and an agenda for future research. In G.R. Ferris (Ed.), *Research in personnel and human resources management* (Vol. 17, pp. 1–39). Stamford, CT: JAI Press.

Kacmar, K., & Carlson, D. (1997). Further validation of the Perceptions of Politics Scale (POPS): A multi-sample approach. *Journal of Management, 23*, 627–658.

Kapoutsis, I., Papalexandris, A., Nikolopoulos, A., Hochwarter, W.A., & Ferris, G.R. (2011). Political skill and job performance prediction: Politics perceptions as a contextual moderator in two-studies. *Journal of Vocational Behavior, 78*, 123–135.

Katz, D., & Kahn, R. (1978). *The social psychology of organizations* (2nd ed.). New York: John Wiley.

Kipnis, D., Schmidt, S.M., & Wilkinson, I. (1980). Intraorganizational influence tactics: Explorations in getting one's way. *Journal of Applied Psychology, 63*, 440–452.

Leary, M. (1995). *Self-presentation: Impression management and interpersonal behavior.* Boulder, CO: Westview Press.

Lee, F., & Tiedens, L.Z. (2001). Is it lonely at the top? The independence and interdependence of power holders. *Research in Organizational Behavior, 23*, 43–91.

Luthans, F., Rosenkrantz, S.A., & Hennessey, H.W. (1985). What do successful managers really do? An observation study of managerial activities. *Journal of Applied Behavioral Science, 21*, 255–270.

Lux, S., Ferris, G., Brouer, R., Laird, M., & Summers, J. (2008). A multi-level conceptualization of organizational politics. In C. Cooper & J. Barling (Eds.), *Handbook of organizational behavior* (pp. 353–371). Thousand Oaks, CA: Sage Publications.

Lykken, D. T. (1968). Statistical significance in psychological research. *Psychological Bulletin, 70*, 151–159.

Machiavelli, N. (1940). *The prince.* New York: Modern Library.

Madison, D., Allen, L., Porter, L., Renwick, P., & Mayes, B. (1980). Organizational politics: An exploration of managers' perceptions. *Human Relations, 33*, 79–100.

Mayes, B., & Allen, R. (1977). Toward a definition of organizational politics. *Academy of Management Review, 4*, 672–677.

McIntyre, M.G. (2005). *Secrets to winning at office politics: How to achieve your goals and increase your influence at work.* New York: St. Martin's Press.

Mintzberg, H. (1983). *Power in and around organizations.* Englewood Cliffs, NJ: Prentice-Hall.

Mowday, R.T., & Sutton, R.I. (1993). Organizational behavior: Linking individuals and groups to organizational contexts. *Annual Review of Psychology, 44*, 195–229.

Packer, M.J. (1985). Hermeneutic inquiry in the study of human conduct. *American Psychologist, 40*, 1081–1093.

Perrewé, P., Zellars, K., Ferris, G., Rossi, A., Kacmar, C., & Ralston, D. (2004). Neutralizing job stressors: Political skill as an antidote to the dysfunctional consequences of role conflict stressors. *Academy of Management Journal, 47*, 141–152.

Pfeffer, J. (1981). *Power in organizations.* Boston: Pitman.

Pfeffer, J. (1992). *Managing with power: Politics and influence in organizations.* Boston: Harvard Business School Press.

Porter, L., Allen, R., & Angle, H. (1981). The politics of upward influence in organizations. In L.L. Cummings & B.M. Staw (Eds.), *Research in organizational behavior* (Vol. 3, pp. 109–149). Greenwich, CT: JAI Press.

Ranker, G., Gautrey, C., & Phipps, M. (2008). *Political dilemmas at work: How to maintain your integrity and further your career.* Hoboken, NJ: John Wiley.

Reardon, K.K. (2005). *It's all politics: Winning in a world where hard work and talent aren't enough.* New York: Doubleday.

Reardon, K.K. (2000). *The secret handshake: Mastering the politics of the business inner circle.* New York: Doubleday.

Riley, P. (1983). A structurationist account of political culture. *Administrative Science Quarterly, 28,* 414–437.

Rosen, C., Chang, C., & Levy, P. (2006). Personality and politics perceptions: A new conceptualization and illustration using OCBs. In E. Vigoda-Gadot & A. Drory (Eds.), *Handbook of organizational politics* (pp. 29–52). Cheltenham: Edward Elgar.

Rosen, C., Chang, C., Johnson, R., & Levy, P. (2009). Perceptions of the organizational context and psychological contract breach: Assessing competing perspectives. *Organizational Behavior and Human Decision Processes, 108,* 202–217.

Rousseau, D.M., & Fried, Y. (2001). Location, location, location: Contextualizing organizational research. *Journal of Organizational Behavior, 22,* 1–13.

Sanders, T. (2005). *The likeability factor.* New York: Crown Publishers.

Scarr, S. (1985). Constructing psychology: Making facts and fables for our times. *American Psychologist, 40,* 499–512.

Schlenker, B. (1980). *Impression management: The self-concept, social identity, and interpersonal relations.* Monterey, CA: Brooks/Cole Publishing.

Sederberg, P. (1984). *The politics of meaning: Power and explanation in the construction of social reality.* Tucson: University of Arizona Press.

Shell, G.R., & Moussa, M. (2007). *The art of woo: Using strategic persuasion to sell your ideas.* New York: The Penguin Group.

Shore, L.M., Tetrick, L.E., Taylor, M.S., Coyle Shapiro, J.A.-M., Liden, R.C., McLean Parks, J., et al. (2004). The employee–organization relationship: A timely concept in a period of transition. In J.J. Martocchio & G.R. Ferris (Eds.), *Research in personnel and human resources management* (Vol. 23, pp. 291–370). New York: Elsevier.

Silvester, J. (2008). The good, the bad, and the ugly: Politics and politicians at work. *International Review of Industrial and Organizational Psychology, 23,* 107–148.

Smith, A., Plowman, D., Duchon, D., & Quinn, A. (2009). A qualitative study of high-reputation plant managers: Political skill and successful outcomes. *Journal of Operations Management, 27*(6), 428–443.

Stengel, R. (2000). *You're too kind: A brief history of flattery.* New York: Simon & Schuster.

Strong, M., Jeanneret, P., McPhail, S., Blakley, B., & D'Egidio, E. (1999). Work context: Taxonomy and measurement of the work environment. In N. Peterson, M. Mumford, W. Borman, P. Jeanneret, & E. Fleishman (Eds.), *An occupational information system for the 21st century: The development of the O* NET* (pp. 127–145). Washington, DC: American Psychological Association.

Treadway, D., Adams, G., & Goodman, J. (2005). An evaluation of political sub-climates: Predictions from social identity, structuration, and symbolic interactionism. *Journal of Business and Psychology, 20,* 201–209.

Treadway, D.C., Adams, G.L., Ranft, A.L., & Ferris, G.R. (2009). A meso-level conceptualization of CEO celebrity effectiveness. *Leadership Quarterly, 20,* 554–570.

Treadway, D.C., Ferris, G.R., Perrewé, P.L., Hochwarter, W.A., Witt, L.A., & Goodman, J.M. (2005). The role of age in the perceptions of politics–job performance relationship: A three-study constructive replication. *Journal of Applied Psychology, 90,* 872–881.

Treadway, D., Ferris, G., Duke, A., Adams, G., & Thatcher, J. (2007). The moderating role of subordinate political skill on supervisors' impressions of subordinate ingratiation and ratings of interpersonal facilitation. *Journal of Applied Psychology, 92,* 848–855.

Treadway, D.C., Breland, J.W., Williams, L.A., Williams, L., & Yang, J. (in press). Political skill, relational control, and the relational self in the process of relational leadership. In M. Uhl-Bien & S.M. Ospina (Eds.), *Advancing relational leadership theory: A conversation among perspectives: Leadership horizons series.* Charlotte, NC: Information Age Publishing.

Treadway, D.C., Breland, J.W., Williams, L.M., Yang, J., & Shaughnessy, B.A. (2010). It's all in how you use it: The interactive effects of political skill and narcissism on social network positioning. Manuscript under review.

Treadway, D.C., Breland, J.W., Williams, L.M., Cho, J., Yang, J., & Ferris, G.R. (in press). Social influence and interpersonal power in organizations: Roles of performance and political skill in two studies. *Journal of Management.*

Treadway, D.C., Ferris, G.R., Douglas, C., Hochwarter, W.A., Kacmar, C.J., Ammeter, A.P., & Buckley, M.R. (2004). Leader political skill and employee reactions. *The Leadership Quarterly, 15,* 493–513.

Treadway, D.C., Ferris, G.R., Duke, A.B., Adams, G., & Thatcher, J.B. (2007). The moderating role of subordinate political skill on supervisors' impressions of subordinate ingratiation and ratings of interpersonal facilitation. *Journal of Applied Psychology, 92,* 848–855.

Tsui, A.S. (1999). From the editor. *Academy of Management Journal, 42,* 589–590.

Van Maanen, J., Sorensen, J.B., & Mitchell, T.R. (2007). The interplay between theory and method. *Academy of Management Review, 32,* 1145–1154.

Vigoda-Gadot, E. (2003). *Developments in organizational politics: How political dynamics affect employee performance in modern work sites.* Cheltenham, UK: Edward Elgar.

Vigoda-Gadot, E., & Drory, A. (Eds.). (2006). *Handbook of organizational politics.* Northampton, MA: Edward Elgar.

Voyer, J. (1994). Coercive organizational politics and organizational outcomes: An interpretive study. *Organization Science, 5,* 72–85.

Weber, M. (1947). *The theory of social and economic organizations.* New York: Oxford Press.

Weber, M. (1954). *Max Weber on law in economy and society* (E. Shils & M. Rheinstein, Trans.). New York: Simon and Schuster.

Whetten, D. (2009). An examination of the interface between context and theory applied to the study of Chinese organizations. *Management and Organization Review, 5*(1), 29–55.

2

The Positive Side of Organizational Politics

Wayne A. Hochwarter
Florida State University

To many, the word *politics* is viewed with disdain, conjuring up visions of shady behavior that is manipulative, divisive, and exclusively self-serving. In just one of countless examples, Mencken noted that "a good politician is quite as unthinkable as an honest burglar." Vocational and public policy researchers corroborate society's increasingly negative opinions by documenting politicians' status as one of the least trusted occupations (Bottery, 2003; Grint, 2005; Hay, 2007). Noting their treacherous status, Qvortrup (2009) argued that "alongside car salesmen and lobbyists, politicians are probably the least trusted profession" (p. 63). Finally, Stoker (2010) advocated for research in social politics despite the fact that it represents "a subject matter that many of our fellow citizens assert to despise" (p. 43).

Research in the organizational sciences largely has run parallel to other academic disciplines, opting for a less than flattering treatment of the construct (Yang, 2009). Specifically, political behavior has been cast in a largely pejorative light, with research focusing on its pervasiveness (Buchanan & Badham, 2008; Ferris, Adams, Kolodinsky, Hochwarter, & Ammeter, 2002; Gandz & Murray, 1980) and adverse influence on individuals as well public and private entities (Ferris & Hochwarter, 2011; Koehler & Rainey, 2008). As a practical example, von Pechman (1953) noted that advancement attempts based on political wrangling, rather than merit, were impractical and were to be swiftly reprimanded. With few exceptions, this view has been espoused by the majority of those occupying decision-making positions over the years.

In this chapter, a uniquely different approach is taken. Specifically, the focus is placed on the characteristics of political activity (i.e., perceptions and actor behaviors) that favorably impact individuals, groups, and organizations (Gotsis & Kortezi, 2010; Vredenburgh & Shea-VanFossen, 2010) rather than on their recognized destructive influences (Ferris et al., 2002). Building on recent discussions (Fedor, Maslyn, Farmer, & Bettenhausen, 2008; Ferris & Hochwarter, 2011; Kurchner-Hawkins & Miller, 2006), a multidisciplinary approach (e.g., psychology, personality, stress and trauma, neuroscience, social influence, intra- and interpersonal dynamics, and anthropology) is incorporated to the explanation of positive political behavior in organizations.

In particular, the complexity associated with the politics process (Ferris et al., 2002), which recognizes the absorption of both person and situational elements, requires an expansive approach to be of any consequence to science and practice (Hochwarter, Ferris, Zinko, Arnell, & James, 2007). As a consequence, scholarship is enhanced by making more explicable a phenomenon typically avoided by scholars in contemporary thought (Fedor & Maslyn, 2002). Likewise, practitioners benefit by gaining a richer appreciation of the intricacies associated with political behavior that unquestionably take place and add considerable value when viewed in the appropriate light (Buchanan, 2008; Dubrin, 2009). In this regard, industry leaders profit by understanding what it is, what it can do, and what can be done with it (Pfeffer, 2010a, 2010b) to maximize employee and organizational benefit. In spite of popular support for its demise (Buchanan, 2008), scholars and practitioners recently have become aware that sweeping politics under the rug causes more damage than simply creating lumpy carpets (Brandon & Seldman, 2004).

Admittedly, this chapter focuses on the conceptual underpinnings, interactions, and outcomes of positive politics in organizations (Buchanan & Badham, 1999; Hochwarter, 2003). As a result, caveats inherent in such a focus warrant brief discussion. First, with the exceptions of recounting historic underpinnings, only limited treatment is given to the negative aspects of politics established in prior studies. Scholarly discussions of destructive politics (e.g., Fairholm, 2009; Hall, Hochwarter, Ferris, & Bowen, 2004) are readily available (Cropanzano & Li, 2006; Klein, 1988), as are popular conversations of the topic (Serven, 2002).

Second, the focus is on politics at the individual level. Burns and Stalker's (1961) seminal work recognized the firm as a political system, pitting individuals against the larger organization for resources, whereas Pfeffer (1981) described business entities in terms of a collection of political actors. Over the years, a common impediment in developing a program of study has been the inability to disentangle the people from the place, both of which are critical. Admittedly, group- and organization-level research focusing on politics perceptions and behaviors is both important and vastly underrepresented in the literature when compared to its influence in practice (Lux, Crook, & Woehr, 2011). In this chapter, macrolevels (e.g., group, organization, and system) serve predominantly as additional degrees of support for individual-level arguments rather than a focal emphasis. If interested, multilevel conceptualizations of politics exist in the published literature and are worthy of consideration (Ferris et al., 2002; Lux, Ferris, Brouer, Laird, & Summers, 2008).

ORGANIZATIONAL POLITICS—WHY THE BAD RAP?

From a societal standpoint, *politics* evokes images of cigar smoke plumes, impassioned backroom negotiations, and final brokerage of deals that benefit the few at the expense of the many (Elden, 1981). Over 120 years ago, Atkinson (1888) prophetically argued that most political enterprises end up being ravaged by actors best described as rogues and rascals (p. 13). Images of Boss Tweed corruptly leading the Democratic Party's political machine in New York during the late-nineteenth century remain vivid to public administration scholars (Ackerman, 2005) and lay students of civic history.

Chicago's Richard J. Daley, the last of the big-city machine politicians, relied on his associations with local precinct captains for electoral success, who, incidentally, held patronage jobs with the city as long as the voting outcomes remained supportive (Cohen & Taylor, 2001). In criticizing the ascension to higher office shared by many, both at the time of publication and at present, Karl (1973) noted, "But it is politics, among the oldest and certainly the lowliest of American professions, which must produce them. That dung heap which is patronage, corruption, partisanship, and self-serving aggrandizement of raw power must generate an absolute minimum of two lilies every four years" (p. 416).

Building on this view, discussions of workplace politics of the early-twentieth century served as the road map for research that continues in contemporary settings. For example, Bojack's (1922) book, aptly titled *Dumbells of Business*, noted that "pin-headedness, tale peddling, and office politics are barnacles on the barque of Business, and the Firm that does not scrap them off is doomed to decay" (p. 17). In describing the experience of others' behavior, Barrett (1918) counseled, "When you come in contact with an establishment where each man's eye is centered only on his pay-envelope, there you will find petty jealousy, office politics, sycophancy, and back biting. If you're working in such an atmosphere, get out: that's my advice" (p. 60).

Dalton (1959) argued that an individual's success in both settings is predicated largely on the "organization he has been able to gather around him" (p. 57) rather than consistent contributions to the sponsoring enterprise. In a more contemporary sense, media depictions (e.g., reality television, self-help books) egregiously overinflate the frequency and intensity of work politicking (Thackaberry, 2003) as a thinly veiled mechanism to increase viewership and sales.

From a scholarly perspective, theory development has been shaped by the prominent writings of Machiavelli (1998), who regarded influence as manipulation and exploitation, and Hobbes (1651/1985), who believed that social interactions are motivated largely by the need to secure favorable advantage at all costs (e.g., "every man against every man," p. 64). In contemporary research, reviews and meta-analytic studies (Ferris et al., 2002; Miller, Rutherford, & Kolodinsky, 2008) have offered consistent (albeit not overwhelming) support for negative politics–outcomes bivariate relationships (Buchanan & Badham, 2008; Kacmar, Bacharach, Harris, & Zivnuska, 2010). Collectively, these findings have allowed scholars to classify organizational politics perceptions as a hindrance stressor (Chang, Rosen, & Levy, 2009), capable of causing and exacerbating strain reactions (LePine, Podsakoff, & LePine, 2005; Rosen, Harris, & Kacmar, 2009).

Coupled with the *bad-side* research emphasis adopted in the behavioral sciences (Schaufeli & Greenglass, 2001; Wright, 2003), the aforementioned factors (i.e., political science theory, adherence to leadership writings that focused on self-interests, early business writer's view of office politics, and media depictions) have reinforced the implicitly negative perception of organizational politics (Vredenburgh & Shea-VanFossen, 2010). However, despite the accumulated evidence, arguing for consensus (i.e., politics perceptions or political behavior remains unremittingly undesirable) would be highly objectionable given the narrow focus embraced in most research to date (Drory & Vigoda-Gadot, 2010).

Neglect notwithstanding, support for studying positive politics is well recognized in both science (Fedor et al., 2008) and practice (Pfeffer,

2010a, 2010b). As a result of the heightened control, politically active employees may view others' egocentric activity as a challenge stressor capable of increasing personal growth and motivation (Parker, Jimmieson, & Amiot, 2010).

THE PURSUIT OF BALANCE: WHY IT WON'T GO AWAY, WHY IT SHOULDN'T GO AWAY

Largely unspoken and considered fractionally segmented in prior research (Ferris et al., 2002), scholars have recognized political activity as a principal component of a firm's social context. Gotsis and Kortezi (2010) argued that politics epitomizes a multilevel work reality with the potential to influence myriad organizational actions and decisions. Chang et al. (2009) acknowledged the universality and wide-ranging influence of political behavior. Finally, Hochwarter and Thompson (2010) described the widespread phenomenon essential to company success.

Others have described political activity as an instinctive characteristic of social interaction (Vredenburgh & Shea-VanFossen, 2010) and an accepted reality invariant across individuals and situations (Ferris, Bowen, Treadway, Hochwarter, Hall, & Perrewé, 2006). Drory and Vigoda-Gadot (2010) classified organizational politics as an innately human activity driven by both self- and social motivations. Confirming its prevalence, Buchanan's (2008) study found that only 12% of surveyed British managers reported that "my organization is relatively free of politics" (p. 8). Taken in their entirety, these studies reinforce Ferris and Kacmar (1992), who argued that "politics in organizations is simply a fact of life" (p. 93).

RECENT SUPPORT FOR THE CONSIDERATION OF POSITIVE POLITICS

Beyond simply documenting its pervasiveness, scholars have argued for the positive impact of organizational politics (Drory & Vigoda-Gadot, 2010; Liu, Liu, & Wu, 2010) in both applied and academic settings. Practically speaking, how many newly minted PhDs have received particular consideration for a faculty position because of a highly respected advisor's influence? Similarly, how many employees have retained their jobs because of their chief executive officer's (CEO's) ability to secure state and federal grants relative to others less adept? Lastly, how many entry-level employees have risen to executive levels by knowing which ropes to jump along the way? In support of its practicality, Fairholm (2009, p. xiv) concluded that "all of us most of the time engage in organizational politics as we negotiate our way through our career."

In terms of career efficacy, Bacharach and Lawler (1998) argued that political behavior is required for recognition and advancement. Hochwarter and Thompson (2010) suggested that political behavior is endemic to healthy employee functioning, in many cases as a result of its self-sacrificing motives (Buchanan & Badham, 2008). In support of a positive influence–occupational success link, meta-analytic research (Ng, Eby, Sorensen, & Feldman, 2005) documented relationships between political knowledge and skills (i.e., supervisor-focused political tactics) and both salary and career satisfaction.

Sullivan, Forret, and Mainiero's (2007) study found that laid-off workers experienced greater regret with regard to their discretionary political behavior (i.e., limited networking, limited social wisdom) compared with those still employed. In other research, political behavior was positively correlated with job performance (Hochwarter, Ferris, Zinko, James, & Platt, 2007; Study 1), while over 90% of managers in Buchanan's (2008) study agreed that "most managers, if they want to succeed, have to play politics at least part of the time" (p. 57).

Finally, Fedor et al. (2008) examined the relationship between perceived negative and perceived positive politics as well as their unique ability to predict job satisfaction, supervisor satisfaction, coworker satisfaction, and psychological contract fulfillment. Described as political behavior that benefits rather than harms the employees, the associated activities of positive politics (e.g., communication, working behind the scenes) closely mirror those found in negative scales. Results established two distinctive politics constructs and found that positive politics perceptions explained outcome variance beyond that attributed to those considered negative. Consistent with prior studies (Fedor & Maslyn, 2002; Hochwarter, 2003; Hochwarter, Ferris, Laird, Treadway, & Gallagher, 2010), Fedor et al.'s research substantiates the existence of politics perceptions, capable of triggering favorable rather than undesirable outcomes.

Although positive politics research has gained considerable momentum (and acceptance) in recent years (Butcher & Clarke, 2006; Ferris & Hochwarter, 2011; Gotsis & Kortezi, 2010), research remains more descriptive than exploratory. In response to scholars' failure to more ardently consider favorable politics (Ferris et al., 2002), Fedor et al. (2008) concluded, "We are still missing a significant portion of the story concerning the effects of political behavior in organizations" (p. 77). In the next several sections, the objective is to extend the discussion of positive politics beyond the specific tactics to an explication of motives, underlying cognitive process, and contextual factors associated with its inherent use. In doing so, the intention is to submit a conceptualization of positive politics that characterizes it as an indispensable component of organizational life, worthy of accelerated scientific consideration.

POLITICAL BEHAVIOR AS HUMAN NATURE

Aristotle stated that "man is by nature a political animal," a quote implying that participation in political behavior, to varying degrees, is characteristic of one's DNA (Cheng, Tracy, & Henrich, 2010). Evolutionary theories, based on the view that interpersonal problems are unraveled by tactics molded principally by natural selection processes (Neuberg, Kenrick, & Schaller, 2010; Sundie, Cialdini, Griskevicius, & Kenrick, 2006), have had limited involvement in social influence studies despite the omnipotence of inheritability. Instead, developmental views of workplace behavior have adopted a Darwinian perspective (Ilies, Arvey, & Bouchard, 2006; Nicholson & White, 2006), which maintains that person–situation resource adaptations divorce those who prosper from those who decay (Ehrlich & Feldman, 2003).

Correspondingly, investigations focusing on the "human characteristics" associated with political activity largely have been scant (Darr & Johns, 2004), despite recognition that instinct and biological makeup influence all social interactions (i.e., from the most trivial to the most imperative; Nicholson, 1997). For example, genetics research has established political engagement's collective biological and sociological underpinnings (Ebstein, Israel, Chew, Zhong, & Knafo, 2010), noting "even seemingly situational variables often have a genetic source" (Judge, Piccolo, & Kosalka,

2009, p. 860). George (2009) concluded that "it is vastly exciting to consider how theorizing and research in organizational behavior might be transformed by taking into account automaticity and the workings of the nonconscious mind" (p. 1335). Accordingly, Nicholson (1997, 2005) argued that scholarship would benefit by isolating the inborn characteristics that predict patterns of human behavior in organizations, irrespective of contextual realities.

In terms of influence motivation, Mintzberg (1985) reasoned that political behavior represents a behavior undertaken to ensure that the fittest will rise to leadership positions in organizations. Vredenburgh and Shea-VanFossen (2010) advocated that our "inherited natures and the internal environments of our work organizations deserve analytic consideration in connection with organizational politics" (p. 28). Evolutional psychology theories, which place particular emphasis on the bidirectional gene–environment interaction (Bjorklund & Pellegrini, 2011), unquestionably play a predominant role in determining when positive politics is calculated and when it is instinctive. Recognizing its deep-rooted human motives, which include influencing and leading (Roberts & Robins, 2000), also provides justification for considering the heritable characteristics of political behavior.

In support of this approach, reviews have supported the developmental and perpetuating role of biology on social behaviors that include exchange (Freese, Li, & Wade, 2003), situational awareness (Chiao, 2011), prosocial behavior (McCullough & Tabak, 2010; Wilson & Wilson, 2007), and empathy (Davis, Luce, & Kraus, 1994), all of which have documented associations with political behavior (Fandt & Ferris, 1990; Grant & Mayer, 2009). Cheng et al. (2010) confirmed that dominance and prestige, motives cooperatively associated with political activity (Nicholson, 1997; Vredenburg & Shea-VanFossen, 2010), represented biological underpinnings of human social order.

Additionally, scholars also have maintained that status and resource pursuits (Adkins & Vaisey, 2009; Taylor, 2009), motives endemic to political participation at work, are neurologically embedded. Moreover, many human predispositions (e.g., coalition management, conflict, empathy, facial communication, manipulation, reciprocity) outlined in prior research (Brown, 1991; Pinker, 2002) often signal the onset and success of politicking (Kiewitz, Restubog, Zagenczyk, & Hochwarter, 2009; Perrewé, Zellars, Ferris, Rossi, Kacmar, & Ralston, 2004).

Finally, among Lawrence and Nohria's (2002) human instincts that shape cognition and conduct are uncertainty reduction and protection motives, both of which represent definitional motives of political behavior (Treadway, Breland, Williams, Wang, & Yang, 2008; Vigoda, 2002). For example, when conflict is seen as the appropriate reaction to perceived resource threat, implementing positive political tactics (e.g., ingratiation, rationalization) may symbolize a more collaborative approach (Nicholson, 1997) relative to those promoting long-term acrimony.

Building on these discussions, Cialdini (2008; Cialdini & Griskevicius, 2010) argued for the existence of six cognitively managed influence principles—authority, commitment and consistency, liking, reciprocity, scarcity, and social proof—thoughtfully deployed to increase persuasion effectiveness. This conceptualization, according to Cialdini and Goldstein (2004), views social influence as a largely automatic (i.e., nonconscious) goal-striving process, which becomes more adept with use over time (Bargh & Chartand, 2000). Research in the organizational politics realm offers appropriate levels of relatedness to characteristics of Cialdini's taxonomy.

For example, the initiation of political behavior rests largely on principles of exchange (Randall, Cropanzano, Bormann, & Birjulin, 1999), perceived liking between dyad partners (Harrell-Cook, Ferris, & Dulebohn, 1999), the accumulation and protection of scarce resources (Hillman, Withers, & Collins, 2009; Liu et al., 2010), and the reduction of social ambiguity (Hochwarter, Ferris, Zinko et al., 2007). At a minimum, these principles promote the realization of affiliation, consistency, and accuracy (Cialdini & Trost, 1998), inherent goals that increase adaptability and improve self-concept regulation (Cialdini & Griskevicius, 2010).

When the aforementioned arguments are considered, it is evident that genetic predispositions influence positive political behaviors in innumerable ways, many of which have yet to receive adequate research attention. Perhaps the strongest evidence for a genetic–political behavior link was outlined by Barkley (2001), who argued that the human phenotype is best viewed as an exchange participant with an impulse for self-control, an instinct for social influence, and a predilection for self-protection. Only by adopting the perspective argued above will science be able to determine, with any certainty, whether the aphorism of the *born politician* has any merit.

POLITICAL BEHAVIOR AS AN ADAPTIVE MECHANISM

In work environments, discrepancies in knowledge and protocol for successful contribution often provoke considerable anxiety (Lord, Diefendorff, Schmidt, & Hall, 2010). Political behaviors represent a practical response, capable of constructively influencing behaviors and outcomes afflicted by organizational ambiguity (Ferris et al., 2002). As a scholarly response to a practical problem, uncertainty reduction has been the most frequently cited benefit of political behavior (Ferris & Hochwarter, 2011). Stated more directly, "the ability to secure information through political behavior has been shown to minimize much of the ambiguity-generated strain experienced on the job" (Hochwarter, Ferris, Zinko et al., 2007, p. 567).

Defined as the exercise of aligning the self with chosen and preferred standards (Vohs & Baumeister, 2004), self-regulation merges the individual and the shifting environment for the purpose of developing focused, goal-directed behavior (Karoly, 1993). At the core of virtually all discussions of successful self-regulation is volition (Baumeister & Heatherton, 1996; Grant & Sonnentag, 2010), which allows for adequate attention to be focused on external constituents (i.e., context) rather than exclusively on the self (Crocker, Moeller, & Burson, 2010). Recently, it has been argued that prosocial individuals are more likely to exercise self-regulation (Balliet & Joireman, 2010) and as a result possess a greater capacity to buffer contextually generated ego-depletion threat (Seeley & Gardner, 2003).

As a self-determination activity, political behavior has drive theory as a conceptual basis (Hull, 1943). As an example, Lawrence (2010) outlined inherent drives possessed by all humans, namely, drives to acquire resources for survival, to defend resources, to develop social relationships, and to understand one's influence in occupied environments. Consistent with the theory, political behavior represents a protective reaction when unsatisfied needs provoke restoration efforts (Treadway et al., 2004). Moreover, its discretionary nature promotes responsibility adoption, initiation, and behavioral restraint when executed appropriately in threat-generating social environments (Baumeister & Vohs, 2007; Hochwarter, Rogers, Summers, Meurs, Perrewé, & Ferris, 2009). Moreover, Drory and Vigoda-Gadot (2010) argued that political behavior has the potential to facilitate ego nurturing and self-regulation.

Predictably, prior research has documented relationships between political behavior and both intrinsic motivation and need for achievement (Treadway et al., 2005), which are person attributes strongly associated with preferred self-regulation outcomes (Bartels & Magun-Jackson, 2009; Deci & Ryan, 2000; Diehl, Semegon, & Schwarzer, 2006). Ferris and colleagues (Ferris, Russ, & Fandt 1989; Ferris, Harrell-Cook, & Dulebohn, 2000) maintained that engagement in organizational politics can serve a multitude of roles, including the maintenance or accumulation of control typically unobtainable as a result of impeding formalities, bureaucracies, or other obstructions.

A valid, and theoretically substantiated (Carver & Scheier, 2005; Dane, 2011; Hochwarter et al., 2010), consequence of contextual engagement is the development of attentional control (see Matthews, Warm, Reinerman, Langheim, & Saxby, 2010 for a review). Defined as "… the ability to organize incoming stimuli in order to maintain a calm state of mind, delay gratification, tolerate change, and create the cognitive and behavioral responses to selected stimuli exclusively" (Luszczynska, Diehl, Gutiérrez-Doña, Kuusinen, & Schwarzer, 2004, p. 556), attention control has been associated with favorable adaptive response to external stress (Eysenck, 2010; Posner & Rothbart, 1998). Alternatively, an inability to generate attentional control has been coupled with dysfunctional rumination (Treynor, Gonzales, & Nolen-Hoeksema, 2003) and heightened anxiety (Wells, 2002).

Given its omnipotence across individuals (i.e., very low–very high) and well-established importance, attentional control represents a behavior considered necessary for self-regulation success (Baskin-Sommers, Zeier, & Newman, 2009; Baumeister & Heatherton, 1996; Hochwarter, Meurs, Perrewé, Royle, & Matherly, 2007). Accordingly, Lord et al. (2010) maintained that "effective self-regulation must allow for both focused attention on current goal-related activities and for rapid reorientation toward new, important information" (p. 546). In terms of managing potentially unsettled work environments, Diehl et al. (2006) argued that attentional control promotes one's ability to directly focus on a particular task or stressor, to manage both internal and external disruptions, and to work toward a desired objective.

Extending this discussion, Hochwarter, Meurs, et al. (2007) confirmed that regulation in the form of attention control (Karoly, 2010) was associated with increased satisfaction, expanded prosocial behavior, decreased tension, and improved mood. A consequence of attentional effectiveness is the ability to successfully manage knowledge gaps present in social environments that are perceived as taxing (Maitlis & Sonenshein, 2010; Sitkin, 2010). More specifically, active participation in this form of influence leads to heightened awareness by impacting sensemaking and sensegiving (Hope, 2010), both of which have been described as aspects of political processes at work (Maitlis & Lawrence, 2007).

Definitionally, sensemaking involves deliberate social engagement undertaken to recognize and adapt to environmental ambiguities (Maitlis, 2005). On the other hand, sensegiving represents behaviors designed to influence others' information collection and construal of meaning and to redirect their pursuit of reality toward a preferred state (Gioia & Chittipeddi, 1991). Objectively, both sensemaking and sensegiving have the pursuit of shared meaning at their core (Balogun & Johnson, 2004), often described as the glue of organizational culture (Weick, 1995, p. 188). In support, Weick (1979) argued that "through the development and structuring of shared meaning and understanding, cycles of interlocked behavior become sensible" (p. 62). According to Lamertz (2002), one viable approach to increase sensemaking is through the activation of socially acceptable influence behavior.

Definitions of organizational politics directly reference the importance of shared meaning (Ammeter, Douglas, Gardner, Hochwarter, & Ferris, 2002; Sederberg, 1984), recognizing its influence on interpretation and shaping of normative behavior (Smircich, 1983). One objective typically sought by political actors when attempting to manage the shared meaning arena is to develop externally perceived legitimacy, especially when it relates to decision making and idea generation (Fedor et al., 2008; Pettigrew, 1977). Buchanan (2008) found that personal reputation at work was attributed largely to perceived effectiveness of political activity. When realized by others, legitimacy has the potential to promote favorable outcomes, affecting the individual, peers, and the organization (Brown, 1998; Buchanan, 2008). In support, Hochwarter, Ferris, Zinko et al. (2007) found that political behavior demonstrated positive effects on uncertainty, emotional exhaustion, and job performance when coupled with favorable levels of reputation.

Complimenting this research, Hoon (2007) found that political behavior, in the form of mobilizing resources and supporting interests deemed most beneficial, helped shape firm strategy. Hope's (2010) qualitative study determined that the political behavior of middle managers (e.g., notably managing resources) influenced transformation by sculpting the sensemaking activities of those responsible for change implementation. Buchanan (2008) documented a number of favorable change-related consequences associated with agent political activity including sensemaking initiatives, such as the pursuit of constructive proposals and managing resistance. Finally, Silvester (2008) argued that political behavior serves an invaluable sensemaking role in increasingly ambiguous environments by expanding belief sharing and building consensus.

MAKING SURE THE WORLD IS A FAIR PLACE THROUGH POLITICAL BEHAVIOR

Vastly underrepresented in the literature is the role that social influence activity, including political behavior, has in restoring what is perceived to be equitable, fair, and just (Fedor et al., 2008). Instead, research has focused largely on the disreputable pursuit of resources and rewards beyond what most would consider deserved (Chang et al., 2009). This neglect is perplexing given the research documenting the predictive influence of perceived reward incongruities on the development and execution of political behavior (Ferris & Hochwarter, 2011; Hochwarter, 2003). Taken one step further, Fedor et al. (2008) inferred "perceptions of organizational justice might come into play in determining whether individuals actually see certain political behavior as positive or not" (p. 89).

Furthermore, O'Leary-Kelly and Griffin (2004) argued that organizational politics represents a response, often triggered by perceived injustice affecting either the focal individual or those in the immediate work environment (Ferris et al., 1989). Ostensibly, both supervisors and subordinates will initiate political behavior to correct an unjust decision (e.g., repeatedly passed over for deserved promotions, wrongly terminated or demoted), especially if the breach is excessive enough to provoke unwarranted distributions of rewards or sanctions (Wei, Liu, Chen, & Wu, 2010).

Evidence for inequity-neutralizing properties of political behavior permeates the existing literature (Drory & Vigoda-Gadot, 2010). Ferris et al. (1989) conceptualized three plausible reactions to perceived politics and unfairness in the workplace, one of which was engagement in the social environment to identify potential opportunities (the others are withdrawal and immersion in work). In environments where justice becomes questioned as a result of others' self-serving activities (Ferris & Hochwarter, 2011), actors have the opportunity to redefine the situation and to mold their behaviors to maximize the acquisition of contextually available outcomes.

In support, Harrell-Cook et al. (1999) confirmed that reactive political activity (i.e., self-promotion) favorably influenced politics perceptions–work outcomes relationships. Similarly, Hochwarter (2003) found that individuals who responded to environments mired with egocentric behavior benefited by participating in political activity (e.g., higher commitment and satisfaction scores). Finally, research has established that an inability to influence decision-making outcomes (e.g., a withdrawal from politics) in environments laden with individualistic behavior predicted declines in job satisfaction (Witt, Andrews, & Kacmar, 2000).

Moreover, the pursuit of fairness restoration via political behavior is consistent with the basic tenets of justice motive theory (Lerner, 2003), which argues that individuals possess a belief in a just world, where deservedness dictates the distribution of rewards and sanctions (Lopes, 2008). When it is perceived that fairness standards have become imbalanced, justice-motivated behaviors, including political tactics, are initiated automatically and heuristically to restore equilibrium (Reichle & Schmitt, 2002). Research acknowledges that these restoration strategies may be considered harmful to social relationships in situations where offensive tactics are exploited (i.e., derogation or blame; van Prooijen, 2010). Given the omnipotence and heritability of other-serving behavior tendencies (Rushton, Russell, & Wells, 1984), it is equally likely that selfless remedies are pursued that are both constructive and externally focused (Gotsis & Kortezi, 2010; Strelan, 2007).

Finally, justice motivation research argues that strategies aimed to restore fairness manifest more evocatively in *high-impact situations*, defined as environments involving considerable deprivation or confiscation of desired resources (Lerner, 2003). Described as an innate need for uncertainty reduction (Thau, Aquino, & Wittek, 2007), uncertainty management theory (Lind & Van den Bos, 2002) argues that information salience directly predicts the onset of ambiguity-reduction behaviors, often in the form of social influence (McGarty, Turner, Oakes, & Haslam, 1993; Westphal & Stern, 2006).

In terms of specific fairness-restoring behavior, Dulebohn and Ferris (1999) found that voice served as a form of influence that favorably affected perceptions of justice. When inequity is perceived, "political conduct, then, may involve efforts to restore justice" (O'Leary-Kelly & Griffin,

2004, p. 484). In support, scholars have recognized the influential role of political behavior, both formal and informal (Ammeter et al., 2002), in the development and maintenance of equity relationships in organizations (Chang et al., 2009; Ferris et al., 2002).

In sum, a review of the existing research base confirms that studies linking politics perceptions and fairness are abundant (Cropanzano, Howes, Grandey, & Toth, 1997; Vigoda-Gadot & Talmud, 2010; Chapter 5 in this volume), with considerably less work focusing on positive political behaviors as potential remedies. Despite its underrepresented status in the literature, modeling positive political behavior–fairness relationships represents an important scholarly and practical endeavor (Ferris & Hochwarter, 2011). In this regard, researchers may find value in extending Fedor et al. (2008), who maintained that perceived fairness may serve as a conduit for helping employees determine the extent and influence of leader's positive political behaviors, assessing the extent to which they are beneficial or detrimental.

WHAT HAPPENS WHEN THE POLITICAL LANDSCAPE IS A DESERT?

Making sense and restoring justice, as noted already, are predicated on the accrual of contextual information. Accordingly, Dierdorff, Rubin, and Bachrach (in press) confirmed that the immediate task environment possesses informational elements, including availability, cue agreement, ambiguity, and self-direction accumulated to gauge fairness. Presumably, instances exist where the context offers few (or no) signals to direct behavior (Kelley, 1973; Buenger, Daft, Conlon, & Austin, 1996), potentially leading to detrimental individual outcomes (Rusbult & Van Lange, 2003).

By extension, these effects become increasingly pronounced when examined within the context of newcomer adjustment behavior (Simosi, 2010). For example, Miller and Jablin (1991) argued that the ambiguity and conflict associated with information inadequacies influences satisfaction, productivity, and intention to remain. More recently, Saks, Gruman, and Cooper-Thomas (2011) found that newcomers who proactively sought to reduce information incongruities received outcomes predictive of career success.

Rather than assuming passivity, cognitive gaps can be filled in information-deficient environments through self-directed means. Gong, Cheung, Wang, and Huang (in press) found that forward-thinking employees used feedback-seeking strategies, took control of opportunities, and avoided settings that hindered goal achievement. Similarly, Aspinwall and Taylor (1997) argued that proactive employees accumulate information and support resources in advance of potentially demanding events that bring about rapid depletion.

Berger and Calabrese (1975) reported that "high levels of uncertainty cause increases in information-seeking behavior. As uncertainty levels decline, information-seeking behavior decreases" (p. 103). Also, Morrison and Bies (1991) contended that employees can garner heightened levels of control over both processes and results by purposefully seeking contextual feedback. Similarly, proactively pursuing information can escalate contextual awareness and familiarity, thereby stimulating innovation and resourceful problem solving (Kammeyer-Mueller, Livingston, & Liao, 2011; Ruscio, Whitney, & Amabile, 1998).

As a form of impression management motive (Bozeman & Kacmar, 1997), political behavior represents a self-regulatory approach to securing information when the context is devoid of such information (Ferris, Treadway, Perrewé, Brouer, Douglas, & Lux, 2007; Seibert, Kraimer, & Crant, 2001). In this regard, political behavior possesses several of the rudiments of proactive coping described in the literature (Aspinwall, 2005). For example, Aspinwall and Taylor's (1997) five-stage model has resource accumulation as its first step. The objective here is to gather the skills and resources (e.g., personal skills, social skills, and abilities) necessary to ward off the effects of future stressors.

Resource accrual represents an important element in proactive political behavior, such that "aggressively mobilizing resources to match or exceed environmental demands is preferred" (Ferris & Hochwarter, 2011, p. 451), relative to passive reactions to information deprivation. Buchanan and Badham (1999) argued that situations characterized by information uncertainty tend to trigger political behavior. Appropriately, active political behavior contributes to the acquisition of scarce resources including information (Dulebohn & Ferris, 1999).

Attention and recognition and initial appraisal of stressors, which represent the next two stages, involve the increased use of environmental screening to determine whether a threat is imminent. These are explained largely as a result of heightened engagement (Buchanan, 2008), and research has documented the favorable relationship between political behavior and the identification and interpretation of social cues (Treadway et al., 2004). Preliminary coping behaviors, observably, are implemented to either eliminate or minimize threat or information-based ambiguity. Political behavior, too, has been described as a control-seeking series of activities undertaken to minimize threat (Ferris, Fedor, & King, 1994). In support, Vredenburgh and Shea-VanFossen (2010) asserted that employees will augment conventional workplace influence strategies with political behavior to minimize ambiguity in settings devoid of informational signals considered necessary.

The final step involves stressor elicitation and use, which is critical in appraisal revision and strategy modification (Aspinwall, 2011). Hochwarter (2003) noted that an important objective of exercising political behavior in information-deficient settings is to ensure confidence that a level of knowledge exists that is commensurate with peers. In terms of particular behaviors, Miller and Jablin's (1991) theoretical model contains testing limits, indirect approaches, surveillance, observation, disguising conversations, the use of third parties, and overt methods as specific information-seeking tactics, each of which is easily blended into a political behavior repertoire (Buchanan, 2008; Dean & Sharfman, 1993).

I GET BY (AND SO DO MANY OTHERS) WITH A LOT OF HELP FROM MY FRIENDS—I

From the moment that undergraduates set foot on hallowed university grounds, the intrinsic merit of networking is accentuated, garnering *overkill* status by many. In terms of scholarly treatment, the role of relationship building has been the subject of considerable cross-disciplinary discussion, much of which can be traced back approximately 100 years (Burgess, 1916; Hilton, 1914). As noted by Barnes (1906), "Well-controlled and intelligently directed action has much to do with controlling the self and others" (p. 73). Contemporary treatments offer a similar account of the capital-generating process (Lin & Erickson, 2008), describing network development as a vehicle to secure desired resources and outcomes (Zhang, 2010). Cheung and Chan (2010) argued that social capital is essential to personal accomplishment, most notably, when it promotes opportunities for resource exchange and accrual.

Furthermore, Luthans, Hodgetts, and Rosenkratz (1988) reported that successful managers spent the majority of work time involved in network-building activities. In terms of success prediction, Seibert, Kraimer, and Liden (2001) found that network-developed social resources were favorably associated with salary, the number of promotions, and career satisfaction. Likewise, Blickle, Witzi, and Schneider (2009) documented the positive relationship between employee networking activity and income, hierarchical standing, and career contentment, whereas Fang, Duffy, and Shaw's (2011) socialization model predicts that networking promotes career success through learning and assimilation. Finally, networking was identified as a political approach characterized as less blatant, more socially appropriate, reliant on expertise, and legitimate (Zanzi, Arthur, & Shamir, 1991) relative to more caustic strategies.

In both description and practice, political behavior represents an important component of network building, especially when the impact of resource exchange is considered (Ferris & Hochwarter, 2011). Foundationally, much of the research can be traced to Froman's (1962) resource conceptualization of politics (Farrell & Petersen, 1982). As an extension, Pfeffer (1981) described political behavior in terms of tactics deployed to gain, enhance, and manipulate power and other resources to ensure favored results. Moreover, Luthans et al. (1988) reported interacting with outsiders and political behavior as networking strategies designed to influence asset accumulation.

Hunt and Osborn (1980) noted that the exchanges occurring among peers may be better described as political behavior, developed to manage the flow of uncertainty-reducing resources. Willem and Scarbrough (2006) argued that networking outcomes promote contextual information gathering often used to develop, exploit, and evaluate political strategies. Finally, Cohen and Bradford (1990) argued that political behavior promotes reciprocity-based mutual exchanges that help establish dyadic relationships, which are most accurately described as dutiful and obligatory.

As confirmed, disentangling the complex political behavior–capital accrual relationship remains a challenge worthy of a researcher's attention (Ammeter et al., 2002). For example, Ferris and Hochwarter (2011) recently argued for a perpetually evolving relationship (e.g., political skill ↔ social capital), amenable to spontaneous and abrupt reshaping. Less ambiguous is the reality that political behavior is essential to the accumulation of social capital (Ferris, Perrewé, Anthony, & Gilmore, 2000; Liu et al., 2010), given its documented instrumentality on resource accrual (e.g., support, information access, beneficial referrals; Oh, Labianca, & Chung, 2006).

As examples of such an effect, Ammeter et al. (2002) argued that leaders who effectively use political behavior are more adept at developing and using comprehensive networks to better manage resources. Ferris et al. (2007) outlined the inherent relationship between social development and influence behavior, whereas others recognize network building as one of many positive political behaviors (Gunn & Chen, 2006). Finally, Vredenburg and Shea-VanFossen (2010) argued that social capital, developed as a result of positive political behavior, promotes relationship building, conflict resolution, and effective persuasion.

I GET BY (AND SO DO MANY OTHERS) WITH A LOT OF HELP FROM MY FRIENDS—II

To date, most research has focused on outcomes associated with either perceptions or actual participation in political activity (Ferris & Hochwarter, 2011). Receiving considerably less attention is the effect of influential other's political perceptions and behaviors on the target employees. In this regard, workplace realities suggest that a supervisor's active management of the social milieu can produce a wide range of subordinate rewards (or punishments), some of which only are loosely associated with actual contribution. Moreover, it is assumed that there are situations where subordinates simply do not possess the influence capabilities needed to maximally contribute to the social domain, and, thus, subsequently realize outcomes considered desirable without some form of assistance.

Supervisors may be particularly helpful in this regard, given their documented ability to manage the accumulation and distribution of company resources (Spreitzer, 1996). In support of such an association, Podolny and Baron (1997) contended that "many organizational ties, such as relations to supervisors and mentors, involve access to resources and conferral of social identity, insofar as normative expectations of superiors and mentors have strong implications for how an individual perceives his or her identity in the organization" (p. 675). Additionally, Bowles (2006) described a situation of network reciprocity in which individuals work for the benefit of others, assuming that these good deeds would result in heightened collaboration and effectiveness.

The few studies that have examined the phenomenon found that supervisors' negative political behavior (e.g., "when my supervisor communicates with me, it is to make himself/herself look better, not to help me") demonstrated injurious effects on dyadic relationships (Ferris & Kacmar, 1992), largely as a result of increasing subordinate job anxiety and dissatisfaction (Ferris, Frink, Bhawuk, Zhou, & Gilmore, 1996). Accordingly, Jablin (1981) reported that subordinates were less communicative and more dissatisfied with supervisors perceived as political. Finally, research has found that perceived supervisor politics contributed to the deterioration of leader–member exchange relationships (Hochwarter, Kacmar, Treadway, & Watson, 2003).

With few exceptions, this research has cast supervisors and subordinates in adversarial situations, identifying how political behavior can be used as a repressive weapon (e.g., "speaking up may lead to retaliation"; Fedor, Ferris, Harrell-Cook, & Russ, 1998). In contrast, other scholars (i.e., Drory & Vigoda-Gadot, 2010) have advocated a more auspicious view, assuming that some informal acts of influence are less malevolent than documented in past research (Buchanan & Badham, 2008).

Theoretically, the view that leaders participate in political activity to benefit subordinates is consistent with the tenets of social exchange theory (Cropanzano et al., 1997), which maintain that subordinate–supervisor interactions (Liden, Sparrowe, & Wayne, 1997) are mutually supporting. In terms of subordinate benefits associated with supervisor political behavior, Cropanzano and Mitchell (2005) argued, "Social exchange relationships evolve when employers 'take care of employees,' which thereby engenders beneficial consequences" (p. 882).

Based on the assumption that an employee's immediate superior serves as a representation of the organization (Eisenberger, Stinglhamber, Vandenberghe, Sucharski, & Rhoades, 2002), perceived supervisor support theory (PSS) argues that a leadership objective is to seek ways to provide subordinates functional benefits (Maertz, Griffeth, Campbell, & Allen, 2007). The theory further contends that supervisors find value in helping employees (e.g., job completion and personal concerns), offering assistance in the form of support and other resources that contribute to personal welfare and work contribution (Shanock & Eisenberger, 2006).

Reinforcing a direct effect of employee health, Kobasa and Puccetti's (1983) physiological study of high-stress executives found that supervisor support (e.g., "supervisor really stand up for their employees"; Moos, Insel, & Humphrey, 1974) predicted lower illness scores.

Moreover, the objective in developing high PSS relationships is both developmental and obligation forming (Stinglhamber, De Cremer, & Mercken, 2006). However, supervisors' access to resources worthy of redistribution often is unattainable by way of organizationally recognized means. As a result, supervisors are expected to make use of both formal and informal behaviors to establish dyadically supportive relationships (Wayne, Shore, & Liden, 1997). Acknowledging value in such an approach, Behson (2005) reported that informal support was more predictive of employee well-being than formal mechanisms. Similarly, research has recognized that informal mentoring relationships benefit employees more, in terms of effectiveness and compensation, than those in formal relationship arrangements (Ragins & Cotton, 1999).

Podolny and Baron (1997) conceptualized informal political assistance as a resource initiated to develop trust and support, necessary to secure mutually beneficial resources (Hollander & Offerman, 1990). Research has confirmed the importance of informal influence, and its subsequent impact on network development, as a necessary component of high-quality exchange relationships (Graen & Uhl-Bien, 1995; Roberson & Colquitt, 2005). In support, Mehra, Kilduff, and Brass (1998) noted that successful employees require access to both instrumental resources (i.e., job-relevant counsel and advising) and emotional resources (i.e., social backing), which are available predominantly in informal networks.

In most organizations, employees are able to generate formal resources (e.g., explicated rules for conduct, rewards, and participation; Ibarra, 1993) with minimal facilitation from others. On the other hand, access to informal network resources often is complicated, given the ill-defined nature of their creation and maintenance (Ferris, 1979; Han, 1983). If pervasive, inconsistencies in informal resource accessibility can promote a "have" and "have-not" culture (Hoffman, 2008; Smith-Doerr, & Powell, 2005). Consistent with perceived organizational support research (POS; Eder & Eisenberger, 2008), leader political behavior that generates and distributes resources reinforces subordinates' belief that the supervisor is both concerned and appreciative of employee contributions (Aselage & Eisenberger, 2003; Kottke & Sharafinski, 1988).

In this regard, political behavior represents a set of "other-serving" behaviors (Buchanan & Badham, 2008) that increases subordinates' job contentment and ability to contribute. Although maintenance of the exchange relationship benefits each party, the use of informal influence is designed to benefit the subordinate in ways that are likely consistent with the objectives of the organization (i.e., increased performance, lower turnover, reduced stress, higher commitment; Fedor et al., 2008) rather than solely favoring the beneficiary.

This realization calls into question the often assumed view that political behavior causes some to win (i.e., resource benefactors) and some to lose (i.e., companies that must recoup or repair) (Ferris et al., 1989). Further questioning the "rob-Peter-to-pay-Paul" perspective, leader political behavior that benefits subordinates is argued to create resources that did not originally exist, or would otherwise lay dormant without activation. Hence, it is unlikely that others were aggrieved because the likelihood of accruing nonexistent or unexploited resources is minimal.

Finally, recognizing that leader political behavior can increase subordinates' work life quality supports recent discussions linking leader influence behavior and altruism (Moss & Barbuto, 2010; Sparrowe, Soetjipto, & Kraimer, 2006). Defined broadly by Simon (1995) as "behavior that contributes to the fitness of others at the sacrifice of self's fitness" (p. 55), altruism represents one of the most frequently examined human values in social psychology (de Waal, 2008; Piliavin & Charng, 1990). In most research to date, coupling other-serving perspectives with political behavior tends to be viewed as inappropriate along both scholarly and practical lines. However, when considered within a framework based on obligation, mutual benefit, and exchange (Cropanzano & Mitchell, 2005), the importance of other-serving political behavior to initiate and maintain favorable dyadic relationships becomes increasingly evident (Sturmer, Kiel, Snyder, & Omoto, 2005).

SUMMARY

In the previous section, the attempt was to draw attention to the positive aspects of organizational politics, addressing focal issues that have not received research attention to date. Specifically, it was argued that politics should be viewed through rose-colored lenses on several fronts. For example, it was suggested that politics has physiological and genetic underpinnings, leading to reactions that are instinctive rather than calculative, that political behavior serves myriad adaptive purposes affecting contribution and well-being, that participation in political activity possesses justice-restoring properties, that political engagement can fill information gaps that trigger anxiety, that social capital can be generated and used most effectively when coupled with positive political behaviors, and that the political acuity of supervisors likely allows subordinates to secure outcomes unattainable via self-generated tactics.

Obviously, this list is far from complete, as the benefits of political behavior extend well beyond this chapter. Despite this admonition, it is hoped that scholars will find something useful here to guide subsequent research. Building on this discussion, measurement issues are addressed, and empirical support is provided for some of the inferences previously theorized in the next section.

WHAT YOU GET DEPENDS ON WHAT YOU ASK FOR AND HOW YOU ASK

In recent years, scholars have paid more attention to the methods used to assess views of political behavior than to the actual participation in politics itself (Ferris & Hochwarter, 2011). The first generation focused on negative organizational politics (Kacmar & Carlson, 1997; Kacmar & Ferris, 1991), followed by nondirectional work (Hochwarter, Kacmar, Perrewé, & Johnson, 2003) and then, more recently, by positive conceptualizations (Fedor et al., 2008; Hochwarter, 2003). Keeping within the content of this chapter, the results of two preliminary studies are reported that focus on participation in political behavior and supervisor other-serving political activity. These findings are more descriptive (i.e., simple–bivariate) than publication oriented (i.e., moderation–mediation, modeling); hence, they fail to address the complexity of most work settings. Despite their simplicity, the hope is that these findings will stimulate the next generation of research.

The first study consisted of 118 manufacturing employees attending a professional conference. Political behavior was measured using items such as "I spend time at work politicking" and "I use politicking at work to ensure that things get done" (see Hochwarter, 2003; Hochwarter, Ferris, Zinko et al., 2007). Positive relationships between political behavior and several variables existed, which included higher levels of control, personal reputation, adaptability to change, fit, voice, job satisfaction, pay satisfaction, and commitment. Lower levels of turnover intent, depressed mood, and supervisor abuse also were reported. Finally, political behavior was positively associated with socially prescribed perfectionism (e.g., others are expecting perfection of oneself; Sherry, Hewitt, Sherry, Flett, & Graham, 2010). Generated from these simple relationships is the potential to more fully explain the contextual and individual factors that predict the onset and effectiveness of political behavior.

The second study examined the influence of supervisor political behavior that is both proactive and perceived as beneficial to subordinate outcomes. The six-item scale had "My boss has knocked down many of the roadblocks that I have faced by manipulating the system," and "My boss works behind the scenes to make sure that I have what I need to be effective" (Kane, Hampton, Hochwarter, & Ferris, 2011). The sample consisted of 211 largely white-collar employees working in a variety of environments. Individuals reporting benefit from supervisors' politicking also indicated increased autonomy, work engagement, citizenship behavior, job security, effort, and accessibility to resources. Career and job satisfaction were higher, while depressed mood at work and politics perceptions were lower. The processes of initiation, as well as a deeper recognition of benefits accrued by both the subordinates and supervisors, represent issues requiring a systematic, and longitudinal, program of study.

THE ROAD LESS TRAVELED—WHERE DO WE GO FROM HERE?

The existing positive politics research domain has considerable opportunities for cross-disciplinary expansion, some of which are briefly noted. Potentially impactful avenues for research are too numerous to discuss. However, several core issues require attention to catalyze research and build a foundation for subsequent evaluation and expansion. First, the nascent stage of the constructs' development requires research to disentangle the relationship between subordinate-benefiting political behaviors and similar constructs that encapsulate actions that are both organizationally informal and other-serving (Child, Elbanna, & Rodrigues, 2010; Kipnis, Schmidt, & Wilkinson, 1980; Porter, Allen, & Angle, 1981).

Most obvious is to distinguish the properties of positive politics (i.e., individual political behavior and supervisors' subordinate-serving tactics) from the well-established citizenship behaviors that permeate the literature (LePine, Erez, & Johnson, 2002; Organ, 1997). For example, scholars often have included an altruism dimension (Smith, Organ, & Near, 1983), which is defined as helping behavior intended to assist a specific person (e.g., upward, downward, lateral) (Organ, 1988). Support for examining such an association was advanced by Podsakoff, MacKenzie, and Hui (1993), who encouraged research assessing political influences on citizen enactment, irrespective of intentions.

In terms of assessment, Smith et al.'s (1983) measure contains "Helps others who have a heavy work load." Similarly, Hochwarter, Ferris, Zinko et al. (2007) measured political behavior with "I work behind the scenes to see that my work group is taken care of." Despite the obvious overlap, these constructs largely have occupied parallel streams of research (Ferris et al., 1995). In a recent study linking the constructs, Graham and Van Dyne (2006) linked positive political participation with a specific form of citizenship identified as civic virtue. For research to move forward, unrestrained thinking is necessary to capture the intricacies of the positive politics phenomenon.

Second, research would benefit from closer scrutiny of the motives associated with positive politics, and in this chapter some explanations were offered. However, given the universality of human motives (Chulef, Read, & Walsh, 2001), the majority have yet to be scrutinized. Scholars devoted to investigating the motivation–positive politics relationship likely will find that the simple answers remain elusive, obscured by the complexities of both human reasoning and influence behavior. For example, there is considerable evidence suggesting that altruism and other forms of other-serving behavioral orientations are complex, malleable constructs (Smith et al., 1983), with both genetic and situational underpinnings (Koenig, McGue, Krueger, & Bouchard, 2007; Simon, 1990). As a logical step in development, scholars may find value in looking beyond the *how* (i.e., tactics) and *what* of positive politics (i.e., outcomes) by committing greater attention to the *why* (i.e., motives, values, objectives).

Similar to other studies (Buchanan & Badham, 1999; Ferris & Hochwarter, 2011), increased use of idiographic research approaches is advocated to establish foundations while simultaneously allowing for original knowledge to be generated. Survey designs are limited in that they immediately construct boundaries around a particular phenomenon, most of which have been generated as a result of looking back rather than looking ahead or to the sides. This criticism is not directed at politics research alone, as many of the most researched topics in the organizational sciences have been hindsight driven. However, this reality is at least somewhat surprising given scholars' frequently promoted objective of progressive thought.

CONCLUSION

Unquestionably, the dominant conceptualization of politics as a negative experience is warranted, impactful, and expected to generate meaningful research for years to come. The goal of this chapter was not to advocate a complete paradigmatic shift in the way that organizational politics and political behavior are viewed in organizations. Instead, the objective was to offer a balanced view, building on recent studies that advocate positive benefits of political activity. At this point in its development, organizational politics research requires new and insightful approaches that promote richer interpretations of this important phenomenon. It is hoped that this chapter will serve in this capacity.

REFERENCES

Ackerman, K. (2005). *Boss Tweed: The rise and fall of the corrupt pol who conceived the soul of modern New York*. New York: Carroll & Graf Publishers.

Adkins, D., & Vaisey, S. (2009). Toward a unified stratification theory: Structure, genome, and status across human societies. *Sociology Theory, 27*, 99–121.

Ammeter, A., Douglas, C., Gardner, W., Hochwarter, W., & Ferris, G. (2002). Toward a political theory of leadership. *Leadership Quarterly, 13*, 751–796.

Aselage, J., & Eisenberger, R. (2003). Perceived organizational support and psychological contracts: A theoretical integration. *Journal of Organizational Behavior, 24*, 491–509.

Aspinwall, L. (2011). Future-oriented thinking, proactive coping, and the management of potential threats to health and well-being. In S. Folkman (Ed.), *The Oxford handbook of stress, health and coping*. New York: Oxford University Press.

Aspinwall, L. (2005). The psychology of future-oriented thinking: From achievement to proactive coping, adaptation, and aging. *Motivation and Emotion, 29,* 203–235.

Aspinwall, L., & Taylor, S. (1997). A stitch in time: Self-regulation and proactive coping. *Psychological Bulletin, 121,* 417–436.

Atkinson, W. (1888). *The study of politics: An introduction lecture.* Boston: Roberts Brothers.

Bacharach, S., & Lawler, E. (1998). Political alignments in organizations: Contextualization, mobilization, and coordination. In R. Kramer & M. Neale (Eds.), *Power and influence in organizations* (pp. 67–88). Thousand Oaks, CA: Sage Publications.

Balliet, D., & Joireman, J. (2010). Ego deletion reduces pro-selfs' concern with the well-being of others. *Group Processes and Intergroup Relations, 13,* 227–239.

Balogun, J., & Johnson, G. (2004). Organizational restructuring and middle manager sensemaking. *Academy of Management Journal, 47,* 523–549.

Bargh, J., & Chartand, T. (2000). A practical guide to priming and automaticity research. In H. Reis & C. Judd (Eds.), *Handbook of research methods in social psychology* (pp. 253–285). New York: Cambridge.

Barkley, R. (2001). The executive functions and self-regulation: an evolutionary neuropsychological perspective. *Neuropsychology Review, 11,* 1–29.

Barnes, W. (1906). *Personal influence (practical psychology): An aid to health, success, and happiness.* Boston: Foreign Language Press Company.

Barrett, H. (1918). *Modern methods in the office: How to cut corners and save money.* New York: Harper.

Bartels, J., & Magun-Jackson, S. (2009). Approach-avoidance motivation and metacognition self-regulation: The role of need for achievement and fear of failure. *Learning and Individual Differences, 19,* 459–463.

Baskin-Sommers, A., Zeier, J., & Newman, J. (2009). Self-reported attentional control differentiates the major factors of psychopathology. *Personality and Individual Differences, 47,* 626–630.

Baumeister, R., & Heatherton, T. (1996). Self-regulation failure: An overview. *Psychological Inquiry, 7,* 1–15.

Baumeister, R., & Vohs, K. (2007). Self-regulation, ego depletion, and motivation. *Social and Personality Psychology Compass, 1,* 1–14.

Behson, S. (2005). The relative contribution of formal and informal organizational work-family support. *Journal of Vocational Behavior, 66,* 487–500.

Berger, C., & Calabrese, R. (1975). Some exploration in initial interaction and beyond: Toward a developmental theory of communication. *Human Communication Research, 1,* 99–112.

Bjorklund, D., & Pellegrini, A. (2011). Evolutionary perspectives on social development. In P. Smith & C. Hart (Eds.), *The Wiley-Blackwell handbook of childhood social development* (pp. 64–83). Chichester, UK: John Wiley.

Blickle, G., Witzki, A., & Schneider, P. (2009). Mentoring support and power: A three-year predictive field study of protégé networking and career success. *Journal of Vocational Behavior, 74,* 181–189.

Bojack, O. (1922). *Dumbbells of business.* Boston: Stratford.

Bolino, M. (1999). Citizenship and impression management: Good soldiers or good actors? *Academy of Management Review, 24,* 82–98.

Bottery, M. (2003). The management and mismanagement of trust. *Educational Management Administration Leadership, 31,* 245–261.

Bowles, S. (2006). Group competition, reproductive leveling, and the evolution of human altruism. *Science, 314,* 1569–1572.

Bozeman, D., & Kacmar, K. (1997). A cybernetic model of impression management processes in organizations. *Organizational Behavior and Human Decision Processes, 69,* 9–30.

Brandon, R., & Seldman, M. (2004). *Survival of the savvy: High-integrity political tactics for career and company success.* New York: Free Press.

Brown, A. (1998). Narrative, politics and legitimacy in an IT Implementation. *Journal of Management Studies, 35,* 35–58.

Brown, D. (1991). *Human universals.* New York: McGraw-Hill.

Buchanan, D. (2008). You stab my back, I'll stab yours: Management experience and perceptions of organizational political behaviour. *British Journal of Management, 19,* 49–64.

Buchanan, D., & Badham, R. (1999). Politics and organizational change: The lived experience. *Human Relations, 52,* 609–629.

Buchanan, D., & Badham, R. (2008). *Power politics and organizational change: Winning the turf game.* London: Sage Publications.

Buenger, V., Daft, R., Conlon, E., & Austin, J. (1996). Competing values in organizations: Contextual influences and structural consequences. *Organization Science, 7,* 557–576.

Burgess, E. (1916). *The function of socialization in social evolution.* Chicago: University of Chicago.

Burns, T., & Stalker, G. (1961). *The management of innovation.* London: Tavistock.

Butcher, D., & Clarke, M, (2006). The symbiosis of organizational politics and organizational democracy. In E. Vigoda-Gadot & A. Drory (Eds.), *Handbook of organizational politics* (pp. 286–300). Cheltenham, UK: Elgar.

Carver, C., & Scheier, M. (2005). Engagement, disengagement, coping, and catastrophe. In A. Elliot & C. Dweck (Eds.), *Handbook of competence and motivation* (pp. 527–547). New York: Guilford Press.

Chang, D., Rosen, C., & Levy, P. (2009). The relationship between perceptions of organizational politics and employee attitudes, strain, and behavior: A meta-analytic examination. *Academy of Management Journal, 52,* 779–801.

Cheng, J., Tracy, J., & Henrich, J. (2010). Pride, personality, and the evolutionary foundations of human social status. *Evolution and Human Behavior, 31,* 334–347.

Cheung, C., & Chan, R. (2010). Social capital as exchange: It's contribution to morale. *Social Indicators Research, 96,* 205–227.

Chiao, J. (2011). Towards a cultural neuroscience of empathy and prosociality. *Emotion Review, 3,* 111–112.

Child, J., Elbanna, S., & Rodrigues, S. (2010). The political aspects of strategic decision making. In P. Nutt & D. Wilson (Eds.), *The handbook of decision making* (pp. 105–138). Chichester: Wiley.

Chulef, A., Read, S., & Walsh, D. (2001). A hierarchical taxonomy of human goals. *Motivation and Emotion, 25,* 191–232.

Cialdini, R. (2008). *Influence: Science and practice.* Needham Heights, MA: Allyn & Bacon.

Cialdini, R., & Goldstein, N. (2004). Social influence: Compliance and conformity. *Annual Review of Psychology, 55,* 591–621.

Cialdini, R., & Griskevicius, V. (2010). Social influence. In R. Baumeister & E. Finkel (Eds.), *Advanced social psychology: The state of the science* (pp. 385–418). New York: Oxford Press.

Cialdini, R., & Trost, M. (1998). Social influence: Social norms, conformity, and compliance. In: D. Gilbert, S. Fiske, & G. Lindzey (Eds.), *The handbook of social psychology* (pp. 151–192). Boston: McGraw-Hill.

Cohen, A., & Bradford, D. (1990). *Influence without authority.* New York: Wiley & Sons.

Cohen, A., & Taylor, E. (2001). *American pharaoh: Mayor Richard J. Daley—His battle for Chicago and the nation.* Chicago: Back Bay.

Crocker, J., Moeller, S., & Burson, A. (2010). The costly pursuit of self-esteem: Implications for self-regulation. In R. Hoyle (Ed.), *Handbook of personality and self-regulation* (pp. 403–429). Chichester, UK: Wiley.

Cropanzano, R., Howes, J., Grandey, A., & Toth, P. (1997). The relationship of organizational politics and support to work behaviors, attitudes, and stress. *Journal of Organizational Behavior, 18,* 159–180.

Cropanzano, R., & Li, A. (2006). Organizational politics and workplace stress. In E. Vigoda-Gadot & A. Drory (Eds.), *Handbook of organizational politics* (pp. 139–160). Cheltenham, UK: Elgar.

Cropanzano, R., & Mitchell, M. (2005). Social exchange theory: An interdisciplinary review. *Journal of Management, 31,* 1–27.

Dalton, M. (1959). *Men who manage.* New York: John Wiley.

Dane, E. (2011). Paying attention to mindfulness and its effects on task performance in the workplace. *Journal of Management, 37,* 997–1018.

Darr, W., & Johns, G. (2004). Political decision-making climates: Theoretical processes and multi-level antecedents. *Human Relations, 57,* 169–200.

Davis, M., Luce, C., & Kraus, S. (1994). The heritability of characteristics associated with dispositional empathy. *Journal of Personality, 62,* 369–391.

Dean, J., & Sharfman, M. (1993). The relationship between procedural rationality and political behavior in strategic decision making. *Decision Sciences, 24,* 1069–1083.

Deci, E., & Ryan, R. (2000). The "what" and "why" of goal pursuits: Human needs and the self-determination of behavior. *Psychological Inquiry, 11,* 227–268.

de Waal, F. (2008). Putting the altruism back into altruism: The evolution of empathy. *Annual Review of Psychology, 59,* 279–300.

Diehl, M., Semegon, A., & Schwarzer, R. (2006). Assessing attention control in goal pursuit: A component of dispositional self-regulation. *Journal of Personality Assessment, 86,* 306–317.

Dierdorff, E., Rubin, R., & Bacharach, D. (in press). Role expectations as antecedents of citizenship and the moderating effects of work context. *Journal of Management.*

Drory, A., & Vigoda-Gadot, E. (2010). Organizational politics and human resource management: A typology and the Israeli experience. *Human Resource Management Review, 20,* 194–202.

Dubrin, A. (2009). *Political behavior in organizations.* Thousand Oaks, CA: Sage Publications.

Dulebohn, J., & Ferris, G. (1999). The role of influence tactics in perceptions of performance evaluations' fairness. *Academy of Management Journal, 42,* 288–303.

Ebstein, R., Israel, A., Chew, S., Zhong, S., & Knafo, A. (2010). Genetics of human social behavior. *Neuron Review, 65,* 831–843.

Eder, P., & Eisenberger, R. (2008). Perceived organizational support: Reducing the negative influence of coworker withdrawal behavior. *Journal of Management, 34,* 55–68.

Ehrlich, P., & Feldman, M. (2003). Genes and cultures. *Current Anthropology, 44,* 87–108.

Eisenberger, R., Stinglhamber, R., Vandenberghe, C., Sucharski, I., & Rhoades, L. (2002). Perceived supervisor support: Contributions to perceived organizational support and retention. *Journal of Applied Psychology, 87,* 565–573.

Elden, J. (1981). Political efficacy at work: The connection between more autonomous forms of workplace organizations and a more participatory politics. *American Political Science Review, 75,* 43–58.

Elliot, A., & Thrash, T. (2002). Approach-avoidance motivation in personality: Approach and avoidance temperaments and goals. *Journal of Personality and Social Psychology, 82,* 804–818.

Eysenck, M. (2010). Attentional control theory of anxiety: Recent developments. In A. Gruszka, G. Matthews, & B. Szymura (Eds.), *Handbook of individual differences in cognition: Attention, memory, and executive control* (pp. 195–204). New York: Springer.

Fairholm, G. (2009). *Organizational power politics: Tactics in organizational leadership.* Santa Barbara, CA: Praeger.

Fandt, P., & Ferris, G. (1990). The management of information and impressions: When employees behave opportunistically. *Organizational Behavior and Human Decision Processes, 45,* 140–158.

Fang, R., Duffy, M., & Shaw, J. (2011). The organizational socialization process: Review and development of a social capital model. *Journal of Management, 37,* 127–152.

Farrell, D., & Petersen, J. (1982). Patterns of political behavior in organizations. *Academy of Management Review, 7,* 403–412.

Fedor, D., Ferris, G., Harrell-Cook, G., & Russ, G. (1998). The dimensions of politics perception and their organizational and individual predictors. *Journal of Applied Social Psychology, 28,* 1760–1797.

Fedor, D., & Maslyn, J. (2002). Politics and political behavior: Where else do we go from here? In F. Dansereau & F. Yammarino (Eds.), *Research in multi-level issues, Volume 1: The many faces of multi-level issues* (pp. 287–294). Oxford, UK: Elsevier Science/JAI Press.

Fedor, D., Maslyn, J., Farmer, S., & Bettenhausen, K. (2008). The contribution of positive politics to the prediction of employee reactions. *Journal of Applied Social Psychology, 38,* 76–96.

Ferris, G. (1979). The informal organization in strategic decision-making. *International Studies of Management and Organization, 9,* 37–62.

Ferris, G., Adams, G., Kolodinsky, R., Hochwarter, W., & Ammeter, A. (2002). Perceptions of organizational politics: Theory and research directions. In F. Yammarino & F. Dansereau (Eds.), *The many faces of multi-level issues* (pp. 174–254). Oxford, UK: Elsevier Science/JAI Press.

Ferris, G., Bowen, M., Treadway, D., Hochwarter, W., Hall, A., & Perrewé, P. (2006). The assumed linearity of organizational phenomena: Implications for occupational stress and well-being. In P. Perrewé & D. Ganster (Eds.), *Research in occupational stress and well-being* (pp. 205–232). Oxford, UK: Elsevier Science Ltd.

Ferris, G., Fedor, D., & King, T. (1994). A political conceptualization of managerial behavior. *Human Resource Management Review, 4,* 1–34.

Ferris, G., Frink, D., Bhawuk, D., Zhou, J., & Gilmore, D. (1996). Reactions of diverse groups to politics in the workplace. *Journal of Management, 22,* 23–44.

Ferris, G., Harrell-Cook, G., & Dulebohn, J. (2000). Organizational politics: The nature of the relationship between politics perceptions and political behavior. In S. Bacharach & E. Lawler (Eds.), *Research in the sociology of organizations* (pp. 89–130). Stamford, CT: JAI Press.

Ferris, G., & Hochwarter, W. (2011). Organizational politics. In S. Zedeck (Ed.), *APA handbook of industrial and organizational psychology* (Vol. 3, pp. 435–459). Washington, DC: American Psychological Association.

Ferris, G., & Kacmar, K. (1992). Perceptions of organizational politics. *Journal of Management, 18,* 93–116.

Ferris, G., Perrewé, P., Anthony, W., & Gilmore, D. (2000). Political skill at work. *Organizational Dynamics, 28,* 25–37.

Ferris, G., Russ, G., & Fandt, P. (1989). Politics in organizations. In R. Giacalone & P. Rosenfeld (Eds.), *Impression management in the organization* (pp. 143–170). Hillsdale, NJ: Lawrence Erlbaum.

Ferris, G., Treadway, D., Perrewé, P., Brouer, R., Douglas, C., & Lux, S. (2007). Political skill in organizations. *Journal of Management, 33,* 290–320.

Freese, J., Li, J., & Wade, L. (2003). The potential relevances of biology to social inquiry. *Annual Review of Sociology, 29,* 233–256.

Froman, L. (1962). *People and politics.* Englewood Cliffs, NJ: Prentice-Hall.

Gandz, J., & Murray, V. (1980). The experience of workplace politics. *Academy of Management Journal, 23,* 237–251.

George, J. (2009). The illusion of will in organizational behavior research: Nonconscious processes and job design. *Journal of Management, 35,* 1318–1339.

Gioia, D., & Chittipeddi, K. (1991). Sensemaking and sense-giving in strategic change initiation. *Strategic Management Journal, 12,* 433–448.

Gong, Y., Cheung, S., Wang, M., & Huang, J. (in press). Unfolding the proactive process for creativity: Integration of the employee proactivity, information exchange, and psychological safety perspectives. *Journal of Management.*

Gotsis, G., & Kortezi, Z. (2010). Ethical considerations in organizational politics: Expanding the perspective. *Journal of Business Ethics, 93,* 497–517.

Graen, G., & Uhl-Bien, M. (1995). Relationship-based approach to leadership: Development of leader–member exchange (LMX) theory of leadership over 25 years: Applying a multi-level multi-domain perspective. *Leadership Quarterly, 6,* 219–247.

Graham, J., & Van Dyne, L. (2006). Gathering information and exercising influence: Two forms of civic virtue organizational citizenship behavior. *Employee Responsibilities and Rights Journal, 18,* 89–109.

Grant, A., & Mayer, D. (2009). Good soldiers and good actors: Prosocial and impression management motives as interactive predictors of affiliative citizenship behavior. *Journal of Applied Psychology, 94,* 900–912.

Grant, A., & Sonnentag, S. (2010). Doing good buffers against feeling bad: Prosocial impact compensates for negative task and self-evaluations. *Organizational Behavior and Human Decision Processes, 111,* 13–22.

Grint, K. (2005). Problems, problems, problems: The social construction of "leadership." *Human Relations, 58,* 1467–1495.

Gunn, J., & Chen, S. (2006). A micro-political perspective of strategic management. In E. Vigoda-Gadot & A. Drory (Eds.), *Handbook of organizational politics* (pp. 209–229). Cheltenham, UK: Elgar.

Hall, A., Hochwarter, W., Ferris, G., & Bowen, M. (2004). The dark side of politics in organizations. In R. Griffin & A. O'Leary-Kelly (Eds.), *The dark side of organizational behavior* (pp. 237–261). San Francisco: Jossey-Bass.

Han, P. (1983). The informal organization you've got to live with. *Supervisory Management, 28,* 25–28.

Harrell-Cook, G., Ferris, G., & Dulebohn, J. (1999). Political behaviors as moderators of the perceptions of organizational politics-work outcomes relationships. *Journal of Organizational Behavior, 20,* 1093–1105.

Hay, C. (2007). *Why we hate politics.* Cambridge, UK: Polity Press.

Higgins, E. (2000). Making a good decision: Value from fit. *American Psychologist, 55,* 1217–1230.

Hillman, A., Withers, M., & Collins, B. (2009). Resource dependence theory: A review. *Journal of Management, 35,* 1404–1427.

Hilton, W. (1914). *Applied psychology: Power of mental imagery.* San Francisco: Applied Psychology Press.

Hobbes, T. (1651/1985). *Leviathan.* London: Penguin.

Hochwarter, W. (2003). The interactive effects of pro-political behavior and politics perceptions on job satisfaction and affective commitment. *Journal of Applied Social Psychology, 33,* 1360–1378.

Hochwarter, W., Ferris, G., Laird, M., Treadway, D., & Gallagher, V. (2010). Non-linear politics perceptions - work outcome relationships: A three-study, five-sample investigation. *Journal of Management, 36,* 740–763.

Hochwarter, W., Ferris, G., Zinko, R., James, M., & Platt, B. (2007). Reputation as a moderator of the political behavior–work outcomes relationships: A two-study investigation with convergent results. *Journal of Applied Psychology, 92,* 567–576.

Hochwarter, W., Kacmar, C., Perrewé, P., & Johnson, D. (2003). Perceived organizational support as a mediator of the relationship between politics perceptions and work outcomes. *Journal of Vocational Behavior, 63,* 438–465.

Hochwarter, W., Kacmar, K., Treadway, D., & Watson, T. (2003). It's all relative: The distinction and prediction of politics perceptions across levels. *Journal of Applied Social Psychology, 33,* 1995–2016.

Hochwarter, W., Meurs, J., Perrewé, P., Royle, T., & Matherly, T. (2007). Attention control as a neutralizer of the anxiety-provoking consequences of others' perceived entitlement behavior. *Journal of Managerial Psychology, 22,* 506–528.

Hochwarter, W., Rogers, L., Summers, J., Meurs, J., Perrewé, P., & Ferris, G. (2009). Personal control antidotes to the strain consequences of generational conflict as a stressor. *Career Development International, 14,* 465–486.

Hochwarter, W., & Thompson, K. (2010). The moderating role of optimism on politics-outcomes relationships: A test of competing perspectives. *Human Relations, 63,* 1–24.

Hoffman, E. (2008). The "haves" and "have-not's within the organization. *Law and Contemporary Problems, 71,* 53–64.

Hollander, E., & Offerman, L. (1990). Power and leadership in organizations. *American Psychology, 45,* 179–189.

Hoon, C. (2007). Committees as strategic practice: The role of strategic conversation in a public administration. *Human Relations, 60,* 921–952.

Hope, O. (2010). The politics of middle management sensemaking and sensegiving. *Journal of Change Management, 10,* 195–215.

Hull, C. (1943). *Principles of behavior.* New York: Appleton-Century-Crofts.

Hunt, J., & Osborn, R. (1980). A multiple-influence approach to leadership for managers. In P. Hersey & J. Stinson (Eds.), *Perspectives in leadership effectiveness* (pp. 47–72). Athens: Ohio University Press.

Ibarra, H. (1993). Personal networks of women and minorities in management: A conceptual framework. *Academy of Management Review, 18,* 56–87.

Ilies, R., Arvey, R., & Bouchard, T. (2006). Darwinism, behavioral genetics, and organizational behavior: A review and agenda for future research. *Journal of Organizational Behavior, 27,* 121–141.

Jablin, F. (1981). An exploratory study of subordinates' perceptions of supervisory politics. *Communication Quarterly, 29,* 269–275.

Judge, T., Piccolo, R., & Kosalka, T. (2009). The bright and dark sides of leader traits: A review and theoretical extension of the leader trait paradigm. *Leadership Quarterly, 20,* 855–875.

Kacmar, K., Bacharach, D., Harris, K., & Zivnuska, S. (2011). Fostering good citizenship through ethical leadership: Exploring the moderating role of gender and organizational politics. *Journal of Applied Psychology, 96,* 633–642.

Kacmar, K., & Carlson, D. (1997). Further validation of the Perceptions of Politics Scale (POPS): A multi-sample approach. *Journal of Management, 23,* 627–658.

Kacmar, K., & Ferris, G. (1991). Perceptions of Organizational Politics Scale (POPS): Development and construct validation. *Educational and Psychological Measurement, 51,* 193–205.

Kammeyer-Mueller, J., Livingston, B., & Liao, H. (2011). Perceived similarity, proactive adjustment, and organizational socialization. *Journal of Vocational Behavior, 78,* 225–236.

Kane, R., Hampton, H., Hochwarter, W., & Ferris, G. (2011). *Contextual boundaries of the political environment: The role of supervisor political support.* Paper presented at the Academy of Management, 70th Annual National Meeting, San Antonio.

Karl, B. (1973). Review: The politics of leadership. *Reviews in American History, 1,* 415–422.

Karoly, P. (1993). Mechanisms of self-regulation: A systems view. *Annual Review of Psychology, 44,* 23–52.

Karoly, P. (2010). Psychopathology as dysfunctional self-regulation: When resilience resources are compromised. In J. Reich, A. Zautra, & J. Hall (Eds.), *Handbook of adult resilience* (pp. 146–180). New York: Guilford Press.

Kelley, H. (1973). The process of causal attribution. *American Psychologist, 28,* 107–128.

Kiewitz, C., Restubog, S., Zagenczyk, T., & Hochwarter, W. (2009). The interactive effects of psychological contract breach and organizational politics on perceived organizational support: Evidence from two longitudinal studies. *Journal of Management Studies, 46,* 806–834.

Kipnis, D., Schmidt, S., & Wilkinson, I. (1980). Intraorganizational influence tactics: Explorations in getting one's way. *Journal of Applied Psychology, 65,* 440–452.

Klein, J. (1988). The myth of the corporate political jungle: Politicization as a political strategy. *Journal of Management Studies, 25,* 1–12.

Kobasa, S., & Puccetti, M. (1983). Personality and social resources in stress resistance. *Journal of Personality and Social Psychology, 45,* 839–850.

Koehler, M., & Rainey, H. (2008). Interdisciplinary foundations of public service motivation. In J. Perry & A. Hondeghem (Eds.), *Motivation in public management: The call of public service* (pp. 33–55). Oxford, UK: Oxford University Press.

Koenig, L., McGue, M., Krueger, R., & Bouchard, T. (2007). Religiousness, antisocial behavior, and altruism: Genetic and environmental mediation. *Journal of Personality, 75,* 265–290.

Kottke, J., & Sharafinski, C. (1988). Measuring perceived supervisory and organizational support. *Educational and Psychological Measurement, 48,* 1075–1079.

Kurchner-Hawkins, R., & Miller, R. (2006). Organizational politics: Building positive political strategies in turbulent times. In E. Vigoda-Gadot & A. Drory (Eds.), *Handbook of organizational politics* (pp. 328–351). Cheltenham, UK: Elgar.

Lamertz, K. (2002). The social construction of fairness: Social influence and sense making in organizations. *Journal of Organizational Behavior, 23,* 19–37.

Lawrence, P. (2010). The key job design problem is still Taylorism. *Journal of Organizational Behavior, 31,* 412–421.

Lawrence, P., & Norhia, N. (2002). *Driven: How human nature shapes our choices.* San Francisco, CA: Jossey-Bass.

LePine, J., Erez, A., & Johnson, D. (2002). The nature and dimensionality of organizational citizenship behavior: A critical review and meta-analysis. *Journal of Applied Psychology, 87,* 52–65.

LePine, J., Podsakoff, N., & LePine, M. (2005). A meta-analytic test of the challenge stressor-hindrance stressor framework: An explanation for inconsistent relationships among stressors and performance. *Academy of Management Journal, 48,* 764–775.

Lerner, M. (2003). The justice motive: Where psychologists found it, how they lost it, and why they may not find it again. *Personality and Social Psychology Review, 7,* 388–399.

Liden, R., Sparrowe, R., & Wayne, S. (1997). Leader–member exchange theory: The past and potential for the future. In G. Ferris (Ed.), *Research in personnel and human resources management* (Vol. 15, pp. 47–119). Greenwich, CT: JAI Press.

Lin, N., & Erickson, B. (2008). Theory, measurement, and the research enterprise on social capital. In N. Lin & B. Erickson (Eds.), *Social capital: An international research program* (pp. 1–24). Oxford, UK: Oxford University Press.

Lind, E., & Van den Bos, K. (2002). When fairness works: Toward a general theory of uncertainty management. In B. Staw & R. Kramer (Eds.), *Research in organizational behavior* (pp. 181–223). Greenwich, CT: JAI Press.

Little, B. (2000). Free traits and personal contexts: Expanding a social ecological model of well-being. In W. Walsh, K. Craik, & R. Price (Eds.), *Person–environment psychology* (pp. 87–116). New York: Guilford Press.

Liu, Y., Liu, J., & Wu, L. (2010). Are you willing and able? Roles of motivation, power, and politics in career growth. *Journal of Management, 36,* 1432–1460.

Lopes, H. (2008). From self-interest motives to justice motives: The challenge of some experimental results. *American Journal of Economics and Sociology, 67,* 287–313.

Lord, R., Diefendorff, J., Schmidt, A., & Hall, R. (2010). Self-regulation at work. In S. Fiske (Ed.), *Annual review of psychology* (pp. 543–568). Chippewa Falls, WI: Annual Reviews.

Luszczynska, A., Diehl, M., Gutiérrez-Doña, B., Kuusinen, P., & Schwarzer, R. (2004). Measuring one component of dispositional self-regulation: Attention control and goal pursuit. *Personality and Individual Differences, 37,* 555–566.

Luthans, F., Hodgetts, R., & Rosenkrantz, S. (1988). *Real managers.* Cambridge, MA: Ballinger.

Lux, S., Crook, T., & Woehr, D. (2011). Mixing business with politics: A meta-analysis of the antecedents and outcomes of corporate political activity. *Journal of Management, 37,* 223–247.

Lux, S., Ferris, G., Brouer, R., Laird, M., & Summers, J. (2008). A multi-level conceptualization of organizational politics. In C. Cooper & J. Barling (Eds.), *The SAGE handbook of organizational behavior* (pp. 353–371). Thousand Oaks, CA: Sage Publications.

Machiavelli, N. (1998). *The prince.* Chicago: University of Chicago Press. (Translated and introduction by Harvey C. Mansfield; original work published 1513.)

Maertz, C., Griffeth, R., Campbell, N., & Allen, D. (2007). The effects of perceived organizational support and perceived supervisor support on employee turnover. *Journal of Organizational Behavior, 28,* 1059–1075.

Maitlis, S. (2005). The social processes of organizational sensemaking. *Academy of Management Journal, 48,* 21–49.

Maitlis, S., & Lawrence, T. (2007). Triggers and enables of sensemaking in organizations. *Academy of Management Journal, 50,* 57–84.

Maitlis, S., & Sonenshein, S. (2010). Sensemaking in crisis and change: Inspiration and insights from Weick (1988). *Journal of Management Studies, 47,* 551–580.

Matthews, G., Warm, J., Reinerman, L., Langheim, L., & Saxby, D. (2010). Task engagement, attention, and executive control. In A. Gruszka, G. Matthews, & B. Szymura (Eds.), *Handbook of individual differences in cognition: Attention, memory, and executive control* (pp. 205–230). New York: Springer.

McCullough, M., & Tabak, B. (2010). Prosocial behavior. In R. Baumeister & E. Finkel (Eds.), *Advanced social psychology: The state of the science* (pp. 263–302). Oxford, UK: Oxford Press.

McGarty, C., Turner, J., Oakes, P., & Haslam, S. (1993). The creation of uncertainty in the influence process: The roles of stimulus information and disagreement with similar others. *European Journal of Social Psychology, 23,* 17–38.

Mehra, A., Kilduff, M., & Brass, D. (1998). At the margins: A distinctiveness approach to the social identity and social networks of underrepresented groups. *Academy of Management Journal, 4,* 441–452.

Miller, V., & Jablin, F. (1991). Information seeking during organizational entry: Influences, tactics, and a model of the process. *Academy of Management Review, 16,* 92–120.

Miller, B., Rutherford, M., & Kolodinsky, R. (2008). Perceptions of organizational politics: A meta-analysis of outcomes. *Journal of Business and Psychology, 22,* 209–222.

Mintzberg, H. (1985). The organization as political arena. *Journal of Management Studies, 22,* 133–154.

Moos, R., Insel, P., & Humphrey, B. (1974). *Family, work and group environment scales manual.* Palo Alto, CA: Consulting Psychologists Press.

Morrison, E., & Bies, R. (1991). Impression management in the feedback seeking process: A literature review and research agenda. *Academy of Management Review, 16,* 522–541.

Moskowitz, D., & Cote, S. (1995). Do interpersonal traits predict affect? A comparison of three models. *Journal of Personality and Social Psychology, 69,* 915–924.

Moss, J., & Barbuto, J. (2010). Testing the relationship between interpersonal political skills, altruism, leadership success and effectiveness: A multilevel model. *Journal of Behavioral and Applied Management, 11,* 155–174.

Neuberg, S., Kenrick, D., & Schaller, M. (2010). Evolutionary social psychology. In S. Fiske, D. Gilbert, & G. Lindzey (Eds.), *Handbook of social psychology* (pp. 761–796). Hoboken, NJ: Wiley.

Ng, T., Eby, L., Sorensen, K., & Feldman, D. (2005). Predictors of objective and subjective career success: A meta-analysis. *Personnel Psychology, 58,* 367–408.

Nicholson, N. (1997). Evolutionary psychology: Toward a new view of human nature and organizational society. *Human Relations, 50,* 1053–1079.

Nicholson, N. (2005). Objections to evolutionary psychology: Reflections, implications, and the leadership exemplar. *Human Relations, 58,* 393–409.

Nicholson, N., & White, R. (2006). Darwinism—A new paradigm for organizational behavior? *Journal of Organizational Behavior, 27,* 111–119.

Oh, H., Labianca, G., & Chung, M. (2006). A multilevel model of group social capital. *Academy of Management Review, 31,* 569–582.

O'Leary-Kelly, A., & Griffin, R. (2004). Dark side issues: Concluding observations and directions for future research. In R. Griffin & A. O'Leary-Kelly (Eds.), *The dark side of organizational behavior* (pp. 462–487). San Francisco, CA: Jossey-Bass.

Organ, D. (1988). *Organizational citizenship behavior: The good soldier syndrome.* Lexington, MA: Lexington Books.

Organ, D. (1997). Organizational citizenship behavior: It's construct clean-up time. *Human Performance, 10,* 85–97.

Parker, S., Jimmieson, N., & Amiot, C. (2010). Self-determination as a moderator of demands and control: Implications for employee strain and engagement. *Journal of Vocational Behavior, 76,* 52–67.

Perrewé, P., Zellars, K., Ferris, G., Rossi, A., Kacmar, C., & Ralston, D. (2004). Neutralizing job stressors: Political skill as an antidote to the dysfunctional consequences of role conflict stressors. *Academy of Management Journal, 47,* 141–152.

Pettigrew, A. (1977). Strategy formulation as a political process. *International Studies of Management and Organization, 7,* 78–87.

Pfeffer, J. (1981). *Power in organizations.* Boston: Pitman.

Pfeffer, J. (2010a). *Power: Why some people have it—and others don't.* New York: HarperCollins.

Pfeffer, J. (2010b). Power play. *Harvard Business Review, 88,* 84–92.

Piliavin, J., & Charng, H. (1990). Altruism: A review of recent theory and research. *American Sociological Review, 16,* 27–65.

Pinker. S. (2002). *The blank slate.* New York: Viking.

Podolny, J., & Baron, J. (1997). Resources and relationships: Social networks and mobility in the workplace. *American Sociological Review, 62,* 673–693.

Podsakoff, P., MacKenzie, S., & Hui, C. (1993). Organizational citizenship behaviors and managerial evaluations of employee performance: A review and suggestions for future research. In G. Ferris (Ed.), *Research in personnel and human resources management* (Vol. 11, pp. 1–40). Greenwich, CT: JAI Press.

Porter, L., Allen, R., & Angle, H. (1981). The politics of upward influence in organizations. In L. Cummings & B. Staw (Eds.), *Research in organizational behavior* (Vol. 3, pp. 109–149). Greenwich, CT: JAI Press.

Posner, M., & Rothbart, M. (1998). Attention, self-regulation, and consciousness. *Philosophical Transactions of the Royal Society of London, 353,* 1915–1927.

Qvortrup, M. (2009). Rebels without a cause? The Irish Referendum on the Lisbon Treaty. *Political Quarterly, 80,* 59–66.

Ragins, B., & Cotton, J. (1999). Mentor functions and outcomes: A comparison of men and women in formal and informal mentoring relationships. *Journal of Applied Psychology, 84,* 529–550.

Randall, M., Cropanzano, R., Bormann, C., & Birjulin, A. (1999). Organizational politics and organizational support as predictors of work attitudes, job performance, and organizational citizenship behavior. *Journal of Organizational Behavior, 20,* 159–174.

Reichle, B., & Schmitt, M. (2002). Helping and rationalization as alternative strategies for restoring the belief in a just world: Evidence from longitudinal change analyses. In M. Ross & D. Miller (Eds.), *The justice motive in everyday life* (pp. 127–148). New York: Cambridge University Press.

Roberson, Q., & Colquitt, J. (2005). Shared and configural justice: A social network model of justice in teams. *Academy of Management Review, 30,* 595–607.

Roberts, B., & Robins, R. (2000). Broad dispositions, broad aspirations: The intersection of the Big Five dimensions and major life goals. *Personality and Social Psychology Bulletin, 26,* 1284–1296.

Rosen, C., Harris, K., & Kacmar, K. (2009). The emotional implications of organizational politics: A process model. *Human Relations, 62,* 27–57.

Rusbult, C., & Van Lange, P. (2003). Interdependence, interaction, and relationships. *Annual Review of Psychology, 54,* 351–375.

Ruscio, J., Whitney, D., & Amabile, T. (1998). Looking inside the fishbowl of creativity: Verbal and behavioral predictors of creative performance. *Creativity Research Journal, 11,* 243–263.

Rushton, J., Russell, R., & Wells, P. (1984). Genetic similarity theory: Beyond kin selection altruism. *Behavioral Genetics, 14,* 179–193.

Saks, A., Gruman, J., & Cooper-Thomas, H. (2011). The neglected role of proactive behavior and outcomes in newcomer socialization. *Journal of Vocational Behavior, 79,* 36–46.

Schaufeli, W., & Greenglass E. (2001). Introduction to special issue on burnout and health. *Psychology and Health, 16,* 501–510.

Sederberg, P. (1984). *The politics of meaning: Power and explanation in the construction of social reality.* Tucson: University of Arizona Press.

Seeley, E., & Gardner, W. (2003). The "selfless" and self-regulation: The role of chronic other-orientation in averting self-regulatory depletion. *Self and Identity, 2,* 103–117.

Serven, L. (2002). *The end of organizational politics as usual: A complete strategy for creating a more productive and profitable organization.* New York: AMACOM.

Seibert, S., Kraimer, M., & Crant, J. (2001). What do proactive people do? A longitudinal model linking proactive personality and career success. *Personnel Psychology, 54,* 845–874.

Seibert, S., Kraimer, M., & Liden, R. (2001). A social capital theory of career success. *Academy of Management Journal, 44,* 219–237.

Shanock, S., & Eisenberger, R. (2006). When supervisors feel supported: Relationships with subordinates' perceived supervisor support, perceived organizational support and performance. *Journal of Applied Psychology, 91,* 689–695.

Sherry, S., Hewitt, P., Sherry, D., Flett, G., & Graham, A. (2010). Perfectionism dimensions and research productivity in psychology professors: Implications for understanding the (mal)adaptiveness of perfectionism. *Canadian Journal of Behavioral Science, 42,* 273–283.

Silvester, J. (2008). The good, the bad, and the ugly: Politics and politicians at work. *International Review of Industrial and Organizational Psychology, 23,* 107–148.

Simon, H. (1990). Invariants of human behavior. *Annual Review of Psychology, 41,* 1–19.

Simon, H. (1995). Rationality in political behavior. *Political Psychology, 16,* 45–61.

Simosi, M. (2010). The role of social socialization tactics in the relationship between socialization content and newcomers' affective commitment. *Journal of Managerial Psychology, 25,* 301–327.

Smircich, L. (1983). Organizations as shared meanings. In L. Pondy, P. Frost, G. Morgan, T. Dandridge, & S. Bacharach (Eds.), *Organizational symbolism* (pp. 55–65). Stamford, CT: JAI Press.

Smith, C., Organ, D., & Near, J. (1983). Organizational citizenship behavior: Its nature and antecedents. *Journal of Applied Psychology, 68,* 653–663.

Smith-Doerr, L., & Powell, W. (2005). Networks and economic life. In N. Smelser & R. Swedberg (Eds.), *The handbook of economic sociology* (pp. 379–402). Princeton: Princeton University Press.

Sitkin, S. (2010). Sensemaking in organizational research. In M. Lounsbury (Ed.), *Research in the sociology of organizations* (pp. 409–418). London: Emerald.

Sparrowe, R., Soetjipto, B., & Kraimer, M. (2006). Do leaders' influence tactics relate to members' helping behavior? It depends on the quality of the relationship. *Academy of Management Journal, 49,* 1194–1208.

Spreitzer, G. (1996). Social structural characteristics of psychological empowerment. *Academy of Management Journal, 39,* 483–504.

Stinglhamber, F., De Cremer, D., & Mercken, L. (2006). Perceived support as a mediator of the relationship between justice and trust: A multi foci approach. *Group and Organization Management, 31,* 442–468.

Stoker, G. (2010). The rise of political disenchantment. In C. Hay (Ed.), *New directions in political science* (pp. 43–63). Basingstoke, UK: Macmillan.

Strelan, P. (2007). The prosocial, adaptive qualities of just world beliefs: Implications for the relationship between justice and forgiveness. *Personality and Individual Differences, 43,* 881–890.

Sturmer, S., Kiel, K., Snyder, M., & Omoto, A. (2005). Prosocial emotions and helping: The moderating role of group membership. *Journal of Personality and Social Psychology, 88,* 532–546.

Sullivan, S., Forret, M., & Mainiero, L. (2007). No regrets? An investigation of the relationship between laid off and experiencing career regret. *Journal of Managerial Psychology, 22,* 787–804.

Sundie, J., Cialdini, R., Griskevicius, V., & Kenrick, D. (2006). Evolutionary social influence. In M. Schaller, J. Simpson, & D. Kenrick (Eds.), *Evolutionary and social psychology* (pp. 287–316). New York: Psychology Press.

Tamir, M. (2009). Differential preferences for happiness: Extraversion and trait-consistent emotion regulation. *Journal of Personality, 77,* 447–470.

Taylor, K. (1968). H.L. Mencken: Rhetorical critic of presidents. *Today's Speech, 16,* 27–30.

Taylor, P. (2009). Infrastructure and scaffolding: Interpretations and change of research involving human genetic information. *Science as Culture, 18,* 435–459.

Thackaberry, J. (2003). Mutual metaphors of *Survivor* and office politics: Images of work in popular *Survivor* criticism. In M. Smith & A. Wood (Eds.), *Survivor lessons: Essays on communication and reality television* (pp. 153–181). New York: McFarland.

Thau, S., Aquino, K., & Wittek, R. (2007). An extension of uncertainty management theory to the self: The relationship between justice, social comparison orientation, and antisocial work behaviors. *Journal of Applied Psychology, 92,* 250–258.

Treadway, D., Breland, J., Williams, L., Wang, L., & Yang, J. (2008). The role of politics and political behavior in the development of performance of LMX relationships. In G. Graen & J. Graen (Eds.), *Knowledge-driven corporation: Complex creative destruction* (pp. 145–180). Charlotte, NC: Information Age.

Treadway, D., Hochwater, W., Kacmar, C., & Ferris, G. Political will, political skill, and political behavior. *Journal of Organizational Behavior, 26,* 226–245.

Treynor, W., Gonzalez, R., & Nolen-Hoeksema, S. (2003). Rumination considered: A psychometric analysis. *Cognitive Behavior and Therapy, 27,* 247–259.

van Prooijen, J. (2010). Retributive versus compensatory justice: Observers' preference for punishing in response to criminal offenses. *European Journal of Social Psychology, 40,* 72–85.

Vigoda, E. (2002). Stress-related aftermaths to workplace politics: The relationships among politics, job distress, and aggressive behavior in organizations. *Journal of Organizational Behavior, 23,* 571–591.

Vigoda-Gadot, E., & Talmud, I. (2010). Organizational politics and job outcomes: The moderating effect of trust and social support. *Journal of Applied Social Psychology, 40,* 2829–2861.

Vohs, K., & Baumeister, R. (2004). Understanding self-regulation: An introduction. In R. Baumeister & K. Vohs (Eds.), *Handbook of self-regulation: Research, theory, and applications* (pp. 1–9). New York: Guilford Press.

von Pechman, W. (1953). Working toward promotion. *Industrial and Engineering Chemistry, 4,* 103A–106A.

Vredenburgh, D., & Shea-VanFossen, R. (2010). Human nature, organizational politics, and human resource development. *Human Resource Development Review, 9,* 26–47.

Wayne, S., Shore, L., & Liden, R. (1997). Perceived organizational support and leader-member exchange: A social exchange perspective. *Academy of Management Journal, 40,* 82–111.

Wei, L., Liu, J., Chen, Y., & Wu, L. (2010), Political skill, supervisor-subordinate *guanxi* and career prospects in Chinese firms. *Journal of Management Studies, 47,* 437–454.

Weick, K. (1979). *The social psychology of organizing* (2nd ed.). Reading, MA: Addison-Wesley.

Weick, K. (1995). *Sense making in organization.* Thousand Oaks, CA: Sage Publications.

Wells, A. (2002). GAD, metacognition, and mindfulness: An information-processing analysis. *Clinical Psychology, 9,* 95–100.

Westphal, J., & Stern, I. (2006). The other pathway to the boardroom: Interpersonal influence behavior as a substitute for elite credentials and majority status in obtaining board appointments. *Administrative Science Quarterly, 51,* 169–204.

Willem, A., & Scarbrough, H. (2006). Social capital and political bias in knowledge sharing: An exploratory study. *Human Relations, 59,* 1343–1370.

Wilson, D., & Wilson, O. (2007). Rethinking the theoretical foundation of sociobiology. *Quarterly Review of Biology, 82,* 327–348.

Witt, L., Andrews, M., & Kacmar, K. (2000). The role of participation in decision-making in the organizational-politics-job satisfaction relationship. *Human Relations, 53,* 341–358.

Wright, T. (2003). Positive organizational behavior: An idea whose time has truly come. *Journal of Organizational Behavior, 24,* 437–442.

Yang, K. (2009). Examining perceived honest performance reporting by public organizations: Bureaucratic politics and organizational practices. *Journal of Public Administration, 19,* 81–105.

Zanzi, A., Arthur, M., & Shamir, B. (1991). The relationship between career concerns and politics in organizations. *Journal of Organizational Behavior, 12,* 219–233.

Zhang, J. (2010). The problems of using social networks in entrepreneurial resource acquisition. *International Small Business Journal, 28,* 338–361.

3

Politics in Perspectives: On the Theoretical Challenges and Opportunities in Studying Organizational Politics

Douglas A. Lepisto
Boston College

Michael G. Pratt
Boston College

> It [Politics] takes both passion and perspective.
>
> **—Max Weber**

Organizational politics is a concept that both benefits and suffers by its ubiquity. It is commonplace for individuals to recognize terms such as *playing the game, working the system,* and more recently closing deals *off-line.* Likewise, it is also a central concept in theories of organizations and organizational behavior, both at very micro- and very macro-levels. Organizational politics has been implicated in classical work out of the Carnegie School (Cyert & March, 1963; March & Simon, 1958), strategic decision making (Dean & Sharfman, 1996; Eisenhardt & Bourgeois, 1988; Eisenhardt & Zbaracki, 1992), resource dependence (Pfeffer & Salancik, 1978), and institutional theory (Selznick, 1957, 1966) and has been the direct object of interest in recent research on political perceptions and skills (e.g., Ferris & Kacmar, 1992; Ferris, Russ, & Fandt, 1989; Ferris, Treadway, Perrewé, Brouer, Douglas, & Lux, 2007; Gandz & Murray, 1980). Recent research shows that perceptions of organizational politics are critical for organizational outcomes, such as turnover intentions, job satisfaction, affective commitment, task performance, and organizational citizenship behaviors (see Chang, Rosen, & Levy, 2009 for recent meta-analysis).

We were invited to write this chapter to identify key theoretical gaps, issues, and directions for research on organizational politics. We have taken that charge to heart. As "interested outsiders" to the field of organizational politics, we were surprised to find that despite its centrality to theorizing and everyday functioning in organizations, there is a relative paucity of theoretical and empirical research focused *directly* on organizational politics appearing in top-management journals. Though we see exciting avenues for future research, we also see three obstacles that have hindered research in this area. First, our understanding of organizational politics is somewhat fragmented across several literatures. Politics often is used in theorizing related to power, social networks, coalitions, decision making, top-management teams, and social influence tactics; each offers different angles of understanding, but typically there are few conversations linking these fields of research.

Second, much of the research to date has *invoked* organizational politics, but often in service of an alternative focus of theorizing. Research on perceptions of organizational politics by Ferris and colleagues, however, serves as a notable exception. Related to this issue is that research on politics tends to focus on the antecedents and outcomes of political behavior. Therefore, knowledge about what politics "do" in a supporting role (e.g., mobilize coalitions, enhance personal standing, decision making, and "getting things done") tends to eclipse a more fundamental question of what it "is."

Consequently, a third obstacle is that, whether viewed directly or not, organizational politics suffers from a dizzying number of definitions and conceptualizations. As a result, similar evidence is seen today of what Kacmar and Baron (1999) lamented about 12 years ago: "Over the last thirty years, virtually as many definitions of organizational politics have been offered as there are articles on the topic" (p. 3). In this chapter, we attempt to address these obstacles.

We are well aware that we are not the first to review and attempt to define organizational politics (e.g., Drory & Romm, 1990; Kacmar & Baron, 1999; Mayes & Allen, 1977; Provis, 2006; Tushman, 1977). However, the present approach differs from these earlier attempts in two key ways. First, research on organizational politics has been somewhat bifurcated into macro- (e.g., organizations as coalitions, social networks, and power) and micro-camps (e.g., individual political skills and behaviors) with very little cross-pollination. By drawing on core elements from both camps, one can better see what is central and unique about this construct vis-à-vis similar ones. Second, before defining the term, this chapter begins by briefly revisiting its historical development to reveal what core question or what core theoretical domain organizational politics attempts to address. In other words, we first ask—"Why do we have a concept such as organizational politics?"—before attempting to outline some key elements of its definition.

Our experience with organizational identity is illustrative (Pratt, 2003). Like politics, *identity* is a fundamental concept that has been central to many disciplines prior to its adoption by organizational studies. Moreover, its uses span levels of analysis, and its definitions are many. However, organizational identity revolves around a key question or domain: Who are we? Disagreements occur over how that question is answered and what that answer "means" (e.g., is it stable or fleeting?), but the core question remains. Thus, the first objective was to seek this core question or domain area for organizational politics. Once this domain area was identified, it was clearer which elements of organizational politics appear to be core, how organizational politics is different from similar constructs, and which avenues for future research are the most fruitful.

Before identifying the domain area for organizational politics we want to identify a few provisos and boundary conditions. First, we fully admit to being new to this area and suspect that this was one of the reasons the invitation was extended to write this chapter. We hope that our potential lack of nuance is compensated by seeing the field with "fresh" eyes. That said, having done work on identity, meaning of work, and intuition, all of which are broad, multidisciplinary areas, we do have some experience dealing with messy and somewhat unwieldy literatures. Second, although we believe we have covered much of the literature, given how dispersed it is in its current state, there undoubtedly is research that was missed. The review focused primarily on the highly cited works on organizational politics.

Third, as noted, we did not limit ourselves to one level of analysis or one subfield of organizational politics (e.g., political behavior, perceptions of politics, political skill). The hope is that this *broad* versus *deep* strategy helps to point out some of the commonalities and tensions that reside across the field, but we recognize there are trade-offs to such an approach. Fourth, and finally, the intent—whether it be in defining the core of politics, offering a definition, or mapping out new research domains—is not to be dogmatic. For example, in coming up with a synthetic definition for organizational politics, we do not mean to present this as *the* definition. Rather, its purpose is to help identify the *central* and *necessary* elements of the concept to help the field move forward effectively and collectively. In this way, a middle ground between strict paradigmatic consensus and conceptual anarchy is sought.

SEEKING THE CORE: WHAT IS ORGANIZATIONAL POLITICS ABOUT?

As noted already, organizational politics is widely recognized across a variety of literatures. We begin by offering a view at 10,000 feet of the concept's history. By looking at its origins, we attempt to examine the core domain area that organizational politics intends to address. These classic works are linked to subsequent research at both micro- and macro-levels of analysis.

Organizational Politics: A Brief History

A political perspective on organizations often is credited as emanating from theoretical assumptions grounded in the Carnegie School (e.g., Cyert & March, 1963; March & Simon, 1958; Simon, 1947), as well as in resource dependence theory (Pfeffer & Salancik, 1978). In contrast to economic perspectives on organizations, which have tended to focus on normative claims regarding efficiency, utility maximization, and conflict-free decision making, the Carnegie School (e.g., Simon, 1957) conceived of actors as having *bounded rationality* (i.e., having limited knowledge of alternatives and consequences of decisions) and emphasized how organizations influence decision making through information, value premises, routines, and disaggregation of goals. Thus, *economic man* was replaced with *administrative man*.

The disaggregation of broad organizational goals into interdependent subgoals, coupled with actors' bounded rationality and identification with these subgoals, raised issues of coordination and potential conflict between and among departments. Therefore, Cyert and March (1963) considered organizations in terms of competing coalitions determined to secure resources and to perpetuate their influence in the organization. Here, organizations are not singular actors with singular goals but instead are composed of multiple actors with multiple goals.

Though organizations overcome the paralyzing effects of competing goals due to *satisficing* (i.e., never reaching optimal solutions), they nevertheless exist with residual tension between competing coalitions with varying interests: "Most organizations most of the time exist and thrive with considerable latent conflict of goals" (Cyert & March, 1963, p. 117). The central assumptions of bounded rationality, decision making, vying coalitions, and interdependence underlie the work of other theorists that more explicitly conceived of decision making as political behavior (e.g., March, 1962; Pettigrew, 1973).

Whereas the Carnegie School focused on decision making, Selznick's (1957, 1966) work in institutional theory invoked similar notions of organizational politics but focused on the relationship to the management of values and competing interests. Selznick described the role of leadership in the process of institutionalization, or how organizations become "infused with value" (Selznick, 1957, p. 17) beyond their technical means. Leaders were central to the process of developing a distinctive character of the organization but also had to contend with organizational rivalry. In the process of developing this distinctive character, various internal interests surfaced, each competing to develop its own prestige and power and ultimately to shape the character of the organization.

Therefore, institutionalization also was a political process. As Selznick (1957) noted, "Creative men are needed—more in some circumstances than in others—who know how to transform a neutral body of men into a committed polity. These men are called leaders; their profession is politics" (p. 61). Likewise, in his classic work on the Tennessee Valley Authority, Selznick (1966) described how relevant external interests were formally and informally co-opted in the leadership and policy domains of the organization. Selznick's research highlights that politics not only is about decision making but also implicates the management of values, leadership, and power.

Although these classic works included notions of politics, subsequent research theorized about political activity more directly through discussions of the role of *power*. We focus on two foundational works: Pfeffer's (1981) *Power in Organizations* and Mintzberg's (1983) *Power in and Around Organizations*. Integrating assumptions from the Carnegie School and notions derived from resource dependence theory, Pfeffer (1981) offered a perspective on organizational politics that emphasized the role of power. Following Dahl (1957) and Emerson (1962), power was conceived as the ability of actors to overcome resistance and to bring about the outcomes they desire. Power was viewed as being inversely proportional to an actor's dependence on another actor (Emerson, 1962).

More specifically, Pfeffer (1981) equated power explicitly with an actor's ability to acquire and control valued *resources* vis-à-vis others. Thus, power here is considered more *structural* than personal (e.g., charisma). If power is the property of relationships based on resources and dependencies, politics was viewed as "power in action" (Pfeffer, 1981, p. 7). Actors can use a variety of tactics (e.g., controlling information, developing coalitions, incorporating outside experts) to increase or manipulate their relative power to influence decisions, particularly under conditions of uncertainty or dissensus about choices. The outcomes of decision making in political contexts are a function of power, where decisions are reflections of the preferences of the powerful.

Mintzberg (1983) viewed politics as an alternative system of influence within organizations that is used in conjunction with, in contrast to, or as a substitute for other systems of influence including formal authority, ideology, and expertise, all three of which are based on relatively legitimate sources of power. Formal authority is equated to power that is formally legitimated (e.g., holding a particular job title); ideology focuses on power related to shared values and beliefs; and expertise is legitimized power derived from specialized knowledge and skill in a particular domain.

Therefore, Mintzberg (1983) perceived power as integral to notions of politics yet offered a slightly different perspective from Pfeffer (1981). For Mintzberg, politics were more analogous to informal power and often illegitimate in nature: "behavior outside of the legitimate systems of influence (or at least outside their legitimate uses), and often in opposition to them" (p. 172). Additionally, actors needed power, but also they needed the political will (Chapter 17 in this volume) and political skill (Chapter 16 in this volume) to successfully engage in and to effectively execute politics.

Subsequent research has drawn from these theoretical roots on decision making and power. Politics has been examined as it relates to top-management teams, strategic decision making (Dean & Sharfman, 1996; Eisenhardt & Bourgeois, 1988; Eisenhardt & Zbaracki, 1992), and strategic planning (Mintzberg, 1990). In addition, research on social networks (e.g., Krackhardt, 1990) has invoked politics and has drawn on notions of social structure and power to examine how individuals develop reputational power. Related research also has examined the political tactics actors use in these structures (e.g., Gargiulo, 1993).

Micro-level approaches to organizational politics has recently increased primarily due to Ferris and colleagues (e.g., Ferris & Kacmar, 1992; Ferris et al., 1989; Ferris et al., 2005; Ferris et al., 2007). Drawing on Gandz and Murray (1980), this area broadly examines *perceptions of organizational politics*, which is concerned with the antecedents, moderating factors, and outcomes of perceiving one's environment as political (Ferris & Kacmar, 1992). Additionally, Ferris and others have drawn on Mintzberg's (1983) notions of *political will* and *political skill* to assess how individuals function effectively in organizations. Though different from their more macrolevel colleagues, research in this area amassed a significant body of systematic, empirical research that focuses on the political actors themselves.

Taken together, a few key themes emerge. First, politics is a way of getting things done in a group, so it is an inherently social phenomenon. Second, getting things done is accomplished via power or social influence. While some equate the two, the perspective taken here follows Ibarra and Andrews (1993), who recognized that power often is tied to formal authority, networks, and structures (Pfeffer, 1981), whereas influence tends to be more localized, relying on "informal" bases of gaining compliance, such as reciprocity or liking. Because the emphasis on using power and gaining conformity via influence are critical to conceptualizations of politics, both are included here.

Third, power is self-interested and goal directed. Although some have argued that all willful (i.e., goal-directed) behavior is to some degree self-interested (Mayes & Allen, 1977), it is important to note that for political behavior, self-interest is not simply one component of behavior but is presumed to be the most important component. Moreover, whether it refers to coalitions or individual actors, politics describes a process of social influence for the purpose of meeting some goal. Thus, politics involves activity and process, is by nature social, and is goal oriented.

Fourth, politics seems most prevalent when officially sanctioned practices (e.g., standard operating procedures, routines, rites, rituals) either are not available or are seen as less effective or less efficient for goal attainment. Indeed, Mintzberg (1983) pointed to this element most directly. Also, evidence can be seen from the Carnegie School, which described the conflict that results from discrepant goals and ineffective or unavailable formal means for their coordination and resolution. Thus, the core domain question of organizational politics appears to be: *How do actors use power and social influence in a group to achieve self-interested goals when officially sanctioned means are unavailable or undervalued?* We now extend and refine this core domain question in offering a definition of organizational politics.

KEY DEFINITIONAL ELEMENTS OF ORGANIZATIONAL POLITICS

In this section, the numerous definitions related to organizational politics are synthesized. Table 3.1 offers a sampling of a variety of commonly used definitions across literatures. From our review, we identify five clusters of characteristics or *elements* that capture what we believe are both necessary and sufficient elements of a definition of organizational politics. While other definitions may have more elements to them, it is thought that once any of the five elements are missing, organizational politics starts to look very similar to related constructs.

It is argued that organizational politics represents (1) an actor's (individual) or actors' (group) (2) self-interested, goal-directed (3) power and social influence actions* that are performed (4) in relation to two or more interdependent social actors (5) by means that are not officially sanctioned. Characterized in this way, organizational politics represents a series of necessary but not sufficient conditions. Furthermore, organizational politics is differentiated from concepts that share similar conceptual space.

Actor or Actors (Individual or Group)

A single individual, groups of actors, and larger collective aggregates can enact organizational politics. Although some definitions recognize this fact (e.g., Pettigrew, 1973), many do not explicitly address whether single

---

* While Weber (1978) distinguished between action, which is subjectively meaningful—either to the actor themselves or attributed by others—and behavior, which is not, we follow Vaisey (2009), who examined patterns of action. Thus, action and behavior both are used to mean what people do.

TABLE 3.1

Common Definitions of Organizational Politics

Source	Definition of Organizational Politics
Ferris, Russ, and Fandt (1989, p. 145)	Social influence process in which behavior is strategically designed to maximize short-term or long-term self-interest, which is either consistent with or at the expense of others' interests (where self-interest maximization refers to the attainment of positive outcomes and prevention of negative outcomes)
Mintzberg (1983, p. 172)	Individual or group behavior that is informal, ostensibly parochial, typically divisive, and, above all, in the technical sense, illegitimate—sanctioned not by formal authority, accepted ideology, or certified expertise
Valle and Perrewé (2000, p. 361)	The exercise of tactical influence, which is strategically goal directed, rational, conscious, and intended to promote self-interest, either at the expense of or in support of others' interests
Pfeffer (1981, p. 7)	Activities taken within organizations to acquire, develop, and use power and other resources to obtain one's preferred outcomes in a situation in which there is uncertainty or dissensus about choices
Bacharach and Lawler (1980, p. 1)	The tactical use of power to retain or obtain control of real or symbolic resources
Bacharach and Lawler (1998, p. 69)	The efforts of individuals or groups in organizations to mobilize support for or opposition to organizational strategies, policies, or practices in which they have a stake or interest
Mayes and Allen (1977, p. 675)	The management of influence to obtain ends not sanctioned by the organization or to obtain sanctioned ends through nonsanctioned influence means
Tushman (1977, p. 207)	The structure and process of the use of authority and power to effect definitions of goals, directions, and other major parameters of the organization
Pettigrew (1973, p. 17)	Behavior by individuals, or, in collective terms by subunits, within an organization that makes a claim against the resource-sharing system of the organization
Kacmar & Baron (1999, p. 4)	Individuals' actions that are directed toward the goal of furthering their own self-interest without regard for the well-being of others or their organization
Ferris et al. (2005, p. 127)	[*Political skill*] The ability to effectively understand others at work and to use such knowledge to influence others to act in ways that enhance one's personal or organizational objectives

continued

TABLE 3.1 (continued)

Common Definitions of Organizational Politics

Source	Definition of Organizational Politics
Ferris, Fedor, and King (1994, p. 4)	The management of shared meaning, which focuses on the subjective evaluation and interpretations of meaning rather than on the view that meanings are inherent, objective properties of situations; from the standpoint of managerial political behavior, the objective is to manage the meaning of situations in such a way as to produce desired, self-serving responses or outcomes
Randall, Cropanzano, Bormann, and Birjulin (1999, p. 161)	Unsanctioned influence attempts that seek to promote self-interest at the expense of organizational goals

actors, collectives, or both can engage in politics. Some have suggested that politics is more fundamentally a group activity constituted by competing coalitions (e.g., Salancik & Pfeffer, 1977). Indeed, systems that are constituted as political often have multiple actors working together and against each other to influence one another and to achieve their goals.

Though politics can be initiated by a group, a single actor also can engage in politics. For example, a manager could set up golfing arrangements with an influential senior executive to sway a strategic decision in favor of his department. Indeed, Ferris and colleagues typically have investigated politics by examining the perspectives of individual actors (e.g., Ferris & Kacmar, 1992; Ferris et al., 1989).

Self-Interested and Goal Directed

Another core component of organizational politics is self-interest. Self-interest has been included (Ferris et al., 1989) or implied in a variety of ways, in a number of definitions, including references to *preferred* (Pfeffer, 1981), *a stake or interest* (Bacharach & Lawler, 1998), and *personal objectives* (Ferris et al., 2005). What is central to many of the definitions in Table 3.1 is not that self-interest is a component of political behavior (economists might argue all behavior is somewhat self-interested) but that it is a primary motive.

This emphasis is captured in treatments that view politics as antithetical to others' interests, such as another work group or one's organization (e.g., Dean & Sharfman, 1996; Kacmar & Baron, 1999; Randall,

Cropanzano, Bormann, & Birjulin, 1999). Indeed, several scholars have strongly delineated self-interest from organizational interest in their definitions and operationalizations of organizational politics (e.g., Dean & Sharfman, 1996; Walter, Kellermanns, & Lechner, in press; Walter, Lechner, & Kellermanns, 2008). For example, Walter et al. (2008) operationalized one element of organizational politics in a survey by asking, "Were people primarily concerned with *their own goals* or with the *goals of their organizations?*" (p. 543). Thus, politics sometimes is viewed as mutually exclusive with the organization's goals and is focused very narrowly upon one individual's interest apart from others (i.e., the goals of the organization).

Self-interest need not be oppositional or mutually exclusive to "organizational" interests. As Cyert and March (1963) noted, organizations are composed of self-interested actors that band together to create coalitions to further their ends. Thus, organizational interests can come from self-interest. More generally, self-interest may align with organizational interests, especially when individuals view their organization as self-defining (Pratt, 1998). Therefore, while it is agreed that self-interest is the primary motive in political behavior, there are times when individual and organizational interests may be compatible.

Such self-interested behavior also is not random or impulsive; rather, it is exhibited with a goal in mind. That is, organizational politics is *goal directed* (e.g., Kacmar & Baron, 1999; Valle & Perrewé, 2000) regardless of the specific content of those goals, such as whether they involve the procurement of resources, promotions, or outcomes of decision making. While in a very general sense, one can argue that all self-interested behavior is goal directed (i.e., to their object of interest), both terms are used because not all goal-directed behavior is primarily self-interested (e.g., advocating for a colleague's interest), and some self-interested behavior is impulsive and thus typically not within the purview of *political* (e.g., impulsively skipping a meeting to go out to lunch with colleagues). With regard to the latter, goal-directed is viewed in this sense as well planned, akin to *strategic* (see Table 3.1), which is central to some definitions of politics.

Power and Social Influence Actions

Organizational politics are manifested through enactments explicitly related to "acquiring, developing, or expending" *power* (Pfeffer, 1981, p. 7). However, power often is conceived as one's latent capacity or potential ability to influence others (French & Raven, 1959) rather than what is actually enacted. Though macro-conceptions often focus on structural elements of power (e.g., formal position, interdependence, and the ability to wield, control, and acquire resources), power also derives from a variety of sources including referent (i.e., charisma) and expert (i.e., knowledge) bases. Hence, French and Raven (1959) integrated more personal bases (e.g., expert and referent) with more structural bases such as reward (i.e., incentives), coercive (i.e., punishment), and legitimate (i.e., formal, norms, authority).

By contrast, although social influence often is seen as the actual use of power, the two concepts often are confounded. This is perhaps not surprising given that the bases of influence (e.g., liking, scarcity, reciprocity, consistency; Cialdini, 1993) tend to mirror bases similar to those of power. However, for the sake of clarification, it is suggested that if influence is the process whereby power is enacted, then political behavior draws on bases of power to influence others to meet their self-interested goals.

The second critical element of power and social influence in politics is *action*. Here, we follow Pfeffer (1981), who characterized organizational politics as "power in action," which is reflected in the action-oriented elements of many definitions including *behavior* (Ferris et al., 1989; Mintzberg, 1983; Pettigrew, 1973), *effort* (Bacharach & Lawler, 1998), *actions* (Kacmar & Baron, 1994), and *activities* (Pfeffer, 1981). Scholars have outlined a number of behavioral tactics that constitute politics including ingratiation (Liden & Mitchell, 1988), withholding of information, using experts, co-optation (Gargiulo, 1993; Pfeffer, 1981; Selznick, 1966), controlling agendas, developing coalitions (e.g., Pfeffer, 1981; Mintzberg, 1983), and managing impressions (e.g., Ferris et al., 2005). These behaviors have been further categorized as short-term (i.e., tactical), long-term (i.e., strategic), proactive (i.e., assertive), or reactive (i.e., defensive) (Ashforth & Lee, 1990; Tedeschi & Melburg, 1984, as cited in Ferris et al., 1989).

In Relation to Two or More Interdependent Social Actors

An emphasis on power, social influence, and coalitions suggest that politics is an inherently *social* process. Moreover, definitions of power have underscored that these social actors also are dependent on each other for power to exist (Emerson, 1962). Without relevant interdependence, there is no potential for the use of power and thus no potential for politics. Thus, it is argued that actors in a political situation are to some extent interdependent.

As noted in Table 3.1, while some definitions of organizational politics recognize the importance of others, many more do not. However, those that do (e.g., Ferris et al., 1989; Valle & Perrewé, 2000) tend to not distinguish the number of others involved. Drawing on early treatments of politics, we argue that organizational politics fundamentally involves a collection of actors, at least *three* or more, with at least one enacting political behavior. The importance of at least three social actors is clear when viewing work on coalition building, which suggests that a coalition cannot be built with only two parties. Moreover, even political situations that are seemingly dyadic, implicitly or explicitly, involve third parties.

Drawing on a scenario from Jackall's (1983) treatise on "Moral Mazes," pretend a plant manager wants to be viewed positively by the chief executive officer (CEO) and diverts an inordinate amount of money from her tight budget prior to the CEO's visit to paint the facility and develop glossy brochures. Some may see this as dyadic in nature—that is, a boss and a subordinate. However, this would ignore the others who likely are central to this action. For example, there are the plant manager's subordinates (i.e., the "fiefdom") whom the plant manager may want to impress or to cement her power over with a successful interaction with the CEO. There are other perceived (i.e., real or imagined) actors that the plant manager is enacting her behavior in relation to. These could be competitors (e.g., a rising star) within their own department or perhaps a rival in another department. Also, there are interested outside observers who see the political actions but are not directly implicated in them.

Each of these others transforms a seemingly dyadic encounter to one involving three or more social actors. However, this third *must* be implicitly or explicitly invoked for it to be political. If the situation was between the CEO and a plant manager and no others were involved—that is, if the plant manager did not have subordinates, did not have any real or imagined competitors, and no one besides the CEO and plant manager observed this—then this would not be a political situation. Rather, it would be better understood as an illegitimate social influence attempt or possibly just an impression management attempt but not political in how the term historically has been used. In short, political activity not only captures the influencer and target of influence but also is always enacted vis-à-vis a third party.

Simmel's (1950) theorizing about social dynamics that involve third parties illustrates conditions that are often construed as political. Simmel suggested that, as parties move from two to three actors, relationships become altered such that two actors can be *indirectly* connected through a third party. In this situation, actors can be conceived of as mediating and brokering relations between actors. Conversely, this third actor can be sought out and lobbied by two conflicting actors to settle disputes. Here, the underpinnings of mobilization and coalition formation are seen. In addition, the inclusion of a third also allows for majorities, and thus voting becomes a means of making decisions. The third also can serve as an *audience*, making behaviors that are perhaps dyadic and behind closed doors more public.

Those playing the mediating or brokering roles can act in a nonpartisan fashion, seeking opportunities to secure a more advantageous position for themselves. In general, this is what Simmel (1950) referred to as *tertius gaudens,* or the third who benefits. For example, by playing a tertius role, this third party may set the two conflicting parties against each another, thus allowing the tertius to pursue his interests unencumbered. Those in a tertius role can also use their mediating position to their advantage. Actors can obtain power via their role as gatekeepers of information and resources between actors. Such examples call to mind commonly held images of what would be constituted as political. In short, while research often has implicitly invoked the notion that politics involves multiple actors, making this notion explicit is a critical element that distinguishes politics from closely related constructs. As argued later, this also opens possibilities for future empirical and theoretical work.

Not Officially Sanctioned Means

Prior theorizing, colloquial understanding, and logic are used to advance this final component. Some definitions of organizational politics call attention to actions that are *unsanctioned* (Randall et al., 1999), *not sanctioned* (Mayes & Allen, 1977), *illegitimate* (Mintzberg, 1983), *informal* (Tushman, 1977), or in a *shadow system* (Kanter, 1977). This follows colloquial images and adages of organizational politics involving "smoky back rooms," "going behind to get ahead," and "working behind the scenes." These elements call attention to notions not only that organizational politics involves actions related to self-interest and power but also that the means are somehow not formally authorized as being legitimate. However, given that the term *legitimate* means very different things in different literatures, the phrase *not officially sanctioned* is used here

Means that are not officially sanctioned can be of two types. First, organizational politics can involve actions that are unofficially sanctioned. That is, even though a given means is not authorized by official operating procedures, formal job duties, reporting structures, and the like, it may nonetheless enjoy some informal sanctioning or even recognition that "this is the way things are done around here." Thus, individuals informally may know that they have to schmooze executives at office social gatherings if they want to win the next promotion, even if such methods are not recognized formally. Such means may be especially likely to receive unofficial sanction when officially sanctioned means are chronically unavailable or undervalued.

Second, political behavior may involve means that are not sanctioned at all. For example, the use of blackmail or withholding valuable information to make one appear more knowledgeable may not be authorized in any circumstances in some organizations but nonetheless may be used in political behavior. These more extreme and unsavory means likely are the source of discomfort and unease that individuals often have when thinking about organizational politics.

In sum, it is suggested that organizational politics can be conceptualized as an actor's or actors' (i.e., individual's or group's) self-interested, goal-directed power and social influence actions that are performed in relation to two or more interdependent social actors by means that are not officially sanctioned. As mentioned in the introduction, although these are viewed as the necessary elements of organizational politics, this is not the one and only definition; some definitions may have additional elements. However, this synthesis is helpful in developing a common understanding that can be used across literatures, whether politics is the direct object of study or theorized in relation to an alternative focus of interest (e.g., politics as a part of strategic decision making).

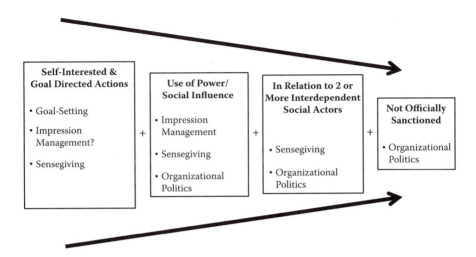

FIGURE 3.1
The unique domain of organizational politics.

Differentiating Organizational Politics From Other Constructs

Identifying the core elements of politics helps differentiate it from similar constructs and thereby enhances its theoretical utility. Many of the proposed arguments build on set theory logic that some constructs are by definition subsets of other constructs, but the reverse is not always true. For example, whereas all organizational politics will involve power and influence, not all power and influence actions will involve organizational politics. It is possible to wield power and influence primarily for the greater good as well as exclusively for self-centered means. Further, organizational politics also is a construct that involves *multiple* necessary, but not sufficient, conditions.

Building on earlier arguments, other concepts may have some but not all of these necessary conditions. Figure 3.1 illustrates the differences between organizational politics and related constructs. The next section examines some concepts that often have been discussed together with politics, such as impression management (Leary & Kowalski, 1990) and goal setting (Locke & Latham, 2002), as well as a newer concept, sensegiving (Gioia & Chittipeddi, 1991), which seems to share similar space in a nomological net. Thus, Figure 3.1 is used illustratively. We recognize there is variance in how these terms are defined, and therefore, our representation may not align perfectly with all existing perspectives.

Figure 3.1 demonstrates that as the various elements of organizational politics are included, other similar terms tend to fall out, ultimately revealing the unique conceptual space of organizational politics. To illustrate, starting at the leftmost box, each of these terms refers to behaviors that are goal directed, with one possible exception. Impression management involves controlling how individuals are perceived (Leary & Kowalski, 1990). For example, during an employment interview, individuals might dress very well, be neat and clean, and arrive on time to persuade the recruiter that they are professional. However, a question mark is added here because while impression management can be goal directed, it may not be always as planned, as argued is the case regarding politics. In fact, impression management often is preattentive and nonconscious (Leary & Kowalski, 1990). However, it is included here given its centrality in some perspective on politics. The case for sensegiving is clearer. Sensegiving involves attempts to alter someone's interpretive scheme, such as to facilitate the acceptance of an organizational change attempt (Gioia & Chittipeddi, 1991). Thus, sensegiving is goal directed. Finally, goal-setting is by definition goal directed.

Some differentiation can begin to be seen among constructs as the element of "use of power and social influence" is added. In particular, goal setting drops from the list because typically it does not involve the use of power or influence over others. Rather, it is the goals—or, more specifically, the property of goals such as its content and intensity—that are the "immediate regulators of human action" (Locke, Shaw, Saari, & Latham, 1981, p. 126). The other contenders remain. Impression management involves social influence, such as improving one's attractiveness to create a sense of liking. Similarly, sensegiving most often is evoked in extant literature as a top-down process, whereby someone in authority is attempting to influence how individuals make sense of the world around them (e.g., Gioia & Chittapeddi, 1991; Pratt, 2000). Even when sensegiving does not involve leaders, it still involves influence tactics, although perhaps not the use of power bases (Maitlis & Lawrence, 2007).

As "in relation to two or more social actors" is added, only sensegiving remains. While not conceptualized necessarily as involving more than dyads, empirical work on sensegiving tends to view it as occurring in larger collectives, be they academic departments (Gioia & Chittipeddi, 1991), symphony orchestras (Maitlis & Lawrence, 2007), or Amway distributor groups (Pratt, 2000). Furthermore, each involves different stakeholders, be they administration and faculty, management teams, conductors and players, or active and inactive distributors, respectively.

At this point, impression management definitely drops out. While impression management may be exhibited in front of an audience, the audience also represents those who are to be directly influenced by the impression manager. Thus, there are only two roles in impression management: (1) the agent; and (2) the target. Consequently, whether impression management is conceptualized as actually dyadic, it often is theorized as functionally dyadic—that is, considering impression management as "only in terms of fostering impressions in the eyes of others" (Leary & Kowalski, 1990, p. 34). As noted previously, political actions always are conduced vis-à-vis others, whether they be allies, competitors, or even indifferent observers (i.e., bystanders).

Alternatively, impression management may play a similar intersecting role as does power and social influence; that is, while politics always may involve some impression management, broadly defined, not all impression management need be political in nature. The qualifier *may* is used here because, as stated earlier, impression management differs from politics in that it is often nonconscious and therefore does not have the more conscious and deliberate qualities implied by *goal directed*. That said, conceiving of politics as goal-directed actions involving at least three parties best distinguishes it from impression management.

Finally, organizational politics differs from sensegiving in that the former uses means that are not officially sanctioned, but the latter does not. Again, although research in this area is still in its early stages, sensegiving primarily has been depicted as a means of furthering organizational ends* (Gioia & Chittipeddi, 1991; Maitlis & Lawrence, 2007), often through officially sanctioned means. Hence, formally sanctioned vehicles such as visioning (Gioia & Chittipeddi, 1991) or dream building (Pratt, 2000) often are used for sensegiving but not for organizational politics.

---

* It is important to note that, to date, most sensegiving depictions are done in the interests of the organization. This is not to say that sensegiving cannot also be self-interested, as was the case in Pratt's (2000) Amway distributors, or that it can be solely or primarily self-interested. If the concept develops such that organizational interests are a primary motive, then this will be another distinguishing feature between sensegiving and organizational politics.

UNANSWERED QUESTIONS AND FUTURE DIRECTIONS

With the domain area for organizational politics identified and some key definitional elements proposed, the second part of our original charge is now addressed: to delineate new areas for research. By investigating what organizational politics is and comparing this with extant work, two broad yet related questions for future research to address emerged: (1) How does perception and perspective factor into organizational politics; and, more generally, (2) what methods could we use to advance our understanding of organizational politics?

These questions are driven principally by two components of the proposed definition: (1) the involvement of three or more social actors; and, to a lesser degree, (2) actions that are not officially sanctioned. More broadly, future research on organizational politics would benefit from more fully embracing its social nature, its fluid, situationally based character, and its ongoing impact on perceptions of self and others and by identifying and utilizing methodological tools to capture such qualities.

How Does Perception and Perspective Factor Into Organizational Politics?

Though many of the critical definitional elements included have been mentioned by others (see Table 3.1), the present perspective perhaps varies most from extant views by explicitly detailing the social nature of politics. This explication is critical as it opens up new and exciting areas for research in an area that appears to enjoy the lion's share of recent attention in this field: perceptions of organizational politics.

If three or more parties are involved in politics, the process can be examined from each of their perspectives. Thus, as Max Weber suggested in the epigraph, the importance of both perception and perspective becomes critical. At a general level, this movement would extend work of Ferris and colleagues on the importance of how individuals perceive their organizations in terms of its *politicalness*. However, these and similar studies tend to focus on an unidentified observer on a rather undifferentiated political context (e.g., "People in this organization attempt to build themselves up by tearing others down" and "Agreeing with powerful others is the best alternative in this organization") (Kacmar & Carlson, 1997). By adding perspective to perception, this general stream of politics research can be enriched in at least five ways.

First, political actions can be examined from different *positions* of actors within a given political process or situation. Recalling the aforementioned example from Jackall's (1983) "Moral Mazes," where a plant manager spends scarce resources on seemingly superfluous things (e.g., making glossy brochures) to impress her CEO, there are potentially a number of actors involved in this situation, including the CEO, the plant manager, the manager's subordinates, and perceived competition. These actors hold different positions as they relate to any political action: *the politician* or the initiator of political action (plant manager); *the voter* or the target of the political influence attempt (CEO); *the interested audience* or someone directly impacted by the success or failure of the political action, either as an ally (protégé) or competitor (manager of different department); and people who may not have any direct stake in the political action or *the bystanders* (workers in different plants who hear about this action) but may nonetheless be influenced by the presence of overt political behavior in their organization. Individuals in each of these positions (e.g., politicians vs. voters) may perceive and interpret the same political activity quite differently (e.g., positive, negative, ambivalent) and thus respond differently. In short, considering the role of position allows the social and socially constructed nature of perceptions and interpretations of politics in organizations to be more fully captured. See Table 3.2 for illustrative examples.

Second, it might be important not only to examine how people in specific positions view and interpret political actions but also how they might perceive and act when in the presence of actors in different positions. Such a focus would more fully embrace the shifting, situationally based nature of organizational politics. For example, how do voters or targets of influence interpret political activities when in the presence of the politicians' allies or competitors? Would bystanders be confused or possibly anxious when interacting with a group composed of politicians, targets, allies, and competitors?

Similarly, how do perceptions change based on the configuration of positions represented in a given political process? Politics must be involved, but perceptions may play out quite differently if there are even numbers of allies and competitors in the mix or if there are more bystanders than members of an interested audience. By more specifically identifying the position of those involved in the political process, a more nuanced

TABLE 3.2

Illustrative Examples of How Positions May Influence Political Perceptions

Political Position	Potential Perceptions and Interpretations
Politician(s)	Political activity is good or a necessary evil? A distraction from getting one's "real work" done? A "game" I am versed in playing? How do I/we expect the "game" to play out? How do I/we manage the "optics" of this situation?
Voter(s)	Political action may be good, bad, or cause ambivalence. Are these actions political? Does such illegitimate influence behaviors make me anxious? Disappointed? Flattered? What are the ramifications of my decision? How will others view my actions in this political situation? What example am I/we setting for others?
Interested Audience: Ally/Allies	Political behavior is acceptable "overall"? What does my role of "ally" entail? What will I owe the politician if they succeed? What do I/we do if the political action fails? What opportunity costs have I/we incurred with this alliance?
Interested Audience: Competitor(s)	Political behavior is bad "overall"? What will I/we do if the politician succeeds or fails? What needs to be done to mitigate the politician's actions? Can I take "the high road" regarding political action given that I may need to rely on it in the future?
Bystander	Political behavior is …? What does this mean about my organization that this political behavior is happening? Succeeding? Failing? How might this eventually impact me/us?

understanding of perceptions and interpretations of political actions, situations, and actors can be gained.

Third, future work also can benefit from turning the perspective from perceptions of *others* (i.e., whether that be of situations or actors) inward to perceptions of one's *self*. While there has been some work in this area (see Table 3.3), it is relatively rare and much more can be done. Table 3.3 provides illustrative examples of topics and methods used in the study of organizational politics. To illustrate, research suggests that identity and work behavior are inherently intertwined; that is, what one does affects who one is and vice versa (Pratt, Rockmann, & Kaufmann, 2006). When actors (individual or collective) engage in organizational politics, how does this affect their self-definition? In what ways, if any, do political actors attempt to balance the needs of their constituents who not only want them to reflect their (i.e., the constituent's) values but also to have integrity (see "the politician's dilemma," Kraatz & Block, 2008)? That is, in what ways might political behaviors be brought to bear in defense of, or

TABLE 3.3

Methods in Organizational Politics Research

Method	Perspective	Author
Survey	Perceptions of environment	Kacmar and Carlson (1997)
		Randall et al. (1999)
		Cropanzano, Howes, Grandey, and Toth (1997)
		Witt, Patti, and Farmer (2002)
		Ferris and Kacmar (1992)
		Parker, Dipboye, and Jackson (1995)
		Rosen, Harris, and Kacmar (2009)
		Darr and Johns (2004)
		Gandz and Murray (1980)
	Perceptions of environment Self-reported political behaviors	Valle and Perrewé (2000)
	Perceptions of political activity (self and others)	Buchanan (2008)
	Perceptions of environment Self-reported political behaviors	Harrell-Cook, Ferris, and Dulebohn (1999)
	Self-reported political behavior	Treadway, Hochwarter, Kacmar, Ferris (2005)
	Perceptions of politics around research and development projects	Markham (2000)
	Perceptions of political activity in strategic alliances	Walter, Lechner, and Kellermanns (2008)
	Perceptions of political activity in top-management teams	Dean & Sharfman (1996)
		Elbanna & Child (2007)
Meta-analysis of Surveys	Perceptions of environment	Chang, Rosen, and Levy (2009)
		Miller, Rutherford, and Kolodinsky (2008)
Participant Observation and Interviews	Actors' interpretations and behaviors	Bradshaw-Camball & Murray (1991)
Primarily Interviews	Perceptions of political situations and other actors	Eisenhardt & Bourgeois (1988)
	Perceptions of environment	Riley (1983)
	Change agent perceptions of politics	Buchanan & Badham (1999)
Interviews, Participant Observation, Cognitive Mapping	Perceptions of specific political behavior	Voyer (1994)
Observation, Interviews, Survey	Respondents' political alliances	Gargiulo (1993)

as a threat to, a politician's integrity? In what ways, if any, and under what conditions might political behavior diminish the actor or actors' identity? Conversely, and perhaps more interestingly, in what ways, if any, and under what conditions might these actions enrich (e.g., increase efficacy of) the political actor?

Turning to an individual-level example, research suggests that some individuals may see politics as a vocation or a calling (Mahler, 2006). Likewise, others suggest that some individuals predominantly may view work as a means to develop power and prestige (Pratt, Pradies, & Lepisto, forthcoming). C. Wright Mills (1951) offered a provocative image of potentially political activity: "'getting ahead' becomes 'a continual selling job'.... Whether you are seeking a new position or are aiming at the job just ahead. In either case you must sell yourself and keep on selling ... you have a product and that product is yourself" (p. 264). Future research should examine the ramifications of this activity on actors' identity and sense of self-worth. Finally, not only might political behavior influence one's identity; the converse also may be true. The notion of *identity politics* or politics based on a social category (e.g., nationality, race, gender, sexual orientation) has some cache in political science, but could it also play a role in organizational politics?

Fourth, though the focus to this point predominantly has examined perceptions and interpretations, perception, interpretation, and action are iterative cycles (Weick, 1995). Thus, scholars also are encouraged to more deeply investigate the *actions* individuals take as they play different positions. While some scholars have moved in the direction of identifying types of political actions, a more fine-grained analysis would involve cataloguing these actions depending on the position one plays. Indeed, research to date appears to have focused more exclusively on the actions of politicians, with seemingly less attention paid to *voters* and *interested audiences*.

Moreover, research also seems to have considered political action in relatively atomized ways, without considering action *relative* to the constellation of other actors. However, Gargiulo (1993) provided a notable exception in his examination of the strategic actions actors take to reduce their dependence on other actors. He described a situation involving three actors, where actor A is dependent on actor B, who is dependent on actor C. One could think of an employee (actor A), a boss (actor B), and the boss's boss (actor C). *Two-step leverage* occurs when actor A establishes relations with actor C. This relationship can serve to limit the influence of actor B on A given that actor C constrains actor B. There are similarities here to our prior discussion of different political positions. Actor A represents the *politician*; actor B is an *interested audience*; and actor C is the *voter*. Although this research focused on the strategic actions of politicians, future research that considers the tactics of others' positions would be illuminating.

This example also implicitly highlights that one's position and associated perceptions and tactics are not always individually determined but that contextual and structural factors (e.g., formal reporting structures and dependencies) are important in shaping them as well (see, e.g., Brass, 1984; Brass & Burkhardt, 1993). Social network methodologies have been particularly useful in this regard. In short, a consideration of action, perception, and interpretation based on the position and composition of actors will better capture the complicated dynamics of political behavior in organizations.

Fifth and finally, highlighting the importance of various positions in a political scenario also raises troubling issues of intent and verification. While we acknowledge this implication, we also realize that inserting these issues into conversations about organizational politics may be akin to opening a conceptual Pandora's box. For example, if someone perceives an actor as engaging in a political activity, is it political even if the actor never intended it to be so? Ultimately, who decides or verifies whether an action is political? Is it in the eye of the beholder? The actor? Or possibly the researcher? In particular, the latter raises broader issues of methodology.

What Methods Could We Use to Advance Our Understanding of Organizational Politics?

While the proposed definition of organizational politics offers potentially new theoretical insights and directions for future research, these should be accompanied by new, or possibly even a return to older, methodological approaches. Before turning to these, it is instructive to quickly review the dominant approaches. Early work on organizational politics (see, e.g., Mintzberg, 1983; Pfeffer, 1981) largely was theoretical, although it relied on observations and case examples to inform thinking.

Subsequent work on politics, particularly related to decision making, tended to use surveys (e.g., Dean & Sharfman, 1996; Walter et al., 2008, in press) with Eisenhardt and Bourgeois's (1988) and Pettigrew's (1973) qualitative case analyses as notable exceptions. Survey methodology also is the dominant paradigm for studies examining the antecedents (e.g., formalization, centralization, job characteristics, demographics) and outcomes (e.g., job satisfaction, anxiety, turnover intentions) of perceptions of politics. Illustrative examples of studies, their topics, and methods used are provided in Table 3.3.

Conceptualizing politics in terms of multiple, interacting, and potentially coalition-forming entities raise some interesting methodological challenges for the study of organizational politics. To be sure, the focus on various political positions could be adapted in a relatively straightforward way to the survey approach taken by those who study the perceptions of organizational politics. These studies may wish to survey individuals' positions in the political action and to compare perceptions across positions. However, even this approach may be problematic.

To begin, positions may shift with the initiation of a given political action and may change over time with respect to that political action (e.g., converting an individual or group from a competitor into an ally). Moreover, any given organization may comprise multiple political actions, and at any given moment individuals may hold multiple positions. This begs the question: What does an overall impression of politics in an organization miss? Finally, given the dynamism of politics (e.g., multiple interdependent actors acting by means not officially sanctioned), it seems unlikely that a single snapshot will get at how these perceptions form or change.

More generally, surveys may be ill-equipped to get at other questions related to politics, such as how political processes are enacted in organizations. As was discussed in the introduction of this chapter, much more is known about the antecedents and consequences of some aspects of organizational politics, but much less is understood about what organizational politics actually are (in action). This is especially true when examining organizational politics as a longitudinal process. These challenges suggest new or renewed interest in some methodological approaches regarding organizational politics.

Starting most generally, research examining political processes might consider taking a more process versus a more variance approach (Langley, 1999; Mohr, 1982) for exploring how organizational politics unfolds, over time, in groups and in organizations. While process research often is qualitative in nature, it need not be (see Van de Ven & Poole, 1990). Whatever specific methods it entails, this research should consider (1) nonlinear, nondeterministic approaches; (2) the role of experience; (3) more relational ontologies; and (4) the role of time, especially as it relates to ongoing processes (Langley & Tsoukas, 2010). In particular, it would be interesting to see how actors (i.e., either individual or collective) in different positions relate to each other as the political process or *organizational politicking* unfolds.

In addition, given the officially unsanctioned character of political action, the role of interviews or surveys—especially of those initiating in or participating in such activity—may be limited due to social desirability effects. This suggests that less invasive approaches (e.g., nonparticipant and participant observations) may be useful in understanding how political action plays out in organization. To date, only a handful of studies have incorporated observational techniques into the examination of political action (see Table 3.3).

In a similar vein, more inductive approaches, especially those that are ethnographic (Pratt & Kim, in press), also may be useful to better comprehend how politics are defined and understood in groups and organizations by those engaging in these practices. Not only can such approaches enrich how the term is conceptualized, but also, returning to the domain statement, it would be interesting to see how actors attempt to achieve self-interested goals when legitimate means are either undesirable or ineffective. As evident in early work on politics, politicking is all about getting things done in collectives. However, it is not clear whether and how this is done *today* is similar to, and different from how it has been done in the past (e.g., Jackall, 1983). For example, in what ways, if any, might social media and similar technologies play a role in politicking? How might advances in employee monitoring (e.g., increase use of security cameras, monitoring of phones and computers) influence the political milieu? Given the paucity of research in this area, more inductive research may be warranted.

Inductive approaches also might be effective in understanding how politics relates to actors' identity and perceptions of meaning. Here qualitative interviews would be helpful. Moreover, specific political processes, such as identity politicking or how actors may find meaning in engaging in politicking at work, are not well understood in organizations and thus are more amenable to theory building and elaborating approaches.

Finally, given the emphasis on examining perspectives and perceptions, methods have been suggested that gain more micro-level insights. However, methods that capture more macro-level dynamics would be welcome, too, especially those that position politics as figure and not ground. Examples of such methods are rich, single, and comparative organizational cases of politicking, network analyses of actors, actions, coalition formation and movement in political processes, and archival or historical analyses of political actions.

CONCLUSION

Organizational politics represent ubiquitous phenomena in organizations, but the topic is not a central focus of current research appearing in top-tier journals. This chapter began by suggesting that this may be due to a fragmentation of understanding and definitions across disparate literatures as well as how politics often are studied as ground rather than figure in both theorizing and empirical research. Thus, much more is known about what organizational politics does than what it is. Although there have been other attempts to review and integrate research in organizational politics, we hope that this cross-level review of the history of the term, subsequent identification of a unique domain area for politics, and articulation of what is believed are core elements of a organizational politics definition will be helpful in navigating its dizzying number of extant definitions, conceptualizations, and applications.

We further hope that through this process, especially in recognition of its social properties, the field will be more fully open to and invigorated to address understudied research areas, such as a more refined view of perspectives and action in the political process. This should be done by examining the various perspectives of those influenced by politics (e.g., voters, interested audiences, bystanders), as well as by turning perspectives inward to examine politics and the self. Also, new methodological issues were raised, such as the difficulty of examining unsanctioned actions, and how more process-oriented, more inductive, and less invasive (e.g., observation) approaches may complement surveys, which has been the dominant methodology in this area. The final conclusion is that organizational politics, despite being an area of inquiry for decades in organizational research, is nonetheless ripe for renewed theoretical and empirical examinations.

ACKNOWLEDGMENT

We would like to thank Jerry Ferris, Mary Ann Glynn, and Candace Jones for their comments on earlier drafts of this chapter.

REFERENCES

Ashforth, B.E., & Lee, R.T. (1990). Defensive behavior in organizations: A preliminary model. *Human Relations, 43*, 621–648.

Bacharach, S., & Lawler, E. (1980). *Power and politics in organizations.* San Francisco: Jossey-Bass.

Bacharach, S., & Lawler, E. (1998). Political alignments in organizations: Contextualization, mobilization, and coordination. In R.M. Kramer & M.A. Neale (Eds.), *Power and politics in organizations* (pp. 67–88). San Francisco: Jossey-Bass.

Bradshaw-Camball, P., & Murray, V. (1991). Illusions and other games: A trifocal view of organizational politics. *Organization Science, 2,* 379–398.

Buchanan, D., & Badham, R. (1999). Politics and organizational change: The lived experience. *Human Relations, 52,* 609–629.

Buchanan, D.A. (2008). You stab my back, I'll stab yours: Management experience and perceptions of organization political behaviour. *British Journal of Management, 19,* 49–64.

Brass, D.J. (1984). Men's and women's networks: A study of interaction patterns and influence in an organization. *Academy of Management Journal, 28,* 327–343.

Brass, D.J., & Burkhardt, M.E. (1993). Potential power and power use: An investigation of structure and behavior. *Academy of Management Journal, 36,* 441–470.

Chang, C., Rosen, C., & Levy, P. (2009). The relationship between perceptions of organizational politics and employee attitudes, strain, and behavior: A meta-analytic examination. *Academy of Management Journal, 52,* 779–801.

Cialdini, R. (1993). *Influence: The psychology of persuasion.* New York: Quill.

Cropanzano, R., Howes, J., Grandey, A., & Toth, P. (1997). The relationship of organizational politics and support to work behaviors, attitudes, and stress. *Journal of Organizational Behavior, 18,* 159–180.

Cyert, R., & March, J. (1963). *A behavioral theory of the firm.* New Jersey: Prentice-Hall.

Dahl, R. (1957). The concept of power. *Behavioral Science, 2,* 201–215.

Darr, W., & Johns, G. (2004). Political decision-making climates: Theoretical processes and multi-level antecedents. *Human Relations, 57,* 169–200.

Dean Jr., J., & Sharfman, M. (1996). Does decision process matter? A study of strategic decision-making effectiveness. *Academy of Management Journal, 39,* 368–396.

Drory, A., & Romm, T. (1990). The definition of organizational politics: A review. *Human Relations, 43,* 1133–1154.

Eisenhardt, K., & Bourgeois III, L. (1988). Politics of strategic decision making in high-velocity environments: Toward a midrange theory. *Academy of Management Journal, 31,* 737–770.

Eisenhardt, K., & Zbaracki, M. (1992). Strategic decision making. *Strategic Management Journal, 13,* 17–37.

Elbanna, S., & Child, J. (2007). Influences on strategic decision effectiveness: Development and test of an integrative model. *Strategic Management Journal, 28*, 431–453.

Emerson, R. (1962). Power-dependence relations. *American Sociological Review, 27*, 31–41.

Ferris, G.R., Russ, G.S., & Fandt, P. (1989). Politics in organizations. In R.A. Giacalone & P. Rosenfeld (Eds.), *Impression management in the organization* (pp. 143–170). Hillsdale, NJ: Lawrence Erlbaum.

Ferris, G.R., & Kacmar, K.M. (1992). Perceptions of organizational politics. *Journal of Management, 18*, 93–116.

Ferris, G.R., Fedor, D.B., King, T.R. (1994). A political conceptualization of managerial behavior. *Human Resource Management Review, 4*, 1–34.

Ferris, G.R., Treadway, D.C., Kolodinsky, R.W., Hochwarter, W.A., Kacmar, C.J., Douglas, C., et al. (2005). Development and validation of the political skill inventory. *Journal of Management, 31*, 126–152.

Ferris, G.R., Treadway, D.C., Perrewé, P.L., Brouer, R.L., Douglas, C., & Lux, S. (2007). Political skill in organizations. *Journal of Management, 33*, 290–320.

French, J., & Raven, B. (1959). The bases of social power. In D. Cartwright & A. Zander (Eds.), *Group dynamics* (pp. 150–167). New York: Harper & Row.

Gandz, J., & Murray, V.V. (1980). The experience of workplace politics. *Academy of Management Journal, 23*, 237–251.

Gargiulo, M. (1993). Two-step leverage: Managing constraint in organizational politics. *Administrative Science Quarterly, 38*, 1–19.

Gioia, D., & Chittipeddi, K. (1991). Sensemaking and sensegiving in strategic change initiation. *Strategic Management Journal, 12*, 433–448.

Harrell-Cook, G., Ferris, G.R., & Dulebohn, J.H. (1999). Political behaviors as moderators of the perceptions of organizational politics–work outcomes relationships. *Journal of Organizational Behavior, 20*, 1093–1105.

Ibarra, H., & Andrews, S. (1993). Power, social influence, and sense making: Effects of network centrality and proximity on employee perceptions. *Administrative Science Quarterly, 38*, 277–303.

Jackall, R. (1983). Moral mazes: Bureaucracy and managerial work. *Harvard Business Review, 61*, 118–130.

Kacmar, K.M., & Baron, R. (1999). Organizational politics: The state of the field, links to related processes, and an agenda for future research. In G.R. Ferris (Ed.), *Research in personnel and human resources management* (Vol. 17, pp. 1–39). Stamford, CT: JAI Press.

Kacmar, K.M., & Carlson, D. (1997). Further validation of the perceptions of politics scale (POPS): A multiple sample investigation. *Journal of Management, 23*, 627–658.

Kanter, R.M. (1977). *Men and women of the corporation*. New York: Basic Books.

Krackhardt, D. (1990). Assessing the political landscape: Structure, cognition, and power in organizations. *Administrative Science Quarterly, 35*, 342–369.

Kraatz, M., & Block, E. (2008). Organizational implications of institutional plurism. In R. Greenwood, C. Oliver, R. Suddaby, & K. Sahlin-Andersson (Ed.), *Handbook of organizational institutionalism* (pp. 243–275). London: Sage Publications.

Krackhardt, D. (1990). Assessing the political landscape: Structure, cognition, and power in organizations. *Administrative Science Quarterly, 35*, 342–369.

Langley, A. (1999). Strategies for theorizing from process data. *Academy of Management Review, 24*, 691–710.

Langley, A., & Tsoukas, H. (2010). Introducing perspectives on process organizational studies. In T. Hernes & S. Maitlis (Eds.), *Process sensemaking and organizing* (pp. 1–26). London: Oxford University Press.

Lawrence, T., Mauws, M., Dyck, B., & Kleysen, R. (2005). The politics of organizational learning: integrating power into the 4I framework. *Academy of Management Review, 30,* 180–191.

Leary, M., & Kowalski, R. (1990). Impression management: A literature review and two-component model. *Psychological Bulletin, 107,* 34–47.

Lepisto, D., Pradies, C., & Pratt, M. (2010). *Reconceptualizing work orientation: On its origins, meanings, and outcomes.* Working paper, Boston College, Chestnut Hill.

Liden, R., & Mitchell, T. (1988). Ingratiatory behaviors in organizational settings. *Academy of Management Review, 13,* 572–587.

Locke, E., & Latham, G. (2002). Building a practically useful theory of goal setting and task motivation: A 35-year odyssey. *American Psychologist, 57,* 705–717.

Locke, E., Shaw, K., Saari, L., & Latham, G. (1980). Goal setting and task performance: 1969-1980. *Psychological Bulletin, 90,* 125–152.

Mahler, M. (2006). Politics as a vocation: Notes toward a sensualist understanding of political engagement. *Qualitative Sociology, 29,* 281–300.

Maitlis, S., & Lawrence, T. (2007). Triggers and enablers of sensegiving in organizations. *Academy of Management Journal, 50,* 57–84.

March, J. (1962). The business firm as a political coalition. *Journal of Politics, 24,* 662–678.

March, J., & Simon, H. (1958). *Organizations.* Cambridge, UK: Blackwell.

Markham, S. (2000). Corporate championing and antagonism as forms of political behavior: An R&D perspective. *Organization Science, 11,* 429–447.

Mayes, B.T., & Allen, R.W. (1977). Toward a definition of organizational politics. *Academy of Management Review, 2,* 672–678.

Miller, B., Rutherford, M., & Kolodinsky, R. (2008). Perceptions of organizational politics: A meta-analysis of outcomes. *Journal of Business and Psychology, 22,* 209–222.

Mills, C. (1953). *White collar.* New York: Oxford University Press.

Mintzberg, H. (1983). *Power in and around organziations.* Englewood Cliffs, NJ: Prentice-Hall.

Mintzberg, H. (1990). Strategy formulation: Ten schools of thought. In J. Fredrickson (Ed.), *Perspectives on strategic management* (pp. 105–235). Cambridge, MA: Ballinger.

Mohr, L.B. (1982). *Explaining organizational behavior.* San Francisco: Jossey-Bass.

Parker, C., Dipboye, R., & Jackson, S. (1995). Perceptions of organizational politics: An investigation of antecedents and consequences. *Journal of Management, 21,* 891–912.

Pettigrew, A. (1973). *The politics of organizational decision-making.* London: Tavistock.

Pfeffer, J. (1981). *Power in organizations.* Boston: Pitman.

Pfeffer, J., & Salancik, G.R. (1978). *The external control of organizations.* New York: Harper & Row.

Pratt, M.G. (1998). To be or not to be? Central questions in organizational identification. In D.A. Whetten & P.C. Godfrey (Eds.), *Identity in organizations: Building theory through conversations* (pp. 171–207). Thousand Oaks, CA: Sage.

Pratt, M. (2000). The good, the bad, and the ambivalent: Managing identification among Amway distributors. *Administrative Science Quarterly, 45,* 456–493.

Pratt, M. (2003). Disentangling collective identities. In J. Polzer, E. Mannix, & M. Neale (Eds.), *Identity issues in groups: Research in managing groups and teams* (Vol. 5, pp. 161–188). Stamford, CT: Elsevier Science Ltd.

Pratt, M.G., & Kim, N. (in press). Designing for drift: Planning ethnographic qualitative research on groups. In A. Hollingshead & M.S. Poole (Eds.), *Research methods for studying groups: A behind-the-scenes guide*. Boca Raton, FL: Taylor & Francis/Routledge.

Pratt, M.G., Pradies, C., & Lepisto, D.A. (forthcoming). Doing well, doing good, doing with: Organizational practices for effectively cultivating meaningful work. In B.J. Kik, Z.S. Byrne, & M.F. Steger (Eds.), *Purpose and meaning in the workplace*. New York: American Psychological Association.

Pratt, M., Rockmann, K., & Kaufmann, J. (2006). Constructing professional identity: The role of work and identity learning cycles in the customization of identity among medical residents. *Academy of Management Journal, 49,* 235–262.

Provis, C. (2006). Organizational politics, definitions, and ethics. In E. Vigoda-Gadot & A. Drory (Eds.), *Handbook of organizational politics* (pp. 89–106). Cheltenham: Edward Elgar.

Randall, M., Cropanzano, R., Bormann, C., & Birjulin, A. (1999). Organizational politics and organizational support as predictors of work attitudes, job performance, and organizational citizenship behavior. *Journal of Organizational Behavior, 20,* 159–174.

Riley, P. (1983). A structurationist account of political culture. *Administrative Science Quarterly, 28,* 414–437.

Rosen, C., Harris, K., & Kacmar, K. (2009). The emotional implications of organizational politics: A process model. *Human Relations, 62,* 27–57.

Salancik, G.R., & Pfeffer, J. (1977). Who gets power and how they hold on to it: A strategic-contingency model of power. *Organizational Dynamics*, Winter, 3–21.

Selznick, P. (1957). *Leadership in administration: A sociological interpretation*. Berkeley: University of California Press.

Selznick, P. (1966). *TVA and the grass roots: A study in the sociology of formal organization*. New York: Harper & Row.

Simmel, G. (1950). *The sociology of Georg Simmel*. New York: Free Press.

Simon, H.A. (1957). *Models of man*. New York: Wiley.

Tedeschi, J., & Melburg, V. (1984). Impression management and influence in the organization. In S. Bacharach & E.J. Lawler (Eds.), *Research in the sociology of organizations* (Vol. 3, pp. 31–58). Greenwich, CT: JAI Press.

Treadway, D.C., Hochwater, W.A., Kacmar, C.J., & Ferris, G.R. (2005). Political will, political skill, and political behavior. *Journal of Organizational Behavior*, 26(3), 229–245.

Tushman, M. (1977). A political approach to organizations: A review and rationale. *Academy of Management Review, 2,* 206–216.

Vaisey, S. (2009). Motivation and justification: A dual-process model of culture in action. *American Journal of Sociology, 114,* 1675–1715.

Valle, M., & Perrewe, P.L. (2000). Do politics perceptions relate to political behaviors? Tests of an implicit assumption and expanded model. *Human Relations*, 53(3), 359–386.

Van de Ven, A., & Poole, M.S. (1990). Methods for studying innovation and development in the Minnesota Innovation Research Program. *Organization Science, 1,* 313–335.

Voyer, J. (1994). Coercive organizational politics and organizational outcomes: An interpretive study. *Organization Science, 5,* 72–85.

Walter, J., Kellermanns, F., & Lechner, C. (in press). Decision making within and between organizations: Rationality, politics, and alliance performance. *Journal of Management*.

Walter, J., Lechner, C., & Kellermanns, F. (2008). Disentangling alliance management processes: decision making, politicality, and alliance performance. *Journal of Management Studies, 45,* 530–560.

Weick, K.E. (1995). *Sensemaking in organizations.* Thousand Oaks, CA: Sage Publications.

Weber, M. (1978). *Economy and society.* Berkeley: University of California Press.

Witt, L., Patti, A., & Farmer, W. (2002). Organizational politics and work identity as predictors of organizational commitment. *Journal of Applied Social Psychology, 32,* 486–499.

4

Measurement and Methodology in Organizational Politics Research

Lynn A. McFarland
Clemson University and Human Capital Solutions, Inc.

Chad H. Van Iddekinge
Florida State University

Robert E. Ployhart
University of South Carolina

Understanding the nature, antecedents, and consequences of organizational politics requires a cohesive relationship among theory, measures, methods, and analyses. A researcher's choices about the measures and methodology used to test a theory undoubtedly will affect the outcome of that investigation and, cumulatively, the amount of support for a given theory. The challenge is to choose the most appropriate measures and methods to study the theory or phenomenon of interest so that the true relationships are revealed and science advances.

Issues of measurement and research methodology are particularly complex within organizational politics research because definitional (Gunn & Chen, 2006), design and measurement (Ferris, Adams, Kolodinsky, Hochwarter, & Ammeter, 2002), and level of analysis (Dipboye & Foster, 2002) issues have been inconsistently applied. Organizational politics encompasses a wide range of potential psychological processes and behaviors. Further, inherent in most definitions of organizational politics are one's motives for engaging in the behaviors that may be seen as political. Therefore, it is not a simple case of observing behavior and determining if someone is acting in a certain way, because the same overt behavior may be caused by different motives. Add to this that politics may occur within any level of the organization (i.e., employee, supervisor, group, organization), and any of those levels may exert influence on other levels. All of these issues account for the inherently complex nature of organizational politics research, yet at the same time incredible opportunities for future research exist to be pursued.

In this chapter, the complexities of designing and selecting adequate measures and methods in organizational politics research are examined. To begin, some popular conceptualizations of organizational politics are discussed, and, in so doing, it is explained why measuring organizational politics may be difficult in many instances. Next, the most popular measurement and methodological approaches in this literature are described, and the strengths and weaknesses of each are noted. Finally, the chapter concludes with methodological directions for future research.

Specifically, measurement, methodological, and analytical approaches are discussed, which have to date been rarely implemented in organizational politics research but have the potential to offer some useful insights. In addition to this, take-away recommendations are provided throughout the chapter. The intention is to briefly summarize the current status of measurement and research methodology in organizational politics research so that considerable attention can be devoted to providing recommendations for future research. However, in the process, the intention is not to criticize any specific author or study but instead to attempt to provide constructive suggestions to help advance work in the future in this important area of inquiry.

DOMAINS AND DEFINITIONS OF ORGANIZATIONAL POLITICS

The measures used in organizational politics are only as good as the definitions on which they are based. If the definition fails to capture the entire construct domain, then the measure of that construct will fail as well. The dominant approach for developing measures of psychological constructs is known as a *domain sampling* approach (Nunnally & Bernstein, 1994). A latent construct domain is first defined so that its nature, boundaries, and characteristics are specified. Then, manifest item sampling from this latent domain are developed so that there exists broad coverage of the domain's content. The item sampling should be comprehensive to ensure construct validity, and there should be enough items to ensure good levels of reliability.

Construct validity refers to whether a measure assesses the theorized psychological construct that it purports to measure (Messick, 1995), and it is based on scores and their intended purpose rather than on the measure itself. This distinction between manifest scores and latent constructs is important because it emphasizes that scores may contain different sources of variance. Scores are fallible representations of latent constructs, and any manifest scores will have both contamination and deficiency. *Contamination* refers to variance within the scores that is systematic but unrelated to the latent construct one is trying to assess. For example, a group of direct reports completing a survey of organizational politics under the watchful eye of their supervisor are likely to respond in a socially desirable manner. Social desirability then becomes a source of contamination because it is systematic yet distinct from latent organizational politics variance. *Deficiency* refers to manifest scores that fail to tap aspects of the latent construct domain. For example, the latent organizational politics domain may have both positive and negative elements, but if the measure captures only the negative elements then the scores will be deficient.

Thus, organizational politics first must be comprehensively defined before it can be adequately measured. Unfortunately, that is no easy task because there is little in the way of consensus on what constitutes organizational politics. Consider the quote by Ferris and Hochwarter (2011, p. 442):

> Scholars have questioned whether a single definition can adequately capture the complexities of organizational politics (Dipboye & Foster, 2002; Fedor et al., 2008). We contend that its establishment will depend on the level of depth and breadth sought by the researcher. If inclusivity is coveted, a definition, based largely on the quantity of accumulated research, would need to consider the following characteristics: volitional behavior versus automatic behavior; self-serving versus other-serving versus group-serving versus organization-serving versus society-serving; triggered by perceived scarce resources (threat) versus abundant resources (opportunity); formal versus informal job responsibility; at the expense of others versus to the benefit of others; negative versus neutral versus positive tone; occurring at one level versus multiple levels (and all combinations contained within); exercising versus conserving influence resources; obtaining rewards versus minimizing sanctions versus maintaining the status quo; primary work location versus remote location, and all combinations and gradations of those stated above.

These are thorny, complex, and interrelated issues to consider and will not be resolved in a single empirical study but will evolve through time as theory and empirical research accumulate. Indeed, modern treatments of construct validity consider it as theoretical and empirical evidence that is acquired, accumulated, and synthesized over time (American Educational Research Association, American Psychological Association, & National Council on Measurement in Education, 1999). Validity is an evolving concept, as is the definition of organizational politics.

It is beyond the scope of this chapter to add to the discussion of definitional issues. Indeed, the first three chapters of this book review this issue in great detail. For the present purposes, it is sufficient to emphasize that *good measures start with good theory about the latent nature of the construct.* This simple statement is deceptively difficult to implement. In the review of the published organizational politics literature, little work was found that focused solely on clarifying the underlying conceptualization of organizational politics. Therefore, the first three chapters in this book are likely to be very helpful in prompting this kind of research.

In general, it appears that once basic measures of organizational politics became available researchers spent more time and energy studying the consequences of organizational politics rather than attending deeply to the underlying theoretical issues. To illustrate, one important dimension of organizational politics measures (i.e., the negativity of the domain) is considered in the following section.

Negativity as an Illustration

Previous chapters have noted that some definitions of organizational politics focus on the negative elements of this construct. For example, organizational politics often is conceptualized as work behaviors that are self-serving and not sanctioned by authority (Ferris, Harrell-Cook, & Dulebohn, 2000; Ferris, Russ, & Fandt, 1989; Kacmar & Baron, 1999; Mayes & Allen, 1977; Mintzberg, 1983). These conceptualizations of organizational politics have shaped the theoretical frameworks of this construct, and, consequently, most of these frameworks operate on the assumption that the outcomes of organizational politics will be negative. Therefore, it is not surprising that these frameworks, which predict negative effects on outcome variables (e.g., stress and job satisfaction), largely have been supported (e.g., Ferris, Frink, Galang, Zhou, Kacmar, & Howard, 1996; Harris, Harris, & Harvey, 2007; Miller, Rutherford, & Kolodinsky, 2008).

For example, consider the development of the Perceptions of Organizational Politics Scale (POPS; Kacmar & Ferris, 1991). This measure contains items that tap five specific dimensions of politics: (1) going along to get ahead; (2) self-serving orientation; (3) coworkers; (4) cliques; and (5) pay and promotion. Participants use a five-point Likert-type scale and indicate the extent to which they agree or disagree with each statement as it reflects their current work environment. The POPS includes such items as "If a co-worker offers to lend some assistance, it is because they expect to get something out of it, not because they really care" and "I have seen changes made here that only serve the purposes of a few individuals, not the work unit or organization." The majority of items refer to negative aspects of politics. Therefore, it is not surprising that a recent meta-analysis showed that perceptions of organizational politics (i.e., largely assessed by the POPS or scales like it) are negatively related to job satisfaction and organizational commitment and are positively related to job stress and turnover intentions (Miller et al., 2008).

No doubt, there are negative aspects of organizational politics, and they should be measured. However, it might be more reasonable to define organizational politics as something that might be bad but might also sometimes be good or, at the very least, neutral (Burns, 1961; Porter, Allen, & Angle, 1981). It has been suggested that individuals might even engage in organizational politics for positive reasons (Kurchner-Hawkins & Miller, 2006). For instance, an individual might engage in political behavior to make the pay and promotion system used by an organization fairer. Researchers who have conducted studies based on measures developed with a positive conceptualization of politics in mind tend to find more positive outcomes of political behavior (e.g., Butcher & Clarke, 1999; Frost & Egri, 1991).

In fact, research in areas such as impression management, self-presentation, and influence tactics, which all address aspects of political behavior, take a more neutral or even positive stance on the nature of these behaviors. Accordingly, research in this literature has tended to find more mixed results regarding the outcomes of these types of political behaviors (e.g., Kacmar, Wayne, & Wright, 2009; Kristof-Brown, Barrick, & Franke, 2002; McFarland, Yun, Harold, Viera, & Moore, 2005; Stevens & Kristof, 1995).

For example, Stevens and Kristof (1995) found that the more impression management tactics one used the more positively the target of the tactics felt toward the tactic user. Further, Kacmar et al. (2009) examined the use of impression management tactics by supervisors during performance appraisals. They found positive outcomes from both the actor and the target of impression management tactics. This was reflected in higher liking, similarity, and leadership ability ratings for the leader provided by the subordinates who experienced impression management tactics.

Thus, if political behavior can range from negative to positive, this range must be recognized within the theory and definition of the latent construct so that the measure can likewise contain items of both negative and positive orientation. Therefore, as noted by previous chapters in this book, measures of organizational politics that capture both the positive and negative aspects of politics will be the most useful because they will be less deficient and more representative of politics in general across situations.

Yet raising this point opens other interpretive questions, such as whether the negative and positive elements are ends on a continuum or different latent dimensions. How scholars choose to answer this question will affect the way they write items for the measure and the way they then create scales and evaluate construct and criterion-related validity. The potentially multidimensional nature of politics may prohibit a focus on all aspects of this construct in one study. Thus, researchers should specify which dimensions of organizational politics they are seeking to understand in a given study, recognizing that other dimensions may lead to entirely different findings. The appropriate definition used for a particular study will depend on the relevance of a definition of organizational politics for the particular theory being investigated.

Recommendations

Researchers should clearly state the definition that is being used and should note that the results may generalize only to the dimensions of organizational politics examined in that study. Researchers also should carefully describe how their measure provides adequate coverage of the relevant construct domain and how contamination and deficiency are minimized. This need not be a lengthy section of a paper; even a couple of sentences should provide sufficient detail. Clearer and more focused construct definitions not only will improve the precision of organizational politics research but also will enhance the ability to compare and contrast studies and meta-analytically summarize these findings.

MEASUREMENT AND RESEARCH DESIGN

After clearly defining organizational politics, it is important to determine how to measure the aspects of politics relevant for the study's purpose. There are many ways to assess politics, each with advantages and disadvantages. This chapter focuses on the three dominant ways politics perceptions and behaviors have been measured: self-reports, retrospective accounts, and direct observation. In practice, these measures are closely tied with the methodology in which they are embedded, and it is difficult to disentangle the research designs from the measures used in those designs. Consequently, the most common research designs used to administer the measures are then described: cross sectional, longitudinal, experimental, and qualitative research.

Measurement

Measurement describes the assignment of numbers, via some assessment, to index one's standing on the latent construct of interest. Psychological phenomena cannot be directly observed, and hence measures are like microscopes that allow us to "see into" psychological phenomena. Yet just as microscopes differ in their clarity and magnification all psychological measures are fallible to some degree. As the three main types of measures used in the organizational politics literature are reviewed, they are compared and contrasted in terms of potential sources of contamination and deficiency.

Note that our treatment of contamination includes consideration of *method bias*, which is systematic variance in a measure that is attributable to the type of measurement method or the context within which the measure was administered (Podsakoff, MacKenzie, Lee, & Podsakoff, 2003). For example, *common-source bias* can occur when the same participants complete all of the measures, whereas *common-method bias* can occur when all measures are of the same type (e.g., self-report) or assessed at the same time. It is thought that method bias will inflate the effect sizes observed, but in some instances the effect sizes may be attenuated (Schmitt, 1994).

Because Podsakoff et al. (2003) provided a "must-read" article describing different types of method bias and how to examine them, the meaning, consequences, or control of method bias here is not belabored. However, to summarize some of the main points, measures are likely to be most susceptible to method bias when the same types of measures (e.g., self-report) are completed by the same people at the same time. To limit method bias, efforts should be made to ensure that antecedent and outcome measures are assessed via different sources or other methods. For instance, employees might fill out a survey indicating their perceptions of politics, whereas a supervisor provides performance ratings on each of those individuals. Or the outcome measures might be assessed using a more objective indicator such as sales performance or turnover.

Self-Reports

The majority of organizational politics research has been conducted using self-report measures, which ask questions about an individual's perceptions and behaviors. For example, the POPS described earlier is a self-report measure that asks participants to indicate the extent to which they perceive organizational politics to be present in their organization (Kacmar & Ferris, 1991). Such measures are relatively easy to use and can be administered via paper and pencil, Internet, or interview methodologies. For example, written or web-based self-report questions usually are placed on Likert-type scales, so both the question and response are constrained.

All perceptions of politics measures used to date have been self-report. Miller et al. (2008) conducted a meta-analysis of outcomes of perceptions of organizational politics that contained 79 independent samples from 59 studies involving over 25,000 individual participants. All of the studies they analyzed included self-reported perceptions of organizational politics, with most using the POPS developed by Kacmar and Ferris (1991).

Self-reports are necessary to use when the goal is to assess individual perceptions and related psychological states. However, self-report measures also have limitations. Given that political behavior is highly driven by the person's underlying motives, it becomes difficult to disentangle organizational politics perceptions from social desirability forms of contamination. That is, people may not respond honestly because they fear that indicating politics are present might reflect badly on them (e.g., perhaps suggesting "sour grapes" on the respondents' part). Therefore, respondents would rather indicate no bad politics in the hopes it makes them look better. Furthermore, respondents might be concerned that responses will be shared with others and therefore will result in some negative consequences for them. Therefore, they are less likely to provide information on their true perceptions. Indeed, "gaming" a survey of politics very well may be an important indicator of political behavior.

Self-reports also may suffer from deficiency. For example, suppose the construct definition of organizational politics emphasizes the effective behavioral manifestation of political behavior. Self-reports may be useful for measuring perceptions, but they may be deficient in the measurement of behavioral effectiveness. Individuals might believe they are "savvy" political strategists but in reality are ineffective and obvious. Also, as noted already, to the extent the latent construct is not comprehensively defined the self-report measure necessarily will be incomplete. Finally, in the item development process, it is typical for items to be dropped because they do not correlate strongly with similar items. One must be careful that dropping items does not inadvertently result in incomplete coverage of the construct domain (see Little, Cunningham, Shahar, & Widaman, 2002).

RECOMMENDATIONS

Self-report measures are the best way to assess internal psychological states, perceptions, processes, and motives, but they are less useful for measuring behavioral effectiveness. Following the best practices of item writing is still the best place to start (e.g., Anastasi & Urbina, 1997; Nunnally & Bernstein, 1994). However, the key challenge for using self-reports in organizational politics research is to ensure the motives can be meaningfully assessed. To reduce contamination due to social desirability, ensure participants recognize that their responses are entirely confidential, and, when possible, anonymous. Phrasing the items so that they are not controversial, and balanced between positive and negative framing may help increase the chances participants will respond honestly and will be less concerned with political fallout from responding honestly. Reducing deficiency requires being able to map all items onto the construct domain so that it is fully covered.

Retrospective Measures

Retrospective measures ask participants what they have done or felt in the past or to recount what others have done in the past. Often, these measures are self-report in nature, but their emphasis on recalling past events from memory makes them distinct from the more "typical" self-report measures described already. They may measure either perceptions or behavioral effectiveness and likely measure behavioral effectiveness more accurately than self-reports because the outcomes of the behavior are likely known. For example, employees might be asked what influence tactics their boss has used and the effectiveness of those tactics. Researchers often use retrospective reports because they are unable to obtain multiple measurements over time or because they desire to study an event whose timing could not have been anticipated.

Much of the research that has examined political behaviors, such as influence tactic use and impression management, has relied on retrospective accounts. For example, Dulebohn, Murray, and Ferris (2004) examined subordinate influence tactic use in relation to performance evaluation outcomes over time. To capture subordinate influence tactic use, supervisors were asked to indicate the extent to which subordinates had previously engaged in self-promotion and ingratiation. Perceptions and ratings of influence tactic use were assessed at two points in time, 1 year apart. Results revealed that self-promotion led to poor performance evaluations and that the poor performance evaluations resulted in a greater use of self-promotion in the future (thus potentially increasing the likelihood of another negative performance evaluation). On the other hand, subordinate use of ingratiation resulted in more positive performance evaluations.

Thus, retrospective measures are a popular way to measure organizational politics perceptions or behavior when the focus is on the past. However, such measures also possess several potential limitations. Clearly, the main problem is that the respondent may not be able to accurately recall the past. As Golden (1992) and others have suggested (e.g., Huber & Power, 1985; Wolfe & Jackson, 1987), inaccurate recall in retrospective reporting can result from inappropriate rationalizations, oversimplifications, faulty post hoc attributions, and simple lapses of memory. It seems that memories are both constructive and reconstructive. Therefore, recall measures may be both contaminated and deficient. A secondary problem with retrospective reports is that respondents may try to present a socially desirable image of themselves or the referent. This invokes the same concerns about contamination noted in self-reports.

RECOMMENDATIONS

Fortunately, there are methods for improving the validity of retrospective reports. First, one might use free reports rather than forced reports. With free reports, informants are encouraged to say that they do not remember (i.e., if in fact that is the case). With forced reports, informants are not allowed to skip questions. Although loss of data from the free-report approach reduces sample size, the free-report option is associated with reasonably high accuracy, whereas the forced-report option is associated with lower accuracy (Koriat & Goldsmith, 1994). Second, researchers should use multiple knowledgeable individuals to allow the information provided by any one individual to be checked against the information provided by the others (e.g., Phillips, 1981; Seidler, 1974; Williams, Cote, & Buckley, 1989). This allows assessments of interrater reliability and agreement. Third, researchers should ask about simple facts or concrete events rather than past opinions or beliefs (Chen, Farh, & MacMillan, 1993; Glick, Huber, Miller, Doty, & Sutcliffe, 1990; Golden, 1992). In constructing the response, it is best to ask for the recall to be as detailed as possible. Fourth, researchers should keep the recall period reasonably short and avoid asking questions about the distant past (Huber & Power, 1985). Fifth, researchers should motivate their informants to provide accurate information. As with self-reports, confidentiality should be ensured, the duration and inconvenience of data collection should be minimized, and rich explanations of the importance and usefulness of the research should be given (Huber & Power, 1985).

Direct Observation

Direct observation of phenomena involves observing behavior as it occurs, such as a person's impression management tactic use. In such instances, researchers typically record the type and frequency with which a behavior has occurred. For example, McFarland et al. (2005) videotaped participants during an assessment center and then observed and recorded participants' use of several different types of impression management behaviors (e.g., ingratiation, self-promotion, excuses). Results revealed that impression management tactics were used more frequently and that there was more variability in impression management use for those exercises requiring candidates to display interpersonal competencies (i.e., the role-plays and mock presentation) relative to the exercise that did not (i.e., the tactical exercise). The relationship between impression management use and assessor evaluations was also influenced by the competencies assessed by the exercises.

A main advantage of direct observation is that it measures behavior directly, not using mere reports of behavior or intentions. Although direct observation still requires judgment, the raters can be blind to the purpose of the study and trained, thereby reducing contamination. The main disadvantage of direct observation is that it is limited to behavioral variables and cannot be used to study perceptions or affective variables (e.g., job satisfaction). Further, this type of measure may be deficient because it cannot capture all the political behaviors that are being used, and it may be contaminated because a researcher may incorrectly code some behaviors as political when they are not. In fact, the underlying motives of the target, which are so critical in understanding political behaviors, are difficult to infer from direct observation.

RECOMMENDATIONS

Effectively using direct observation depends on (1) clear operational definitions of the constructs, (2) behavioral examples linked to the underlying constructs, (3) simple rating scales, and (4) training of raters. On this latter point, rater training approaches from the performance appraisal literature are extremely valuable (Bernardin & Buckley, 1984; McIntyre, Smith, & Hassett, 1984; Woehr & Huffcutt, 1994). Furthermore, using multiple raters is critical for establishing validity, reliability, and agreement. When appropriate, raters should be blind to the purpose and conditions of the study (Schraeder, Becton, & Portis, 2007).

Research Designs

Each of the types of measures just described (i.e., self-reports, retrospective accounts, and direct observation) can be administered in a variety of ways. The type of research design chosen has implications for the inferences drawn from the relationships examined, and the extent to which contamination, in the form of method bias, may be present. Therefore, each of the research designs most commonly used within organizational politics research is discussed, and within each section the implications of the approach when used with the aforementioned measures are described.

Cross Sectional Designs

Most research conducted on organizational politics has used cross sectional designs, which examine relationships among variables or constructs at a single point in time. In the typical organizational politics study, participants are given a self-report measure and are asked to indicate their perceptions of politics and, at that time, to respond to measures of various other antecedent (e.g., work context, organizational influences) and outcome variables (e.g., job satisfaction, stress). For example, Harris et al. (2007) examined competing models of the relationships among perceptions of organizational politics, perceived organizational support, and individual outcomes. Over 400 employees from different levels and departments within one organization were surveyed and asked to report their perceptions of politics, perceived organizational support, job satisfaction, pay satisfaction, job strain, role conflict, and intent to turnover. Measures were completed by participants in one administration. Results revealed that perceived organizational support and perceived organizational politics were negatively correlated. Further, perceptions of organizational politics were negatively correlated with satisfaction and positively correlated with job strain, role conflict, and intent to turnover.

Cross sectional designs are popular because they are an efficient way to collect data and are relatively easy to implement in real organizations. Despite the popularity of cross sectional research designs (Miller et al., 2008), such designs have limitations that can distort the nature of relationships among variables. First, cross sectional designs can cause contamination when only one type of measurement method or source is used. Such designs compound the potential for method bias because there is not time or space between the administrations of these measures. Further, such studies also tend to collect data for all measures from the same individuals; thus, common source bias is also a concern. These concerns are particularly acute in organizational politics research because the motives that underlie political behavior are likely to taint the entire measurement process. Second, cross sectional designs make it difficult, if not impossible, to determine causality.

For example, Cole and Maxwell (2003) showed that cross sectional tests of mediation are severely biased and that relationships may even change in sign when examined longitudinally. Much of the research on organizational politics has attempted to provide support for the antecedents and consequences of political perceptions or behavior. However, very little of this research has used the longitudinal designs necessary to increase inferences regarding the causal direction of the relationships. For example, Ferris et al. (1996) tested the perceptions of organizational politics model proposed by Ferris et al. (1989). This study employed a cross sectional research design whereby measures (i.e., antecedents, perceptions of politics, and outcome measures) were administered to all participants at one point in time. Although the study provided support for the predicted model, the authors themselves noted that "the inability to make causal inferences due to the correlational nature of the data" is a limitation of that work.

RECOMMENDATIONS

It may seem that a point being made here is to advocate that researchers avoid cross sectional designs, and in an "ivory tower" way, that may be true. Yet, as *organizational* researchers, one must live with the practical realities of data collection and with the fact that a well-designed cross sectional study still can be informative and useful. Therefore, when using cross sectional designs, researchers should take steps to minimize method bias. The best solution is to simultaneously use different sources and methods. For example, self-reports of political motives can be linked to other reports of political perceptions, which can in turn be linked to a company's archival records (e.g., turnover, promotion rates). Of the two types of method bias, it is probably most critical to use different sources of information than to use different measurement methods. Statistical approaches for modeling method bias in cross sectional designs tend to not work well (e.g., Conway & Lance, 2010; Podsakoff et al., 2003). That said, often it is helpful to offer some empirical support ruling out method bias concerns. For example, Lindell and Whitney (2001) suggested including a measure (i.e., a "marker variable") that is theoretically unrelated to the constructs being assessed. Then, one can estimate the relationships (if any) between the marker variable and the substantive variables of interest to gauge the extent to which method bias may be present. Another option is to conduct confirmatory factor analysis (CFA) to rule out factor structures "simpler" than the hypothesized structure. However, such an approach clearly is post hoc, and if the hypothesized factor structure is less parsimonious than the method bias factor structure the hypothesized structure will almost always fit better. Still, the magnitude of the difference between the two structures can be used as a rough gauge of method bias.

Longitudinal Research

Separating the timing of measures can be an important means to reduce method bias. However, temporal spacing does not make the study longitudinal or inform questions of change. Rather, at least three repeated time periods on the same variable are needed to provide adequate inferences of change (Ployhart & Vandenberg, 2010). Such studies are rare in organizational politics research. It is much more common for studies to separate the timing of measures, but each measure is administered only at one time period. This design is a variant of the cross sectional design, and the spacing of measurement occasions is done mainly to draw stronger inferences of causality and reduce method bias concerns.

For example, Higgins and Judge (2004) examined self-reported applicant influence–tactic use and recruiter perceptions of fit. Participants completed an initial survey during a placement office orientation meeting and then completed a post interview survey (time 2) and another survey 3 months after the start of the recruiting season (time 3). They found that applicant self-monitoring predicted applicant impression management and that impression management had a weak relationship with hiring recommendations. Given how Higgins and Judge timed the measures (i.e., self-monitoring was assessed prior to impression management), their findings indicate that applicant self-monitoring is one of the causes of applicant impression management.

One might expect longitudinal research to be the primary research design in organizational politics research because organizational politics is largely a social phenomenon and because social phenomena are largely reciprocal and ever changing. Only over time can changes and reciprocal relationships be captured. Further, organizational politics is thought to have numerous antecedents and outcomes, and without longitudinal work strong statements about causality cannot be made. However, little work to date has examined organizational politics and its relationships with other variables over time, much less longitudinally.

RECOMMENDATIONS

It is recognized that conducting longitudinal research is difficult. It is challenging to develop the design and hard to find organizations willing to participate in the study. Nevertheless, cross sectional research, and even research that separates the timing of measures, can take us only so far. To provide stronger inferences of causality, to understand how politics perceptions originate and change, and to study the evolution and effectiveness of political behavior, longitudinal research with three or more repeated measurements on the relevant constructs is necessary. When thinking of the design of longitudinal research, the review by Ployhart and Vandenberg (2010) may be particularly helpful. To summarize their main points, researchers should first develop a theory as to why political perceptions and behavior should change over time. This is easier said than done because most theories are vague with respect to time, duration, and dynamic relationships (Mitchell & James, 2001). Researchers should plan on collecting at least three waves of data, but more is usually better. They should expect attrition that can be over 50% by the conclusion of the study. Furthermore, they should analyze the data using growth models capable of studying change over time and predictors of such change.

Experimental Research Designs

Experimental research designs generally involve manipulating one or more independent variables to determine their effect on one or more dependent variables. For example, van Knippenberg and Steensma (2003) used a laboratory experiment to examine the expectation of future interaction on the use of hard and soft influence tactics. In the first condition, participants could use only hard tactics or only soft tactics to persuade another person. In the second condition, participants were told either that they would have future interactions with the person they were trying to persuade or that they would not have future interactions with that person. Results revealed that the expectation of future interactions diminished the use of influence in general and of hard influence tactics in particular.

In another experiment, Kacmar et al. (2009) had participants work on a task in which a confederate supervisor either used or did not use impression management tactics. Further, the participants received either negative or positive feedback from the supervisor. Findings indicated that both impression management and feedback exhibited a significant main effect on supervisory ratings. Subordinate reactions to the supervisor were higher when the supervisor used impression management during the interactions and when positive feedback cues were provided.

Experimental designs have many advantages. They often can provide reasonably strong inferences of causality because of randomization, control, and manipulation. In this regard, a well-conducted experimental study can be used to offset some of the challenges associated with conducting longitudinal research. Also, they can be administered fairly quickly to students, and hence it is possible to have a continuous program of experimental research. Finally, they can be used to manipulate factors that cannot be ethically or legally manipulated in organizational settings.

However, experimental designs often are criticized for a lack of external validity. Because the experiments are conducted in simulated environments, the results may not generalize to field contexts. The belief here is that such criticisms are frequently overstated. For example, many experiments are criticized because of the artificial nature of the task. Yet if the theory does not propose a specific type of task or even reference the key elements of the task, then it is hard to understand why experimental results would lack external validity. Unfortunately, many organizational scholars appear to assume that laboratory experiments do not generalize, and they mistake identical task elements as the index of generalizability. The opinion held by these authors is that it is more critical that the experiment tests the key parts of the theory because it is the theory that generalizes to the real world. If one believes that task elements must be identical, then this same criticism could be relevant to field studies conducted within a single organization.

Of course, the main question for this chapter is whether experimental designs are appropriate for the study of organizational politics, and it is our belief that the answer depends on the nature of the theory and hypothesis in question. Clearly, it is unlikely that an experiment can capture the variety of influences on political behavior in organizations and, hence, that experimental results are unlikely to have direct implications for practice. For example, contamination still may be present if the experiment lacks realism or if participants respond in an acquiescent manner. Measurements obtained from experiments also may be deficient if, for example, many of the self-report items reference phenomena unfamiliar to the participants (e.g., students without work experience). Fortunately, the use of experimental studies and field studies is not an either–or question. We believe that experimental methods provide a critical complement to field studies and that they should be used jointly and interactively to better understand phenomena.

RECOMMENDATIONS

The design of experimental studies in organizational politics research can benefit from the same guidelines used for experimental design in general. For example, it is important that the design of the manipulations and tasks allow for appropriate tests of the study hypotheses. Thus, *realism* should not come at the expense of *rigor*. Likewise, including manipulation checks and measures that could help address likely reviewer concerns can be helpful. One also might ask questions about how serious participants took the study, their motivation, and so on. More specific to organizational politics, the following advice seems reasonable. First, experiments lack serious, long-term consequences, so there is probably not much utility in trying to understand the prevalence or consequences of political behavior. Rather, experiments should focus on characteristics that cannot be easily studied in the field, namely, the psychological factors that underlie political behavior, the nature and structure of perceptions of politics, political behavior in small groups, and so on. Second, construct validation of organizational politics measures actually may be better conducted in the laboratory. Here, lacking serious consequences, participants can be more honest in their responses, so well-designed manipulations can create different political environments and psychological states within which participants complete organizational politics measures.

Qualitative Research Designs

Qualitative methodologies gather data through observation, open-ended questions, or interviews that provide direct quotations. The major benefit of this approach is that it results in more in-depth, comprehensive information about a phenomenon. A second benefit is that it can lead to new insights that may not be recognized in existing theoretical work. Qualitative designs typically use subjective information and participant observation to describe the context or natural setting of the variables under consideration as well as the interactions of the different variables in the context. Therefore, this approach seeks a wide understanding of the entire situation.

Because qualitative research, by nature, is "open-ended," different approaches exist for conducting this type of research. For example, Ferris, Fedor, Chachere, and Pondy (1989) made inferences about the relationship between myths and politics in organizational contexts based on their experiences with the implementation of a new performance appraisal system in a division of a large corporation. Their findings suggest that organizational members often invoke multiple myths to resist or co-opt change. Further, Riley (1983) examined behavior in two organizations that differed in routinization. She found that the organization with less routinization had more politics. In neither case did the authors quantify the qualitative data in any way but instead used what might be considered a case study approach. Specifically, they used examples and critical incidents from their observations to draw conclusions.

On the other hand, some qualitative research turns the qualitative information that is collected into data that can be more easily analyzed. For instance, Smith, Plowman, Duchon, and Quinn (2009) observed and conducted field interviews with high-reputation plant managers from 11 manufacturing plants. The authors transcribed all the data collected and followed several coding steps to identify dimensions of high-reputation plant managers, including (1) identifying broad themes, (2) developing codes within each broad theme, (3) identifying similar categories of codes across the themes, and (4) assessing content within each category. Their results revealed that effective plant managers possessed certain dispositional traits (e.g., self-motivation, humility) and systematically applied interpersonal behaviors that resembled influence tactic use (e.g., creating accountability, leading by example, developing trust).

Given the nature of organizational politics, one would expect qualitative research to be a more common research tool in this area, but it is a rarely used technique. Perhaps this is due to some of the difficulties associated with this type of research. First, the very subjectivity of the inquiry leads to difficulties in establishing the reliability and validity of the approaches and information obtained. Second, it is very difficult to prevent or detect researcher-induced bias. Third, it can be incredibly time-consuming and difficult to convince organizations to allow for the collection of these types of data. Finally, even with following the best practices in qualitative research design, it can be difficult to get this kind of research published.

RECOMMENDATIONS

Steps can be taken to address some of the difficulties of conducting qualitative research. First, all records should be maintained in the form of detailed notes or recordings. These records also should be developed during or before, rather than after, the data-gathering session. Second, a study's "trustworthiness" is increased when data analysis and conclusions are triangulated. That is, participants' perceptions should be verified in a systematic manner. This may be achieved with the use of, for example, multiple data collection devices, sources, and analysts to establish the validity of findings (Lincoln & Guba, 1985). As noted already, one problem with qualitative research is that it can be difficult to publish this type of research. This difficulty may reflect the fact that qualitative studies usually focus on a limited number of participants (because the collection of qualitative data is particularly arduous), and therefore the generalizability of such studies may be questioned. To address this issue, researchers must be able to show that the sample examined is similar to the population to which they are trying to generalize. If this is not possible, they should be sure to demonstrate clear links to existing theory. Further, researchers conducting qualitative research are oftentimes ambiguous about data collection and coding details. Therefore, it is incumbent upon researchers doing qualitative research to clearly articulate precisely how the data were collected and analyzed (as would be the case with the use of any research design).

DATA ANALYTICAL APPROACHES

The definition of organizational politics determines the appropriate measures and methodology, which in turn determine the appropriate data analytical approaches. There are already numerous articles and chapters that provide broad overviews of data analytical methods (e.g., Ployhart, 2008). Therefore, the purpose of this section is to summarize the application of data analytical approaches to the study of organizational politics. First, it summarizes analytical approaches for the assessment of measures, followed by data analytical approaches for the relationships among measures. The purpose is to provide a broad snapshot of existing data analytical practices within the organizational politics literature.

Measurement Model

As noted previously, all measures of organizational politics will contain variance attributable to both contamination and deficiency in addition to true score variance. Given an appropriate design, it is possible to estimate the presence of these different forms of variance and hence to determine the construct validity of a measure. Analyzing the quality of organizational politics measures usually falls into two types: classical test theory and CFA. Classical test theory is based on the premise that the variance in any given score (i.e., item or scale) is a function of true score variance and error variance.

Multitrait-multimethod (MTMM) correlation matrices may be used where measures both similar to and different from the organizational politics measure may be administered. The pattern of correlations can be used to make inferences regarding convergent and discriminant validity. CFA approaches provide a more rigorous manner for investigating construct validity. CFA allows one to specify different latent structures and hence to test different forms of true score variance, error variance, and by extension, contamination and deficiency variance. Further, CFA models can be used to estimate and test different types of method bias. The combination of classical test theory approaches and CFA approaches is illustrated nicely in the development of the POPS (Kacmar & Ferris, 1991). In their study, they first used classical test theory to evaluate the quality of the items and then used CFA to confirm the underlying latent structure. Item refinements were made using a blend of both approaches, and the measure was evaluated in different samples.

One finding that tends to occur in the measurement of organizational politics is that multiple latent factors represent different types of politics perceptions or behaviors. This was found in Kacmar and Ferris (1991) and has been used frequently in other studies. However, sometimes scholars focus on only a single overall measure of politics (e.g., Maslyn & Fedor, 1998). It should be noted that whether organizational politics is treated as multiple, homogeneous constructs, an overall homogeneous construct, or an overall multidimensional construct is a theoretical question. Methods such as CFA can help test the theoretical question, but they cannot answer it because these different models are not nested.

In general, it is preferable for researchers to use more rigorous methods like CFA to evaluate the adequacy of their measures. However, researchers need to remember that validity does not "stick" to a measure. Validity is fundamentally about whether the inferences one makes from a set of scores is appropriate for their intended purposes (Messick, 1995, 1998; American Educational Research Association, American Psychological Association, & National Council on Measurement in Education, 1999). This means that a measure developed in one organization cannot be assumed to be "valid" for every organization. Even if researchers use CFA or modern-test theory approaches (e.g., item–response theory), it is important for scholars to critically reevaluate the validity evidence for a measure in their specific study. This does not mean they must conduct a MTMM analysis but rather that they evaluate the factor structure and determine whether that structure is consistent with theory and existing research. Such an approach has been used in this literature (e.g., Dulebohn et al., 2004; Higgins & Judge, 2004), but it is still not done on a widespread basis. Until there is a sufficiently large database of empirical validity support for organizational politics measures, it is vital for scholars to evaluate the adequacy of their measures.

Provided sample sizes are appropriate, it is helpful to use CFA to evaluate the adequacy of measures in a given study. Such information helps ensure the measures are operating similarly to other studies and facilitates the accumulation of construct validity evidence. When describing the CFA results, it is important to report a range of fit indices that provide information about both relative and absolute fit. Of course, researchers also should always report means, standard deviations, intercorrelations, and reliability evidence. Any changes to the instructions or wording of items from prior research also need to be conveyed.

Statistical Models

All popular statistical models used in the organizational politics literature are focused on accounting for variance in a dependent variable. When the predictors are categorical, the variance is explained by between-group differences. When the predictors are continuous, the variance is explained by between-observation differences (i.e., observations are usually individuals, and hence variability in the dependent variable is explained by individual differences in psychological characteristics). Thus, regardless of whether one uses analysis of variance (ANOVA) or regression, the basic model and statistical inference are the same. Indeed, the vast majority of organizational politics research uses one of these two methods.

However, the nature of the organizational politics construct and the research design will affect the specific data analytical approach that should be used. It was noted earlier how most research is cross sectional, and as a result correlation and regression analyses remain the dominant approaches. Yet it is worth emphasizing that when testing more elaborate theories of organizational politics, these traditional approaches become limiting because they can model data with only a single dependent variable. When the theory involves multiple independent, mediating, and dependent variables, only methods such as path analysis or structural equation models (SEMs) can test the theory in a holistic manner.

An excellent illustration is provided by Dulebohn et al. (2004), who used latent path analysis to model 8 mediators and 19 mediated relationships. Testing such a model using regression analysis would only approximate the SEM results because regression cannot model all the relationships and dependences among the variables. A further benefit of using SEM is its ability to model and remove measurement error from the latent constructs.

However, it is important to remember that such benefits occur only to the extent the data are appropriately modeled and that SEM cannot estimate all forms of measurement error (DeShon, 1998).

It was noted earlier that there is little longitudinal research in organizational politics and virtually no research using growth models. There is a similar lack of any research using multilevel models. Researchers must remember that regression-based approaches assume residuals are independent and normally distributed, with a mean of zero and constant variance. Violations to these assumptions will frequently produce type I errors. Such violations are most likely to occur when (1) there is a nesting to the data (e.g., supervisor political behavior is evaluated by their direct reports) or (2) there are repeated measurements from the same respondents (e.g., surveying the direct reports multiple times). In both instances, the residuals will be correlated, and standard errors will shrink, thus producing type I errors.

It is quite likely that perceptions of politics and political behavior change across levels of analysis. Maslyn and Fedor (1998) demonstrated that self-report questions that differ in their foci (i.e., organizational politics versus work-group politics) result in different latent factors. However, their study was not multilevel in that all responses and analyses were limited to the individual level.

RECOMMENDATIONS

The review of the organizational politics literature suggests that scholars are using appropriate analytical approaches. However, as their theories become multilevel and longitudinal, the "old workhorses" under the general linear model (i.e., regression and ANOVA) become limiting. Thus, as researchers increasingly incorporate more multilevel research designs or longitudinal research designs, the data analytical methods necessarily must change. Fortunately, a variety of methodologies capable of handling modeling such data are readily available. For example, hierarchical linear modeling (HLM) can model either nested or longitudinal data structures (see Raudenbush & Bryk, 2002). SEM also is incredibly flexible and offers the possibility of also modeling and removing different forms of measurement error (see Chan, 1998a, 1998b). These issues are discussed further in the next section.

FUTURE RESEARCH DIRECTIONS

The study of organizational politics is vibrant and continues to evolve into ever more complex theories, measures, and designs. Despite such evolution, most empirical studies rely on field research designs that try to control method bias by using different sources, methods, and time periods. Such research has led to many insights, but we may be reaching an asymptote in what these designs can tell us about organizational politics. The study of organizational politics needs to advance by adopting new measurement methods and longitudinal and multilevel designs and analyses, because these better reflect the context within which organizational politics unfold. Given the scope of this chapter, the presentation of future research directions is limited to those methodological in nature.

Develop Comprehensive Definitions of Organizational Politics

Definitions of organizational politics have been used loosely (Buchanan & Badham, 1999), and currently there is very little consensus reached across studies (Fedor & Maslyn, 2002; Ferris et al., 2002). This is particularly true between the perceptions of politics literature, which largely views politics as a negative phenomenon, and the self-presentation and influence tactic literature, which tends to view political behavior as largely positive. It is incumbent upon researchers to consider the various dimensions and issues posed by Ferris and Hochwarter (2011) to ensure that the construct chosen is clearly defined and that the measures used capture the entire domain specified. This is easier said than done, and two approaches are presented to stimulate such research.

First, scholars need to write their construct definitions completely and comprehensively. One may start by reviewing items from various measures purporting to assess the same construct, but this by itself will not guarantee that the construct is adequately defined. In the experience of the present authors, incredible value has been found with an old-fashioned thesaurus. Write as many words that describe the construct, and then for each word, examine its synonyms and antonyms. Often, this will lead to a more nuanced and precise definition of the construct and to recognition that many existing items in popular measures are deficient.

Rather than have scholars "battle it out for the ultimate measure," we believe it is in the profession's best interest to conduct this measurement approach in an "open-source" format, where the item development is done collaboratively with scholars at different institutions. To our knowledge, such an open-source approach to scale development has not been used (see, e.g., the work in the GLOBE project). Wouldn't it be great, though, if it was done first in the organizational politics area?

Second, researchers should implement qualitative research designs. This might take the form of participant observation, in-depth interviews with employees in different levels and roles, and highly involved case studies. A benefit of this approach is that, if open-minded, the analysis might reveal political behavior not initially considered. That is, unlike survey measures that determine what behavior falls into the political realm, qualitative research allows for a more fluid interpretation. Researchers may see things that they had not considered previously. In other words, a qualitative approach may offer insights into political behavior that have been missed to date.

Definitions Should Clarify the Foci of Interest

The fact that definitions may change depending on the level of analysis that is the focus of the study absolutely must be acknowledged and addressed in future work in this area. Politics perceptions and behavior may differ in quantity and quality, when the target is a supervisor, peer, direct report, or customer. Yet existing definitions of politics scarcely reflect these potential differences. The study by Maslyn and Fedor (1998) demonstrated that perceptions of politics differ between group and organizational foci. However, much more work needs to be done to understand whether the differences also relate to differences in construct domains (e.g., type and number of factors) as well as antecedents and consequences.

Incorporate New Approaches to Measurement

A major challenge in the measurement of organizational politics perceptions is one of reducing contamination due to social desirability. Because this issue is not so different from controlling faking in the personnel selection literature, the findings from that literature may be used to improve the measurement of organizational politics. For example, the use of conditional reasoning approaches may represent more effective ways to assess underlying motives (e.g., James, McIntyre, Glisson, Bowler, & Mitchell, 2004). Likewise, computer-based or adaptive measures that assess response latencies could prove useful for detecting socially desirable response patterns (Holden, 1998; Holden & Hibbs, 1995).

Incorporate Context

Along the same lines as the second suggestion, research in the area of organizational politics needs to take context more seriously. In effect, there is no "organization" in the study of organizational politics. Most recognize that behavior is a function of the person and situation (context), yet the context part of the function remains understudied in the organizational politics area. The use of the term *context* here is broad, including national culture, organizational climate, work-group norms, and related factors. Also, it can include such nonpsychological variables as competitive environment and employment rates. Johns (2006) provided a compelling description for why context should be included in the study of organizational behavior and a framework within which to frame future research.

For example, the perception, manifestation, and consequences of political behavior may differ across levels of analysis. Politics may be more socially accepted, perhaps even career critical, with more senior leadership roles in large organizations. At the same time, one might question whether politics perceptions are equated with leadership perceptions. The word *politics* often takes a negative meaning, but to be effective some political behavior is expected of senior leaders.

Thus, one way that researchers more effectively can incorporate context is by studying it at higher levels of analysis. Another way is to examine cross-level models. For example, organizational climate is likely to be a strong facilitator or dampener of political behavior. In this manner, organizational differences in climate might influence the relationship between psychological variables and political behavior as well as the expression of political behavior directly. Likewise, different human resources policies and practices might produce differences in political perceptions and behavior. For example, compensation systems that emphasize individual performance may increase political behavior over systems that emphasize collective behavior. In the cross-level study of organizational politics, researchers will need to attend to issues of emergence, aggregation, and multilevel modeling. The book by Kozlowski and Klein (2000) has become a standard introduction to these issues.

Think Longitudinally

Organizational politics researchers are encouraged to pay closer attention to longitudinal issues. Despite great theoretical advancements, there is still insufficient attention paid to how organizational politics perceptions and behavior originate, change, and evolve over time. Mitchell and James (2001) noted that most organizational behavior research fails to consider issues of timing (e.g., when an effect occurs), duration (e.g., how long does an effect occur), and magnitude (e.g., does an effect or relationship change in magnitude over time). Given the highly malleable nature of organizational politics, the neglect of such longitudinal issues is troubling.

Therefore, an important first step is to take existing theories and view them from a longitudinal lens. The next step is to then design studies to test these longitudinal questions. It is necessary to measure variables with as many repeated occasions as possible so that more complex forms of change can be identified. Should one find variability in change over time, then it becomes reasonable to examine what might predict or explain such change. For example, how might the political behavior of new hires occur over time? Does political behavior start immediately, or is there a slow but steady increase in such behavior over time? Are there certain kinds of people who more quickly and frequently engage in such behavior, and if so, do they maintain this difference or do they decline in such behavior over time? Answering these questions requires the adoption of longitudinal data analytic methods, which are easily incorporated using HLM and SEM (see Ployhart & Vandenberg, 2010, for an introduction).

CONCLUSION

There is no question that political behavior is an important phenomenon in organizations. It is encouraging that researchers are studying this phenomenon in a variety of ways and using a variety of methods. However, for the field to continue to evolve, some significant developments need to take place. A concerted attempt was made to identify the definitional, measurement, methodological, and data analytical developments believed to most significantly move the field forward. Again, the intention is not to criticize the research that already has been conducted, because it has been valuable and insightful. Instead, the purpose here was to push the boundaries and thinking about organizational politics and to suggest methodological approaches that might offer even greater understanding of these important phenomena.

REFERENCES

American Educational Research Association, American Psychological Association, & National Council on Measurement in Education (1999). *Standards for educational and psychological testing*. Washington, DC: American Educational Research Association.

Anastasi, A., & Urbina, S. (1997). *Psychological testing*. Upper Saddle River, NJ: Prentice-Hall.

Bernardin, H.J., & Buckley, M.R. (1984). Strategies in rater training, *Academy of Management Review, 6*, 205–221.

Buchanan D., & Badham, R. (1999). Politics and organizational change: The lived experience. *Human Relations, 52*, 609–629.

Burns, T. (1961). Micro politics: Mechanisms of institutional change. *Administrative Science Quarterly, 6*, 257–281.

Butcher, D., & Clarke, M. (1999). Organizational conflict: The missing discipline of management. *Industrial and Commercial Training, 31*, 9–12.

Chan, D. (1998a). Functional relations among constructs in the same content domain at different levels of analysis: A typology of composition models. *Journal of Applied Psychology, 83*, 234–246.

Chan, D. (1998b). The conceptualization and analysis of change over time: An integrative approach incorporating longitudinal mean and covariance structures analysis (LMACS) and multiple indicator latent growth modeling (MLGM). *Organizational Research Methods, 1*, 421–483.

Chen, M.-J., Farh, J.-L., & MacMillan, I.C. (1993). An exploration of the expertness of outside informants. *Academy of Management Journal, 36*, 1614–1632.

Cole, D.A., & Maxwell, S.E. (2003). Testing meditational models with longitudinal data: Questions and tips in the use of structural equation modeling. *Journal of Abnormal Psychology, 112*, 558–577.

Conway, J.M., & Lance, C.E. (2010). What reviewers should expect from authors regarding common method bias in organizational research. *Journal of Business and Psychology, 25*, 325–334.

DeShon, R.P. (1998). A cautionary note on measurement error corrections in structural equation modeling. *Psychological Methods, 3*, 412–423.

Dipboye, R.L., & Foster, J. (2002). Multi-level theorizing about perceptions of organizational politics. In F.J. Yammarino & F. Dansereau (Eds.), *Research in multi-level issues, Volume 1: The many faces of multi-level issues* (pp. 255–227). Oxford, UK: JAI Press/Elsevier Science.

Dulebohn, J.H., Murray, B., & Ferris, G.R. (2004). The vicious and virtuous cycles of influence tactic use and performance evaluation outcomes. *Organizational Analysis, 12*, 53–74.

Fedor, D.B., & Maslyn, J.M. (2002). In F. Yammarino & F. Dansereau (Eds.), *Politics and political behavior: Where else do we go from here?* US: Elsevier Science/JAI Press.

Fedor, D.B., Maslyn, J., Farmer, S., & Bettenhausen, K. (2008). The contributions of positive politics to prediction of employee reactions. *Journal of Applied Social Psychology, 38*, 76–96.

Ferris, G.R., Adams, G., Kolodinsky, R.W., Hochwarter, W.A., & Ammeter, A.P. (2002). Perceptions of organizational politics: Theory and research directions. In F.J. Yammarino & F. Dansereau (Eds.), *Research in multi-level issues, Volume 1: The many faces of multi-level issues* (pp. 179–254). Oxford, UK: JAI Press/Elsevier Science.

Ferris, G.R., Fedor, D.B., Chachere, J.G., & Pondy, L.R. (1989). Myths and politics in organizational contexts. *Group and Organization Studies, 14*, 83–103.

Ferris, G.R., Frink, D.D., Galang, M.C., Zhou, J., Kacmar, K.M., & Howard, J.L. (1996). Perceptions of organizational politics: Prediction, stress-related implications, and outcomes. *Human Relations, 49*, 233–266.

Ferris, G.R., Harrell-Cook, G., & Dulebohn, J.H. (2000). Organizational politics: The nature of the relationship between politics perceptions and political behavior. In S. Bacharach & E. Lawler (Eds.), *Research in the sociology of organizations* (Vol. 17, pp. 89–130). Stamford, CT: JAI Press.

Ferris, G.R., & Hochwarter, W.A. (2011). Organizational politics. In S. Zedeck (Ed.), *APA handbook of industrial and organizational psychology* (Vol. 3, pp. 435–459). Washington, DC: American Psychological Association.

Ferris, G.R., Russ, G.S., & Fandt, P.M. (1989). Politics in organizations. In R.A. Giacalone & P. Rosenfeld (Eds.), *Impression management in the organization* (pp. 143–170). Hillsdale, NJ: Lawrence Erlbaum.

Frost, P., & Egri, C. (1991). The political process of innovation. In L.L. Cummings & B.M. Staw (Eds.), *Research in organizational behavior* (Vol. 13, pp. 229–295). Greenwich, CT: JAI Press.

Glick, W.H., Huber, G.P., Miller, C.C., Doty, D.H., & Sutcliffe, K.M. (1990). Studying changes in organizational design and effectiveness: Retrospective event histories and periodic assessments. *Organization Science, 1*, 293–312.

Golden, B.R. (1992). The past is the past—or is it? The use of retrospective accounts as indicators of past strategy. *Academy of Management Journal, 35*, 848–860.

Gunn, J., & Chen, S. (2006). A micro-political perspective of strategic management. In E. Vigoda-Gadot & A. Drory (Eds.), *Handbook of organizational politics* (pp. 209–229). Northampton, MA: Edward Elgar Publishing.

Harris, R.B., Harris, K.J., & Harvey, P. (2007). A test of competing models of the relationships among perceptions of organizational politics, perceived organizational support, and individual outcomes. *Journal of Social Psychology, 147*, 631–655.

Higgins, C.A., & Judge, T.A. (2004). The effect of applicant influence tactics on recruiter perceptions of fit and hiring recommendations: A field study. *Journal of Applied Psychology, 89*, 622–632.

Holden, R.R. (1998). Detecting fakers on a personnel test: Response latencies versus a standard validity scale. *Journal of Social Behavior and Personality, 13*, 387–398.

Holden, R.R., & Hibbs, N. (1995). Incremental validity of response latencies for detecting fakers on a personality test. *Journal of Research in Personality, 29*, 362–372.

Huber, G.P., & Power, D.J. (1985). Research notes and communications retrospective reports of strategic-level managers: Guidelines for increasing their accuracy. *Strategic Management Journal, 6*, 171–180.

James, L.R., McIntyre, M.D., Glisson, C.A., Bowler, J.L., & Mitchell, T.R. (2004). The conditional reasoning measurement system for aggression: An overview. *Human Performance, 17*, 271–295.

Johns, G. (2006). The essential impact of context on organizational behavior. *Academy of Management Review, 31*, 386–401.

Kacmar, K.M., & Baron, R.A. (1999). Organizational politics: The state of the field, links to related processes, and an agenda for future research. In G.R. Ferris (Ed.), *Research in personnel and human resources management* (Vol. 17, pp. 1–39). Stamford, CT: JAI Press.

Kacmar, K.M., & Ferris, G.R. (1991). Perceptions of organizational politics scale (POPS): Development and construct validation. *Educational and Psychological Measurement, 51*, 193–205.

Kacmar, K.M., Wayne, S.J., & Wright, P.M. (2009). Subordinate reactions to the use of impression management tactics and feedback by the supervisor. *Journal of Managerial Issues, 21,* 498–517.

Koriat, A., & Goldsmith, M. (1994). Memory in naturalistic and laboratory contexts: Distinguishing the accuracy-oriented and quantity-oriented approaches to memory assessment. *Journal of Experimental Psychology: General, 123,* 297–315.

Kozlowski, S.W.J., & Klein, K.J. (2000). *Multilevel theory, research, and methods in organizations: Foundations, extensions, and new directions.* San Francisco: Jossey-Bass.

Kristof-Brown, A., Barrick, M.R., & Franke, M. (2002). Applicant impression management: Dispositional influences and consequences for recruiter perceptions of fit and similarity. *Journal of Management, 28,* 27–46.

Kurchner-Hawkins, R., & Miller, R. (2006). Organizational politics: Building positive political strategies in turbulent times. In E. Vigoda-Gadot & A. Drory (Eds.), *Handbook of organizational politics* (pp. 328–351). Northampton, MA: Edward Elgar Publishing.

Lincoln, Y.S., & Guba, E.G. (1985). *Naturalistic inquiry.* Beverly Hills, CA: Sage Publications.

Lindell, M.K., & Whitney, D.J. (2001). Accounting for common method variance in cross-sectional research designs. *Journal of Applied Psychology, 86,* 114–121.

Little, T.D., Cunningham, W.A., Shahar, G., & Widaman, K.F. (2002). To parcel or not to parcel: Exploring the question, weighing the merits. *Structural Equation Modeling, 9,* 151–173.

Maslyn, J.M., & Fedor, D.B. (1998). Perceptions of politics: Does measuring different foci matter? *Journal of Applied Psychology, 84,* 645–653.

Mayes, B.T., & Allen, R.W. (1977). Toward a definition of organizational politics. *Academy of Management Review, 2,* 672–678.

McFarland, L.A., Yun, G., Harold, C.M., Viera Jr., L., & Moore, L.G. (2005). An examination of impression management use and effectiveness across assessment center exercises: The role of competency demands. *Personnel Psychology, 58,* 949–980.

McIntyre, R.M., Smith, D.E., & Hassett, C.E. (1984). Accuracy of performance ratings as affected by rater training and perceived purpose of rating. *Journal of Applied Psychology, 69,* 147–156.

Messick, S. (1995). Validity of psychological assessment: Validation of inferences from person's responses and performances as scientific inquiry into score meaning. *American Psychologist, 50,* 741–749.

Messick, S. (1998). Test validity: A matter of consequence! *Social Indicators Research, 45,* 35.

Miller, B., Rutherford, M., & Kolodinsky, R. (2008). Perceptions of organizational politics: A meta-analysis of outcomes. *Journal of Business and Psychology, 22,* 209–222.

Mintzberg, H. (1983). *Power in and around organizations.* Englewood Cliffs, NJ: Prentice-Hall.

Mitchell, T.R., & James, L.R. (2001). Building better theory: Time and the specification of when things happen. *Academy of Management Review, 26,* 530–547.

Nunnally, J.C., & Bernstein, I.H. (1994). *Psychometric theory* (3rd ed.). New York: McGraw-Hill.

Phillips, L.W. (1981). Assessing measurement error in key informant reports: A methodological note on organizational analysis in marketing. *Journal of Marketing Research, 18,* 395–415.

Ployhart, R.E. (2008). Work motivation methods, measures, and assessment strategies. In R. Kanfer, G. Chen, & R. Pritchard (Eds.), *Work motivation: Past, present, and future* (pp. 17–61). New York: Routledge.

Ployhart, R.E., & Vandenberg, R.J. (2010). Longitudinal research: The theory, design, and analysis of change. *Journal of Management, 36,* 94–120.

Podsakoff, P.M., MacKenzie, S.B., Lee, J., & Podsakoff, N.P. (2003). Common method biases in behavioral research: A critical review of the literature and recommended remedies. *Journal of Applied Psychology, 88,* 879–903.

Porter, L.W., Allen, R., & Angle, H. (1981). The politics of upward influence in organizations. In L.L. Cummings & B.M. Staw (Eds.), *Research in organizational behavior* (Vol. 3, pp. 109–149). Greenwich, CT: JAI Press.

Raudenbush, S.W., & Bryk, A.S. (2002). *Hierarchical linear models: Applications and data analysis methods* (2nd ed.). Newbury Park, CA: Sage Publications.

Riley, P. (1983). A structurationist account of political culture. *Administrative Science Quarterly, 28,* 414-437.

Schmitt, N. (1994). Method bias—The importance of theory and measurement. *Journal of Organizational Behavior, 15,* 393–398.

Schraeder, M., Becton, J., & Portis, R. (2007). A critical examination of performance appraisals. *Journal for Quality and Participation, 30,* 20–25.

Seidler, J. (1974). On using informants: A technique for collecting quantitative data and controlling measurement error in organization analysis. *American Sociological Review, 39,* 816–831.

Smith, A.D., Plowman, D.A., & Duchon, D. (2010). Everyday sensegiving: A closer look at successful plant managers. *Journal of Applied Behavioral Science, 46,* 220–244.

Smith, A.D., Plowman, D., Duchon, D., & Quinn, A.M. (2009). A qualitative study of high-reputation plant managers: Political skill and successful outcomes. *Journal of Operations Management, 27*(6), 428–443.

Stevens, C., & Kristof, A.L. (1995). Making the right impression: A field study of applicant impression management during job interviews. *Journal of Applied Psychology, 80,* 587–606.

van Knippenberg, B.B., & Steensma, H.H. (2003). Future interaction expectation and the use of soft and hard influence tactics. *Applied Psychology: An International Review, 52,* 55–67.

Williams, L.J., Cote, J.A., & Buckley, M.R. (1989). Lack of method variance in self-reported affect and perceptions at work: Reality or artifact? *Journal of Applied Psychology, 74,* 462–468.

Woehr, D.J., & Huffcutt, A.I. (1994). Rater training for performance appraisal: A quantitative review. *Journal of Occupational and Organizational Psychology, 67,* 189–205.

Wolfe, J., & Jackson, C. (1987). Creating models of the strategic decision making process via participant recall: A free simulation examination. *Journal of Management, 13,* 123–134.

Section II

Critical Research Issues in Organizational Politics

5

It's Fairly Political Around Here: Relationship Between Perceptions of Organizational Politics and Organizational Justice

Maureen L. Ambrose
University of Central Florida

It seems obvious that perceptions of organizational politics and perceptions of organizational fairness should be related. Organizational politics involves informal behaviors that are self-serving, aimed at influencing another party, and designed to promote individual goals that are not sanctioned by the organization (Drory & Romm, 1990). Politicking involves activities such as working around formal organizational rules, influencing decision makers, and obtaining special favors—that is, activities that seem to fly in the face of conventional beliefs about fairness in organizations. Both organizational politics and organizational fairness play a central role in organizational life, yet remarkably few researchers explicitly have examined the relationship between them.

In this chapter, the current literature on perceptions of organizational politics and organizational justice is reviewed, with due consideration given to what is known, what is not yet known, and where research might go from here in these important areas of inquiry. The chapter begins with the examination of two foundational works on politics and justice. Next, empirical research is reviewed that considers justice as an antecedent of politics, a parallel influence to politics, a consequence of politics, and a moderator of the relationship between politics and outcomes. Finally, stock is taken of the current level of understanding concerning the relationship between these politics and justice, and opportunities for future research are discussed.

FOUNDATIONAL WORK

The focus of this chapter is on perceptions of organizational politics, which refer to individuals' subjective evaluation of politics. The link between perception of politics and perceived fairness is implicit in early work on organizational politics. However, explicit and careful consideration of the relationship between the two occurred relatively recently. Research on organizational politics and justice spans only about 15 years. Two works emerge as central to the current state of the field: Ferris, Frink, Beehr, and Gilmore (1995) and Andrews and Kacmar (2001). Ferris, Frink et al. provided a theoretical foundation for examining the relationship between perceived politics and justice. Andrews and Kacmar provided the empirical foundation for the distinctness of the constructs.

Conceptual Integration of Politics and Justice

Ferris, Frink, et al. (1995) provided the first comprehensive consideration of the relationship between organizational fairness and organizational politics. They noted, "most would likely argue that politics inherently reflects unfairness" (p. 21). However, they suggested a more complex relationship between the two constructs. Specifically, they proposed that perceptions of politics and fairness may be positively related, negatively related, or independent, depending on contextual and situational contingencies.

Several observations from Ferris, Frink, et al. (1995) warrant attention and provide more detailed suggestions about possible relationships between perceived politics and fairness. First, Ferris, Frink, et al. reiterated the role of attributions of intentionality in labeling behavior as political (see Ferris, Bhawuk, Fedor, & Judge, 1995). They suggested that labeling is associated with a negative relationship between politics and fairness. Specifically, whether a behavior is labeled as fair or as political depends on whether it is viewed as beneficial (an opportunity) or detrimental (a threat) to the target. According to Ferris, Frink, et al., behaviors that are beneficial will be labeled as fair; those that are detrimental will be labeled as politics. Here, politics and justice are positioned as opposite ends of the same continuum.

Second, Ferris, Frink, et al. (1995) suggested that aiding employees in understanding and managing political processes in organizations serves to level the playing field. Rather than eschewing politics, Ferris, Frink et al. suggested that providing employees the opportunities to develop their political skills, acknowledging politics is a part of organizational life, and legitimatizing political behavior will enhance perceptions of fairness. Indeed, they stated, "As everyone becomes more political, the likelihood that someone will be surprised by an influence attempt is lessened and fairness is more likely to prevail" (p. 29). Thus, embracing politics (increased political behavior) is associated with increased perceived fairness.

Third, Ferris, Frink et al. (1995) proposed a typology of organizations depending on the total amount of political activity and the percentage of individuals engaged in political activity. Consistent with their overall analysis, Ferris, Frink et al. suggested that organizations in which political activity is high and the number of individuals engaging in political behavior is high (labeled *highly participatory* organizations) as well as organizations in which political activity is low and the percentage of individuals engaging in political activity is low (labeled *pure bureaucracy*) will be perceived as fair. In contrast, organizations in which political activity is high but only a few individuals engage in political activity will be perceived as the most unfair. Ferris, Frink et al. suggested that the relationship between the amount of political activity and fairness will be moderated by the dispersion of the political behavior.

Fourth, although not explicitly considered by Ferris, Frink et al. (1995), their analysis of the relationship between perceptions of politics and justice also suggests that procedural fairness may moderate the relationship between perceived politics and outcomes. Drawing on Ferris, Russ, and Fandt (1989), Ferris, Frink et al. (1995) suggested that control moderates the relationship between politics and outcomes. Ferris et al. (1989) suggested that whether politics is viewed as an opportunity (beneficial) or a threat (detrimental) is a function of the degree of control the individual feels over the political and work environment. Control plays an important role in the justice literature as well. Early research on justice by Thibaut and Walker (1975) conceptualized process control (i.e., often operationalized as voice) as central to perceptions of procedural fairness. Thus, one might extrapolate from Ferris, Frink et al.'s (1995) argument that procedural fairness would moderate the relationship between perceptions of politics and outcomes.

Finally, Ferris, Frink et al. (1995) acknowledged that their analysis of the relationship between politics and fairness is based on the view of the bystander. Actors and observers see things differently. As politics and fairness are perceptual phenomena, it is likely individuals engaged in political behavior (or as described already, benefiting from such behavior) will view the situation differently from observers (or those disadvantaged by such behavior). In other words, the relationship between perceived politics and fairness depends on the role of the evaluator.

Empirical Distinctiveness of Politics and Justice

Andrews and Kacmar (2001) investigated the empirical distinctiveness of organizational politics and organizational justice. Although previous research had treated these as distinct constructs, Andrews and Kacmar were the first to systematically evaluate this assumption. To establish the distinctiveness of the constructs, Andrews and Kacmar examined the relationship between perceptions of politics, organizational support, distributive justice, and procedural justice as well as differences in their antecedents. The focus here is on the comparisons of politics and fairness. Results of confirmatory factor analyses demonstrated that perceived politics, procedural justice, and distributive justice were distinct constructs. Further, as predicted, they found differences in the relationship between antecedents of politics perceptions and perceptions of procedural and distributive justice. Formalization differentially predicted politics and procedural justice and locus of control differentially predicted politics and distributive justice.

Two aspects of Andrews and Kacmar's (2001) study deserve further mention. First, the authors demonstrated that justice and politics are distinct, but they are also related. They concluded that the variables shared "at least to some extent, one mutual underlying construct" (p. 361). Second, Andrews and Kacmar demonstrated politics differs from both forms of justice but asserted that it is more distinctive from procedural justice than from distributive justice. They suggested that the unfair distribution of rewards may be perceived as a political activity, making political activity and distributive justice more closely related.

Summary

The research by Ferris, Frink et al. (1995) and Andrews and Kacmar (2001) provided a foundation for work on politics and justice. Ferris, Frink et al.

provided the first detailed discussion of the relationship between organizational politics and organizational justice. Although only a few studies have explicitly examined the proposed relationships detailed in Ferris et al., the chapter provided a springboard for subsequent work in the area. Andrews and Kacmar established the empirical foundation for the distinctiveness of the constructs, clarifying the similarities among and differences between politics and justice.

One additional paper requires mention. The first 15 years of research on organizational politics was guided by a conceptual model of the antecedents and consequences of perceptions of politics developed by Ferris et al. (1989). About 13 years later, Ferris, Adams, Kolodinsky, Hochwarter, and Ammeter (2002) provided a review of organizational politics research and, based on their review, developed a revised perceptions of politics model. Fairness perceptions are included in the revised model as a consequence of politics perceptions. Although their discussion of politics and justice is brief, the Ferris et al. (2002) model is widely cited in subsequent research on politics and justice, as it provides a basis for the legitimacy and importance of the topic.

In the following sections, published research is reviewed that explicitly examines the relationship between politics and justice. The search of the literature identified 24 publications that have explicitly addressed this relationship.* This work is grouped into four categories based on the author's conceptualization of the relationship between politics and justice. First, studies are described that conceptualize justice as an antecedent of politics. Second, research is reviewed that considers politics and justice as constructs that work in parallel to affect outcomes. Third, research is examined conceptualizing fairness as a consequence of politics. Fourth, research is examined that conceptualizes justice as a moderator of the relationship between politics and outcomes.

---

* To identify relevant research I searched the ABI and PsychInfo databases using the following key words for politics: *organizational politics, politics perceptions, perceived politics, political skill,* and *perception of politics scale.* For justice I used the key words *organizational justice, distributive justice, procedural justice, interactional justice informational justice, interpersonal justice, organizational fairness, distributive fairness, procedural fairness, interactional fairness, informational fairness,* and *interpersonal fairness.* Each politics key word was paired with each justice key word. The search was completed in spring 2010. A total of 24 articles were identified. For six articles (e.g., Schminke, Ambrose, & Cropanzano, 2000; Miller, Rutherford, & Kolodinsky, 2008) politics and justice were not a central theme and are not included among those summarized.

ORGANIZATIONAL JUSTICE AS AN
ANTECEDENT OF ORGANIZATIONAL POLITICS

Three articles have considered justice as an antecedent of perceptions of politics. In conceptual work, Dipboye (1995) examined the relationships among politics, empowerment, organizational support, and fairness in human resource management systems. He suggested that managers engage in political behavior as an attempt to restore control over procedures and policies that they see as inflexible and impersonal. Dipboye asserted that managers "destructure" procedures in an attempt to develop a satisfying work environment for their employees. That is, they engage in political behavior to create or maintain fairness.

Parker, Dipboye, and Jackson (1995) examined a range of antecedents and consequences of perceptions of politics. They investigated organizational influences (e.g., involvement in decision making, hierarchical level), personal influences (e.g., age, education), and job influences (e.g., intergroup cooperation, fairness of rewards), and they found that the perceived fairness of rewards (i.e., distributive fairness) and involvement in decision making (which can be classified as a proxy for procedural justice) were significant predictors of politics perceptions. Further, when organizational, personal, and job factors were taken into account, the perceptions of politics were unrelated to all of the employee attitudes they examined (i.e., perceived effectiveness of senior management, overall satisfaction, positive values, loyalty) with the exception of perceived innovation. In contrast, after accounting for perceptions of politics, involvement in decision making (i.e., procedural justice), significantly predicted all employee attitudes, and fairness of reward (i.e., distributive fairness) significantly predicted overall satisfaction.

Othman (2008) examined trust, justice, job ambiguity, perceptions of politics, and turnover intentions in a Malaysian finance company. Job ambiguity was conceptualized as an antecedent of justice and trust, justice as an antecedent of trust, and trust, justice, and job ambiguity as antecedents of perceptions of politics. Perceptions of politics were hypothesized to predict turnover intentions. Although Othman adapted Moorman's (1991) measure of distributive, procedural, and interactional fairness, he did not differentiate among the fairness facets. Rather, all items were summed to create a single measure of fairness. Using structural equation modeling (SEM), Othman found support for his conceptualization. Job ambiguity was significantly related to justice and trust, and justice was a significant predictor of trust. All three antecedents also significantly predicted perceptions of politics and perceptions of politics predicted turnover intentions. Of the three predictors, justice exhibited the greatest influence on politics perceptions.

JUSTICE AND PERCEPTIONS OF POLITICS AS INDEPENDENT PREDICTORS

Two studies conceptualized justice and politics as independent antecedents of outcomes. First, Aryee, Chen, and Buhwar (2004) focused primarily on the distinctiveness of perceptions of politics and organizational justice. Aryee et al.'s primary purpose was to examine the relationship between organizational justice and perceptions of politics and to extend the work of Andrews and Kacmar (2001). Specifically, Aryee et al. examined organizational structural antecedents, procedural justice, perceptions of politics, and task and contextual performance. They reported the results of three studies. The first focused on the distinctiveness of the constructs. Using two samples, Aryee et al. demonstrated the distinctiveness of perceptions of politics, assessed by a shortened version of Kacmar and Ferris's (1991) Perceptions of Organizational Politics Scale (POPS), and procedural justice, assessed by Moorman's (1991) seven-item scale.

Aryee et al.'s (2004) second study examined differences in antecedents of justice and perception of politics. They found formalization and participation in decision making predicted both procedural justice and perceptions of politics, whereas authority hierarchy and spatial distance predicted only perceptions of politics. Finally, in Study 3, they examined justice and perceptions of politics as predictors of task and contextual performance and found justice to be a significant predictor of both. Additionally, when justice was included in the model, perceptions of politics did not significantly predict either task performance or contextual performance. Aryee et al. noted that previous research reporting significant relationships between perceptions of politics and performance did not control for perceived procedural fairness. They called for future longitudinal research to assess whether procedural justice mediates the relationship between perceptions of politics and performance.

In the next study, Rosen, Chang, Johnson, and Levy (2009) also examined the relationship between politics and justice. Specifically, they were interested in perceived politics, procedural justice, psychological contract violation, work attitudes, and contextual performance. For simplicity, only the relationship among the three focal constructs is considered here (i.e., psychological contract violation, perception of politics, and procedural fairness). Rosen et al. examined four competing models: (1) perceived politics and procedural justice as moderators of the relationship between psychological contract violation and outcomes; (2) psychological contract violation as a predictor of perceived politics and procedural justice; (3) perceived politics and procedural justice as predictors of psychological contract violation; and (4) perceived politics, procedural justice, and psychological contract violation as indicators of a latent general (un)fairness factor.

The results from three studies provide support for two of the models: Politics and justice as antecedents of psychological contract violation (and psychological contract violation as a mediator of the relationship between perceptions of politics and procedural justice and attitudes and contextual performance) and psychological contract violation, perceptions of politics, and procedural justice as indicators of a global evaluation of the (un) fairness of the organization (i.e., which in turn predicts attitudes and contextual performance).

Several attributes of these findings deserve comment. First, in both conceptualizations, perceptions of politics and procedural justice play an equivalent role in their influence on outcomes (i.e., psychological contract violation or the latent global unfairness factor). Second, in the first conceptualization the effects of politics perceptions on outcomes are fully mediated by psychological contract violation, whereas procedural justice is partially mediated. Third, the conceptualization of psychological contract violation, perceptions of politics, and procedural justice as indicators of a general unfairness impression is consistent with Andrews and Kacmar's (2001) findings that perceptions of politics and justice share an underlying mutual construct. Additionally, perceptions of politics and procedural justice as indicators of general unfairness evaluation reflects a theme articulated in the politics and justice literatures but typically not explicitly examined (e.g., Cropanzano, Kacmar, & Bozeman, 1995).

JUSTICE AS A CONSEQUENCE OF POLITICS

The most common approach to the relationship between politics and justice conceptualizes justice as a consequence of political behavior. In general, research on justice as a consequence of politics perceptions reflects greater complexity than research on justice as an antecedent or as parallel influences.

Ambrose and Harland (1995) addressed the relationship among influence tactics, procedural fairness, and influence tactic use and effectiveness. Drawing on Leventhal's (1980) six procedural rules (i.e., consistency, accuracy, correctability, representativeness, bias suppression, and ethicality), Ambrose and Harland suggested that different influence tactics are perceived as more or less fair. They evaluated each tactic's adherence to the Leventhal rules and created a fairness index for each tactic, proposing that tactics perceived as more fair will be used more frequently. Additionally, they proposed that tactic fairness will be positively associated with tactic effectiveness (assessed by target compliance and target commitment). Analyzing the results of previous research on influence tactics, they found support for their predictions. Implicit in the Ambrose and Harland conceptualization is perceived fairness as a consequence of political behavior and as a mediator between political behavior and the effectiveness of that behavior.

Dulebohn (1997) also examined influence tactics and justice. In the development of a theoretical framework integrating influence tactics and justice evaluations in human resource systems, Dulebohn suggested that political behavior (i.e., influence tactics) may serve as informal voice mechanisms that can enhance actors' perceptions of fairness. Dulebohn and Ferris (1999) provided an empirical test of this idea where they found that actors' supervisor-focused influence tactics* (e.g., volunteering to help the supervisor, praising the supervisor for his or her accomplishments) were associated with positive perceptions of procedural fairness.

Contrary to expectations, Dulebohn and Ferris (1999) found that job-focused influence tactics (e.g., working harder when they know the supervisor is watching, taking responsibility for positive events when they aren't solely responsible) were associated with lower (i.e., rather than the expected higher) perceptions of procedural fairness. Further, influence

---

* Influence tactics were assessed by supervisors.

tactics interacted with formal attributes of a performance appraisal system (i.e., decision control, formal opportunity for voice). The effects of influence tactics on perceptions of procedural fairness was found to be weaker when the formal system incorporated attributes that enhanced fairness.

Several aspects of Dulebohn's (Dulebohn, 1997; Dulebohn & Ferris, 1999) work are of particular interest. First, this research examines perceptions of fairness from the political actors' perspective. Most research considers the fairness perceptions of observers of political behavior. Second, consistent with the actor's perspective, this research proposed a positive relationship between political behavior and perceived fairness. That is, from the actor's perspective, political behavior allows individuals to pursue their goals, and this freedom to pursue one's interest is perceived as fair. In contrast, when political behavior is examined from the observer's perspective, it is viewed as a violation of fairness rules (e.g., consistency and bias suppression) and interpreted as unfair. Third, the two types of political behavior exhibited different effects on procedural fairness. Supervisor-focused tactics were positively related to procedural fairness, but job-focused tactics were negatively related. Dulebohn and Ferris (1999) suggested that the use of job-focused tactics may reflect a lack of confidence in the formal appraisal system. These differences reflect yet another layer of complexity in the relationship between politics and justice, as the type of political behavior and the type of fairness must be considered in evaluating the relationship.

Zellars and Kacmar (1999) also examined the relationship between influence tactics and fairness. In a laboratory study, they manipulated coworker ingratiation and coworker reward. They found that when a coworker's ingratiation was paired with reward for that coworker (i.e., at the expense of the participant), participants reported higher perceptions of favoritism (i.e., an indicator of unfairness). These findings are consistent with Ferris, Frink, et al.'s (1995) suggestion that when behavior is detrimental to an individual it will be perceived as political and interpreted as unfair.

In theoretical work on the relationship between politics and fairness, Beugré and Liverpool (2006) suggested that perceptions of politics will negatively affect perceptions of distributive, procedural, and interactional fairness. They also suggested that justice perceptions will affect perceptions of politics, although their discussion focused on politics as an antecedent of justice and moderators of the relationship between perceived politics and justice. They proposed three moderators. First, consistent with Ferris,

Frink, et al. (1995), they suggested that the impact of the political behavior is an important moderator. Specifically, they suggested that evaluations of fairness will be shaped by whether an individual is a beneficiary or a victim of the political behavior.

Second, Beugré and Liverpool (2006) suggested that political behavior can occur at the individual, group, or organizational level, and they proposed that different sources of the political behavior may impact different types of fairness. For example, they suggested that individual-level politics may affect perceptions of interactional justice, whereas organization-level political behavior may affect procedural justice perceptions. Third, Beugré and Liverpool suggested that the proximity of political behavior may moderate the relationship between perceptions of politics and fairness. They proposed that politics in one's own work group is more strongly negatively associated with fairness than politics in a distal work unit.

The remaining studies examining justice as a consequence of politics have suggested a straightforward negative relationship between perceived politics and fairness. In a scenario study evaluating the perceived fairness of allocation rules, Conlon, Porter, and Parks (2004) found that allocation decisions based on political considerations were evaluated as the least fair. In an examination of leadership, politics, and fairness, Miller and Nicols (2008) found perceptions of organizational politics to be negatively related to perceptions of distributive fairness.

JUSTICE AS A MODERATOR OF THE RELATIONSHIP BETWEEN POLITICS AND OUTCOMES

Four studies have conceptualized justice as a moderator of the relationship between politics and outcomes. Byrne (2005) examined the moderating effect of procedural and interactional justice on the relationship between perceptions of organizational politics and employee outcomes (i.e., turnover intentions, organizational citizenship behavior targeted at the organization [OCBO], organizational citizenship behavior targeted at the supervisor [OCBS], and job performance). Byrne predicted that justice would mitigate the negative relationship between perceived political behavior and turnover intentions and job performance. For citizenship behavior, she expected procedural justice to mitigate the relationship between perceived politics and OCBO and interactional justice to mitigate the negative relationship between perceived politics and OCBS.

Byrne (2005) found limited support for her hypotheses. Procedural justice and interactional justice moderated the relationship between covert political behavior—assessed by the "Go Along to Get Ahead" items of Kacmar and Carlson's (1997) revised POPS—and OCBO, although the moderating effect of procedural justice differed from that of interactional justice. Further, neither procedural justice nor interactional justice moderated the relationship between overt political behavior and OCBO or turnover—assessed by the "General Political Behavior" items of the POPS. Nor did either type of justice moderate the relationship between overt or covert political behavior and OCBS or job performance.

Harris, Andrews, and Kacmar (2007) also examined justice as a moderator of the relationship between perceptions of organizational politics and outcomes. They investigated the moderating effect of distributive and procedural justice on the relationship between perceived politics and turnover intentions and job satisfaction. Harris et al. hypothesized that the relationship between perceived politics and attitudes would be weaker when perceived fairness was higher. Further, they predicted a three-way interaction among distributive justice, procedural justice, and perceptions of politics such that the negative relationship between perceived politics and attitudes would be weakest when both procedural justice and distributive justice were high.

Harris et al. (2007) found significant three-way interactions for both turnover intentions and job satisfaction. Contrary to expectations, the weakest relationship occurred when distributive justice and procedural justice were low,* and the strongest relationship was found when distributive justice was low and procedural justice was high. These results suggest politics has little impact on turnover and satisfaction when both procedures and outcomes are unfair. In contrast, perceived politics has its

---

* In evaluating support for the interaction hypotheses, Harris et al. (2007) compare the strength of the relationship between perceived politics and outcomes for high and low procedural justice when distributive justice is high. Under high distributive justice, the weakest relationship between perceived politics and outcomes is for high procedural justice. However, the full pattern of results (comparing the strength of the relationship between perceived politics and outcomes for high and low distributive justice and high and low procedural justice) revealed the weakest relationship when distributive justice was low and procedural justice was low and the strongest relationship when distributive justice was low and procedural justice was high.

strongest influence on outcomes when there is mixed information about fairness (e.g., when procedures are fair and outcomes are unfair).

In the third study to examine the moderating effect of justice, Salimäki and Jämsén (2010) investigated political behavior associated with pay systems. Specifically, they examined the moderating effect of procedural justice (i.e., voice in the development of the system) and distributive justice (i.e., fairness of rewards) on the relationship between perceived politics and pay system effectiveness. Salimäki and Jämsén found that the negative relationship between perceived politics in pay decisions and pay system effectiveness was stronger when distributive justice was low. For procedural justice, this negative relationship was stronger when voice was high.* Salimäki and Jämsén did not investigate a three-way interaction among distributive justice, procedural justice, and perceived politics.

The final study to examine justice as a moderator of the relationship between politics and outcomes investigated political skill (Andrews, Kacmar, & Harris, 2009). Political skill refers to "the ability to effectively understand others at work, and to use such knowledge to influence others to act in ways that enhance one's personal and/or organizational objectives" (Ferris et al., 2005, p. 127). Andrews et al. drew on Mischel's (1968) situationalist perspective, arguing that fair treatment reflects a strong situation and unfair treatment reflects a weak situation. Because political skill is an individual difference, it is likely to be displayed and effective in weak situations. Thus, Andrews et al. predicted that the relationship between political skill and task performance would be negative when justice is high (i.e., a strong situation) and positive when justice is low (i.e., a weak situation).

For citizenship behavior, Andrews et al. (2009) predicted a stronger positive relationship when justice is low. They examined the moderating effects of both procedural and distributive justice, and when the

---

* Salimäki and Jämsén's (2010) interpretation of the interactions focus on the endpoints (the values 1 sd above and below the mean that were used to plot the figure). They noted ratings of pay system effectiveness is lowest when distributive justice is low and politics is high and highest when politics is high and procedural justice is high. Although these end points are an important aspect of the pattern of results, regression analyses address slopes, not means. An examination of slopes indicates distributive justice mitigates the negative impact of politics. However, no such mitigation is found for procedural justice. Rather, the negative relationship between politics and pay system effectiveness is stronger when procedural justice is high. This effect may reflect a contrast effect. Perhaps when individuals are provided high voice in the development of the system they expect a fair pay system (i.e., one free of political behavior). These expectations may make them more sensitive to politics and lead to stronger negative reactions to the pay system when they are faced with political behavior in pay decisions.

interactions were examined separately the results supported their predictions for task performance. For citizenship behavior, only distributive justice was a significant moderator. When both interactions were included in the analyses, the only significant interaction was for political skill and procedural justice for task performance. Andrews et al. suggested that this change in results likely was a function of multicollinearity. They did not consider a three-way interaction among political skill, distributive justice, and procedural justice.

SUMMARY OF CURRENT LITERATURE

Several conclusions can be drawn from the existing research on perceived politics and justice. First, nearly all research in this area acknowledges the intuitive relationship between politics and fairness. Politics are self-serving and "work" by going outside existing structures and systems. Such behavior lends itself to the use of decision processes and to decision outcomes that are inconsistent and biased and, consequently, unfair. Yet, despite the close conceptual connection between the two constructs, there is relatively little empirical research examining their relationship. Further, there is little agreement about the conceptual relationship between the two constructs. As described in the preceding review, justice has been conceptualized as an antecedent of perceived politics, a parallel predictor with perceived politics, a consequence of perceived politics, and a moderator of the relationship between perceived politics and outcomes. In all, its conceptual status in the field is unclear.

One might expect that the conceptual relationship between justice and politics would have evolved over time. For example, one might expect early research to see justice as a parallel process with politics, followed by a shift to a role as an antecedent, then a shift to its role as a consequence and moving to a role as a moderator. Yet an examination of the literature shows that work on justice as an antecedent, a parallel process, a consequence, and a moderator spans the last 15 years. There has been neither a clear evolution of thought nor a consensus regarding the conceptual role justice plays. In fact, the most recent articles in each of the previously mentioned subareas were published in 2008, 2009, 2006, and 2010.

In some ways, this lack of consensus is not surprising, because clearly the relationship between politics and justice is complex. It is likely that the relationship between justice and politics is reciprocal, with politics affecting perceptions of justice and justice affecting perceptions of politics. Similarly, the moderating influence of justice on the relationship between perceived politics and outcomes is consistent with other research on contextual influences. Perhaps only one relationship can be eliminated. Empirical research that simultaneously examines justice and politics has demonstrated that perceptions of politics do not predict significant variance in outcomes once perceptions of fairness or justice are accounted for (Aryee et al., 2004; Parker et al., 1995). This result suggests that models in which the effect of justice on outcomes is mediated by perceptions of politics are not likely to be accurate.

Second, the research on politics and justice is characterized by a lack of strong theoretical foundation, thus contributing to conceptual ambiguity. Additionally, research on politics and justice typically has been conducted by politics researchers. Given the clear connection between the two areas, it is surprising that few justice researchers have sought to understand the relationship. Perhaps greater integration with justice research would help identify relevant theoretical perspectives that might move the field forward. For example, justice research typically draws on theories of social exchange, identity, or uncertainty to explain fairness effects. Some politics researchers have acknowledged the relevance of these theoretical perspectives (Byrne, 2005; Rosen et al., 2009; Salimäki & Jämsén, 2010). However, there are few systematic and comprehensive applications of these perspectives in the current literature. Yet, such application might be fruitful.

For example, uncertainty management theory (UMT; van den Bos & Lind, 2002) suggests that fairness is powerful because individuals dislike uncertainty, and fairness is important in the process of uncertainty management because it minimizes uncertainty. In contrast, political activity increases uncertainty. Thus, fairness could be a mechanism for offsetting the negative effects of politics perceptions. However, other individual and situational characteristics also could minimize uncertainty. Political skill could serve a similar uncertainty reduction function. Thus, drawing on UMT, one might expect fairness to be most powerful in mitigating the negative effects of politics perceptions when political skill is low, but not when political skill is high. Indeed, given the central role of uncertainty in politics, a consideration of UMT might prove especially useful. In general, further exploration and application of the theoretical foundations underlying justice effects might be useful for understanding the relationship among justice, politics, and outcomes.

Third, most research has examined either procedural justice (i.e., 10 articles) or distributive justice (i.e., 5 articles). Only two papers have investigated interactional justice. Yet most organizational research on politics has focused on individual-level perceptions of politics and political activities that are inherently relational (e.g., influence tactics, impression management, political skill). Interactional justice should play a key role for such activities. Further, the research that examines multiple types of fairness typically finds different effects for different types of fairness (e.g., Byrne, 2005; Harris et al., 2007). This suggests that a more nuanced approach might be needed, with particular reference to one that considers differential effects based on the type of justice, the type of political behavior, and situational and individual factors.

Finally, the diversity of conceptual models, diversity of operationalizations of politics (e.g., impression management, influence tactics, POPS), and diversity of the type of operationalization of justice (e.g., distributive justice, procedural justice, general fairness) hinder the development of cumulative knowledge. Although there are a substantial number of empirical studies investigating both politics and justice, the diversity of approaches to this investigation limits the conclusions that can be drawn. It can be stated with some confidence that politics and justice are distinct but related constructs. Further, when both politics and justice are examined in the same analyses, the magnitude of the effect of justice on outcomes typically is larger than and may subsume the effect of politics. Yet, overall, the research remains fragmented.

EXTENSIONS OF CURRENT RESEARCH

Several areas of potential integration have not yet been fully explored in the politics and justice literature. As noted already, one area of overlap that could serve as a foundation for future research is uncertainty. Researchers suggest political behavior is more likely to occur when there is environmental uncertainty (Cropanzano et al., 1995; Ferris et al., 1989; Ferris et al., 2002; Othman, 2008). Yet, paradoxically, uncertainty increases the importance of fairness. This creates an interesting dilemma for managers. The circumstances that facilitate political behavior are precisely the circumstances in which it is likely to be most damaging.

Cropanzano et al. (1995) suggested that fairness (i.e., specifically adherence to the rules of procedural fairness) is a way to manage dysfunctional politics. UMT suggests that managing perceptions of politics and fairness may be most critical in uncertain environments. Systematically considering the influence of uncertainty on perceptions of politics and organizational justice may improve understanding of the relationship between the two constructs and outcomes.

Politics research also has recognized the impact of organizational structure on political behavior (Andrews & Kacmar, 2001; Aryee et al., 2004; Beugré & Liverpool, 2006; Ferris, Frink, et al., 1995). A substantial number of studies examined the relationship between structure and perceptions of politics (Fedor, Ferris, Harrell-Cook, & Russ, 1998; Kacmar, Bozeman, Carlson, & Anthony, 1999; Parker et al., 1995). Considerable research on justice also has considered the influence of structure on justice perceptions (Ambrose & Schminke, 2001; Schminke, Ambrose, & Cropanzano, 2000; Schminke, Cropanzano, & Rupp, 2002). Justice research has demonstrated that procedural justice is more influential in mechanistic organizations, whereas interactional justice is more influential in organic organizations (Ambrose & Schminke, 2003). Thus, there seems to be fertile ground for considering the interactions among perceived politics, justice, and structure.

Finally, recent research on organizational justice has focused on global perceptions of fairness (Ambrose & Schminke, 2009; Choi, 2008; Holtz & Harold, 2009; Jones & Martens, 2009; Kim & Leung, 2007). This work examines the relationship between justice facet judgments (i.e., distributive, procedural, interactional) and overall justice judgments or between event judgments and global entity judgments of fairness. The work by Rosen et al. (2009) offers an alternative, and intriguing, perspective. Rosen et al.'s work demonstrates that modeling perceptions of politics, psychological contract violations, and procedural justice as indicators of a general impression of fairness provides as good a fit to the data as more complicated, mediated, or moderated models involving the three constructs.

Rosen et al.'s (2009) conceptualization is simple but potentially powerful. First, it highlights the similarity among three related yet unique constructs. It suggests that these phenomena have similar effects because each provides an indication of the type of organization in which the employee works. Consequently, each has implications for the employee's relationship with the organization. From an organizational fairness perspective, it addresses the finding that facet measures of fairness typically account for about 50–60% of the variance in overall fairness judgments. This suggests that current conceptualizations of fairness facets may be too narrow.

Unfortunately, it is difficult to draw strong conclusions from Rosen et al.'s (2009) study, because, for example, they did not consider all facets of justice. It is unclear what unique variance each justice construct accounts for if all types of fairness, as well as psychological contract violation and perceived political behavior, were considered simultaneously. Further, Rosen et al. did not consider more complicated relationships among the indicators of fairness. Is a general impression of (un)fairness simply an additive function of (un)fairness facets? Or does research on more complex models of politics and justice, such as moderation, better describe the relationship?

Nonetheless, considering perceived political behavior and facet justice judgments as indicators of a general impression of unfairness is an intriguing idea that warrants further investigation. Moreover, as Rosen et al. (2009) noted, these results have important implications for how researchers model the relationships among variables, such as perceptions of politics and facets of justice that have developed separately, but are joined by a common theme. It is important for researchers to be clear about their particular interest. Is the research about a specific attribute, such as perceptions of politics? Or is the research question about the general (fairness) impression, or climate, of the organization, of which multiple constructs might serve as indicators?

An additional issue associated with a global impression of fairness also is relevant to research on perceptions of politics. The justice literature distinguishes between event judgments versus entity judgments (Cropanzano, Byrne, Bobocel, & Rupp, 2001). Event judgments are specific assessments of fairness associated with a particular event (e.g., an employee's most recent performance appraisal). Entity judgments are global assessments about an entity, such as overall fairness of a supervisor or overall fairness of an organization. In their discussion of the measurement issues associated with the perception of politics, Ferris et al. (2002) raised the question of the appropriate focus for measures of perceptions of politics. They identified a similar distinction between assessments of organizational politics in general versus the politics associated with particular policies or systems.

Although little justice research has been explicit about this distinction between event and entity judgments, it is becoming clear that these two types of judgments are fundamentally different. For example, recent research on employee reactions to organizational justice demonstrates that global entity judgments moderate the relationship between specific event judgments and outcomes (Choi, 2008). The event/entity distinction may be useful for organizational politics research as well.

FUTURE RESEARCH DIRECTIONS

Fundamental Issues

Perhaps the most critical issue for future research on organizational politics and justice surrounds the ontology of the organizational politics and justice constructs. To make progress in understanding the relationship between organizational politics and justice, we need to have a clear understanding of the nature of the constructs. Substantial research on organizational justice has grappled with codifying and classifying what justice is and what it is not. For example, justice research recognizes fairness is composed of several independent but related facets and has considered the relationship between the facets. Further, research has identified three primary motives for fairness: instrumental, relational, and deontic. Of course, conceptual issues remain. There is not complete agreement on whether justice is best represented by three facets (i.e., distributive, procedural, interactional) or four (i.e., distributive, procedural, interpersonal, informational). Also, there is discussion about the possibility of other facets that may have been overlooked (Ambrose & Schminke, 2010; Colquitt & Shaw, 2005). However, in general, the conceptual space occupied by organizational justice is well defined.

Research on organizational politics has yet to develop as clear an understanding of what organizational politics is and is not (see Ferris and Hochwarter, 2011 for a thorough and thoughtful discussion of this issue). Indeed, as already noted, one of the barriers to the synthesis of research on politics and justice is the broad range of definitions and operationalizations of organizational politics. In the previous section, some ways current research on organizational justice might inform research on organizational politics were suggested. Perhaps justice research also can lend a hand in researchers thinking about the ontological status of the politics construct.

Indeed, perhaps using a justice template might serve both to clarify the politics construct and to further integrate politics and justice. For example, what might we learn about politics if we were to examine it through the three motivational lenses for justice? Is it useful to think about instrumental political behavior, relational political behavior, and deontic political behavior? Similarly, are there different facets of politics that are relevant to distributions, procedures, and interactions? Do such categorization templates provide a way of classifying the diverse conceptualizations and operationalizations of political behavior?

Of course, it may be that the frameworks that help us understand organizational justice do little to inform us about organizational politics. If this is the case, then politics researchers must find a way to develop their own frameworks for capturing the conceptual construct domain space for organizational politics. For meaningful progress to be made on understanding the relationship between organizational politics and justice, future research must grapple with the ontology of the politics and justice constructs.

Perceived Politics and Increased Fairness

The current research on organizational politics and justice provides a foundation for the examination of some new research questions. Research on politics is clear that politics can be both positive and negative (Fedor, Maslyn, Farmer, & Bettenhausen, 2008; Ferris & Hochwarter, 2011; Treadway et al., 2004). However, researchers have focused primarily on the negative side of political behavior. In contrast, it would be interesting to consider the conditions under which perceived political behavior is associated with greater perceptions of fairness. Hochwarter's (Chapter 2 in this volume) arguments about positive politics would seem to hold out potential for such a conceptualization relating to justice perceptions. Also, Dulebohn and Ferris (1999) examined this idea from the perspective of the actor, conceptualizing political behavior as a form of informal voice. Other researchers consider how the harm or benefit of the political activity influences employee reactions (Beugré & Liverpool, 2006; Ferris, Frink, et al., 1995). However, no empirical research has examined the positive influence of political behavior on perceived fairness for observers of politics.

Justice research suggests several possible moderators for the relationship between perceived politics and perceived fairness. First, drawing on justice research (Greenberg, 1987), politics researchers have noted that favorable outcomes are perceived as more fair than unfavorable outcomes (Beugré & Liverpool, 2006; Ferris, Frink et al., 1995; Ferris et al., 2002). Thus, political behavior that benefits the actor but that also benefits the observer may be associated with positive perceptions of fairness. For example, Treadway et al. (2004) suggested that managers who are "good politicians" may access resources that benefit their subordinates. Here, outcome favorability may moderate the relationship between perceived politics and fairness.

Additionally, drawing on Folger's (1998, 2001) deontic view of fairness, political behavior might be associated with increased perceptions of fairness when it is used to right a wrong. Nadisic (2008) demonstrated that supervisors may try to correct injustice they feel their subordinates have suffered as a result of organizational actions. These corrective actions include "invisible remedies" that compensate subordinates by allowing them to take company-owned time or items. One might argue that this behavior is prosocial, but the compensation may benefit the supervisor as well, thus increasing the loyalty, satisfaction, and performance of the compensated employee.

This idea is similar to Dipboye's (1995) discussion of the destructuring of human resources systems, where the manager's political behavior is aimed at increasing fairness. A similarly positive relationship between politics and justice may stem from Tripp, Bies, and Aquino's (2002) work on the aesthetics of revenge. Political behavior used to seek justifiable revenge may increase perceived fairness. Given the generally negative relationship between politics and fairness, examining conditions under which the relationship is positive should provide new insights about the relationship between politics and justice.

Multilevel Politics and Justice

A second area that deserves greater attention is multilevel issues. Ferris et al. (2002) explicitly addressed multilevel issues in organizational politics research. Research on politics and justice sometimes acknowledges multilevel influences (e.g., Beugré & Liverpool, 2006), but no empirical research has examined these issues.

Implicit in some work on politics and justice (e.g., Andrews et al., 2009; Salimäki & Jämsén, 2010) is the role of justice climate, which is defined as a shared group-level cognition regarding the extent to which group members are treated fairly (Naumann & Bennett, 2000). Climate is a group-level construct that affects both group-level and individual-level outcomes (see Chapter 9 in this volume for a discussion of the relationship between organizational climate and politics).

Research has demonstrated that justice climate is distinct from individual-level justice perceptions and predicts outcomes above and beyond individual-level justice perceptions. Justice climate is a significant predictor of job attitudes, helping, team performance, team absence, group-level OCBs, group-level burnout, and customer service (Chen, Lam, Naumann, & Schaubroeck, 2005; Colquitt, Noe, & Jackson, 2002; Liao & Rupp, 2005; Moliner, Martínez-Tur, Peiró, Ramos, & Cropanzano, 2005; Mossholder, Bennett, & Martin, 1998; Naumann & Bennett, 2000; Simons & Roberson, 2003). Although politics and justice research has drawn on the idea of fair organizational climates, researchers have considered only individual-level perceptions of fairness.

The most obvious application of justice climate is simply including it when the conceptual model calls for an assessment of fairness climate. However, interesting research questions that go beyond this straightforward application also exist. For example, as described before, Andrews et al. (2009) draw on Mischel's (1968) strong and weak situations argument to develop hypotheses about the relationship between political skill and outcomes. Andrews et al. measured individual-level perceptions of fairness. They argued that an individual's perception of unfair treatment reflects a weak situation, whereas the perception of fair treatment reflects a strong situation. Strong situations constrain behavior whereas weak situations allow greater variance in behavior.

A more direct assessment of the hypotheses would be generated by considering justice climate, with specific reference to climate strength. By definitions, strong climates (i.e., climate for which there is a high-level of agreement among group members) are strong situations. Weak climates (i.e., climates for which there is low agreement among group members) are weak situations. Examining justice climate directly would allow for the consideration of both level (fair/unfair) and strength. It might be that climate strength matters for fair climates. When there is a high level of agreement that fair behavior is "how we do things around here," this limits the effectiveness of political skill. However, when there is a low level of agreement (i.e., weak fair climate), greater variance in behavior should be tolerated, allowing for political skill to exert an influence. In contrast, there might be no difference between strong unfair climates and weak unfair climates. In either case, unfair climate opens the door for political behavior and, consequently, the influence of political skill.

Why Do People Behave Unfairly

The current research on organizational politics and organizational justice provides a foundation for some new justice inquiries as well. Most research on organizational fairness considers fairness from the perspective of the recipient. That is, organizational justice research has focused on individuals' reactions to fair or unfair treatment. Recently, several scholars have identified the need to also consider why managers behave fairly or unfairly (Ambrose & Schminke, 2009; Masterson, Byrne, & Mao, 2005; Scott, Colquitt, & Paddock, 2009). That is, rather than investigate recipients, these researchers have suggested that to fully understand fairness in organizations actors need to be studied as well.

To date, research on the fairness of actors has drawn on research on ethics, cognitive and affective motives, and communication. Research on organizational politics provides an additional perspective. For example, research on politics has identified situational and individual characteristics associated with political behavior. These characteristics may play a role in individuals' decisions to engage in fair or unfair behavior as well. Further, understanding the motivation behind political behavior can provide insight about the motivation for fair and unfair behavior.

Political Skill and Fairness

Justice research also could benefit from examining the relationship between political skill and justice. Ferris et al. (2005) found that political skill was associated with socially acceptable influence tactics (i.e., upward appeal and coalition building tactics) but not those typically viewed as caustic (i.e., assertiveness). These results can be coupled with Ambrose and Harland's (1995) finding that the perceived procedural fairness of influence tactics is associated with their frequency of use and effectiveness. Individuals high in political skill are likely to recognize the importance of perceived fairness, and manage their political activity such that it follows norms of fairness. Thus, individuals high in political skill are likely to be perceived as fairer.

Given the likely relationship between political skill and perceived fairness, it is interesting to consider a more complex set of relationships involving justice and political skill. For example, one might begin by conceptualizing perceived fairness as mediating the relationship between political skill and positive outcomes. Additionally, individual and situational characteristics might moderate the relationship between political skill and perceived fairness. For example, one could conceptualize a moderated mediation model with organizational structure. The relationship between political skill and fairness might be stronger in organic organizations. Organic organizations are characterized by flexible, loose, decentralized structures. Formal lines of authority are less clear, and communication channels are open and more flexible (Burns & Stalker, 1961; Lawrence & Lorsch, 1967). In these settings, there are fewer rules and regulations, and also there is greater face-to-face interaction. These situational characteristics should provide greater behavioral flexibility and should strengthen the relationship between political skill and fairness, with fairness mediating this interactive effect on outcomes. Of course, this raises the issue of whether individuals high in political skill *are* fairer or are simply *perceived* as fairer, which is a question worthy of investigation as well.

CONCLUSION

In this chapter, existing research on organizational politics and organizational justice was summarized, and avenues for extension as well as new paths were considered. Despite an intuitively appealing antithetical relationship, the research on politics and justice suggests that the relationship is anything but simple. However, the complexity provides fertile ground for the development of theory-based models and interesting new research directions. The hope is that this chapter will stimulate further thought and investigation of perceptions of politics and organizational justice.

REFERENCES

Ambrose, M.L., & Harland, L. (1995). Procedural justice and influence tactics: Fairness, frequency, and effectiveness. In R. Cropanzano & K.M. Kacmar (Eds.), *Organizational politics, justice, and support: Managing the social climate of the workplace* (pp. 97–130). Westport, CT: Quorum.

Ambrose, M.L., & Schminke, M. (2001). Are flexible organizations the death knell for the future of procedural justice? In R. Cropanzano (Ed.), *Justice in the workplace II: From theory to practice* (pp. 229–244). Hillsdale, NJ: Erlbaum.

Ambrose, M.L., & Schminke, M. (2003). Organization structure as a moderator of the relationship between procedural justice, interactional justice, POS and supervisory trust. *Journal of Applied Psychology, 88,* 295–305.

Ambrose, M.L., & Schminke, M. (2009). The role of overall justice judgments in organizational justice: A test of mediation. *Journal of Applied Psychology, 94,* 491–500.

Ambrose, M.L., & Schminke, M. (2010). *Measuring justice: An examination of indirect, direct and overall justice.* Presented at the annual meeting of the Academy of Management, Montreal.

Andrews, M.C., & Kacmar, K.M. (2001). Discriminating among organizational politics, justice, and support. *Journal of Organizational Behavior, 22,* 347–366.

Andrews, M.C., Kacmar, K.M., & Harris, K.J. (2009). Got political skill? The impact of justice on the importance of political skill for job performance. *Journal of Applied Psychology, 94,* 1427–1437.

Aryee, S., Chen, Z.X., & Buhwar, P.S. (2004). Exchange fairness and employee performance: An examination of the relationship between organizational politics and procedural justice. *Organizational Behavior and Human Decision Processes, 94,* 1–14.

Beugré, C.D., & Liverpool, P.R. (2006). Politics as determinants of fairness perceptions in organizations. In E. Vigoda-Gadot & A. Drory (Eds.), *Handbook of organizational politics* (pp. 122–135). Northampton, MA: Edward Elgar Publishing.

Burns, T., & Stalker, G.M. (1961). *The management of innovation.* London: Tavistock.

Byrne, Z. (2005). Fairness reduces the negative effects of organizational politics on turnover intentions, citizenship behavior, and job performance. *Journal of Business and Psychology, 20,* 175–200.

Chen, X., Lam, S.S.K., Naumann, S.E., & Schaubroeck, J. (2005). Group citizenship behaviour: Conceptualization and preliminary tests of its antecedents and consequences. *Management and Organization Review, 1,* 273–300.

Choi, J. (2008). Event justice perceptions and employees' reactions: Perceptions of social entity justice as a moderator. *Journal of Applied Psychology, 93,* 513–528.

Colquitt, J.A., Noe, R.A., & Jackson, C.L. (2002). Justice in teams: Antecedents and consequences of procedural justice climate. *Personnel Psychology, 55,* 83–109.

Colquitt, J.A., & Shaw, J.C. (2005). How should organizational justice be measured? In J. Greenberg & J. Colquitt (Eds.), *The handbook of organizational justice* (pp. 113–152). Mahwah, NJ: Erlbaum.

Conlon, D.E., Porter, C.O.L.H., & Parks, J.M. (2004). The fairness of decision rules. *Journal of Management, 30,* 329–349.

Cropanzano, R., Byrne, Z.S., Bobocel, D.R., & Rupp, D.E. (2001). Moral virtues, fairness heuristics, social entities, and other denizens of organizational justice. *Journal of Vocational Behavior, 58,* 164–209.

Cropanzano, R.S., Kacmar, K.M., & Bozeman, D.P. (1995). The social setting of work organizations: Politics, justice and support. In R.S. Cropanzano & K.M. Kacmar (Eds.), *Organizational politics, justice, and support: Managing the social climate of the workplace* (pp. 1–18). Westport, CT: Greenwood Publishing Co.

Dipboye, R.L. (1995). How politics can destructure human resource management in the interest of empowerment, support, and justice. In R.S. Cropanzano & K.M. Kacmar (Eds.), *Organizational politics, justice, and support: Managing the social climate of the workplace* (pp. 55–80). Westport, CT: Greenwood Publishing Co.

Drory, A., & Romm, T. (1990). The definition of organizational politics: A review. *Human Relations, 43,* 1133–1154.

Dulebohn, J.H. (1997). Social influence in justice evaluations of human resources systems. In G.R. Ferris (Ed.), *Research in personnel and human resources management* (Vol. 15, pp. 241–291). Greenwich, CT: JAI Press.

Dulebohn, J.H., & Ferris, G.R. (1999). The role of influence tactics in perceptions of performance evaluations' fairness. *Academy of Management Journal, 42,* 288–303.

Fedor, D.B., Ferris, G.R., Harrell-Cook, G., & Russ, G.S. (1998). The dimensions of politics perceptions and their organizational and individual predictors. *Journal of Applied Social Psychology, 28,* 1760–1797.

Fedor, D., Maslyn, J., Farmer, S., & Bettenhausen, K. (2008). The contributions of positive politics to prediction of employee reactions. *Journal Applied Social Psychology, 38,* 76–96.

Ferris, G.R., Adams, G., Kolodinsky, R.W., Hochwarter, W.A., & Ammeter, A.P. (2002). Perceptions of organizational politics: Theory and research directions. In F. Yammarino & F. Dansereau (Eds.), *Research in multi-level issues, Volume 1: The many faces of multi-level issues* (pp. 179–254). Oxford, UK: JAI Press/Elsevier Science.

Ferris, G.R., Bhawuk, D.P.S., Fedor, D.B., & Judge, T.A. (1995). Organizational politics and citizenship: Attributions of intentionality and construct definition. In M.J. Martinko (Ed.), *Advances in attribution theory: An organizational perspective* (pp. 231–252). Delray Beach, FL: St. Lucie Press.

Ferris, G.R., Frink, D.D., Beehr, T.A., & Gilmore, D.C. (1995). Political fairness and fair politics: The conceptual integration of divergent constructs. In R.S. Cropanzano & K.M. Kacmar (Eds.), *Organizational politics, justice, and support: Managing the social climate of the workplace* (pp. 21–36). Westport, CT: Greenwood Publishing.

Ferris, G.R., & Hochwarter, W.A. (2011). Organizational politics. In S. Zedeck (Ed.), *APA handbook of industrial and organizational psychology, Vol. 3: Maintaining, expanding, and contracting the organization* (pp. 435–459). Washington, DC: American Psychological Association.

Ferris, G.R., Russ, G.S., & Fandt, P.M. (1989). Politics in organizations. In R.A. Giacalone & P. Rosenfeld (Eds.), *Impression management in the organization* (pp. 143–170). Hillsdale, NJ: Lawrence Erlbaum.

Ferris, G.R., Treadway, D.C., Kolodinsky, R.W., Hochwarter, W.A., Kacmar, C.J., Douglas, C., et al. (2005). Development and validation of the political skill inventory. *Journal of Management, 31,* 126–152.

Folger, R. (1998). Fairness as moral virtue. In M. Schminke (Ed.), *Managerial ethics: Moral management of people and processes* (pp. 13–34). Mahwah, NJ: Lawrence Erlbaum.

Folger, R. (2001). Fairness as deonance. In S.W. Gilliland, D.D. Steiner, & D.P. Skarlicki (Eds.), *Research in social issues in management* (pp. 3–31). Greenwich, CT: Information Age.

Greenberg, J. (1987). A taxonomy of organizational justice theories. *Academy of Management Review, 12,* 9–22.

Harris, K.J., Andrews, M.C., & Kacmar, K.M. (2007). The moderating effects of justice on the relationship between organizational politics and workplace attitudes. *Journal of Business Psychology, 22,* 135–144.

Holtz, B.C., & Harold, C.M. (2009) Fair today, fair tomorrow? A longitudinal investigation of overall justice perceptions. *Journal of Applied Psychology, 94,* 1185–1199.

Jones, D.A., & Martens, M.L. (2009). The mediating role of overall fairness and the moderating role of trust certainty in justice-criteria relationships: The formation and use of fairness heuristics in the workplace. *Journal of Organizational Behavior, 30,* 1025–1051.

Kacmar, K.M., Bozeman, D.P., Carlson, D.S., & Anthony, W.P. (1999). A partial test of the perceptions of organizational politics model. *Human Relations, 52,* 383–416.

Kacmar, K.M., & Carlson, D.S. (1997). Further validation of the Perceptions of Politics Scale (POPS): A multi-sample approach. *Journal of Management, 23,* 627–658.

Kacmar, K.M., & Ferris, G.R. (1991). Perceptions of Organizational Politics Scale (POPS): Development and construct validation. *Educational and Psychological Measurement, 51,* 193–205.

Kim, T., & Leung, K. (2007). Forming and reacting to overall fairness: A cross-cultural comparison. *Organizational Behavior and Human Decision Processes, 104,* 83–95.

Lawrence, P.R., & Lorsch, J.W. (1967). *Organization and environment.* Homewood, IL: Irwin.

Leventhal, G.S. (1980). What should be done with equity theory? In K.J. Gergen, M.S. Greenberg, & R.H. Willis (Eds.), *Social exchange: Advances in theory and research* (pp. 27–55). New York: Plenum.

Liao, H., & Rupp, D.E. (2005). The impact of justice climate and justice orientation on work outcomes: A cross-level multi-foci framework. *Journal of Applied Psychology, 90,* 242–257.

Masterson, S.S., Byrne, Z.S., & Mao, H. (2005). Interpersonal and informational justice: Identifying the differential antecedents of interactional justice behaviors. In S.W. Gilliland, D.D. Steiner, D.P. Skarlicki, & K. van den Bos (Eds.), *What motivates fairness in organizations* (pp. 79–103). Greenwich, CT: Information Age Publishing.

Miller, B.K., & Nicols, K.M. (2008). Politics and justice: A mediated moderation model. *Journal of Managerial Issues, 20,* 214–237.

Miller, B.K., Rutherford, M.A., & Kolodinsky, R.W. (2008). Perceptions of organizational politics: A meta-analysis. *Journal of Business Psychology, 22,* 209–222.

Mischel, W. (1968). *Personality and assessment.* New York: Wiley.

Moliner, C., Martínez-Tur, V., Peiró, J.M., Ramos, J., & Cropanzano, R. (2005). Relationships between organizational justice and burnout at the work-unit level. *International Journal of Stress Management, 12,* 99–116.

Moorman, R.H. (1991). Relationship between organizational justice and organizational citizenship behaviors: Do fairness perceptions influence employee citizenship? *Journal of Applied Psychology, 76,* 845–855.

Mossholder, K.W., Bennett, N., & Martin, C.L. (1998). A multilevel analysis of procedural justice context. *Journal of Organizational Behavior, 19,* 131–141.

Nadisic, T. (2008). The Robin Hood Effect: Antecedents and consequences of managers using invisible remedies to correct workplace injustice. In S.W. Gilliland, D.D. Steiner, & D.P. Skarlicki (Eds.), *Justice, morality and social responsibility* (pp. 125–153). Greenwich, CT: Information Age Publishing.

Naumann, S.E., & Bennett, N. (2000). A case for procedural justice climate: Development and test of a multilevel model. *Academy of Management Journal, 43,* 881–890.

Othman, R. (2008). Organizational politics: The role of justice, trust, and job ambiguity. *Singapore Management Review, 33,* 43–53.

Parker, C., Dipboye, R., & Jackson, S. (1995). Perceptions of organizational politics: An investigation of antecedents and consequences. *Journal of Management, 21,* 891–912.

Rosen, C.C., Chang, C. Johnson, R.E., & Levy, P.E. (2009). Perceptions of the organizational context and psychological contract breach: Assessing competing perspectives. *Organizational Behavior and Human Decision Processes, 108,* 202–217.

Salimäki, A., & Jämsén, S. (2010). Perceptions of politics and fairness in merit pay. *Journal of Managerial Psychology, 25,* 229–251.

Schminke, M., Ambrose, M.L., & Cropanzano, R.S. (2000). The effect of organizational structure on perceptions of procedural fairness. *Journal of Applied Psychology, 85,* 294–304.

Schminke, M., Cropanzano, R.S., & Rupp, D.E. (2002). Organization structure and fairness perceptions: The moderating effects of organizational level. *Organizational Behavior and Human Decision Processes, 89,* 881–905.

Scott, B.A., Colquitt, J.A., & Paddock, E.L. (2009). An actor-focused model of justice rule adherence and violation: The role of managerial motives and discretion. *Journal of Applied Psychology, 94,* 756–769.

Simons, T., & Roberson, Q. (2003). Why managers should care about fairness: The effects of aggregate justice perceptions on organizational outcomes. *Journal of Applied Psychology, 88,* 432–443.

Thibaut, J., & Walker, L. (1975). *Procedural justice: A psychological analysis.* Hillsdale, NJ: Lawrence Erlbaum.

Treadway, D.C., Hochwarter, W.A., Ferris, G.R., Kacmar, C.J., Douglas, C., Ammeter, A.P., et al. (2004). Leader political skill and employee reactions. *Leadership Quarterly, 15,* 493–513.

Tripp, T.M., Bies, R.J., & Aquino, K. (2002). Poetic justice or petty jealousy? The aesthetics of revenge. *Organizational Behavior and Human Decision Processes, 89,* 966–984.

van den Bos, K., & Lind, E.A. (2002). Uncertainty management by means of fairness judgments. In M.P. Zanna (Ed.), *Advances in experimental social psychology* (Vol. 34, pp. 1–60). San Diego, CA: Academic Press.

Zellars, K.L., & Kacmar, K.M. (1999). The influence of individual differences on reactions to co-workers' ingratiatory behaviors. *Journal of Managerial Issues, 11,* 234–248.

6

Organizational Citizenship Behavior: A Review of the Political Perspective

Mark C. Bolino
University of Oklahoma

William H. Turnley
Kansas State University

Organizational citizenship behavior (OCB) is defined as "individual behavior that is discretionary, not directly or explicitly recognized by the formal reward system, and in the aggregate promotes the efficient and effective functioning of the organization" (Organ, Podsakoff, & MacKenzie, 2006, p. 3). Specifically, OCBs include instances in which employees go above and beyond the call of duty by helping out their colleagues and supervisors, tolerating impositions at work, defending the organization when others criticize it, and volunteering to take on special assignments. Since their introduction in 1983, OCBs have been the focus of considerable research attention. Indeed, more than 650 articles have been written about OCBs or related constructs like extrarole behavior, contextual performance, or prosocial organizational behavior (Podsakoff, Whiting, Podsakoff, & Blume, 2009).

Generally speaking, research on OCBs has tended to emphasize their positive aspects (Bolino, Turnley, & Niehoff, 2004), and, undeniably, OCBs are beneficial in many respects. In particular, researchers have found that OCBs are predicted by a variety of desirable traits (e.g., conscientiousness, concern for others, prosocial personality), job attitudes (e.g., job satisfaction, organizational commitment), and leadership styles (e.g., transformational leadership, high-quality leader–member exchange [LMX]; Organ et al., 2006). Furthermore, employees tend to engage in OCBs when they are treated fairly (Moorman, 1991) and when the organization lives up to its promises (Turnley, Bolino, Lester, & Bloodgood, 2003).

OCBs are associated with a variety of positive consequences as well (Podsakoff et al., 2009). At the organizational level, OCBs are positively related to a number of indicators of success, including productivity, efficiency, and customer satisfaction. Moreover, employees who exhibit OCBs tend to receive higher performance ratings and rewards from their supervisors, to have fewer absences, and to be less likely to quit their jobs. In short, the idea that OCBs are associated with a number of desirable antecedents and consequences is backed by nearly 30 years of research.

In recent years, though, a small but growing body of research has challenged the idea that OCBs are unambiguously positive (e.g., Bergeron, 2007; Bolino, 1999; Bolino et al., 2004; Bolino & Turnley, 2005; Halbesleben, Harvey, & Bolino, 2009; Munyon, Hochwarter, Perrewé, & Ferris, 2010). Fandt and Ferris (1990) were perhaps the first to point out that the behaviors studied by citizenship researchers bear a strong resemblance to the behaviors investigated by researchers interested in organizational politics. Specifically, they noted that while OCBs appear to be prosocial on the surface, they also may be self-serving and driven by instrumental and impression-management motives. Since that time, organizational researchers have responded by examining citizenship behaviors from a political perspective in a number of conceptual and empirical papers. This chapter seeks to provide an overview and enhanced understanding of this work.

The chapter is organized into three sections. In the first section, the key papers are identified and discussed, starting with Fandt and Ferris (1990), which provides the foundation for much of the research investigating the political aspects of OCBs. In doing so, the interest is in describing the origins of this perspective and in providing a sense for how this line of work has developed. Second, a number of papers that have viewed citizenship using a political lens are reviewed. In particular, studies are reviewed that have focused on identifying and understanding political, instrumental, and impression-management motives of OCBs. Also, research is reviewed that has sought to better understand the attributions that observers make about employees' motives for engaging in OCBs. In the third and final section of the chapter, recommendations are made to researchers who want to better understand OCBs, particularly their political aspects, and some directions for future research in this area are outlined.

ORIGINS OF THE POLITICAL VIEW OF OCBS

In early work on citizenship, the notion that employees might perform OCBs for self-serving, image-enhancing, or political concerns was never completely ruled out. Indeed, Organ (1988) noted that some motives for engaging in OCBs may be "more admirable than others" (p. 4) and indicated that OCBs are not necessarily "limited to those gestures that are utterly and eternally lacking in any tangible return to the individual who demonstrates them" (p. 5). Nevertheless, research on OCBs clearly implied that citizenship behavior was performed for prosocial reasons. Indeed, Organ described citizenship behaviors as analogous to altruism (or other prosocial behaviors) and relied heavily on prior work in this area in his early theorizing about OCBs.

At roughly the same time that research on OCBs was rapidly expanding, organizational scholars also were showing increasing interest in understanding politics and impression management in organizations (e.g., Ferris & Judge, 1991; Ferris & Mitchell, 1987; Ferris, Russ, & Fandt, 1989). Arguably, Fandt and Ferris (1990) were the first to point out that the distinction between OCBs and political behavior may not be as clear-cut as it would appear to be. Specifically, they called for research that would more carefully examine the similarities and distinctions between prosocial behaviors and opportunistic behaviors and noted that it was "unclear whether what appear to be prosocial behaviors on the surface, are intended to help oneself (e.g., the mere appearance of being altruistic can be quite self serving), not others" (p. 156).

In a subsequent article, Ferris, Judge, Rowland, and Fitzgibbons (1994) noted that many citizenship behaviors and impression-management behaviors "appear to be quite similar, if not identical" (p. 129). Furthermore, they argued that motive or intent is the key factor that distinguishes acts of citizenship from acts of impression management. In other words, helping one's supervisor to curry favor is a political behavior, while helping one's supervisor to become more effective is citizenship behavior.

Commenting on the work of Ferris and his colleagues (1994), Podsakoff, MacKenzie, and Hui (1993) agreed that motives may be important in understanding *why* employees engage in behaviors that may be construed as citizenship or impression management. However, they argued that employees' *true* intentions are less relevant in understanding how supervisors respond to employee citizenship than supervisors' *perceptions* of employees' motives for engaging in OCBs. Likewise, they maintained that it is irrelevant if acts of helpfulness, conscientiousness, courtesy, and so on are defined as citizenship or political behaviors because such actions should enhance organizational performance regardless of employees' motives for engaging in the behaviors. Their view, then, differed from that of Schnake (1991) who, in a review of the OCB literature, noted that politically-motivated citizenship behaviors may appear to be constructive and may even have positive consequences in the short run but might have destructive and dysfunctional effects in the long run.

This initial dialogue among researchers investigating organizational politics and researchers investigating organizational citizenship stimulated a number of conceptual and empirical papers concerning citizenship and politics. In particular, using a scenario study, Eastman (1994) found that supervisors evaluating the same extrarole behaviors were more likely to reward employees when their behavior was seen as citizenship behavior than when it was seen as ingratiation (i.e., a specific type of impression management).

In a conceptual paper, Ferris, Bhawuk, Fedor, and Judge (1995) developed a model of intentionality and construct labeling that outlined a number of factors—characteristics of the actor (e.g., political skill), the situation (e.g., employment interview), and the perceiver (e.g., bystanders or beneficiary); the specific extrarole behavior exhibited (e.g., helping); and prior interactions between the actor and perceiver (e.g., perceiver liking of the actor)—that affect the attributions that perceivers make regarding extrarole behavior and how such attributions influence perceiver reactions. Thus, their model suggests that a variety of factors determine whether employees' extrarole behavior will be seen as good citizenship or as self-interested political behavior.

Instead of focusing on attributions of OCB motives, Bolino (1999) developed a conceptual model explaining how impression-management motives might lead employees to engage in OCBs. For instance, he argued that employees will be motivated to engage in an OCB when it will be noticed by others, when they have an upcoming performance appraisal, and when such behavior can be used to offset poor in-role performance. He also proposed that impression-management motives will lead employees to perform OCBs that are preferred by influential targets, that will be noticed and valued by influential observers, and that are timed to occur at image-enhancing moments. Finally, similar to Schnake's (1991) argument, his model suggests that OCBs motivated by impression management will have a less positive impact on the effectiveness of work groups and organizations than OCBs motivated by traditional motives (e.g., job satisfaction, conscientiousness).

In summary, the idea that OCBs may be motivated by instrumental, political, or impression-management concerns was noted by a number of authors throughout the 1990s, and these papers provided the foundation for much of the subsequent work investigating (1) the ways instrumental, political, or impression-management motives influence the occurrence of OCBs, (2) the situational factors that affect the performance or effectiveness of OCBs used for instrumental gain, and (3) the attributions that supervisors and colleagues make about citizenship motives. In the next section of this chapter, these streams of research are reviewed.

POLITICAL MOTIVES FOR OCBS

In this section, conceptual and empirical work that has examined OCBs using a political lens is discussed. To the best of our knowledge, this research has not been previously reviewed. The papers included in this review were identified by searching various databases, including *ABI-INFORM* and *PsycArticles*. Generally speaking, papers were sought that included *organizational citizenship behavior* and *politics*. However, in addition to searching for the key words *organizational citizenship behaviors*, *OCBs*, and *citizenship*, terms describing a number of related constructs (e.g., *extrarole behavior, contextual performance, citizenship performance*) also were searched.

Likewise, because politics is a very general term, a number of more specific terms (e.g., *impression management, self-presentation, self-enhancement, self-serving, instrumental*) that have been used in research investigating political motives and OCBs also were investigated. Finally, the findings of a number of studies indicate that perceptions of organizational politics are negatively related to OCBs (see Chang, Rosen, & Levy, 2009 for a recent meta-analysis). These studies investigate the negative effects of perceptions of organizational politics on OCBs rather than the political view of OCBs; therefore, these papers are not included in the review.

Political, Instrumental, and Impression-Management Motives for OCBs

In response to research that suggested that OCBs might occur due to instrumental or impression-management motives (e.g., Fandt & Ferris, 1990; Ferris et al., 1994), several influential studies set out to provide empirical evidence that citizenship behaviors were indeed motivated by such concerns. These studies are summarized in Table 6.1.

In one of the earliest studies in this area, Hui, Lam, and Law (2000) conducted a quasi-field experiment that examined the level of employee citizenship behavior before and after individuals received a promotion. This study found that those employees who believed that OCBs were instrumental for promotion were more likely to reduce their level of OCBs following promotion. Clearly, such a finding implies that citizenship behaviors are being performed to enhance one's standing in the organization rather than as a repayment for positive organizational treatment (as would be expected by social exchange theory; Organ, 1990).

In another early empirical study examining the political side of citizenship behavior, Rioux and Penner (2001) outlined the functional approach to the study of OCBs. This approach suggests that individuals engage in behaviors (i.e., including OCBs) in an effort to meet their needs or goals. Moreover, it also suggests that there may be multiple motives behind any specific action. With regard to the political perspective of OCBs, this study developed a framework of motives for citizenship behavior that has since been frequently used. Specifically, Rioux and Penner developed and refined the Citizenship Motives Scale (CMS), which examined the influence of three motives for OCBs: (1) prosocial values, which focuses on employee desires to help and build relationships with others; (2) organizational concern, which focuses on employee feelings of attachment and commitment to the organization; and (3) impression management, which in this study focused mainly on employee attempts to avoid looking bad.

Although Rioux and Penner (2001) found that prosocial values and organizational concern motives were more strongly related to OCBs than impression-management motives, it nevertheless suggested that impression-management motives might explain incremental variance in citizenship behaviors when other motives were considered. Moreover, by creating a scale that allowed for the examination of impression-management motives for OCBs, this study laid the foundation for future studies that

TABLE 6.1

Studies of Political Motives for Organizational Citizenship Behavior (OCB)

Author(s) (Year)	Political Motive/Behavior	OCB	Key Findings
Hui, Lam, & Law (2000)	Promotion/Instrumentality	Altruism, Compliance	Employees who believe OCBs are instrumental reduced citizenship after they received a promotion.
Rioux & Penner (2001)	Impression Management (IM) Motives	Altruism, Conscientiousness, Courtesy, Sportsmanship, Civic Virtue	IM motives accounted for only incremental variance in OCB—much less than did prosocial or organizational motives. Development of Citizenship Motives Scale (CMS).
Finkelstein & Penner (2004)	IM Motives	OCB-I and OCB-O	IM motives explained incremental variance in OCB, but less than prosocial or organizational motives.
Bolino, Vareda, Bande, & Turnley (2006)	Ingratiation, Self-promotion	Overall OCB	Ingratiation was positively related to OCB; self-promotion was negatively related to OCB.
Bowler & Brass (2006)	Dependence	Interpersonal Citizenship Behavior (i.e., Helping)	Performance of OCB was positively related to dependence on target.
Finkelstein (2006)	IM Motives	OCB-I and OCB-O	IM motives were related to coworker-directed OCB not organizationally-directed to OCB.
Becker & O'Hair (2007)	Machiavellianism	OCB-I and OCB-O	Employees high in Machiavellianism perform OCBs for IM reasons, not prosocial or organizational reasons.
Chen, Lin, Tung, & Ko (2008)	Ingratiation	Job-focused, Coworker-focused, and Supervisor-focused OCB	Ingratiation was positively related to supervisor-focused OCB, but not to job-focused OCB.
Nguyen, Seers, & Hartman (2008)	Ingratiation, Self-promotion	Altruism, Conscientiousness	Both ingratiation and self-promotion were positively related to helping.
Grant & Mayer (2009)	IM Motives	Helping, Courtesy, Initiative, Voice	Prosocial and IM motives interacted to predict affiliative forms of OCB.

more strongly supported the idea that impression-management motives influence the performance of certain citizenship behaviors. Indeed, the CMS since has been used in a number of research efforts designed to examine impression-management motives for OCB.

For example, in a subsequent paper, Finkelstein and Penner (2004) refined the impression-management motives scale developed by Rioux and Penner (2001) so that it focused more specifically on employee desires for extrinsic rewards. Similar to Rioux and Penner, Finkelstein and Penner examined the functional perspective of OCBs among employees working for a municipal agency and found that all three motives (i.e., pro-social, organizational concern, and impression management) were associated with some types of citizenship behavior. In particular, Finkelstein and Penner found that impression-management motives were associated with citizenship behaviors directed at colleagues (OCB-I) but not at the organization as a whole (OCB-O). Thus, in contrast to prior research that had established prosocial motives as predictors of OCB, Finkelstein and Penner's study provided empirical support for the idea that OCBs were performed for politically oriented motives in at least some cases.

Finkelstein (2006) further extended this line of inquiry by examining the functional perspective of OCBs among a sample of private-sector employees working in a variety of organizations and industries. Examining the same three motives that had been studied previously, she again found that impression-management motives were related to citizenship behaviors directed at other individuals but not citizenship behaviors directed at the organization as a whole.

In the aggregate, the functional perspective (Finkelstein, 2006) highlighted two important findings relative to the political view of citizenship behaviors. First, it empirically documented that OCBs result from multiple, often overlapping, motives, including impression management. Second, it suggested that individuals who are inclined to perform citizenship behaviors to manage impressions are more likely to engage in behaviors targeted at specific individuals (i.e., who might be able to repay such actions) than behaviors intended to benefit the organization as at large.

In an extension of prior research, Bolino, Varela, Bande, and Turnley (2006) examined whether three types of impression management influenced the OCB ratings given to employees by their supervisors. This study examined supervisor-focused, self-focused, and job-focused impression-management behaviors as identified by Wayne and Ferris

(1990). Supervisor-focused tactics generally involve ingratiatory behaviors designed to make the employee look helpful. Self-focused tactics typically involve exemplification-type actions designed to make the employee look dedicated and hard-working. In contrast, job-focused tactics often involve activities like self-promotion, which are intended to make the person appear more competent but which often backfire and make the person appear less likable. The results of this study indicate that supervisor-focused impression management (ingratiation) was positively related to evaluations of OCBs, whereas job-focused impression management (self-promotion) was negatively related to OCBs. Moreover, this study further suggested that OCB ratings mediate the relationship between employee impression-management attempts and the extent to which employees are seen as likable by their supervisor.

Using an approach that varied slightly from those previously discussed, Becker and O'Hair (2007) investigated the relationships among Machiavellianism, OCB motives, and the performance of citizenship behaviors. Individuals with Machiavellian tendencies are willing to manipulate situations for their own benefit and usually are concerned with their own extrinsic rewards more than intrinsic rewards or the betterment of the organization as a whole (Christie & Geis, 1970). Consistent with this viewpoint, Becker and O'Hair (2007) found that Machiavellianism was positively correlated with employees' impression-management motives for engaging in OCBs and negatively associated with employees' prosocial and organizational-concern motives for citizenship. Additionally, and consistent with the research discussed earlier, this study found that those with Machiavellian tendencies were more likely to engage in citizenship directed at others than they were to engage in citizenship intended to benefit the overall organization.

Although most prior research has examined the effects of the different types of motives on various types of citizenship behavior, prevailing theory in this area (e.g., Bolino, 1999; Rioux & Penner, 2001) always has suggested that there may be multiple motives for the same citizenship behaviors. Building on that idea, Grant and Mayer (2009) conducted two studies that focused on the interaction of prosocial and impression-management motives in predicting OCBs. In line with prior research, they found that both types of citizenship had independent effects on citizenship behavior, at least in some cases. However, in an interesting extension of prior work, they also found that prosocial and impression-management motives interacted to predict affiliative forms of OCBs. Affiliative forms of citizenship include actions like helping and courtesy, which are designed to assist colleagues and foster better relationships among coworkers.

Because such behaviors are jointly motivated (i.e., employees want to help their colleagues, but they also want to make themselves look good by doing so), it makes sense that impression-management motives strengthen the positive relationship between prosocial motives and these types of citizenship behaviors. In contrast, challenging forms of OCBs, like voice and taking charge, can be politically risky because they may threaten or upset one's colleagues; thus, employees with impression-management concerns may avoid such actions. Consistent with these expectations, impression-management concerns were found to strengthen the relationship between prosocial motives and affiliative, but not challenging, forms of citizenship.

More recent extensions of this line of research tend to provide support for the basic idea that impression-management concerns motivate OCBs and that when citizenship is motivated by instrumental concerns it tends to be targeted at specific individuals (i.e., those most likely to be able to reward such gestures). For example, while working from a framework that suggests that OCBs can be targeted at supervisors, colleagues, or the organization (Barr & Pawar, 1995; Staw, 1983), Chen, Lin, Tung, and Ko (2008) found that the motive of ingratiation was associated with OCBs directed only at one's supervisor but not with OCBs directed at colleagues or the organization as a whole. In addition, Nguyen, Seers, and Hartman (2008) found that ingratiation was correlated with the extent to which individuals engaged in altruistic (i.e., helping) behavior directed at their teammates in the context of a group project conducted in an academic institution. Interestingly, and in contrast to prior research (e.g., Bolino et al., 2006), Nguyen et al. found that self-promotion also was positively associated with helping behavior.

Although Bowler and Brass (2006) did not examine impression-management motives directly, they found support for the impression-management-based idea that individuals perform more citizenship behaviors when they are dependent on the target of such behaviors. Specifically, asymmetric influence (i.e., being relatively more or less dependent on another individual) was associated with the performance and receipt of interpersonal citizenship behavior. The more influence persons had, the more likely they were to be the recipient of citizenship behavior from less influential persons and the less likely they were to engage in citizenship behavior directed at less influential persons. Moreover, individuals also were more likely to be the target of interpersonal citizenship behavior if they had an influential friend.

However, even though impression-management motives often increase the incidence of citizenship behavior, it remains unclear whether such actions actually are beneficial to the organization—or at least whether they are as beneficial to the organization as more prosocially motivated OCBs. As noted previously, early theoretical work suggested that citizenship motivated by impression management could be of lower quality and value, which might weaken its positive effects (e.g., Bolino, 1999). More recent theoretical work suggests that OCBs motivated by impression-management actually may hurt group cohesion and performance rather than help it (Banki, 2010). As discussed later, though, empirical studies are needed to resolve differing views about the effects of citizenship motives.

Before turning to the issue of situational influences on the use of citizenship behavior, one additional conceptual piece deserves mention here that takes a different approach to demonstrating the political nature of citizenship behavior. Specifically, in a departure from the aforementioned line of research, Salamon and Deutsch (2006) proposed an alternative lens through which to view the political nature of OCBs. Using an evolutionary perspective on such behavior, they examined particularly "costly" OCBs as a form of voluntary handicap that some employees willingly take on.

In contrast to notions of social exchange, which view the performance of OCBs as an extra cost or burden that is undertaken either to repay prior positive treatment or a functional behavior for which future repayment is expected, this perspective views OCBs as behaviors that individuals undertake precisely because the costs associated with them signal that employees are more competent than their colleagues. Two issues are paramount in terms of the kinds of OCBs that employees engage in for this reason. First, the OCB must convey reliable information about the competence of the employee. Second, the OCB must come at some cost to the individual (i.e., impose a handicap) that is recognized by others. In doing so, performing the OCB is assumed to signal that employees are so gifted that they can engage in the OCB in addition to their regular duties, a burden that their less gifted colleagues are not able to pull off effectively.

Although the previously discussed studies vary in terms of the frameworks from which they draw, generally they paint a fairly consistent picture. All of them provide evidence that there is a political side to OCB by demonstrating that impression-management concerns are commonly associated with the performance of such behavior. However, impression-management concerns do not appear to be equally associated with all types of citizenship. Specifically, the findings indicate that employees who engage in OCBs for political purposes appear to be more likely to target their citizenship behaviors at specific individuals (often supervisors) who are able to provide some reward for these efforts rather than engaging in citizenship behaviors for the good of the organization as a whole.

Situational Analysis: Moderators Affecting the Use and Effectiveness of OCBs

The prior section reviewed research that fell mainly within the functional perspective by suggesting that employees have multiple motives for engaging in citizenship behavior. In particular, these studies indicate that OCBs are not always performed purely to help others or to repay the receipt of positive treatment. Instead, they suggest that employees sometimes engage in OCBs for instrumental and self-serving reasons. In this section, research that takes a somewhat different approach to examining the political nature of OCB is reviewed.

Specifically, work is reviewed that shows how OCBs tend to occur in situations where such actions provide a benefit to those who engage in citizenship. These studies are summarized in Table 6.2. Collectively, this stream of research is more disconnected in nature and shares fewer commonalities than the research described in the prior section. However, the following studies all examine important moderating factors that influence the use and effectiveness of OCBs and reflect the basic underlying idea that citizenship behaviors are being used in an instrumental fashion.

Bowler, Halbesleben, Stodnick, Seevers, and Little (2009) do a nice job of summarizing the basic idea shared by most of the following studies. Specifically, Bowler and his colleagues argued that prosocial and organizational-concern motives for citizenship tend to be value expressive, meaning that they reflect enduring individual values and thus are likely to occur regardless of the specific situation. In contrast, OCBs motivated

TABLE 6.2

Studies of Moderators of the Political Motive—Organizational Citizenship Behavior (OCB) Relationship

Author(s) (Year)	Political Motive/Behavior	OCB	Moderator of Political Motive—OCB	Findings
Fuller, Barnett, Hester, Relyea, & Frey (2007)	Self-monitoring	Voice	Self-monitoring	High self-monitors used voice as a means of self-promotion following good performance, but rarely engaged in voice when they performed poorly.
Yun, Takeuchi, & Lin (2007)	Self-enhancement motives	OCB-I and OCB-O	Role Ambiguity	Self-enhancement motives were positively related to OCB-I and OCB-O when role ambiguity was high, but this relationship was negative when role ambiguity was low.
Blatt (2008)	IM Motives	Helping Accounts	Temporary/ Permanent Employment Status	IM was rarely the motive for OCB among temporary knowledge workers because they have little to gain from such actions.
Tang, Sutarso, Davis, Dolinski, Ibrahim, & Wagner (2008)	Intrinsic and Extrinsic Helping Motives	Altruism (i.e., Helping)	Culture	The relationship between instrumental motives and the performance of OCB was culture specific.
Andrews, Kacmar, & Harris (2009)	Political Skill	Supervised- focused OCB	Organizational Justice	Political skill was positively related to OCB when distributive justice was low but had little effect on OCB when distributive justice was high.
Bowler, Halbesleben, Stodnick, Steevers, & Little (2009)	IM Motives	Interpersonal Citizenship Behavior (i.e., Helping)	Network Centrality	IM motives were more strongly associated with OCBs for individuals with low network centrality (i.e, who had a greater need to acquire social capital).

by impression-management concerns are likely to be much more variable across situations. When motivated by impression-management concerns, then employees will engage in only OCBs that are likely to result in positive consequences for those performing them.

In this regard, Bowler et al. (2009) examined network centrality as a moderator of the relationship between motives for citizenship and the performance of interpersonal citizenship behavior (i.e., helping behavior). In general, those in more central network positions performed more OCBs than those occupying more peripheral positions within the network. However, when impression-management motives were considered, their results suggested that there is a stronger positive relationship between impression-management motives and citizenship for individuals with low network centrality because these individuals believe that they need to engage in helping behavior to foster better relationships and to acquire social capital.

Andrews, Kacmar, and Harris (2009) examined the moderating effects of organizational justice on the relationship between political skill and OCBs. Using a situationist perspective (Mischel, 1968), they suggested that political skill would be more important in "weak situations" where strong norms that govern employee behavior were lacking. In this study, that meant situations in which procedural and distributive justice were low and where there was an absence of widely accepted organizational procedures that were perceived to be fair to all. In such cases, those with high political skill are assumed to be more likely to resort to using OCBs to get ahead, and their findings tended to support this idea. Specifically, though the results were not significant for procedural justice, political skill was positively related to OCB when distributive justice was low and had little effect on OCB when distributive justice was high.

Somewhat similarly, Yun, Takeuchi, and Lin (2007) examined the influence of self-enhancement motives on OCBs in another context. Specifically, they argued that self-enhancement motives would be more strongly linked to the performance of OCBs when role ambiguity was high (i.e., in another relatively "weak" situation in which performance norms were unclear). They found support for the moderating effect of role ambiguity on the relationship between self-enhancement motives and OCBs. Additionally, this study further suggested that managerial perceptions of employee commitment to the organization moderated the influence of OCBs on reward allocation decisions, such that employees were more likely to reap rewards for their acts of citizenship when managers perceived that the employees were highly committed to the organization.

In another study, Fuller, Barnett, Hester, Relyea, and Frey (2007) examined self-monitoring and how it relates to the use of employee voice (i.e., a particular type of OCB). High self-monitors pay closer attention to situational and interpersonal cues and are better able to control their expressive behaviors than are low self-monitors (Snyder, 1974). As a result, they tend to be able to use impression management to create the image they desire more effectively than low self-monitors (Turnley & Bolino, 2001). Fuller and colleagues studied voice as an expression of citizenship behavior and found that high self-monitors used this type of OCB as a form of self-promotion when they had performed well but rarely engaged in this form of OCB when they had performed poorly.

Tang, Sutarso, Davis, Dolinski, Ibrahim, and Wagner (2008) examined motives for citizenship behavior across four cultures—United States, Taiwan, Poland, and Egypt. Their model suggested two potential motives for citizenship. The good Samaritan effect examined relatively traditional predictors of citizenship by focusing on intrinsic motivations for the behavior. This approach suggests that employees engage in such behaviors out of concern for their colleagues (e.g., prosocial motives) or for their organization (e.g., organizational concern).

In contrast, Tang and colleagues (2008) also examined whether the love of money might lead to a focus on extrinsic motivation, which could either increase or decrease the extent to which employees engage in citizenship. Their study found that the good Samaritan effect was supported in all four countries. However, extrinsic motivation was unrelated to the performance of citizenship in three of the four countries. Specifically, the love of money led to extrinsic motivation, which was positively related to citizenship only in Poland. Thus, this study highlights the fact that motivations for citizenship and, in particular, instrumental motives for citizenship may be culture-specific.

Finally, Blatt (2008) conducted interviews with temporary knowledge workers to examine their motives for engaging in OCBs. Based on the motives reported by the temporary employees themselves, impression management was rarely listed as a reason the individuals engaged in citizenship, although it should be noted that social exchange and organizational identification also were rarely reported as motives for citizenship in this study. Blatt suggested that the motives for citizenship are likely to vary between temporary and permanent (or core) workers.

In particular, Blatt (2008) posited that impression management is seldom the motive for citizenship among temporary knowledge workers because they have little to gain from such actions; at least in this context, it was unlikely that the positions would be made permanent or that the individuals would be rewarded for their extra efforts. Thus, this study highlights another key situational aspect (i.e., employment status) that should perhaps be considered to more fully understand the circumstances in which political motives are most likely to influence the performance of citizenship behavior.

Attributional Analysis: When Do Others See OCBs as Politically Motivated?

As noted earlier, Eastman (1994) investigated the attributions of supervisors with regard to extrarole behavior, and Ferris et al. (1995) developed a conceptual model explaining the process by which perceivers make attributions of intentionality regarding employees' OCBs. Building on this work, a number of studies have investigated the attributions that supervisors and colleagues make when employees engage in OCBs and have examined how such attributions affect important decisions in organizations. Table 6.3 provides an overview of the studies, and they are summarized in greater detail in this section.

Allen and Rush (1998) hypothesized that supervisors would give employees higher performance evaluations and would be more likely to recommend them for common organizational rewards (e.g., salary increases, promotions) when they attributed employees' OCBs to altruistic motives rather than instrumental motives. In a field study using a sample of managers, they found that altruistic, but not instrumental, motive attributions mediated the relationship between OCBs and evaluations of performance. However, the motives attributed to OCBs did not mediate the relationship between OCBs and reward recommendations. Another noteworthy finding of their study was that altruistic motive attributions were positively related to the frequency of OCBs; likewise, supervisors were more likely to ascribe instrumental motives to the citizenship of employees who engaged in relatively low levels of OCBs.

The role of attributions was investigated further by Johnson, Erez, Kiker, and Motowidlo (2002). In their study, undergraduate students watched

TABLE 6.3

Studies of Third-Party Attributes of Organizational Citizenship Behavior (OCB) Motives

Author(s) (Year)	Political Motive/Behavior	OCB	Findings
Allen & Rush (1998)	Altruistic, Instrumental	Altruism, Conscientiousness, Courtesy, Sportsmanship, Civic Virtue	Altruistic, not instrumental, motive attributions mediated the relationship between OCBs and performance evaluations. However motive attributions did not mediate the relationship between OCB and reward recommendations.
Johnson, Erez, Kiker, & Motowidlo (2002)	Altruistic, Instrumental	Perceived Helpfulness	Attributions of altruistic, but not instrumental, motives partially mediated the relationship between helping and reward decisions. Observers are less likely to make altruistic attributions for individuals with unfavorable reputations.
Farell & Finkelstein (2007)	Gender Congruency of OCB	Helping, Civic Virtue	Observers were more likely to attribute female helping to traditional/social exchange motives and more likely to attribute male helping to IM motives.
Snell & Wong (2007)	Citizenship-related IM	Conscientiousness, Helpfulness, Harmoniousness, Stewardship	Respondents tended to attribute colleagues' OCBs to organizational concern or prosocial motives rather than impression-management motives, and they were most likely to ascribe impression-management motives to their coworkers' OCBs when OCBs were inconsistent or exaggerated.
Halbesleben, Bowler, Bolino, & Turnely (2010)	IM Motives	Not Measured	Supervisors responded angrily when they attributed OCBs to IM motives.

videotaped performance vignettes in which an employee's helping behavior and reputation (favorable or unfavorable) were manipulated, and they were then asked to make reward decisions (e.g., regarding promotions, pay increases). Like Allen and Rush (1998), Johnson and colleagues found that attributions of altruistic motives (but not instrumental motives) partially mediated the relationship between helping and reward decisions. In addition, their findings suggest that observers are less likely to attribute altruistic motives to individuals with unfavorable reputations (i.e., abrasive, insincere, and self-promoting). Their study, then, provides some support for the model described by Ferris et al. (1995), which proposed that helping behavior is judged differently based on who performs it and that citizenship attributions have a meaningful impact on important outcomes. Specifically, individuals appear to get more credit for their acts of citizenship when they are attributed to prosocial or pro-organization motives.

Snell and Wong (2007) conducted a qualitative study that focused on differentiating *good soldiers* and *good actors* by interviewing 20 employees in Hong Kong. The respondents in their study were more likely to attribute the OCBs of their colleagues to organizational concern or prosocial motives than to impression-management motives. Furthermore, they were most likely to ascribe impression-management motives to their coworkers' OCBs when they noted inconsistencies in the occurrence of their citizenship (i.e., coworkers engaged in OCBs only in selective contexts) and when they felt like their colleagues were claiming to engage in OCBs that were exaggerated or false (i.e., pseudo-OCBs). Similar to the findings of other studies, OCBs that were seen as motivated by impression management were viewed negatively, whereas OCBs attributed to prosocial values or pro-organizational motives were viewed positively.

Farrell and Finkelstein (2007) argued that gender-role expectations may affect observers' attributions about why employees engage in OCBs that are considered feminine (i.e., helping) or masculine (i.e., civic virtue). Specifically, they hypothesized that observers would be more likely to attribute citizenship to traditional motives (i.e., conscientiousness, positive social exchange) when OCBs were gender congruent and to impression-management motives when OCBs were gender incongruent. In a series of scenario studies, they found partial support for their hypotheses. Specifically, they found that undergraduate student "observers" were more likely to attribute the helping behavior of female employees to traditional and social exchange motives than to impression-management motives.

In contrast, observers were more likely to ascribe impression-management motives to the helping behavior of males. The findings with regard to civic virtue behavior, though, were not significant.

Using Weiner's (1995) social responsibility theory of attribution as a conceptual framework, Halbesleben, Bowler, Bolino, and Turnley (2010) sought to build on earlier work by proposing a broader view of the attributional process regarding OCBs. Specifically, they developed and tested a structural model that linked cognitions, ascribed motives, emotional responses, and supervisor evaluations. Based on the citizenship motives identified by Rioux and Penner (2001), they examined three different motives that supervisors might assign to citizenship (i.e., impression management, prosocial motives, and organizational concern).

Using responses obtained from a sample of supervisors working in a number of industries, they found that citizenship attributions were related to supervisors' emotional reactions to OCBs, which were, in turn, related to performance ratings. In particular, their findings indicate that when OCBs were ascribed to impression-management motives, supervisors responded angrily; conversely, feelings of happiness were associated with attributions of prosocial values and organizational concern. They also found that the negative reactions associated with impression-management motives were less intense than the positive reactions associated with attributions of prosocial motives and organizational concern.

Finally, Bowler, Halbesleben, and Paul (2010) developed a conceptual model examining the ways LMX relationships in the workplace shape citizenship attributions. Specifically, they proposed that employees will tend to attribute the OCBs of their supervisors to prosocial and organizational-concern motives and will be unlikely to attribute them to impression-management motives. Likewise, they argued that supervisors will ascribe positive motives to the OCBs of subordinates with whom they have high-quality LMX relationships. However, their model also suggests that coworkers will tend to view the OCBs of their peers as driven by impression management and will be unlikely to attribute their OCBs to prosocial values and organizational concern. As such, their conceptual model simultaneously considers the citizenship attributions of multiple parties.

Taken together, this line of work indicates that observers do not simply accept the performance of OCBs at face value. Rather, they make judgments about the motives that account for acts of citizenship, often based on the frequency, consistency, and perceived authenticity of the behavior.

Furthermore, the motives that observers ascribe to acts of citizenship affect how they evaluate those who engage in OCBs and how they feel about such behaviors. In the final section of this chapter, some of the ways future research might build on the work that was just reviewed are discussed.

WHERE TO FROM HERE? RECOMMENDED DIRECTIONS FOR FUTURE RESEARCH

Since Fandt and Ferris (1990) first noted the similarity between OCBs and political behaviors, a great deal has been learned about how OCBs may be driven by instrumental and impression-management motives. Likewise, research also has revealed that when supervisors and coworkers attribute employees' OCBs to self-serving motives, such judgments affect the ways employees are evaluated. Nevertheless, the dominant view of OCB continues to emphasize that it stems from social exchange (e.g., job satisfaction, organizational justice) or positive dispositional motives (e.g., conscientiousness, prosocial personality; Organ, 1990).

In fact, instrumental or political motives for OCBs have been mentioned only briefly, if at all, in comprehensive reviews of the literature. For instance, in their book on the nature, antecedents, and consequences of OCBs, Organ et al. (2006) did not mention some of the more compelling empirical studies highlighted in this review, such as the one by Hui et al. (2000), which found that employees who believed OCBs were helpful for getting ahead in their organizations tended to reduce their OCBs after they had been promoted. Likewise, there is no discussion of the study by Rioux and Penner (2001), which identified impression management as a key motive behind the performance of OCBs, along with prosocial values and organizational concern.

In their brief discussion of impression-management motives and OCB, Organ et al. (2006) did make reference to researchers who "have argued that the only reason that many employees engage in OCB is to create a good impression..." (p. 220). However, such statements do not seem to accurately characterize the studies that have raised questions about employees' motives for engaging in citizenship behaviors. As noted by Grant and Mayer (2009), most researchers investigating the possibility that employees have political motives for performing OCBs have suggested that self-serving motives occur in addition to (not instead of) traditional motives. Indeed, impression management was only one of three citizenship motives identified by Rioux and Penner (2001). Similarly, Bolino (1999) noted that, in most cases, employees' motives for performing OCBs are likely to be mixed, and his conceptual model incorporates both impression-management motives and traditional motives (i.e., social exchange and dispositional characteristics) as predictors of OCBs.

In short, then, the prevailing view of OCBs tends to emphasize their positive aspects and downplays the idea that citizenship may stem from self-serving motives or that it may have dysfunctional consequences within organizations (Bolino et al., 2004). As described in this chapter, though, a political lens is useful for gaining additional insight into why employees engage in OCBs and how others react to such behaviors. Even still, while our understanding of the political aspects of citizenship behavior clearly has increased over the past 20 years, additional work in this area still is needed. In this final section, some of these ongoing areas of concern are addressed.

Political Motives and OCBs

As noted earlier, most research suggests that political motives account for OCBs in addition to, not in place of, other motives that are traditionally associated with OCBs (e.g., job satisfaction, conscientiousness). With the exception of Grant and Mayer (2009), though, few studies have examined how these different motives work in tandem. In future studies, it would be interesting to examine how political and traditional citizenship motives may work together, or perhaps in opposition, in determining the occurrence of OCBs. In some cases, employees may be most inclined to go the extra mile when they can both express their genuine commitment to the organization and, at the same time, earn the admiration of their boss and colleagues.

In addition, at certain stages in an employee's career, some motives may be more dominant than others. Such variations would be interesting to explore as well. For instance, when employees first join an organization, their OCBs may be driven more by instrumental motives as they see engaging in extrarole behavior as a way to get ahead and advance more quickly. However, as individuals settle into their roles and begin to identify more with their organizations, their extrarole efforts may be driven less by self-interest and more by organizational concern.

Conceptual and empirical work in this area might also explore the implications of different combinations of motives. For example, based on a 2 × 2 framework, researchers might seek to identify how citizenship performance differs among employees who are highly motivated to perform OCBs for both political and traditional reasons, employees who are more motivated by political motives than by traditional motives, employees who are more motivated by traditional motives than political motives, and employees who are largely unmotivated to engage in OCBs. It is possible that different combinations of motives could affect the frequency, targeting, timing, consistency, or quality of citizenship as well (Bolino, 1999). In sum, there are still a number of issues to explore with regard to citizenship motives, their antecedents, their consequences, and how they interrelate.

Citizenship Attributions

Additional work also is needed to better understand the attributions that others make with regard to citizenship behavior. In particular, studies have found that high self-monitors (Turnley & Bolino, 2001) and individuals who possess political skill (Harris, Kacmar, Zivnuska, & Shaw, 2007) are more effective at managing impressions than low self-monitors or those with poor political skill. It is possible, then, that some individuals may be better at using OCBs to create more favorable images of themselves. Thus, employees' political skill or their self-monitoring abilities may determine whether their supervisors and colleagues view them as good soldiers when they engage in citizenship behaviors or whether such actions get them labeled as opportunists. More generally, it would be interesting to know how accurate citizenship attributions are and what factors determine their accuracy. For instance, some supervisors may possess certain traits or have accrued certain experiences that enable them to make more accurate citizenship attributions.

Although it is clear that certain attributions can affect the ways those who engage in OCBs are perceived, these attributions might have broader effects as well. For instance, if employees ascribe the OCBs of their peers to political motives, the workplace itself may come to be seen as more political. In this way, OCBs could contribute to perceptions of politics that, ironically, tend to be negatively associated with OCBs (Chang et al., 2009). Thus, when employees believe that their peers are engaging in OCBs for political reasons, they may become resentful and cut back on their own OCBs, or such attributions may alter their own motives for performing OCBs.

Furthermore, there may be a meaningful interplay between employees' citizenship motives and the attributions that they make about the OCBs of others. In particular, those who perform OCBs due to instrumental concerns may tend to ascribe the OCBs of others to political motives. Likewise, employees who engage in OCBs because of their prosocial values or concern for the organization may assume that the same is true of their colleagues as well. Or employees who engage in OCBs for pro-social motives may be especially resentful when they perceive that others are engaging in OCBs for instrumental reasons. In short, there are clearly additional avenues for future research on citizenship attributions as well.

Measuring OCBs

Ferris et al. (1994) noted that impression-management behaviors and OCBs bear a strong resemblance. Bolino and Turnley (1999) further pointed out that some of the items used to measure OCBs and impression management are nearly identical. For example, whereas the item "Assists supervisor with his or her work" is intended to measure an OCB (Smith, Organ, & Near, 1983), the item "Volunteer to help your immediate supervisor on a task" is intended to measure impression-management behavior (Wayne & Ferris, 1990). To differentiate their measure of impression management from measures of OCBs, Bolino and Turnley included the motive for engaging in the behavior within the item itself. For example, some of the items in their impression-management measure include "Do personal favors for your colleagues to show them that you are friendly" and "Stay at work late so people will know you are hard working." In this way, they sought to more clearly differentiate impression-management behaviors from OCBs.

Although including the motives for the behaviors within the items themselves raises some legitimate concerns (Bolino & Turnley, 1999), it might be tempting to see if items measuring citizenship also could be altered in a way that would better capture the spirit of the citizenship construct. For instance, rather than simply measuring the degree to which employees assist their supervisors, one could measure the degree to which employees help their supervisors to contribute to the overall success of the organization.

Such an approach might be problematic, though, because measures of impression management usually are self-reported by individuals who are aware of their own motives, whereas measures of OCBs are typically obtained from supervisors or peers who would have to infer the motives of the focal employee. Given the argument made by some researchers that OCBs motivated by political concerns may be of lower quality than those motivated by traditional motives, it might be more practical, instead, to develop measures of citizenship that also provide a better assessment of the quality of OCBs. In this way, both the frequency and quality of citizenship could be examined in a meaningful way.

Political Motives and Organizational Effectiveness

Perhaps the most central question with regard to citizenship and politics has yet to be resolved; namely, in terms of organizational functioning, does it even matter if OCBs result from political motives? As noted earlier, Podsakoff et al. (1993) argued that OCBs are likely to have the same effect on organizational performance regardless of whether employees engage in citizenship behaviors for prosocial reasons or because they want to look good or get ahead. Others, though, have suggested that OCBs might be of lower quality and thus have a less positive impact on the performance of the organization, when they are motivated by self-interest (e.g., Bolino, 1999; Schnake, 1991).

Organ et al. (2006) have been quite critical of this idea and argued that employees could not derive image-enhancing benefits from low-quality OCBs. Moreover, they suggested that supervisors providing ratings of OCBs are not likely to give employees credit for low-quality OCBs. For example, they argued that supervisors evaluating the degree to which employees have "actively participated in a meeting" (p. 219) will rate employees who merely show up to the meeting and do not contribute significantly lower on this aspect of OCBs than those who have made substantive contributions. Finally, they noted that prior studies show that OCB is positively related to unit-level performance and argue that it is difficult to explain such findings if "OCB is all for show and is of no real value" (Organ et al., 2006, p. 220).

Although Organ et al. (2006) raised three compelling points, they neglected to acknowledge any potential counterarguments. First, they dismissed the possibility that someone might be able to perform low-quality OCBs and still derive benefits from it. This assumes that potential raters invariably realize it when the OCBs of those they are rating are of low quality. For instance, an employee could volunteer to serve on a task force to impress his or her supervisor yet could make very few substantive contributions to its mission. If the supervisor has little knowledge of the inner workings of the task force, it is plausible that the employee could get credit for volunteering to help out with the task force nonetheless.

Moreover, because measures of OCBs tend to assess the frequency of citizenship rather than its quality, it is likely that the nature of the employee's contribution would not be fully captured by existing measures. For instance, items used to measure civic virtue simply ask supervisors to agree or disagree that a subordinate "attends meetings that are not mandatory but are considered important" or "attends functions that are not required but help the company image" (Podsakoff, MacKenzie, Moorman, & Fetter, 1990). Items such as these provide very little, if any, indication of the quality of contributions that employees make at such meetings or functions; instead, they focus merely on the degree to which employees attend them.

Second, as Organ et al. (2006) pointed out, the findings of a number of studies show that OCBs are positively related to the effective functioning of groups and organizations. However, the correlation between OCBs and unit-level performance is not particularly strong. For instance, a recent meta-analytic study of this work found that the average correlation between OCBs and objective measures of unit performance was .29 (or .37 when corrected for measurement and sampling error; Podsakoff et al., 2009). Moreover, in some studies, it has been found that certain OCBs have non-significant or even negative effects on unit-level performance (e.g., Podsakoff & MacKenzie, 1994; Podsakoff, Ahearne, & MacKenzie, 1997).

It seems possible that the quality of OCBs might account for at least some of these results. For instance, OCBs could yield inconsistent effects if, as Hui et al. (2000) found, employees perform OCBs until they achieve their goal (e.g., a promotion) and then subsequently reduce their OCBs. In addition, variance in citizenship quality also could help to explain why OCBs are more strongly related to organizational performance in some situations than in others.

Third and finally, in spite of the assertions presented by Organ et al. (2006), research on the political view of OCBs does not suggest that such behaviors are "all for show" or "of no value" (p. 220) whatsoever. Instead, such research merely suggests that organizations may be more likely to benefit when employees go beyond the call of duty because they feel a genuine sense of satisfaction and commitment to the organization than because they want to look good, curry favor with others, or get ahead more quickly in the organization.

Indeed, while some managers may not really care why employees engage in OCBs, particularly in the short run, it does not seem unreasonable to believe that extrarole performance may be more impactful and enduring when it is motivated by prosocial concerns. Likewise, it does not seem unreasonable to expect peers to react more favorably when they perceive that their colleagues' OCBs are performed for relatively selfless rather than self-serving motives. In short, while there is compelling evidence that OCBs generally contribute to the effective functioning of organizations, future studies should seek to determine if this relationship is stronger when employees' motives are less political.

CONCLUSION

Over 20 years ago, Ferris and his colleagues first raised some provocative questions about the construct of OCB. Specifically, they noted that although OCBs typically appear to be prosocial on the surface, they also may be self-serving and driven by instrumental and impression-management motives. Since that time, organizational researchers have responded by examining OCBs from a political perspective in a number of conceptual and empirical papers. In this chapter, the emergence of the political view of OCB was discussed, and papers were reviewed that have examined citizenship using this lens. Based on the review and the areas of future research identified, it is hoped that researchers will continue to investigate the political aspects of OCBs and their implications for employees and organizations.

ACKNOWLEDGMENT

The authors gratefully acknowledge the assistance of Anthony Klotz in identifying the articles reviewed in this chapter and are thankful, as well, for his help in developing the tables that summarize this work.

REFERENCES

Allen, T.D., & Rush, M.C. (1998). The effects of organizational citizenship behavior on performance judgments: A field study and a laboratory experiment. *Journal of Applied Psychology, 83*, 247–260.

Andrews, M.C., Kacmar, K.M., & Harris, K.J. (2009). Got political skill? The impact of justice on the importance of political skill for job performance. *Journal of Applied Psychology, 94*, 1427–1437.

Banki, S. (2010). Is a good deed constructive regardless of intent? Organization citizenship behavior, motive, and group outcomes. *Small Group Research, 41*, 354–375.

Barr, S.H., & Pawar, B. (1995). Organizational citizenship behavior: Domain specifications for three middle range theories. *Academy of Management Best Paper Proceedings*, 302–306.

Becker, J.A.H., & O'Hair, H.D. (2007). Machiavellians' motives in organizational citizenship behavior. *Journal of Applied Communication Research, 35*, 246–267.

Bergeron, D.M. (2007). The potential paradox of organizational citizenship behavior: Good citizens at what cost? *Academy of Management Review, 32*, 1078–1095.

Blatt, R. (2008). Organizational citizenship behavior of temporary knowledge employees. *Organization Studies, 29*, 849–866.

Bolino, M.C. (1999). Citizenship and impression management: Good soldiers or good actors? *Academy of Management Review, 24*, 82–98.

Bolino, M.C., & Turnley, W.H. (1999). Measuring impression management in organizations: A scale development based on the Jones and Pittman taxonomy. *Organizational Research Methods, 2*, 187–206.

Bolino, M.C., & Turnley, W.H. (2005). The personal costs of citizenship behavior: The relationship between individual initiative and role overload, job stress, and work-family conflict. *Journal of Applied Psychology, 90*, 740–748.

Bolino, M.C., Turnley, W.H., & Niehoff, B.P. (2004). The other side of the story: Reexamining prevailing assumptions about organizational citizenship behavior. *Human Resource Management Review, 14*, 229–246.

Bolino, M.C., Varela, J.A., Bande, B., & Turnley, W.H. (2006). The impact of impression-management tactics on supervisor ratings of organizational citizenship behavior. *Journal of Organizational Behavior, 27*, 281–297.

Bowler, W.M., & Brass, D.J. (2006). Relational correlates of interpersonal citizenship behavior: A social network perspective. *Journal of Applied Psychology, 91*, 70–82.

Bowler, W.M., Halbesleben, J.R.B., & Paul, J.R.B. (2010). If you're close with the leader, you must be a brownnose: The role of leader–member relationships in follower, leader, and coworker attributions of organizational citizenship behavior motives. *Human Resource Management Review, 20*, 309–316.

Bowler, W.M., Halbesleben, J.R.B., Stodnick, M., Seevers, M.T., & Little, L.M. (2009). The moderating effect of communication network centrality on motive to perform interpersonal citizenship. *Journal of Managerial Issues, 21*, 80–96.

Chang, C., Rosen, C.C., & Levy, P.E. (2009). The relationship between perceptions of organizational politics and employee attitudes, strain, and behavior: A meta-analytic examination. *Academy of Management Journal, 52*, 779–801.

Chen, Y., Lin, C., Tung, Y., & Ko, Y. (2008). Associations of organizational justice and ingratiation with organizational citizenship behavior: The beneficiary perspective. *Social Behavior and Personality, 36*, 289–302.

Christie, R., & Geis, F.L. (1970). *Studies in Machiavellianism*. New York: Academic Press.

Eastman, K.K. (1994). In the eyes of the beholder: An attributional approach to ingratiation and organizational citizenship behavior. *Academy of Management Journal, 37*, 1379–1391.

Fandt, P.M., & Ferris, G.R. (1990). The management of information and impressions: When employees behave opportunistically. *Organizational Behavior and Human Decision Processes, 45*, 140–158.

Farrell, S.K., & Finkelstein, L.M. (2007). Organizational citizenship behavior and gender: Expectations and attributions for performance. *North American Journal of Psychology, 9*, 81–96.

Ferris, G.R., Bhawuk, D.P.S., Fedor, D.F., & Judge, T.A. (1995). Organizational politics and citizenship: Attributions of intentionality and construct definition. In M.J. Martinko (Ed.). *Advances in attribution theory: An organizational perspective* (pp. 231–252). Delray Beach, FL: St. Lucie Press.

Ferris, G.R., & Judge, T.A. (1991). Personnel/human resources management: A political influence perspective. *Journal of Management, 17*, 447–488.

Ferris, G.R., Judge, T.A., Rowland, K.M., & Fitzgibbons, D.E. (1994). Subordinate influence and the performance evaluation process: Test of a model. *Organizational Behavior and Human Decision Processes, 58*, 101–135.

Ferris, G.R., & Mitchell, T.R. (1987). The components of social influence and their importance for human resources research. In K.M. Rowland & G.R. Ferris (Eds.), *Research in personnel and human resources management* (Vol. 5, pp. 103–128). Greenwich, CT: JAI Press.

Ferris, G.R., Russ, G.S., & Fandt, P M. (1989). Politics in organizations. In R.A. Giacalone & P. Rosenfeld (Eds.), *Impression management in the organization* (pp. 143–170). Hillsdale, NJ: Lawrence Erlbaum Associates.

Finkelstein, M.A. (2006). Dispositional predictors of organizational citizenship behavior: Motives, motive fulfillment, and role identity. *Social Behavior and Personality, 34*, 603–616.

Finkelstein, M.A., & Penner, L.A. (2004). Predicting organizational citizenship behavior: Integrating the functional and role identity approaches. *Social Behavior & Personality: An International Journal, 32*, 383–398.

Fuller, J.B., Barnett, T., Hester, K., Relyea, C., & Frey, L. (2007). An exploratory examination of voice behavior from an impression management perspective. *Journal of Managerial Issues, 19*, 134–151.

Grant, A.M., & Mayer, D.M. (2009). Good soldiers and good actors: Prosocial and impression management motives as interactive predictors of affiliative citizenship behaviors. *Journal of Applied Psychology, 94*, 900–912.

Halbesleben, J.R.B., Bowler, W.M., Bolino, M.C., & Turnley, W.H. (2010). Organizational concern, prosocial values, or impression management? How supervisors attribute motives to organizational citizenship behavior. *Journal of Applied Social Psychology, 40*, 1450–1489.

Halbesleben, J.R.B., Harvey, J., & Bolino, M.C. (2009). Too engaged? A conservation of resources view of the relationship between work engagement and work interference with family. *Journal of Applied Psychology, 94*, 1452–1465.

Harris, K.J., Kacmar, K.M. Zivnuska, S., & Shaw, J.D. (2007). The impact of political skill on impression management effectiveness. *Journal of Applied Psychology, 92,* 278–285.

Hui, C., Lam, S.S.K., & Law, K.K.S. (2000). Instrumental values of organizational citizenship behavior for promotion: A field quasi-experiment. *Journal of Applied Psychology, 85*, 822–828.

Johnson, D.E., Erez, A., Kiker, D.S., & Motowidlo, S.J. (2002). Liking and attributions of motives as mediators of the relationships between individuals' reputations, helpful behaviors and raters' reward decisions. *Journal of Applied Psychology, 87*, 808–815.

Mischel, W. (1968). *Personality and assessment.* New York: Wiley.

Moorman, R.H. (1991). Relationship between organizational justice and organizational citizenship behaviors: Do fairness perceptions influence employee citizenship? *Journal of Applied Psychology, 76*, 845–855.

Munyon, T.P., Hochwarter, W.A., Perrewé, P.L., & Ferris, G.R. (2010). Optimism and the nonlinear citizenship behavior–job satisfaction relationship in three studies. *Journal of Management, 36*, 1505–1528.

Nguyen, N.T., Seers, A., & Hartman, N.S. (2008). Putting a good face on impression management: Team citizenship and team satisfaction. *Journal of Behavioral and Applied Management, 9*, 148–168.

Organ, D.W. (1988). *Organizational citizenship behavior: The good soldier syndrome.* Lexington, MA: Lexington Books.

Organ, D.W. (1990). The motivational basis of organizational citizenship behavior. *Research in Organizational Behavior, 12*, 43–72.

Organ, D.W., Podsakoff, P.M., & MacKenzie, S.B. (2006). *Organizational citizenship behavior: Its nature, antecedents, and consequences.* Thousand Oaks, CA: Sage Publications.

Podsakoff, P.M., Ahearne, M., & MacKenzie, S.B. (1997). Organizational citizenship behavior and the quantity and quality of work group performance. *Journal of Applied Psychology, 82*, 262–270.

Podsakoff, P.M., & MacKenzie, S.B. (1994). Organizational citizenship behaviors and sales unit effectiveness. *Journal of Marketing Research, 31*, 351–363.

Podsakoff, P.M., MacKenzie, S.B., & Hui, C. (1993). Organizational citizenship behaviors and managerial evaluations of employee performance: A review and suggestions for future research. In G.R. Ferris & K.M. Rowland (Eds.), *Research in personnel and human resources management* (Vol. 11, pp. 1–40). Greenwich, CT: JAI Press.

Podsakoff, P.M., MacKenzie, S.B., Moorman, R.H., & Fetter, R. (1990). Transformational leader behaviors and their effects on followers' trust in leader, satisfaction, and organizational citizenship behaviors. *Leadership Quarterly, 1*, 107–142.

Podsakoff, N.P., Whiting, S.W., Podsakoff, P.M., & Blume, B.D. (2009). Individual- and organizational-level consequences of organizational citizenship behaviors: A meta-analysis. *Journal of Applied Psychology, 94*, 122–141.

Rioux, S.M., & Penner, L.A. (2001). The causes of organizational citizenship behavior: A motivational analysis. *Journal of Applied Psychology, 86*, 1306–1314.

Salamon, S.D., & Deutsch, Y. (2006). OCB as a handicap: An evolutionary psychological perspective. *Journal of Organizational Behavior, 27*, 185–199.

Schnake, M. (1991). Organizational citizenship: A review, proposed model, and research agenda. *Human Relations, 44*, 735–759.

Smith, C.A., Organ, D.W., & Near, J.P. (1983). Organizational citizenship behavior: Its nature and antecedents. *Journal of Applied Psychology, 68*, 653–663.

Snell, R.S., & Wong, Y.L. (2007). Differentiating good soldiers from good actors. *Journal of Management Studies, 44*, 883–909.

Snyder, M. (1974). Self-monitoring of expressive behavior. *Journal of Personality and Social Psychology, 30*, 526–537.

Staw, B.M. (1983). Motivation research versus the art of faculty management. *Review of Higher Education, 6*, 301–321.

Tang, T., Sutarso, T., Davis, G., Dolinski, D., Ibrahim, A., & Wagner, S. (2008). To help or not to help? The good Samaritan effect and the love of money on helping behavior. *Journal of Business Ethics, 82*, 865–887.

Turnley, W.H., & Bolino, M.C. (2001). Achieving desired images while avoiding undesired images: Exploring the role of self-monitoring in impression management. *Journal of Applied Psychology, 86*, 351–360.

Turnley, W.H., Bolino, M., Lester, S., & Bloodgood, L. (2003). The impact of psychological contract fulfillment on the performance of in-role and organizational citizenship behaviors. *Journal of Management, 29*, 187–206.

Wayne, S.J., & Ferris, G.R. (1990). Influence tactics, affect, and exchange quality in supervisor-subordinate interactions: A laboratory experiment and field study. *Journal of Applied Psychology, 75*, 487–499.

Weiner, B. (1995). *Judgments of responsibility: A foundation for a theory of social conduct.* New York: Guilford Press.

Yun, S., Takeuchi, R., & Liu, W. (2007). Employee self-enhancement motives and job performance behaviors: Investigating the moderating effects of employee role ambiguity and managerial perceptions of employee commitment. *Journal of Applied Psychology, 92*, 745–7.

7

Abusive Supervision as Political Activity: Distinguishing Impulsive and Strategic Expressions of Downward Hostility

Bennett J. Tepper
Georgia State University

Michelle K. Duffy
University of Minnesota

Denise M. Breaux-Soignet
University of Arkansas

The words *abusive supervisor* conjure up varying images such as former Indiana University basketball coach Bobby Knight's explosive outbursts toward his own players (as well as the media and officials) and Steve Jobs's infamous temper tantrums. The term also brings to mind depictions of hostile organizational authorities in feature films. For example, at a pivotal moment in David Mamet's *Glengarry, Glen Ross*, an abusive manager played by Alec Baldwin reproaches a struggling group of salespeople. Profanity, insults, and threats permeate his address, but he delivers it calmly and in the service of a well-defined goal: to motivate the underperforming group through fear. A nonfictional episode of supervisory abuse is depicted in the well-known film *Patton*, depicting the life and military exploits and contributions of the renowned General George S. Patton (played by the actor George C. Scott). During a visit to a field hospital, General Patton slaps and verbally derogates a soldier in an impulsive fit of rage toward what Patton perceives to be a "malingerer."

In the last dozen years, scholars have brought the tools of scientific inquiry to study the phenomena these cases illustrate (see Tepper, 2007, for a review). This work suggests that abusive supervision is not merely anecdotal but instead plays out every day in work organizations, and the effects of exposure are quite predictable. Researchers have conceptualized abusive supervision as nonphysical forms of hostility perpetrated by supervisors against their direct reports (Tepper, 2000).

Repeated manifestations of hostility, as opposed to one-shot episodes, are the focus of this research, and the work excludes physical forms of aggression such as hitting and slapping. The content domain includes a diverse portfolio of behaviors including explosive outbursts (i.e., "loses his/her temper with me"), actions designed to undermine subordinates' ability to achieve positive regard (e.g., "blames me for his/her failures"), and derogatory comments ("tells me I am stupid"). Exposure to these kinds of behaviors has been linked with diminished well-being, displaced aggression against other targets, and the performance of actions that undermine organizational effectiveness.

With few exceptions, scholars have treated abusive supervision as a dysfunctional form of work behavior that organizational authorities should make every effort to eliminate (for an alternative perspective, see Ferris, Zinko, Brouer, Buckley, & Harvey, 2007). It is with that goal in mind that researchers have undertaken studies designed to identify factors that predict the occurrence of abusive supervision—that is, to answer the question, why do supervisors engage in abusive behavior toward their subordinates? To date, researchers have framed abusive supervision as stemming from frustrating and provocative events at work as well as the tendency for some supervisors to lash out when provoked (Tepper, 2007).

The precursors of abusive supervision that have been examined include personality factors that generally dispose high-power individuals to derogate low-power counterparts (e.g., impulse hostility), mistreatment of those in supervisory positions by higher organizational authorities (e.g., psychological contract breach, interpersonal and procedural injustices), conflictive relationships in which supervisors and subordinates see themselves as adversaries rather than allies, and subordinate characteristics and actions that evoke frustration in supervisors (e.g., dissimilarity, conflictive behavior, poor work performance, and high negative affect; Aryee, Chen, Sun, & Debrah, 2007; Hoobler & Brass, 2006; Tepper, Duffy, Henle, & Lambert, 2006; Tepper, Moss, & Duffy, 2011).

Essentially, current theorizing tends to frame abusive supervision as *hot*, or emanating from aggravating and frustrating circumstances in which supervisors who are dispositionally inclined to hostility flip their lid in response to a variety of noxious environmental stimuli (Fox & Spector, 2010). However, this may be an overly narrow characterization of what drives abusive supervision. Instances of supervisory abuse may appear to be more impulsive and less controlled than they actually are. The legendary coach of the Green Bay Packers Vince Lombardi was well known for yelling at his players. However, those close to the coach understood that these tirades did not reflect uncontrolled anger: "Lombardi's histrionics were, at least in part, a calculated act. One Green Bay administrative employee recalls catching the coach practicing scowls and grimaces in a mirror" (Garvin, 2010).

Consider also a well-publicized incident in which Meg Whitman, chief executive officer of eBay, yelled at, shoved, and physically escorted from the room a former assistant. When questioned by the media, Whitman characterized the incident as resulting from tensions that surface in any high-pressure work environment. To many who observed or heard about the event, Whitman's behavior was perceived to be an impulsive episode of "limbic lava" in which the emotion centers of the brain explode in "out of control activity" (Siegel, 2010, p. 26). At the same time, however, Whitman was known as a demanding leader who often expressed displeasure with employees who did not meet standards.

An equally reasonable inference is that Whitman's behavior was calculated to push her employee and signal other employees to perform to a higher standard. Indeed, the media reported that Whitman believed that her employee had not performed adequately. We do not know whether Whitman's behavior was an expression of limbic lava or a coldly calculated ploy designed to push her employees to enhance their performance. However, the possibility that expressions of abusive supervision reflect distinguishable and varied motivations suggests the need for more nuanced theorizing than what has appeared in contemporary work.

Precedent for the notion that abusive supervision reflects distinguishable motivations and processes comes from both the neurobiology and psychology literatures. Neurobiological research suggests that hot and cold.forms of aggression are mediated by distinct brain mechanisms. Whereas hot aggression appears to be associated with impaired functioning in the orbital frontal cortex, cold aggression is linked with dysfunction in the amygdala (Blair, 2004). Social and personality psychologists have "distinguished between instrumental (proactive) and hostile (reactive) aggression. The former is a relatively nonemotional display of injurious power that clearly is aimed at some external goal.... Hostile aggression is a less controlled outburst of anger and frenzy that appears to be a defensive reaction to some goal blocking, provocation, or frustration" (Dodge & Coie, 1987, p. 1147). Recent contributions to the organizational psychology literature have suggested that hot and cold forms of workplace aggression reflect distinct psychosocial responses to a focal person's work environment (Fox & Spector, 2010; Scott, Colquitt, & Paddock, 2009).

In this chapter, it is proposed that abusive supervision derives from distinguishable underlying motives, which are referred to here as *impulsive* and *strategic*. Impulsive abuse is conceptualized as automatic and uncontrolled actions that may occur outside the supervisor's awareness. Strategic abuse refers to thoughtful and deliberate expressions of hostility that are performed with specific objectives in mind. Because much of the work to date has been anchored in a hot and impulsive perspective on abusive supervision, the primary objective here is to complicate current thinking by introducing the grounding for a cold and strategic perspective.

Therefore, most of this review focuses on abusive supervision as planned, goal-directed activity, whereby behaviors are performed in the service of specific objectives. A strategic perspective on abusive supervision is developed by weaving together theory and research on (1) organizational politics, which refers to the influence processes organizational members employ in the service of personal and organizational objectives; (2) the motivations that individuals seek to satisfy through aggressive behavior; (3) the cognitive processes associated with the performance of deliberate acts; and (4) the cognitive mechanisms that "free" individuals to perform potentially harmful actions.

ABUSIVE SUPERVISION AS POLITICAL ACTIVITY IN WORK ORGANIZATIONS

It is proposed that managers may perform cold, calculated displays of hostility to influence workers' perceptions, attitudes, and behaviors (i.e., abusive supervision may reflect political activity in work organizations). Varying definitions of organizational politics have been proposed. For example,

Mayes and Allen (1977) defined organizational politics as influence attempts designed to achieve (1) organizationally sanctioned objectives using nonsanctioned means or (2) objectives not sanctioned by the organization. Organizationally sanctioned objectives are goals whose successful attainment has been deemed important to the success of the organization, whereas nonsanctioned objectives represent more selfishly motivated goals that are not considered central to organizational functioning.

Pfeffer (1981) also viewed politics as a process by which employees accomplish personal and organizational objectives, but from his perspective political behavior is not necessarily counterproductive. Indeed, Pfeffer argued that politics is simply the process by which things get done in organization, good and bad. What these definitions have in common is the notion that politics constitutes a social influence process, that is, a mechanism by which agents change target persons' cognitions, affective states, or behaviors (Ferris, Russ, & Fandt, 1989).

In a number of studies, scholars have examined the influence tactics that people use to get their way in organizational settings (Kipnis, Schmidt, & Wilkinson, 1980; Schilit & Locke, 1982; Yukl, Lepsinger, & Lucia, 1991). The influence tactic typologies vary from study to study, but there are some recurring themes. For example, most typologies include rational persuasion (i.e., explaining the reasons for the request), ingratiation (i.e., putting the target in a favorable mood as the agent makes the request), and exchange (i.e., offering something of value in exchange for compliance). Of direct relevance to the focus of this chapter, actors tailor their use of influence tactics to meet strategic objectives. Yukl, Guinan, and Sottolano (1995) found that managers relied primarily on rational persuasion to elicit compliance but also that they used (1) pressure tactics to change the behavior of subordinate targets, (2) inspirational appeals to assign work, and (3) ingratiation, personal appeals, and exchange tactics to get assistance.

No research has explored supervisory abuse as an independent influence tactic, although some of the specific behaviors that appear in other tactic categories overlap with the abusive supervision content domain (e.g., threats, lying, and coercion; Kipnis & Schmidt, 1988). In proposing that abusive supervision captures politically motivated behavior, it is suggested that abuse may be viewed as a distinguishable form of interpersonal influence that managers use to accomplish various strategic objectives.

In making a case for abusive supervision as politically driven and in differentiating it from hot or impulsive motives, it is not suggested that all instances of abuse fall neatly into one category or the other. As Scott et al. (2009) pointed out, the cognitive drivers of cold and calculated hostility and the affective drivers of hot and impulsive hostility are "interlinked, as cognition can influence affect and vice-versa [sic]" (p. 761). For the sake of clarity in this presentation, the two sets of motives are treated separately, but it is recognized that specific instances of abusive supervision may reflect varying levels of both hot and cold motives. Some instances of downward hostility primarily are driven by uncontrolled anger, some primarily by a rational weighing of the costs and benefits associated with abuse, and some by a more balanced mix of hot and cold drivers.

Also, it is noted that in acknowledging a strategic side to abusive supervision, the position that such behavior should be tolerated is not embraced. This feature of the present perspective departs from Ferris et al. (2007), who theorized that the strategic and tactical drivers of leader bullying potentially could contribute to organizational effectiveness. Ferris et al. argued that "politically skilled leaders may use bullying in a manner that can result in positive consequences" (p. 203).

The position taken here is that socially skilled people choose interpersonal behaviors other than hostility to get things done and that whatever "good" comes from abusive supervision pales in comparison to its many downsides (see Tepper, 2007 for a thorough review of the consequences of abusive supervision). Consequently, notwithstanding the unfortunate tendency for third parties to be accepting of abusive and high-performing managers (Shaffer, Courtright, Colbert, & Darnold, 2009), civility need not be sacrificed in the pursuit of legitimate organizational objectives (Sutton, 2007). It is to those objectives that attention is now turned.

STRATEGIC OBJECTIVES ACHIEVED THROUGH ABUSIVE SUPERVISION

Scott et al. (2009) proposed a model of justice rule adherence and violation that describes the hot and cold motives underlying the performance of injurious acts across organizational levels and targets. The authors based their conceptual work on Tedeschi and Felson's (1994) social interaction theory of aggression, and the same theoretical foundation is employed here because it provides a useful foundation for identifying and examining the strategic objectives that managers may accomplish by abusing their direct reports. According to the theory, actors may aggress to fulfill three general kinds of objectives: (1) to force compliance; (2) to manage impressions; and (3) to redress perceived injustices.

Forcing compliance refers to the motivation to assert control over uncooperative players in one's social environment. The second objective captures the motivation to create and maintain social identities the actor desires (Schlenker, 1980), which may include impressions people have of themselves or the impressions that others have of them. The third objective refers to the basic human need to balance the scales of justice when norms or rules are violated (Lerner, 1980). All three motives have implications for adaptation.

Experiencing greater control in one's work and nonwork lives is associated with better heath and greater longevity; individuals who successfully manage impressions are more likely to fulfill social goals compared with those who do not create desired social identities; and successfully redressing injustices gives people a sense of order and stability. Consequently, the motivation to accomplish these objectives resides in many people. Of direct relevance to the focus on abusive supervision, to achieve these objectives managers may abuse subordinates to control them, to manage impressions others form and maintain of them, or to balance the scales when subordinates transgress.

Controlling Subordinates

Three kinds of situations are likely to evoke in managers the motivation to exert control over subordinates is likely evoked in managers when subordinates resist performance of downward requests, when subordinates fail to meet performance standards, and when subordinates perform acts of workplace deviance. The first of the three situations involves responses to interpersonal influence attempts in which subordinates refuse to perform requests that their managers make of them. Resistance or nonconformity is unusual in that subordinates ordinarily enthusiastically commit to, or reluctantly comply with, manager requests (Falbe & Yukl,

1992). However, subordinate resistance does occur, and its manifestations may be counterproductive (e.g., outright refusal, ignoring the supervisor) or well intended (e.g., pointing out potential problems, offering better suggestions; Tepper, Uhl-Bien, Kohut, Rogelberg, Lockhart, & Ensley, 2006). Counterproductive resistance (and to a lesser extent well-intended resistance) creates power dynamics with which managers may not be comfortable. This is because when subordinates resist, they assert control over influence episodes such that their behavior is more self-determined compared with when subordinates conform to manager requests, either enthusiastically or reluctantly. In simple terms, resisting subordinates do what they want to do, not what their managers want them to do. This may explain why managers perceive subordinate resistance unfavorably and why managers try to reassert control over resisting subordinates by employing increasingly coercive and controlling, follow-up influence tactics (Falbe & Yukl, 1992; Yukl, Kim, & Falbe, 1996). Consistent with our position that managers use abusive supervision to control resisting subordinates, Tepper, Duffy, and Shaw (2001) found that abusive supervision correlated positively with subordinate resistance. Although these authors framed resistance as a consequence of abusive supervision, the correlational nature of their work does not rule out the possibility that subordinate resistance is a cause of managerial abuse.

The second type of situation that evokes managers' motivation to assert control occurs when subordinates fail to meet performance standards. A poorly performing subordinate may create nontrivial problems by thwarting a manager's pursuit of personal and unit performance objectives and by damaging the manager's reputation as a capable leader (Bass, 1990). Therefore, managers will be motivated to assert control when their subordinates perform poorly. Ideally, managers would address performance problems by adopting a developmental perspective, for example, by serving as a coach or mentor to poor performers. However, managers who lack the resources or inclination to develop subordinates and who believe in the efficacy of a vigorous chastening may choose instead to abuse poor performers (Scott et al., 2009). Consistent with the argument that managers use hostility to control low-performing subordinates, Tepper et al. (2011) found that subordinate performance was negatively related to abusive supervision.

A third situation in which managers will be motivated to assert control is when subordinates perform actions that undermine unit and organizational effectiveness (referred to in the literature as workplace deviance; Robinson & Bennett, 1995). Workplace deviance consists of actions that are targeted at coworkers (e.g., spreading rumors, undermining others, public humiliation) or the organization (e.g., theft, sabotage, shirking responsibilities).

Like resistant and poorly performing subordinates, those who regularly perform deviant acts create management challenges for their superiors (e.g., disrupted workflows, decreased morale). Managers may attempt to control workplace deviance through legitimate means, using the organization's formal disciplinary systems to discourage further antisocial behavior. However, at other times, managers may perceive those systems to be insufficient and inefficient responses to employee deviance. In these instances, managers may assert control by abusing their direct reports.

Managing Impressions

A second strategic objective that managers may pursue via abusive supervision is impression management. Specifically, managers may abuse subordinates to create or to maintain desired identities. In their pioneering work, Jones and Pittman (1982) described the perceptions that people may want others to have of them as well as the self-presentation strategies that people use to achieve those impression management goals. For example, a person who wants to be seen as likable will use ingratiatory strategies (e.g., opinion conformity, favors, other enhancement) to elicit affection; a person who desires to be seen as competent will use self-promotion strategies (e.g., performance claims, performance accounts) to elicit respect and awe.

Jones and Pittman (1982) also identified intimidation as an impression management goal that some people may want to achieve. Managers may wish to be perceived as tough and ruthless, and they will use strategies that align with the abusive supervision content domain (i.e., threats and anger displays) to create those impressions. For example, to make the "pecking order" clear, managers may ignore or treat rudely subordinates who display signs that they do not respect the managers' authority. The motivation to avoid appearing weak may be triggered when subordinates perform deviant or dysfunctional acts. The revenge literature suggests that third parties may perceive targets of hostility to be weak and vulnerable if they do not retaliate when injured (Tripp, Bies, & Aquino, 2002).

Therefore, managers may believe that in relationships with deviant subordinates, failing to give as good as they get may produce a weak image.

The notion that managers may believe that there is value in being perceived as intimidating is consistent with McGregor's (1960) Theory X; that is, the managerial assumption that workers generally are lazy and do not exert high effort without external inducements (i.e., contingent reward and punishment). Although there appears to be no research that has examined the notion that managers use abusive supervision to cultivate an image of ruthlessness, Ashforth (1997) found that managers who embraced a theory X management philosophy were perceived to be more tyrannical by their immediate subordinates.

Managers also may use downward hostility to improve their self- and social-image relative to subordinates who they envy. Envy refers to the unpleasant emotional state that accompanies the perception that a referent other possesses superior personal qualities (e.g., intelligence, ability, attractiveness) or resources (e.g., possessions, access to a strong social network; Parrott & Smith, 1993). Ordinarily, managers have control over a variety of work-related resources, so it might seem unlikely that they would have reason to envy their less powerful direct reports. However, as Cohen-Charash and Mueller (2007) pointed out, "The experience of envy can occur when individuals experience even a single disadvantage relative to a comparison other…as long as this disadvantage is in a domain that is important to the person's sense of self" (p. 666).

Rank-and-file employees may bring with them to the workplace a variety of personal characteristics and skills that have the potential to trigger envy in managers (e.g., superior social skills, career prospects, upward mobility). A manager may envy a subordinate's (1) close relationship with the manager's own superior, (2) ability to make contributions to the organization that the manager is unable to make, or (3) general likeability. Unflattering comparisons like these may motivate managers to harm envied subordinates to reduce or eliminate perceived disadvantages (Wert & Salovey, 2004).

To the extent managers believe that damaging the reputation of an envied subordinate can improve the envier's image, abusive supervision may appear to be a strategically sound impression management tool. Of course, managers who employ abuse to improve their social image (relative to envied subordinates) must be surreptitious. This is because being perceived as an abuser may do damage to a manager's own reputation.

Redressing Injustices

Abusive supervision may be instrumental in redressing injustices perpetrated by subordinates. The concept of retributive justice underlies this cold motive for abusive supervision, where retributive justice refers to the belief that, in the wake of harm-doing, those who are blameworthy should be punished. People experience anger with, and develop grievances toward, the blameworthy, and they satisfy these grievances or restore justice by punishing the perpetrator. It is proposed that some manifestations of abusive supervision reflect conscious attempts to restore justice when subordinates transgress. It has been argued that subordinates' deviance evokes frustration that can activate both managers' motivation to assert control and manage impressions. Here, it is proposed that subordinates' deviance also triggers the motivation to redress injustices.

The norm of *homeomorphic reciprocity* (Gouldner, 1960) stipulates that supervisors should respond in kind when they sustain injuries resulting from subordinates' deviance (e.g., subordinate shirking causes supervisors to miss project deadlines and appear incompetent to higher authorities). Negative reciprocity, or returning harms to those who are responsible for performing injurious acts, helps to ensure the stability of social systems. This is because people are deterred from mistreating others when doing so leads to redress (Bies & Tripp, 2001). Therefore, managers may abuse deviant subordinates as a conscious way of satisfying the norm of homeomorphic reciprocity and discouraging subordinate deviance in the future.

Redressing injustices also plays a role in maintaining what Lerner (1980) referred to as a *belief in a just world*, which is an understanding that the world is a fundamentally fair place and that people generally get what they deserve, both good and bad. Managers who have a strong belief in a just world embrace the notion that subordinates who meet and exceed performance expectations should be appropriately rewarded and those who transgress by performing deviant acts should be punished. A reasonable question, then, is what form of punishment might managerial redress take? Scott et al. (2009) argued that "managers may be motivated to violate the rules of justice to balance the scales.... The need to believe in a just world motivates individuals to rectify what they perceive to be offensive, norm-violating behavior by others" (p. 760). Hence, managers may use abusive supervision to injure deviant subordinates to protect their belief in a just world.

COGNITIVE PROCESSES UNDERLYING STRATEGIC ABUSE

Having described the strategic goals that abusive supervision may satisfy, attention now is turned to describing the cognitive processes underlying the execution of abusive supervisory behaviors. Fox and Spector's (2010) model of instrumental counterproductive work behavior (CWB) is invoked to explain the cognitive features of strategic abuse. Abusive supervision may be viewed as managerial CWB, defined as intentional acts that threaten the legitimate interests of organizational stakeholders (Spector, Fox, Penney, Bruursema, Goh, & Kessler, 2006). Consequently, Fox and Spector's model of cold and calculated CWB seems well suited to framing cold and calculated managerial abuse.

Fox and Spector's (2010) model is rooted in Ajzen's (2002) theory of planned behavior and Ajzen and Fishbein's (1970) theory of reasoned action, according to which the immediate precursor of deliberate action is the intention to perform said action. In turn, behavioral intention is a joint function of the actors' attitudes toward the behavior and subjective norms. Actors form favorable attitudes toward acts that are instrumental in achieving terminal goals. Fox and Spector illustrated this feature of the model with an analysis of an incident involving coworker bullying. A medical researcher, Koren, engaged in bullying tactics to silence and discredit a colleague, Olivieri, whose research results called into question the efficacy of a drug Koren touted and thus jeopardized the support Koren received from the drug's manufacturer.

Fox and Spector (2010) theorized that Koren had developed a favorable attitude toward bullying Olivieri, because undermining her would restore his reputation and protect the stream of financial support he had been receiving from the drug company. It is proposed that supervisors will hold more favorable attitudes toward abusive supervision when they are convinced that abusive supervision will be instrumental in achieving one or more of the strategic goals described earlier (i.e., controlling subordinates, managing impressions, and redressing injustices). Attitudes toward specific acts also are influenced by the perceived "rightness" of the behavior (i.e., whether the actor perceives the behavior to be morally justifiable). This point is revisited later.

The second precursor of behavioral intention in the theories of planned behavior and reasoned action, subjective norms, captures the acceptability of the behavior from the perspective of relevant members of the social environment (Ajzen, 2002; Ajzen & Fishbein, 1970). People contemplating performing a specific action look for cues from others to evaluate the legitimacy and appropriateness of the action. In the bullying incident Fox and Spector (2010) described, Koren would have been convinced that his colleagues and higher authorities were supportive of his (bullying) efforts to silence Olivieri.

It is theorized that supervisors will perceive abuse of subordinates to be normatively appropriate when organizational authorities signal that abuse is acceptable. Furthermore, it is suggested that those signals may be explicit or implicit. Hence, for example, hostility toward direct reports may be ingrained in an organization's culture, or culture may place a premium on getting the job done without regard to the means by which managers secure subordinate compliance (Glomb, Steel, & Arvey, 2002). Supervisors also will look to their peers for clues about the acceptability of abusive behavior. When individuals in similar managerial roles abuse their direct reports or encourage each other to do the same, a focal supervisor is likely to believe that abusive supervision is normative.

Ajzen's (2002) theory of planned behavior further specifies that intentions to perform specific acts do not always translate into performance of those acts. Actors express their behavioral intentions when they have. People experience a sense of control when they believe that they have the ability to perform the act and that performing the act is within their personal control. Fox and Spector (2010) speculated that Koren believed himself to be a powerful organizational actor whose bullying tactics would not be questioned. Collective application of these ideas to the present focus on abusive supervision, it is proposed that managers will develop an intention to abuse subordinates when abuse is beneficial and normative. Furthermore, the intention to abuse will translate into abusive behavior when managers see the behavior as being within their ability and control.

MORAL DISENGAGEMENT AND STRATEGIC ABUSE

The focus now shifts to describing the cognitive processes that "free" those in supervisory positions to treat subordinates with hostility. Individuals do not always perform actions that satisfy their underlying motivations. One of the constraints on goal-directed behavior is the extent to which such behavior has the potential to injure others. For example, the belief in a just world, which was discussed earlier, creates an interesting paradox because it stipulates that in their own behavior people should uphold the principles of justice. Hence, the motivation to maintain a belief in a just world evokes a behavioral dilemma for managers contemplating hostile responses to subordinates' transgressions. On one hand, managers are motivated to violate justice rules to punish deviant subordinates and to return approximately equal levels of harm. On the other hand, the belief in a just world motivates the same manager to avoid performing actions that may be harmful to others. For answers to how managers resolve this dilemma, Bandura's (1990, 1999) social cognitive theory is used for guidance.

According to social cognitive theory, self-regulatory mechanisms are activated when individuals contemplate performing injurious acts. The prospect of performing personally and socially objectionable actions (e.g., abuse of subordinates) invites self-sanctions (e.g., self-condemnation, self-loathing). Consequently, to engage in abusive supervision, managers must first construe abusive behavior as justifiable. One way to make objectionable behavior acceptable is to disengage the normal self-sanctions against harm-doing, which is a process that Bandura (1991) referred to as *moral disengagement.* Moral disengagement refers to a set of cognitive justifications or mechanisms that allow one to commit injurious acts while avoiding the self-sanctions that ordinarily deter such behavior (Bandura, Barbaranelli, Caprara, & Pastorelli, 1996; Bandura, Caprara, Barbaranelli, Pastorelli, & Regalia, 2001; Detert, Trevino, & Sweitzer, 2008; McFarland, Aquino, & Duffy, 2010).

Once free of the self-sanctions that abusive supervision might activate, managers are able to perceive abuse as a viable strategy for achieving their goals (Bandura, 1991). Indeed, the activation of moral disengagement mechanisms can encourage self-approval for abusive supervision, as hostile behaviors come to be perceived as necessary in the pursuit of higher goals (Brief, Buttram, & Dukerich, 2001). Social cognitive theory identifies eight mechanisms of moral disengagement that operate via agents' construals of their own injurious conduct (i.e., moral justification, euphemistic language, and advantageous comparison), the level of personal responsibility for their harmful behavior (i.e., displacement and diffusion of responsibility), the level of harm that their behavior causes (i.e., minimizing or ignoring the consequences), and the characterization of the target of their harmful behavior (i.e., dehumanization and attribution of blame; Bandura, 1990).

Reconstrual of the Conduct Itself

Managers may morally justify abusive supervision, reconstruing harmful behaviors as valued, righteous, and socially acceptable. For example, a manager might perceive a subordinate's actions to be counterproductive and a threat to organizational effectiveness and survival. Harming subordinates to prevent them from continuing to threaten the organization may become a moral imperative and hence morally justifiable. Managers also might use euphemistic language to sanitize what normally would be considered injurious conduct (e.g., "I'm not abusing my subordinate; I am protecting the organization") or construe their abusive behavior as less deplorable compared with actions that others have taken (e.g., shutting down a manufacturing plant on which an entire community depends).

Reconstrual of the Agent's Responsibility

When people do not see themselves as responsible for injurious conduct, they do not experience the self-sanctions that follow transgressive behavior. Personal responsibility for injurious conduct will be minimized when perpetrators can attribute their actions to the demands or expectations of higher authorities. Milgram's (1974) obedience studies illustrate this phenomenon. In those studies, research subjects committed what they believed to be life-threatening actions against a defenseless target because an authority figure ordered them to do so and indicated that they would take responsibility for injuries the victims sustained.

Of course, it would not be expected that organizational authorities openly would advocate abuse of subordinates: "Only obtuse authorities would leave themselves accusable of authorizing destructive acts" (Bandura, 2002, p. 106). Instead, higher authorities will use insidious and subtle messages to convey their approval of abusive supervision as a legitimate management tool (e.g., you have to break some eggs to make an omelet). These messages allow managers to distance themselves from the responsibility for having performed injurious acts and thereby to disengage the self-sanctions that harmful behavior evokes.

Reconstrual of the Effects of the Agent's Behavior

The third set of moral disengagement practices operate by obfuscating or distorting the effects of the harmful behavior. Managers may convince themselves that the harm abusive supervision causes subordinates "is not that big of a deal." One reason for this is that the injuries abusive supervision causes may not be readily apparent to the perpetrator (e.g., subordinate depression) or that the link between the abuse and outcomes may not be obvious. For example, exposure to abuse at work may be a primary cause of problem drinking that takes place away from the workplace and that may persist long after the abuse has ended (Bamberger & Bacharach, 2006). As Bandura (2002) pointed out, "It is easier to harm others when their suffering is not visible and when destructive actions are physically and temporally remote from their injurious effects" (p. 108).

Reconstrual of the Target of Injurious Behavior

The last set of moral disengagement mechanisms operates by dehumanizing or blaming the victim of injurious behavior. Perpetrators of injurious behavior do not experience self-censure if they perceive their victims as undeserving of humane treatment or responsible for having provoked the perpetrator's behavior. Support for these ideas comes from studies that have explored links between abusive supervision and subordinate characteristics, such as dissimilarity, negative affectivity, and performance (Tepper et al., 2006, 2011). The relationships uncovered in these studies have been interpreted to mean that supervisors view some subordinates as unworthy of fair treatment normally afforded coworkers.

―――――――

FUTURE RESEARCH DIRECTIONS

Before closing, directions for future research are highlighted that build on the proposed conceptualization. As noted already, this conceptualization of politically motivated abusive supervision is distinct from hot and impulsive abuse and as such highlights several key issues in need of future work, including examination of abusive supervision as an interpersonal influence tactic, examination of the role the organization plays in supporting strategic abuse, and target and third-party attributions for abuse that is perceived to come from hot versus cold motivations.

Abusive Supervision as an Interpersonal Influence Tactic

It was argued that abusive supervision constitutes a form of interpersonal influence that may be distinguished from the previously examined influence tactics. An obvious direction for future research is to augment extant measures of organizational influence behavior (e.g., Kipnis and Schmidt, 2009 Profile of Organizational Influence Strategies; Yukl et al., 1992 Influence Behavior Questionnaire) by including items that capture abuse of direct reports.

Armed with such instruments, scholars would be able to build on previous influence tactic research by examining questions like the following:

1. Under what circumstances do managers use abuse (as opposed to some of the other more common and less coercive means of influence) to get their way?
2. Do managers use abuse in combination with other influence tactics and, if so, which ones?
3. Do dispositional characteristics of managers predict their use of abuse as an influence strategy?

Addressing questions like these would contribute to what is known both about abusive supervision in general and abuse as a cold and calculating way of getting things done in particular.

Organizational Support for Abusive Supervision

Another direction for future research is to explore the role that higher-organizational authorities play in the occurrence of abusive supervision at lower hierarchical levels. Anecdotal evidence suggests that higher authorities outwardly may endorse abusive behavior (e.g., clearly communicating that abuse of the powerless is an acceptable way of getting things done), but for reasons mentioned earlier it is likely that such examples are the exception rather than the norm. Instead, it would be expected that organizations will encourage abusive supervision indirectly by failing to discipline abusers when those opportunities arise, rewarding high-performing managers who are known for abusing subordinates, and by modeling abuse themselves.

These actions implicitly communicate that abuse is normatively appropriate, even if is not the intention of higher authorities to convey such messages. Indeed, it is conceivable that organizational authorities will publicly condemn managerial abuse while surreptitiously protecting abusers. Studies should be undertaken to identify the conditions under which, through both their words and deeds, organizational authorities actively discourage abuse of direct reports (e.g., adopting and enforcing zero-tolerance policies) and the conditions under which authorities eschew discipline (e.g., when abusers are perceived to be irreplaceable or when abusers have strong ties to powerful players inside or outside the organization).

Hot Versus Cold Attributions for Abusive Supervision

The third direction for future research involves examining observers' attributions for supervisory abuse. Generally, it will be important to address whether targets and third parties respond differently when they believe that supervisory abuse comes from a cold place rather than a hot place. Also, even within the domain of cold abuse, research should investigate whether others distinguish between self-serving supervisory hostility (e.g., undermining subordinates to get ahead) and supervisory hostility that is motivated by more honorable goals (e.g., improving unit performance output or to develop the ability of their direct reports. That supervisory abuse may be an expression of tough love (i.e., abrasive behavior that is intended to develop rather than degrade subordinates) is a notion that warrants attention in future research as well.

CONCLUSION

It has been proposed that managers may abuse subordinates as a cold and calculating way of achieving strategic objectives and that some manifestations of abusive supervision constitute a form of political activity. The notion that abusive supervision may be politically driven represents a departure from the primary emphasis in current theory and research, in which abusive supervision is framed as a hot and impulsive reaction to anger-provoking events at work. Using Tedeschi and Felson's (1994) social interaction model of aggression as a foundation, three strategic objectives were identified that managers may achieve through abusive supervision (i.e., controlling subordinates, managing impressions, and redressing injustices). Then, Fox and Spector's (2010) application of the theory of planned behavior (Ajzen, 2002) was invoked to explain the cognitive processes associated with managers' abuse of subordinates.

Finally, Bandura's (1990, 1999) social cognitive theory was employed to explain how managers overcome the usual self-sanctions against transgressive behavior to abuse subordinates or to retrospectively justify previous occasions of abuse. Three directions for future research also were outlined that build on the proposed conceptualization of politically motivated abusive supervision as distinct from hot and impulsive abuse. The hope is that by taking up these research agendas, the field will develop a more comprehensive understanding of abusive supervision in work organizations.

REFERENCES

Ajzen, I. (2002). Perceived behavioral control, self-efficacy, locus of control, and the theory of planned behavior. *Journal of Applied Social Psychology, 32,* 665–663.

Ajzen, I., & Fishbein, M. (1970). The prediction of behavior from attitudinal and normative variables. *Journal of Experimental Social Psychology, 6,* 466–487.

Aryee, S., Chen, Z.X., Sun, L., & Debrah, Y.A. (2007). Antecedents and outcomes of abusive supervision: Test of a trickle-down model. *Journal of Applied Psychology, 92,* 191–201.

Ashforth, B.E. (1997). Petty tyranny in organizations: A preliminary examination of antecedents and consequences. *Canadian Journal of Administrative Sciences, 14,* 126–140.

Bamberger, P.A., & Bacharach, S.B. (2006). Abusive supervision and subordinate problem drinking: Taking resistance, stress, and subordinate personality into account. *Human Relations, 59,* 1–30.

Bandura, A. (1990). Selective activation and disengagement of moral control. *Journal of Social Issues, 46,* 27–46.

Bandura, A. (1991). Social cognitive theory of moral thought and action. In W.M. Kurtines & J.L. Gewirtz (Eds.), *Handbook of moral behavior and development: Theory, research and applications* (Vol. 1, pp. 71–129). Hillsdale, NJ: Lawrence Erlbaum.

Bandura, A. (1999). Moral disengagement in the perpetuation of inhumanities. *Personality and Social Psychology Review, 3,* 193–209.

Bandura, A. (2002). Social cognitive theory in cultural context. *Journal of Applied Psychology: An International Review, 51,* 269–290.

Bandura, A., Barbaranelli, C., Caprara, G., & Pastorelli, C. (1996). Mechanisms of moral disengagement in the exercise of moral agency. *Journal of Personality and Social Psychology, 71,* 364–374.

Bandura, A., Caprara, G., Barbaranelli, C., Pastorelli, C., & Regalia, C. (2001). Sociocognitive self-regulatory mechanisms governing transgressive behavior. *Journal of Personality and Social Psychology, 80,* 125–135.

Bass, B.M. (1990). *Bass and Stogdill's handbook of leadership.* New York: Free Press.

Bies, R.J., & Tripp, T.M. (2001). A passion for justice: The rationality and morality of revenge. In R. Cropanzano (Ed.), *Justice in the workplace: From theory to practice.* Mahwah, NJ: Lawrence Erlbaum.

Blair, R.J.R. (2004). The roles of orbital frontal cortex in the modulation of antisocial behavior. *Brain and Cognition, 55,* 198–208.

Brief, A.P., Buttram, R. T., & Dukerich, J. M. (2001). Collective corruption in the corporate world: Toward a process model. In M. E. Turner (Ed.), *Groups at work: Theory and research* (pp. 471–499). Mahwah, NJ: Lawrence Erlbaum.

Cohen-Charash, Y., & Mueller, J.S. (2007). Does perceived unfairness exacerbate or mitigate interpersonal counterproductive work behaviors related to envy? *Journal of Applied Psychology, 92,* 666–680.

Detert, J.R., Trevino, L.K., & Sweitzer, V.L. (2008). Moral disengagement in ethical decision making: A study of antecedents and consequences. *Journal of Applied Psychology, 93,* 374–391.

Dodge, K.A., & Coie, J.D. (1987). Social-information-processing factors in reactive and proactive aggression in children's peer groups. *Journal of Personality and Social Psychology, 53,* 1146–1158.

Falbe, C. M., & Yukl, G. (1992). Consequences for managers of using single influence tactics and combinations of tactics. *Academy of Management Journal, 35,* 638–652.

Ferris, G.R., Russ, G.S., & Fandt, P.M. (1989). Politics in organizations. In R.A. Giacalone & P. Rosenfeld (Eds.), *Impression management in the organization* (pp. 143–170). Hillsdale, NJ: Lawrence Erlbaum.

Ferris, G.R., Zinko, R., Brouer, R.L., Buckley, M.R., & Harvey, M.G. (2007). Strategic bullying as a supplementary, balanced perspective on destructive leadership. *Leadership Quarterly, 18,* 195–206.

Fox, S., & Spector, P. E. (2010). Instrumental counterproductive behavior and the theory of planned behavior: A "cold cognitive" approach to complement "hot affective" theories of CWB. In C.A Schriesheim & L.L. Neider (Eds.), *Research in management: The dark side of management* (pp. 93–114). Charlotte, NC: Information Age.

Garvin, G. (2010). Documentaries offer big news from little obscure places. *Miami Herald,* Saturday, December 12.

Glomb, T.M., Steel, P.D.G., & Arvey, R.D. (2002). Office sneers, snipes, and stab wounds: Antecedents, consequences, and implications of workplace violence and aggression. In R. Lord, R. Klimoski, & R. Kanfer (Eds.), *Emotions in the workplace* (pp. 227–259). San Francisco: Jossey Bass.

Gouldner, A.W. (1960). The norm of reciprocity: A preliminary statement. *American Sociological Review, 25,* 161–178.

Hoobler, J., & Brass, D. (2006). Abusive supervision and family undermining as displaced aggression. *Journal of Applied Psychology, 91,* 1125–1133.

Jones, E.E., & Pittman, T.S. (1982). Toward a general theory of strategic self-presentation. In J. Suls (Ed.), *Psychological perspectives on the self* (pp. 231–262). Hillsdale, NJ: Lawrence Erlbaum.

Kipnis, D., & Schmidt, S.M. (1988). Upward-influence styles: Relationship with performance evaluations, salary, and stress. *Administrative Science Quarterly, 33,* 528–542.

Kipnis, D., & Schmidt, S.M. (2009). *Profiles of Organizational Influence Strategies (POIS) Form S.* Menlo Park, CA: Mindgarden.

Kipnis, D., Schmidt, S.M., & Wilkinson, I. (1980). Intra-organizational influence tactics: Explorations in getting one's way. *Journal of Applied Psychology, 65,* 440–452.

Lerner, M.J. (1980). *The belief in a just world: A fundamental delusion.* New York: Plenum Press.

Mayes, B., & Allen, R. (1977). Toward a definition of organizational politics. *Academy of Management Review, 4,* 672–677.

McFarland, B., Aquino, K., & Duffy, M. (in press). Individual predictors of the commitment to integrity: The role of personality and moral identity. *Business Ethics Quarterly.*

McFerran, B., Aquino, K., & Duffy, M.K. (2010). Individual predictors of the commitment to integrity: The role of personal and moral identity. *Business Ethics Quarterly, 20,* 35–56.

McGregor, D. (1960). *The human side of enterprise.* New York: McGraw-Hill.

Milgram, S. (1974). *Obedience to authority: An experimental view.* New York: Harper & Row.

Parrott, W.G., & Smith, R.G. (1993). Distinguishing the experiences of envy and jealousy. *Journal of Personality and Social Psychology, 64,* 906–920.

Pfeffer, J. (1981). *Power in organizations.* Pitman: Boston.

Robinson, S.L., & Bennett, R.J. (1995). A typology of workplace deviant behaviors: A multidimensional scaling study. *Academy of Management Journal, 38,* 555–572.

Schilit, W.K., & Locke, E.A. (1982). A study of upward influence in organizations. *Administrative Science Quarterly, 27,* 304–316.

Schlenker, B.R. (1980). *Impression management: The self-concept, social identity, and interpersonal relations.* Monterey, CA: Brooks/Cole.

Scott, B.A., Colquitt, J.A., & Paddock, E.L. (2009). An actor-focused model of justice rule adherence and violation: The role of managerial motives and discretion. *Journal of Applied Psychology, 94,* 756–769.

Shaffer, J., Courtright, C. H., Colbert, A., & Darnold, T. C. (2009). *Perpetuating abusive supervision: Reactions of third-party observers.* Paper presented at the Annual Meeting of the Society for Industrial/Organizational Psychology, New Orleans, LA.

Siegel, D. (2010). *Mindsight: The new science of personal transformation.* New York: Bantam.

Spector, P.E., Fox, S., Penney, L.M., Bruursema, K., Goh, A., & Kessler, S. (2006). The dimensionality of counterproductivity: Are all counterproductive behaviors created equal? *Journal of Vocational Behavior, 68,* 446–460.

Sutton, R.I. (2007). *The no asshole rule: Building a civilized workplace and surviving one that isn't.* New York: Warner Business Books.

Tedeschi, J.T., & Felson, R.B. (1994). *Violence, aggression, and coercive actions.* Washington, DC: American Psychological Association.

Tepper, B.J. (2000). Consequences of abusive supervision. *Academy of Management Journal, 43,* 178–190.

Tepper, B.J. (2007). Abusive supervision in work organizations: Review, synthesis, and directions for future research. *Journal of Management, 33,* 261–289.

Tepper, B.J., Duffy, M.K., Henle, C.A., & Lambert, L.S. (2006). Procedural injustice, victim-precipitation, and abusive supervision. *Personnel Psychology, 59,* 101–123.

Tepper, B.J., Duffy, M.K., & Shaw, J. (2001). Personality moderators of the relationship between abusive supervision and subordinates' resistance. *Journal of Applied Psychology, 86,* 974–983.

Tepper, B.J., Moss, S.E., & Duffy, M.K. (2011). Predictors of abusive supervision: Supervisor perceptions of deep-level dissimilarity, relationship conflict, and subordinate performance. *Academy of Management Journal*, 279–294.

Tepper, B.J., Uhl-Bien, M.A., Kohut, G.A., Rogelberg, S.G., Lockhart, D., & Ensley, M.D. (2006) Subordinates' resistance and managers' evaluations of subordinates' performance. *Journal of Management, 32*, 185–209.

Tripp, T., Bies, R.J., & Aquino, K. (2002). Poetic justice or petty jealousy? The aesthetics of revenge. *Organizational Behavior and Human Decision Processes, 89*, 966–984.

Wert, S.R., & Salovey, P. (2004). A social comparison account of gossip. *Review of General Psychology, 8*, 122–137.

Yukl, G., Guinan, P. J., & Sottolano, D. (1995). Influence tactics used for different objectives with subordinates, peers, and superiors. *Group and Organization Management, 20*, 272–296.

Yukl, G., Kim, H., & Falbe, C.M. (1996). Antecedents of influence outcomes. *Journal of Applied Psychology, 81*, 309–317.

Yukl, G., Lepsinger, R., & Lucia, T. (1992). Preliminary report on the development and validation of the influence behavior questionnaire. In K.E. Clark, M.B. Clark, & D.P. Campbell (Eds.), *The impact of leadership* (pp. 417–427). Greensboro, NC: Center for Creative Leadership.

8

Organizational Politics and Stress: The Development of a Process Model

Pamela L. Perrewé
Florida State University

Christopher C. Rosen
University of Arkansas

Christina Maslach
University of California–Berkeley

This chapter focuses on the relationship of organizational politics to stress, beginning with a review of research that has investigated how politics relates to stress. As mentioned in Ferris and Treadway's introduction to this volume in Chapter 1, organizational politics has been defined and operationalized in a variety of ways. This is also the case with research that has investigated how politics relates to work stress because researchers have considered how job stress relates to perceptions of organizational politics political behavior and political skill.

Also, a process model is developed that integrates the literature, with a focus on the roles that perceptions of organizational politics, political behavior, and political skill each play in determining how organizational politics relates to different stress-related outcomes, including psychological and physiological well-being as well as job burnout. In addition, also following from a theme identified in Ferris and Treadway's introductory chapter, not only is the relationship of politics to distress considered, but also politics is examined with respect to its potential to elicit *eustress* (i.e., stress that is healthy or that gives a feeling of fulfillment). Finally, after the model presentation and discussion, recommendations are provided, and directions for future research are identified.

ORGANIZATIONAL POLITICS AND STRESS

Over the past 3 decades, research examining the relationship between organizational politics and job stress has flourished, with empirical research demonstrating that perceptions of organizational politics, political behavior, and political skill have direct, moderated, and mediated effects on stress-related outcomes, including job anxiety and tension, helplessness, victimization, burnout, depression, and diminished control over personal outcomes (e.g., Brouer, Ferris, Hochwarter, Laird, & Gillmore, 2006; Chang, Rosen, & Levy, 2009; Ferris, Frink, Galang, Zhou, Kacmar, & Howard, 1996; Ferris, Adams, Kolodinsky, Hochwarter, & Ammeter, 2002; Kacmar & Baron, 1999; Mayes & Ganster, 1988; Miller, Rutherford, & Kolodinsky, 2008; Perrewé, Zellars, Ferris, Rossi, Kacmar, & Ralston, 2004; Vigoda, 2002).

Interestingly, research has shown that, depending on how it is operationalized, organizational politics will demonstrate different types of effects on employees, including countervailing effects on stress-related outcomes (Ganster, Rosen, & Mayes, 2011). Moreover, as argued in this chapter, there is reason to believe that these constructs are each part of an ongoing process, whereby employees perceive politics at work, they appraise the extent to which such perceptions are personally threatening, and they engage in activities intended to control the extent to which they are affected by the political activities of others.

Although various approaches to studying stress are not specifically examined in this chapter, it is acknowledged that the process model presented in this chapter was, to a large extent, inspired by the popular and classic work of Richard Lazarus. In particular, Lazarus's transactional model (Folkman & Lazarus, 1990; Lazarus, 1966) suggests that stress cannot be found in the person or the environment alone but also in the *interaction* between the two. The model views stressors subjectively, meaning that what is stressful to one individual may not be stressful to another individual. Therefore, stress is cognitively determined. Lazarus was more concerned about the appraisal and cognitive components of stress as opposed to medical and physiological approaches. Based on Lazarus's (1991) belief in the primacy of cognition, the transactional model of stress posits that two processes (i.e., cognitive appraisal and coping) mediate between environmental stressors and resulting responses.

According to the model, environmental conditions (e.g., organizational politics) engage the cognitive appraisal process (i.e., the *primary* appraisal), which consists of an evaluation of whether the event is a threat to the individual's well-being or whether it can be dismissed as benign or perhaps challenging. If the individual perceives a threat to well-being, the *secondary* appraisal process is engaged to determine if anything can be done to handle the situation. In this secondary appraisal stage, individuals are said to evaluate available options for coping with the stressor. An individual may use either *problem-focused* or *emotion-focused* coping. The perception that the stressful situation cannot be changed is argued to lead to emotion-focused coping, whereby the individual engages in strategies (e.g., political behaviors) to help alleviate the negative effects of the situation on well-being. If the stressful situation is deemed controllable, the individual is predicted to use problem-focused coping, whereby the individual attempts to alter the stressful situation in some way.

Organizational politics is identified as representing a stimulus that, when perceived by individual employees, has the potential to elicit the appraisal and coping process. In addition, the role that political behavior and political skill play in the process of relating organizational politics to psychological well-being, physiological well-being, and burnout is considered. In the following sections, the focal constructs (i.e., perceptions of organizational politics, political behavior, and political skill) are reviewed. Then, an integrated process model is presented, which, consistent with the transactional model of stress, identifies how aspects of the person and situation interact to explain the effects of politics on stress-related outcomes.

Perceptions of Organizational Politics

Organizational politics refers to a group of activities that are not formally sanctioned by organizations; are associated with attempts to benefit, protect, or enhance self-interest; and are engaged in without regard for the welfare of the organization or its members (Chang et al., 2009; Ferris, Russ, & Fandt, 1989; Mayes & Allen, 1979). In their seminal chapter, Ferris et al. (1989) identified organizational politics as an environmental stressor and suggested that employees who *perceive* that other members of the organization are acting politically tend to experience higher levels of psychological strain and, in turn, demonstrate increased levels of organizational withdrawal as they attempt to avoid this aversive stimulus. Extending these ideas, Ferris and colleagues (Ferris et al., 1989; Ferris, Adams, Kolodinsky, Hochwarter, & Ammeter, 2002) identified three characteristics of perceptions of organizational politics that serve to integrate this construct with the broader work stress literature.

First, perceptions of organizational politics have been conceptualized as an individually experienced phenomenon rather than a specific feature of the work environment, as events, people, and activities are perceived and interpreted in different ways by different people. Thus, similar to other stressors (Schuler, 1980), how employees perceive and respond to perceptions of organizational politics rests in the eye of the beholder (Harris & Kacmar, 2005).

Second, uncertainty and ambiguity are central to understanding processes and outcomes associated with perceptions of organizational politics (Ferris et al., 1996). For example, nontransparent human resource (HR) practices increase the ambiguity and uncertainty that surround employment decisions. As a result, self-serving biases may lead employees to attribute unfavorable outcomes (e.g., failure to receive a promotion) to political processes. In addition, actual or perceived political activities of others (e.g., making HR decisions based on subjective criteria, such as favoritism) may increase the amount of uncertainty in the environment, which may lead employees to engage in politicking to get ahead. Thus, perceptions of organizational politics are inexorably intertwined with ambiguity and uncertainty, which are primary determinants of individual stress reactions (Beehr & Bhagat, 1985).

Finally, perceptions of organizational politics can be interpreted as either a threat or opportunity. For example, employees who feel that they have a high degree of understanding and control over political processes are likely to view perceptions of organizational politics as an opportunity to get ahead, whereas employees who have less understanding and control tend to view perceptions of organizational politics as more threatening. Thus, perceptions of organizational politics have several characteristics (i.e., they are individually experienced, its association with uncertainty and ambiguity, and they can represent an opportunity or threat) that are common to other stressors. Therefore, it seems appropriate to categorize these perceptions as a source of stress emanating from the work environment (Ferris et al., 2002).

Political Behavior

Political behavior has been broadly defined as informal (i.e., not sanctioned by the employer) activities aimed at protecting or promoting self-interest by influencing the thinking, perceptions, or behavior of other members of the organization (Allen, Madison, Porter, Renwick, & Mayes, 1979; Bass, 1968; Farrell & Peterson, 1982; Ferris & Judge, 1991; Hochwarter, 2003; Kipnis & Schmidt, 1988; Martin & Sims, 1974; Mayes & Ganster, 1988; Mechanic, 1962; Newman, 1968; Patchen, 1974; Pettigrew, 1973; Strauss, 1962). Over 20 years ago, Ashforth and Lee (1990) suggested that the literature on organizational politics and political behavior has focused more on the proactive promotion of self-interest, whereas the reactive or defensive promotion of self-interest has been virtually ignored. It appears that current research also has emphasized proactive political behaviors over reactive behaviors.

Reactive behaviors consist of avoiding action (e.g., passing the buck, playing dumb, stalling), avoiding blame (e.g., playing safe, justifying, scapegoating, misrepresenting), and avoiding change (e.g., resisting change, protecting one's turf; Ashforth & Lee, 1990). Reactive political behaviors include those actions (i.e., influence tactics) that individuals take in response to a perceived threat to manage any personal damage that may come about or to forestall future negative outcomes. Proactive political behaviors consist of those actions (i.e., influence tactics) individuals undertake in response to a perceived opportunity to influence outcomes on their behalf.

Several types of political behaviors, mostly proactive, have been identified in the literature (e.g., assertiveness, ingratiation, rationality, sanctions, exchange, upward appeals, blocking, and coalition building), and there is evidence that many of these activities relate positively to work outcomes, including salary, promotions, and performance assessments (for a review, see Higgins, Judge, & Ferris, 2003). However, at the same time, researchers have suggested that political behaviors may feed back and give rise to political work environments, which may be detrimental to the well-being of employees, as work groups that are characterized by employees who frequently engage in more political behaviors will be objectively more political (Ganster et al., 2011).

Political Skill

Compared with perceptions of organizational politics and political behaviors, political skill (Ferris et al., 1999) is a relatively new construct in the organizational sciences. Nonetheless, political skill has its origins in the work of Mintzberg (1983) and Pfeffer (1981) who suggested that, to be effective in organizations, employees must possess the ability to influence others and have an intuitive sense of how to use power to achieve desired outcomes. Recent conceptualizations of political skill have defined it as "the ability to effectively understand others at work and to use such knowledge to influence others to act in ways that enhance one's personal and/or organizational objectives" (Ahearn, Ferris, Hochwarter, Douglas, & Ammeter, 2004, p. 311).

Politically skilled individuals possess high degrees of social astuteness, interpersonal influence, networking ability, and an ability to project sincerity in their actions and words (Ferris et al., 2005). Thus, political skill has been characterized as a pattern of social competencies that provide individuals with a heightened ability to assess social cues and understand the behavioral motivations of others, to influence others and match behavior to fit situations, and to attain personal and professional goals using interpersonal influence (Ferris, Treadway, Perrewé, Brouer, Douglas, & Lux, 2007). Therefore, political skill, as an individual difference variable, is a critical construct to consider in a comprehensive model of organizational politics and stress.

PERCEPTIONS OF POLITICS, POLITICAL BEHAVIOR, AND POLITICAL SKILL: AN INTEGRATIVE PROCESS MODEL

The preceding review indicates that perceptions of organizational politics, political behavior, and political skill are thematically related, as each is linked to self-serving attempts to influence others. Specifically, perceptions of organizational politics are associated with an observer's perspective of the extent to which an environment is political. Political behavior refers to strategic attempts by an actor to influence a target. Political skill plays a role in determining the efficacy of political actors' behavior and influences observers' appraisals, in terms of threat or opportunity, of political situations. Building on this review, a process model of organizational politics and stress (Figure 8.1) is developed in which political behaviors and political skill play important roles in determining the extent to which perceptions of organizational politics elicit stress responses from employees.

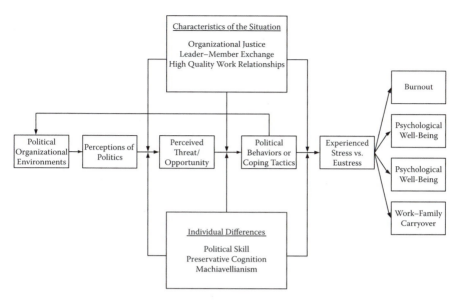

FIGURE 8.1
Process model of organizational politics and stress.

The model in Figure 8.1 serves to integrate the literature and extend fundamental thinking about these relations by examining cognitive processes, contextual factors (e.g., organizational justice, leader–member exchange, and high-quality work relationships), and individual differences that can serve as a personal resource (e.g., political skill) or a personal liability (e.g., perseverative cognition) to the effects of perceptions of organizational politics. Finally, implications for both positive and negative personal outcomes are examined, as well as implications for spillover to the home and crossover to family members.

Political Organizational Environments and Perceptions of Organizational Politics

Consistent with previous research that considered how politics relates to stress (see Cropanzano & Li, 2006), it is suggested that there is an explicit link between the political environment and perceptions of organizational politics. In particular, there is likely to be a strong correspondence between the objective level of political activity in an environment and employees' perceptions of politics (Ferris & Kacmar, 1992). For example, environments in which employees frequently engage in and are rewarded for political behaviors are likely to create a work context, or climate, which is perceived as more political and employee perceptions of the political environment are likely to link politics to employee outcomes. This chain of relationships is reflected in the proposed model, which specifies that the effects of political organizational environments on employee outcomes are mediated by perceptions of organizational politics and that political behavior, which is identified as a potential coping response to politics, contributes to the formation of political environments.

Stress-Based Responses to Perceptions of Organizational Politics

Drawing from the stress literature, researchers have presented two theoretical explanations for why perceptions of organizational politics elicit stress-based responses from employees. First, perceptions of organizational politics are thought to trigger a primary appraisal (Lazarus & Folkman, 1984) that the work environment is threatening because politics interfere with employees' ability to achieve personal and professional goals. In particular, politics exert influence on reward structures, making it difficult for employees to predict which behaviors lead to success at work (Cropanzano, Howes, Grandey, & Toth, 1997).

Similarly, politics is detrimental to the formation of high-quality employee–organization exchange relationships (Rosen, Chang, Johnson, & Levy, 2009), which has an impact on employees' feelings of safety and job security (i.e., they do not have a clear sense of where they stand in their organization). Thus, politics makes the work environment less predictable. This unpredictability is linked to decreased feelings of understanding and control, both of which may elicit an appraisal that the work context is more threatening.

Second, excessive levels of politics place demands on employees' coping resources. In particular, employees who work in environments that are perceived as more political are likely to feel pressure to engage in political activities themselves to get ahead, or defend themselves, in their organizations. For example, highly political organizations tend to reward employees who engage in upward influence tactics (e.g., impression management) or other informal means of influence, who take credit for the work of others, who are members of powerful coalitions, or have connections to high-ranking allies in the organization (Harrell-Cook, Ferris, & Dulebohn, 1999; Treadway, Hochwarter, Kacmar, & Ferris, 2005).

As organizations reward these activities, additional job demands are placed on already overtaxed workers to engage in political behaviors to compete for limited organizational resources. Similarly, political climates also are characterized by elevated levels of interpersonal conflict, which puts additional demands on employees' resources for conflict resolution (Vigoda, 2002). Thus, in addition to eliciting an appraisal that the work context is threatening, politics also are likely to drain employees' coping resources, which may lead to heightened levels of strain (Hobfoll, 1988, 1989).

Given that perceptions of organizational politics refer to employees' perceptions of "actions by individuals which are directed toward the goal of furthering their own self-interest without regard for the well-being of others" (Kacmar & Baron, 1999, p. 4), it is not surprising that research has demonstrated that perceived politics shares considerable domain space with other workplace stressors (Ferris et al., 1996) and also is associated with a number of stress-related outcomes. For example, research has shown that perceptions of organizational politics demonstrate moderate to high relationships with job anxiety and tension, fatigue, somatic tension, helplessness, victimization, burnout, and depression (Brouer et al., 2006; Chang et al., 2009; Ferris et al., 1996; Ferris et al., 2002; Kacmar & Baron, 1999; Miller et al., 2008; Vigoda, 2002).

Beyond simple bivariate associations, there is evidence that psychological strain mediates the effects of perceptions of organizational politics on work attitudes and job performance (Chang et al., 2009) and that understanding and control buffer the negative effects of politics perceptions on various affect and stress-based outcomes, including job anxiety, general job satisfaction, and satisfaction with supervision (Ferris et al., 1993, 1996; Kacmar, Bozeman, Carlson, & Anthony, 1999; Witt, Andrews, & Kacmar, 2000).

In sum, researchers have suggested that perceptions of organizational politics are a source of stress because they create uncertainty about the future and places demands on employee resources. Research has supported this perspective, demonstrating that perceptions of organizational politics are associated with heightened levels of stress and, in turn, undesirable employee outcomes (Chang et al., 2009). Unfortunately, empirical studies have failed to consider the positive implications of perceptions of organizational politics, as research has not explicitly evaluated Ferris et al.'s (1989) idea that politics may present an opportunity for gains for certain employees. A potential explanation for why empirical studies focused only on the negative implications of perceiving politics is that almost all studies that have examined perceived politics have operationalized the construct using some version of Kacmar and Ferris's (1991) Perceptions of Organizational Politics Scale (POPS), which has received criticism for not being a neutral measure of organizational politics.

The lack of a neutral measure of perceptions of organizational politics, along with the difficulties organizational scientists have had with regard to defining organizational politics, may explain why researchers generally have construed politics as a threatening aspect of the work environment, without considering how some employees may see working in a political context as a challenge (or opportunity). This description of politics also is consistent with the emerging challenge or hindrance stress literature, which suggests that, depending on how a particular stressor affects an employee, it can be classified as a challenge or hindrance stressor that has either positive or negative effects on employee outcomes (see Cavanaugh, Boswell, Roehling, & Boudreau, 2000; LePine, LePine, & Saul, 2007; LePine, Podsakoff, & LePine, 2005).

Hindrance stressors refer to demands that people tend to appraise as constraining their personal growth, development, and work-related accomplishments. Examples of hindrance stressors identified in past research include perceptions of organizational politics, role ambiguity, and role conflict (LePine et al., 2007). Challenge stressors refer to demands that people tend to appraise as potentially promoting their personal growth and work-related achievement. Examples of challenge stressors include responsibility and job complexity.

In contrast to challenge and hindrance stress research but consistent with the extant stress literature (e.g., Lazarus & Folkman, 1984; McGrath, 1976; Schuler, 1980), it is argued that it is not the event itself that determines whether individuals experience a hindrance or a challenge stressor but the way the event is interpreted. Thus, in a later section, situational and individual boundary conditions that help to explain how and why the same political phenomenon may be perceived as either a threat or hindrance or an opportunity or challenge are considered.

Political and Coping Behaviors

In addition to suggesting that employees engage in political behaviors as a means of securing valuable work and career outcomes (Higgins et al., 2003), researchers have characterized political behavior as a coping response through which employees attempt to reduce different forms of uncertainty at work by exerting control over the environment (Deluga, 1989; Harrell-Cook et al., 1999; Hochwarter, 2003; Mayes & Ganster, 1988; Nonis, Sager, & Kumar, 1996; Valle & Perrewé, 2000). Though examined in only a limited number of studies, empirical research generally has supported this perspective, demonstrating that employees respond to certain work stressors (e.g., role stressors) by engaging in political behavior. For example, Kipnis and Schmidt (1988) found that employees who reported the highest levels of job tension also had the highest scores across six of the upward influence behaviors (i.e., reason, friendliness, assertiveness, coalition, higher authority, and bargaining) that were investigated.

Similarly, Mayes and Ganster's (1988) results were consistent with their hypothesis that engaging in political influence behaviors is one way that employees cope with job-related stress. Mayes and Ganster's (1988) research also provided evidence for a direct relationship between role stressors and personal political activity, indicating a statistically significant ($p < .05$), positive relationship between role conflict and political activity and a marginally significant ($p < .06$), and positive relationship between role ambiguity and political activity. These correlations support the perspective that political behavior is a coping response that is triggered by workplace stress. Similarly, DeLuga (1989) and Nonis et al. (1996) demonstrated that role stressors are associated with an increased use of influence tactics (e.g., assertiveness, upward appeals, exchange, and coalition building), which provides additional support for the notion that political behavior is a coping response.

The literature also has provided some support for the efficacy of political behavior as a coping response. In particular, research (Chen & Fang, 2007; Harrell-Cook et al., 1999) has demonstrated that political behavior may alleviate the negative effects of workplace stressors on employee outcomes. For example, political behaviors such as impression management, self-promotion, and ingratiation attenuate the effects of perceived politics on work attitudes, job performance, satisfaction with the supervisor, and intent to leave (Harrell-Cook et al., 1999; Hochwarter, 2003; Zivnuska, Kacmar, Witt, Carlson, & Bratton, 2004).

Interestingly, one study (Nonis et al., 1996) was identified that indicated that political behavior may *accentuate* the negative effects of stressors. Specifically, Nonis et al. hypothesized that employees were most likely to overcome the negative effects of role stress if they engaged in proactive coping strategies, such as upward influence tactics aimed at acquiring support from available sources and gaining control over the environment. However, Nonis et al.'s results indicated that upward influence tactics strengthened the relationship between role stress and two outcomes—propensity to leave and satisfaction with supervisor.

With the exception of Nonis et al.'s (1996) study, however, research has indicated that political behavior is an effective coping mechanism through which employees reduce uncertainty and exert control over the environment (Harrell-Cook et al., 1999). Thus, in contrast to perceptions of organizational politics, which generally are identified as a source of stress (Ferris et al., 2002; Chang et al., 2009), it appears that engaging in political activities may have some benefit for employees. However, as previously mentioned, one's own political activity could potentially contribute to the formation of a political climate, which may demonstrate more negative long-term effects.

Nonetheless, when employees are capable of successful politicking, they tend to experience less stress and to receive superior job performance ratings, greater salary increases, and quicker advancement; that is, all conducive to what commonly is thought of as career success (e.g., Liu, Ferris, Zinko, Perrewé, Weitz, & Xu, 2007; Treadway, Ferris, Duke, Adams, & Thatcher, 2007). Indeed, politics is an engrained component of virtually all work settings (Gandz & Murray, 1980), and without the ability to exercise political influence at appropriate times the likelihood of acquiring favorable career outcomes would be limited significantly (Mintzberg, 1983; Pfeffer, 1992). However, there is relatively little consensus with regard to which political activities will be most (or least) effective in terms of attenuating the effects of stressors on outcomes. Also, the long-term side effects of engaging in these activities, such as damage to one's own reputation or the impact of redirecting resources from performance-oriented activities, are not well understood.

Finally, as discussed in the following section, it does not appear that political behavior translates into similar outcomes for all employees, as certain individuals (e.g., those who are more politically skilled) may reap greater rewards from engaging in self-serving political influence tactics. As evidence, one study (Treadway et al., 2007) found that subordinates high on political skill who engaged in ingratiation were not perceived by their supervisors as using manipulation for personal gain. The role of political skill and other individual difference variables is now examined in greater detail.

Individual Differences

As mentioned already, empirical and theoretical work has suggested that political skill is an individual difference that is particularly relevant to understanding how employees perceive and respond to workplace stressors. Ferris and colleagues (Ferris et al., 2007; Perrewé, Ferris, Frink, & Anthony, 2000) have argued that political skill reduces the amount of strain that individuals experience as a result of environmental stressors, as individuals high in political skill possess heightened levels of "social astuteness, savvy, and understanding of people, along with a fundamental belief that they can control the processes and outcomes of interactions with others" (Perrewé et al., 2000, p. 7).

As such, political skill serves as a unique and effective coping resource because it predisposes individuals to feel that they have more control over the social environment and enhances their understanding of the work context. As a result, politically skilled individuals tend to interpret stressors in different ways. For example, politically skilled employees are predisposed to interpret environmental stimuli related to interpersonal interactions as an opportunity rather than a threat (Perrewé, Zellars, Ferris, Rossi, Kacmar, & Ralston, 2004).

With regard to its ability to neutralize the effects of stressors, political skill has been described as a personal resource that individuals use for coping with stressors and that facilitates the acquisition of other resources in the organization (Ferris et al., 2007). Thus, political skill is an internal resource that assists individuals in managing (i.e., accumulating and protecting) resources from the external environment. Psychological resource theories, such as Hobfoll's (1998) conservation of resource (COR) theory, would suggest that political skill has the potential to neutralize the effects of stressors because it provides employees with additional resources (both internal and external) that can be used to cope with stressors. Consistent with this perspective, a growing body of empirical research (e.g., Harvey, Harris, Harris, & Wheeler, 2007; Hochwarter, Ferris, Gavin, Perrewé, Hall, & Frink, 2007; Meurs, Gallagher, & Perrewé, 2010; Perrewé et al., 2004, 2005) has demonstrated that political skill moderates the effects of workplace stressors, including role conflict, role overload, and felt accountability on employee outcomes (e.g., job tension, job satisfaction, career satisfaction).

Also, there is evidence that political skill plays a role in determining how employees react to social stressors, such as organizational politics (Brouer et al., 2006; Harvey et al., 2007). For example, Brouer et al. identified perceptions of organizational politics as a workplace stressor and demonstrated that political skill attenuates the relationship between perceptions of organizational politics and feelings of depression. In addition to determining how employees react to perceptions of organizational politics, there also is evidence that political skill enhances the effectiveness of political behaviors. For example, Harris et al. (2007) used social influence theory, which suggests that the ability of actors to understand the dynamics of their relationship with the target of influence is critical for success, to support their hypothesis that political skill moderates the relationship between political behavior and supervisor ratings of performance. Their results demonstrated that all five political behaviors examined (i.e., intimidation, exemplification, ingratiation, self-promotion, and supplication) contributed to positive outcomes for employees who were higher in political skill.

Similarly, Kolodinsky, Treadway, and Ferris (2007) demonstrated that the relationship between subordinate rationality (i.e., the use of reasoning and rational persuasion to influence others) and two outcomes (i.e., supervisor liking and perceived similarity to the subordinate) was stronger for politically skilled employees. Finally, and as discussed in a previous section, Treadway et al. (2007) reported that the use of ingratiation by politically skilled employees favorably influenced their supervisors' reactions, whereas ingratiation attempts by employees low in political skill were perceived by their supervisors as manipulation and reacted less favorably.

Taken together, the literature indicates that political skill serves as an antidote to many job-related stressors (e.g., Perrewé et al., 2004), including perceptions of organizational politics. A plausible explanation of these effects is that politically skilled employees have more resources (both internal and external) available for coping with stressors. Also, there is evidence that political skill enhances the extent to which an actor's political behaviors influence the thoughts and actions of others, as political skill provides the influencer with the skill to enact influence tactics for positive outcomes. As discussed later in this chapter, these findings suggest that perceptions of organizational politics, political behavior, and political skill should not be examined separately, as consideration of each is necessary for understanding the relationship between organizational politics and stress.

In addition to political skill, other individual difference variables are likely to play a role in determining how perceptions of organizational politics affect employees (see Rosen, Chang, & Levy, 2006). Unfortunately, a comprehensive examination of relevant individual differences that might serve as a boundary condition in the relationship between perceptions of organizational politics and outcomes is simply beyond the scope of this chapter, given length consideration. Nonetheless, the role of two individual differences is mentioned as particularly important to understanding the processes that link organizational politics to stress-based outcomes. One personality construct was chosen that has been theoretically and empirically tied with the stress experience (i.e., perseverative cognition), and another personality construct is examined that has been theoretically and empirically tied with politics (i.e., Machiavellianism).

Perseverative cognition is evidenced in worry and rumination over current or even perceived future stressors. Perseverative cognition is thought to be related to the delayed disengagement from threatening information (Pieper & Brosschot, 2005). Some research (i.e., Pieper, Brosschot, Van der Leeden, & Thayer, 2007) supports the belief that worry might have a stronger relationship with health than stressful events, because the experience of worry about a stressor generally is longer than that of the event itself. Worry and rumination also have been linked either directly or indirectly to important health outcomes, such as sleep quality, increased cortisol, higher heart rate, and increased mortality (see Brosschot, Gerin, & Thayer, 2006; Brosschot & Thayer, 2004). Individuals who focus or ruminate over stressors in their environment may be more likely to experience more negative psychological as well as physiological effects from perceptions of organizational politics.

As both an Italian philosopher and politician, Niccolo Machiavelli provided his detailed thoughts in his book *The Prince* on how a ruler may maintain and even increase power. When responding to the question about whether it is better to be feared or loved, Machiavelli wrote, "It may be answered that one should wish to be both, but, because it is difficult to unite them in one person, it is much safer to be feared than loved, when, of the two, either must be dispensed with" (p. 90). Therefore, it should come as no surprise that individuals who exhibit Machiavellian tendencies typically engage in deceitful and manipulative behaviors to achieve their desired goals (Geis, 1978; Hunt & Chonko, 1984).

Those high in Machiavellianism are highly motivated by gaining as much power as possible to maintain success and control. Consequently, those high in Machiavellianism have been reported as more likely to be opportunistic, to cheat, to deceive, and to manipulate to achieve their goals (Christie & Geis, 1970). In addition, behaviors of individuals high in Machiavellianism tend to demonstrate interpersonal consideration and sincerity, resulting in enhanced apparent authenticity. However, these behaviors, more often than not, represent strategic tactics aimed at achieving personal agendas (Dahling, Whitaker, & Levy, 2009). As such, those high in Machiavellianism should be more acutely aware of organizational politics (Valle & Perrewé, 2000) and should be more likely to engage in political behaviors when they perceive politics in the organization.

The discussion of these three individual differences (i.e., political skill, perseverative cognition, and Machiavellianism) illustrates the essential role that characteristics of the individual play in the process that links perceptions of organizational politics to stress-related outcomes. Clearly, a plethora of individual difference variables may serve to affect the linkages between perceptions of organizational politics and stress, and there are various points in this process where individual differences are likely to intervene. For example, political skill, owing to its relationship with intrapersonal resources, is likely to play a large role in determining whether politics is perceived as a threat or an opportunity. On the other hand, perseverative cognition may play a greater role in determining how perceptions of organizational politics relate to more downstream outcomes, such as physiological and psychological well-being, which are linked to long-term exposure to stressors. In addition to individual differences, a number of situational characteristics are likely to intervene in the process that links politics to outcomes. These are discussed in detail in the following section.

Situational Characteristics

As noted by Johns (2006), considering the context surrounding organizational phenomena enriches the understanding of organizational behavior. Unfortunately, relatively little research has considered situational characteristics that may impose boundary conditions on the effects of perceptions of organizational politics. Therefore, an attempt to further

contextualize politics research is made by identifying situational characteristics that may affect the extent to which perceptions of organizational
politics are appraised as a threat or opportunity and that subsequently
have the potential to either attenuate (when present) or accentuate (when
absent) the effects of perceptions of organizational politics on more distal
stress-based reactions.

Though a number of situational characteristics are likely to intervene in
the processes that link perceptions of organizational politics to employee
outcomes, attention is focused on three aspects of the situation that exem-
plify characteristics of organizations (i.e., organizational justice), supervisors (i.e., leader-member exchange), and work groups (i.e., high-quality
work relationships) that are particularly important to understanding how
individuals interpret and respond to their perceptions of politics.

The first situational characteristic discussed is organizational justice,
which typically is associated with employees' treatment by their employer.
Organizational justice involves employees' perceptions of fairness in the
workplace (Folger & Cropanzano, 1998). Different sources of information
are used when forming these perceptions, including the perceived fairness of
previous organizational decisions and outcomes (distributive justice; Adams,
1965), the processes that organizations use to make decisions and allocate
outcomes (procedural justice; Thibaut & Walker, 1975), and interpersonal
treatment by agents of the organization (interactional justice; Bies, 2001).

Previous research suggests that one reason organizational justice is
relevant to employee outcomes is because fairness-related information
impacts the processes through which employees make sense of their
experiences in the organization (Lind & van den Bos, 2002; Tangirala &
Alge, 2006; Thau, Aquino, & Wittek, 2007; van den Bos & Lind, 2002). For
example, uncertainty management theory (UMT), which has been used
to explain the effects of justice, suggests that employees seek predictability
and a sense of security in their immediate environment (Lind & van den
Bos, 2002) and that when it is missing individuals feel anxious about their
ability to control their surroundings and become especially attentive to
fairness-related information, which can be used to reduce uncertainty.

Lind and van den Bos (2002) further speculated that, when faced with
uncertainty, the fairness of one's previous treatment by an employer serves
as a source of information, such that employees who perceive that they
have been treated in a fair manner in the past will have more confidence
that they ultimately will receive positive outcomes. Moreover, being treated

fairly in the past makes the possibility of a loss less anxiety-provoking, as employees who have received fair treatment in the past will be more confident that their organization will act in a good faith manner to protect them from being exploited (van den Bos & Lind, 2002). Thus, Lind and van den Bos (2002) speculated that "firmly constructed fairness judgments either remove uncertainty or alleviate much of the discomfort that uncertainty would otherwise generate" (p. 6).

Empirical research has supported the central tenets of UMT, as both laboratory and field studies have demonstrated that fairness-related information is most salient when uncertainty is high (Tangirala & Alge, 2006; Thau et al., 2007; van den Bos, Wilke, & Lind, 1998). There is also evidence that people rely heavily on fairness information when forming evaluations of a target when they do not have enough information to make a judgment regarding whether an authority can be trusted (van den Bos, Lind, Vermunt, & Wilke, 1997; van den Bos et al., 1998). Recent studies also have demonstrated that organizational justice interacts with different forms (e.g., job insecurity) and sources of uncertainty (e.g., organizational politics) to explain work outcomes (Diekmann, Barsness, & Sondak, 2004; Harris, Andrews, & Kacmar, 2007).

Therefore, given its close relationship with uncertainty and the impact of uncertainty on stress (Beehr & Bhagat, 1985; O'Driscoll & Beehr, 1994), as well as evidence that fairness information acts as a heuristic that affects how employees interpret and respond to uncertainty in the environment, it is posited that organizational justice is important for how perceptions of organizational politics affect employees. Specifically, UMT suggests that employees working in environments that are characterized by fair outcomes, processes, and interpersonal treatment are less likely to appraise politics as a threat because employees working in environments that are characterized by high levels of fairness will have more confidence that their employer is concerned for their well-being, and that politics will not influence decision-making processes that directly affect them. As such, politics is likely to demonstrate weaker relationships with stress-based outcomes in fair organizational contexts because employees working in fair environments feel that they have greater control over their own destiny and, because of this sense of control, transient uncertainties (e.g., changing political dynamics of the office) are perceived as less threatening than they might otherwise be (van den Bos & Lind, 2002).

On the other hand, environments that are characterized as both political and unfair are likely to be viewed as highly threatening and thus have the potential to be detrimental to worker well-being as they are likely to elicit stronger stress reactions from employees. Unfortunately, empirical research has not provided strong or consistent evidence that organizational justice moderates the effects of perceptions of organizational politics on employee outcomes (Byrne, 2005), and researchers have not explicitly considered whether justice moderates the effects of perceptions of organizational politics on stress-based reactions. Thus, additional research is needed to explore the complex relationship that exists between perceptions of organizational politics and organizational justice. For more on the nature of organizational politics and justice, see Chapter 5 in this volume.

A second aspect of the social context that is likely to influence how employees experience and appraise perceptions of organizational politics is the nature of the exchange relationship that is developed between leaders and followers (or supervisors and subordinates). Leader–member exchange (LMX) theory suggests that supervisors form relationships of differential quality with subordinates (Graen & Uhl-Bien, 1995), such that employees who are part of the ingroup are treated in a different way from employees who are viewed as members of the outgroup. Members of the ingroup realize high-quality exchanges with their leaders and form relationships characterized by mutual trust, liking, loyalty, professional respect, and reciprocal behaviors with others. Moreover, ingroup members tend to have access to higher-quality feedback and more information regarding their employment and standing in their organization (Sias, 2005). For example, Gerstner and Day's (1997) meta-analysis demonstrated that LMX quality is negatively associated with role conflict and positively associated with role clarity.

Together, these findings indicate that employees who have high-quality LMX relationships with their supervisors are likely to develop a clearer understanding of what is expected from them in their jobs and may be better able to anticipate which behaviors will be rewarded in their organization. On the other hand, low-quality LMX subordinates tend to receive less assistance (i.e., physical and mental effort, resources, and social support) and information from their supervisors; Erdogan, Kraimer, & Liden, 2002) and, as a result, often experience more negative outcomes relative to their high-quality LMX counterparts (Gerstner & Day, 1997; Schriesheim, Castro, & Cogliser, 1999). Thus, because supervisors represent a proximal and accessible source of information, the quality of the LMX relationship that employees develop with their supervisors is likely to influence the inferences that employees make about how they will be affected by ambiguous features of the work context, such as organizational politics (Rosen, Harris, & Kacmar, 2010).

Empirical studies have supported this perspective, indicating that LMX plays a role in determining how employees are affected by politics. Rosen et al. (2010) demonstrated that perceptions of organizational politics positively affect the performance of high-quality LMX employees. However, this finding was unanticipated as the authors hypothesized that LMX would change the magnitude, not the sign, of the relationship between perceptions of organizational politics and performance. Rosen et al. speculated that these unexpected findings could be attributed to high-quality LMX employees being the beneficiaries of organizational politics; thus these employees may feel that their long-term prospects in the organization are better and may be willing to put more time and effort into their job to make their employer look good.

With regard to the relationship between perceptions of organizational politics and stress, Harris and Kacmar (2005) proposed that LMX acts as an antidote to strains stemming from political work environments because subordinates in high-quality relationships are likely to receive more information and support from their supervisors. These benefits enable employees in high-quality LMX relationships to understand and make sense of situations and behaviors that appear to be political and that may be viewed as threatening. Harris and Kacmar's results supported their hypotheses, demonstrating a pattern that was consistent with their hypothesis that LMX decreases the perceived seriousness of threats from politics. Together, these studies (i.e., Rosen et al., 2010; Harris & Kacmar, 2005) provide evidence that LMX quality plays a central role in determining how employees interpret and respond to perceptions of organizational politics.

Finally, characteristics of the work group also play an important role in determining how employees experience and cope with politics. One work group characteristic that is particularly relevant is the extent to which work groups are characterized by high-quality relationships and connections (Carmeli, 2009; Dutton & Heaphy, 2003; Ferris, Liden, Munyon, Summers, Basik, & Buckley, 2009). High-quality relationships at work are characterized by high levels of (1) emotional carrying capacity, which allows employees to express more emotions and a greater range of emotions in the relationship; (2) tensility, which is the ability of relationships to bend and withstand strain in the face of challenges or threats; and (3) connectivity, which reflects an openness to new ideas and influences and an ability to block behaviors that counter generative processes (Dutton & Heaphy, 2003; Ragins & Dutton, 2007).

These characteristics of high-quality relationships at work lead people to experience greater subjective feelings of vitality (i.e., feelings of positive arousal and a heightened sense of positive energy), positive regard (i.e., feelings of being known or being loved), and mutuality (i.e., a sense that members of a relationship engaged and actively participating), and research from a number of areas indicates that higher-quality relationships with others enhances employee well-being (Heaphy & Dutton, 2008) and diminishes burnout (Fernet, Gagne, & Austin, 2010).

A potential reason work group relationships are positively associated with employee well-being is that, similar to other forms of support, high-quality relationships help people cope more effectively with stress by changing how individuals view stressful stimuli and providing resources that allow individuals to better manage and control stressful situations. Moreover, high-quality relationships among members of organizational units may facilitate the development of psychological safety (Carmeli, Brueller, & Dutton, 2009; Carmeli & Gittell, 2009) and trust (Ferrin, Bligh, & Kohles, 2008), which also affect how employees experience and cope with workplace stressors (Dollard & Bakker, 2010)

High-quality work relationships at the level of the collective should be particularly important to understanding the appraisal and coping processes that link psychosocial stressors (e.g., organizational politics) to employee well-being. In particular, it is posited that perceptions of organizational politics will demonstrate weaker negative effects on employees working in groups that collectively have higher-quality work relationships, as members of high-quality work groups may be more likely to view organizational politics as a challenge that their group needs to work together to overcome as opposed to a threat to them individually.

Additionally, employees who have more high-quality connections with others in the group will have access to more social, emotional, informational, and material resources that will allow them to better cope with the stress generated by perceptions of organizational politics. Unfortunately, empirical research has not explicitly considered how high-quality relationships, as a group-level construct, affect outcomes related to perceptions of organizational politics. However, Valle and Witt (2001) provided evidence, albeit indirectly, for this perspective by demonstrating that perceptions of organizational politics have a weaker negative effect on the satisfaction of employees who perceive higher levels of team orientation and cooperation in their department and organization.

These three aspects of the context (i.e., organizational justice, LMX, and high-quality relationships) illustrate the role situational characteristics at the level of the organization, supervisor, and work–group play in linking organizational politics to stress-related outcomes. As with individual differences, a number of situational characteristics are likely to affect the linkage between perceptions of organizational politics and stress, and these characteristics intervene at various points in this process. As noted in the previous discussion, each situational characteristic is likely to demonstrate an impact on how employees interpret perceptions of organizational politics in terms of a threat or opportunity. In addition, situational characteristics also may impact the effectiveness of various coping strategies.

For example, political behaviors may be more likely to stand out and thus may create tension in organizations that have climates characterized by high levels of justice. On the other hand, as noted by Rosen, Harris, et al. (2010), employees who have high-quality exchange relationships with their supervisors may be rewarded for engaging in political activities. Finally, collective factors, such as group-level relationship quality, may play a broader role in terms of determining how perceptions of organizational politics ultimately relate to worker well-being. Thus, the preceding review suggests that a complex process is involved in determining how employees perceive and interpret perceptions of organizational politics and that characteristics of the individual and the situation may play a role in determining perceptions of organizational politics are experienced in a more negative (i.e., distress) or positive (i.e., eustress) way, which is discussed in the following section.

Experienced Stress versus Eustress

Experiencing and perceiving politics at work may be perceived as a threat that has been argued to be important instigators of the stress response (Quick, Quick, Nelson, & Hurrell, 1997). However, a number of factors that might mitigate this relationship have been considered. Specifically, both situational and individual difference variables that may affect the manner in which individuals react to perceived politics have been examined. For example, under certain circumstances, individuals may perceive politics as an opportunity to enhance their reputation and their performance, which may lead to experienced eustress. The challenge of coping with political environments by engaging in political behaviors may be particularly rewarding under the proper circumstances.

Coping has been defined as a set of strategies that people use to manage stressful demands and the emotions that are associated with the demands (Folkman, Lazarus, Dunkel-Schetter, Delongis, & Gruen, 1986). Although coping can take many specific forms, most organizational scholars agree that it is important to separate coping intended to manage the demand (*proactive coping*) from coping intended to regulate emotions associated with the demand (*escape coping*; Lazarus & Folkman, 1984). Proactive coping involves purposeful, take-charge behaviors and cognitions (e.g., engaging in political behaviors, thinking positively about capabilities), whereas escape coping involves withdrawing from the situation to create emotional distance (Latack & Havlovic, 1992).

Clearly, the choice of coping strategy has important implications for employee effectiveness and the experienced strain. Specifically, whereas proactive coping allows individuals to manage demands they encounter (e.g., perceived politics), escape coping allows individuals to accept only that they are not able to manage the demands. Thus, proactive coping (e.g., engaging in political behaviors) is more likely to lead to eustress, whereas escape coping is more likely to lead to strain. Of course, this relationship changes depending on both situational and individual factors as previously discussed. Thus, individuals may perceive and interpret political environments as opportunities, which leads to eustress, or threats, which leads to experienced stress.

One way viewing political environments as opportunities may lead to eustress is through subjective occupational success, which is the positive and meaningful work events that are related to individual work goals (Grebner, Elfering, & Semmer, 2010). When individuals believe they can successfully navigate their interpersonal and politically laden environment, they are more likely to experience subjective occupational success and eustress. There is theoretical and empirical evidence suggesting that subjectively experienced success at work promotes well-being and health (Grebner et al.). The outcomes associated with experienced stress and eustress are now examined.

Strain Outcomes

Psychological Strain

Psychological strain refers to ineffective cognitive function or disturbed affective states that are associated with exposure to a stressor (Bhagat, Krishnan, Nelson, Leonard, Ford, & Billing, 2010; Beehr & Glazer, 2005; Jackson & Schuler, 1985). Though psychological strain has been operationalized in a variety of ways, generally it is assessed using instruments that measure feelings of anxiety, tension, depression, and frustration (Spector & Jex, 1998), all of which are indicators of psychological well-being.

Anything that places demands on employees or that prevents goal achievement has the potential to elicit feelings of psychological strain (Rodell & Judge, 2009). However, the relationship between a particular stressor and psychological strain is a function of individuals' coping styles. For example, there is evidence that people who engage in proactive efforts to manage stressors (i.e., problem-focused coping) experience less psychological strain than those who focus solely on emotion-focused coping (Gow & Litchfield, 2002; Leiter, 1991), which involves efforts to manage distress following a stressful experience (Lazarus & Folkman, 1984).

In contrast to physical health status and mental illness, levels of psychological strain show relatively quick changes in response to stress (Frese & Zapf, 1988) and therefore have been particularly useful in research that has examined stress–strain relationships in shorter time frames (e.g., Daniels & Guppy, 1994). This research has provided consistent evidence that exposure to organizational stress and resulting psychological strain have strong negative associations with work attitudes, such as job satisfaction and organizational commitment, and positive associations with organizational withdrawal (Podsakoff, LePine, & LePine, 2007). Also, there is some evidence that psychological strain has modest relationships with job performance (Rodell & Judge, 2009; Rosen, Chang, Djurdjevic, & Eatough, 2010) and measures of physiological well-being (Licht et al., 2009).

Theorists have suggested that politics is linked to employee anxiety, tension, frustration, and negative emotions because politics threaten the ability of employees to achieve meaningful personal and career goals (Ferris et al., 2002; Rosen, Harris, & Kacmar, 2009). Therefore, it is not surprising that psychological strain is one of the most commonly investigated outcomes of perceptions of organizational politics. Numerous studies, including recent meta-analyses (Chang et al., 2009; Miller et al.,

2008), have demonstrated that perceptions of organizational politics show strong, positive relationships with job anxiety and tension as well as other indicators of psychological well-being. Moreover, consistent with the perspective that perceptions of organizational politics reflect a source of stress in the work environment, research has highlighted that perceived control (Ferris et al., 1993) and understanding (Ferris et al., 1994, 1996) moderate the effects of perceptions of organizational politics on job anxiety.

Something that has not been considered in the literature is that, in certain situations, politics have the potential to improve psychological well-being by making work more fulfilling, engaging, or interesting. For example, Xie and Johns's (1995) research demonstrated a U-shaped relationship between emotional exhaustion and self-reported job characteristics across a variety of professional, managerial, clerical, and blue-collar employees. These results suggest that stress in blue-collar and clerical settings is a function of understimulation and boredom, whereas stress is more a function of overstimulation and heightened responsibility in professional and managerial settings (Johns, 2006; Xie & Johns, 1995).

Thus, the organizational context and job complexity may play a role in determining the amount of psychological strain associated with organizational politics, as employees in certain situations may view politics as an exciting aspect of their job that allows them to escape the boredom of mundane job tasks. Politics also may present employees with an opportunity to autonomously engage in behaviors that allow them to connect with others through the formation of coalitions aimed at achieving common goals and to demonstrate competence in terms of managing political aspects of their environment. As such, working in a political climate may facilitate the satisfaction of basic psychological needs (i.e., autonomy, competence, and relatedness), which is known to have positive effects on psychological well-being (Reis, Sheldon, Gable, Roscoe, & Ryan, 2000; Ryan, Huta, & Deci, 2008).

Physiological Strain

There are a number of perspectives regarding the impact of environmental stressors on physiological strain. This discussion begins with an examination from the physiology literature and a focus on the recent research on the allostatic load model (McEwen, 1998), which represents the latest in an evolution of models proposed by Cannon (1932) and Selye (1955).

The notion of homeostasis states that the body maintains a steady state in various physiological systems, and this has been at the core of explanations for how individuals react to environmental demands.

According to Cannon (1932), experienced stress was the result of external environmental demands that were disturbing to individuals' natural homeostatic balance. The fundamental process that occurs when one is confronted with an environmental demand or threat is one of defending oneself (i.e., fight) or fleeing (i.e., flight). Cannon placed the concept of stress within a stimulus–response framework and emphasized the importance of outside demands external to the person.

Selye (1955) conceptualized the stress experience as a process of adaptation that he termed the *general adaptation syndrome* (GAS). Selye argued that the human body goes through three stages when confronted with an intense demand. First is the alarm reaction, characterized by hormonal changes in the body, similar to Cannon's *fight or flight* response. The second stage is the adaptation that is characterized by diminishing symptoms as the body adapts to the demands. However, if the exposure to the stressor is prolonged, adaptation is impossible, and the third stage, exhaustion, sets in. Selye argued that this last stage would lead to death unless there was some aid from an outside source.

According to Selye (1974), the adaptability of an organism is finite. In general, he argued that stress is the nonspecific response of the body to a demand, regardless of whether the demand resulted in pleasant or unpleasant conditions. When demands resulted in unpleasant conditions, he termed this *distress*, and when demands resulted in pleasant conditions, he termed this *eustress*. Of course, most of the damage occurs when individuals are under distress rather than eustress (Selye).

More recently, physiologists have noted limitations of the homeostasis concept which refers to the body's attempt to maintain a stable internal environment through a complex system of feedback mechanisms. The concept of *allostasis* was first proposed by Sterling and Eyer (1988) and is referred to as *stability through change*. Allostasis refers to physiological response systems that supplement the basic homeostatic systems and respond to environmental demands and anticipated demands.

Allostasis, then, refers to the process of adjustment of various effector systems (e.g., cardiovascular, neuroendocrine) to cope with real or imagined challenges to homeostatic systems. Unlike Selye's (1955) model, which defines stress as a nonspecific response of the body, the allostasis model allows for a wide variation of physiological responses. Often, multiple effectors are used to control values for a given homeostatic variable. For example, blood glucose levels can be affected by insulin, adrenaline, and cortisol. This is an example of the range of physiological responses that the body can make to internal homeostatic systems.

Further, there can be a number of different physiological responses to environmental demands. The variety of allostatic mechanisms makes stress research more complicated, because it suggests we cannot rely on single indicators. Finally, the allostatic model emphasizes the importance of the mind–body connection to the stress process. For organizational stress researchers, this means that many of the stressors in the workplace, and most (if not all) of the psychosocial stressors exert their influence through individual cognitive processing.

Compared with earlier homeostasis conceptualizations, the allostasis perspective views the individual (human or otherwise) not solely as a reactive organism, but as one who perceives aspects of the environment and initiates allostatic responses in *anticipation* of predicted needs. The transactional model, discussed earlier, is entirely consistent with this allostatic perspective (Lazarus, 1966). Of course, the actual measurement of physiological responses opens up another area in need of additional research.

Interestingly, physiological measures of experienced stress and well-being generally have little relationship with self-reported psychological stress and well-being measures (Ganster, Fox, & Dwyer, 2001). Generally, individuals are unaware of many physiological stress responses that occur within them. Of course, some physiological responses to stress are more easily noticed, such as a rapid heartbeat. However, other physiological responses provide no obvious cues about their increasing or decreasing levels, such as blood pressure.

There is abundant evidence that systolic and diastolic blood pressure respond to psychological stressors at work (Perrewé et al., 2004) as well as laboratory stressors (Schaubroeck & Ganster, 1993). Further, research has demonstrated that high blood pressure is associated with chronic exposure to stressful conditions (Semmer, Grebner, & Elfering, 2004). Given that individuals generally are not aware of their own blood pressure, either in terms of its normal resting level or how it responds to acute stressful events, this makes elevated blood pressure a particularly dangerous risk.

Research connecting organizational politics and political skill to physiological strain is extremely limited. Perrewé and colleagues (2004) demonstrated that individuals with political skill reacted less negatively (i.e., physiologically) to perceived role conflict at work. Specifically, under conditions of role conflict, their research supported the moderating effects of political skill such that lower political skill was associated with increased systolic and diastolic blood pressure. Political skill acted as a buffer or neutralizer to the negative physiological effects of perceived role conflict.

In a recent study, Rosen and colleagues (2011) examined the psychological as well as physiological consequences of working in a political climate. They found significant positive effects of political climate on systolic and diastolic blood pressure. However, political climate failed to significantly explain any of the variance in the self-reported psychological well-being measures. Thus, their research is supportive of the notion that individuals may not be able to detect changes in certain physiological outcomes, such as blood pressure. Clearly, examining both psychological and physiological responses to stressors is an important area for continued research.

Burnout

Burnout is a psychological syndrome that involves a prolonged response to chronic interpersonal stressors on the job. The three key dimensions of this response are an overwhelming exhaustion, feelings of cynicism and detachment from the job, and a sense of ineffectiveness and lack of accomplishment (Cordes & Dougherty, 1993; Maslach, 1982, 1993; Maslach & Leiter, 1997). These three dimensions have a structured interrelationship in which exhaustion, occurring in response to environmental demands, leads to cynicism, which in turn diminishes professional efficacy. This structured relationship defines burnout as a syndrome rather than as a coincidental cluster of symptoms. A distinguishing feature of burnout is a general feeling of hopelessness experienced by the individual (Zellars, Perrewé, & Hochwarter, 1999). Burnout tends to manifest itself in normal persons who do not suffer from prior psychopathology or an identifiable organic illness. As such, burnout seems to fit the diagnostic criteria for job-related neurasthenia (Schaufeli, Bakker, Hoogduin, Schaap, & Kladler, 2001).

Burnout is one end of a continuum in the relationship that people establish with their jobs and stands in contrast to the opposite pole of engagement, which has been variously defined in terms of energy, involvement with work, and effectiveness (Leiter & Maslach, 1998) or vigor, dedication, and absorption (Schaufeli & Bakker, 2004; Munyon, Breaux, & Perrewé,

2009). A greater focus on the positive goal of work engagement and how to promote it has gained increasing research attention (see Bakker & Leiter, 2010). Although job engagement and burnout are theoretically and empirically related, they can have different predictors (Schaufeli & Bakker, 2004). It is argued that engagement is the personal outcome most likely to occur when individuals experience eustress at work.

As a job stress phenomenon, burnout is assumed to play a mediating role between the occurrences of external job demands (stressors) and work-related outcomes. This mediation model has identified critical areas of the work environment in which incongruencies, or mismatches, between the job and the person have the potential of either aggravating burnout or promoting engagement. In turn, the experience of burnout or engagement has an impact on the individual's job performance, health, and well-being (Leiter & Maslach, 2005).

In particular, research has identified six key areas of work life: workload, control, reward, community, fairness, and values. The first two areas are reflected in the demand–control model of job stress (Karasek & Theorell, 1990), and reward refers to the power of reinforcements to shape behavior. Community captures all of the work on social support and interpersonal conflict, whereas fairness emerges from the literature on equity and social justice. Finally, the area of values picks up the cognitive-emotional power of job goals and expectations.

Research on the interrelationships of these six areas suggests that there is a consistent and complex pattern that predicts the level of experienced burnout or engagement. Workload and control each plays critical roles (thus replicating the demand–control model) but is not sufficient. Reward, community, and fairness add further power to predict values, which in turn was the critical predictor of the three dimensions of burnout or engagement (see Leiter & Maslach, 2004, 2005, for a complete description of these relationships and relevant empirical evidence). More recently, longitudinal research has found that assessments of these six areas of work life at time 1 can help predict which individuals are more likely to experience burnout a year later, at time 2 (Maslach & Leiter, 2008).

So far, only one study (Vigoda, 2002) has examined the relationship between organizational politics and burnout. This study demonstrated that burnout, operationalized using a version of the Maslach Burnout Inventory (MBI; Maslach & Jackson, 1986) that was expanded to include job distress items, mediated the effects of perceptions of organizational politics on aggressive behaviors engaged in by employees (e.g., involvement in verbal or physical confrontations with coworkers and clients). Although Vigoda's (2002) study did not explicitly focus on burnout as it has been operationalized in the literature, the results of this study suggest that further empirical and theoretical examination of the politics and burnout link is warranted.

Presently, it is hypothesized that negative perceptions of organizational politics experiences with colleagues or organizational practices (e.g., the perception that others are cheating to get ahead, or wrongly blaming others for their own mistakes; the perception that a promotion was denied because of favoritism) would be reflected in greater mismatches in the areas of community, fairness, or control. If unresolved, such mismatches would lead to burnout. In support of such a hypothesis, prior research has found that employees' reports of abusive interactions on the job are related to the exhaustion and cynicism components of burnout (Leiter, Frizzell, Harvie, & Churchill, 2001).

A key premise of the mediation model is that burnout should not be viewed simply as an endpoint in itself but instead as an important pathway by which the organizational environment can lead to changes in individual behavior and in psychological and physical well-being. As would be expected from the research literature on stress and health, the exhaustion dimension of burnout (which is closest to an orthodox stress variable) has been correlated with various self-reported physical symptoms of stress: headaches, gastrointestinal disorders, muscle tension, hypertension, cold and flu episodes, and sleep disturbances (see Leiter & Maslach, 2000, for a review). Few studies have included independent measures of health outcomes, such as the use of health-care services or the filing of workers' compensation claims (a recent exception is a study that found that higher levels of exhaustion at time 1 were predictive of rates of workplace injuries during the following year; Leiter & Maslach, 2009).

However, it is behavioral outcomes, rather than health ones, that are especially relevant for consideration of the links between burnout and organizational politics. In this regard, research has found that burnout is associated with various forms of negative responses to the job, including job dissatisfaction, low organizational commitment, absenteeism, intention to leave the job, and turnover (see Schaufeli & Enzmann, 1998, for a review). Burnout also is linked to poorer quality of work, as people shift to doing the bare minimum, rather than performing at their best. They make more errors, become less thorough, and exhibit less creativity for solving problems. For example, studies have found that greater burnout among nurses is linked to a lower level of patient care and to a higher risk of patient mortality (Aiken, Clarke, Sloane, Sochalski, & Silber, 2002; Vahey, Aiken, Sloane, Clarke, & Vargas, 2004).

Thus, people who are experiencing burnout are changing their job behaviors in ways that might be protective for themselves but that could negatively impact their colleagues. For example, being absent from work or otherwise withdrawing from the job means that other employees must shoulder the extra workload. Burnout also can be expressed in personal behaviors (e.g., rudeness) that can exacerbate social conflicts and disrupt the flow of work. In other words, the risk is that burnout can be "contagious" and perpetuate itself through informal interactions on the job. Although no research has been done on this issue, it seems possible that people who are experiencing burnout may be more likely to engage in organizational politics, particularly reactive behaviors (e.g., passing the buck, scapegoating, or protecting one's turf). Thus, it may be that in a more reciprocal model burnout might be a causal factor in organizational politics as well as an outcome.

Work–Family Carryover

Research on the work–family interface (i.e., carryover) has been clear that the roles filled are not independent of each other and that participation in one role creates stressful demands that have implications for other roles that may be positive or negative (e.g., Kirchmeyer, 1995). For example, engaging in successful impression management tactics may trigger appraisals that foster positive emotions, which may be transferred to and thereby enrich the employee's nonwork roles. However, coping with the expectations and demands of impression management might require working extra hours, which reduces the time available for meeting important demands of the nonwork roles. Being able to understand and predict the full range of positive and negative effects that role demands have may be important to the extent that the roles in which people engage are becoming more intertwined (LePine et al., 2007) and the number and intensity of stressful demands that people face in their lives are on the rise (e.g., Miller & Miller, 2005).

Spillover theory describes a process by which feelings, attitudes, and behaviors spill over from one role to another for the same individual

(Piotrkowski, 1979). Spillover also has been described as the transference of moods, skills, values, and behaviors from one role to another (Carlson, Kacmar, Wayne, & Grzywacz, 2006). Crossover theory describes the process by which the workplace stress of one individual crosses over to his or her partner at home (Westman, 2006). This goes beyond the stressed employee by describing the interplay *between* individuals. Westman (2001, 2006) developed a model of the crossover process that informs how crossover occurs. Crossover is rooted in a role theoretic framework where roles are negotiated socially among multiple environments (Westman, 2001; Westman, Brough, & Kalliath, 2009); thus, individuals in one domain exert an influence in defining roles for others in another domain (Westman, 2001).

The core assumption of the crossover process is "one's stress has an impact on others in different settings, indicating a complex causal relationship between stress and strain in the individual arena and between stress and strain of the dyads" (Westman, 2006, p. 166). In other words, when an employee experiences stress at work (e.g., from a negative political climate), this stress may spill over into the home environment, and this experienced stress influences the partner's experienced stress through the contagion of creating more demands (Westman, 2001). Experienced stress may illicit emotional reactions that create empathy and crossover from one person to another in recognition of the partner's feelings (Bakker, Demerouti, & Schaufeli, 2005).

Less research has examined the positive spillover and crossover from experienced eustress. Positive spillover refers to an increase in the homogeneity of two role domains through the transfer of moods, skills, values, and behaviors (Crouter, 1984). As an example, an individual who is satisfied in the context of her work role will experience feelings of well-being that will translate to satisfaction in the context of her family role (e.g., Rice et al., 1992). Finally, enrichment (Carlson et al., 2006; Greenhaus & Powell, 2006) refers to the extent to which experiences in one role improve the quality of life and affect in the other role through either instrumental (i.e., direct) or affective (i.e., indirect) paths.

Similar to negative crossover, positive emotions from the workplace may spill over and subsequently crossover to the partner. Thus, the benefits from eustress are not limited only to the person experiencing it. Unfortunately, research linking organizational politics to the work–family interface is not available. Although there has been work on the effects of formal and informal work–family practices in organizations on work–family conflict (e.g., Anderson, Coffey, & Byerly, 2002), perceptions of politics have not been directly examined as to the potential impact on spillover and crossover stress.

CONCLUSION AND DIRECTIONS FOR FUTURE RESEARCH

In this chapter, the attempt was made to demonstrate that perceptions of organizational politics, political behavior, and political skill are thematically related to each other, as each is linked to self-serving attempts to influence others. Building on this literature review, a process model of organizational politics and stress was developed in which political behaviors and political skill play important roles in determining the extent to which perceptions of organizational politics elicit stress responses from employees. This model serves to integrate the literature and to extend fundamental thinking about these relations by examining the role of both contextual factors and individual differences that can serve to affect the role of perceptions of organizational politics on experienced stress responses.

Several areas need to be addressed in future research. First, although the role of contextual and individual factors in the relationship between perceptions of organizational politics and stress is discussed, how these factors might work together was not considered. Specifically, how do contextual factors and individual differences interact, and what roles do these interactions play in the organizational politics and stress relationship? Further, although distress and eustress were discussed, very little research has examined the role of politics in determining eustress. Perhaps engaging in politics tactics successfully (unsuccessfully) might lead to experienced eustress (distress).

Further, there is virtually no published empirical research examining the role of POP and indicators of physiological well-being. Given that psychological and physiological measures of experienced stress do not generally coincide, much research is still needed in this area. In addition, the relationship between politics and burnout is intriguing. It is possible that people who experience burnout at work may be more likely to engage in organizational politics, particularly reactive behaviors such as passing the buck and scapegoating. Thus, it may be that in a more reciprocal model, burnout might be a causal factor in organizational politics as well as an outcome. Clearly, this is an area ripe for research.

Finally, no research was found examining organizational-level versus group-level politics and their differential role predicting employee stress and well-being. Specifically, do employees who experience organizational and group-level politics differ in qualitatively different ways? This chapter likely raises more questions about the relationship between organizational politics and stress than it answers. However, by developing a process model of perceptions of organizational politics and employee stress and well-being, the hope is that a means to systematically examine this important phenomenon has been provided. Organizational politics is a fact of life in organizations; the question becomes when, and under what circumstances, do organizational politics harm employees and when do politics help employees. As should be evident from this review, much more research is needed before this important question can be answered.

REFERENCES

Adams, J.S. (1965). Inequity in social exchange. In L. Berkowitz (Ed.), *Advances in experimental social psychology* (Vol. 2, pp. 267–299). New York: Academic Press.

Ahearn, K.K., Ferris, G.R., Hochwarter, W.A., Douglas, C., & Ammeter, A.P. (2004). Leader political skill and team performance. *Journal of Management, 30*, 309–327.

Aiken, L.H., Clarke, S.P., Sloane, D.M., Sochalski, J., & Silber, J.H. (2002). Hospital nurse staffing and patient mortality, nurse burnout, and job dissatisfaction. *Journal of the American Medical Association, 288*(16), 1987–93.

Allen, R.W., Madison, D.L., Porter, L.W., Renwick, P.A., & Mayes, B.T. (1979). Organizational politics: Tactics and characteristics of its actors. *California Management Review, 22*, 77–83.

Anderson, S.E., Coffey, B.S., & Byerly, R.T. (2002). Formal organizational initiatives and informal workplace practices: Links to work–family conflict and job-related outcomes, *Journal of Management, 28*, 787–810.

Ashforth, B.E., & Lee, R.T. (1990). Defensive behavior in organizations: A preliminary model. *Human Relations, 43*, 621–648.

Bakker, A.B., Demerouti, E., & Schaufeli, W.B. (2005). The crossover of burnout and work engagement among working couples. *Human Relations, 58*, 661–689.

Bakker, A.B., & Leiter, M.P. (Eds.). (2010). *Work engagement: A handbook of essential theory and research*. New York: Psychology Press.

Bass, B.M. (1968). How to succeed in business according to business students and managers. *Journal of Applied Psychology, 52*, 254–262.

Beehr, T.A., & Bhagat, R.S. (1985). *Human stress and cognition in organizations: An integrated perspective*. New York: John Wiley & Sons.

Beehr, T.A., & Glazer, S. (2005). Organizational role stress. In J. Barling, E.K. Kelloway, & M.R. Frone (Eds.), *Handbook of work stress* (pp. 7–33). Thousand Oaks, CA: Sage Publications.

Bhagat, R.S., Krishnan, B., Nelson, T.A., Leonard, K.M., Ford Jr., D.L., & Billing, T.K. (2010). Organizational stress, psychological strain, and work outcomes in six national contexts. *Cross Cultural Management: An International Journal, 17*, 10–29.

Bies, R.J. (2001). Interactional (in)justice: The sacred and the profane. In J. Greenberg & R. Cropanzano (Eds.), *Advances in organizational justice* (pp. 89–118). Stanford, CA: Stanford University Press.

Brosschot, J.F., Gerin, W., & Thayer, J.F. (2006). The perseverative cognition hypothesis: A review of worry, prolonged stress-related physiological activation, and health. *Journal of Psychosomatic Research, 60*, 113–124.

Brosschot, J.F., & Thayer, J.F. (2004). Worry, perseverative thinking and health. In I. Nyklicek, L.R. Temoshok, & A.J.J.M. Vingerhoets (Eds.), *Emotional expression and health: Advances in theory, assessment and clinical applications* (pp. 99–115). London, UK: Taylor and Francis.

Brouer, R.L., Ferris, G.R., Hochwarter, W.A., Laird, M.D., & Gillmore, D.C. (2006). The strain-related reactions to perceptions of organizational politics as a workplace stressor: Political skill as a neutralizer. In E. Vigoda-Gadot, & A. Drory (Eds.), *Handbook of organizational politics* (pp. 187–206). Northhampton, MA: Edward Elgar Publishing.

Byrne, Z.S. (2005). Fairness reduces the negative effects of organizational politics on turnover intentions, citizenship behavio, and job performance. *Journal of Business and Psychology, 20*, 175–200.

Cannon, W.B. (1932). *The wisdom of the body* (2nd ed.). New York: Norton.

Carlson, D.S., Kacmar, K.M., Wayne, J.H., & Grzywacz, J.G. (2006). Measuring the positive side of the work–family interface: Development and validation of a work–family enrichment scale. *Journal of Vocational Behavior, 68*, 131–164.

Carmeli, A. (2009). High-quality relationships, individual aliveness and vitality, and job performance at work. In N. Ashkanasy, W.J. Zerbe, & C.E.J. Hartel (Eds.), *Research on emotion in organizations*. Oxford, UK: Elsevier JAI Press.

Carmeli, A., Brueller, D., & Dutton, J.E. (2009). Learning behaviours in the workplace: The role of high-quality interpersonal relationships and psychological safety. *Systems Research and Behavioral Science, 26*, 81–98.

Carmeli, A., & Gittell, J.H. (2009). High quality relationships, psychological safety, and learning from failures in work organizations. *Journal of Organizational Behavior, 30*, 709–729.

Cavanaugh, M.A., Boswell, W.R., Roehling, M.V., & Boudreau, J.W. (2000). An empirical examination of self-reported work stress among U.S. managers. *Journal of Applied Psychology, 85*, 65–74.

Chang, C.-H., Rosen, C.C., & Levy, P.E. (2009). The relationship between perceptions of organizational politics and employee attitudes, strain, and behavior: A meta-analytic examination. *Academy of Management Journal, 52*, 779–801.

Chen, T.-T., & Fang, W. (2007). The moderating effect of impression management on the organizational politics–performance relationship. *Journal of Business Ethics, 79*, 263–277.

Christie, R., & Geis, F. (1970). *Studies in Machiavellianism*. San Diego, CA: Academic Press.

Cordes, C.L., & Dougherty, T.W. (1993). A review and integration of research on job burnout. *Academy of Management Review, 18,* 621–656.

Cropanzano, R., & Li, A. (2006). Organizational politics and workplace stress. In E. Vigoda-Gadot & A. Drory (Eds.), *Handbook of organizational politics* (pp. 136–160). Cheltenham, UK: Edward-Elgar.

Cropanzano, R., Howes, J.C., Grandey, A.A., & Toth, P. (1997). The relationship of organizational politics and support to work behaviors, attitudes, and stress. *Journal of Organizational Behavior, 18,* 159–180.

Crouter, A.C. (1984). Spillover from family to work: The neglected side of the work–family interface. *Human Relations,* 37, 425–441.

Dahling, J.J., Whitaker, B.G., & Levy, P.E. (2009). The development and validation of a new Machiavellianism scale. *Journal of Management, 35,* 219–257.

Daniels, K., & Guppy, A. (1994). Occupational stress, social support, job control, and psychological well-being. *Human Relations, 47,* 1523–1544.

DeLuga, R. (1989). Employee-influence strategies as possible stress-coping mechanisms for role conflict and role ambiguity. *Basic and Applied Social Psychology, 10,* 329–335.

Diekmann, K., Barsness, Z.I., & Sondak, H. (2004). Uncertainty, fairness perceptions, and job satisfaction: A field study. *Social Justice Research, 17,* 237–255.

Dollard, M.F., & Bakker, A.B. (2010). Psychosocial safety climate as a precursor to conducive work environments, psychological health problems, and employee engagement. *Journal of Occupational and Organizational Psychology, 83,* 579–599.

Dutton, J.E., & Heaphy, E.D. (2003). The power of high-quality connections. In K. Cameron, J.E. Dutton, & R.E. Quinn (Eds.), *Positive organizational scholarship* (pp. 263–278). San Francisco: Berrett-Koehler Publishers.

Erdogan, B., Kraimer, M.L., & Liden, R.C. (2004). Work value congruence and intrinsic career success: The compensatory roles of leader–member exchange and perceived organizational support. *Personnel Psychology, 57,* 305–332.

Farrell, D., & Peterson, J.C. (1982). Patterns of political behavior in organizations. *Academy of Management Review, 45,* 403–412.

Fernet, C., Gagne, M., & Austin, S. (2010). When does quality of relationships with coworkers predict burnout over time? The moderating role of work motivation. *Journal of Organizational Behavior, 31,* 1163–1180.

Ferrin, D.L., Bligh, M.C., & Kohles, J.C. (2008). It takes two to tango: An interdependence analysis of the spiraling of perceived trustworthiness and cooperation in interpersonal and intergroup relations. *Organizational Behavior and Human Decision Processes, 107,* 161–178.

Ferris, G.R., & Judge, T.A. (1991). Personnel/human resources management: A political influence perspective. *Journal of Management, 17,* 447–488.

Ferris, G.R., & Kacmar, K.M. (1992). Perceptions of organizational politics. *Journal of Management, 18,* 93–116.

Ferris, G.R., Russ, G.S., & Fandt, P.M. (1989). Politics in organizations. In R. Giacalone & P. Rosenfeld (Eds.), *Impression management in the organization* (pp. 143–170). Hillsdale, NJ: Lawrence Erlbaum.

Ferris, G.R., Adams, G., Kolodinsky, R.W., Hochwarter, W.A., & Ammeter, A.P. (2002). Perceptions of organizational politics: Theory and research directions. In F. Dansereau, & F. J. Yammarino (Eds.), *Research in multi-level issues.* Oxford, UK: Elsevier Science/JAI Press.

Ferris, G.R., Liden, R.C., Munyon, T.P., Summers, J.K., Basik, K.J., & Buckley, M.R. (2009). Relationships at work: Toward a multidimensional conceptualization of dyadic work relationships. *Journal of Management, 35,* 1379–1403.

Ferris, G.R., Treadway, D.C., Kolodinsky, R.W., Hochwarter, W.A., Kacmar, C.J., Douglas, C., et al. (2005). Development and validation of the political skill inventory. *Journal of Management, 31,* 126–152.

Ferris, G.R., Berkson, H.M., Kaplan, D.M., Gilmore, D.C., Buckley, M.R., Hochwarter, W.A., et al. (1999). *Development and initial validation of the political skill inventory.* Paper presented at the Academy of Management 59th Annual National Meeting, Chicago, IL.

Ferris, G.R., Frink, D.D., Galang, M.C., Zhou, J., Kacmar, K.M., & Howard, J.L. (1996). Perceptions of organizational politics: Predictors, stress-related implications, and outcomes. *Human Relations, 49,* 233–266.

Ferris, G.R., Frink, D.D., Gilmore, D.C., & Kacmar, K.M. (1994). Understanding as an antidote for the dysfunctional consequences of organizational politics as a stressor. *Journal of Applied Social Psychology, 24,* 1204–1220.

Ferris, G.R., Treadway, D.C., Perrewé, P.L., Brouer, R.L., Douglas, C., & Lux, S. (2007). Political skill in organizations. *Journal of Management, 33,* 290–320.

Ferris, G.R., Brand, J.F., Brand, S., Rowland, K.M., Gilmore, D.C., King, T.R., et al. (1993). Politics and control in organizations. In E.J. Lawler, B. Markovsky, J. O'Brien, & K. Heimer (Eds.), *Advances in group processes* (Vol. 10, pp. 83–111). Greenwich, CT: JAI Press.

Folger, R., & Cropanzano, R. (1998). *Organizational justice and human resource management.* London: Sage.

Folkman, S., & Lazarus, R.S. (1990). Coping and emotion. In N.L. Stein, B. Leventhal, & T. Trabasso (Eds.), *Psychological and biological approaches to emotion* (pp. 313–332). Hillsdale, NJ: Lawrence Erlbaum.

Folkman, S., Lazarus, R.S., Dunkel-Schetter, C., Delongis, A, & Gruen, R.J. (1986). Dynamics of a stressful encounter: Cognitive appraisal, coping, and encounter outcomes. *Journal of Personality and Social Psychology, 50,* 992–1003.

Frese, M., & Zapf, D. (1988). Methodological issues in the study of work stress: Objective vs subjective measurement of work stress and the question of longitudinal studies. In C. L. Cooper & R. Payne (Eds.), *Causes, coping, and consequences of stress at work* (pp. 375–411). New York: John Wiley & Sons, Ltd.

Gandz, J., & Murray, V. (1980). The experience of workplace politics. *Academy of Management Journal, 23,* 237–251.

Ganster, D.C., Fox, M., & Dwyer, D. (2001). Explaining employee health care costs: A prospective examination of stressful job demands, personal control, and physiological reactivity. *Journal of Applied Psychology, 86,* 954–964.

Ganster, D.C., Rosen, C.C., & Mayes, B.T. (2011). *Organizational politics and blood pressure: Divergent effects of political behavior and political climate.* Paper presented at the American Psychological Association's 9th International Conference on Occupational Stress and Health, Orlando, FL.

Geis, F.L. (1978). Machiavellianism. In H. London & J. Exner (Eds.), *Dimensions of personality* (pp. 305–363). New York: Wiley.

Gerstner, C.R., & Day, D.V. (1997). Meta-analytic review of leader–member exchange theory: Correlates and construct issues. *Journal of Applied Psychology, 82,* 827–844.

Gow, K., & Litchfield, K. (2002). Coping strategies as predictors of strain. *Journal of Applied Health Behaviour, 41,* 36–45.

Graen, G.B., & Uhl-Bien, M. (1995). Relationship-based approach to leadership: Development of leader–member exchange (LMX) theory of leadership over 25 years: Applying a multi-level multi-domain perspective. *Leadership Quarterly, 6,* 219–247.

Grebner, S., Elfering, A., & Semmer, N.K. (2010). The success resource model of job stress. In P.L. Perrewé & D.C. Ganster (Eds.), *Research in occupational stress and well being. Volume 8: New developments in theoretical and conceptual approaches to job stress research* (pp. 61–108). Bingley, UK: Emerald Group Publishing Limited.

Greenhaus, J., & Powell, G. (2006). When work and family are allies: A theory of work–family enrichment. *Academy of Management Review, 31,* 72–92.

Harrell-Cook, G., Ferris, G.R., & Dulebohn, J.H. (1999). Political behaviors as moderators of the perceptions of organizational politics–work outcomes relationships. *Journal of Organizational Behavior, 20,* 1093–1105.

Harris, K.J., Andrews, M.C., & Kacmar, K.M. (2007). The moderating effects of justice on the relationship between organizational politics and workplace attitudes. *Journal of Business and Psychology, 22,* 135–144.

Harris, K.J., & Kacmar, K.M. (2005). An investigation of supervisor constructs as buffers on the perceptions of politics–strain relationship. *Journal of Occupational and Organizational Psychology, 78,* 337–354.

Harvey, P., Harris, R.B., Harris, K.J., & Wheeler, A.R. (2007). Attenuating the effects of social stress: The impact of political skill. *Journal of Occupational Health Psychology, 12,* 105–115.

Heaphy, E., & Dutton, J. (2008). Positive social interactions and the human body at work: Linking organizations and physiology. *Academy of Management Review, 33,* 137–162.

Higgins, C.A., Judge, T.A., & Ferris, G.R. (2003). Influence tactics and work outcomes: A meta-analysis. *Journal of Organizational Behavior, 24,* 89–106.

Hobfoll, S. E. (1988). *The ecology of stress.* Washington, DC: Hemisphere.

Hobfoll, S.E. (1989). Conservation of resources: A new attempt at conceptualizing stress. *American Psychologist, 44,* 513–524.

Hochwarter, W.A. (2003). The interactive effects of pro-political behavior and politics perceptions on job satisfaction and affective commitment. *Journal of Applied Social Psychology, 33,* 1360–1378.

Hochwarter, W.A., Ferris, G.R., Gavin, M.B., Perrewé, P.L., Hall, A.T., & Frink, D.D. (2007). Political skill as a neutralizer of felt accountability–job tension effects on job performance ratings: A longitudinal investigation. *Organizational Behavior and Human Decision Processes, 102,* 226–239.

Hunt, S.D., & Chonko, L.B. (1984). Marketing and Machiavellianism. *Journal of Marketing, 48,* 30–42.

Jackson, S.E., & Schuler, R.S. (1985). A meta-analysis and conceptual critique of research on role ambiguity and role conflict in work settings. *Organizational Behavior and Human Decision Processes, 36,* 16–78.

Johns, G. (2006). The essential impact of context on organizational behavior. *Academy of Management Review, 31,* 386–408.

Kacmar, K.M., & Baron, R.A. (1999). Organizational politics: The state of the field, links to related processes, and an agenda for future research. In G.R. Ferris (Ed.), *Research in personnel and human resources management* (Vol. 17, pp. 1–39). Stanford, CT: JAI Press.

Kacmar, K.M., & Ferris, G.R. (1991). Perceptions of organizational politics scale (POP): Development and construct validation. *Educational and Psychological Measurement, 51,* 193–205.

Kacmar, K.M., Bozeman, D.P., Carlson, D.S., & Anthony, W.P. (1999). An examination of the perceptions of organizational politics model: Replication and extension. *Human Relations, 52*, 383–416.

Karasek, R., & Theorell, T. (1990). *Stress, productivity, and the reconstruction of working life.* New York: Basic Books.

Kipnis, D., & Schmidt, S.M. (1988). Upward-influence styles: Relationship with performance evaluations, salary, and stress. *Administrative Science Quarterly, 33*, 528–542.

Kipnis, D., Schmidt, S.M., & Wilkinson, I. (1980). Intraorganizational influence tactics: Explorations in getting one's way. *Journal of Applied Psychology, 65*, 440–452.

Kirchmeyer, C. (1995). Managing the work–nonwork boundary: An assessment of organizational responses. *Human Relations, 48*, 515–536.

Kolodinsky, R.W., Treadway, D.C., & Ferris, G.R. (2007). Political skill and influence effectiveness: Testing portions of an expanded Ferris and Judge (1991) model. *Human Relations, 60*, 1747–1777.

Latack, J.C., & Havlovic, S.J. (1992). Coping with job stress: A conceptual evaluation framework for coping measures. *Journal of Organizational Behavior, 13,* 479–508.

Lazarus, R.S. (1966). *Psychological stress and the coping process.* New York: McGraw-Hill.

Lazarus, R.S. (1991). *Emotions and adaptation.* New York: Oxford University Press.

Lazarus, R.S., & Folkman, S. (1984). *Stress, appraisal, and coping.* New York: Springer.

Leiter, M.P. (1991). The dream denied: Professional burnout and the constraints of service organizations. *Canadian Psychology, 32*, 547–558.

Leiter, M.P., Frizzell, C., Harvie, P., & Churchill, L. (2001). Abusive interactions and burnout: Examining occupation, gender, and the mediating role of community. *Psychology and Health, 16*, 547–563.

Leiter, M.P., & Maslach, C. (1998). Burnout. In H. Friedman (Ed.) *Encyclopedia of mental health* (pp. 202–215). New York: Academic Press.

Leiter, M.P., & Maslach, C. (2000). Burnout and health. In A. Baum, T. Revenson, & J. Singer (Eds.) *Handbook of health psychology* (pp. 415–426). Hillsdale, NJ: Lawrence Erlbaum.

Leiter, M.P., & Maslach, C. (2004). Areas of worklife: A structured approach to organizational predictors of job burnout. In P.L. Perrewe & D.C. Ganster (Eds.), *Research in occupational stress and well-being* (Vol. 3, 91–134). Oxford, UK: Elsevier.

Leiter, M.P., & Maslach, C. (2005). A mediation model of job burnout. In A.S.G. Antoniou & C.L. Cooper (Eds.), *Research companion to organizational health psychology* (pp. 544–564). Cheltenham, UK: Edward Elgar.

Leiter, M.P., & Maslach, C. (2009). Burnout and workplace injuries: A longitudinal analysis. In A.M. Rossi, J.C. Quick, & P.L. Perrewe (Eds.), *Stress and quality of working life: The positive and the negative* (3–18). Greenwich, CT: Information Age.

LePine, J.A., LePine, M.A., & Saul, J.R. (2007). Relationships among work and non-work challenge and hindrance stressors and non-work and work criteria: A model of cross-domain stressor effects. In P.L. Perrewé & D.C. Ganster (Eds.), *Research in occupational stress and well being. Volume 6: Exploring the work and non-work interface* (pp. 35–72). Amsterdam: Elsevier Ltd.

LePine, J.A., Podsakoff, N.P., & LePine, M.A. (2005). A meta-analytic test of the challenge stressor-hindrance stressor framework: An explanation for inconsistent relationships among stressors and performance. *Academy of Management Journal, 48*, 764–775.

Licht, C., de Gues, E., Seldenrijk, A., van Hout, H., Zitman, F., van Dyck, R. et al. (2009). Depression is associated with decreased blood pressure, but antidepressant use increases the risk for hypertension. *Hypertension, 53*, 631–638.

Lind, E.A., & van den Bos, K. (2002). When fairness works: Toward a general theory of uncertainty management. *Research in Organizational Behavior, 24,* 181–223.

Liu, Y., Ferris, G.R., Zinko, R., Perrewé, P.L., Weitz, B., & Xu, J. (2007). Dispositional antecedents and outcomes of political skill in organizations: A four-study investigation with convergence. *Journal of Vocational Behavior, 71,* 146–165.

Machiavelli, N. *The Prince,* http://www.constitution.org/mac/prince00.htm.

Martin, N.H., & Sims, J.H. (1974). Power tactics. In D.A. Kolb, I.M. Rubin, & J.M. McIntyre (Eds.), *Organizational psychology: A book of readings.* Englewood Cliffs, NJ: Prentice-Hall.

Maslach, C. (1982). *Burnout: The cost of caring.* Englewood Cliffs, NJ: Prentice-Hall.

Maslach, C. (1993). Burnout: A multidimensional perspective. In W.B. Schaufeli, C. Maslach, & T. Marek (Eds.), *Professional burnout: Recent developments in theory and research* (19–32). Washington, DC: Taylor & Francis.

Maslach, C., & Leiter, M.P. (1997). *The truth about burnout.* San Francisco, CA: Jossey-Bass.

Maslach, C., & Leiter, M.P. (2008). Early predictors of job burnout and engagement. *Journal of Applied Psychology, 93,* 498–512.

Maslach, C., & Jackson, S.E. (1986). *MBI: The Maslach Burnout Inventory Manual, Research Edition.* Palo Alto, CA: Consulting Psychologists Press.

Maslach, C., Schaufeli, W.B., & Leiter, M.P. (2001). Job burnout. *Annual review of Psychology, 52,* 397–422.

Mayes, B.T. & Allen, R.W. (1977). Toward a definition of organizational politics. *Academy of Management Review, 2,* 672–678.

Mayes, B.T., & Ganster, D.C. (1988). Exit and voice: A test of hypotheses based on fight/flight responses to job stress. *Journal of Organizational Behavior, 9,* 199–216.

McEwen, B.S. (1998). Stress, adaptation, and disease. Allostatis and allostatic load. *Annals of the New York Academy of Sciences, 840,* 33–44.

McGrath, J.E. (1976). Stress and behavior in organizations. In M.D. Dunnette (Ed.), *Handbook of industrial and organizational psychology* (pp. 1351–1395). Chicago: Rand McNally Co., Inc.

Mechanic, D. (1962). Sources of power of lower level participants. *Administrative Science Quarterly, 7,* 349–364.

Meurs, J.A., Galagher, V.C., & Perrewe, P.L. (2010). The role of political skill in the stressor-outcome relationship: Differential predictions for self- and other-reports of political skill. *Journal of Vocational Behavior, 76,* 520–533.

Miller, B.K., Rutherford, M.A., & Kolodinsky, R.W. (2008). Perceptions of organizational politics: A meta-analysis of outcomes. *Journal of Business and Psychology, 22,* 209–222.

Miller, J., & Miller, M. (2005). Get a life! *Fortune, 152*(11), 109–117.

Mintzberg, H. (1983). *Power in and around organizations.* Englewood Cliffs, NJ: Prentice-Hall.

Munyon, T.P., Breaux, D.M., & Perrewé, P.L. (2009). Implications of burnout for health professionals. In A. Antoniou, G. Chrousos, C.L. Cooper, M.W. Eysenck, & C.D. Spielberger (Eds.), *Handbook of managerial behavior and occupational health* (pp. 264–277). London: Edward Elgar.

Newman, W.H. (1968). Strategic considerations in planning. In D.R. Hampton, C.E. Summer, & R.A. Webber (Eds.), *Organizational behavior and the practice of management.* Glenview, IL: Scott, Foresman, & Co.

Nonis, S.A., Sager, J.A., & Kumar, K. (1996). Salesperson use of upward influence strategies in coping up role stress. *Academy of Marketing Science Journal, 24,* 44–56.

O'Driscoll, M.P., & Beehr, T.A. (1994). Supervisor behaviors, role stressors and uncertainty as predictors of personal outcomes for subordinates. *Journal of Organizational Behavior, 15*, 141–155.

Patchen, M. (1974). The locus and basis of influence on organizational decisions. *Organizational Behavior and Human Decision Performance, 11*, 195–221.

Pettigrew, A.M. (1973). *The politics of organizational decision-making.* London: Tavistock Publications Ltd.

Perrewé, P.L., Ferris, G.R., Frink, D.D., & Anthony, W.P. (2000). Political skill: An antidote to workplace stressors. *The Academy of Management Executive, 14*, 115–123.

Perrewé, P.L., Zellars, K.L., Ferris, G.R., Rossi, A.M., Kacmar, C.J., & Ralston, D.A. (2004). Neutralizing job stressors: Political skill as an antidote to the dysfunctional consequences of role conflict stressors. *Academy of Management Journal, 47*, 141–152.

Perrewé, P.L., Zellars, K.L., Rossi, A.M., Ferris, G.R., Kacmar, C.J., Liu, Y., et al. (2005). Political skill: An antidote in the role overload–strain relationship. *Journal of Occupational Health Psychology, 10*, 239–250.

Pfeffer, J. (1981). *Power in organizations.* Boston: Pitman.

Pfeffer, J. (1992). *Managing with power: Politics and influence in organizations.* Boston: Harvard Business School Press.

Pieper, S., & Brosschot, J.F. (2005). Prolonged stress-related cardiovascular activation: Is there any? *Annals of Behavioral Medicine, 30*, 91–103.

Pieper, S., Brosschot, J.F., Van der Leeden, R., & Thayer, J.F. (2007). Cardiac effects of momentary assessed worry episodes and stressful events. *Psychosomatic Medicine, 69*, 901–909.

Piotrkowski, C.S. (1979). *Work and the family system: A naturalistic study of the working-class and lower-middle-class families.* New York: Free Press.

Podsakoff, N.P., LePine, J.A., & LePine, M.A. (2007). Extending the challenge stressor–hindrance stressor framework: A meta-analytic test of differential relationships with job attitudes and retention criteria. *Journal of Applied Psychology, 92*, 438–454.

Quick, J.C., Quick, J.D., Nelson, D.L., & Hurrell, J.J. (1997). *Preventative stress management in organizations* (2nd Ed.). Washington, DC: American Psychological Association.

Ragins, B.R., & Dutton, J.E. (2007). Positive relationships at work: An introduction and invitation. In J.E. Dutton & B.R. Ragins (Eds.) *Exploring positive relationships at work: building a theoretical and research foundation.* Mahwah, NJ: Lawrence Erlbaum.

Reis, H.T., Sheldon, K.M., Gable, S., Roscoe, J., & Ryan, M. (2000). Daily well-being: The role of autonomy, competence, and relatedness. *Personality and Social Psychological Bulletin, 25*, 419–435.

Rice, R.W., Frone, M.R., & McFarlin, D.B. (1992). Work–family conflict and the perceived quality of life. *Journal of Organizational Behavior, 13*, 155–168.

Rodell, J.B., & Judge, T.A. (2009). Can "good" stressors spark "bad" behaviors? The mediating role of emotions in links of challenge and hindrance stressors with citizenship and counterproductive work behaviors. *Journal of Applied Psychology, 94*, 1438–1451.

Rosen, C.C., Chang, C.-H., Djurdjevic, E., & Eatough, E. (2010). Occupational stressors and job performance: An updated review and recommendations. In P.L. Perrewé & D.C. Ganster (Eds.), *Research in occupational stress and well-being* (pp. 1–60). Amsterdam: Elsevier.

Rosen, C.C., Chang, C.-H., Johnson, R.E., & Levy, P.E. (2009). Perceptions of the organizational context and psychological contract breach: Assessing competing perspectives. *Organizational Behavior and Human Decision Processes, 108*, 202–217.

Rosen, C.C., Chang, C.-H., & Levy, P.E. (2006). Organizational politics and personality: Past, present, and future. In E. Vigoda-Gadot & A. Drory (Eds.) *Handbook of organizational politics* (pp. 29–52). Cheltenham, UK: Edward-Elgar.

Rosen, C.C., Harris, K.J., & Kacmar, K.M. (2009). The emotional implications of perceived organizational politics: A process model. *Human Relations, 62*, 27–57.

Rosen, C.C., Harris, K.J., & Kacmar, K.M. (2010). LMX, context perceptions, and performance: An uncertainty management perspective. *Journal of Management.*

Ryan, R.M., Huta, V., & Deci, E.L. (2008). Living well: A self-determination theory perspective on eudaimonia. *Journal of Happiness Studies, 9*, 139–170.

Schaubroeck, J. & Ganster, D.C. (1993). Chronic demands and responsivity to challenge. *Journal of Applied Psychology, 78*, 73–85.

Schaufeli, W.B., & Bakker, A.B. (2004). Job demands, job resources, and their relationship with burnout and engagement. *Journal of Organizational Behavior, 25*, 293–315.

Schaufeli, W.B., Bakker, A.B., Hoogduin, K., Schaap, C., & Kladler, A. (2001). The clinical validity of the Maslach Burnout Inventory and the Burnout Measure. *Psychology and Health, 16*, 565–582.

Schaufeli W.B., & Enzmann D. (1998). *The burnout companion to study & practice: A critical analysis.* Philadelphia: Taylor & Francis.

Schriesheim, C.A., Castro, S.L., & Cogliser, C.C. (1999). Leader–member exchange (LMX) research: A comprehensive review of theory, measurement, and data-analytic practices. *Leadership Quarterly, 10*, 63–113.

Schuler, R.S. (1980). Definition and conceptualization of stress in organizations. *Organzational Behavior and Human Performance, 25*, 184–215.

Selye, H. (1955). Stress and disease. *Science, 122*, 625–631.

Selye, H. (1974). *Stress without distress.* Philadelphia: JB Lippincott.

Semmer, N., Grebner, S., & Elfering, A. (2004). Beyond self-report: Using observational, physiological, and situation-based measures in research on occupational stress. In P.L. Perrewé & D.C. Ganster (Eds.), *Research in occupational stress and well-being, Volume 3: Emotional and physiological processes and positive intervention Strategies* (pp. 205–263). Amsterdam: Elsevier.

Sias, P.M. (2005). Workplace relationship quality and employee information experiences. *Communication Studies, 56*, 375–395.

Spector, P.E., & Jex, S.M. (1998). Development of four self-report measures of job stressors and strain: Interpersonal conflict at work scale, organizational constraints scale, quantitative workload inventory, and physical symptoms inventory. *Journal of Occupational Health Psychology, 3*, 356–367.

Sterling, P., & Eyer, J. (1988). Allostasis: A new paradigm to explain arousal pathology. In S. Fisher & J. Reason (Eds.), *Handbook of life stress, cognition, and health* (pp. 629–649). New York: Wiley.

Strauss, G. (1962). Tactics of lateral relationships: The purchasing agent. *Administrative Science Quarterly, 7*, 161–168.

Tangirala, S., & Alge, B.J. (2006). Reactions to unfair events in computer-mediated groups: A test of uncertainty management theory. *Organizational Behavior and Human Decision Processes, 100*, 1–20.

Thau, S., Aquino, K., & Wittek, R. (2007). An extension of uncertainty management theory to the self: The relationship between justice, social comparison orientation, and antisocial work behaviors. *Journal of Applied Psychology, 92*, 250–258.

Thibaut, J., & Walker, L. (1975). *Procedural justice: A psychological analysis.* Hillsdale, NJ: Lawrence Erlbaum.

Treadway, D.C., Hochwarter, W.A., Kacmar, C.J., & Ferris, G.R. (2005). Political will, political skill, and political behavior. *Journal of Organizational Behavior, 26,* 229–245.

Treadway, D.C., Ferris, G.R., Duke, A.B., Adams, G.L., & Thatcher, J.B. (2007). The moderating role of subordinate political skill on supervisors' impressions of subordinate ingratiation and ratings of subordinate interpersonal facilitation. *Journal of Applied Psychology, 92,* 848–855.

Vahey, D.C., Aiken, L.H., Sloane, D.M., Clarke, S.P., & Vargas, D. (2004). Nurse burnout and patient satisfaction. *Medical Care, 24*(2), 57–66.

Valle, M., & Perrewé, P.L. (2000). Do politics perceptions relate to political behaviors? *Human Relations, 53,* 359–386.

Valle, M., & Witt, L.A. (2001). The moderating effect of teamwork perceptions on the organizational politics–job satisfaction relationship. *Journal of Social Psychology, 141,* 379–388.

van den Bos, K., & Lind, E.A. (2002). Uncertainty management by means of fairness judgments. In M. P. Zanna (Ed.), *Advances in experimental social psychology* (Vol. 34, pp. 1–60). San Diego, CA: Academic Press.

van den Bos, K., Lind, E.A., Vermunt, R., & Wilki, H.A.M. (1997). How do I judge my outcome when I do not know the outcome of others? The psychology of the fair process effect. *Journal of Personality and Social Psychology, 72,* 1034–1046.

van den Bos, K., Wilke, H.A.M., & Lind, E.A. (1998). When do we need procedural fairness? The role of trust in authority. *Journal of Personality and Social Psychology, 72,* 95–104.

Vigoda, E. (2002). Stress-related aftermaths of workplace politics: The relationship among politics, job distress, and aggressive behaviors in organizations. *Journal of Organizational Behavior, 23,* 571–591.

Westman, M. (2001). Stress and strain crossover. *Human Relations, 54,* 717–751.

Westman, M. (2006). Crossover of stress and strain in the work–family context. In F. Jones, R.J. Burke, & M. Westman (Eds.), *Work–life balance: A psychological perspective* (pp. 163–184). New York: Psychology Press.

Westman, M., Brough, P., & Kalliath, T. (2009). Expert commentary on work–life balance and crossover of emotions and experiences: Theoretical and practice advancements. *Journal of Organizational Behavior, 30,* 587–595.

Witt, L.A., Andrews, M.C., & Kacmar, K.M. (2000). The role of participation in decision-making in the organizational politics–job satisfaction relationship. *Human Relations, 53,* 341–358.

Xie, J.L., & Johns, G. (1995). Job scope and stress: Can job scope be too high? *Academy of Management Journal, 38,* 1288–1309.

Zellars, K., Perrewé, P.L., & Hochwarter, W.A. (1999). Mitigating burnout among high NA employees in health care: What can organizations do? *Journal of Applied Social Psychology, 29,* 2250–2271.

Zivnuska, S., Kacmar, K.M., Witt, L.A., Carlson, D.S., & Bratton, V.K. (2004). Interactive effects of impression management and organizational politics on job performance. *Journal of Organizational Behavior, 25,* 627–640.

9

How Organizational Climates Reflect the Motives of Those in Power

Lawrence R. James
Georgia Institute of Technology

Rustin D. Meyer
Georgia Institute of Technology

The initial intent of this chapter was to discuss how organizational climates reflect the motives of those in power. We remain somewhat on course in regard to this objective, in that the chapter discusses how some powerful leaders engender several types of climate. This discussion focuses on what is referred to as *channeling models*. As used here, channeling models begin with the hypothesis that the greater the desire for power, the greater the likelihood of engaging in political behaviors (i.e., tactics intended to accrue, exercise, and sustain influence). However, the channels through which this influence is exercised primarily are dependent on personality factors other than the need for power; that is, the expression of leaders' need for power is channeled through their other motives.

To elucidate precisely how this process works, the focus is on the channeling influence of two additional motives. First, it is argued that people who are high in need for power and are *also* aggressive will prefer influence tactics that bring harm to others, such as when leaders act as catalysts for interdepartmental conflict. The end result of this "high–high" motive profile is a toxic organizational climate wherein subordinates are exploited and competitors eliminated. Second, it is argued that people who are high in need for power but have a strong social awareness and concern for others will prefer influence tactics that bring cohesion to the group, such as when leaders act as catalysts for cooperation. The end result of this "high–low" motive profile is a developmental organizational climate wherein subordinates are nurtured.

Thus, the primary point is that a strong need for power should not be vilified as an inherently unsavory characteristic. Instead, it is posited here that the combination of a high need for power and aggressiveness engenders toxic organizational climates, which then lead to a downward spiral of political retribution and dehumanization. However, when a high need for power is coupled with a sense of concern and social awareness, climates are created that typify the very essence of what is healthy and good about effective leadership.

As we began to search the extant literature in politics to build our channeling models, it became clear that the study of organizational politics may be heading down the same road that leadership has traveled. That is, considerable effort has been devoted to documenting what it is that leaders do with little or no understanding of why they do it. In particular, the field of leadership has been strangely quiet as to what motivates people to be leaders in the first place. This is a problem because until we understand why people seek a particular objective, we will never fully understand why they engage in the behaviors that they use to obtain it (Allport, 1937; Murray, 1938).

Simply describing those who seek to exercise influence and those who do not, the methods and techniques of gaining and exercising influence, and the political skill a person has is a useful start, but not a psychologically meaningful end state (Vroom & Jago, 2007). Also, as with leadership, such a strategy will miss a main component of the essence of political behavior in organizations. So, the focus was shifted to aim at beginning to build an explanation of why, within the set of those who seek power and influence in organizations, different leaders use different influence (political) tactics.

THE DESIRE FOR POWER OR THE POWER MOTIVE

Human personality is often shaped by how people deal with basic conflicts both within and between conscious and unconscious motives (Allport, 1937; Murray, 1938; Westen, 1990, 1991). An example is the basic conflict between fight versus flight. In the face of danger or challenge, a small proportion of people are predisposed to fight whereas the majority of people are predisposed to seek safety. Over time, some of those predisposed to fight develop a fondness for fighting and hurting others, which evolves into an implicit motive to harm others. This is the basis for the aggressive personality (James & LeBreton, 2010; James et al., 2005).

In the realm of power, leadership, and organizational politics, an additional conflict is dominance versus submissiveness. Research findings have demonstrated that effective leaders often are socially skilled individuals who strive to be dominant (Foti & Hauenstein, 2007; Judge, Bono, Ilies, & Gerhardt, 2002; McClelland & Boyatzis, 1982; Stricker & Rock, 1998; Veroff, 1992; Winter, 1973, 1992). These individuals want to be leaders (Chan & Drasgow, 2001) and are willing to devote years to attaining the experience and knowledge required to be effective and successful leaders (Yukl, 2009). As they gain knowledge and experience, effective leaders undergo increasing internal pressures to exert their will on decisions that determine the directions taken by their organizations (Resick, Whitman, Weingarden, & Hiller, 2009; Veroff, 1992; Winter, 1973). They believe that their organizations should follow the most rational and strategic courses of action, and they are increasingly confident that they know what these courses are (McClelland, 1985; Winter, 1992).*

On the surface, strategic decision making is pretty much as it appears. Throughout human evolution, leaders have been responsible for strategic decisions that affect the survival of their social collectives (e.g., family, clan, kingdom, government, military organization, social institution, business; see Finkelstein & Hambrick, 1996; Hambrick, Finkelstein, & Mooney, 2005; Van Vugt, Hogan, & Kaiser, 2008). This broad mission is dependent on leaders' abilities to reason and solve problems in ways that engender the safety and security of the collective (e.g., protect the collective from enemies), assist the collective in acquiring resources (e.g., food, donations, raw materials, financing), promote efficient coordination and cooperation among components of the collective (e.g., design an organizational structure), oversee human relations issues (e.g., selection, promotion, administration of justice), and provide for effective delivery of a product (e.g., knowledge dissemination, art, health care, warfare, transportation, investments).

However, what is missing is an explanation of why only some people seek to exert their wills via positions of dominance in organizations when others do not. Specifically, what is it psychologically that motivates a person to seek influence and impact? Why do only some people attempt to attain positions where they can affect courses of events by influencing how people think (e.g., decisions they make), feel (e.g., how stressed are

---

* We have drawn liberally on a recent discussion of the power motive by James et al. (in press; to appear in Landis and Cortina). Also, we have added new material to the present discussion.

they), and act (e.g., how they perform; Foti & Hauenstein, 2007; House, Spangler, & Woycke, 1991; Judge et al., 2002; McClelland & Boyatzis, 1982; Winter, 1973)? These authors believe the answer is the need for power, often referred to as the *power motive* (Winter, 1973).

Our research, which is in the early stages, suggests that approximately 20% of people are predisposed to seek positions of influence and dominance in organizations. Underlying this tendency appears to be a desire to exert one's will over others, which draws sustenance from a sense of inner strength, forcefulness, and personal efficacy (e.g., intellectual, physical, devotional) that qualify the person to command the attention of others and to lead them (McClelland, 1985; Veroff, 1992; Winter, 1973, 1992). This is the essence of the power motive; it involves an intense desire to exert one's will over others because one is personally potent and forceful, superior in one or more ways, and thus highly qualified to influence others. It is accompanied by desires to control events or at least to have considerable influence over them. Also, it is accompanied by the desire to act effectively and to lead others to successful accomplishments (Winter, 1973).

Not surprisingly, the power motive is thought to be primarily implicit (McClelland, 1985; Veroff, 1992; Winter, 1973). Motives tend to be implicit (i.e., not accessible to introspection) because they involve desires that, if known to the possessors of the motive, would cause them to experience guilt, anxiety, disbelief, or embarrassment (Bandura, 1999; Baumeister, Campbell, Krueger, & Vohs, 2003; Cramer, 1998, 2000, 2006). The norms of society for socially adaptive behavior focus on personal rights, equality, egalitarian power sharing, teamwork, participative decision making, and the avoidance of selfish, self-aggrandizing activities, such as the seeking of status, privilege, entitlements, and personal power as primary goals.

Most people, including those with strong power motives, tend to internalize the ideologies and arguments that support these socially normative behaviors and beliefs as part of being socialized (James et al., 2005). Their conscious thinking about what constitutes reasonable and socially appropriate behavior in social situations, including work situations, is shaped by these internalized ideologies and arguments. It is simply not acceptable to most people with strong power motives to consciously think of themselves as having intense desires to exert their wills over others, because their inner strength, superior intelligence (or attractiveness, strength, devotion), and skills at persuasion entitle them to dominate and control others (an exception would be narcissists with strong power motives).

Nonetheless, the power motive does assert itself because people who possess the motive are strongly attracted to positions of dominance, influence, and control (Bargh & Alvarez, 2001; Chen, Lee-Chai, & Bargh, 2001; House et al., 1991; Winter, John, Stewart, Klohnen, & Duncan, 1998). What makes the seeking of these positions consciously acceptable to people with strong power motives is the use of biases to cover the true driving force of their desires to exert their wills. Specifically, people with strong power motives often engage in the use of cognitive biases that allow them to disengage ideologies and arguments against the seeking of power (see Bandura, 1999 on moral disengagement), to neutralize societal norms that disapprove of the seeking of power (see Sykes & Matza, 1957 on neutralization techniques), and to build self-illusionary logical rationales (i.e., rationalizations) for seeking to control others (see the following discussion).

In the discussion that follows, these cognitive biases are referred to as *justification mechanisms* (JMs). Also, an attempt is made to show that the understanding of the power motive is perhaps best accomplished by studying the operation of the self-deceptive biases that people who possess the motive use to rationalize the seeking of power. Then, it is argued that the specific form of these self-deceptive biases influence the specific political tactics that individuals use to attain and maintain power, which in turn help to shape organizational climate.

However, first there is a need to address the fact that discussions of the power motive seldom consider the latent driving forces behind the seeking of influence. Rather, they tend to focus on the extrinsic rewards that accrue to leaders who hold positions of influence. We do not deny that extrinsic rewards play an important role in the acquisition of power; indeed, it is posited that they influence the channeling process by helping to provide a type of rational cover under which one's true motives can be concealed. Position and power bestow a leader with status, prestige, privilege, access to an unequal distribution of resources, and, frequently, enlarged wealth (Overbeck, 2010). Increases in status and prestige help to satisfy ego needs and to enhance a person's sense of self-worth (Maslow, 1954). The privileges, prestige, and resources that accrue from attaining rank and position in an authority hierarchy also are conducive to feelings of significance, pride, accomplishment, and mastery (Kipnis, 1976; see also McClelland, 1985; McClelland, Koestner, & Weinberger, 1989; Winter, 1973, 1992).

Status, prestige, privilege, unequal distributions of resources, and the like are natural byproducts of the evolutionary proclivity of humans to arrange themselves into hierarchical authority structures (Bargh & Alvarez, 2001; McAdams & Pals, 2006; Van Vugt et al., 2008). Presumably, these incentives came about as means for the group to attract and reward competent and trustworthy people who were willing to step forward and take on the responsibilities of initiating and directing actions that promote group welfare and keep the group safe and secure.

The *evolved leader psychology* (Van Vugt et al., 2008, p. 182) is that good leaders are also willing to share their resources generously with their followers. Moreover, they are expected to engage in egalitarian (e.g., democratic, delegated, participative) forms of leadership whenever possible. Also, they are expected to make strategic decisions that place the welfare of the group ahead of their personal ambitions and gains. It is acceptable to have status and privilege in the evolved leader psychology as long as one is not ostentatious about it and perhaps is even a bit uncomfortable with it.

Unfortunately, the seeking of power often is attributed to leaders' placing their personal ambition ahead of group welfare (see Bargh & Alvarez, 2001), which is not acceptable in the evolved leader psychology model. This negative attribution stimulates visions of leaders who are willing to engage in force, threat, and coercion to gain power, privileges, and resources. According to the evolved leader psychology (Van Vugt et al., 2008), when it appears that leaders are motivated by personal gain, individuals hark back to domains ruled by chieftains and warlords. These domains often were (are) subject to tyranny, threat, exploitation, greed, class warfare, and oppression by aggressive individuals representing soldier classes and narcissistic ruling elites. It is a vision of dominance and oppression that conflicts strongly with implicit theories of what constitutes good leadership (see Lord, Foti, & DeVader, 1984), and it may fuel a sense of reactance toward the idea that a high-power motive can serve as a healthy and beneficial characteristic among leaders.

We agree with scholars such as Bargh and Alvarez (2001) who argued that a general tendency exists, especially in some social science circles, to denigrate power motives because the motives are thought to be energized primarily by self-centered if not aggressive desires (e.g., the seeking of status, privilege, and unequal resources, or worse, by desires to oppress, force, corrupt, and tyrannize). However, it is believed that vilifying the power motive has stifled scientific interest in it and retarded attempts to develop objective ways to measure it. As a result, the field of leadership has done little to advance understanding of a key motivational factor that drives and shapes the reasoning and behaviors of leaders (Hogan & Kaiser, 2005; Kaiser, Hogan, & Craig, 2008; Vroom & Jago, 2007). Indeed, Winter (1992) was one of the first to note that the field of leadership misses the mark, when he observed that the seeking of power in the United States is associated with "suspicions, doubts, and denials" (p. 302). Winter (p. 302) went on to state:

> Leaders almost never say that their actions are motivated by a desire for power; instead they talk of "service" or "duty." As a result, one might expect Americans to be defensive or unaware of their power motivation....

People with strong power motives may be defensive or unaware of what motivates them, but they nonetheless feel compelled to exert their will over others. How then do they deal with the prevailing social stereotype that power should be treated with suspicion, because it is associated with exploitation, inevitable corruption, and coercion? At least as important is how do they deal with the fact that the motivation for the seeking of power does involve socially disagreeable characteristics, namely, the belief that one's inner strength and superior characteristics place one ahead of others in regard to commanding the attention of others and leading them? How do they disengage ideologies and arguments against the seeking of power and neutralize societal norms that disapprove of the seeking of power?

A strong part of the answers to these questions is that, like any motive that has garnered social disapproval, the exercise of the power motive is protected by defense mechanisms (see Cramer, 2006). It is believed that the defense mechanism of rationalization is of particular interest in regard to the power motive. This is because people with strong power motives often justify exerting their wills by embedding their actions in strategic decision making. The propensity to select their own personal strategies is attributed to the objective merit and rational superiority of these strategies over the strategies proposed by others (see Pfeffer, 1994).

In most cases, people with a strong power motive do not think that they are seeking or exercising power. Rather, they see themselves as thinking rationally and arriving at the best strategic decisions, which is the primary evolutionary function of leadership (Van Vugt et al., 2008). In fact, their decision making often does have objective and rational components. In addition, however, it often is molded by unseen forces that serve the defense mechanism of rationalization. This means that the reasoning gives rational support to the release of the implicit power motive. Another way of saying this is that people for whom the power motive directs behavior have developed ways of reasoning that make exerting *their* wills appear to be rational and sensible.

Again, these ways of reasoning help to enhance the rational appeal of power, and therefore, are referred to as *justification mechanisms* (James, 1998; James & LeBreton, 2010; James et al., in press), which operate from below the level of consciousness (i.e., implicitly) to direct reasoning in predetermined ways (a bias). Reasoning focuses on building logical support (i.e., a defense) for releasing an underlying desire to use power. It is this desire to exert one's will over others that serves the motivation to lead and gives impetus to achieving significant outcomes as a leader.

Justification Mechanisms for Power

Individual differences in desires to exercise power have received comparatively little scientific attention (see Overbeck, 2010). James et al. (in press) studied the extant but scant professional literature to gain insights into how people with strong power motives build seemingly objective and rational cases for exercising their wills. This search involved attempts to uncover the implicit or unconscious biases that shape the interpretations people with strong power motives place on power activities and the slants in logic they use to argue for the rationality of strategic decisions that involve a personal use of power.

James et al. (in press) indentified four justification mechanisms for power, each of which helps people with strong power motives (hereafter referred to as POs) to build strategic decisions that rationalize their use of power. These four justification mechanisms comprise an initial but developable set of biases that enable the release of the power motive. No claim was made that these four justification mechanisms exhaust the entire set of salient justification mechanisms for power. However, they do appear to offer a reasonable base on which to begin studies of how to measure the strength of a person's power motive.

Agentic Bias

When attempting to think rationally and objectively about strategic decisions, POs instinctively take the perspective of the agents or initiators of actions (see Moskowitz, 1994; Overbeck, 2010; Veroff, 1992; Winter, 1992). Consequently, their thinking often reflects a propensity to confirm (e.g., build logical support for) the agents' ideas, plans, and solutions. These ideas, plans, and solutions are viewed as providing logically superior strategic decisions. Whether others embrace these superior decisions is seen as determined by the agents' political skills to persuade, convince, and convert people to their ideas (House et al., 1991; Veroff, 1992). The adoption of strategic decisions is thus judged to be contingent on the superiority of the agents' reasoning skills and how effectively they influence others to follow their plans (see Hogan & Kaiser, 2005; Van Vugt et al., 2008; Yukl, 2009).

The key to the *agentic bias* is the *perspective* from which people frame and reason. POs instinctively look down; that is, they identify with the people who reside in management positions, create strategic plans, and then lead others to carry out the plans. People with weak or nonexistent power motives (referred to as NPs) instinctively look up; that is, when thinking about strategic decisions, they take the perspectives of those lower in the organization who are affected by the decisions and actions. Naturally, they think in terms of the implications and consequences of the decisions on the feelings and actions of followers like themselves.

To illustrate, suppose a group of people is told that employee theft usually decreases after surveillance cameras are installed in workplaces, but the cameras also make many employees nervous and unhappy. Individuals in the group are then asked to draw what they think represents the most salient and reasonable inference based on the information given. The NPs among the group instinctively will see this problem through the eyes of employees, and many will infer that employees are unhappy because surveillance cameras are perceived to be an invasion of privacy. In contrast, the POs in the group instinctively will see the problem through the eyes of those who must decide whether to install surveillance cameras. To them, the primary issue, based on the information given, is the seriousness of employee theft in a given company.

An implicit bias to think like a PO (or an NP) does not denote error, for one's predisposition to reason from the perspective of those in power, the agents or initiators of action, often engenders a plausible way of examining the problem. However, a purely rational model calls for dialectics, where the pros and cons of each of several possible points of view are considered (see James, 1998). The connotation of bias here is that one favors the point of view that is consistent with one's latent personality. POs may well subscribe consciously to the idea of multiple points of view and even may express strong beliefs that the pros and cons of each of these views need to be objectively evaluated. However, when tasked with analyzing specific real-world problems, POs instinctively and consistently will lean toward seeing the problems through the lens of an agent or initiator or controller of action.

However, NPs do not view the problem through the lens of a leader. This is because a considerable proportion of people, perhaps the majority, possess low or very modest power motives and typically neither seek nor enjoy leadership responsibilities (Chan & Drasgow, 2001; McClelland, 1985; Winter, 1973, 1992). A weak power motive denotes a low need to exercise one's will by attaining positions of influence, which indicates that a desire to exhibit impact and influence on others is not especially salient as a work career goal (Winter et al., 1998).

In more specific behavioral terms, a weak power motive often is manifested by not taking the initiative to lead groups and avoiding jobs that have supervisory responsibilities (Chan & Drasgow, 2001); never having run for office in school, clubs, or teams (Stricker & Rock, 1998); seldom if ever taking strong, forceful actions that affect others (Winter, 1992); avoiding situations which require taking responsibility for the welfare of others (Winter et al., 1998); passing on opportunities to plan and organize projects (Moskowitz, 1994); experiencing discomfort when attempting to persuade others that one's ideas are objectively superior (House et al., 1991); and seldom expressing disagreements with or criticism of those in authority (Moskowitz, 1994).

The data suggest that not all or even most people want to be leaders (Chan & Drasgow, 2001; Stricker & Rock, 1998). Some of these people have not only low power motives but also desire to be led (i.e., a full submissive). That is, some people prefer to be dependent on leaders for their survival and social welfare (Moskowitz, 1994; Winter, 1992; Winter et al., 1998). Others have strong desires to be independent or to be unharried by leadership responsibilities in order to pursue other types of objectives (e.g., create, write, build).

Many additional possibilities exist, but the key is that as a group these people share the common attribute of little to no aspiration toward power and leadership. The data support the idea that these people are unlikely to emerge as leaders (Kenny & Zaccaro, 1983) and that when placed in leadership positions they tend not to perform well because they lack the motivational and behavioral characteristics required to be effective leaders (Chan & Drasgow, 2001; Foti & Hauenstein, 2007; Judge et al., 2002; McClelland & Boyatzis, 1982; Stricker & Rock, 1998; Yukl, 2009).

Social Hierarchy Orientation

Reasoning from this orientation reflects implicit acceptance of hierarchical authority structures as the primary form of human organization. Reasoning often is based on the unstated, and for many POs unrecognized, premise that disproportionate influence, privilege, and distribution of resources are rational ways of organizing and leading (as opposed to egalitarian power structures; see Buss, 2005; Overbeck, 2010; Sidanius & Pratto, 1999; Simon & Oakes, 2006). As an example of this way of thinking, consider the following premise: Decision making in most companies is effective when managers are organized in terms of graded levels of authority, where they have a sphere of influence in which they are responsible for making decisions.

Members of a group of managers are asked to analyze this premise and, individually, to identify an unstated assumption on which it is based. POs in the group are predisposed to accept the premise that graded levels of authority and spheres of influence are rational ways of organizing many companies. The unstated assumptions they identify thus are likely to be supportive of the premise. An assumption such as the following is illustrative: Decisions can be made quickly without lengthy discussion or dissent.

NPs on the other hand are unlikely to be supportive of the premise because they do not implicitly accept hierarchical authority structures as the primary and most natural form of human organization (see Bargh & Alvarez, 2001; Van Vugt et al., 2008). In fact, they may be disposed to reason that power structures that involve disproportionate influence, privilege, and distributions of resources often produce less than optimal decisions. The unstated assumptions they identify thus are likely to be critical of the premise. An illustration of a subtle and indirect criticism is that the premise assumes that individuals can make better decisions than groups composed of diverse and knowledgeable individuals (place *incorrectly* in front of *assumes* to capture the true meaning of NPs).

Presumably, NPs are critical because they, like a great many people, subscribe to the evolved leader psychology that leadership is best when it is based on egalitarian (e.g., democratic, participative) forms of decision making (Lord et al., 1984; Van Vugt et al., 2008). Such thinking evolved from hunter–gatherer societies, where people experienced a sense of "empathetic responsiveness" to one another, a product of having experienced pleasures and suffered pain together (Bandura, 1999, p. 200). This sense of common togetherness and empathy engendered perceptions of similarity and common social obligations (Bandura, 1969), which is to say an egalitarian society. Their preferred leadership pattern also reflected empathetic responsiveness and was characterized by transitory, democratic, consensually appointed leaders whose power was limited to their areas of expertise (see Van Vugt et al., 2008). Hierarchical authority structures are viewed as necessary evils that need not have a permanent basis, when they are considered necessary for such things as defense of the collective (Van Vugt et al.).

Note that NP's preferred form of leadership allows people without strong desires to be leaders to be dependent on strong leadership when conditions call for strong leaders (e.g., the group is in peril of being attacked) and to have a voice in decisions that affect them in more stable and tranquil contexts. NPs will be receptive to reasoning that supports this form of leadership. On the other hand, POs may give explicit recognition to this leveling of the authority structures in stable and tranquil conditions, but their true, unstated, and often unrecognized allegiance is to hierarchically graded systems of power.

Power Attribution Bias

Reasoning with this bias reflects a predisposition to logically connect the use of power with positive behavior, values, and outcomes. Acts of power are interpreted in positive terms, such as taking initiative, assuming responsibility, and being decisive (McClelland, 1985; Russell, 1938; Veroff, 1992; Winter, 1973, 1992). These same acts logically are associated with positive outcomes, such as organizational survival, stability, effectiveness, and success. The powerful are viewed as talented, experienced, and successful leaders. In like manner, successful leadership rationally is attributed to the use of power.

The *power attribution bias* stands in contrast to the tendency of society, including a great many NPs, to correlate the exercise of power with entitlement, corruption, and tyranny (Kipnis, 1976; Lord Acton, 1865). More specifically, the power motive is held culpable for (1) placing personal gain ahead of group welfare; (2) the seeking of influence simply to dominate others; (3) the willingness to use threat and coercion to gain power, status, and entitlements; and (4) the building of organizations ruled by narcissistic tyrants who oppress, exploit, and victimize subordinates and employees (see Bargh & Alvarez, 2001; Chen et al., 2001; Kipnis, 1972; Lord Acton, 1865; Resick et al., 2009; Van Vugt et al., 2008).

NPs who make attributions that those seeking power are dishonest or corrupt believe their framing and analyses are logical and rational. Often, they bolster their arguments by pointing to specific examples from history where individuals sought power for corrupt, criminal, or self-serving purposes. On the other hand, POs are predisposed to infer that seeking power is necessary for the survival of the collective and the achievement of important goals. Also, they believe that their framing and analyses are logical and rational, and may point to examples from history supportive of their inferences (e.g., Abraham Lincoln).

Basically, POs' desire to engage in power clearly places them on the defensive in a climate that tends to frame power in derogatory terms. Justification mechanisms, such as the *Power attribution bias*, are needed to give POs ostensibly objective and rational reasons for engaging in acts of power (e.g., use of power *is necessary* [in the minds of POs] for organizational survival). It is the apparent objectivity and rationality of this reasoning that deflects the proclivities of NPs to seek less attractive attributions for POs' use of power.

Leader Intuition Bias

Decisions and actions appear more reasonable (to POs) when they are based on resources and strategies that confer power to the leader. A great many managers solve problems in much the same way as expert decision makers, analogous to grand chess masters who simply look at a chessboard and see potential winning strategies (see Kahneman & Klein, 2009). The experience and training of more mature leaders allows them to see promising strategies quickly. They differ from less experienced and less well-trained leaders in their "unusual ability to appreciate the dynamics of complex [situations] and quickly judge whether a [strategy] is promising or fruitless" (Kahneman & Klein, 2009, p. 515).

These "expert" decision makers often think of this process as reflecting their (leader) intuition (Klein, 1998). What these expert decision makers do not realize is that the ones among them who are POs are predisposed to intuitively think of strategies that confer power to themselves (i.e., or people like themselves, see McClelland, 1985; Winter, 1973, 1992). Among these expert decision makers, NPs will be significantly less prone to intuitively identity these same types of strategies as promising.

What likely has happened here is that, over the years, POs selectively attended to patterns and decisions that not only were efficacious, but also that involved resources that conveyed power to the leader. Examples of such resources include: (a) receiving recognition for such things as being an expert or a first-mover (French & Raven, 1959; Van Vugt et al., 2008; Winter, 1973); (b) being able to inflict pleasure (rewards) or pain (punishment) on subordinates (French & Raven, 1959); (c) being in the nexus of communication or influence structures (French & Raven, 1959); (d) being in control of resources (French & Raven, 1959); (e) functioning in hierarchical authority structures where one has personal responsibility for important decisions (Overbeck, 2010); and (f) working in cultures where the accumulation and exercise of power via forming alliances and coalitions is expected, even encouraged. The result of selective attention and learning is that strategies and actions that allow POs to develop a power base become part of their tacit knowledge structure. This tacit knowledge is accessed automatically (i.e., without awareness, Schneider & Shiffrin, 1977), which makes it appear as experience-based intuition of how to solve strategic problems (see Kahneman & Klein, 2009).

Like the *Agentic bias* above, it is important to note that the *Leader intuition bias* inherently involves organizational politics. As described by Pfeffer (1981) and reiterated by Ferris and Treadway (Chapter 1 in this volume), power, politics, and influence are intertwined. Power refers to the exercise of influence, politics refer to the means used to exercise influence (as illustrated in the preceding paragraph), and political skill refers to how accomplished one is in the use of the political influence strategies. Clearly, skilled use of political influence tactics is critical to the effective use of at least two of the four justification mechanisms. To use the *Agentic bias* to build a justification for exercising power is dependent upon the POs being able to persuade others to adopt their strategic decisions, and this requires the use of skilled influence tactics.

The *Leader intuition bias* suggests that POs develop and internalize these skilled influence tactics as they develop a tacit knowledge structure of how best to lead. Then, the tactics are used automatically as part of what appears to POs to be an intuitive understanding of leadership. NPs also may develop tacit knowledge structures, and then rely on experienced-based intuition to solve strategic decisions. However, these knowledge structures are unlikely to involve cognitive associations between effective leadership and resources that enhance the NPs' power. This is because NPs have no power motive to direct their perceptual process toward selectively attending to opportunities to exercise power.

Implications of JMs for Organizational Climate

It is important to note that these JMs set the stage for a basic organizational climate that reflects the fact that influence is being wielded by powerful individuals. That is, the climate that results from the mere fact that an organization is being led by a PO is qualitatively different from an organizational climate that would result if an NP were in-power (i.e., which does sometimes happen, typically via patrimony, appointment, small organization size, or chance). Specifically, the default organizational climate that develops out of the influence of POs and the relevant JMs they utilize includes: (a) a climate that favors the interests of those at the top, which stems of their use of the *Agentic bias*; (b) a certain level of insulation from the perspectives of those at lower levels, which stems from their use of the *Social hierarchy orientation*; (c) a climate wherein decisions are expected to be accepted without formal discussion or recourse, which comes from their use of the *Power attribution bias*; and (d) a climate wherein a given course of action is assumed to be just, correct, and so forth, simply because it represents the position of the status quo, which comes from their use of the *Leader intuition bias*. As seen later, there is nothing inherently wrong or evil about this baseline climate. Instead, what determines whether this power structure yields a positive or negative organizational climate largely is dictated by the additional motives that characterize those at the top. Again, this shaping of power by other personality variables is referred to as a "channeling model."

Channeling the Power Motive and Organizational Climates

As outlined previously, a strong power motive often sets in motion behaviors toward acquiring positions of leadership, exerting one's will over others, and the foundations of the baseline organizational climate outlined previously. However, the relationship between the power motive and how one actually exerts one's will, which is to say their politics or methods and techniques of influence (Ferris & Treadway, Chapter 1 in this volume), is not direct. There are many ways that the desire to exert oneself can be channeled into methods and techniques of influence, or as some would say, a style of leading. These styles include transformational (methods and techniques), charismatic, empowering, transactional, interpersonal, task oriented, laissez faire, and toxic. What direction this channeling takes largely is determined by personality variables other than the power motive (Bargh & Alvarez, 2001; Chen et al., 2001; House et al., 1991; James et al., in press; Winter et al., 1998).

To illustrate briefly, people who want to exert their wills and also are aggressive tend to channel their power motives into abusive and threatening behaviors that create toxic environments for their subordinates (Bargh & Alvarez, 2001; James et al., in press). People who are narcissistic tend to channel their power motives into arrogant and imperious forms of leadership (Resick et al., 2009). People who are nurturing, communal, and charismatic are prone to channel their power motives into transformational forms of leadership (Bargh & Alvarez, 2001; House et al., 1991). Extraverted people with strong power motives tend to value relationships with others as they attempt to fulfill their desires for impact. Introverted people with strong power motives tend to place less value on relationships and to avoid impactful careers that require extensive interactions with others (Winter et al., 1998).

Two forms of channeling are the focus of attention in this chapter. One form of channeling model focuses on how nurturing, communal, socially concerned and aware leaders channel their power motives into influence (political) strategies that advance the common good of the organization and society (e.g., Collins, 2001). They exercise their influence instrumentally; that is, they use influence to create climates that promote cooperation, maintain order, dispense justice, avoid conflict, develop people, and enhance productivity and profits—again, characteristics that are not inconsistent with the baseline climate outlined previously. This type of leader has been described as high in socialized power (McClelland & Boyatzis, 1982; Winter, 1973, 1992; Winter et al., 1998). The term *instrumental influence* is used to describe the strategies of these leaders and the climates they seek to create (i.e., a climate characterized by instrumental influence; see James & LeBreton, in press).

Another form of channeling model focuses on how aggressive leaders channel their power motives into influence (political) strategies that create toxic organizational climates. This channeling model was recently described in James et al. (in press) and James and LeBreton (in press). Aggression was chosen as a personality variable for channeling power because it was believed that power has been held culpable for abuses that were actually perpetrated by aggression. The countless abuses of power documented in papers and books over the history of humankind are noted. It is believed that power often is not the culprit for these abuses, and throughout history people have attributed to power what truly belongs to channeling variables involving other motives, such as aggression and narcissism. Aggression is a particularly worthy candidate for study. The description of the channeling models is initiated by considering aggressive people with strong power motives.

Toxic Leaders and Toxic Organizational Climates

The defining characteristic of aggressive people with strong power motives is that they seek and use power in ways that prove to be detrimental to those around them, organizations, or even themselves (e.g., Hogan & Kaiser, 2005; Kaiser et al., 2008; Kellerman, 2004). These are leaders who abuse their authority and engage in illegitimate uses of vested powers, often for self-aggrandizing reasons, such as the seeking of status and privilege (Bargh & Alvarez, 2001). These leaders are referred to as *toxic* when their abuses of power unfairly frustrate and hinder the performance, development, and advancement of qualified and motivated individuals, cause short- or long-term harm to the organization, or lead to self-destructive behaviors (Resick et al., 2009; Van Vugt et al., 2008). Organizations are referred to as having *toxic climates* when the abuses of the leader create situations characterized by unfair hindrance of the performance, development, and advancement of qualified and motivated individuals, which result in short- or long-term harm to the organization.

There are some who believe that access to, and sustained use of, power inherently is corrupting (e.g., Kipnis, 1976). In agreement with Bargh and Alvarez (2001), we believe this implicit theory is unsupportable. If it were valid, then it would follow logically that all leaders who accrue power necessarily become corrupt, which is not the case. Toxic leaders are not created by giving people power and allowing them to keep or to enhance it. Instead, toxic leaders are created by the fact that some people have a high need not only for power but also for aggression. The result of this *combination* is that they seek power in aggressive ways, and if they are successful in attaining power then they use it in aggressive ways, which is to say in ways that harm others. Examples of harmful behaviors include decisions that (1) unfairly frustrate and hinder the performance, development, and advancement of qualified and motivated individuals, (2) damage the organization's reputation or viability, or (3) endanger employees or customers.

In the following sections, this position is developed by providing an overview of the typical pattern of influence strategies used by toxic leaders, the biased types of reasoning that underlie their strategic decision making, and the idea that this engenders a toxic organizational climate.

The (Political) Influence Strategies Used by Toxic Leaders

People who seek and use power in aggressive ways (i.e., toxic leaders) often attempt to control others by use of intimidation, threat, force, and bribery. They frequently are viewed as bullies who exploit their followers for personal gain. If they do express interest in or concern for their subordinates, usually it is for an ulterior motive, such as gaining insight into their subordinates' views to better manipulate them. They have little real concern for people, their chief desire being to enhance their own power and entitlements. They may appear to be attentive and caring, but this is almost always done to make themselves "look good" so they can enhance their power and status (McClelland, 1985; Winter, 1973). Almost inevitability, their true nature eventually will be manifest in ways that harm the development or performance of their subordinates.

Toxic leaders evaluate tasks in terms of opportunities to gain recognition and power. Similarly, they evaluate risk in terms of the effects of outcomes on their personal power and reputation. Such leaders serve others primarily to extend their own power and status and are often proficient at manipulating and managing impressions of their superiors. They use their power to advance personal interests (e.g., wealth, prestige, prominence), and they evaluate others in terms of their title, status, pedigree, and reputation. Toxic leaders network and form relationships with others to enhance their opportunities to take dominant roles, with any consideration given to the effectiveness of their organizations taking a backseat to their personal ambitions and agenda (Winter, 1992).

Toxic leaders often exert their power just for the pleasure of seeing others submit. They tend to set impossible standards and then fire those who fail to satisfy them, to demand unquestioning loyalty and submission, to claim to be entitled to treatment that exceeds legitimate bounds of leader–subordinate relationships, and to actively create the false perception of conflict for scarce resources. These tactics often are exercised under the guise of order, justice, and success, but the true intent is to evoke a sense of unease among followers.

This toxicity may escalate to the level of hostility; illustrations include leaders who constantly ridicule and degrade subordinates, act as catalysts for dissension and conflict among peers and subordinates, or engage in harassment, including sexual harassment (Judge et al., 2006; Rosenthal & Pittinsky, 2006). Not surprisingly, not only do these actions create an environment of fear among subordinates, but they also communicate messages about what is considered appropriate behavior. Thus, when supervisors engage in these influence tactics, it eventually comes to be viewed as normative.

The willingness to cause injury and injustice to gain or retain power also may extend to unethical if not corrupt actions, such as breaking the law (e.g., financial transgressions) and then demanding that subordinates condone it and cover it up. Also, toxic leaders may place subordinates in harm's way for selfish gain (e.g., taking unwarranted and self-interested risks with employee pensions, setting subordinates up to "take the fall" for the leader's indiscretions). Toxic leaders' penchant for causing injury may turn inward and engender self-destructive behaviors, such as abuse of drugs and alcohol, excessive spending, sexual escapades, petty larceny (e.g., shoplifting), and increases in serious traffic violations, often the result of road rage (Hogan & Kaiser, 2005; Resick et al., 2009).

The Conditional Reasoning of Toxic Leaders

Toxic leaders think of power and strategic decision making in terms of their personal potency—that is, their ability to personally dominate, control, intimidate, assert their will, and instill fear (Winter, 1973). What they want from others is deference and submission, which they often frame as allegiance and respect. This proclivity to think of interactions with others as dominance contests, in which the objective is to take control by making others submit, is known as a *potency bias* (James et al., 2005).

Reasoning shaped by a potency bias furnishes toxic leaders with what to them is a rational basis for attaining and using personal power. Toxic leaders often frame people such as themselves as strong, assertive, brave, powerful, bold, and in control. These positive characterizations suggest that attempts to gain control over others by accruing personal power is not only reasonable but also laudatory. Perhaps at least as telling is toxic leaders' framing of leaders who do not seek personal potency. They think of such leaders as weak, impotent, timid, fearful, and not in control (James & Mazerolle, 2002). Thus, the presence of a climate wherein subordinates operate in fear and do not express their own will is viewed not only as acceptable but also as the norm associated with how to effectively manage others.

Such reasoning suggests that one of the great fears of toxic leaders is being seen as weak (Veroff, 1992). It indicates further that if their quest for dominance is frustrated and they are at risk of being seen as weak, then toxic leaders are prepared to use injurious and unjust methods to show that they are strong, powerful, bold, and in control (Baumeister et al., 2003; James & Mazerolle, 2002). In fact, their pride, honor, and self-respect are tied to their personal potency and status (Baumeister et al., 2003). Anything that threatens such potency and status is regarded as a form of personal disrespect and dishonor that is deserving of immediate retribution. Losing an argument or not being accorded the office with the greatest status are examples of triggers for retaliation. This proclivity for retaliation is known as the *retribution bias* (James et al., 2005).

Toxic leaders are not interested in sharing or delegating authority. Indeed, they regard questions about their ideas or plans, or any hesitation to implement them, as signs of mutiny (Winter, 1992). Moreover, toxic leaders believe that they are much more able than others to decipher hostility and disrespect in the words and actions of others. They think of themselves as having great skills to see clearly and intuitively into the true nature of human behavior. People with less insight and perceptiveness are thought to be blinded by their naiveté and goodness and thus fail to discern the dark side of human behavior (Hogan & Kaiser, 2005). However, the self-ascribed insight, perceptiveness, and intuitiveness of toxic leaders are illusionary. The true, but unrecognized, explanation for toxic leaders seeing hostility and disrespect in the actions of others is that they are paranoid, or in more contemporary terms, suffer from a *hostile attribution bias* (Dodge & Coie, 1987).

Proclivities to see hostile intentions in the actions of others and a desire to dominate relationships with these others often result in callous leadership styles and hostile work environments. An authoritarian, dictatorial, domineering style is especially likely if toxic leaders sense disloyalty, for they now feel the need to quell potential rebelliousness and to seek retribution for traitors to the cause. Paranoia, a desire to dominate, and a proclivity to seek retribution also can trigger other forms of unethical behavior, especially if these biases are accompanied by other biases, such as the judgment that one is being unfairly victimized by powerful others such as government agencies, a competitor, or organized labor (Bandura, 1999; Frost, Ko, & James, 2007).

To illustrate, a proclivity to believe that competitors use unfair business tactics to gain advantage to intentionally create financial distress for one's company (i.e., a hostile attribution bias) may be thought to justify issuing false reports of earnings to counteract potential damage. To toxic leaders, this is not an act of corruption but rather a justifiable act of self-defense. The illusion of rationality for corrupt behavior is strengthened if the unethical leader also is prone to think of regulations or even laws as rules built by bureaucrats that place unfair and often dysfunctional restrictions on competition. While toxic leaders may be of sufficient emotional intelligence to stifle their disdain for regulations and laws in typical circumstances, in times of stress, especially very intense stress triggered by survival instincts, they may give in to a natural proclivity to seek retribution in whatever way is necessary (James et al., 2005).

In sum, toxic leaders are driven by a desire for *personal* power or potency. Their reasoning is shaped by biases such as the potency bias, the retribution bias, and the hostile attribution bias. These biases allow them to justify engaging in toxic behaviors to enhance the self-perception that they are not weak but in fact are dominant and in control. Their toxicity often takes the form of the four types of unethical leader behaviors identified by Kellerman (2004): corruption, callousness, evil, and insularity. Several of these behaviors were illustrated, to which other activities (e.g., misinformation about costs, miscalculation of resources, lying about market demands, sabotage of competitors, exaggeration of earnings, not paying taxes, gambling employee pensions, dissolving healthy companies for short-term profits, and misinforming the public about the safety of a product) would be added (Kipnis, 1976).

The products of these activities are organizations with climates that are toxic to the people who work in them. That is, chronic exposure to corruption, callousness, sabotage, and general recklessness have direct and indirect negative effects on the lives and well-being of followers. This includes, but is not necessarily limited to stress, tension, collusion, paranoia and, perhaps worst of all, acceptance that toxic political maneuvers are not only acceptable but are also necessary means of survival in a dog-eat-dog world. Moreover, these organizations tend to be ineffective largely because they are full of alienated and demoralized followers (Van Vugt et al., 2008).

Identifying Toxic Leaders

Acts of aggression are protected by a unique set of justification mechanisms, which differ from those for power. The objective of the aggression justification mechanisms is to create the self-deception that acts of aggression can be justified as self-defense, attempts to restore honor, or legitimate strikes against injustice, disloyalty, or oppression. These rationalizations conceal from awareness the true but unacceptable cause of aggressive actions, namely, a willingness to harm others in pursuit of self-centered goals. The aggression justification mechanisms thus protect aggressive persons from realizing that they are truly hostile, malicious, or malevolent individuals (James & LeBreton, 2010; James et al., 2005).

Over the last 15 years, we have engaged in over 20 studies designed to develop and validate a conditional reasoning test that identifies aggressive individuals. The Conditional Reasoning Test for Aggression (CRT-A) has been the subject of more than 40 peer-reviewed papers and articles in respected scientific journals. It is now recognized as a leading instrument for identifying aggressive individuals in organizational settings (Landy, 2008). The ways aggression-based items have been melded with those designed to assess power motives to better detect potentially toxic leaders is described in James et al. (in press).

Leaders and Climates Characterized by Instrumental Influence

The key personality variable that channels the power motive into instrumental influence is social awareness and concern (McClelland, 1985; Winter, 1973, 1992). As noted earlier, leaders fitting this pattern use their influence to promote cooperation, maintain order, dispense justice, avoid conflict, develop people, and enhance productivity and profits. This socialized use of power suggests that the leaders serve as catalysts for successful accomplishments by others (McClelland, 1985).

Such leaders seek responsibility for directing others in the interest of seeing that the collective's goals are accomplished (Bass, 1985, 1990). They are willing to commit intense effort, over long periods of time if necessary, to helping people accomplish the collective's objectives. These leaders experience a sense of accomplishment and take pride not so much in their personal achievements as in the achievements of the collectives whose success they have taken responsibility for engineering (McClelland & Boyatzis, 1982). These leaders are referred to as *instrumental influencers* or simply *influencers.*

Instrumental influence carries with it a cost, namely, huge responsibilities for the welfare and success of the people whom one influences. Influencers must accept responsibility for maintaining a safe, stable, and secure climate, where people are treated with integrity, equity, and justice. They know that they will be held liable for the failures of their people and thus must develop, implement, and maintain influence networks that result in the overall success of their collectives. It is the process of satisfying these responsibilities that creates a sense of intrinsic satisfaction. The essence of instrumental influence lies in the commitments and sacrifices that a leader is willing to make to promote cooperation, maintain order, dispense justice, avoid conflict, develop people, and enhance productivity and profits (Avolio, Sosik, Jung, & Berson, 2003; Podsakoff, MacKenzie, Moorman, & Fetter, 1990).

Influencers are aware that people within the collective have values and goals that differ from their own. They seek to understand the needs, values, and hopes of their people (Bono & Judge, 2004). Being attentive to the moods, concerns, and ideas of others allows them to conceive and articulate visions that will be consistent with followers' needs, values, and hopes, thereby motivating the followers toward collective goals rather the leader's own self-interest (House et al., 1991). Influencers want people to be committed to their strategic vision and to work toward goals with enthusiasm and passion but in ways that make them feel a sense of morale and to be concerned about the overall success of the collective. Accordingly, influencers work hard at gaining insight into what motivates others and then at developing the planning and persuasive skills they need to win these others over (House et al., 1991).

The Conditional Reasoning of Influencers

When reasoning about strategic decisions, influencers tend to rely on their own ideas, visions, solutions, and strategies. What is referred to by *their own* are the ideas, visions, solutions, and strategies that they developed themselves, had assistance in developing, or adopted as their own. Influencers consistently reason that the chance of success is greater if they personally define problems, build visions, and make, or at least have strong influence on, final strategies (Eden, 1992). It is this sense of efficacy in their own reasoning and strategic problem solving that motivates influencers to take on leadership responsibilities, seek out leadership opportunities, and attempt to persuade others that their visions and goals will be effective (Bass, 1985; House et al., 1991).

The preferred leadership style of influencers is persuasion based on promoting the subordinates' own needs, values, and interests (Bass, 1985; Van Vugt et al., 2008). Influencers want to provide value-added contributions to subordinates' effectiveness, sense of self-confidence, and feelings of morale if not commitment to the collective. Influencers feel a sense of reward when subordinates are successful, and this success can be attributed, in part, to how the subordinates were led. Also, they are pleased when subordinates display high morale and commitment (e.g., high retention rates, minimal grievances, interdepartmental cooperation).

Concern for the success of subordinates reflects both a desire to be instrumental in guiding the collective toward success and a genuine interest in having impact in how the people in the collective are treated (Judge et al., 2002; Winter, 1992). Through their direction, influencers want to ensure that justice is administered fairly, that rewards are distributed equitably, that the people in the collective are safe and protected from threat, that the leadership is sensitive to follower's needs and values, that people believe in the mission of the collective, and that followers are given the opportunities to develop and maximize their skills (Bono & Judge, 2004; Van Vugt et al., 2008). Influencers also want to guarantee that the collective adheres to ethical principles, which means that they should serve as role models (Kaiser et al., 2008). Here again, strong personal investments are seen in what is right and good for the collective (i.e., rather than just focusing on what is good for the self).

In sum, leaders who fit the pattern of instrumental influence design strategies to benefit their collectives. The result is that their collectives tend to be composed of people who view their work environment as being instrumental in serving the needs of the collective as well as their social and personal needs (i.e., a climate of instrumental influence) and to be more effective than collectives led by toxic leaders (Kellerman, 2004; Resick et al., 2009). Greater effectiveness is related directly to influencers' attempts to understand the needs of their people and to use this understanding to win the people over to their visions and strategies.

Of course, the leaders must have the political skills required to understand others and to design effective methods of persuasion. If successful in this persuasion, then influencers believe that people will work toward strategic goals with enthusiasm and passion. Psychologically, successful influencers tend to have strong self-confidence in their abilities to define problems, to build visions and strategies, and to show their people how to realize these visions. This sense of efficacy is coupled with a strong desire to be instrumental in seeing that their people are safe and treated fairly and with respect.

Identifying Influencers

Currently, problems are in the process of being added to the CRT-L to distinguish between toxic leaders and (instrumental) influencers. An illustrative problem is presented and discussed in James and LeBreton (in press). Preliminary results suggest that between 12.3 and 19.4% of the variance in monthly store profits can be predicted by using conditional reasoning to assess the constructs outlined in this chapter, namely, need for power and aggression. Although much developmental and validation work is still necessary before finalizing these instruments, we are confident that ultimately they will not only be able to continue to be used to predict outcomes such as profits but, more importantly, the political styles that leaders will be most likely to demonstrate and whether they will engender a toxic climate characterized by deceit and distrust or a supportive climate characterized by mutual respect and shared commitment. We believe that this has important implications not only for organizations' financial functioning but also for subordinates' quality of life derived from their experiences in different organizational climates.

CONCLUSIONS

One of psychology's main benefits is that it provides empirically verifiable explanations of why certain individuals do and do not behave in particular ways. The study of politics, influence and power as well as the effects of these forces on follower perceptions of organizational climate is no exception. First, however, psychologists must avoid making premature value judgments about the effects of one's need for power. Instead, a more nuanced perspective is encouraged, where the need for power is not inherently viewed as a negative attribute. Also, thinkers are encouraged to critically examine the ways other motives, *in combination with* a high need for power, consciously and unconsciously encourage the use of political tactics in either prosocial or antisocial ways. Specifically, it is argued that the distinction between *aggression* on the one hand and *concern* on the other hand is a useful means not only to predict the behavior of individual leaders but also to begin to understand the ways their conditional reasoning influences the organizational climates they create.

REFERENCES

Allport, G.W. (1937). *Personality: A psychological interpretation.* New York: Holt.

Avolio, B., Sosik, J., Jung, D., & Berson, Y. (2003). Leadership models, methods, and applications. In W.C. Borman (Ed.), Handbook of psychology: Industrial and organizational psychology (Vol. 12, pp. 277–307). New York: John Wiley & Sons.

Bandura, A. (1999). Moral disengagement in the perpetration of inhumanities. *Personality and Social Psychology Review, 3,* 193–209.

Bass, B.M. (1985). Leadership: Good, better, best. *Organizational Dynamics, 13,* 26–40.

Bass, B.M. (1990). *Bass and Stogdill's handbook of leadership: Theory, research, and managerial applications* (3rd ed.). New York: Free Press

Bargh, J.A., & Alvarez, J. (2001). The road to hell: Good intentions in the face of non-conscious tendencies to misuse power. In A.Y. Lee-Chai & J.A. Bargh (Eds.), *The use and abuse of power: Multiple perspectives on the causes of corruption* (pp. 42–55). New York: Taylor & Francis.

Baumeister, R.F., Campbell, J.D., Krueger, J.I., & Vohs, K.D. (2003). Does high self-esteem cause better performance, interpersonal success, happiness, or healthier lifestyles? *Psychological Science in the Public Interest, 4,* 1–44.

Bono, J.E., & Judge, T.A. (2004). Personality and transformational and transactional leadership: A meta-analysis. *Journal of Applied Psychology, 89,* 901–910.

Buss, D.M. (2005). *Handbook of evolutionary psychology.* Hoboken, NJ: Wiley.

Chan, K., & Drasgow, F. (2001). Toward a theory of individual differences and leadership: Understanding the motivation to lead. *Journal of Applied Psychology, 86,* 481–498.

Chen, S., Lee-Chai, A.Y., & Bargh, J.A. (2001). Relationship orientation as a moderator of the effects of social power. *Journal of Personality and Social Psychology, 80*, 173–187.

Collins, J. (2001). *Good to great: Why some companies make the leap...and others don't.* New York: HarperCollins.

Cramer, P. (1998). Defensiveness and defense mechanisms. *Journal of Personality, 66*, 880–894.

Cramer, P. (2000). Defense mechanisms in psychology today: Further processes for adaptation. *American Psychologist, 55*, 637–646.

Cramer, P. (2006). *Protecting the self: Defense mechanisms in action.* New York: Guilford Press.

Dodge, K.A., & Coie, J.D. (1987). Social-information-processing factors in reactive and proactive aggression in children's peer groups. *Journal of Personality and Social Psychology, 53*, 1146–1158.

Eden, D. (1992). Leadership and expectations: Pygmalion effects and other self-fulfilling prophecies. *Leadership Quarterly, 3*, 271–305.

Finkelstein, S., & Hambrick, D.C. (1996). *Strategic leadership: Top executives and their effects on organizations.* Minneapolis, MN: West Educational Publishing.

Foti, R.J., & Hauenstein, N.M. (2007). Pattern and variable approaches in leadership emergence and effectiveness. *Journal of Applied Psychology, 92*, 347–355.

French, J.R., & Raven, B. (1959). The bases of social power. In D. Cartwright (Ed.), *Group dynamics.* New York: Harper & Row.

Frost, B.C., Ko, C.E., & James, L.R. (2007). Implicit and explicit personality: A test of a channeling hypothesis for aggressive behavior. *Journal of Applied Psychology, 92*, 1299–1319.

Galotti, K.M. (1989). Approaches to studying formal and everyday reasoning. *Psychological Bulletin, 105*, 331–351.

Greenwald, A.G., & Banaji, M.R. (1995). Implicit social cognition: Attitudes, self-esteem, and stereotypes. *Psychological Review, 102*(1), 4–27.

Hahn, U., & Oaksford, M. (2007). The rationality of informal argumentation: A Bayesian approach to reasoning fallacies. *Psychological Review, 114*, 704–732.

Haidt, J. (2001). The emotional dog and its rational tail: A social intuitionist approach to moral judgment. *Psychological Review, 108*, 814–834

Hambrick, D.C., Finkelstein, S., & Mooney, A.C. (2005). Executive job demands: New insights for explaining strategic decisions and leader behaviors. *Academy of Management Review, 30*, 472–491.

Hogan, R., & Kaiser, R.B. (2005). What we know about leadership. *Review of General Psychology, 9*, 169–180.

House, R.J., Spangler, W.D., & Woycke, J. (1991). Personality and charisma in the U.S. presidency: A psychological theory of leader effectiveness. *Administrative Science Quarterly, 36*, 364–396.

James, L.R. (1998). Measurement of personality via conditional reasoning. *Organizational Research Methods, 1*(2), 131–163.

James, L.R., & LeBreton, J.M. (2010). Assessing aggression using conditional reasoning. *Current Directions in Psychological Science, 19*(1), 30–35.

James, L.R., & LeBreton, J.M. (in press). *Assessing the implicit personality via conditional reasoning.* Washington DC: American Psychological Association.

James, L.R., LeBreton, J.M., Mitchell, T.R., Smith, D.R., DeSimone, J.A., Cookson, R. et al. (in press). Use of conditional reasoning to measure the power motive. In R. Landis & J.M. Cortina (Eds.), *Advances in methodology* (SIOP Frontiers Series volume). San Francisco: Jossey-Bass.

James, L.R., & Mazerolle, M.D. (2002). *Personality in work organizations.* Thousand Oaks, CA: Sage Publications.

James, L.R., McIntyre, M.D., Glisson, C.A., Bowler, J.L., & Mitchell, T.R. (2004). The conditional reasoning measurement system for aggression: An overview. *Human Performance, 17*(3), 271–295.

James, L.R., McIntyre, M.D., Glisson, C.A., Green, P.D., Patton, T.W., LeBreton, J.M. et al. (2005). A conditional reasoning measure for aggression. *Organizational Research Methods, 8*(1), 69–99.

Judge, T.A., Bono, J.E., Ilies, R., & Gerhardt, M.W. (2002). Personality and leadership: A qualitative and quantitative review. *Journal of Applied Psychology, 87*, 765–780.

Judge, T.A., LePine, J.A., & Rich, B.L. (2006). Loving yourself abundantly: Relationship of the narcissistic personality to self- and other perceptions of workplace deviance, leadership, and task and contextual performance. *Journal of Applied Psychology, 91*, 762–776.

Kaiser, R.B., Hogan, R., & Craig, S.B. (2008). Leadership and the fate of organizations. *American Psychologist, 63*, 96–110.

Kahneman, D., & Klein, G. (2009). Conditions for intuitive expertise. *American Psychologist, 64*, 515–526.

Kenny, D.A., & Zaccaro, S J. (1983). An estimate of variance due to traits in leadership. *Journal of Applied Psychology, 68*, 678–685.

Kellerman, B. (2004). *Bad leadership: What it is, how it happens, why it matters.* Boston: Harvard Business School Press.

Kipnis, D. (1972). Does power corrupt? *Journal of Personality and Social Psychology, 24*(1), 33–41.

Kipnis, D. (1976). *The powerholders.* Chicago: University of Chicago Press.

Klein, G. (1998). *Sources of power: How people make decisions.* Cambridge, MA: MIT Press.

Kuhn, D. (1991). *The skills of argument.* New York: Cambridge University Press.

Landis, R., & Cortina, J.M. (Eds.). (in press). *Advances in methodology* (SIOP Frontiers Series volume). San Francisco: Jossey-Bass.

Landy, F.J. (2008). Stereotypes, bias and personnel decisions: Strange and stranger. *Industrial and Organizational Psychology: Perspectives on Science and Practice, 1*, 379–392.

LeBreton, J.M., Barksdale, C.D., Robin, J., & James, L.R. (2007). Measurement issues associated with conditional reasoning tests: Indirect measurement and test faking. *Journal of Applied Psychology, 92*(1), 1–16.

Lord Acton. (1865). Letter to Bishop Mandell Creighton.

Lord, R.G., Foti, R.J., & DeVader, C.L. (1984). A test of leadership categorization theory: Internal structure, information processing, and leadership perceptions. *Organizational Behavior and Human Performance, 34*, 343–378.

Maslow, A. (1954). *Motivation and personality.* New York: Harper.

Moskowitz, D.S. (1994). Cross-situational generality and the interpersonal circumplex. *Journal of Personality and social Psychology, 66*, 921–933

McAdams, D.P., & Pals, J.L. (2006). A new big five. *American Psychologist, 61*(3), 201–217.

McClelland, D.C. (1985). *Human motivation.* Glenview, IL: Scott, Foresman, and Company.

McClelland, D.C., & Boyatzis, R.E. (1982). Leadership motive pattern and long-term success in management. *Journal of Applied Psychology, 67*(6), 737–743.

McClelland, D.C., Koestner, R., & Weinberger, J. (1989). How do self-attributed and implicit motives differ? In F. Halisch & J.H.L. van den Bercken (Eds.), *International perspectives on achievement and task motivation* (pp. 259–289). Lisse, Netherlands: Swets & Zeitlinger Publishers.

Murray, H.A. (1938). *Explorations in personality*. New York: Oxford University Press.

Overbeck, J.R. (2010). Concepts and historical perspectives on power. In A. Guinote & T.K. Vescio (Eds.), *The social psychology of power*. New York: Guilford.

Pfeffer, J. (1981). *Power in organizations*. Boston: Pitman.

Pfeffer, J. (1994). *Managing with power*. Boston: Harvard Business School Press.

Podsakoff, P.M., MacKenzie, S.B., Moorman, R.H., & Fetter, R. (1990). Transformational leader behaviors and their effects on follower's trust in leader, satisfaction, and organizational citizenship behaviors. *Leadership Quarterly, 1,* 107–142.

Resick, C.J., Whitman, D.S., Weingarden, S.M., & Hiller, N.J. (2009). The bright-side and the dark-side of CEO personality: Examining core self-evaluations, narcissism, transformational leadership, and strategic influence. *Journal of Applied Psychology, 94,* 1365–1381.

Rosenthal, S.A., & Pittinsky, T.L. (2006). Narcissistic leadership. *Leadership Quarterly, 17,* 617–633.

Russell, B. (1938). *Power: A new social analysis*. London: Routledge Classics.

Schneider, W., & Shiffrin, R.M. (1977). Controlled and automatic human information processing: I. Detection, search, and attention. *Psychological Review, 84,* 1–66.

Sidanius, J., & Pratto, F. (1999). *Social dominance: An intergroup theory of social hierarchy and oppression*. New York: Cambridge University Press.

Simon, B., & Oakes, P. (2006). Beyond dependence: An identity approach to social power and domination. *Human Relations, 59,* 105–139.

Sykes, G.M., & Matza, D. (1957). Techniques of neutralization: A theory of delinquency. *American Sociological Review, 22,* 664–670.

Stricker, L.J., & Rock, D.A. (1998). Assessing leadership potential with a biographical measure of personality traits. *International Journal of Selection and Assessment, 6,* 164–184.

Van Vugt, M., Hogan, R., & Kaiser, R.B. (2008). Leadership, followership, and evolution: Some lessons from the past. *American Psychologist, 63,* 182–196.

Veroff, J. (1992). Power motivation. In C.P. Smith (Ed.), *Motivation and personality: Handbook of thematic content analysis* (pp. 278–324). New York: Cambridge University Press.

Vroom, V.H., & Jago, A.G. (2007). The role of the situation in leadership. *American Psychologist, 62,* 17–24.

Westen, D. (1990). Psychoanalytic approaches to personality. In L.A. Pervin (Ed.), *Handbook of personality: Theory and research* (pp. 21–65). New York: Guilford Press.

Westen, D. (1991). Social cognition and object relations. *Psychological Bulletin, 109,* 429–455.

Winter, D.G. (1973). *The power motive*. New York: Free Press.

Winter, D.G. (1992). Power motivation revisited. In C.P. Smith (Ed.), *Motivation and personality: Handbook of thematic content analysis*. New York: Cambridge University Press.

Winter, D.G., John, O.P., Stewart, A.J., Klohnen, E.C., & Duncan, L.E. (1998). Traits and motives: Toward an integration of two traditions in personality research. *Psychological Review, 105,* 230–250.

Yukl, G.A. (2009). *Leadership in organizations* (7th ed.). Boston: Prentice-Hall.

10

Politics in and Around Teams: Toward a Team-Level Conceptualization of Organizational Politics

Eran Vigoda-Gadot
University of Haifa

Dana R. Vashdi
University of Haifa

Theory and research on organizational politics has expanded rapidly in recent decades, and it is reflected in many journal articles, books, and book chapters as well as conference presentations in management and organizational studies. A quick literature search was conducted and resulted in more than 100 journal articles mentioned in the *Social Sciences Citation Index (SSCI)* during the years 1968–2010 with the precise term *organizational politics* in its title. A rough breakdown by decades indicates a growing trend. The numbers rise from 19 between 1981 and 1990 to 31 between 1991 and 2000 and up to 36 between 2001 and 2010. When extending the search to include variants of the term organizational politics, the total number of studies found that have dealt with such issues is even more impressive and reaches several hundred, with many of them published in the recent decade only.

However, whereas vast attention has been given to individual aspects of this phenomenon, there is relatively little knowledge about the politics in and around teams. Another look into the *SSCI* resulted in no study that specifically and explicitly dealt with organizational politics within teams or workgroups. Several studies, however, have discussed some aspects of organizational politics and team activity, and are reviewed in this chapter.

In the early 1990s, Pfeffer (1992) reargued that organizations, particularly large ones, are like governments in that they are fundamentally political entities. To understand them, one needs to understand organizational politics, just as to understand governments one needs to understand governmental politics. This similarity between larger national and governmental entities and the workplace is of great value to those who are interested in the psychological nature of individuals and, more so, team activity and behavior. As high politics largely is an action field for parties, pressure-groups, interest-groups, and political movements, so is politics in organizations an action field for various types of teams and groups, beyond the interests of individuals.

One of the major assumptions directing this chapter is that the basic motivation to become engaged in workplace politics, by individuals and teams, is quite similar to those motivations of politicians and activists at the national level. This activity is individually derived but also largely group and team derived. The quest for acknowledgment of specific interests, the willingness to play a "give-and-take" game, and the rationality of actions during build-up, construction, deconstruction, and reconstruction of coalitions and teams are all part of a political code of action occurring inside organizations and around them in the wider society.

Although there is no doubt that internal politics is a common phenomenon in every organization, too little is known about the exact nature and boundaries of such politics among teams of various structures, nature, cultures, and orientations. Uncovering some of the missing links in this direction may contribute to the generalization power of the field and to its scholarly robustness and may point to promising avenues for future empirical research. The major goal of this chapter is to effectively integrate what we know today about team-related organizational politics and to suggest a few directions for future theoretical development. In other words, the focus is on ideas for the extension of current knowledge on teams in general and on organizational politics and to illuminate a potential track for developing the knowledge of workplace politics in the direction of group-level and teamwork analysis.

REVIEW OF TEAM-LEVEL ORGANIZATIONAL POLITICS AND POLITICAL SKILL

Increasingly, teams are being used as a primary work unit within organizations (Cohen & Bailey, 1997; Guzzo & Dickson, 1996). Many organizations now set up work teams to improve task coordination, communication, and knowledge transfer in organizations. One of the questions concerning researchers and practitioners today is whether any group of people working together constitutes a team and whether such a group will actually produce performance that is more than the sum of the individuals' contributions. Katzenbach and Smith (1993, p.112) defined a team as "a small number of people with complementary skills who are committed to a common purpose, set of performance goals, and approach for which they hold themselves mutually accountable."

Although there are several other definitions, all are quite similar and emphasize the interdependence between team members (Sundstrom, De Meuse, & Futrell, 1990). As underlined by the aforementioned definition, teams, as opposed to groups, produce through *joint* contributions of their members and require individual and *mutual* accountability. Teams require not only that team members share a common purpose but also that this purpose is translated into specific performance goals and that there is an agreement and commitment to a common approach of how the team work will be completed.

Over the years, several taxonomies regarding types of teams have emerged (e.g., Cohen & Bailey, 1997; Devine, 2002; Hackman, 1990; Sundstrom, 1999). These taxonomies distinguish between teams based on issues such as (1) the duration of the existence of the team distinguishing between short-term mission teams and long-term continuous teams, (2) the functional homogeneity versus the heterogeneity of the team members, and (3) the complexity and stability of the environment in which the teams perform (Pepinsky, Pepinsky, & Pavlik, 1960). Obviously, these taxonomies should be considered when weighting the impact and meaning of power, influence, and organizational politics in teams, and they will be, at least partially, discussed further in this chapter.

Many of the theories regarding teams draw from the basic framework proposed by McGrath (1964), which constitutes the input-process-outcome (I-P-O) model. The inputs include antecedents at the individual level (e.g., team members' competencies or personalities), at the team level (e.g., leadership style or task structure), and at the organizational level (e.g., environmental complexity or attributes of the organizational design). The processes are defined by Marks, Mathieu, & Zaccaro (2001, p. 357) as "members' interdependent acts that convert inputs to outcomes through cognitive, verbal, and behavioral activities directed toward organizing task-work to achieve collective goals." Examples of such team processes are team communication and team-shared mental models (i.e., an organized understanding or mental representation of knowledge that is shared by team members; see, e.g., Cannon-Bowers, Salas, & Converse, 1993).

Finally, outcomes usually are framed as team effectiveness and include performance (e.g., quality and quantity) and members' affective states (e.g., satisfaction, commitment, and viability). Hackman (1987) emphasized that team effectiveness must be examined both in regards to current effectiveness (i.e., present performance) and future team effectiveness (i.e., capability to continue working together) to achieve a comprehensive assessment of team success. As elaborated later, the I-P-O model has been extended to include more than just processes as mediating factors and feedback loops that connect outputs to future inputs. However, this classic I-P-O model has been the basis for many studies on teams.

As mentioned in Chapter 1 in this volume, two general perspectives are adopted when examining organizational politics: (1) as negative phenomena; or (2) as natural, evolving phenomena without a negative connotation. According to Burns's (1961), politics in organizations is deemed, at best, as a necessary evil and is consequently associated with a variety of negative actions that are harmful and dangerous from the organizational point of view (e.g., Ferris & Kacmar, 1992; Ferris & King, 1991; Mintzberg, 1983; Parker, Dipboye, & Jackson, 1995; Vigoda, 2000, 2001, 2002). Examples of political acts include concealing important information, lobbying for preferred alternatives, favoritism, taking credit for other people's contributions, and scapegoating (e.g., Eisenhardt & Bourgeois, 1988; Ferris & Kacmar, 1992).

Studies that examined the effect of such organizational politics perceptions on various work outcomes concluded that organizations rife with internal politics usually evince low performance on various scales, from attitudes such as satisfaction and commitment to self-reports of lower performance and a lesser inclination to engage in organizational citizenship behaviors. In the same vein, elevated levels of stress, negligent behaviors, and aggression tend to be found as consequences of politics perceptions (e.g., Cropanzano, Howes, Grandey, & Toth, 1997; Maslyn & Fedor, 1998; Vigoda, 2000, 2002).

When taking this perspective and elevating it to the team level, it is likely that teams perceived as highly political will be perceived as such due to rivalry political behaviors within the team or if the team as a whole presents rivalry political behavior toward other teams in the organization. One important implication is that the capacity of a team to work together in the future is, among other things, subject to the prevalence of power relations, influence behaviors, and politics within the team.

Particularly by those who view politics as negative and destructive phenomena, it may be assumed that higher levels of politics perceptions at the team level may lead to lower levels of team coherence, increased frustration among some team members, higher level of stress and cynicism, and eventually lower levels of team performance and productivity. Although research in this area is scarce, one study by Elron and Vigoda-Gadot (2006) studied the meaning of politics, from this viewpoint, in multicultural virtual teams. At the team level, they found that the prevalence of politics increases the level of detrimental conflicts in top-management teams (TMTs) and lowers their performance (Eisenhardt & Bourgeois, 1988; Elron, 2000).

When adopting the perspective suggested by Kipnis, Schmidt, and Wilkinson (1980), political behavior and political skill in organizations are best reflected by influential activities and tactics engaged in by members to maximize their interests and goals in the workplace. For example, building coalitions in favor of specific decisions or creating support for one's needs and aspirations using collective group or team pressures represent legitimate ways to build organizational politics and to enhance influence or power. Hence, the meaning of political skill is using one's assets to increase power or influence abilities to advance specific interests. Similarly, workplace politics of teams is an elementary and legitimate influential behavior directed at others to gain advantages that cannot be achieved otherwise (i.e., by formal and routine procedures).

Taken both at the individual or team level, such behaviors involve various tactics (e.g., the influence tactics discussed already among them) aimed at affecting such processes and outcomes as resource distribution and decision making as well as goal setting and goal attainment (e.g., Mayes & Allen, 1977). Higher political skill at the team level may lead to higher competencies against other teams and to higher motivation to seek far-reaching goals and aspirations of the team. This "super motivation" and highly skillful political orientation at the team level may be viewed as a source of power and uniqueness. In addition, heightened political skill may be apparent within the team when its members try to influence the team to go in a specific direction.

As can be understood, it is important to define which approach one takes when investigating team politics, specifying whether team politics are viewed as a negative team phenomenon or as a neutral behavior apparent in any team. Second, team politics can refer to political behaviors within the team, among the team members or to the political behaviors of the team toward external entities such as other teams, management or customers. These external activities are referred to as boundary-spanning activities including the extent and type of team external activities (Ancona & Caldwell, 1992). This latter point is elaborated next.

Chapter 1 in this volume mentioned the social roots of the organizational politics theory and study and suggested the work by Cyert and March (1963) as a milestone in this direction. According to this view, individual behavior in organizations is driven by coalitions, as are the establishment of goals and the implementation of strategy. Through the alignment of interest groups' resources, coalitions build power and develop methods to influence others. Such power and influence are meaningful and affect organizations as a whole (Bacharach & Lawler, 1980).

It has been suggested that greater emphasis should be put on social network analysis to explain politics in the workplace (Ibarra & Andrews, 1993; Vigoda-Gadot & Drory, 2006). This social anchor of human activity is extremely important when trying to explain how teams are engaged in politics and how politics are engaged in the actions of teams. Chapter 1 in this volume suggested that social network patterns in organizations can yield quite useful information for existing coalitions as well as for the key individuals critical to their formation. Moreover, employees with better organizational political skills are more likely to be centrally located in social networks (Brass, 1984; Brass & Burkhardt, 1993), have more friendship ties (Lee & Tiedens, 2001), and thus more intensively affect the team and the organization.

Looking at the potential opposite effect (i.e., how the social group influences the individual), Porter, Allen, and Angle (1981) recognized that the social norms surrounding any influence attempt would affect both the tactic choice and the chosen tactic's effectiveness by the individual. Therefore, the reciprocal relations between the individual and the team are of high value when trying to analyze the meaning of politics for teams and for teamwork. Moreover, the performance of those teams may be affected when teams are engaged in "power games" instead of in achieving the team goals. Hence, it is argued that organizational politics is part of almost every stage in team activity. It is part of the team-building and development processes, team maintenance, and team behavior during normal times and times of crisis. Also, politics is part of the stage of team disengagement.

WITHIN-TEAM POLITICAL BEHAVIOR

Team Development and Internal Politics

Tuckman (1965) identified four distinct stages of team development: forming, storming, norming, and performing. The forming stage is characterized by team members sharing information about themselves and their task explicitly through discussions or implicitly through nonverbal cues, such as status symbols or physical traits. In this stage, team members get to know each other as individuals and ideally to establish trust, clarify group goals, and develop shared expectations. In the storming stage, conflicts emerge as team members work to identify appropriate roles and responsibilities.

Competition among ideas is apparent, and the duality of being an autonomous person and at the same time a team member characterizes the psychological atmosphere. In the norming stage, teams recognize and agree on ways of working together, strengthen relationships, and solidify understanding of member obligations, all of which increase levels of trust, mission clarity, and coordination. Finally, in the performing stage, team members work toward project completion, actively helping and encouraging each other (Furst, Reeves, Rosen, & Blackburn, 2004).

It is interesting to examine these stages from an internal-politics perspective. Team members may use the forming stage to map the political terrain within the team. This stage is characterized by understanding who the leader is and whether there is a chance to dominate within this team despite the leader. Team members with high political skill are likely to use this stage to learn about the other team members' agendas, strengths, and weaknesses. In the storming stage, coalitions may be formed. This is the stage where team members try to exert their agendas and styles and to influence the way thing should be done in this team.

People are likely to seek out those who see things similarly to them as opposed to those who don't and to try to create subgroups around similar points of view. The conflict representing this stage is very much a power game. The flow into the norming stage is contingent upon either a dominant position being accepted by a majority or an agreed midlevel path that was agreed on through some form of negotiations between different subgroups. From a political perspective, the norming and performing stages enable team members to score points as they lead or influence the team in the direction of high performance and provide an opportunity to score points for future decision making and team activities.

The IMOI Model

In a recent review of research and theory on organizational teams, Ilgen and colleagues (Ilgen, Hollenbeck, Johnson, & Jundt, 2005) proposed that the classic I-P-O framework is insufficient for characterizing teams. One reason that is very relevant for the current chapter is that many of the mediational factors that intervene and transmit the influence of inputs to outcomes are not processes but rather emergent cognitive or affective states. An example of an emergent state is team cohesion: "the tendency for a group to stick together and remain united in the pursuit of its instrumental objectives and/or for the satisfaction of member affective needs" (Carron, Brawley, & Widmeyer, 1998, p. 213). This is likely to be affected by inputs, such as the political skill of team members, or by the extent to which team members exert political behaviors.

Ilgen et al. (2005) proposed the IMOI (input-mediator-output-input) model, whereby "substituting 'M' for 'P' reflects the broader range of variables that are important mediational influences with explanatory power for explaining variability in team performance and viability" (p. 520). Adding the extra I at the end of the model invokes the notion of cyclical causal feedback, and the elimination of the hyphen between letters signifies that the causal linkages may not be linear or additive but rather nonlinear or conditional.

When examining within team political behaviors (i.e., political skill and strategies exerted by team members to gain power or dominance within the team), the IMOI model may provide a framework for understanding the roles played by these behaviors. First, team members' political skill may serve as an input affecting team processes and emergent states. For example, the use of political skill may influence such team processes as workload sharing and helping or emergent states such as team efficacy or potency. The nature of this relationship may be positive if the exertion of political skill within the team is aimed at pulling team members together around an individual's or subteam's goal or negative if it is directed at creating divides between subgroups with competing goals or when focused at gaining personal advantages to one of the team members at the expense of others.

Second, these processes and emergent states resulting from such political activity may impact team outcomes, with the relationship between these mediators and outcomes labeled *team functioning* (Ilgen et al., 2005). Finally, these outcomes may impact consequent inputs. Thus, team members belonging to a team executing low performance may try to use political behaviors to try to influence future agendas or work standards. In the next sections, the components of the IMOI as a framework for understanding within team political behaviors are further elaborated.

Inputs

Team Composition and Diversity

Team composition refers to the nature and attributes of group members and demonstrates a powerful influence on team processes and outcomes (Kozlowski & Bell, 2003). Team composition concerns what individual members bring to the team in terms of demography, skill, ability, and disposition (Driskell, Hogan, & Salas, 1987; Hollenbeck, Ilgen, Sego, Hedlund, Major, & Phillips, 1995; Tesluk & Mathieu, 1999). Diversity refers to dissimilarity among members in regards to these attributes. Team composition has been included in studies of team effectiveness for more than 50 years (e.g., Mann, 1959) and has been conceptualized as including job-related (Webber & Donahue, 2001) as well as surface- and deep-level attributes (Harrison, Price, & Bell, 1998).

Job-related diversity relates to diversity in experiences, skills, or perspectives pertinent to cognitive work tasks. Surface-level diversity relates to differences among team members in overt, biological characteristics that typically are reflected in physical features such as age, gender, and race/ethnicity. Finally, deep-level diversity refers to differences in attitudes, beliefs, and values that can be learned only through extended interaction and information gathering.

Much of the research has concluded that diversity can be a double-edged sword (Webber & Donahue, 2001). Specifically, examinations of diversity in teams have found that it can lead to more high-quality solutions while also decreasing cohesion (McLeod & Lobel, 1992; Milliken & Martins, 1996;

O'Reilly, Caldwell, & Barnett, 1989; Watson, Kumar, & Michaelsen, 1993). In addition, different types of diversity have been found to demonstrate different effects on team effectiveness (Williams & O'Reilly, 1998), and, even within the same dimension of diversity, there have been considerable contradictory findings regarding the relationship of such diversity to performance.

One stream of research attempting to settle these inconsistencies examined moderating variables. For example, Polzer, Milton, and Swann (2002) found that interpersonal congruence (i.e., the degree to which a person's self-views and others' appraisals of that person coincide) moderated the impact of demographic diversity on group processes and performance. They found that in groups that achieved high interpersonal congruence, demographic diversity enhanced creative task performance, whereas in groups that failed to achieve interpersonal congruence, diversity impaired performance.

Another stream of research has claimed that the relationship between diversity and performance is not necessarily a linear one. For example, Earley and Mosakowski (2000) examined the effect of cultural diversity in teams and found a U-shaped relationship. That is, they found that given sufficient opportunity or time to work together, homogeneous and highly heterogeneous teams are more effective than moderately heterogeneous ones. The relationship between highly heterogeneous teams and performance is explained by the formation of a hybrid team culture, which is apparent when a simplified set of rules, norms, expectations, and roles that team members share and *enact* emerge. This emergent culture facilitates team interaction and performance by offering a common sense of identity and by providing a basis for team member self-evaluation (Casmir, 1992; Klimoski & Mohammed, 1994). One important implication of this study is the understanding that the formation of a hybrid culture may enable heterogeneous teams on other dimensions to perform well.

Hence, and in regards to politics within the team, diversity on different dimensions may serve as a basis for internal coalitions. People attempting to gain power within the team initially may turn to team members who are more similar to themselves. Such coalitions may be problematic as they may prevent (1) the natural occurrence of a team hybrid culture, (2) the opportunity to achieve high interpersonal congruence, collaboration, and acceptance of others' views to questions in dispute, and (3) the reduction of stereotyping. In such cases, power dynamics and political processes within the team may be moderating factors influencing the impact of diversity on performance over time.

Structure: Team Roles

A fundamental question that arises when studying teams is how individual inputs aggregate and emerge to influence collective actions and outcomes (Kozlowski & Klein, 2000). One potential mechanism linking individuals and team-level characteristics is the concept of team roles (Stewart, Fulmer, & Barrick, 2005). Says Stewart et al.:

> A role is defined as a set of behaviors that are interrelated with the repetitive activities of others and characteristic of the person in a particular setting (Biddle, 1979; Forsyth, 1990; Katz & Kahn, 1978). From this definition, it can be seen that roles represent patterns of individual behavior resulting from interaction with other team members. These individual roles collectively combine to form aggregate constructs that represent stable patterns of group process (Kozlowski, Gully, Nason, & Smith, 1999; Morgeson & Hofmann, 1999). Roles thus reflect consistent patterns of behavior at the individual level, and role configuration reflects collective interaction at the team level (Kozlowski & Klein, 2000; Morgeson & Hofmann, 1999). (p. 344).

Based on the this definition, when discussing team roles, researchers do not refer to the functional roles people have (i.e., job role and function in the organization) as these do not help understand how team members will interact with one another, how they will approach a problem, or how they generally will behave (Senior, 1997). Belbin (1993) observed management teams and identified nine different roles that emerge in successful teams. According to Belbin, these roles must emerge *naturally* and be spread or *balanced* among team members for the team to perform effectively. Belbin's work also points out that the availability of team members who are more people than task oriented is vital for successful team work.

Roles and politics are strongly related. Role negotiation (i.e., the understanding of who will fill which role) starts at the formative stage of team development. This process of understanding whether individuals can fill the role they are accustomed to or is required for them in this specific team may involve both political skill and political behavior. Usually unconsciously, individuals try to understand if the required role is available and either consciously or unconsciously exert power, influence, or impression management tactics to acquire the specific role. Also, specific roles involve more power toward the team, such as Belbin's (1993) coordinator role, which requires a team member who is mature, confident, and a good administrator. The coordinator is the team member in charge of clarifying goals, promoting decision making and delegating responsibilities.

It is important to understand that the team itself has power and can prevent a person from acquiring a desired role. For example, if the team does not feel like a specific person should play the coordinator role, the team will disregard the person's attempts to delegate responsibilities and respond to the member that is preferred by the team. Thus, the political behavior of the individuals within the team is apparent in the attempt to maneuver the team to accept the required role.

Tasks

One critical factor influencing the processes and outcomes of any team is the types of tasks the team performs (e.g., Hackman, 1990; McGrath, 1984; Steiner, 1972). Hyatt and Ruddy (1997) claimed that the type of task performed is important to consider when studying team effectiveness because it determines, at least partially, what the definition of effectiveness entails; it determines the criteria against which group effectiveness is measured; and the task can affect the importance of some characteristics of effective groups such as if communication is required for effective performance.

Hackman (1990) divided team tasks into five categories:

1. *Management tasks,* which characterize the tasks of top-management teams (such as setting organizational directions and making decisions that are critical for the organization as a whole)
2. *Special product tasks,* which are the tasks of task forces and project teams that attempt to create a one-of-a-kind or one-time-only team product
3. *Assistance tasks,* which are characteristic of professional support groups that aim to give expert assistance to those generating the organizations primary product or service
4. *Performance tasks,* which are characteristic of sport or music teams in which the task is to "play" well for an audience
5. *Service tasks,* which include providing internal services characteristic of human service teams or external services characteristic of customer service teams

Hackman (1990) elaborated on the task the team performs and referred to it as the *stuff* with which the team works: "Top management teams, for example, dealt constantly with power and influence; Task forces worked with ideas and plans; Support teams traded in expertise..." (p. 487). It is obvious that the substance of a team's task significantly impacts the interactions that take place among team members. Thus, when examining internal team politics, one factor that can influence the extent to which political behaviors dominate the team process, and the extent to which such behavior is positive or negative in nature, may be the type of task the team performs, or the *stuff* with which the team deals.

Top-management teams, which are composed of experienced senior managers, may be especially prone to exert higher levels of political behaviors because each member of this team is used to demonstrating, take charge, and opinion-oriented behavior toward others. In contrast, in teams where the conductor or coach is the leader, political behaviors may be less apparent and may influence the performance of the team to a lesser extent. This is not to say there is no politics in performing teams but rather that it may have less strength in its effects on the internal team dynamics.

Leadership

Leadership involves influencing others to achieve organizational goals (Robbins, 2003), and leaders have more formal and informal power and influence in organizations compared with other organizational members. Hence, it is more likely that leaders will be involved in organizational politics compared with lower-ranked employees. Power and influence are transformed into political skill, which is defined as one's ability to understand social interactions at work and to use this understanding to influence others to act in ways that enhance one's personal or organizational goals (Ahearn, Ferris, Hochwarter, Douglas, & Ammeter, 2004; Ferris, et al., 2005).

Thus, effective leadership appears to require high political skill and being perceived by other individuals as well as by teams as highly politically involved in workplace decisions. Indeed, Douglas and Ammeter (2004) found leader political skill to be a significant predictor of ratings of leader effectiveness. The most extensive study to date examining the impact of political skill on leaders' job performance indicated that political skill was the strongest predictor of managerial performance when compared with self-monitoring, emotional intelligence, and leadership self-efficacy (Semadar, Robins, & Ferris, 2006).

Possessing high political skill means that such leaders can change followers' behaviors as the situation demands and find it easy to influence others (Brouer, 2007). These leaders are able to adjust their behavior in ways appropriate for each of their followers and as the situation demands (Ferris et al., 2005). In turn, such leadership skill should encourage follower trust, job satisfaction, and organizational citizenship behaviors (Ahearn et al., 2004; Ferris et al., 2005).

Ahearn et al. (2004) investigated the impact of the political skill of leaders on team performance. More specifically, their study examined the role of leader political skill in the performance of casework teams in a large state child welfare system. Team performance was operationalized as *permanency rate*, or the successful placement of children into legally final living arrangements (i.e., adoption, successor guardianship, or return to natural parents). After controlling for several contextually important factors (i.e., average caseload, average age of children served, average number of team placements, team member experience, leader experience, and team empowerment), leader political skill was found to explain significant variance in team performance scores. Thus, it seems that high political skill of leaders is a positive contributor to team performance. However, additional research in this direction is needed.

Mediators

Processes

The realization that process plays a pivotal role in team performance has led to the development of theoretical models of team effectiveness, with team processes occupying a central role (e.g., Gist, Locke, & Taylor, 1987; Guzzo & Shea, 1992; Hackman, 1983). In a review of team effectiveness research, Cohen and Bailey (1997) defined team process as "interactions such as communication and conflict that occur among group members and external others" (p. 244). McGrath (1984) referred to team interaction process as "patterned relations among team members" (p. 11).

Marks et al. (2001) defined team process as "members' interdependent acts that convert inputs to outcomes through cognitive, verbal, and behavioral activities directed toward organizing task work to achieve collective goals. Centrally, team process involves members' interacting with other members and their task environment. Team processes are the means by which members work interdependently to utilize various resources, such as expertise, equipment, and money, to yield meaningful outcomes (e.g., product development, rate of work, team commitment, satisfaction)" (p. 357). These processes include workload sharing, mentoring and knowledge sharing, and helping. Workload sharing processes have been demonstrated to be critical for team effectiveness in that they have an important influence on the level of effort team members collectively expend in carrying out task work (Barrick, Stewart, Neubert, & Mount, 1998; Campion, Medsker, & Higgs, 1993). Mentoring and knowledge-sharing processes are likely to influence team effectiveness in that they shape the learning potential of the team (Argote, Ingram, Levine, & Moreland, 2000), the level of knowledge and skills that team members are able to bring to bear on team tasks (Nonaka & Takeuchi, 1995), as well as the degree to which team members can formulate and apply innovative ideas (Hargadon & Sutton, 1997) and solve technical problems (Orr, 1996). Finally, certain patterns of helping among team members may facilitate the implementation of team performance strategies and boost actual group performance (Campion et al., 1993; Podsakoff, Ahearne, & Mackenzie, 1997).

Internal political behavior itself may be a process mediating the relationship between inputs (e.g., roles or tasks) and team performance. This process may be defined in different ways such as the extent to which people use power and influence as opposed to knowledge, skill, or experience to get their way or to get other team members on their side or the extent to which people in the team use *soft* tactics as opposed to assertive tactics (e.g., demand or intimidation) to get their way or to get other team members on their side (Kipnis et al., 1980).

Team politics would be defined as a team process and not an emergent state, because it refers to the nature of the team member interactions and not to the cognitive, motivational, and affective states of teams. As mentioned already, the scarceness of research examining politics at the team level implies that no research has examined team politics as a team-level process affecting team outcomes. This may be a future worthy aim in the attempt to explain variance in the team-level input–output relationship.

Emergent States

Marks et al. (2001) defined emergent states as "constructs that characterize properties of the team that are typically dynamic in nature and vary as a function of team context, inputs, processes, and outcomes" (p. 357). Examples of emergent states include variables such as collective efficacy, potency, cohesion, and situational awareness. Emergent states can be considered both as team inputs and proximal outcomes. As inputs, emergent states may affect different team-level processes such as the political behaviors of team members. As an example of an emergent state and its relationship with team political behaviors, we elaborate on team cohesiveness.

Team Cohesiveness

Team cohesiveness was defined by Festinger (1950, p. 274) as "the resultant of all the forces acting on the members to remain in the group" and was claimed to consist of three facets (i.e., member attraction, group activities or task commitment) and prestige or group pride. However, over the years, other researchers have emphasized only one of the facets. A positive relationship between cohesion and group performance has been shown in several meta-analytic reviews conducted over the past 15 years (Evans & Dion, 1991; Mullen & Copper, 1994; Gully, Devine, & Whitney, 1995).

More recently, Beal, Cohen, Burke, and McLendon (2003) conducted another meta-analysis reviewing the relationship between group cohesion and performance. Their analysis showed that group cohesion was more strongly related to performance behaviors (i.e., what team members do) than to other outcomes and was more strongly related to efficiency than to effectiveness. In addition, all of the cohesion components were significantly related to team performance at the team level of analysis, with task commitment and group pride exhibiting the strongest relations. Finally, they found that when the team task experiences more complex workflow then team cohesion is more strongly related to team performance, thereby making team members more interdependent and placing more emphasis on team member coordination.

Team cohesion is likely to play a key factor when examining politics within and between teams. More cohesive teams are likely to be less preoccupied with political processes. Indeed, Ensley, Pearson, and Amason (2002) found that cohesion in top-management teams was negatively related to affective conflict and positively related to cognitive conflict. Affective conflict is emotional and focused on personal incompatibilities or disputes (Brehmer, 1976; Cosier & Rose, 1977; Jehn, 1992; Priem & Price, 1991; Torrance, 1957). Recently, Summers, Humphrey, and Ferris (in press) found that *flux* in team functioning, caused by team member change, affected both team process and outcomes. This notion of flux appears to have potential to relate to increased use of intrateam politics and should be examined in future research.

In addition, research on groupthink refers to "a mode of thinking that people engage in when they are deeply involved in a cohesive in-group, when the members' strivings for unanimity override their motivation to realistically appraise alternative courses of action...a deterioration of mental efficiency, reality testing and moral judgment that results from in-group pressures" (Janis, 1972, p. 9). Thus, a negative consequence of highly cohesive teams is characterized by minimized conflict within the team or any kind of activity that threatens team unity. Such findings may be the basis for hypotheses claiming that high cohesion minimizes intrateam political behaviors.

Outcomes

Performance

Teams exist to perform tasks, and "performance is the most widely studied criterion variable in the organizational behavior and human resource management literatures" (Bommer, Johnson, Rich, Podsakoff, & Mackenzie, 1995, p. 587). Mathieu, Maynard, Rapp, and Gilson (2008) defined team performance as a three-dimensional concept consisting of:

1. Organizational-level performance: relevant mainly for top-management teams where there is an alignment between team characteristics and organizational outcomes
2. Team performance behaviors and outcomes: behaviors are actions that are relevant to achieving goals such as team process improvement, learning behaviors, and cognitive task performance, and outcomes are the consequences of performance such as accuracy and quality or satisfaction with team service
3. Role-based performance: the extent to which members exhibit the requisite competencies necessary to perform their jobs

In contrast to this division of performance into distinct and measurable dimensions, many studies have used blended or composite measures of team outcomes (Mathieu et al., 2008). For example, Hiller, Day, and Vance (2006) used a measure of effectiveness composed of planning, problem solving, support and consideration, mentoring and development, and overall effectiveness, and Van der Vegt and Bunderson (2005) combined efficiency, quality, overall achievement, productivity, and mission fulfillment.

The relationship between organizational politics and work outcomes, both at the individual and team levels, is important because all organization members have power that can be exercised in unique ways to benefit themselves in their work environment. Power, influence, and politics affect individuals and teams and thus the organization in general. Research examining such a relationship at the team level may seek to answer questions such as:

- What happens when leading teams to specific results collides with the political aspirations of specific team members?
- How do external politics, at the wider organizational environment or even outside the organization, impact team activities toward meeting their goals?
- What happens to team performance when the interests of the individual team members conflict with team interests?

Although research on team politics and team performance is scarce, several propositions can be made based on the literature on teams and organizational politics. For example, when team goals are not clear and uncertainty about procedures is apparent, team members may be more likely to exhibit political behavior. Such behavior may be apparent in an attempt to score organizational points or to acquire their fair share of the available rewards, where, due to uncertainty, the environment does not provide normative guidelines for appropriate behaviors. Such self-interest behaviors may harm team performance because such people do not have the team goals as their priority and the other team members may shift focus from the behaviors needed for achieving team goals toward the political behaviors apparent in the team. Similarly, when others believe an individual is acting in a self-interested or negatively political manner, they may feel the need to engage in their own defensive tactics (Mayes & Allen, 1977) which may hinder performance.

In addition, political behavior may inhibit the development of effective social relationships (Witt, Kacmar, Carlson, & Zivnuska, 2002). Lencioni

(2002) described the ultimate dysfunction as occurring when team members put their individual needs above the collective goal of the team. This tends to shift focus from the relevant team results and impedes the desire to win. In addition, workers less motivated by self-interests may put forth effort toward goals that they genuinely believe to be important to the organization but that in fact are viewed as unimportant by most others (Mayes & Allen, 1977), again hampering organizational performance.

Viability

Team viability is a popular criterion measure, yet it suffers from much construct confusion (Mathieu et al., 2008). Viability has been conceived of as a collective sense of belonging (similar to the notion of social cohesion), as team membership stability over time, or as the extent to which individuals wish to remain as members of the team. Moreover, team viability (Barrick, Bradley, Kristof-Brown, & Colbert, 2007) often is combined with affect or attitudinal measures, such as group member satisfaction, team climate or atmosphere, team commitment, and group cohesion (Balkundi & Harrison, 2006). Balkundi and Harrison regarded team viability as "a team's potential to retain its members through their attachment to the team, and their willingness to stay together as a team" (p. 52). They found that the density of expressive ties between team members is strongly and positively associated with team viability.

Relying on these findings, it seems reasonable to predict that the nature of the political behaviors exhibited by team members will be related to team viability. When team members use power in an attempt to divide the team and form coalitions within the team, competing for acknowledgment of their ideas over those of others, it is unlikely for the team to be viable. Therefore, high team viability is expected to be negatively related to the level of negative team politics. However, team members may use political skill in an attempt to form strong and tight team identification with their goals and through this to create a highly viable team.

Innovation and Learning

Exerting power and influence for personal gain seems to contradict efforts to renew and improve organizational and team processes. Thus, the relationship between inter-team politics and positive team outcomes such as team innovation and learning is likely to be a negative sign. Team innovation is defined as "the intentional introduction and application within a team, of ideas, processes, products or procedures new to the team, designed to significantly benefit the individual, the team, the organization, or wider society" (West & Wallace, 1991, p. 303). Thus, team innovation reflects an integration among people, structures, and interaction processes (Agrell & Gustafson, 1996). To promote team innovation, research has shown the importance of developing a team climate of trust and openness (West, 1990), vision and shared objectives (West), team collaboration (West & Wallace, 1991), and the team's belief in its potency to perform well and attain goals (Farr & Ford, 1990).

Obviously, if the team is overwhelmed by negative politics and dysfunctional political power games within it, trust, openness, and collaboration will not be part of the team atmosphere, which will interfere with the innovation process. On the other hand, teams that feel a high political stance in regards to the organization are likely to feel potency concerning their ability to attain what is needed to achieve their goals and be more innovative.

Team learning is defined as "a process in which a team takes action, obtains and reflects on feedback, and makes changes to adapt or improve" (Edmondson, 2002, p. 129). In a recent review of team learning, Edmondson, Garvin, and Gino (2008) claimed that power dynamics exhibit an important theoretical relationship with learning behavior within teams. Teams are not likely to learn if they operate in a threatening environment not characterized by a shared perception of psychological safety (i.e., the shared belief that a group is safe for interpersonal risk taking; Edmondson, 1999). In such negative environments, people are afraid to bring up and discuss mistakes due to fear of criticism by powerful others and because owning up to mistakes may be used against them in the political "games" of other team members.

Moreover, learning requires open communication and the sharing of knowledge and experience. Individuals in teams with heightened political behavior are likely to share the information and knowledge they have. They are not likely to discuss their own mistakes but are more likely to use others' mistakes as opportunities to "score points." In sum, politics in teams may be detrimental both for team innovation and team learning.

BOUNDARY-SPANNING (INTERTEAM) TEAM POLITICAL BEHAVIOR

Thus far, the discussion has involved examining the political behaviors of the team members within the team. However, as entities within organizations, teams may behave politically toward other teams in the organizations or toward other entities such as management. In addition, teams may interact with forces outside of the organization and may enact power and influence toward them. In fact, Pfeffer (1986) argued that groups must manage relations with outsiders because they often depend on those outsiders for resources or information.

Ancona (1990) discussed a specific role for team members who import technical information from outside the team; this has been referred to as *boundary spanners, stars,* and *gatekeepers.* However, Ancona and Caldwell (1988) theoretically expanded this role and showed that groups or teams use external contacts not only to obtain technical information but also to map resources, support, and trends in organizations, to influence those individuals with key resources, and to synchronize work flow.

Power and influence appear to be major themes in team–environment relations (Ancona, 1990). Based on her exploratory study, Ancona concluded that teams have the strength to influence their environment. In fact, when management was not clear about its goals and directions, teams that knew in what direction they want to go and started moving in that direction actually influenced the decisions made by management. Thus, it seems that the environment and the team have a dual influence such that the "environment influences a team by setting limits on activity and by picking particular teams as models defining the task and performance. In this case, autonomy was easily talked about but not often provided. A team can influence its environment by promoting its activities as the ones that should shape the definition of task and performance" (p. 358).

So, in this mutual relationship between the team and its environment, politics plays an important role. When resources are scarce, teams may use political tactics to win resources over other teams. In addition, just as individuals, teams may use political skill in attempts to move forward their agendas. Such agendas may or may not coincide with management's agendas and create an interesting political arena.

Types of Teams

In the team literature, there are a number of typologies regarding types of teams. For example, Cohen and Bailey (1997) defined four types of teams that can be identified in organizations today: work, parallel, project, and management. Sundstrom et al. (1990) differentiated between advice and involvement teams, production and service teams, project and development teams, and action and negotiation teams. Although distinctive, there are many similarities between these two typologies. In the following sections, we elaborate on different types of teams and have chosen these types because the political behavior within them is especially interesting.

Self-Managing Teams

A self-managing team is defined as a team that has authority and accountability for executing the work and managing the work process, but within a structure and toward purposes set by others (Wageman, 2001). Hackman (1986) claimed that self-managing teams vary to the degree to which they (1) take collective responsibility for the outcomes of their work, (2) monitor their own performance, actively seeking data about how well they are doing, and (3) manage their own performance, making alterations in work strategies when circumstances change or when feedback indicates that a new approach may be needed.

Self-managing teams have become a common organizational entity around which work is structured (Cascio, 1995; Hackman, 1990; Lawler, 1986; Manz & Sims, 1993). Because self-managing teams have a large amount of autonomy and control over their immediate work environments (Cohen, Chang, & Ledford, 1997), they require less hierarchical command and control leadership (Morgeson, 2005). However, these teams often have an externally appointed leader who is in charge of making sure the team is progressing in the intended direction. Such teams may be highly susceptible to political dynamics as team members use the lack of a dominant leader as a chance to move forward their own agendas.

Recent research has explored the evolution of shared leadership within such self-managed teams. This idea has been referred to as distributed leadership and has been defined in very political terms as emergent, fluctuating levels of individual team member influence, or mutual influence of, by, and on team members (Pearce, 2004). In other approaches (e.g., Avolio, Sivasubramaniam, Murry, Jung, & Garger, 2003), distributed leadership extends to the collective influence of the team on individual members (p. 149). One interesting question regarding politics in self-lead teams may be the extent to which political skill of team members influences to who and for how long leadership is distributed. Another question is whether such self-managed, self-lead teams are characterized by higher levels of political behaviors.

Top-Management Teams

Pfeffer (1992) argued that political behavior is more profound in TMTs in comparison with other teams. Because the responsibility of top-management teams to the function of the firm or organization is at times crucial for survival and success, it is more likely that internal politics of decision making and external politics directed at other teams or organizations will be higher in TMTs compared with ordinary teams.

Eisenhardt and Bourgeouis (1988) conducted a qualitative study examining the impact of politics in TMTs and found that the TMTs of the effective firms avoided negative political behaviors, whereas the TMTs of poor-performing firms tended to use negative political behaviors. They claimed that this could be explained in two ways. On one hand, poor firm performance is likely to trigger power centralization, which leads to the emergence of political behaviors. On the other hand, engaging in political behaviors may lead to poor performance as it is time-consuming, restricts information flow, and prevents forming of new alliances based on the issue at hand.

Thus, although TMTs are more profoundly occupied by political behavior, at the same time this political behavior seems to harm performance. Future research should further examine the nature of the quantity and quality of team political behavior and its relationship to team and organization performance.

Ad Hoc Teams

One of the issues concerning research on teams is whether the team members work together continuously or whether the teamwork is a one-time episode. Examples of ad hoc teams are cross-functional project teams or teams formed to solve an urging and critical temporary problem.

Sundstrom et al. (1990) defined *action teams* as short-term mission teams that are formed around a certain task and are dissolved upon its completion. Such action teams conduct each task within the context of a different team in a way that issues such as cohesion and team learning receive different consideration.

An example of research comparing ongoing and short-term teams is that of Mennecke and Valacich (1998) using a short decision-making task. They found that ongoing teams spent less time on the tas and discussed less unique information yet were more satisfied with the team process. In another study, Hall and Williams (1966) found that short-term teams preferred compromise, whereas ongoing teams preferred more creative conflict-handling techniques.

Because long-term teams know the distribution of power within the team, politics may demonstrate less negative effects on performance compared with short-term teams in which people may spend time and effort trying to dominate. Short-term teams may be more focused on the team goals, knowing this is a one-time joint effort, as opposed to ongoing teams who may see a specific task as an opportunity to change the power structure of the team. Therefore, political issues may be toned down and not get central attention by members.

Hierarchical Teams

A primary characteristic of hierarchical teams is that there are status differences among the team members, and responsibility for the final decision lies with the leader (Hollenbeck et al., 1995; Phillips, 2002). Examples of hierarchical teams include military teams, emergency room teams, or managerial teams. When examining the effectiveness of such teams in decision-making tasks, Hollenbeck et al. (1995) incorporated the concept of hierarchical sensitivity.

Hollenbeck et al. (1995) defined hierarchical sensitivity as "the degree to which the team leader effectively weights staff members' judgments in arriving at the team's decision. Although the leader does the weighting, hierarchical sensitivity is conceptualized as arising out of the dyadic level because the staff member can influence the leader in terms of how much weight to put on any one or all of his or her recommendations…. A team that is high in hierarchical sensitivity has a leader who uses the best possible weight for each staff member's opinion when combining these to arrive at the team's decision. A team that is low in hierarchical sensitivity has a leader whose weighting system deviates substantially from the optimum" (pp. 297–298). Thus, team members trying to influence the leader to use their ideas or opinions as heavier weight in the team decision-making processes may cause the team to have lower hierarchical sensitivity, which has been associated with lower team decision accuracy (Hollenbeck et al., 1995).

Virtual Teams

Virtual teams are defined as groups of employees with unique skills, situated in distant locations, whose members must collaborate using technology across space and time to accomplish important organizational tasks (Lipnack & Stamps, 2000). The development of new and improved forms of communication and information technology has created new opportunities for organizations to build and manage virtual teams (Kirkman, Rosen, Tesluk, & Gibson, 2004).

Because virtual teams can rapidly respond to business globalization challenges (Kayworth & Leidner, 2001; Maznevski & Chudoba, 2000; Montoya-Weiss, Massey, & Song, 2001), which is a key factor in today's dynamic, complex, and unpredictable world, their use is expanding exponentially (Kirkman, Rosen, Gibson, Tesluk, & McPherson, 2002). In fact, the *Wall Street Journal* reported that more than half of companies with more than 5,000 employees use virtual teams (de Lisser, 1999). Also, a recent survey by the Gartner group found that more than 60% of professional employees work in virtual teams (Kanawattanachai & Yoo, 2002).

A meta-analysis by Martins, Gilson, and Maynard (2004) reviewed findings related to team inputs, processes, and outcomes and identified areas of agreement and inconsistency in the literature on virtual teams. One consistent finding presented in their study is that virtual interaction increases the amount of time required to accomplish tasks (e.g., Cappel & Windsor, 2000; Daly, 1993; Graetz, Boyle, Kimble, Thompson, & Garloch, 1998; Hollingshead, 1996; Straus, 1996; Weisband, 1992). Therefore, it is possible that during a longer phase of task accomplishment, effort, politics, and power struggles may become more prevalent because there is more time to become involved in coalition building and influence-related actions.

Another interesting question regarding politics and virtual teams is whether the use of less face-to-face meetings decreases the use of political tactics between team members. Indeed, Elron and Vigoda-Gadot (2006) found that influence tactics and political processes in virtual teams are more restrained and mild than in face-to-face teams. Finally, an interesting question, which to the best of our knowledge has not been studied, concerns the relative power such virtual teams have in the organization compared with other teams.

MEASUREMENT AND ANALYSIS ISSUES

One interesting concern related to empirical research on teams and politics is the issue of how to best measure *politics* in teams. First, one must decide whether to examine the perceptions of politics, actual political behavior, or the demonstration of political skill. Three main methods of measurement of team-level constructs are proposed in the literature (Kirkman, Telsuk, & Rosen, 2001). The most commonly used method is the aggregation of individual-level responses. Thus, team members respond to questions regarding individual-level phenomena, and these responses are aggregated to reflect a team-level construct.

The second method is similar to the first, but questions are aimed at team-level phenomena. Such questions capture the perceptions of the individual regarding a characteristic of the team, and these perceptions are too aggregated to the team level. Both of these methods require the researcher to demonstrate agreement among team members concerning the construct being measured individually. The third method for measuring is the consensus method, which involves the team meeting and actually answering the questionnaire together using consensus decision making. Each of these methods has advantages and disadvantages and may impact the conclusions reached in the specific research.

Therefore, when individual political behavior is extended to the team level, one may argue that those individual behaviors should be aggregated to represent the overall team politics, especially when this is compared with the political behavior of other teams. However, if the political behavior of team members differs greatly, this aggregation may be problematic.

Besides aggregation, there are other ways to operationalize concepts at the team level. Humphrey, Hollenbeck, Meyer, and Ilgen (2007) examined the variance between team members regarding specific traits as team-level measures of such traits. According to this approach, team political behavior may be constructed as the variance in perceptions regarding the political behavior of their own political behavior within the team, with high variance indicating strongly differing perceptions of behaviors. Taggar (2002) suggested that it might be that the characteristic of a team may be influenced by individual team members. For example, political skill of the team may be assessed as the political skill of the team leader or by the most political member of the team. Hence, it is important to note that the results of any research trying to understand the relationship between team-level politics and any other variable will be affected by the measurement method.

Finally, the analytical procedures appropriate when quantitative measures are used for team-level constructs also should be mentioned. As much of the research on teams involves variables measured at different levels of analysis (e.g., individual, team, and organizational levels), it is important that the analytical procedure used to analyze the data takes into account the multilevel nature of the data. Hierarchical linear modeling (HLM) allows for precisely this type of examination. The HLM approach permits testing the nesting of individuals within teams and the nesting of teams within organizations. The advantage of HLM is that by modeling residuals at levels two and three (i.e., with the individual serving as the level-one unit of analysis), such models acknowledge that individuals belonging to the same team and teams belonging to the same organization may be more similar to one another than to individuals belonging to different teams or to different organizations (Bryk & Raudenbush, 1992).

DISCUSSION, CONTRIBUTIONS, AND FURTHER RESEARCH

How can organizational politics contribute to the understanding of team processes, and what can team-based knowledge bring into future studies on workplace politics? This chapter takes a first step in exploring this missing link in the literature. It is aimed at exploring the nexus between these realms and has attempted to show that they are highly relevant to one another. Most research on organizational politics has concentrated on the influence politics has on the individual in the organization or on the organization as a whole. It largely has overlooked the role organizational politics plays at the team level, both within the team and in the eternal activities of the team. Similarly, research on teams has focused on many team processes as influencing the performance of teams but largely has missed the impact internal and external organizational politics can exert on team effectiveness.

In addition, if team politics is a team-level phenomenon, then the consequences of such team political behavior must be examined at the team level. In other words, team political behavior, as a team-level process, is likely to impact team-level performance or emergent states such as team cohesion, stability, and resilience. Additionally, such team politics may demonstrate positive or negative effects on such team-level outcomes depending on the constructiveness of the use of the political power the team uses.

Moreover, team politics also may affect outcomes at the organization level. Teams high in political behavior may be alienated by other organizational teams and may use their power to affect organizational decisions. From the organizations' point of view, leaders may find it much harder to disregard requests, threats, or sanctions conducted by highly political teams compared with when such requests, threats, or sanctioned are carried out by individuals.

As mentioned already, the political behavior and style of the team leader also are important issues when discussing team politics. The research conducted to date has indicated that politically skilled leaders are associated with more effective performance. However, the relationship between the political behavior of the leader and the political behavior of the team has yet to be examined. Do highly political leaders create highly political teams? Or perhaps teams with highly political leaders are low in internal political behavior because the leader dominates all power issues? In addition, team politics may intervene in the relationship between leader political skill and performance of the individual, team, or organization. Similarly, future research must begin to examine the antecedents and consequences of team politics as well as the conditions and circumstances that may affect the team politics–performance relationships. The hope is that the ideas presented in this chapter stimulate increased scholarship in this important area of inquiry.

REFERENCES

Agrell, A., & Gustafson, R. (1996). Innovation and creativity in work groups. In M.A. West (Ed.), *The handbook of work group psychology* (pp. 317–344). Chichester, UK: John Wiley.

Ahearn, K.K., Ferris, G.R., Hochwarter, W.A., Douglas, C., & Ammeter, A.P. (2004). Leader political skill and team performance, *Journal of Management, 30,* 309–327.

Ancona, D.G. (1990). Outward bound: Strategies for team survival in organizations. *Academy of Management Journal, 33,* 334–365.

Ancona, D.G., & Caldwell, D.F. (1988). Beyond task maintenance: Defining external functions in groups. *Group and Organization Studies, 13,* 468–494.

Ancona, D.G., & Caldwell, D.F. (1992). Bridging the boundary: External activity and performance in organizational teams. *Administrative Science Quarterly, 37,* 634–665.

Argote, L., Ingram, P., Levine, J.M., & Moreland, R.L. (2000). Knowledge transfer in organizations: Learning from the experience of others. *Organization Behavior and Human Decision Processes, 82,* 1–8.

Avolio, B., Sivasubramaniam, N., Murry, W., Jung, D., & Garger, J. (2003). Assessing shared leadership: Development and preliminary validation of a team multifactor leadership questionnaire. In C. Pearce & J. Conger (Eds.), *Shared leadership: Reframing the hows and whys of leadership.* Thousand Oaks, CA: Sage Publications.

Bacharach, S.B., & Lawler, E.J. (1980). *Power and politics in organizations.* San Francisco: Jossey-Bass.

Balkundi, P., & Harrison, D.A. (2006). Ties, leaders, and time in teams: Strong inference about network structure's effects on team viability and performance. *Academy of Management Journal, 49,* 49–68.

Barrick, M.R., Stewart, G.L., Neubert, M.J., & Mount, M.K. (1998).Relating member ability and personality to work–team processes and team effectiveness. *Journal of Applied Psychology, 83,* 377–391.

Barrick, M.R., Bradley, B.H., Kristof-Brown, A.L., & Colbert, A.E. (2007). The moderating role of top management team interdependence: Implications for real teams and working groups. *Academy of Management Journal, 50,* 544–577.

Beal D. J., Cohen R.R., Burke M.J., & McLendon, C.L. (2003). Cohesion and performance in groups: A meta-analytic clarification of construct relations. *Journal of Applied Psychology, 88,* 989–1004.

Belbin, R.M. (1993). *Team roles at work.* Oxford, UK: Butterworth-Heinemann.

Bommer, W.H., Johnson, J.L., Rich, G.A., Podsakoff, P.M., & Mackenzie, S.B. (1995). On the interchangeability of objective and subjective measures of employee performance: A meta-analysis. *Personnel Psychology, 48,* 587–605.

Brass, D.J. (1984). Being in the right place: A structural analysis of individual influence in an organization. *Administrative Science Quarterly, 29,* 518–539.

Brass, D.J., & Burkhardt, M.E. (1993). Potential power and power use: An investigation of structure and behavior. *Academy of Management Journal, 36,* 441–470.

Brehmer, B. (1976). Social judgment theory and the analysis of interpersonal conflict. *Psychological Bulletin, 83,* 985–1003.

Brouer, R.L. (2007). *The role of political skill in the leadership process-work outcomes relationships.* Unpublished doctoral dissertation, Department of Management, College of Business, Florida State University, Tallahassee.

Bryk, A., & Raudenbush, S. (1992). *Hierarchical linear models: Applications and data analysis methods.* Newbury Park, CA: Sage Publications.

Burns, T. (1961). Micropolitics: Mechanisms of institutional change. *Administrative Science Quarterly, 6,* 257–281.

Campion, M.A., Medsker, G.J., & Higgs, A.C. (1993). Relations between work group characteristics and effectiveness: Implications for designing effective work groups. *Personnel Psychology, 46*, 823–850.

Cannon-Bowers, J.A., Salas, E., & Converse, S.A. (1993). Shared mental models in expert team decision making. In N.J. Castellan, Jr. (Ed.), *Current issues in individual and group decision making* (pp. 221–246). Hillsdale, NJ: Lawrence Erlbaum.

Cappel, J.J., & Windsor, J.C. (2000). Ethical decision making: A comparison of computer-supported and face-to face group. *Journal of Business Ethics, 28*, 95–107.

Carron, A.V., Brawley, L.R., & Widmeyer, W.N. (1998). Measurement of cohesion in sport and exercise. In J.L. Duda (Ed.), *Advances in sport and exercise psychology measurement*, (pp. 213–226). Morgantown, WV: Fitness Information Technology.

Cascio, W.F. (1995). Whither industrial and organizational psychology in a changing world of work? *American Psychologist, 50*, 928–939.

Casmir, F.L. (1992). Third culture building: A paradigm shift for international and intercultural communication. *Communication Yearbook, 16*, 407–428.

Cohen, S.G., & Bailey, D.E. (1997). What makes teams work: Group effectiveness research from the shop floor to the executive suite. *Journal of Management, 23*(3), 239–290.

Cohen, S.G., Chang, L., & Ledford Jr., G.E. (1997). A hierarchical construct of self-management leadership and its relationship to quality of work life and perceived work group effectiveness. *Personnel Psychology, 49*, 643–676.

Cosier, R.A., & Rose, R.L. (1977). Cognitive conflict and goal conflict effects on task performance. *Organizational Behavior and Human Performance, 19*, 378–391.

Cropanzano, R., Howes, J.C., Grandey, A.A., & Toth, P. (1997). The relationship of organizational politics and support to work behaviors, attitudes, and stress, *Journal of Organizational Behavior, 18*, 159–80.

Cyert, R.M., & March, J.G. (1963). *A behavioral theory of the firm*. New York: Prentice Hall.

Daly, B.L. (1993). The influence of face-to-face versus computer-mediated communication channels on collective induction. *Accounting, Management, and Information Technology, 3*, 1–22.

de Lisser, E. (1999). Update on small business: Firms with virtual environments appeal to workers. *Wall Street Journal*, B2.

Devine, D.J. (2002). A review and integration of classification systems relevant to teams in organizations. *Group Dynamics: Theory, Research, and Practice, 6*, 291–310.

Douglas, C., & Ammeter, A.P. (2004). An examination of leader political skill and its effect on ratings of leader effectiveness. *Leadership Quarterly, 15*, 537–550.

Driskell, J.E., Hogan, R., & Salas, E. (1987). Personality and group performance. In C. Hendrick (Ed.), *Review of personality and social psychology* (Vol. 9, pp. 91–112). Newbury Park, CA: Sage Publications.

Earley, P.C., & Mosakowski, E. (2000). Creating hybrid team cultures: an empirical test of transnational team functioning. *Academy of Management Journal, 43*, 26–49.

Edmondson, A. (1999). Psychological safety and learning behavior in work teams. *Administrative Science Quarterly, 44*, 350–383.

Edmondson, A. (2002). The local and variegated nature of learning in organizations: A group-level perspective. *Organization Science, 13*, 128–146.

Edmondson, A.C., Garvin, D.A., & Gino, F. (2008). Is yours a learning organization? *Harvard Business Review*, March, 1–10.

Eisenhardt, K.M., & Bourgeois III, L.J. (1988). Politics of strategic decision making in high-velocity environments: Toward a midrange theory. *Academy of Management Journal, 31,* 737–770.

Elron, E. (2000). *Cultural diversity and political processes in multinational top management teams.* Paper presented at the Academy of Management Meeting, Toronto.

Elron, E., & Vigoda-Gadot, E. (2006). Influence and political processes in cyberspace: The case of global virtual teams. *International Journal of Cross-Cultural Management, 6*(3), 295–317.

Ensley, M., Pearson, A., & Amason, A. (2002). Understanding the dynamics of new venture top management teams: Cohesion, conflict, and new venture performance. *Journal of Business Venturing, 17,* 365–386.

Evans, C.R., & Dion, K.L. (1991). Group cohesion and performance: A meta-analysis. *Small Group Research, 22*(2), 175–186.

Farr, J.L., & Ford, C.M. (1990). Individual innovation. In M.A. West & J.L. Farr (Eds.), *Innovation and creativity at work* (pp. 63–80). Chichester: John Wiley & Sons.

Ferris, G.R., & Kacmar, K.M. (1992). Perceptions of organizational politics. *Journal of Management, 18,* 93–116.

Ferris, G.R., & King, T.R. (1991). Politics in human resources decisions: A walk on the dark side. *Organizational Dynamics, 20,* 59–71.

Ferris, G.R., Treadway, D.C., Kolodinsky, R.W., Hochwarter, W.A., Kacmar, C.J., Douglas, C., et al. (2005). Development and validation of the political skill inventory. *Journal of Management, 31,* 126–152.

Festinger, L. (1950). Informal social communication. *Psychological Review, 57,* 271–282.

Forsyth, D.R. (1990). *Group dynamics* (2nd ed.). Pacific Grove, CA: Brooks/Cole.

Furst, S.A., Reeves, M., Rosen, B., & Blackburn, R.S. (2004). Managing the life-cycle of virtual teams. *The Academy of Management Executive,* 18(2), 6.

Gist, M.E., Locke, E.A., & Taylor, M.S. (1987). Organizational behavior: Group structure, process, and effectiveness. *Journal of Management, 13,* 237–257

Graetz, K.A., Boyle, E., Kimble, C., Thompson, P., & Garloch, J. (1998). Information sharing in face-to-face, teleconferencing and electronic chat groups. *Small Group Research, 29,* 714–743.

Gully, S.M., Devine, D.J., & Whitney, D.J. (1995). A meta-analysis of cohesion and performance: Effects of level of analysis and task interdependence. *Small Group Research, 26,* 497–520.

Guzzo, R.A., & Shea, G.P. (1992). Group performance and intergroup relations in organizations. In M.D. Dunnette & L.M. Hough (Eds.), *Handbook of industrial and organizational psychology* (2nd ed., Vol. 3, pp. 269–313). Palo Alto, CA: Consulting Psychologists Press.

Guzzo, R.A., & Dickson, M.W. (1996). Teams in organizations: Recent research on performance and effectiveness. In J.T. Spence (Ed.), *Annual review of psychology* (Vol. 47, pp. 307–338). Palo Alto, CA: Annual Reviews.

Hackman, J.R. (1983). *A normative model of work team effectiveness.* Technical Report 2, Yale School of Organization and Management, New Haven, CT.

Hackman, J.R. (1986). The psychology of self-management in organizations. In M.S. Pallak & R. Perloff (Eds.), *Psychology and work: Productivity, change, and employment* (pp. 85–136). Washington, DC: American Psychological Association.

Hackman, J.R. (1987). The design of work teams. In J.W. Lorsch (Ed.), *Handbook of organizational behavior* (pp. 315–342). Englewood Cliffs, NJ: Prentice Hall.

Hackman, J.R. (1990). *Groups that work (and those that don't): Creating conditions for effective teamwork.* San Francisco, CA: Jossey-Bass.

Hall, J., & Williams, M.S. (1966). A comparison of decision-making performances in established and ad hoc groups. *Journal of Personality and Social Psychology, 3*(2), 214–222.

Hargadon, A.B., &, Sutton, R.I. (1997). Technology brokering and innovation in a product development firm. *Administrative Science Quarterly, 42*(4), 716–749.

Harrison, D.A., Price, K.H., & Bell, M.P. (1998). Beyond relational demography: Time and the effects of surface and deep-level diversity on work group cohesion. *Academy of Management Journal, 41,* 96–107.

Hiller, N.J., Day, D.V., & Vance, R.J. (2006). Collective enactment of leadership roles and team effectiveness: A field study. *Leadership Quarterly, 17,* 387–397.

Hollenbeck, J.R., Ilgen, D.R., Sego, D., Hedlund, J., Major, D.A., & Phillips, J. (1995). The multi-level theory of team decision-making: Decision performance in teams incorporating distributed expertise. *Journal of Applied Psychology, 80,* 292–316.

Hollingshead, A.B. (1996). Information suppression and status persistence in group decision making. *Human Communication Research, 23,* 193–219.

Humphrey, S.E., Hollenbeck, J.R., Meyer, C.J., & Ilgen, D.R. (2007). Personality configurations in self-managed teams: A conceptual examination of the use of seeding to maximize and minimize trait variance in teams. *Journal of Applied Psychology, 92,* 885–892.

Hyatt, D.E., & Ruddy, T.M. (1997). An examination of the relationship between work group characteristics and performance: Once more into the breech. *Personnel Psychology, 50,* 553–585.

Ibarra, H., & Andrews, S.B. (1993). Power, social influence, and sense making: Effects of network centrality and proximity on employee perceptions. *Administrative Science Quarterly, 38,* 277–303.

Ilgen, D.R., Hollenbeck, J.R., Johnson, M., & Jundt, D. (2005). Teams in organizations: From the input-process-output models to IMOI models. *Annual Review of Psychology, 56,* 517–543.

Janis, I.L. (1972). *Victims of groupthink: A psychological study of foreign policy decisions and fiascoes.* Boston: Houghton Mifflin.

Jehn, K. (1992). *The impact of intragroup conflict on effectiveness: A multimethod examination of the benefits and detriments of conflict.* Unpublished doctoral dissertation, Northwestern University, Evanston, IL.

Kanawattanachai, P., & Yoo, Y. (2002). Dynamic nature of trust in virtual teams. *Journal of Strategic Information Systems, 11,* 187–213.

Katz D., & Kahn R.L. (1978). *The social psychology of organizations* (2nd ed.). New York: Wiley.

Katzenbach, J.R., & Smith, D.K. (1993). The discipline of teams. *Harvard Business. Review, 71,* 111–20.

Kayworth, T.R., & Leidner, D.E. (2001). Leadership effectiveness in global virtual teams. *Journal of Management Information Systems, 18,* 7–40.

Kipnis, D., Schmidt, S.M., & Wilkinson, I. (1980). Intraorganizational influence tactics: Exploration in getting one's way. *Journal of Applied Psychology, 65,* 440–452.

Kirkman, B.L., Tesluk, P.E., & Rosen, B. (2001). Assessing the incremental validity of team consensus ratings over aggregation of individual-level data in predicting team effectiveness. *Personnel Psychology, 54,* 645–667.

Kirkman, B.L., Rosen, B., Gibson, C.B., Tesluk, P.E., & McPherson, S.O. (2002). Five challenges to virtual team success: Lessons from Sabre, Inc. *Academy of Management Executive, 16*(3), 67–79.

Kirkman, B.L., Rosen, B., Tesluk, P.E., & Gibson, C.B. (2004). The impact of team empowerment on virtual team performance: The moderating role of face-to-face interaction. *Academy of Management Journal, 47*(2), 175–192.

Klein, K.J., Ziegart, J.C., Khight, A.P., & Xiao, Y. (2006). Dynamic delegation: Shared, hierarchical, and deindividualized leadership in extreme action teams. *Administrative Science Quarterly, 51*, 590–621.

Klimoski, R.J., & Mohammed, S. (1994). Team mental model: Construct or metaphor. *Journal of Management, 20*(2), 403–437.

Kozlowski, S.W.J., & Bell, B.S. (2003). Work groups and teams in organizations. In W.C. Borman & D.R. Ilgen (Eds.), *Handbook of psychology: Industrial and organizational psychology* (Vol. 12, pp. 333–375). New York: Wiley.

Kozlowski, S.W.J., Gully, S.M., Nason, E.R., & Smith, E.M. (1999). Developing adaptive teams: A theory of compilation and performance across levels and time. In D.R. Ilgen & E.D. Pulakos (Eds.), *The changing nature of work performance: Implications for staffing, personnel actions, and development* (pp. 240–292). San Francisco: Jossey-Bass.

Kozlowski, S.W.J., & Klein, K.J. (2000). A multilevel approach to theory and research in organizations: Contextual, temporal, and emergent processes. In K.J. Klein & S.W.J. Kozlowski (Eds.), *Multilevel theory, research, and methods in organizations: Foundations, extensions, and new directions* (pp. 3–90). San Francisco: Jossey-Bass.

Lawler, E.E. (1986). *High involvement manage*ment. San Francisco: Jossey- Bass.

Lee, F., & Tiedens, L.Z. (2001). Who's being served? "Self-serving" attributions in social hierarchies. *Organizational Behavior and Human Decision Processes, 84*, 254–287.

Lencioni, P. (2002). *The five dysfunctions of a team.* New York: John Wiley and Sons.

Lipnack, J., & Stamps, J. (2000). *Virtual teams: People working across boundaries with technology* (2nd ed.). New York: Wiley.

Mann, R.D. (1959). A review of the relationships between personality and performance in small groups. *Psychological Bulletin, 56*, 241–270.

Manz, C.C., & Sims Jr., H.P. (1993). *Business without bosses: How self-managing teams are building high-performance companies.* New York: Wiley.

Marks, M.A., Mathieu, J.E., & Zaccaro, S.J. (2001). A temporally based framework and taxonomy of team processes. *Academy of Management Review, 26*, 356–376.

Martins, L.L., Gilson, L.L., & Maynard, M.T. (2004). Virtual teams: What do we know and where do we go from here? *Journal of Management, 30*, 805–835.

Maslyn, J.M., & Fedor, D.B. (1998). Perceptions of politics: Does measuring different foci matter? *Journal of Applied Psychology, 84*, 645–653.

Mathieu, J., Maynard, M.T., Rapp, T., & Gilson, L. (2008). Team effectiveness 1997–2007: A review of recent advancements and a glimpse into the future. *Journal of Management, 34*(3), 410–476.

Mayes, B.T., & Allen, R.W. (1977). Toward a definition of organizational politics. *Academy of Management Review, 2*, 672–678.

Maznevski, M.L., & Chudoba, K.M. (2000). Bridging space over time: Global virtual team dynamics and effectiveness. *Organization Science, 11*, 473–492.

McGrath, J.E. (1964). *Social psychology: A brief introduction.* New York: Holt, Rinehart and Winston.

McGrath, J.E. (1984). *Groups: Interaction and performance*. Englewood Cliffs, NJ: Prentice-Hall.

McLeod, P.L., & Lobel, S.A. (1992). The effects of ethnic diversity on idea generation in small groups. *Academy of Management Best Paper Proceedings, 227–231*.

Mennecke, B.E., & Valacich, J.S. (1998). Information is what you make of it: The influence of group history and computer support on information sharing, decision quality, and member perceptions. *Journal of Management Information Systems, 15,* 173–197.

Milliken, F.J., & Martins, L.L. (1996). Searching for common threads: Understanding the multiple effects of diversity in organizational groups. *Academy of Management Review, 21,* 402–433.

Mintzberg, H. (1983). *Power in and around organizations*. Englewood Cliffs, NJ: Prentice-Hall.

Montoya-Weiss, M.M., Massey, A.P., & Song, M. (2001). Getting it together: Temporal coordination and conflict management in global virtual teams. *Academy of Management Journal, 44,* 1251–1262.

Morgeson, F.P. (2005). The external leadership of self-managing teams: Intervening in the context of novel and disruptive events. *Journal of Applied Psychology, 90,* 497–508.

Morgeson, F.P., & Hofmann, D.A. (1999). The structure and function of collective constructs: Implications for multilevel research and theory development. *Academy of Management Review, 24,* 249–265.

Mullen, B., & Copper, C. (1994). The relation between group cohesiveness and performance: An integration. *Journal of Applied Psychology, 115,* 210–227.

O'Reilly, C.A., Caldwell, D.F., & Barnett, W.P. (1989). Work group demography, social integration, and turnover. *Administrative Science Quarterly, 34,* 21–37.

Orr, J. (1996). *Talking about machines: An ethnography of a modern job*. Ithaca, NY: Cornell University Press.

Nonaka, I., & Takeuchi, H. (1995). *The knowledge-creating company*. Oxford University Press: New York.

Parker, C.P., Dipboye, R.L., & Jackson, S.L. (1995). Perceptions of organizational politics: an investigation of antecedents and consequences. *Journal of Management, 21,* 891–912.

Pearce, C.L. (2004). The future of leadership: Combining vertical and shared leadership to transform knowledge work. *Academy of Management Executive, 18(1),* 47–57.

Pepinsky, P., Pepinsky, H., & Pavlik, W. (1960). The effects of task complexity and time pressure upon team productivity. *Journal of Applied Psychology, 44,* 34–38.

Pfeffer, J. (1986). A resource dependence perspective on intercorporate relations. In M.S. Mizruchi & M. Schwartz (Eds.), *Structural analysis of business* (pp. 117–132). New York: Academic Press.

Pfeffer, J. (1992). *Management with power*. Boston: Harvard Business School Press.

Phillips, J.M. (2002). Antecedents and consequences of procedural justice perceptions in hierarchical decision-making teams. *Small Group Research, 33,* 32–64.

Podsakoff, P.M., Ahearne, M., & Mackenzie, S.B. (1997). Organizational citizenship behavior and the quantity and quality of work group performance. *Journal of Applied Psychology, 82,* 262–70.

Polzer, J.T., Milton, L.P., & Swann, W.B.J.R. (2002). Capitalizing on diversity: interpersonal congruence in small work groups. *Administrative Science Quarterly, 47,* 296–324.

Porter, L.W., Allen, R.W., & Angle, H.L. (1981). The politics of upward influence in organizations. In B.M. Staw & L.L. Cummings (Eds.), *Research in organizational behavior* (Vol. 3, pp. 109–149). Greenwich, CT: JAI Press.

Priem, R.L., & Price, K.H. (1991). Process and outcome expectations for the dialectical inquiry, devil's advocacy, and consensus techniques of strategic decision making. *Group and Organization Studies, 16,* 206–225.

Robbins, S.P. (2003). *Organizational behavior: Concepts, controversies, and applications* (10th ed.). Upper Saddle River, NJ: Prentice-Hall.

Semadar, A., Robins, G., & Ferris, G.R. (2006). Comparing the effects of multiple social effectiveness constructs in the prediction of managerial performance. *Journal of Organizational Behavior, 27,* 443–461.

Senior, B. (1997). Team roles and team performance: is there really a link? *Journal of Occupational and Organizational Psychology, 70,* 241–58.

Steiner, I.D. (1972). *Group process and productivity.* New York: Academic Press.

Stewart, G.L., Fulmer, I.S., & Barrick, M.R. (2005). An exploration of member roles as a multilevel linking mechanism for individual traits and team outcomes. *Personnel Psychology, 58*(2), 343–365.

Straus, S.G. (1996). Getting a clue: The effects of communication media and information distribution on participation and performance in computer-mediated and face-to-face groups. *Small Group Research, 27,* 115–142.

Summers, J.K., Humphrey, S.E., & Ferris, G.R. (in press). Team member change and flux in coordination and performance: Effects of strategic core roles, controllability, and cognitive ability. Academy of Management Journal.

Sundstrom, E. (1999). The challenges of supporting work team effectiveness. In E. Sundstrom (Ed.), *Supporting work team effectiveness: Best management practices for fostering high performance.* San Francisco: Jossey-Bass.

Sundstrom, E., De Meuse, M.P., & Futrell, D. (1990). Work teams: Application and effectiveness. *American Psychologist, 45,* 120–133.

Taggar, S. (2002). Individual creativity and group ability to utilize individual creative resources: A multilevel model. *Academy of Management Journal, 45,* 315–330.

Tesluk, P.E., & Mathieu, J.E. (1999). Overcoming roadblocks to effectiveness: Incorporating management of performance barriers into models of work group effectiveness. *Journal of Applied Psychology, 84,* 200–217.

Torrance, E.P. (1957). Group decision making and disagreement. *Social Forces, 35,* 314–318.

Tuckman, B.W. (1965). Developmental sequence in small groups. *Psychological Bulletin, 63,* 384–389.

Van der Vegt, G.S., & Bunderson, J.S. (2005). Learning and performance in multidisciplinary teams: the importance of collective team identification. Academy of Management Journal, 48, 532–47.

Vigoda, E. (2000). The relationship between organizational politics, job attitudes, and work outcomes: Exploration and implications for the public sector. *Journal of Vocational Behavior, 57,* 326–347.

Vigoda, E. (2001). Reactions to organizational politics: A cross-cultural examination in Israel and Britain. *Human Relations, 54,* 1483–1518.

Vigoda, E. (2002). Stress-related aftermaths to workplace politics: An empirical assessment of the relationship among organizational politics, job stress, burnout, and aggressive behavior. *Journal of Organizational Behavior, 23,* 571–591.

Vigoda-Gadot, E., & Drory, A. (Eds.).(2006). *Handbook of organizational politics.* Cheltenham, UK: Edward Elgar.

Wageman, R. (2001). How leaders foster self-managing team effectiveness: Design choices vs. hands-on coaching. *Organization Science, 12,* 559–577.

Watson, W.E., Kumar, K., & Michaelsen, L.K. (1993). Cultural diversity's impact on inter-action process and performance: Comparing homogeneous and diverse task groups. *Academy of Management Journal, 36,* 590–602.

Webber, S.S., & Donahue, L.M. (2001). Impact of highly and less job-related diversity on work group cohesion and performance. *Journal of Management, 27,* 141–162.

Weisband, S. (1992). Group discussion and first advocacy effects in computer-mediated and face-to-face decision making groups. *Organizational Behavior and Human Decision Processes, 53,* 352–380.

Welbourne, T.M., Johnson, D.E., & Erez, A. (1998). The role-based performance scale: Validity analysis of a theory-based measure. *Academy of Management Journal, 41,* 540–555.

West, M.A. (1990). The social psychology of innovation in groups. In M.A. West & J.L. Farr (Eds.), *Innovation and creativity at work* (pp. 309–333). Chichester, UK: Wiley.

West, M.A., & Wallace, M. (1991). Innovation in health care teams. *European Journal of Social Psychology, 21,* 303–315.

Williams, K.Y., & O'Reilly, C.A. (1998). Demography and diversity in organizations. In B.M. Staw & R.M. Sutton (Eds.), *Research in organizational behavior* (Vol. 20, pp. 77–140). Stamford, CT: JAI Press.

Witt, L.A., Kacmar, K.M., Carlson, D.S., & Zivnuska, S. (2002). Interactive effects of person-ality and organizational politics on contextual performance. *Journal of Organizational Behavior, 23,* 911–926.

11

Leadership and Organizational Politics: A Multilevel Review and Framework for Pragmatic Deals

Francis J. Yammarino
State University of New York at Binghamton

Michael D. Mumford
University of Oklahoma

> If you would persuade, you must appeal to interest rather than intellect.
>
> **—Benjamin Franklin (1706–1790)**

The literature on organizational politics including political behavior, perceptions of politics, and political skill (e.g., Ferris, Adams, Kolodinsky, Hochwarter, & Ammeter, 2002; Ferris, Davidson, & Perrewé, 2005; Ferris & Hochwarter, 2011; Ferris, Treadway, et al., 2005; Lux, Ferris, Brouer, Laird, & Summers, 2008; Vigoda-Gadot & Drory, 2006) and the literature on political leadership (e.g., Bass, 2008; Burns, 1978; Silvester, 2008; Tosi, 1992; Valenty & Feldman, 2002) are extensive. In contrast, theoretical work and empirical research at the intersection of leadership and organizational politics is rather new and limited (see Ammeter, Douglas, Gardner, Hochwarter, & Ferris, 2002). In this chapter, the intent is not to review each of those larger literatures separately but rather to first conduct a review of newer work based on levels of analysis at the intersection of leadership and organizational politics.

Next, based on this and related multilevel literatures (see Ammeter et al., 2002; Ferris, Treadway, et al., 2005; Yammarino & Dansereau, 2008, 2009a, 2009b; Yammarino, Dionne, Chun, & Dansereau, 2005), using a pragmatic leadership and a negotiated exchange approach (described in the following section), an inherent multilevel framework is presented for understanding what we call *pragmatic deals* (i.e., our view of the integration of leadership and organizational politics). Briefly, it is proposed that various leader characteristics (skills and network) and key organizational politics dimensions (communication and positioning) generate a pragmatic deal-making process.

The process involves a combination of leader idiosyncrasy credits, visioning, and leader and team ethics and integrity that result in the negotiation of a pragmatic deal. Such deals then undergo an acceptance and evaluation process that ultimately yields various long- and short-term outcomes for both leaders and their teams/units. Five contextual factors affecting the pragmatic negotiated deal-making process also are considered. Overall, 21 multilevel research propositions are asserted, with a number of embedded ideas, for examination in future empirical research.

REVIEW OF LITERATURE ON LEADERSHIP AND ORGANIZATIONAL POLITICS

The review of the theoretical work and empirical research at the intersection of leadership and organizational politics began with Ammeter et al. (2002). An initial review and conceptualization in the area yielded 17 articles that include a number of ideas aimed at multiple levels of analysis, which can provide a basis for the conceptual framework developed in this chapter. Specifically, in Table 11.1, a summary of this literature is presented where each article is identified along with the primary constructs and concepts, levels of analysis involved, and the key notions and ideas formulated in the articles.

A cursory review of the points highlighted in the table reveals that the vast majority of the articles develop ideas associated with leader political skill at the leader (individual) level of analysis and, secondarily, also with political skill for subordinates and employees at the individual level. Several articles also consider antecedents or precursors (e.g., personality traits and prior relationships) and consequences or outcomes (e.g., performance and affective reactions for leaders and their subordinates and teams) of leaders' and others' political skill. Likewise, in a number of the articles, various moderators (e.g., structure, context) and mediators (e.g., leader–member exchange [LMX], trust) of the antecedent-to-political skill and political skill-to-consequences associations at various (e.g., individual, dyad, team)

TABLE 11.1

Literature on Leadership and Organizational Politics

Authors and Date	Constructs and Concepts	Levels of Analysis	Key Points
Ammeter, Douglas, Gardner, Hochwarter, and Ferris (2002)	Political theory of leadership	Primarily individual/ leader, but also team and organization	Develop a model of a political theory of leadership based on constructive management of shared meaning; consider antecedents of political behavior, leader attributes that contribute to political skill, leader political behaviors, and leader and target audience outcomes
Ahearn, Ferris, Hochwarter, Douglas, and Ammeter (2004)	Leader political skill and team performance	Individual/ leader and team	Leader political skill has a positive impact on team performance and empowerment
Beu and Buckley (2004)	Politically astute leaders and subordinate performance	Individual leader and subordinate	Politically astute transactional, personalized charismatic leaders create an environment for subordinate crimes of obedience and immoral performance
Davis and Gardner (2004)	LMX and organizational politics	Individual leader and subordinate, leader–member dyad	Attributional processes within LMX relationships impact perceptions of organizational politics and organizational cynicism
Douglas and Ammeter (2004)	Leader political skill and effectiveness	Individual leader and subordinate	Subordinate perceptions of leader political skill and leader effectiveness are related for individuals within groups
Hall, Blass, Ferris, and Massengale (2004)	Leader reputation and accountability	Individual leader	Leader reputation influences stakeholder trust and leader accountability and, via an attributional process, perceptions of leader effectiveness and performance
Kan and Parry (2004)	Leadership and resistance to change	Individual leader and subordinate	Organizational politics (expressed as identifying, legitimizing, and reconciling paradox) can both facilitate and confound transformational leadership

continued

TABLE 11.1 (continued)

Literature on Leadership and Organizational Politics

Authors and Date	Constructs and Concepts	Levels of Analysis	Key Points
Novicevic and Harvey (2004)	HRM political skill	Organization and TMT	Organization HRM political skill affects degree to which leadership development capital is mapped onto intellectual capital and reputation of organization
Treadway et al. (2004)	Leader political skill and employee reactions	Individual leader and subordinate	Leader political skill can affect perceived support, trust, satisfaction, cynicism, and commitment of subordinates
Ferris, Treadway, et al. (2005)	Political skill inventory	Individual leader and subordinate	Development and validation of multidimensional political skill inventory consisting of social astuteness, interpersonal influence, networking ability, and apparent sincerity
Ferris, Treadway, Perrewé, Brouer, Douglas, and Lux (2007)	Political skill in organizations	Individual leader and subordinate and in relation to group and organization	Identifies construct domain of political skill (social astuteness, interpersonal influence, networking ability, and apparent sincerity) and embeds it in a cognition-affect-behavior multilevel meta-theoretical framework
Ferris, Zinko, Brouer, Buckley, and Harvey (2007)	Leader bullying behavior	Individual leader	Strategic leader bullying behavior as a form of organizational politics; leader bullying can be viewed as a strategic influence process that can yield positive outcomes under some conditions
Treadway, Ferris, Duke, Adams, and Thatcher (2007)	Subordinate political skill and supervisor ingratiation impression	Individual subordinate, supervisor–subordinate dyad	High political skill subordinates are seen by supervisors as less ingratiating and more facilitating interpersonally and with greater interpersonal influence; low political skill subordinates are seen by supervisors as simply ingratiating and self-interested
Silvester (2008)	Politics and political skill at work	Individual leader and subordinate	Workplace politics and political skill in relation to political behavior performance

TABLE 11.1 (continued)

Literature on Leadership and Organizational Politics

Authors and Date	Constructs and Concepts	Levels of Analysis	Key Points
Brouer, Duke, Treadway, and Ferris (2009)	Political skill and demographic dissimilarity	Individual subordinate, leader–member dyad	Subordinate political skill can help overcome supervisor–subordinate racial dissimilarity and develop high-quality LMX relationships
Smith, Plowman, Duchon, and Quinn (2009)	Political skill of plant managers	Individual leader and in relation to subordinates and organization	High reputation plant managers inspire confidence and trust in subordinates; their political skill is associated with an empowering, goal setting, and management by objectives leadership style and employee and plant performance
Treadway, Adams, Ranft, and Ferris (2009)	CEO celebrity	Individual leader and in relation to organization	CEO political skill (actions and behaviors) can result in attributions of celebrity (short-term) and reputation (long-term) status that impact CEO compensation and firm performance

levels of analysis are developed conceptually and tested empirically in this relatively new literature.

Three of the articles summarized in the table are particularly noteworthy. First, based on an extensive literature review, Ammeter et al. (2002) developed a comprehensive model of a political theory of leadership. Their model is based on constructive management of shared meaning and considers antecedents of political behavior, leader attributes that contribute to political skill, leader political behaviors, and leader and target audience outcomes. They indicated that leaders need not be viewed from this political perspective necessarily as manipulative and personally ambitious.

Second, Ferris, Treadway, et al. (2005) developed and extensively validated the Political Skill Inventory (PSI). Their conceptualization and generally supportive results in three studies and seven samples indicated that the multidimensional PSI consists of social astuteness, interpersonal influence, networking ability, and apparent sincerity; was positively related to self-monitoring, political savvy, emotional intelligence, and performance;

was negatively related to trait anxiety; and was not correlated with general mental ability.

Third, Ferris, Treadway, Perrewé, Brouer, Douglas, and Lux (2007) conducted a comprehensive review of the construct domain of political skill and embedded it in a cognition-affect-behavior multilevel metatheoretical framework. Through this framework, they proposed the ways political skill operates to impact both the users of political skill themselves as well as others (individuals, leaders, and groups) in organizations.

In addition to these major articles, an in-depth reading of the literature summarized in Table 11.1 makes clear that the intersection of leadership and organizational politics work is not only new but also rather limited. In particular, the integration of leadership ideas and approaches in general and organizational politics overall, not simply leader political skill, is still relatively unexplored conceptually and certainly lacking in the number of rigorous empirical research studies. The state of the literature at this point in time is that ideas (theory) are ahead of the data (empirical studies), as is often the case for new areas, but multilevel conceptual and empirical work is scant overall. In the remainder of this chapter, an attempt is made to address this void at the intersection of leadership and organizational politics with the development of an integrative multilevel conceptual framework for pragmatic deals that can be examined empirically in future work.

PRAGMATIC DEALS: INTEGRATION OF LEADERSHIP AND ORGANIZATIONAL POLITICS

In particular, the foregoing review based on levels of analysis of the literature on leadership and organizational politics and related literatures suggest an inherent multilevel integration referred to here as pragmatic deals. Using a pragmatic leadership and a negotiated exchange approach as the core of the deal-making process, the proposed framework for understanding the nature of pragmatic deals is presented in Figure 11.1. A general deal-making approach is illustrated in the four boxes across the top of the figure, and below each of these general boxes more specific elements of pragmatic negotiated deals are presented.

It is proposed that the integration of (1) the leader characteristics of skills and network and (2) key organizational politics dimensions of

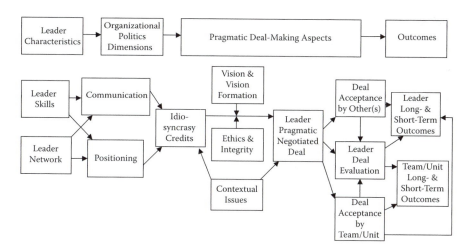

FIGURE 11.1
Framework for pragmatic deals.

communication and positioning generate (3) a pragmatic deal-making process that involves leader idiosyncrasy credits, visioning, and ethical issues as well as deal negotiation, acceptance, and evaluation, and (4) this process ultimately results in various long- and short-term outcomes for both leaders and their teams/units. Contextual issues affecting the pragmatic negotiated deal-making process also are indicated.

Additional details regarding the key constructs for pragmatic deals and the deal-making process are shown in Table 11.2. In particular, for each construct identified in Figure 11.1, the levels of analysis involved along with specific variables and dimensions that comprise the constructs are presented in Table 11.2. In the following sections, the notions shown in Figure 11.1 and Table 11.2 are elaborated, and a series of multilevel propositions for investigation in future work on pragmatic negotiated deals and the deal-making process is presented.

Leader Characteristics and Organizational Politics

The proposed conceptual framework begins with a consideration of key leader characteristics of leader skills, broadly speaking, and leader network and primary organizational politics dimensions of communication and positioning because *who you are, where you are* in an organization or network, and *who you talk to* are critical for making deals. Moreover, although these leader characteristics and organizational politics dimensions are

TABLE 11.2

Constructs and Levels of Analysis for Pragmatic Deals

Key Construct	Levels of Analysis	Variables/Dimensions
Leader Skills	Leader/individual	Conceptual skills (intelligence, creativity, wisdom), experience, and political skills (social astuteness, interpersonal influence)
Leader Network	Leader/individual, leader relative to individuals (dyads) and teams/units	Structural characteristics (connections, centrality) and functional characteristics (boundary spanning) of the network; networking ability
Communication	Leader/individual, leader-to-individuals (dyads) and leader-to-teams/units	Information flows through network and team; can be unidirectional (giving directions, "selling") or bidirectional (consultation, feedback, negotiation) and involve logistics (different modes)
Positioning	Leader/individual, leader relative to individuals (dyads) and teams/units	In physical, psychological, economic, or political "space" to make deals (opportunity, proximity)
Idiosyncrasy Credits	Leader/individual, leader relative to individuals (dyads) and teams/units	Leader's idiosyncrasy credits and credit balance relative to team/unit and other parties (potential deal partners); real and perceived credits are relevant; abilities, likability, and positive impressions; connections to reputation
Leader Pragmatic Negotiated Deal	Leader/individual, leader-to-individuals (dyads) and leader-to-teams/units	Pragmatic leadership as outstanding leadership for deal making; investments and returns in dyadic and group exchanges and negotiations; negotiations for minimum disruption and maximum return to team/unit
Vision (and Vision Formation)	Leader/individual	Vision and assessment of strengths, weaknesses, threats, and opportunities; linkage to mission; vision formation process includes identifying and conceptualizing practical problems and planning, arranging and articulation (selling) practical solutions
Ethics and Integrity	Leader/individual, teams/units	Ethics (professional codes of conduct) and integrity (words and actions consistency) of both leader and team/unit; group norms
Deal Acceptance by Others	Leader/individual, teams/units	Social acceptance of deal by other party (parties) based on credits, prior relations, and benefits

TABLE 11.2 (continued)

Constructs and Levels of Analysis for Pragmatic Deals

Key Construct	Levels of Analysis	Variables/Dimensions
Deal Acceptance by Team/Unit	Teams/units	Social acceptance of deal by leader's team/unit based on credits, leader sensemaking of deal for team/unit, leader building team/unit commitment to deal execution, and benefits
Deal Evaluation	Leader/individual	Leader evaluation and appraisal of deal based on vision, acceptance, and forecasting of short- and long-term outcomes
Leader Outcomes	Leader/individual	Short- and long-term outcomes: primary—performance, productivity, satisfaction, stress reduction, personal growth and development, credit and network building; secondary—reputation, compensation, and promotion
Team Outcomes	Teams/units	Short- and long-term outcomes: primary—performance, productivity, positive affective climate (satisfaction, trust, stress and cynicism reduction), cohesion and efficacy, growth and innovation, network building; secondary—team-based compensation and rewards
Contextual Issues	Leader/individual, teams/units	Leader hierarchical level; time frame over which commitments become due for team/unit; short- and long-term costs and benefits; history of parties and building relations for future deals; salience of deal for team/unit and leader

critical for effective and successful leadership (deal-making), they are intimately connected because positioning and persuasion (communication) require *special knowledge* (i.e., specialized information and skills or expertise and a network from which to access and obtain such information and enhance and develop such skills).

Leader Skills

At the individual-level of analysis, there are individual differences in leader conceptual skills (intelligence, creativity, and wisdom), leader experience, and leader political skill (social astuteness and interpersonal influence; see Ammeter et al., 2002; Bass, 2008; Ferris, Treadway, et al., 2005, 2007; Friedrich, Vessey, Schuelke, Ruark, & Mumford, 2009; Silvester, 2008; Smith, Plowman, Duchon, & Quinn, 2009; Yukl, 2010), which are particularly relevant to making pragmatic deals.

The importance of leader conceptual skills and leader experience for effective leadership are well known and well established (e.g., Bass, 2008; Friedrich et al., 2009; Mumford, 2006; Yukl, 2010). Leader conceptual skills include intelligence, creativity, foresight, intuition, and wisdom, and these skills are critical for problem solving. Leaders identify problems, engage in sensemaking, define problems for the team/unit, and direct others to work toward solutions. Intelligence, or general cognitive ability, is associated with effective problem solving and decision making, and foresight, intuition, and wisdom often contribute to leaders' effective identification of problems, planning and prioritization of tasks, and anticipation of potential pitfalls and outcomes.

Creative problem-solving skills (e.g., idea generation and idea evaluation) help leaders clarify objectives without restricting the problem solving of others. Moreover, general leadership experience provides leaders with an understanding of leadership responsibilities and their distribution, and how to motivate others to accomplish the objectives. Specific time and experience with the team/unit members provide valuable information to recognize and access information and expertise from them.

Tosi (1992) discussed leader political skill in terms of personalized political behavior, especially coercion and manipulation. He asserted that leaders' coercive political behavior toward subordinates is more prevalent in mechanistic organizations, operates through direct confrontation and overt, adversarial relationships, and results in collective protest behavior. In contrast, Tosi proposed that political behaviors are more prevalent in organic organizations and are covert, seeking compliance through rational appeal, persuasion, and manipulation.

Taking a broader perspective, the conceptual and empirical work of Ferris and his colleagues on leader political skill is particularly noteworthy (e.g., Ahearn, Ferris, Hochwarter, Douglas, & Ammeter, 2004; Ammeter et al., 2002; Brouer, Duke, Treadway, & Ferris, 2009; Douglas & Ammeter, 2004; Ferris, Davidson, et al., 2005; Ferris, Treadway, et al., 2005, 2007; Ferris, Zinko, Brouer, Buckley, & Harvey, 2007; Treadway, Adams, Ranft, & Ferris, 2009; Treadway, Ferris, Duke, Adams, & Thatcher, 2007;

Treadway et al., 2004). For these scholars, politically skilled individuals are able to accurately diagnose social contexts and then adapt their behavior to situations such that they select the proper methods and tactics to influence others effectively.

Political skill includes the dimensions of social astuteness, interpersonal influence, networking ability, and apparent sincerity and implies an accurate understanding of the social and task implications of one's behavior and the effective use of social capital to accomplish goals. In particular, social astuteness and interpersonal influence (e.g., including perspective taking, awareness of subordinates' expertise, network awareness and accuracy, and communication) are especially relevant for pragmatic deal making.

Leader Network

The leader's network, or social network, can be thought of as an individual-level phenomenon (e.g., leaders differ in the size and quality of their networks). However, social networks also describe the connections between leaders and other individuals, so various dyads (i.e., special two-person cases of groups and teams) are involved, as well as between leaders and their team/unit or other teams/units, a leader–group phenomenon. These other parties in leaders' networks, both inside and outside of their organizations, may be sources of information, expertise, and resources (e.g., Bass, 2008; Friedrich et al., 2009; Yukl, 2010) or parties with whom deals may be struck. Leaders' ability to perceive and interpret characteristics of a social network and their position in the networks, both internal and external to the organization, are important for effective leadership (Ammeter et al., 2002; Douglas & Ammeter, 2004; Ferris, Treadway, et al., 2005; Hall, Blass, Ferris, & Massengale, 2004; Treadway et al., 2004, 2009).

Social networks focus on the leader's social cognition (network acuity) and then move outward to evaluate the leader's personal (ego) network, the leader's position within the organizational network, and ultimately the leader's position within networks external to the organization (interorganizational network; see Friedrich et al., 2009). These levels of network factors then may have an impact on various outcomes at the leader, team, and organization levels. Particularly relevant dimensions here include structural characteristics (connections and centrality) and functional characteristics (boundary spanning) of the network and the leader's networking ability (e.g., Friedrich et al.).

Communication

Leaders differ in communication skills (i.e., a leader/individual level of analysis) but also communicate with other individuals one to one (i.e., a dyadic level of analysis) and with various teams/units including their own (i.e., which are leader–group phenomena; see Bass, 2008; Yukl, 2010). Communication can be viewed simply as the movement of information throughout a network (internal or external), team/unit, or organization and is a prerequisite for understanding where critical knowledge, expertise, and problems or issues exist.

There is extensive research on the communication style or rhetoric of leaders, how the content of communications can be used to influence followers, and consultation, feedback, direction-giving language, and communication norms (see Bass, 2008; Ferris, Treadway, et al., 2005; Treadway et al., 2004; Yukl, 2010). These communications involve information flows through the leader's network, teams/units, and organization that can be unidirectional (e.g., giving directions and "selling"), bidirectional (e.g., consultation, feedback, and negotiation) and logistics (i.e., different modes of communication; see Friedrich et al., 2009). Consultation is bidirectional communication that occurs at the beginning or during problem solving.

Exchanging feedback is another form of bidirectional communication that often occurs after problem solving and is important for learning and development as well as for goal understanding and attainment. Communication also involves persuasion, influence, and the use of influence tactics (e.g., impression management, political, proactive, and reactive influence tactics) vertically up with superiors and down with subordinates, horizontally with peers, and diagonally with others in organizations (for details, see Yukl, 2010). Moreover, the timing of communication is as relevant here as are the types and forms of communication (e.g., Bass, 2008).

Positioning

As with networks, the leader's positioning can be thought of as an individual-level phenomenon (e.g., leaders differ in their placement in teams and organizations). However, positioning also describes the relative placement between leaders and other individuals, so various dyads are involved, as well as between leaders and their team/unit or other teams/units, a leader–group phenomenon (e.g., Douglas & Ammeter, 2004; Yammarino, 1996). Beyond leader placement in the organizational chart or management (organizational) network (e.g., as linking pins) and within networks external to the organization (e.g., interorganizational network; see Ammeter et al., 2002; Friedrich et al., 2009; Treadway et al., 2009), positioning essentially addresses location in physical, psychological, economic, or political "space" to make deals (i.e., the opportunity for and proximity to deal making).

Leaders' centrality or position within organizational networks has an impact on various outcomes. Regarding their position in an interorganizational network, leaders can alter the network by engaging in boundary-spanning activities or by representation of their organization to other organizations. In addition, leaders may further develop their network by engaging in alliances with others both inside and outside of the organization. Moreover, location and positioning in all these instances need not be viewed simply in terms of physical space.

Leaders occupy a particular psychological space or distance relative to others (Friedrich et al., 2009; Yammarino, 1996; Yammarino & Dansereau, 2009a), and space and location are based on political connections (Ammeter et al., 2002; Ferris, Treadway, et al., 2005, 2007; Hall et al., 2004; Silvester, 2008; Tosi, 1992; Treadway et al., 2009) and resource- and information-based economic space and location (Mumford, 2006). So, leader positioning is a multifaceted phenomenon.

The previous ideas and discussion suggest the following propositions regarding the connections among primary leader characteristics and key organizational politics dimensions:

> Proposition 1: Leader conceptual skills (intelligence, creativity, and wisdom), experience, and political skill (social astuteness and interpersonal influence) will enhance leader one to one (dyadic) and leader-to-group communication.

> Proposition 2: Leader conceptual skills (intelligence, creativity, and wisdom), experience, and political skill (social astuteness and interpersonal influence) will enhance leader positioning and positioning relative to others one to one (dyadic) and in groups/teams.

> Proposition 3: Leader network and networking ability will enhance leader persuasion and communication flows (information, expertise, and resource attainment and allocation) and timing with others, including potential deal partners, one to one (dyadic) and in groups/teams.

Proposition 4: Leader network and networking ability will enhance leader positioning and positioning relative to others one to one (dyadic) and in groups/teams.

Idiosyncrasy Credits

The leader's idiosyncrasy credits (see Hollander, 1958; Phillips, Rothbard, & Dumas, 2009; Stone & Cooper, 2009) can be thought of as an individual-level phenomenon (i.e., leaders differ in the number and type of credits, their credit balances, and their abilities to generate and garner credits). However, idiosyncrasy credits also summarize the connections between leaders and other individuals, so various dyads are involved, as well as between leaders and their team/unit or other teams/units (i.e., a leader–group phenomenon).

For Hollander (1958), idiosyncrasy credits represented a way to capture the total or accumulation of all the positive attributes, characteristics, or resources of a leader. Once leader "debits" were accounted for, the remainder or net (i.e., credits minus debits) was the leader's credit balance. This balance could then be drawn on to allow leaders to deviate from group/team norms, which presumably permitted leaders to do things the team/unit could not that would ultimately benefit the team/unit (in addition to the leader). Phillips et al. (2009) similarly discussed idiosyncrasy credits as the accumulation of positive impressions of leaders acquired through past behaviors and achievements. Stone and Cooper (2009) noted that likely general sources of idiosyncrasy credits are leaders' abilities and skills as well as their talents in inspirational and motivational communication.

In addition to credits and credit balance per se relative to the team/unit and other potential deal partners, particularly relevant issues here are the importance of real and perceived credits, and the abilities and likeableness of, and positive impressions created by, the leader (cf. Ferris, Davidson, et al., 2005; Ferris, Treadway, et al., 2005, 2007). As such, idiosyncrasy credits can also be viewed as similar to, or at least associated with, leader reputation (Ammeter et al., 2002; Hall et al., 2004; Novicevic & Harvey, 2004) and potentially leader celebrity (Treadway et al., 2009). Relatedly, the difficulty of building such credits for leaders and the potential for negative outcomes of the credit-building process for both leaders and their subordinates essentially have been framed by Beu and Buckley (2004) in terms of crimes of obedience and immoral performance, and by Ferris, Zinko, et al. (2007) in terms of strategic bullying.

For our purposes here, leaders build up and then use idiosyncrasy credits, drawing on the credit balance through communication (persuasion) and influence, not only to make or "cut" deals but also to "sell" deals to their own as well as other groups/teams and other leaders. In essence, as in marketing and sales, there is a sales pitch that is communicated to close the deal with other parties involved as well as with leaders' team/unit.

These notions about idiosyncrasy credits, when considered with the prior ideas and discussion, suggest the following propositions:

> Proposition 5: Leader communication abilities and communication flows and timing will enhance leader idiosyncrasy credits and credit balances, both real and perceived, and in connection with others one on one (dyadic) and in groups/teams (both the leader's own and potential deal partners).

> Proposition 6: Leader positioning and positioning relative to others will enhance leader idiosyncrasy credits and credit balances, both real and perceived, and in connection with others one on one (dyadic) and in groups/teams (both the leader's own and potential deal partners).

Leader Pragmatic Negotiated Deal

Pragmatic leadership (e.g., Mumford, 2006) and negotiated exchange (e.g., Yammarino & Dansereau, 2009a) form the core of the deal-making process. Leaders differ in pragmatic styles and skills, a leader/individual level of analysis notion, but also engage in negotiated exchanges (negotiations) with other individuals one to one, a dyadic level of analysis idea, and with various teams/units, a leader–group phenomenon.

Pragmatic Leadership

Pragmatic leadership is a form of outstanding leadership for deal making and an individual-level or individual differences approach to leadership (see Mumford, 2006; Mumford, Hunter, Friedrich, & Caughron, 2009; Mumford & Van Doorn, 2001). Individual differences can focus on leaders and their style but also on the style of others in a team who may have some form of leadership responsibility.

Pragmatic leadership, sometimes referred to as a functional and problem-solving approach to leadership, is outstanding leadership where influence is exercised by identifying and communicating solutions to significant social problems, working through elites or experts in solution generation, creating structures to support solution implementation, and demonstrating the feasibility of these solutions. Essentially, the pragmatic leadership approach asserts that effective leadership behavior fundamentally depends on leaders' ability to solve the kinds of complex social problems that arise in teams (and organizations).

Mumford (2006), Mumford et al. (2009), and Mumford and Van Doorn (2001) provided details on the pragmatic leadership approach and articulated the leader capabilities, knowledge, and skills needed for solving complex social problems. Leaders begin to address complex issues by defining the problems and formulating a solutions framework or set of ideas to understand the problem and develop initial solution strategies. The focus here for leaders is on the problem per se, its significance, origin, and potential solutions. Experience, knowledge of the job/tasks, and understanding of the environment shape the way the leader represents the problem, the kinds of information sought, and the type of concepts applied.

Capabilities such as wisdom and knowledge, perspective taking, creative problem solving, and social judgment skills enable leaders to go beyond themselves to assess how others react to a solution, identify restrictions, develop plans, and build support for implementation (e.g., Mumford, 2006; Mumford et al., 2009; Mumford & Van Doorn, 2001). Ultimately, however, performance depends on the implementation of a plan, and the implementation occurs in a social context when leaders depend on the efforts of others for making proposed solutions happen.

So, social cognition and knowledge of peers, subordinates, and superiors are critical for solution implementation. Flexibility, adaptability, and adjusting plans as dictated by the changing social environment and the ability to communicate a vision, to establish clear and achievable goals, to monitor progress, and to motivate others to implement a given solution also are critical skills (e.g., Mumford, 2006; Mumford et al., 2009).

Moreover, general cognitive abilities, crystallized cognitive abilities, motivation, personality, and prior career experiences all influence leaders' problem-solving skills, social judgment and social skills, and knowledge. These in turn impact actual problem solving, and ultimately performance, subject to outside environmental influences. As noted by Mumford and Van Doorn (2001), pragmatic leadership requires careful observation of people and social systems to identify needs, objective analysis of the situation to identify restrictions and intervention points, and development and implementation of solution strategies designed to maximize benefits at low cost.

Given the importance of expertise and analysis for pragmatic leadership, such leaders try to exert influence by appealing to knowledgeable elites or experts (i.e., influential or prominent individuals for whom the issue is salient and who possess some information about it) actively involved with the issue. Then, under conditions when certain substitutes for leadership exist (e.g., follower expertise, clear goals, consensus; Dionne, Yammarino, Atwater, & James, 2002), pragmatic leadership may flourish. The appeal to these knowledgeable elites or experts is based on direct, objective, persuasive techniques (e.g., position papers, demonstration projects, specific examples; Mumford & Van Doorn, 2001).

Negotiated Exchange

Negotiated exchange with other parties one-on-one, or with another team/unit, can be viewed as investments and returns in dyadic- or group-based relationships, respectively, where the negotiations are designed for and have a goal of minimum disruption and maximum return to the leader's team/unit (see Dansereau et al., 1995; Yammarino, 1996; Yammarino & Dansereau, 2009a). Thus, leaders carefully negotiate deals with other parties.

Dyads can involve negotiated exchange between leader and follower or leader and leader, and leaders can also engage in negotiated exchange with their own (to "sell a deal") or other (to "make" a deal) teams and groups. The leader and the other party (parties) make investments in, and receive returns from, one another. The key investments and returns variables can be anything of value or benefit to the parties, whether economic, psychological, or social in nature (see Yammarino & Dansereau, 2009a).

For example, simply providing attention, support, and assurance for one party often results in a payoff of satisfying or exceptional "performance," broadly defined, above or beyond standards, particularly in terms of quality. For a successful negotiated exchange, the variables or dimensions and their relationships operate in terms of some type of perceived agreement between the parties (Dansereau et al., 1995; Yammarino, 1996; Yammarino & Dansereau, 2009a). Thus, the negotiated exchange is specific to that dyadic- or group-based relationship and deal.

Essentially, investments are what one party gives to another party and returns are what one party receives from another party. The idea of giving and receiving are linked with the principle of reciprocal reinforcement (i.e., investments trigger return, and returns trigger investments), so they are positively related and may be highly dynamic. The parties are thus interdependent, and when in a balanced relationship, where the amounts of giving and receiving for each party are similar, there is agreement in terms of the dyads or groups involved (see Dansereau et al., 1995; Yammarino, 1996; Yammarino & Dansereau, 2009a).

Moreover, dyads and groups involved in negotiated exchange may display relationships that are based on high levels of investments and returns (rich or complex deals), whereas others may be based on low amounts of these variables (poor or simple deals) but in balance nonetheless. This negotiated exchange bonding process in dyads or groups may start with an investment in or a return to either party from the other party (i.e., deals may be started or proposed by either party).

A key element of the negotiated exchange, whether a dyadic- or group-based approach, is the notion of support for self-worth that one party provides another (see Dansereau et al., 1995; Yammarino & Dansereau, 2009a). This concept is defined as supporting another party's actions and ideas; assuring others of confidence in their integrity, ability, and motivation; and paying attention to others' feelings and needs. The focus is on developing the relationship, especially long-term and for potential future deals, at a dyadic or group level. This process relies on interdependence between the parties and may develop over time, evolving from pooled interdependence (i.e., where each party provides a discrete contribution to the dyadic or group relationship) to reciprocal interdependence (i.e., where the contributions to the dyadic and group relationships are two-way).

Additional specific dimensions of investments and returns, which appear to be particularly relevant for pragmatic deal making, can include showing respect, cooperating, being open, being task centered, endorsing values, exhibiting benevolence, being accepting, being authentic, providing learning opportunities, communicating, and allowing self-responsibility and mistakes. Specific behavioral indicators of investments and returns in pragmatic deal making can include head nods (i.e., agreement), direct eye contact (i.e., attention), praise, and questions (by one party) and answers (by the other party). In these behavioral ways, the dyadic- and group-based bonds in negotiated exchange can be enhanced and reinforced to richer (higher or more intense) levels.

These notions about pragmatic leadership, negotiated exchange, and leader pragmatic negotiated deals, when considered with the prior ideas and discussion, suggest the following proposition:

> Proposition 7: Leader idiosyncrasy credits will enhance leader pragmatic negotiated deal making with others (potential partners) both one on one in dyads and one on many in groups/teams. A pragmatic leadership style at the individual/leader level and exchange-based negotiations at a dyadic level (e.g., leader to leader) or at a group level (e.g., leader to group) will enhance the number of beneficial deals made for leaders and their team/unit.

Key Moderators

Vision and Vision Formation

Although numerous moderators are plausible within our framework, vision and the vision formation process are key moderators of the relationship between leader idiosyncrasy credits and the leader pragmatic negotiated deal. Vision and the vision formation process is one of the most widely discussed aspects of leadership (see Bass, 2008; Yammarino et al., 2005; Yukl, 2010). At the individual level of analysis, there are individual differences in leader vision and vision formation skills.

The vision formation process includes identifying and conceptualizing practical problems and then planning, arranging, and articulating ("selling") practical solutions (e.g., Mumford, 2006). The conceptualization and planning phases should include an assessment of strengths, weaknesses, threats, and opportunities to the team/unit (and likely the organization) and the linkage to team/unit (and organization) mission (e.g., Bass, 2008; Yukl, 2010). As such, given careful analysis of the vision and the vision formation process by the leader, some deals will be made, other potential deals will be avoided (e.g., not relevant to the vision), and still others will be revisited for renegotiation or cancellation (e.g., too costly or nonbeneficial to the team/unit or the leader relative to the vision).

When considered with the prior ideas and discussion, the following moderator proposition is suggested:

Proposition 8: Leader vision and vision formation process will moderate the relationship between leader idiosyncrasy credits and the leader pragmatic negotiated deal such that some deals will be made, others avoided, and still others revisited.

Ethics and Integrity

Likewise, ethics and integrity are key moderators of the relationship between leader idiosyncrasy credits and the leader pragmatic negotiated deal. Ethics and integrity represent a growing area of research in the field of leadership (see Bass, 2008; Palanski & Yammarino, 2009; Yukl, 2010). The ethics and integrity of both the leader (individual level of analysis) and the team/unit (group level of analysis) are relevant (see Bass, 2008; Beu & Buckley, 2004; Palanski & Yammarino, 2009; Yukl, 2010).

In both cases, for leaders and their teams/units, ethics or professional codes of conduct, and integrity or words and actions consistency are particularly important as are group norms (Palanski & Yammarino, 2009; Yammarino & Dansereau, 2009a). Essentially, ethics and integrity of leaders and their teams/units place boundaries and limits on deals, which can cause them to shift, change, and even be pushed or encouraged such deals to be made. As such, given ethical and professional considerations, some deals will be made, other potential deals will be avoided (e.g., deemed unethical or unprofessional by leader or team/unit), and still others will be revisited for renegotiation or cancellation (e.g., for reasons of maintaining or restoring leader or team/unit integrity).

Ethics and integrity for both the leader and team/unit can also have a "dark side." For example, recent and past personal and organizational scandals and other ethical violations, well documented in the popular press and scholarly literature, make clear that deals often are made that may benefit solely leaders or perhaps leaders and their immediate team/unit, particularly in the short-term, at the expense of the larger organization or other constituencies and stakeholders (e.g., stockholders, taxpayers, public at large), particularly in the long-term. In less severe yet still problematic situations, there may be a relatively "low bar" or standard for making deals (i.e., simply, "nobody was harmed").

Regardless, these issues enter into the pragmatic deal-making process; although personal, organizational, and professional codes of conduct and ethics-based training and education programs may well help offset these transgressions (both limited and severe in nature) by leaders or their teams/units, empirical research on these issues is lacking and worthy of pursuit in future work.

When considered with the prior ideas and discussion, the following moderator proposition is suggested:

Proposition 9: Leader ethics and integrity, and team/unit ethics and integrity, will moderate the relationship between leader idiosyncrasy credits and the leader pragmatic negotiated deal such that some deals will be made, others avoided, and still others revisited.

Deal Acceptance and Evaluation

Deal Acceptance by Others

After a pragmatic deal has been negotiated and presumably implemented, the issue of the degree of acceptance of the deal by the other parties to the deal becomes relevant. The other parties may be other leaders, so their acceptance is an individual-level phenomenon, or another team/unit, so acceptance by members is a group-level phenomenon.

A primary concern is the social acceptance of deal by other party (parties) (e.g., Friedrich et al., 2009) based on their (target) attributes (cf. Ammeter et al., 2002; Davis & Gardner, 2004), leader idiosyncrasy credits, and prior relations with the deal maker (i.e., real or perceived benefits of the deal to the other parties are involved; see Hollander, 1958; Phillips et al., 2009; Stone & Cooper, 2009). Leaders draw on their credit balances to "sell" deals, through communication and persuasion, and to foster deal acceptance. Perhaps a key issue here is whether other leaders or other groups/teams have been "burned" in the past (how much and how recently), a negative result for others' benefits minus costs, and their willingness to go along with the negotiated deal given leaders' idiosyncrasy credits and credit balance.

When considered with the prior ideas and discussion, the following proposition is suggested about deal acceptance by others:

Proposition 10: Social acceptance of a leader pragmatic negotiated deal by the other party at the individual level, or parties at the group level, will be enhanced by prior relationships with the leader (deal maker) and by real or perceived benefits to the party or parties.

Deal Acceptance by Team/Unit

Likewise, again after negotiation and implementation of a pragmatic deal, the issue of the degree of acceptance of the deal by leaders' team/unit becomes relevant (e.g., Friedrich et al., 2009). In this case, the team/unit's acceptance is a group-level phenomenon.

Primary concerns are the social acceptance of deal by leaders' team/unit based on their (target) attributes (cf. Ammeter et al., 2002; Davis & Gardner, 2004), leaders' idiosyncrasy credits, leaders' sensemaking of the deal for the team/unit, and leaders' ability to build team/unit commitment to deal execution (i.e., real or perceived benefits of the deal to the team/unit are involved; Hollander, 1958; Phillips et al., 2009; Stone & Cooper, 2009). Again, a key issue can be whether leaders' team/unit perceives it has been "burned" in the past (e.g., how much and how recently), a negative result for the team's/unit's benefits minus costs, and their willingness to go along with the negotiated deal given leaders' idiosyncrasy credits and credit balance.

When considered with the prior ideas and discussion, the following proposition is suggested about deal acceptance by the team/unit:

> Proposition 11: Social acceptance of a leader pragmatic negotiated deal by leaders' team/unit at the group level will be enhanced by leaders' idiosyncrasy credit balance with the team/unit and by real or perceived benefits to the team/unit.

Leader Deal Evaluation

After a pragmatic deal has been negotiated and implemented and the degree of acceptance of the deal by the other parties to the deal as well as by leaders' team/unit has been assessed, leaders are in a position to do a thorough evaluation of the deal. In this instance, an individual-level phenomenon is relevant.

Leaders can carefully evaluate deals in a cognitive, quantitative, and decision making approach (see Mumford, 2006; Mumford et al., 2009). Leaders' evaluation and appraisal of the pragmatic negotiated deal is based on the acceptance of the deal by their team/unit as well as acceptance by the other parties, the previously developed vision for their team/unit, and the forecasting of potential short- and long-term outcomes for leaders' team/unit and themselves.

Forecasting, which involves prototyping, testing, refinement, and preparation, is a key part of planning or what might be thought of as mental simulations by pragmatic leaders (see Mumford, 2006) and, as such, is both objective and yet subject to wishful thinking. Pragmatic leaders, as part of their careful consideration and analysis of deals, will attempt to avoid subjective wishful thinking and to plan for and forecast objectively both positive and negative short- and long-term outcomes of existing or potential deals with others. The analysis and forecast might include the sacrifice of short-term performance to make appropriate long-term deals. These forecasts can be thought of as operating in a way analogous to credits and credit balances.

Thus, if the *net forecast* then is primarily negative, pragmatic leaders likely will not make the deal to begin with, will attempt to renegotiate a more favorable set of outcomes for an existing deal, or will end ("kill") an existing deal that is unfavorable for them or their team/unit. In contrast, if planning and forecasting results primarily in a positive net forecast of various outcomes for leaders or their team/unit, they likely will attempt to make a new deal, to continue an existing deal, or to extend in various ways a current deal with the other parties involved.

Beyond cognitions and decision-making approaches, in a more process-oriented and qualitative approach Kan and Perry (2004) focused on reconciling and legitimizing paradox, or what might be called assessing whether appropriate or inappropriate deals were made. In this case, effective leadership and a favorable evaluation of the negotiated deal would be based on reconciling paradox, to use Kan and Perry's term.

When considered with the prior ideas and discussion, the following propositions are suggested about leader deal evaluation:

Proposition 12: At the individual level, leader pragmatic negotiated deals that align with leaders' vision and for which leaders can generate positive net forecasts of long- and short-term outcomes for themselves and their team/unit will be evaluated favorably by them. Deals with negative net forecasts will be evaluated unfavorably by leaders.

Proposition 13: At the individual level, leader pragmatic negotiated deals that are socially accepted by other parties to the deal will be evaluated favorably by leaders. Deals not socially accepted will be evaluated unfavorably by leaders.

Proposition 14: At the individual level, leader pragmatic negotiated deals that are socially accepted by leaders' team/unit will be evaluated favorably by leaders. Deals not socially accepted will be evaluated unfavorably by leaders.

Long- and Short-Term Outcomes

Leader

At the leader (individual) level of analysis, short- and long-term primary outcomes of the pragmatic negotiated deal-making process can include the leader's performance, productivity, satisfaction, stress reduction, personal growth and development, idiosyncrasy credits, and network building, and secondary outcomes include reputation, compensation, and promotion. There is extensive literature on these outcomes and generally well-established relationships at the individual level of analysis, with constructs and concepts discussed here or similar ones (for discussion and review of these outcomes and associations, see Ammeter et al., 2002; Bass, 2008; Brief & Weiss, 2002; Friedrich et al., 2009; Hart & Cooper, 2002; Mumford, 2006; Neal & Hesketh, 2002; Viswesvaran, 2001; Yammarino, 1996; Yammarino & Dansereau, 2009a; Yukl, 2010). Simply put, positive associations (negative associations) are expected among deal acceptance by others, deal acceptance by leaders' team/unit, leaders' deal evaluation, and various positive (negative) outcomes at the individual level for leaders.

When considered with the prior ideas and discussion, the following propositions are suggested about leader long- and short-term outcomes:

Proposition 15: Social acceptance of a leader pragmatic negotiated deal by the other parties will enhance leader short- and long-term outcomes such as performance, productivity, satisfaction, stress reduction, personal growth and development, idiosyncrasy credits, network building, and ultimately reputation, compensation, and promotion.

Proposition 16: Social acceptance of a leader pragmatic negotiated deal by leaders' team/unit will enhance leader short- and long-term outcomes such as performance, productivity, satisfaction, stress reduction, personal growth and development, idiosyncrasy credits, network building, and ultimately reputation, compensation, and promotion.

Proposition 17: Leader favorable evaluation of a pragmatic negotiated deal will enhance leader short- and long-term outcomes such as performance, productivity, satisfaction, stress reduction, personal growth and development, idiosyncrasy credits, network building, and ultimately reputation, compensation, and promotion.

Team/Unit

For leaders' team/unit, at the team/unit (group) level of analysis, short- and long-term primary outcomes of the pragmatic negotiated deal-making process include the team/unit's performance, productivity, positive affective climate (e.g., satisfaction, trust, and stress and cynicism reduction), cohesion and efficacy, growth and innovation, and network building and secondary outcomes of team-based compensation and rewards.

Again, there is extensive literature on these outcomes and generally well-established relationships at the group/team level of analysis with constructs and concepts discussed here or similar ones (for discussion and review of these outcomes and associations, see Ahearn et al., 2004; Ammeter et al., 2002; Bass, 2008; Brief & Weiss, 2002; Friedrich et al., 2009; Hart & Cooper, 2002; Kozlowski & Ilgen, 2006; Mumford, 2006; Neal & Hesketh, 2002; Yammarino, 1996; Yammarino & Dansereau, 2009a; Yukl, 2010). Simply put, positive associations (negative associations) are expected among deal acceptance by leaders' team/unit, leaders' deal evaluation, and positive (negative) outcomes at the team level for leaders' team/unit.

When considered with the prior ideas and discussion, the following propositions are suggested about team/unit long- and short-term outcomes:

Proposition 18: Social acceptance of leader pragmatic negotiated deal by leaders' team/unit will enhance team/unit short- and long-term outcomes such as performance, productivity, positive affective climate (e.g., satisfaction, trust, and stress and cynicism reduction), cohesion and efficacy, growth and innovation, network building, and ultimately team-based compensation and rewards.

Proposition 19: Leader favorable evaluation of a pragmatic negotiated deal will enhance team/unit short- and long-term outcomes such as performance, productivity, positive affective climate (e.g., satisfaction, trust, and stress and cynicism reduction), cohesion and efficacy, growth and innovation, network building, and ultimately team-based compensation and rewards.

Contextual Issues

Although numerous contextual issues could be examined as well as their impact on multiple dimensions in our framework, the focus is limited to five key contextual factors that can operate at multiple levels of analysis and impact the pragmatic deal-making process, especially leader idiosyncrasy credits and the pragmatic negotiated deal per se. Moreover, given the complexity and nuances involved with these factors, we simply offer general propositions about them, leaving specific formulations for future work. These contextual factors are hierarchical level of the leader, time frame over which commitments come due for the team/unit, long- and short-term costs and benefits for the team/unit, history of the parties involved in the deal and building future relationships, and salience of deal for the team/unit.

First, hierarchical level of the leader (e.g., Ammeter et al., 2002; Hall et al., 2004; Hunt, 1991; Jacobs & Jaques, 1987; Smith et al., 2009; Treadway et al., 2009) is a contextual factor to consider in pragmatic deal making. Hunt and Jacobs and Jaques noted that at successively higher hierarchical levels, increasing cognitive and task complexity occur. Hunt's approach extended the work of Jacobs and Jaques on stratified systems theory. He argued that for an organization to perform effectively certain tasks are critical, that these tasks become more complex and qualitatively different as one moves up the hierarchy (levels of management), and that more complex tasks (e.g., vision and strategy creation and development) are reflected in longer time spans for completion.

Hunt (1991) also argued that increasingly complex tasks at successively higher levels of management require increasing levels of leader cognitive capacity. Cognitive capacity assumes that cognitively complex individuals process information different from and perform selected tasks better than do cognitively less complex people, because they use more categories to discriminate among stimuli and see more commonalities among these categories. As such, there should be a match between leader cognitive complexity and critical task complexity at each level of management.

Thus, based on this work, one might suspect that the higher leaders' hierarchical level, the more complex the nature of pragmatic negotiated deals, the more it is necessary to make deals, especially "creative" pragmatic deals, drawing down leader credit balances, and the more likely ethics and integrity boundaries are pushed to limits, again drawing down credit balances, to complete complex pragmatic negotiated deals.

Second, another contextual factor to consider in pragmatic deal making is the time frame over which commitments come due for leaders' team/unit. Time lines and how events play out over time can significantly impact leadership credits and activities, especially with negotiated exchanges in dyads and groups (e.g., Yammarino & Dansereau, 2009a). Short time lines for team/unit commitments coming due might negatively impact leader idiosyncrasy credit balances, drawing them down quicker and adversely affecting the consummation of a negotiated deal or the acceptance of it by the team/unit. Long time lines tend to push team/unit commitments farther into the future where the impact on the team/unit may be less severe and tap into fewer leader idiosyncrasy credits.

Third, long- and short-term costs (e.g., disruption of team/unit activities) and benefits (e.g., enhanced team/unit reputation) for the team/unit is another contextual factor to consider in pragmatic deal making (e.g., Yammarino & Dansereau, 2009a). So, different from typical team/unit outcomes previously discussed, the prior (in time) team/unit-assessed costs and benefits of the pragmatic negotiated deal can alter (i.e., enhancing or hurting) leaders' idiosyncrasy credit balance, the pragmatic negotiated deal per se, future long- and short-term outcomes for the team/unit, and even the team's/unit's forecasting of those potential outcomes.

Fourth, another contextual factor to consider is the history of the parties (e.g., Ammeter et al., 2002), especially trustworthiness and ambiguity among them (Friedrich et al., 2009), involved in the pragmatic negotiated deal and for building future relationships. Prior relationships can result in trust and certainty to form the basis for the current negotiated deal, can build leader credit balances, and can set the tone for potential future relationships and the negotiation of new pragmatic deals (i.e., overall richer relationships and deals). In general, positive prior interactions and favorable deals among the parties should foster leader idiosyncratic credits, positive future interactions, and new pragmatic negotiated deals viewed favorably by all parties involved.

Fifth, a final contextual factor to consider in pragmatic deal making is the salience of the deal, whether of central importance or on the periphery, for the team/unit as well as for the leader (e.g., Mumford, 2006; Yammarino & Dansereau, 2009a). If the potential deal is something on the periphery for the leader and his or her team/unit, salience is limited, leader credit balances are not drawn down dramatically, both costs and benefits would tend to be less for both the leader and the team/unit, risks and rewards are low, and the negotiation (negotiated exchange) process to strike a pragmatic deal may go quickly and smoothly.

In contrast, when a potential deal is of central importance for the leader and his/her team, salience is high, leader credit balances can be drawn down dramatically, potential costs but also potential benefits are high for the leader and team/unit, perceived risks and potential rewards are high, and the negotiated exchange (negotiation) process to strike a pragmatic deal may take an extended amount of time and not progress smoothly or easily.

When considered with the prior ideas and discussion, the following general propositions are suggested about the five contextual issues:

> Proposition 20: Five key contextual factors that operate at multiple levels of analysis will impact, either favorably or adversely (depending on the factor), leader idiosyncrasy credits at the individual level.

> Proposition 21: Five key contextual factors that operate at multiple levels of analysis will impact, either favorably or adversely (depending on the factor), pragmatic negotiated deals in terms of the leader's pragmatic style at the individual level and negotiated exchanges with the other party one on one at the dyadic level or with multiple parties one on many at the group/team level.

CONCLUSION

The main purpose of this chapter was to review the relatively new literature at the intersection of leadership and organizational politics. The result was a conceptual framework for understanding pragmatic deals, a multilevel integration that includes pragmatic leadership and negotiated exchange approaches at the core. It was asserted that leader characteristics of skills and network and organizational politics dimensions of communication and positioning generate a pragmatic deal-making process involving leader idiosyncrasy credits and visioning, leader and team/unit ethics and integrity, and deal negotiation, acceptance by multiple parties, and evaluation by the leader. Also, it was suggested that the pragmatic deal-making process can be impacted by various multilevel contextual factors and, in turn, that pragmatic negotiated deals can result in numerous long- and short-term outcomes for both leaders and their teams/units. The culmination of this review and model was 21 multilevel research propositions, including a number of embedded ideas, for testing in future empirical research.

Clearly, the approach here is merely a beginning for a new and relatively unexplored area of research. The next requirement is the testing of these ideas, which will necessitate the use of some current measures of the concepts but also the development of appropriate new operationalizations of the constructs involved at multiple levels of analysis. Various research designs also will need to be explored as some of these ideas may be better assessed, at least initially, via manipulations in rigorous laboratory experiments and in historiometric case studies of exemplars of leader pragmatic negotiated deals in a variety of arenas. Subsequently, based on promising or supportive results from this initial empirical work, large-scale longitudinal field studies could be conducted to further test and confirm or refute the notions presented here.

As this line of theoretical work and empirical testing proceeds, additional factors not considered here in detail or at all (e.g., attribution processes, emotions, justice factors, accountability, type of organization, organization mission and strategy, and the "dark side" of deals beyond the ethical issues involved) could be incorporated to enhance the proposed framework for understanding pragmatic negotiated deals. These ideas essentially involve the consideration of additional mediators, moderators, and higher-level contextual factors not currently explored.

If this entire line of research, including numerous longitudinal and multilevel tests (because, after all, a set of multilevel process-oriented ideas is presented that enfold over time and that trigger future events and deals), shows promise, then a series of leader and team/unit developmental experiences and training programs to enhance the pragmatic deal-making process can be envisioned. Obviously, that state of affairs remains off in the future, but the hope is that the multilevel integrative ideas proposed here for the understanding of leader pragmatic negotiated deals will stimulate future research in this arena, where leadership and organizational politics intersect.

ACKNOWLEDGMENT

We thank Kristie Shirreffs for her assistance on preparation of this chapter.

REFERENCES

Ahearn, K.K., Ferris, G.R., Hochwarter, W.A., Douglas, C., & Ammeter, A.P. (2004). Leader political skill and team performance. *Journal of Management, 30,* 309–327.

Ammeter, A.P., Douglas, C., Gardner, W.L., Hochwarter, W.A., & Ferris, G.R. (2002). Toward a political theory of leadership. *Leadership Quarterly, 13,* 751–796.

Bass, B.M. (2008). *The Bass handbook of leadership.* New York: Free Press.

Beu, D.S., & Buckley, M.R. (2004). This is war: How the politically astute achieve crimes of obedience through the use of moral disengagement. *Leadership Quarterly, 15,* 551–568.

Brief, A.P., & Weiss, H.M. (2002). Organizational behavior: Affect in the workplace. *Annual Review of Psychology, 53,* 279–307.

Brouer, R.L., Duke, A., Treadway, D.C., & Ferris, G.R. (2009). The moderating effect of political skill on demographic dissimilarity—leader–member exchange quality relationship. *Leadership Quarterly, 20,* 61–69.

Burns, J.M. (1978). *Leadership.* New York: Harper.

Dansereau, F., Yammarino, F.J., Markham, S.E., Alutto, J.A., Newman, J., Dumas, M., et al. (1995). Individualized leadership: A new multiple-level approach. *Leadership Quarterly, 6,* 413–450.

Davis, W.D., & Gardner, W.L. (2004). Perceptions of politics and organizational cynicism: An attributional and leader–member exchange perspective. *Leadership Quarterly, 15,* 439–465.

Dionne, S.D., Yammarino, F.J., Atwater, L.E., & James, L.R. (2002). Neutralizing substitutes for leadership theory: Leadership effects and common-source bias. *Journal of Applied Psychology, 87,* 454–464.

Douglas, C., & Ammeter, A.P. (2004). An examination of leader political skill and its effects on ratings of leader effectiveness. *Leadership Quarterly, 15,* 537–550.

Ferris, G.R., Adams, G., Kolodinsky, R.W., Hochwarter, W.A., & Ammeter, A.P. (2002). Perceptions of organizational politics: Theory and research directions. In F.J. Yammarino & F. Dansereau (Eds.), *The many faces of multi-level issues (Research in Multi-Level Issues, Vol.1)* (pp. 179–254). Oxford, UK: Elsevier Science.

Ferris, G.R., Davidson, S.L., & Perrewé, P.L. (2005). *Political skill at work: Impact on work effectiveness.* Mountain View, CA: Davies-Black Publishing.

Ferris, G.R., & Hochwarter, W.A. (2011). Organizational politics. In S. Zedeck (Ed.), *APA handbook of industrial and organizational psychology* (Vol. 3, pp. 435–459). Washington, DC: American Psychological Association.

Ferris, G.R., Treadway, D.C., Kolodinsky, R.W., Hochwarter, W.A., Kacmar, C.J., Douglas, C., et al. (2005). Development and validation of the political skill inventory. *Journal of Management, 31,* 126–152.

Ferris, G.R., Treadway, D.C., Perrewé, P.L., Brouer, R.L., Douglas, C., & Lux, S. (2007). Political skill in organizations. *Journal of Management, 33,* 290–320.

Ferris, G.R., Zinko, R., Brouer, R.L., Buckley, M.R., & Harvey, M.G. (2007). Strategic bullying as a supplemental, balanced perspective on destructive leadership. *Leadership Quarterly, 18,* 195–206.

Friedrich, T.L., Vessey, W.B., Schuelke, M.J., Ruark, G.A., & Mumford, M.D. (2009). A framework for understanding collective leadership: The selective utilization of leader and team expertise within networks. *Leadership Quarterly, 20,* 933–958.

Hall, A.T., Blass, F.R., Ferris, G.R., & Massengale, R. (2004). Leader reputation and accountability in organizations: Implications for dysfunctional leader behavior. *Leadership Quarterly, 15,* 515–536.

Hart, P.M., & Cooper, C.L. (2002). Occupational stress: Toward a more integrated framework. In N. Anderson, D.S. Ones, H. K. Sinangil, & C. Viswesvaran (Eds.), *Handbook of industrial, work, and organizational psychology* (Vol. 2, pp. 93–114). London: Sage Publications.

Hollander, E. P. (1958). Conformity, status, and idiosyncrasy credit. *Psychological Review, 65,* 117–127.

Hunt, J.G. (1991). *Leadership: A new synthesis.* Newbury Park, CA: Sage Publications.

Jacobs, T.O., & Jaques, E. (1987). Leadership in complex organizations. In J.A. Zeidner (Ed.), *Human productivity enhancement* (Vol. 2, pp. 7–65). New York: Praeger.

Kan, M.M., & Parry, K.W. (2004). Identify paradox: A grounded theory of leadership in overcoming resistance to change. *Leadership Quarterly, 15,* 467–491.

Kozlowski, S.W.J., & Ilgen, D.R. (2006). Enhancing the effectiveness of groups and teams. *Psychological Science in the Public Interest, 7,* 77–124.

Lux, S., Ferris, G., Brouer, R., Laird, M., & Summers, J. (2008). A multi-level conceptualization of organizational politics. In C. Cooper & J. Barling (Eds.), *Handbook of organizational behavior* (pp. 353–371). Thousand Oaks, CA: Sage Publications.

Mumford, M.D. (2006). *Pathways to outstanding leadership: A comparative analysis of charismatic, ideological, and pragmatic leadership.* Mahwah, NJ: Lawrence Erlbaum.

Mumford, M.D., Hunter, S.T., Friedrich, T.L., & Caughron, J.J. (2009). Charismatic, ideological, and pragmatic leadership: An examination of multi-level influences on emergence and performance. In F.J. Yammarino & F. Dansereau (Eds.), *Multi-level issues in organizational behavior and leadership (Research in Multi-Level Issues* (Vol. 8, pp. 79–115). Bingley, UK: Emerald/JAI.

Mumford, M.D., & Van Doorn, J.R. (2001). The leadership of pragmatism: Reconsidering Franklin in the age of charisma. *Leadership Quarterly, 12,* 279–310.

Neal, A., & Hesketh, B. (2002). Productivity in organizations. In N. Anderson, D.S. Ones, H.K. Sinangil, & C. Viswesvaran (Eds.), *Handbook of industrial, work, and organizational psychology* (Vol. 2, 7–24). London: Sage Publications.

Novicevic, M.M., & Harvey, M.G. (2004). The political role of corporate human resource management in strategic global leadership development. *Leadership Quarterly, 15,* 569–588.

Palanski, M.E., & Yammarino, F.J. (2009). Integrity and leadership: A multi-level conceptual framework. *Leadership Quarterly, 20,* 405–420.

Phillips, K.W., Rothbard, N.P., & Dumas, T.L. (2009). To disclose or not to disclose? Status distance and self-disclosure in diverse environments. *Academy of Management Review, 34,* 710–732.

Silvester, J. (2008). The good, the bad, and the ugly: Politics and politicians at work. *International Review of Industrial and Organizational Psychology, 23,* 107–148.

Smith, A., Plowman, D., Duchon, D., & Quinn, A. (2009). A qualitative study of high-reputation plant managers: Political skill and successful outcomes. *Journal of Operations Management, 27*(6), 428–443.

Stone, T.H., & Cooper, W.H. (2009). Emerging credits. *Leadership Quarterly, 20,* 785–798.

Tosi, H. (1992). *The environment/organization/person contingency model: A meso approach to the study of organizations.* Greenwich, CT: JAI Press.

Treadway, D.C., Adams, G.L., Ranft, A.L., & Ferris, G.R. (2009). A meso-level conceptualization of CEO celebrity effectiveness. *Leadership Quarterly, 20,* 554–570.

Treadway, D., Ferris, G., Duke, A., Adams, G., & Thatcher, J. (2007). The moderating role of subordinate political skill on supervisors' impressions of subordinate ingratiation and ratings of interpersonal facilitation. *Journal of Applied Psychology, 92,* 848–855.

Treadway, D.C., Hochwarter, W.A., Ferris, G.R., Kacmar, C.J., Douglas, C., Ammeter, A.P., et al. (2004). Leader political skill and employee reactions. *Leadership Quarterly, 15,* 493–513.

Valenty, L.O., & Feldman, O. (2002). *Political leadership for the new century.* Westport, CT: Praeger.

Vigoda-Gadot, E., & Drory, A. (Eds.) (2006). *Handbook of organizational politics.* Northampton, MA: Edward Elgar Publishing.

Visweswaran, C. (2001). Assessment of individual job performance: A review of the past century and a look ahead. In N. Anderson, D.S. Ones, H.K. Sinangil, & C. Visweswaran (Eds.), *Handbook of industrial, work, and organizational psychology* (Vol. 1, pp. 110–126). London: Sage Publications.

Yammarino, F.J. (1996). Group leadership: A levels of analysis perspective. In M.A. West (Ed.), *The handbook of work group psychology* (pp. 189–224). Chichester, UK: John Wiley & Sons.

Yammarino, F.J., & Dansereau, F. (2008). Multi-level nature of and multi-level approaches to leadership. *Leadership Quarterly, 19,* 135–141.

Yammarino, F.J., & Dansereau, F. (2009a). A new kind of OB (organizational behavior). In F.J. Yammarino & F. Dansereau (Eds.), *Multi-level issues in organizational behavior and leadership (Research in Multi-Level Issues,* Vol. 8, pp. 13–60). Bingley, UK: Emerald/JAI.

Yammarino, F.J., & Dansereau, F. (Eds.) (2009b). *Multi-level issues in organizational behavior and leadership (Research in Multi-Level Issues, Vol. 8).* Bingley, UK: Emerald/JAI.

Yammarino, F.J., Dionne, S.D., Chun, J.U., & Dansereau, F. (2005). Leadership and levels of analysis: A state-of-the-science review. *Leadership Quarterly, 16,* 879–91.

Yukl, G. (2010). *Leadership in organizations.* Upper Saddle River, NJ: Prentice Hall.

12

Power, Politics, and Social Networks in Organizations

Daniel J. Brass
University of Kentucky

David M. Krackhardt
Carnegie Mellon University

"While personal attributes and strategies may have an important effect on power acquisition,... structure imposes the ultimate constraints on the individual" (Brass, 1984, p. 518). If power is indeed, first and foremost, a structural phenomenon (Pfeffer, 1981), it is surprising that so much research on politics in organizations has taken a behavioral or cognitive approach focusing on individual aptitudes and political tactics and strategies (see Chapter 1 in this volume). This chapter attempts to remedy that shortcoming by presenting a structural, social network approach to power and politics in organizations. While not slighting all that has been learned via behavioral and cognitive approaches to politics, it is argued that the structure of social networks strongly affects the extent to which personal attributes, cognition, and behavior result in power in organizations.

A basic introduction to social network analysis is provided, and the social network research relating to power in organizations is reviewed. The focus here is on the context of political activity, the network structure within which political activity occurs. Rather than attempt to integrate the cognitive and behavioral findings with the structural, how behavior and cognition lead to structural positions of power in organizations is explored instead. Rather than focus on political tactics that may be useful or useless within given structures of relationships, the focus is on *social network tactics* that may alter the structural constraints on the acquisition of power in organizations. Moving beyond the interpersonal acquisition of power, the larger network structures are considered that facilitate the effective use of power to bring about large-scale organizational change.

Following Brass (2002), it is assumed that organizations are both cooperative systems of employees working together to achieve goals and political arenas of individuals and groups with differing interests. Furthermore, it is believed that interdependence is necessary and that political activity and the exercise of power most likely occur when different interests (conflict) arise. Though power is relational and situational, perceptions of power are important, and most employees seem to agree on who has general (across situations) power. Despite the negative connotations associated with politics in organizations and opinions as to whether it is a good or bad thing, it is obvious that it needs to be studied and understood to develop an informed understanding of organizations and how they function.

SOCIAL NETWORKS AND POWER

The diagrams in Figure 12.1 (adapted from Brass & Labianca, 2011) are illustrative of social networks and how they might relate to power and politics. A social network is defined as a set of nodes (social actors such as individuals, groups, or organizations) and ties representing some relationship or absence of a relationship among the actors. Although dyadic relationships are the basic building blocks of social networks, the focus extends beyond the dyad to consideration of the structure or arrangement of relationships in addition to the attributes, behaviors, or cognitions of the actors. The pattern of relationships defines actors' positions in the social structure and provides opportunities and constraints that affect the acquisition of power.

Actors can be connected on the basis of (1) similarities (e.g., physical proximity, membership in the same group, or similar attributes such as gender), (2) social relations (e.g., kinship, roles, affective relations such as friendship), (3) interactions (e.g., talks with, gives advice to), or (4) flows (e.g., information, money; Borgatti, Mehra, Brass, & Labianca, 2009). Ties may be binary (present or absent) or valued (e.g., by frequency, intensity, or strength of ties), and some ties may be asymmetric (e.g., A likes B, but B does not like A) or directional (e.g., A goes to B for advice). Most

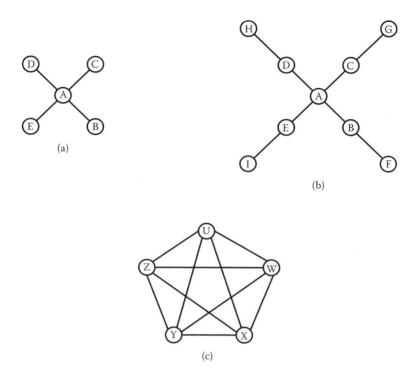

FIGURE 12.1
Networks and power.

organizational researchers explain the outcomes of networks by reference to flows of resources. For example, central actors in the network may benefit because they have greater access to information flows than more peripheral actors. However, networks can serve as *prisms* as well as *pipes* (Podolny, 2001), conveying mental images of the actor's status to others observing the network interactions.

The added value of the network perspective is that it goes beyond individual actors or isolated dyads of actors by providing a way to consider the structural arrangement of many actors. Typically, a minimum of two ties connecting three actors is implicitly assumed to have a network and to establish such notions as indirect ties and paths (e.g., *six degrees of separation* and the common expression *It's a small world*; see Watts, 2003). The focal actor in a network is referred to as *ego*; the other actors with whom ego has direct relationships are called *alters*. Social networks have been related to a variety of important organizational outcomes (see Brass, Galaskiewicz, Greve, & Tsai, 2004, for a review of research findings).

NETWORK CENTRALITY

Considering the simple network diagram in Figure 12.1a, it is not difficult to hypothesize that the central actor (position A in Figure 12.1a) is in a powerful position. That hypothesis is based simply on the pattern or structure of the nodes (actors) and ties, without reference to the cognitive or behavioral strategies or skills of the actors. From a structural perspective, the *patterns* of relationships provide the opportunities and constraints that affect power and politics. The hypothesis that central network positions are associated with power has been confirmed across a variety of setting. These include small, laboratory workgroups (Shaw, 1964), interpersonal networks in organizations (Brass, 1984, 1985; Brass & Burkhardt, 1993; Burkhardt & Brass, 1990; Fombrun, 1983; Krackhardt, 1990; Sparrowe & Liden, 2005; Tushman & Romanelli, 1983), organizational buying systems (Bristor, 1992; Ronchetto, Hun, & Reingen, 1989), intergroup networks in organizations (Astley & Zajac, 1990; Hinings, Hickson, Pennings, & Schneck, 1974), interorganizational networks (Boje & Whetten, 1981; Galaskiewicz, 1979), professional communities (Breiger, 1976), and community elites (Laumann & Pappi, 1976).

Several theoretical explanations can be provided for the relationship between centrality and power. From an exchange theory perspective, actor A has easy, direct access to any resources that might flow through the network (not dependent on any particular actor) and controls the flow of resources to other actors (B, C, D, and E are dependent on actor A). Negotiation researchers might evoke the well-known explanation of relative best alternative to a negotiated agreement (BATNA) determining negotiation power. Actor A has several alternatives, whereas the other actors are dependent on actor A. From a cognitive perspective, central actors have better knowledge of the network than peripheral actors (Krackhardt, 1990). They are more likely to know who knows what or whom to approach or avoid in forming coalitions. From a prism perspective, central actors are viewed by others as more powerful. Whether or not the perception is accurate, central actors may be able to obtain better outcomes or to receive deferential treatment based on that perception.

From a network perspective, actor A in Figure 12.1a is the most central in the network. Measures of actor centrality are not attributes of isolated individuals; rather, they represent the actor's relationship within the network. Actor centrality has been measured in a variety of ways. For example, the number of relationships, or size of one's network, is referred to as degree centrality. Other things being equal, a larger network is a more powerful network (Brass & Burkhardt, 1992). Also, it can be distinguished as to whether one is the source or the object of the relationship. In-degree centrality refers to the number of alters who choose ego, and it is argued that being the object of a relationship (i.e., being chosen by others) is more prestigious than being the source (i.e., choosing others as measured by out-degree; Knoke & Burt, 1983). For example, Burkhardt and Brass (1990) found that all employees increased their centrality (i.e., symmetric measure) following the introduction of new technology. However, the early adopters of the new technology increased their in-degree centrality and subsequent power significantly more than the later adopters.

STRUCTURAL HOLES

Rather than simply building a large network, Burt (1992) has argued that the pattern of ties is more important than the size of one's network. Burt focused his research on *structural holes*, that is, building relationships with those who are not themselves connected (e.g., actor A in Figure 12.1a has several structural holes because B, C, D, and E are not connected to each other). Structural holes provide two advantages. First, the *tertius gaudens* advantage (i.e., the third who benefits) derives from ego's ability to control the information flow between the disconnected alters (i.e., broker the relationship) or to play them off against each other. Such an advantage is particularly apparent in competitive situations, such as negotiations.

The second advantage is less obvious. By connecting to alters who are not themselves connected, ego has access to nonredundant information. Alters who are connected share the same information and are often part of the same social circles. Alters who are not connected likely represent different social circles and are sources of different, non-redundant information. However, the two advantages of control and access to non-redundant information appear to be a trade-off: To play one against the other, the two alters need to be sufficiently similar or redundant to be credible alternatives. In addition, the irony of the structural hole strategy is that connecting to any previously disconnected alter (i.e., one not connected to any of ego's alters) creates structural hole opportunities for the alter as well as for ego (Brass, 2009).

For example, in Figure 12.1b, actor A can broker the relationship between actor C and actor B, but actor C can broker the relationship between actor A and actor G. Likewise, actors B, D, and E can broker the relationships between actor A and actors F, H, and I, respectively. In competitive, exclusionary situations (Borgatti et al., 2009), where forming a relationship with one person excludes the possibility of relationship with another alter (e.g., contract bargaining, interorganizational alliances, marriage), actor A's power is substantially reduced by the addition of actors F, G, H, and I in Figure 12.1b (Cook, Emerson, Gilmore, & Yamagishi, 1983).

However, in cooperative, information sharing situations, actor A's position is enhanced by the addition of indirect ties to alters F, G, H, and I in Figure 12.1b. Networks may produce different outcomes contingent upon the competitiveness of the situation (Kilduff & Brass, 2010). Comparing Figure 12.1a with Figure 12.1b also points out the importance of going beyond the dyadic relationships to focus on indirect ties and the larger network. Global, *whole-network* measures of structural holes (i.e., betweenness centrality) have been associated with power in organizations (Brass, 1984), while local, ego-network measures of structural holes have shown robustness in predicting performance outcomes (Burt, 2007).

A third possible advantage to structural holes is illustrated by a *tertius iungens* strategy (Obstfeld, 2005). Rather than "divide and conquer," the broker (e.g., actor A) may connect two alters (e.g., actors B and C) to the benefit of each (e.g., marriage broker, or banks connecting borrowers with lenders). Within organizations, ego may connect two alters with synergistic skills or knowledge rather than mediate the exchange between the alters. Such *tertius iungens* behavior may enhance the broker's reputation, and create obligations for future reciprocations from the alters. Although little research has investigated the exact mechanisms involved, the evidence indicates advantages to actors who occupy structural holes (see Brass, 2011, for a detailed review).

CLOSED NETWORKS

Whereas Burt's (1992) approach to structural holes focuses on the position of individual actors within the network, Coleman (1990) focuses on the overall structure of the network, addressing the benefits of norms of reciprocity, trust, and mutual obligations as well as monitoring and sanctioning of inappropriate behavior that result from *closed* networks. Closed networks are characterized by high interconnectedness among network actors (often measured as the density of relationships) such as depicted in Figure 12.1c. The actors in Figure 12.1c (U, W, X, Y, and Z) are *structurally equivalent*. In Figure 12.1c, each actor is connected to each other actor, and it is difficult to predict which actor will be most powerful without additional information about the abilities or political skill of the actors. Figure 12.1a presents a strong structural effect, whereas Figure 12.1c represents a weak structural effect on individual power. However, Figure 12.1c represents a strong structural effect on group power (e.g., the effect of unions or coalitions in acquiring power).

Closed networks provide the opportunity for shared norms, social support, and a sense of identity that may prove essential to groups seeking power. In closed networks, such as Figure 12.1c, information circulates rapidly and the potential damage to one's reputation discourages unethical behavior and, consequently, fosters generalized trust among members of the network (Brass, Butterfield, & Skaggs, 1998). However, closed networks can become self-contained silos of redundant, self-reinforcing information that may prove self-defeating in acquiring power in the larger network. For the group, a balance including a local, core group of densely tied, reliable friends as well as external ties to disconnected clusters outside the group may prove most beneficial (Burt, 2005; Reagans, Zuckerman, & McEvily, 2004).

THE STRENGTH OF TIES

Following Granovetter's (1973) seminal research on the strength of weak ties, social network researchers have focused on the nature of the relationship as well as the structure of relationships. Tie strength is a function of its interaction frequency, intimacy, emotional intensity (mutual confiding), and degree of reciprocity (p. 348). Close friends are strong ties, whereas acquaintances represent weak ties. Granovetter argued that strong tie alters are likely to be connected to each other and that weak ties likely extend to disconnected alters in different social circles.

The strength of weak ties results from their bridging to disconnected social circles that may provide useful, nonredundant information. This structural explanation is similar to but preceded Burt's (1992) structural hole arguments, in which he notes that weak ties are a proxy for structural holes. Whereas family and friends may be more accessible and more motivated to provide information, weak tie acquaintances were more often the source of helpful information when searching for jobs (Granovetter, 1973).

Strong ties also have benefits because they can be trusted sources of influence. For example, Krackhardt (1992) showed that strong ties were influential in determining the outcome of a union election. Weak ties are more useful in searching out information, but strong ties are useful for the effective transfer of tacit information (Hansen, 1999). Strong *embedded* ties provide higher levels of trust, richer transfers of information, and greater problem-solving capabilities when compared with arm's-length ties (Uzzi, 1997). Thus, strong ties are more trusted sources of advice and may be more influential in uncertain or conflicting situations. However, strong ties require more time and effort and are likely to provoke stronger obligations to reciprocate than weak ties.

The expected effects of tie strength have been confirmed in research on dyadic level negotiating (Valley & Neale, 1993). Friends achieve higher joint utility than strangers. However, some research suggests that there might be a curvilinear relationship between tie strength and joint utility (e.g., lovers may be overly concerned about avoiding damage to the relationship and be unwilling to press for an adequate resolution to their issues). As Valley, Neale, and Mannix (1995) noted, relationship strength affects not only the outcome but also the process of dyadic negotiation—that is, the quantity of moves available as well as the quality of the interaction.

While friends may prove to be valuable assets in forming coalitions or endorsing controversial changes, negative ties (e.g., enemies or opposing parties) may have more impact than positive ties (Brass & Labianca, 2011; Labianca & Brass, 2006). For example, Labianca, Brass, and Gray (1998) found that strong positive ties to other departments did not reduce perceptions of intergroup conflict but that a negative relationship with a member of another department increased perceptions of intergroup conflict. Moving beyond the strength of the dyadic relationship, it is expected that third-party friends (or enemies) also may facilitate or hinder the acquisition of power. Having a friend with a negative tie to a member of another group also increased perceptions of intergroup conflict (Labianca et al., 1998). These results suggest that avoiding enemies may be more important than soliciting friends in attempting to influence others.

In addition to the affective strength of ties, social network researchers have debated whether one type of tie (e.g., friendship) can be appropriated for a different type of use (e.g., sales, such as in the case of Girl Scout cookies). Can a friend be counted on to support an influence attempt? Though many employees recognize the sales advantages of establishing relationships with customers, some evidence (Ingram & Zou, 2008) suggests that people prefer to keep their affective relationships separate from their instrumental business relationships. Relying on friends for support of influence attempts may prove defeating in the long run if such tactics damage affective relationships.

TIES TO POWERFUL ALTERS

Lin (1999) argued that tie strength and structural holes are less important than the resources possessed by alters. Following Granovetter's (1973) work, Lin, Ensel, and Vaughn (1981) found that weak ties reached higher status alters more often than strong ties and that obtaining a high-status job was contingent on the occupational prestige of the alters. Similarly, having ties to the dominant coalition of executives in an organization was related to power and promotions for nonmanagerial employees (Brass, 1984, 1985). Sparrowe and Liden (2005) extended these findings by focusing on the nature of the tie as well as the network resources of the alters. While confirming that centrality was related to power, they found that subordinates benefited from trusting (LMX) relationships with central, well-connected supervisors who shared their network connections with their subordinates (sponsorship). When leaders were low in centrality, sharing ties in the leader's trust network was detrimental to acquiring influence.

Actual ties to powerful alters may provide useful information and other resources, but the *perception* of being connected to powerful others may be an additional source of power for ego. For example, when approached for a loan, the wealthy Baron de Rothschild replied, "I won't give you a loan myself, but I will walk arm-in-arm with you across the floor of the

Stock Exchange, and you will soon have willing lenders to spare" (Cialdini, 1989, p. 45). Being perceived as having a powerful friend had more effect on one's reputation for high performance than actually having such a friend (Kilduff & Krackhardt, 1994). At the interorganizational level, market relations between firms are affected by how third parties perceive the quality of the relationship (Podolny, 2001). Networks represent prisms observed by others as well as resource flows. Whether accurate or inaccurate, perceptions are relevant indicators and predictors of power (Krackhardt, 1990).

BUILDING POWERFUL NETWORKS

As noted in Chapter 1 in this volume, researchers have focused more on political tactics in organizations and less on the structure or context within which such actions occur. One might view the structure or context as fixed and identify structures within which particular tactics might be effective. For example, it might be hypothesized that political tactics will determine power in a structure such as Figure 12.1c while having little or no effect in a structure such as Figure 12.1a.

In one of the few studies to investigate both network structure and political tactics, Brass and Burkhardt (1993) found that network centrality and political tactics (i.e., assertiveness, ingratiation, exchange, upward appeal, rationality, and coalition formation) both were significantly related to perceptions of power. In addition, political tactics and network centrality each partially mediated the relationship between the other and power. Using network position (i.e., centrality) as an indicator of potential power (i.e., access to resources) and political tactics as a measure of the strategic use of such resources, they concluded that behavioral tactics decreased in importance as network centrality increased. These results are consistent with the introductory diagrams; that is, political tactics will have little importance in Figure 12.1a but will be crucial in Figure 12.1c.

Perhaps researchers and practitioners more practically might spend their efforts on factors that employees can control (e.g., political strategies) rather than on attempts to alter network structure. However, the result of political tactics is not solely within the control of one party because all influence attempts are relational. Similarly, the extent to which individuals have control over network relationships also must be considered. Even one's direct relationships are in part dependent on another party. Not every high school invitation to the dance is accepted.

If important outcomes also are affected by indirect relationships (over which ego has even less control), the ability of ego to build a powerful network is inversely related to the path distance of alters whose relationships may affect ego. For example, Fowler and Christakis (2008) found that a person's happiness was affected by the happiness of alters as many as three path lengths removed in the network. Human agency decreases and structural determinism increases to the extent that relationships many path lengths away affect ego. With this limitation in mind, social network tactics that may be useful in building powerful social networks are examined next.

SOCIAL NETWORK TACTICS

Much has been written on how to win friends and influence people, but relatively little research has investigated building effective networks. Yet research focusing on predictors of network connections provides some clues on how to build powerful networks. For example, Brass (2011) reviewed several network antecedents.

Spatial, Temporal, and Social Proximity

Despite the advent of e-mail and social networking sites such as Facebook, being in the same place at the same time fosters relationships that are easier to maintain, that are more likely to be strong, and that provide more stable links than electronic touch points. A relationship is more likely to form between people who are close in the social network (e.g., acquaintance of a friend) than three or more links removed. Krackhardt (1994) referred to this as the *law of propinquity*, suggesting that the probability of two people forming a relationship is inversely proportional to the distance between them. To the extent that organizational workflow and hierarchy locate employees in physical and temporal space, additional effects of those formal, required relationships on social networks can be expected.

Homophily

Birds of a feather flock together, and there is overwhelming evidence for homophily in social relationships: People prefer to interact with similar alters (see McPherson, Smith-Lovin, & Cook, 2001 for a cogent review). Similarity is thought to ease communication, to increase predictability of behavior, to foster trust and reciprocity, and to reinforce self-identity. Feld (1981) extended homophily by noting that activities often are organized around *social foci*. Actors with similar demographics, attitudes, and behaviors will meet in similar settings, will interact with each other, and will enhance that similarity. However, similarity also can lead to rivalry for scarce resources, differences may be complementary, and people may aspire to form relationships with higher status alters. Similarity is a relational concept, and organizational coordination requirements (e.g., hierarchy and workflow requirements) may provide opportunities or restrictions on the extent to which a person is similar or dissimilar to others.

Balance

A friend of a friend is my friend; a friend of an enemy is my enemy. Cognitive balance (Heider, 1958) often is at the heart of network explanations (see Kilduff & Tsai, 2003 for a more complete exploration). However, the effects of balance are limited; in a perfectly balanced world, everyone would be part of one giant positive cluster or two opposing clusters linked only by negative ties. The adage, "Two's company; three's a crowd," also suggests that two friends may become rivals for ego's time and attention.

Human and Social Capital

As French and Raven (1959) famously noted, human capital in the form of expertise is a source of personal power and likely a source of social capital because those with expertise are sought out by others. Social capital is generally defined as benefits derived from relationships with others (Adler & Kwon, 2002). However, as Casciaro and Lobo (2008) noted, the *lovable fool* is preferable to the *competent jerk*; people choose positive affect over ability. People with social capital also are attractive partners; that is, forming relationships with well-connected alters creates opportunities for indirect flows of information and other resources. The research suggests the following.

1. Be in temporal and physical proximity by intentionally placing yourself in the same place at the same time as others.
2. Recognize the power of homophily and seek out ways in which you are similar to others.
3. Increase your human capital skills and expertise, and in the process, increase your status ("preferential attachment").
4. Leverage existing relationships to create new relationships using balance theory tenets (Brass & Labianca, 2011).
5. Perceptions are important and people are not likely to form relationships with others who are perceived as motivated by calculated self-interest.

Emerging Networks

Considering these findings, Krackhardt (1994) proposed a three-dimensional model (i.e., dependency, intensity, and affect) of the fundamental processes by which networks emerge in organizations. Dependency refers to the extent that one person is dependent on another for the performance of tasks, particularly important from the resource dependency framework. Interdependency is a necessary prerequisite to conflict and subsequent political activity and the exercise of power. A high level of dependency refers to relationships that are critical to task accomplishment. Crozier's (1964) classic study of the dependence of managers and workers on maintenance personnel in a French tobacco plant illustrates the power of dependency. Dependency likely will be affected by formal workflow and hierarchical reporting requirements and is positively associated with temporal, spatial, and social proximity, human capital such as expertise, and social capital such as centrality.

Intensity refers to the frequency and duration of interactions. Intensity may be minimal even in high-dependency situations, and purely social interactions, though low on dependency, may be high or low on intensity. Low-intensity weak ties are low cost in terms of time commitment and may provide useful, nonredundant information from distal parts of the organization. While strong high-intensity ties may be the source of reliable, trustworthy information, low-intensity ties may the source of novel, creative information. The third dimension, affect, refers to how a person feels about the relationship, from strong feelings (love and hate) to weak feelings (politely positive or neutral). Affect likely will be associated with homophily and balance. Relationships can be characterized by any combination of high or low degrees on all three dimensions.

Krackhardt (1994) argued that overall patterns tend to emerge over time as a function of these three dimensions. Dependency tends to promote intensity. Employees with task-related needs for information, resources, or permission seek out alters who can satisfy these needs. Connecting with the alter who fills the need will lead to repeat interactions and will increase intensity. When intensity is high, prolonged frequent interactions induce affective evaluations. Frequent interaction leads to strong emotional bonds, whether they are positive or negative.

Over time, employees learn what to expect from each other, resulting in positive feelings of trust, respect, and even strong friendships. Or employees may learn that others are untrustworthy or unlikable. Whereas strong positive affect will reinforce the relationship, strong negative affect will shorten the life of, or destabilize, the tie. In either case, the proposed model suggests that affect will increase with intensity. Those parts of the network that are reinforced with positive affect will form a stable core, and negative ties will be replaced or disappear over time.

The model suggests that the parts of the network that depend on trust will be stable over time, and evidence suggests that the stable, recurring interactions are the ones that employees see and recall. These are the relationships that people as a matter of habit and preference tend to use. These ties are the old standbys that employees have learned to trust and depend on. The low-dependency, low-intensity, low-affect interactions tend to be more fluid and transitory.

These findings and analysis suggest that the central, powerful players in an organization are neither the competent jerks nor the lovable fools (Casciaro & Lobo, 2008) but rather those who are both competent and likable and become the old standbys. Accomplishing tasks in a reliable, trustworthy, and pleasant fashion increases others' dependency, intensity, and affect. Perceptions are key, and being perceived as unreliable, incompetent, or unpleasant to work with defeats any attempts at increasing centrality. Self-interested, calculative behavior often is labeled *political* and remains a perceptual contrast to merit.

Thus, solely self-interested attempts at influence will be perceived negatively and decrease centrality. Such attempts often are dyadic in nature (e.g., ingratiating oneself to powerful others in hopes of obtaining a promotion or a larger raise). Influencing others to bring about positive organization change also may occur one dyadic relationship at a time, but large-scale change requires moving beyond the dyad to consideration of the larger network needed for the effective use of power. The larger network is addressed in relation to forming coalitions conducive to successful organizational change.

ORGANIZATIONAL CHANGE

Following McGrath and Krackhardt (2003), we begin with the assumption that innovative organizational change begins with a creative idea. Based on the notion that the recombination of diverse ideas leads to creativity, people with diverse networks that span across differentiated clusters of knowledge will be the sources of good ideas. This suggests that weak ties and structural holes (i.e., connections to disconnected sources of nonredundant information) will be instrumental in generating innovative ideas, and research has confirmed this hypothesis (Burt, 2004; Perry-Smith, 2006; Zhou, Shin, Brass, Choi, & Zhang, 2009).

The task, then, is for the creative few to convince the rest of the organization that their ideas are good ones. Innovations that are clearly superior to the status quo will be easily adopted by others, and clearly inferior ideas will be rapidly abandoned. It is the controversial innovations that will likely succeed or fail based on effective or ineffective attempts to influence others. As noted in the introduction, the exercise of power is of greater necessity when conflict occurs.

The task of the creative few is to build a coalition of support for their ideas. We refer to these few as *founders*. Coalitions form around issues and ideas, and politics can make strange bedfellows. The first task of founders is to find someone who likes their ideas. Murnighan and Brass (1991) suggested that founders need a large number of bridging weak ties to accomplish this, although a network of reliable, trusted contacts can provide the template for knowing how people will respond to issues and ideas. Krackhardt (1997) modeled this process, assuming that founders seek out others close to them in the network for feedback on the value of their ideas. Extensive bridging ties can extend this search beyond local connections.

Based on Asch's (1951) conformity experiments, at least one positive response to a founder's idea is necessary to proceed with the innovation. Founders retain their beliefs if they achieve initial support or abandon them if they are surrounded by people who disagree with them. Knowledge of the network is particularly important, and founders are advised to pick the low-hanging fruit first. As previously noted, avoiding negative ties may be particularly important. Founders must know where others stand on issues and approach those who are likely to agree. Because central, powerful alters may be motivated to maintain the status quo, this may mean approaching peripheral actors who are more likely to be open to the merits of the change. Power may be used by the elite to sustain the status quo or to shape perceptions such that alternatives are not considered and existing roles are viewed as beneficial (Lukes, 1974).

Central actors who disagree with the innovation also will be able to mobilize countercoalitions to block the diffusion process, whereas central actors who agree may facilitate the diffusion. By approaching like-minded alters, founders can build numbers, or advocates who can extend the diffusion process until it reaches the tipping point either by virtue of motivated disciples or the persuasiveness of the sheer number of advocates. Infectious disease may spread via a single contact, but behavioral change may require multiple contacts from different sources (Centola, 2010). Targets are more susceptible to persuasion when approached by different advocates at different times, each reinforcing the behavioral change.

Krackhardt's (1997) computer simulation suggests that founders focus on local clusters on the periphery of the organization with few links to the central core, thus avoiding central core positions until requisite numbers are achieved. When the innovation is controversial, nonadvocates are as likely to convert advocates to remain with the status quo as vice versa; ties across clusters tend to give the advantage to the status quo. Thus, founders first need to establish cohesive clusters of support (e.g., Figure 12.1c) so that nonadvocates are not mobilized. While founders' extensive weak ties or structural holes may be helpful in knowledge of the network and whom to approach, founders must be careful not to approach minority advocates in majority nonadvocate clusters, as the majority will quickly convert the minority advocate.

Having established a base, founders and early advocates can slowly and carefully move to adjacent clusters with sufficient numbers to convert more adopters before attempting to convert the central core or the entire organization. Krackhardt (1997) referred to this as the *principle of optimal viscosity*. Organizational change is accomplished when actors in subunits are minimally connected, and "the seed for change is planted at the periphery, not the center, of the network" (McGrath & Krackhardt, 2003, p. 328).

The optimal viscosity model contrasts with the widely held notion that ideal, flat, maximum density organizations can respond rapidly to change. Although such an ideal type may not be possible or even desirable (Krackhardt, 1994), extensive connections across subunits will result in rapid diffusion only when innovation is accepted as clearly superior to the status quo. However, when innovation is clearly superior, political activity and the exercise of power are clearly unnecessary.

CONCLUSION

Overall, the main objective of this chapter was to demonstrate how a social network perspective might contribute to greater understanding of power and politics in organizations. Organizations are designed to be cooperative systems; however, political activity occurs when conflict arises, and those with power have the advantage. Research was summarized relating power to centrality in the organizational network, noting the advantages of ties to both connected others (closed networks) and disconnected others (structural holes). Generating positive organization change requires both the creative ideas and knowledge of the network provided by bridging ties to disconnected clusters (structural holes) and the support for the diffusion and adopting of these ideas provided by closed networks of trusting ties. Tactics for building centrality in the network were suggested, as were ideas regarding bringing about organizational change. The hope is that these ideas will generate research on political strategies that may be effective or ineffective within the context of the structural opportunities and constraints of social networks in organizations.

ACKNOWLEDGMENTS

We are indebted to Steve Borgatti, Joe Labianca, Ajay Mehra, Dan Halgin, and the other faculty and PhD students at the LINKS Center (http://linkscenter.org) for the many interesting and insightful discussions that form the basis for chapters such as this.

REFERENCES

Adler, P.S., & Kwon, S. (2002). Social capital: Prospects for a new concept. *Academy of Management Review, 27*, 17–40.

Asch, S.E. (1951). Effects of group pressure upon the modification and distortion of judgments. In H. Guetzkow (Ed.), *Groups, leadership, and men* (pp. 151–162). Pittsburgh: Carnegie Press.

Astley, W.G., & Zajac, E.J. (1990). Beyond dyadic exchange: Functional interdependence and sub-unit power. *Organization Studies, 11*, 481–501.

Boje, D.M., & Whetten, D.A. (1981). Effects of organizational strategies and contextual constraints on centrality and attributions of influence in interorganizational networks. *Administrative Science Quarterly, 26*, 378–395.

Borgatti, S.P., Mehra, A., Brass, D.J., & Labianca, G. (2009). Network analysis in the social sciences. *Science, 323*, 892–895.

Brass, D.J. (1984). Being in the right place: A structural analysis of individual influence in an organization. *Administrative Science Quarterly, 29*, 518–539.

Brass, D.J. (1985). Men's and women's networks: A study of interaction patterns and influence in an organization. *Academy of Management Journal, 28*, 327–343.

Brass, D.J. (1992). Power in organizations: A social network perspective. In G. Moore & J.A. Whitt (Eds.), *Research in politics and society* (pp. 295–323). Greenwich, CT: JAI Press.

Brass, D.J. (2002). Intraorganizational power and dependence. In J.A.C. Baum (Ed.), *The Blackwell companion to organizations* (pp. 138–157). Oxford: Blackwell.

Brass, D.J. (2009). Connecting to brokers: Strategies for acquiring social capital. In V.O. Bartkus & J.H. Davis (Eds.), *Social capital: Reaching out, reaching in* (pp. 260–274). Northhampton, MA: Elgar Publishing.

Brass, D.J. (2011). A social network perspective on industrial/organizational psychology. In S.W.J. Kozlowski (Ed.), *The Oxford handbook of organizational psychology.* New York: Oxford University Press.

Brass, D.J., & Burkhardt, M.E. (1992). Centrality and power in organizations. In N. Nohria & R. Eccles (Eds.), *Networks and organizations: Structure, form, and action* (pp. 191–215). Boston: Harvard Business School Press.

Brass, D.J., & Burkhardt. M.E. (1993). Potential power and power use: An investigation of structure and behavior. *Academy of Management Journal, 36*, 441–470.

Brass, D.J., Butterfield, K.D., & Skaggs, B.C. (1998). Relationships and unethical behavior: A social network perspective. *Academy of Management Review, 23*, 14–31.

Brass, D.J., Galaskiewicz, J., Greve, H.R., & Tsai, W. (2004). Taking stock of networks and organizations: A multilevel perspective. *Academy of Management Journal, 47,* 795–819.

Brass, D.J., & Labianca, G. (2011). A social network perspective on negotiation. In D. Shapiro & B.M. Goldman (Eds.), *Negotiating in human resources for the 21st century.* Thousand Oaks, CA: Sage Publications.

Breiger, R.L. (1976). Career attributes and network structure: A block model study of biomedical research specialty. *American Sociological Review, 41,* 117–135.

Bristor, J.M. (1993). Influence strategies in organizational buying: The importance of connections to the right people in the right places. *Journal of Business-to-Business Marketing, 1,* 63–98.

Burkhardt, M.E. & Brass, D.J. (1990). Changing patterns or patterns of change: The effects of a change in technology on social network structure and power. *Administrative Science Quarterly, 35,* 104–127.

Burt, R.S. (1992). *Structural holes: The social structure of competition.* Cambridge, MA: Harvard University Press.

Burt, R.S. (2004). Structural holes and good ideas. *American Journal of Sociology, 110,* 349–399.

Burt, R.S. (2005). *Brokerage and closure: An introduction to social capital.* Oxford, Oxford University Press.

Burt, R.S. (2007). Second-hand brokerage: Evidence on the importance of local structure for managers, bankers, and analysts. *Academy of Management Journal, 50,* 110–145.

Casciaro, T., & Lobo, M.S. (2008). When competence is irrelevant: The role of interpersonal affect in task-related ties. *Administrative Science Quarterly, 53,* 655–684.

Centola, D. (2010). The spread of behavior in an online social network experiment. *Science, 329,* 1194–1197.

Cialdini, R.B. (1989). Indirect tactics of impression management: Beyond basking. In R.A. Giacalone & P. Rosenfield (Eds.), *Impression management in the organization* (pp. 45–56). Hillsdale, NJ: Lawrence Erlbaum.

Coleman, J.S. (1990). *Foundations of social theory.* Cambridge, MA: Harvard University Press.

Cook, K.S., Emerson, R.M., Gilmore, M.R., & Yamagishi, T. (1983). The distribution of power in exchange networks: Theory and experimental results. *American Journal of Sociology, 89,* 275–305.

Crozier, M. (1964). *The bureaucratic phenomenon.* Chicago: University of Chicago Press.

Feld, S.L. (1981). The focused organization of social ties. *American Journal of Sociology, 86,* 1015–1035.

Fombrun, C.J. (1983). Attributions of power across a social network. *Human Relations, 36,* 493–508.

Fowler, J.H., & Christakis, N.A. (2008). The dynamic spread of happiness in a large social network. *British Journal of Medicine, 337*(2338), 1–9.

French, J.R.P., & Raven, B. (1959). The bases of social power. In D. Cartwright & A. Zander, *Group dynamics* (pp. 150–167). New York: Harper & Row.

Galaskiewicz, J. (1979). *Exchange networks and community politics.* Beverly Hills, CA: Sage Publications.

Granovetter, M.S. (1973). The strength of weak ties. *American Journal of Sociology, 6,* 1360–1380.

Hansen, M.T. (1999). The search-transfer problem: The role of weak ties in sharing knowledge across organization subunits. *Administrative Science Quarterly, 44,* 82–111.

Heider, R. (1958). *The psychology of interpersonal relations.* New York: Wiley.

Hinings, C.R., Hickson, D.J., Pennings, J.M., & Schneck. R.E. (1974). Structural conditions of intraorganizational power. *Administrative Science Quarterly, 19,* 22–44.

Ingram, P., & Zou, X. (2008). Business friendships. In A.P. Brief & B.M. Staw (Eds.), *Research in organizational behavior* (Vol. 28, pp. 167–184). London: Elsevier.

Kilduff, M., & Brass, D. J. (2010). Organizational social network research: Core ideas and key debates. In J.P. Walsh & A.P. Brief (Eds.), *Academy of Management Annuals* (Vol. 4, pp. 317–357). London: Routledge.

Kilduff, M., & Krackhardt, D. (1994). Bringing the individual back in: A structural analysis of the internal market for reputation in organizations. *Academy of Management Journal, 37,* 87–108.

Kilduff, M., & Tsai, W. (2003). *Social networks and organizations.* London: Sage.

Knoke, D., & Burt, R.S. (1983). Prominence. In R.S. Burt & M.J. Miner (Eds.), *Applied network analysis: A methodological introduction* (pp. 195–222). Beverly Hills, CA: Sage Publications.

Krackhardt, D. (1990). Assessing the political landscape: Structure, cognition, and power in organizations. *Administrative Science Quarterly, 35,* 342–369.

Krackhardt, D. (1992). The strength of strong ties: The importance of Philos. In N. Nohria & R. Eccles (Eds.), *Networks and organizations: Structure, form, and action* (pp. 216–239). Boston: Harvard Business School Press.

Krackhardt, D. (1994). Constraints on the interactive organization as an ideal type. In C. Heckscher & A. Donnellan (Eds.), *The post-bureaucratic organization* (pp. 211–222). Thousand Oaks, CA: Sage.

Krackhardt, D. (1997). Organizational viscosity and the diffusion of controversial innovations. *Journal of Mathematical Sociology, 22,* 177–199.

Labianca, G., & Brass, D.J. (2006). Exploring the social ledger: Negative relationships and negative asymmetry in social networks in organizations. *Academy of Management Review, 31,* 596–614.

Labianca, G., Brass, D.J., & Gray, B. (1998). Social networks and perceptions of intergroup conflict: The role of negative relationships and third parties. *Academy of Management Journal, 41,* 55–67.

Laumann. E.O., & Pappi, F.U. (1976). *Networks of collective action: A perspective on community influence systems.* New York: Academic Press.

Lin, N. (1999). Social networks and status attainment. *Annual Review of Sociology, 25,* 467–487.

Lin, N., Ensel, W.M., & Vaughn, J.C. (1981). Social resources and strength of ties: Structural factors in occupational status attainment. *American Sociological Review, 46.* 393–405.

Lukes, S. (1974). *Power: A radical view.* London: Macmillan.

McGrath, C., & Krackhardt, D. (2003). Network conditions for organizational change. *Journal of Applied Behavioral Science, 39,* 324–336.

McPherson, J.M., Smith-Lovin, L., & Cook, J.M. (2001). Birds of a feather: Homophily in social networks. *Annual Review of Sociology, 27,* 415–444.

Murnighan, J.K., & Brass, D.J. (1991). Intraorganizational coalitions. In M. Bazerman, B. Sheppard, & R. Lewicki (Eds.), *Research on negotiations in organizations* (Vol. 3, pp. 283–307). Greenwich, CT: JAI Press.

Obstfeld, D. (2005). Social networks, the tertius iungens orientation, and involvement in innovation. *Administrative Science Quarterly, 50,* 100–130.

Perry-Smith, J.E. (2006). Social yet creative: The role of social relationships in facilitating individual creativity. *Academy of Management Journal, 49*, 85–101.

Pfeffer, J. (1981). *Power in organizations.* Marshfield, MA: Pitman.

Podolny, J.M. (2001). Networks as the pipes and prisms of the market. *American Journal of Sociology, 107*, 33–60.

Reagans, R., Zuckerman, E., & McEvily, B. (2004). How to make the team: Social networks vs. demography as criteria for designing effective teams. *Administrative Science Quarterly, 49*, 101–133.

Ronchetto, J.R., Hun, M.D., & Reingen, P.H. (1989). Embedded influence patterns in organizational buying systems. *Journal of Marketing, 53*, 51–62.

Shaw, M.E. (1964). Communication networks. In L. Berkowitz (Ed.), *Advances in experimental social psychology* (Vol. 1, pp. 111–147). New York: Academic Press.

Sparrowe, R.T., & Liden, R.C. (2005). Two routes to influence: Integrating leader-member exchange and network perspectives. *Administrative Science Quarterly, 50*, 505–535.

Tushman, M., & Romanelli, E. (1983). Uncertainty, social location and influence in decision making: A sociometric analysis. *Management Science, 29*, 12–23.

Uzzi, B. (1997). Social structure and competition in interfirm networks: The paradox of embeddedness. *Administrative Science Quarterly, 42*, 35–67.

Valley, K.L., & Neale, M.A. (1993). *Intimacy and integrativeness: The role of relationships in negotiations.* Working paper, Cornell University, Ithaca, NY.

Valley, K.L., Neale, M.A., & Mannix, E.A. (1995). Friends, lovers, colleagues, strangers: The effects of relationships on the process and outcome of dyadic negotiations. *Research on Negotiation in Organizations, 5*, 65–93.

Watts, D.J. (2003). *Six degrees: The science of a connected age.* New York: W.W. Norton.

Zhou, J., Shin, S. J., Brass, D.J., Choi, J., & Zhang, Z. (2009). Social networks, personal values, and creativity: Evidence for curvilinear and interaction effects. *Journal of Applied Psychology, 94*, 1544–1552.

13

Organizational Politics in Strategic Management and Entrepreneurship

Robert A. Baron
Oklahoma State University

Sean Lux
University of South Florida

Garry L. Adams
Auburn University

Bruce T. Lamont
Florida State University

> Politics is the art of the possible.
>
> **—Otto Von Bismarck**

> In real life, strategy is actually very straightforward. You pick a general direction and implement like hell.
>
> **—Jack Welch**

> I never perfected an invention that I did not think about in terms of the service it might give others.... I find out what the world needs, then I proceed to invent.
>
> **—Thomas Edison**

Politics, strategy, entrepreneurship—as these quotations imply, these terms seem to refer to very different domains. *Politics* involves the use of various tactics to gain and exercise power (e.g., Silvester, 2008). *Strategy* focuses on devising plans and implementing them to secure and hold competitive advantage, in business, on the battlefield, in sports, and in many other contexts (e.g., Hofer & Schendel, 1978; Mintzberg, 1983). *Entrepreneurship* relates to the complex processes through which new and profitable organizations are created from what Humphrey Bogart once described (in a classic film) as "...the stuff that dreams are made of..." (in this case, the dreams, vision, and passion of entrepreneurs; Cardon, Wincent, Sing, & Drnvosek 2009; Shane & Venkataraman, 2000). However, upon close examination, it becomes clear that these three constructs actually are, in fact, related, although in ways that may not be obvious or immediately apparent. In essence, they all involve a very basic aspect of human life, and especially of "the social side" of life: influence.

Influence has been a topic of major interest for centuries and has been systematically investigated through the methods of modern social science for several decades. Although it has been studied in several different fields (e.g., management, sociology, political science), it is perhaps most central to the field of social psychology, where it is defined as the process through which one or more persons attempt to change the behavior, attitudes, or feelings of one or more others (Baron & Branscombe, 2011; Cialdini, 2008). Influence attempts take many different forms, and, as noted herein, several of these are related to organizations in general and to new ventures and strategy in particular. However, before turning to these tactics, it important to delineate the scope of this chapter by briefly considering the nature of organizational politics as it is treated here.

For many people, the term *organizational politics* has a slightly sinister ring, and in fact, initial definitions of this topic resonated closely with this view. For instance, Mayes and Allen (1977) described it as activity undertaken to secure outcomes not attainable via organizationally sanctioned means. Similarly, Ferris, Russ, and Fandt (1989) described political behavior as inherently self-serving. Other authors have proposed more negative definitions, such as Chanlat (1997), who referred to organizational politics as a *social disease*, and other scholars have emphasized the importance of its control or elimination (e.g., Gioia & Longenecker, 1994).

Certainly, such definitions describe many instances of organizational politics, and often they are enacted to further the interests and selfish motives of the persons who employ them (e.g., Kacmar & Baron, 1999). On the other hand, to the extent that organizational politics represent specific uses of the more general process of *influence*, the situation becomes more complex. Social psychologists agree that influence is an essentially neutral process, and it can be used for promoting personal, selfish ends or for much more altruistic purposes.

Consider the vast range of contexts in which individuals attempt to exert influence over others to change their behavior, attitudes, or feelings. Confidence artists, including their modern representatives who operate on the Web, are intent on changing the behavior of intended victims so that these people give them what they want (i.e., money, valuables, or confidential personal information). Similarly, advertisers use sophisticated techniques of persuasion to induce potential customers to buy their products or services, even if the products or services are not the best or most appropriate for their needs.

However, influence also can be directed toward prosocial or altruistic purposes. For example, public service organizations seek to change the habits and lifestyle of millions of persons to help them achieve better health ("Stop smoking, or don't start"; "Eat healthier foods"; "Don't get too much exposure to the sun"). Also, individuals often seek to exert influence over others to help rather than exploit them. The phrase *this is for your own good* sometimes represents efforts to conceal underlying selfish motives, but on other occasions it reflects genuine desires to help on the part of the persons seeking to exert influence.

Within organizations, influence often takes the form of organizational politics (e.g., Ferris & Hochwarter, 2011). Many of the actions organizational politics involve do appear to reflect selfish motives and efforts to advance the interests of individuals or groups and, importantly, even if these are inconsistent with those of the overall organization (e.g., Pfeffer, 1981). However, as noted in Chapter 1 in this volume, organizational politics, like the basic processes of influence on which it rests, is better defined in more neutral terms that avoid the aura of selfish motives and behaviors with which it often has been linked.

Chapter 1 defines organizational politics very broadly, as involving efforts to create, maintain, modify, or abandon shared meanings within the organization (i.e., efforts to induce the persons in an organization to see the world similarly and, presumably, to work toward shared goals under the guidance of common, approved values). In the remainder of this discussion, a similar approach is adopted—that is, one that avoids implicit acceptance of the idea that organizational politics (e.g., influence) basically is negative or harmful in nature.

An extensive and insightful literature concerned with the nature, causes, perceptions, and effects of organizational politics already exists (see Chapter 1 in this volume for a review). Therefore, the focus here is on the tasks of extending this literature (and the basic concept of organizational politics) to two fields where it has not previously been fully considered: entrepreneurship and strategic management. To accomplish this task, discussion proceeds as follows. First, an initial section examines the nature of influence and the many forms it can take. This is useful because to date the vast literature on influence in social psychology has not been fully integrated into the management literature and research generally and into investigations of organizational politics in particular. In fact, management scholars have directed attention to only a limited range of the phenomena that fall under the general term *influence* (see, e.g., Schreisheim & Neider, 2006).

Second, the potential role of organizational politics in new ventures is examined. Although it might at first be assumed that politics plays only a minor role in this context, there are actually several reasons its impact may actually be considerable. Overall, politics may be relevant both to important activities that occur within new ventures and to the interface of new ventures with many agents and stakeholders outside the venture (e.g., venture capitalists, angel investors, customers, suppliers).

In particular, the potential impact of entrepreneurs' political skill on the success of new ventures—their ability to "effectively understand others and to use such knowledge to influence others to act in ways that enhance one's personal and/or organizational objectives" (Ferris, Treadway, et al., 2005, p. 127)—is more fully examined. Recent evidence indicates that entrepreneurs' political skill does indeed play a significant role in the success of new ventures, so in this respect politics is directly relevant to entrepreneurship and the processes through which new ventures emerge and develop.

Third, we turn our attention to the role of organizational politics and influence in strategic management. Successful strategy formulation and implementation has always been viewed as requiring the effective management of influence by skilled leaders (MacMillan & Jones, 1978). However, recent research in strategic management has favored economic theories of firm success rather than political ones. Where power and influence have been addressed, this has been implicitly rather than explicitly, and usually within a context of developing competitive advantage.

The one area of recent growing attention that offers an exception to this general principle, however, has been among strategy scholars interested in the antecedents and consequences of corporate political activity (CPA). The broader strategy literature is reviewed relevant to understanding the power and politics of firms to better inform the nascent but growing CPA literature. Among other things, the review highlights that power and skills are organizational and interorganizational level phenomena and that top-management teams (TMTs) are central to their development.

These general observations from the broader strategy literature are then used where power and politics are peripheral to extend CPA research. A better understanding of top managers' political proclivities, experiences, and skills can usefully extend CPA research (Lux, Crook, & Woehr, 2011). Also, it is likely that the political skill of organizations goes beyond those of their leaders (Oliver & Holzinger, 2008). These capabilities may be the product of past investments and embedded in organizational routines (Reus, Ranft, Lamont, & Adams, 2009), making them a potential source of competitive advantage (Nelson & Winter, 1982). Therefore, political skill also may be viewed as an organization-level phenomenon that varies across organizations and helps to explain the differential success of CPA. This organization-level view of the political skill construct, where TMTs are central, is a natural extension of the strategy literature. In conclusion, a challenge is issued for strategy and entrepreneurship scholars to further explore the political skills and competencies underlying influence attempts in both new ventures and established firms. Developments in one literature are likely to benefit the others.

THE NATURE AND FORMS OF SOCIAL INFLUENCE: INSIGHTS INTO ORGANIZATIONAL

Politics From Social Psychological Theory and Research

Most people are exposed to attempts at influence many times each day. Requests from friends, advice from coworkers or relatives, and discussions with roommates or a spouse over where to dine or to vacation or what to buy all fall under the same general heading. Similarly, most persons attempt to influence others many times each day, requesting the loan of some item, help with a work project, or their endorsement of some plan for anything from a major initiative within the organization to a social evening or family outing. In short, influence is an important and pervasive fact of social life. As Eric Hoffer (1976) said, "It would be difficult to exaggerate the degree to which we are influenced by those we influence."

Not only is influence pervasive, it also is very much a two-way street in which most people are both the target of influence and seek to exert it themselves. If exerting influence is indeed a basic goal of organizational politics, it is important to understand the nature of influence to apply it to settings such as new ventures or the formulation and implementation of effective strategy. In the past, efforts to examine influence in the context of organizations often have focused on describing the nature and use of specific tactics (e.g., Kipnis, Schmidt, & Wilkinson, 1980; Nutt, 1986). However, a broader perspective is adopted here that focuses on a basic set of principles, established by extensive research in social psychology and related fields, which appear to underlie a large proportion of the specific tactics individuals use for exerting influence in organizations and elsewhere.

Basic Principles of Social Influence

Some years ago, Robert Cialdini, a well-known expert on influence, reasoned that the best way to uncover the basic nature of influence was to carefully observe what he termed *compliance professionals*: people whose success, financial or otherwise, depends on their ability to influence others and, more specifically, to comply with their requests. Such persons include salespeople, advertisers, political lobbyists, fund-raisers, politicians, con artists, and professional negotiators. To study what these people actually do, Cialdini temporarily concealed his true identity and took jobs in various settings where gaining compliance is a way of life. In other words, he worked in advertising, direct (i.e., door-to-door) sales, fund-raising, and other compliance-focused fields. On the basis of these firsthand experiences, he concluded that although techniques for gaining compliance take many different forms, they all rest to some degree on six basic principles (Cialdini, 1984, 2008):

- *Friendship/liking*: In general, individuals are more willing to comply with requests from friends or from people they like than with requests from strangers or people they don't like.
- *Commitment/consistency*: Once individuals have committed themselves to a position or action, they are more willing to comply with requests for behaviors that are consistent with this position or action than with requests that are inconsistent with it because they wish to be consistent in what they say or do.

- *Scarcity*: In general, individuals value and try to secure outcomes or objects that are scarce or decreasing in availability. As a result, they are more likely to comply with requests that focus on scarcity than ones that make no reference to this issue.
- *Reciprocity*: Generally, individuals more willing to comply with a request from someone who previously has provided a favor or concession to them than to someone who has not. In other words, individuals feel obligated to pay people back in some way for what they have done for them.
- *Social validation*: Generally, individuals are more willing to comply with a request for some action if this action is consistent with what they believe persons similar to themselves are doing (or thinking). They want to be correct, and one way to do so is to act and think like others.
- *Authority*: In general, individuals are more willing to comply with requests from someone who holds legitimate authority or simply appears to do so.

According to Cialdini (2008), these basic principles underlie many techniques used by professionals (and also by nonprofessionals) to influence others and gain compliance with their wishes. Table 13.1 presents an overview of some the highly inventive tactics that are based on these principles. As can be seen, each principle can, and does, give rise to a number of different tactics. Further, many of these tactics appear to be quite effective; that is, when used with skill and care, they do cause the target persons to measurably change their actions or underlying attitudes. For instance, the principle of *friendship/liking* (i.e., individuals are more likely to accept influence from people they like or with whom they have an existing relationships than from strangers) underlies the tactics of ingratiation, flattery, and self-promotion.

Similarly, the principle of reciprocity underlies the *door-in-the-face tactic* (i.e., starting with a very large request that is almost certain to be rejected but then "scaling back" to a smaller one, which is the one the influencer wanted all along (Guéguen, 2003), and the *that's-not-all tactic* (i.e., offering the intended target something "extra," albeit trivial, before they can reply to a request; this puts pressure on them to reciprocate by saying yes; see, e.g., Burger, 1986). In short, these principles, which often serve as basic guidelines of social life, often can be effectively turned to the purpose of exerting influence. Because they are so common and so widely accepted, influence attempts based on them is often hard to resist and may, in fact,

TABLE 13.1

Principles Underlying Social Influence and Tactics Based on These Principles

Underlying Principle	Tactics Based on This Principle	Description
Friendship/Liking	Ingratiation	Efforts to induce liking in others
	Flattery	Unjustified praise of others
	Self-promotion	Describing our own virtues
Commitment/ Consistency	Foot in the door	Small request followed by larger one
	Lowball procedure	Change in deal after target person agrees with request
Reciprocity	Door in the door	Large request followed by much smaller
	That's not all tactic	Offering small additional benefit prior to decision by target person
Scarcity	Playing hard to get	Suggesting that the influencer is in great demand
	Deadline technique	Establishing a deadline for acceptance or action
Social Validation	Accepting influence to do what persons similar to ourselves are doing	Influencer suggests that the requested action is what others are doing
Authority	Obedience to commands from authority figures	Direct commands from authority figures who do or do not actually possess authority to make these demands

not even be perceived as such by the persons who succumb to it. Having briefly described the findings of basic research on influence in the field of social psychology, the focus next is turned to a very basic question: Why is organizational politics, which is viewed here primarily as involving organizational applications of influence, relevant to entrepreneurship?

Organizational Politics in New Venture: Why It Occurs

New ventures are small by definition, consisting initially, solely of the founders of the venture. This would seem to suggest that they do not represent fertile ground for organizational politics or the exercise of influence. Generally, founders begin with a shared vision of the kind of company they wish to develop, although of course this often changes greatly very quickly. In addition, generally they know each other well before launching a new company. These conditions would seem to suggest that founders have little need for exerting influence on one another, and little reason to engage in the tactics that together, are often viewed as constituting political behavior in organizations. In fact, though, there are several reasons influence and some forms of organizational politics may play an important role in the operation of new ventures.

First, consider the fact that new ventures, in contrast to large, established organizations, have no well-developed routines, procedures, or rules for operations. On the contrary, as frequently noted (e.g., Baron, 2007), entrepreneurs must make it up as they go along. In other words, they operate in what might, in the context of social influence, be viewed as "weak situations"—that is, ones that are not scripted and in which a great deal of uncertainty exists about what actions or strategies are best or most appropriate. A basic finding of research in this area is that individuals are most susceptible to influence in situations where uncertainty exists over what is most appropriate or effective. For this reason, there are strong grounds for anticipating that founders will engage in efforts to influence one another with high frequency. Essentially, they have few guides, other than themselves, for developing and directing their (hopefully) growing companies.

Second, though conflict is costly in any organization, it may be especially damaging to new ventures. Resources are limited and high levels of collaboration between founders are necessary for the new venture's survival. For this reason, founders often are highly motivated to avoid open confrontations. Therefore, when they discover that they have contrasting views or prefer different courses of action, they often attempt to handle such situations through influence rather than open disagreement or conflict. This is reasonable, since the costs of confrontations, both within the new venture and outside it, are very high (e.g., venture capitalists may withhold further financing if it appears that the founders of the venture are locked in conflict or contests of will). However, it may pave the way for considerable use of influence and political actions, which may be more common in new ventures than initially might be assumed.

Third, new ventures often suffer from a lack of reputation or credibility (e.g., Rindova, Williamson, Petkova, & Sever, 2005); that is, they are new and often unknown in their markets and frequently compete with well-established firms who enjoy the benefits of an established trademark and reputation. Under these conditions, it is crucial that the founding team speak with one voice and at least to external observers, appear to be fully in agreement and working cooperatively as a team to achieve the new venture's goals. Signs of disagreement between the founders may be interpreted by potential customers, suppliers, and other stakeholders as a sign that the new venture is unlikely to survive and to meet its obligations. Recognition of this fact, too, would encourage founders to employ influence and political tactics to settle any actual or latent disagreements to prevent these from developing into open conflict and becoming public knowledge.

Finally, it is widely recognized that the founders of new ventures tend to experience strong levels of emotion (e.g., high levels of both positive affect and negative affect; see, e.g., Baron, 2008; Cardon et al., 2009). Often, they are passionately committed to their companies and have powerful emotional reactions to both advances and setbacks. A large body of evidence indicates that many forms of influence especially are likely to operate and to be effective in the context of strong emotions (e.g., Baron & Branscombe, 2011). Furthermore, additional evidence indicates that strong emotions tend to spread from one person to another, especially if they are similar to each other and have an ongoing social relationship (e.g., Epstude & Mussweiler, 2009)—that is, a process known as *emotional contagion*.

This applies very well to founders, who often work together very closely and have relationships predating the founding of their venture. Thus, it seems likely that they will experience strong tendencies to mirror each other's emotions and consequently that such reactions will increase in intensity through an upward spiral of mutual influence. Recent findings indicate that strong affective reactions on the part of entrepreneurs can have important effects on the success of their new ventures (e.g., Baron, Tang, & Hmieleski, 2011), so this is yet another way the basic process of influence can play an important role in entrepreneurship—even if, as in emotional contagion, it is not the result of conscious, overt efforts to change others' actions or attitudes.

In sum, although new ventures are small, their founders are exposed to powerful situational forces that together may strongly encourage the use of influence (the precursor of organizational politics) between them. Having clarified this point, another basic question is now considered: Does being adept in the "art" of exerting influence, either within and outside the new venture, play a role in the success of these new businesses? A very large literature on the role of such skills, known generally as political skill (see Ferris, Davidson, & Perrewé, 2005) indicates that they indeed play an important role with respect to the outcomes experienced by individuals (e.g., career success). It is suggested that these skills also may be related to the outcomes experienced by entrepreneurs and their new ventures, and in fact several studies have offered support for this view. This research is now briefly reviewed, and its implications for extending knowledge concerning organizational politics to the domain of entrepreneurship are examined.

Political Skill and Its Relevance to New Ventures

Attempts at influence are ubiquitous, as most people encounter them many times each day. However, just as clearly, only some of these attempts are successful. Part of the reason this is so is that human beings possess or quickly develop many techniques for resisting even powerful influence efforts (Baron & Branscombe, 2011). In addition, they also possess a strong motive to be independent—that is, to be unique individuals and not to be influenced by others (e.g., Pronin, Berger & Molouki, 2007) or to follow along with the general herd.

However, another reason attempts to exert influence fail involves the attempts themselves, because they are not carried out effectively or because the most appropriate tactics for a given situation are not employed. Individuals differ greatly in terms of skills closely related to the successful exercise of influence, such as their verbal eloquence and hence persuasiveness. Individuals also differ in their ability to perceive others accurately, and such understanding often is an essential ingredient in choosing and delivering effective efforts at influence. In recent years, Ferris and his colleagues (e.g., Ferris, Davidson, et al., 2005; Ferris, Treadway, et al., 2005) have suggested that the same basic principle applies to organizational politics.

Specifically, individuals differ greatly in terms of their political skill, which involves the ability to accurately understand social contexts and then to adapt their behavior to employ the tactics most likely to be effective in exerting influence in those contexts (Ferris, Treadway, Perrewé, Brouer, Douglas, & Lux, 2007). This general principle suggests that political skill, which can be measured effectively by means of a well-validated measure (Ferris, Treadway, et al., 2005), may play an important role in entrepreneurship. Specifically, entrepreneurs high in political skill may be more effective in influencing others in a wide range of contexts. In turn, this may contribute to their effectiveness in carrying out tasks that play an important role in new venture success.

For example, consider the necessity of acquiring needed resources (e.g., financial, human, informational). Exerting influence on others is important for this task because acquiring essential resources often involves interacting directly with others in a face-to-face context (e.g., personal conversations) or making effective presentations to them (e.g., to venture capitalists). Persons high in political skill would be more effective in these respects than those less politically skilled.

Similarly, consider the task of negotiation, which is an activity that entrepreneurs must perform frequently and with a wide range of other persons (e.g., venture capitalists, prospective suppliers and customers). In such contexts, political skill can translate into greater success in influencing others and thus in obtaining the agreements entrepreneurs desire. Finally, entrepreneurs often must communicate with persons from different backgrounds than themselves and generate enthusiasm in such persons for their new products or services. Once again, a high level of political skill might prove valuable in performing these tasks.

In sum, there are strong grounds for suggesting that entrepreneurs high in political skill, which encompass accurate perceptions of others coupled with the capacity to adjust one's actions and tactics to match the requirements of specific, current situations, will prove valuable to entrepreneurs and their new ventures. Evidence that this is indeed the case has been reported in several recent studies. In the first of these investigations (Baron & Markman, 2003), entrepreneurs working in two different industries (i.e., cosmetics, high-tech) completed a widely used and well-validated measure of social skills (i.e., skills closely related to several aspects of political skill; see, e.g., Riggio, 1986). Entrepreneurs' scores on this measure were then related to one indicator of their financial success (i.e., the income these entrepreneurs earned from their new ventures over each of several years). Results indicated that several social skills (i.e., social perception, social adaptability, expressiveness) were significantly related to this measure of financial success.

A more recent investigation (Baron & Tang, 2009) extended these findings by investigating the relationship of entrepreneurs' political skill not to their personal income but to the financial success of their new ventures and also by investigating underlying (i.e., mediating) mechanisms through which entrepreneurs' social skills might influence indices of new venture performance. Results indicated that two variables (i.e., entrepreneurs' effectiveness in acquiring useful information and their effectiveness in obtaining essential resources) mediated the effects of their social or political skill on widely accepted measures of new venture performance, such as growth in sales, growth in profits, and growth in number of employees (see Zahra, Neubaum, & El-Hagrassey, 2002). Both mediating variables were predicted by the theoretical conceptualization previously noted, which is a framework suggesting that entrepreneurs' political skill plays a role (e.g., acquiring necessary resources) in their performance of important tasks and that these tasks in turn strongly influence new venture performance.

This study was conducted with Chinese entrepreneurs working in many different businesses. Thus, this research extended earlier results to a very different cultural context and to many additional industries. However, as in the earlier research by Baron and Markman (2003), the findings indicated that specific social or political skill (e.g., social perception, social adaptability, expressiveness) were indeed significantly related to measures of new venture success, with r's ranging from .19 to .36.

In sum, existing evidence suggests that in acquiring essential resources for their new companies (e.g., human, financial), entrepreneurs draw heavily on benefits conferred by their individual skills in interacting effectively with others (i.e., their social and political skill). In short, entrepreneurs who possess such skills to a high degree enjoy an important advantage over those who do not, presumably because these skills make them more effective in exerting influence over others. Put in other terms, they are more accomplished and skilled users of various techniques of organizational politics. In the domain of entrepreneurship, they may direct these skills primarily toward influencing persons *outside* their new ventures rather than within them. Despite this fact, however, organizational politics (i.e., broadly conceived as resting primarily on influence) does appear to be highly relevant to entrepreneurship. Indeed, effective use of the tactics it encompasses may be an important factor in the complex equation, which involves many different variables, that predicts new venture survival and success.

A Brief Note on Tactics

Techniques for engaging in organizational politics, like techniques for exerting influence, can range from the overt, such as hard-sell attempts at persuasion and various kinds of pressure tactics (see Kipnis et al., 1980) through much more subtle and indirect procedures like ingratiation, the foot-in-the-door tactic, and the that's-not-all tactic (see Table 13.1). Clearly, entrepreneurs generally lack the resources to demand compliance from others, especially persons outside their new ventures. Thus, they are more likely to use and to obtain success with subtler strategies. For this reason, it is predicted that although political skill can be reflected in many different tactics its most effective application will be found in relatively subtle, low-pressure approaches. This possibility, and many others suggested by the current framework, can readily be investigated in future research. Some especially promising directions for such work are described in the later section Corporate Political Activities. Attention is now focused on the more general phenomenon of organizational politics in strategic management.

POWER AND POLITICS IN STRATEGIC MANAGEMENT

The study of politics in strategic management scholarship has taken on two basic forms over the past 30 years. First, organizational theory scholars often have focused on organizational politics, power, and influence as key components to understanding how firms operate, function, perform, and potentially fail. Second, strategy scholars recently have begun to take an interest in how firms themselves engage in political activities. Corporate political activities (CPAs) are efforts to manage or influence politicians, policy makers, and regulators and include campaign contributions, lobbying, and executive testimony among other politically related activities.

As strategic management emerged from organizational theory into a distinct discipline, strategy scholars possessed divergent levels of interest in these two areas of inquiry. The role of politics in affecting and shaping strategic decisions was once an important area of early strategy inquiry (e.g., Allison, 1971; MacMillan & Jones, 1978; Porter, 1980; Pfeffer, 1981), however, interest in power and politics among strategic management scholars began to decline as the management discipline evolved into organizational behavior and human resources and strategic management fields. Strategy scholars focused largely on explaining differences across firms and largely ceded study of behavior within firms to organizational behavior scholars.

As strategy scholars increasingly focused on why some firms and not others obtain sustainable competitive advantage (Barney & Arikan, 2001), power and politics were applied less as a foundational strategy theory. Psychology- and sociology-based theories explaining phenomena within the firm obtained somewhat limited use in explaining economic competition among firms (Lux, Ferris, Brouer, Laird, & Summers, 2008). On the other hand, CPA scholarship has gone from a niche area of inquiry to gaining broader appeal and interest as strategy scholars seek to explain how firms affect society (Greenwood, Suddaby, & Hinings, 2002).

The state of these two areas of inquiry is highly differentiated. Power and politics scholarship examined a multitude of complex political interactions across a range of internal and external actors. Multiple theoretical perspectives were developed and applied, and rich qualitative and quantitative field studies typified research. This diverse scholarship is to some extent a victim of its own success. The complexity of this scholarship acts as barrier to entry to strategy scholars seeking to use past findings and to further develop this area of inquiry.

This issue has been further exacerbated as strategy scholars have shifted to other areas of inquiry, resulting in relatively few active strategy scholars today engaging in organizational politics scholarship. However, politics scholarship would benefit greatly from review and synthesis. By contrast, CPA scholarship has been narrower in scope, based on a few theoretical approaches, and largely reliant on secondary, archival data. CPA scholarship also has benefited from recent reviews and meta-analysis (Hillman, Keim, & Schuler, 2004; Lux et al., 2011; Oliver & Holzinger, 2008), thus lowering barriers to entry for scholars interested in studying CPA.

Although CPA scholarship is perhaps more developed than power and politics scholarship, at least in the domain of strategic management, CPA scholarship has provided surprisingly limited insight into two core CPA research questions. First, Lux et al.'s (2011) meta-analysis of CPA found that existing research has provided limited insight into *why* firms engaged in CPA. Second, although multiple studies have found empirical support for a positive relationship between CPA and performance, CPA scholars have yet to adequately explain *how* CPA affects performance. Lux et al. believed one of the reasons scholars have provided limited insight into these two core questions was the reliance on economic- and political science-based theories. Applying organizational politics theory developed at the microlevel may provide insightful explanations to both basic research questions at the macrolevel (Staw, 1991).

Building on the review of politics in new ventures, the intention here is to first provide a review and synthesis of organizational politics scholarship in strategic management and then to use insights from that review to specify new research directions in the area of CPA. Specifically, strategic management and organizational politics perspectives are used to provide insight into why firms engage in CPA and how CPA affects performance.

The Pervasive but Peripheral Role of Power and Politics in Strategic Management

Corporate Governance

The corporate governance area serves as one of the few areas where theories of power and politics can be seen most vividly in strategic management research. But even here, power and politics are more assumed than made explicit in most cases. The central issue is about who is in control of firms and what that means for stockholders. Those in control (e.g., managers with power) get to choose directions for their companies and, by extension, their outcomes. Several explanations have been offered for control (or power) dynamics in corporate governance research. Agency theory examines the relational nature of interactions among three organizational entities: (1) stockholders as the legitimate owners of the firm; (2) the board of directors (BOD) as the legally elected representatives of stockholders; and (3) the chief executive officer (CEO) and top-management team (TMT) as the formulators and implementers of firm strategy and direction.

Traditional agency theory assumes that firms exist to maximize returns to stockholders as the legitimate owners of the firm. Furthermore, the BOD is empowered to monitor and control CEO and TMT activities and to align the interests of both entities. Also, the CEO and TMT are employed as agents by the stockholders as they possess specialized, relevant management skills lacked by the owners. In this traditional governance hierarchy, power is assumed to be possessed by stockholders as the legitimate owners of the firm, with the BOD directly exercising this ownership power on behalf of the stockholders. Positive empirical support for the agency theory approach to power relationships in corporate governance has been found in studies such as Mizruchi (1983), Zahra and Pearce (1989), and Haleblian and Finkelstein (1993).

However, other governance theories came into prominence by offering alternative assumptions and explanations of power relationships in governance. Proponents of managerial hegemony theory (Kosnik, 1987; Mace, 1971) argued that the CEO and TMT represent the dominant entity of control in governance relationships, primarily because most BOD lack the knowledge to protect against and control any potential managerial malfeasance. Examples of managerial hegemony-based forces that serve to limit BOD effectiveness in its control function include ongoing trends, such as the dilution of corporate ownership into smaller stockholder blocks, increased CEO duality (i.e., a situation where the firm CEO also serves as the chair of the BOD) in firms, increased CEO participation in BOD member selection, compensation determination and dismissal, BOD dependence on the CEO and TMT members for accurate and timely information regarding the firm operations and internal decision-making processes, and increases in multiple BOD member–CEO interlocks (Herman, 1981; Kosnik, 1987; Vance, 1983; Williamson, 1964).

As a result, managerial hegemony advocates view the CEO and TMT as the dominant power entities in organizations. Empirical validation for the managerial hegemony view of governance can be found in studies such as Kosnik (1987), Daily and Johnson (1997), and Allgood and Ferrell (2000). So, how can these conflicting empirical results be explained regarding the application of power in firm governance relationships? A primary explanation is that environment and context have dramatic impacts on governance interactions. Factors such as past performance, industry, and economic conditions influence stockholder expectations and power allocation in firms. Regardless, the research on corporate governance clearly highlights the importance of TMTs as determinants of organizational outcomes.

Organizational Networks

Another strategic management area where theories of power and politics have been used to explain behaviors and outcomes at the TMT, intra-organizational, and interorganizational levels is that of network dynamics. This section focuses on network dynamics at the TMT and intraorganizational levels, since the competitive dynamics and supply chain sections detail elements of firm and industry network interactions at the interorganizational level. Social network theory proposes that individuals build power through interpersonal and political connections created in organizational interactions. Descriptors such as centrality, strong versus weak ties, structural cohesion, and structural holes have been applied to depict the quality and status of one's position within a social network.

The primary assumption of network theory is that the higher quality of a position one develops within a social network, the greater the accrual of social capital, where social capital is defined as "the sum of the actual or potential resources embedded within, available through, and derived from the network of relationships possessed by an individual or social unit" (Nahapiet & Ghoshal, 1998, p. 243). The possession and application of social capital contribute to increased personal efficiency, effectiveness, and positions of power within an organizational hierarchy.

One area where corporate governance and network theory intersect is that of interlocking directorates. Based in social class theory, managerial hegemony advocates propose that many large corporations are governed and guided by a *managerial elite*, a self-perpetuating network of CEO and BOD members connected by generations of social standing, status, wealth, and elite education (Koenig, Gogel, & Sonquist, 1979; Mizruchi, 1996). The primary implication of the managerial elite and interlocking director-ates is that these networks evolve through governance mechanisms, such as CEO duality, where the CEO can directly influence BOD member selec-tion and compensation. Such BOD stacking effectively limits the ability of the BOD to monitor and control CEO and TMT actions. In addition, aspects of the managerial elite contribute to good old boy networks and glass ceiling effects, where racial and gender minorities often lack status connections and social capital required to crack these hierarchical net-works. Clearly, the organizational network research documents that there is power in relationships.

Competitive Dynamics

Over the past 2 decades, the study of competitive dynamics has become an emerging area of examination as researchers have explored the fre-quency, range, scope, and timing of competitive actions and responses, both within and across industry boundaries (Smith, Grimm, & Gannon, 1992). Aspects of power and politics directly impact competitive dynam-ics, as industry players implement strategic plans while assessing the role of power in the nature and likelihood of competitive response. Actor and respondent power positions impact industry dynamics as industry leaders, other industry firms, and smaller niche players attempt to expand competitive positions or maintain current standings. Environmental factors such as industry life cycle, regulatory freedom or constraint, the industry's relative reliance on and rate of technological change, and also the relative aggression of and proactive versus reactive tone in competitive interactions all influence firm competitiveness (Derfus, Maggitti, Grimm, & Smith, 2008; Grimm & Smith, 1997).

Also, there are secondary means by which issues of power and politics impact competitive dynamics, specifically dealing with aspects of latent power. The issue addressed via latent power explores the extent to which firms refrain from engaging in competitive actions or responses due to concerns of competitive retaliation. Such a balance of power in competitive dynamics is similar to the cold war relationship between the United States and Russia, where each possessed the ability to take strong, competitive actions but each refrained due to concerns regarding surviving retaliatory responses. In such cases, power does not have to be explicitly exercised to serve as a deterrent to competitive action and reaction. Therefore, the competitive dynamics literature documents that the exercise of power and political maneuvering play out in a competitive context where economic and political strategies are intertwined.

Supply Chain Dynamics

Traditional strategic management theorists advocated a power-based approach regarding interactions between focal firms and their buyer and supplier vendors (Porter, 1980). This power-based approach assumed short-term relationships between firms and vendors and proposed that the firm in the favorable power position in the firm–vendor dyadic relationship used its power and leverage to negotiate favorable terms and conditions relative to the weaker dyadic member. However, strong global competitive forces have forced firms to move from this power-based model to more of a strategic sourcing model in which firms may outsource both primary, value-creating activities and support activities in efforts to create best-in-class partnership linkages across supply chain groupings (Cox, 1999; Welch & Nayak, 1992).

Global competitive forces also have driven firms to shift from power-based vendor interactions to collaboration-based vendor partnerships. The collaboration-based, win–win approach typically calls for the establishment of long-term partnerships across supply chain groupings, where partners share knowledge and resources in attempts to lower costs while increasing linkage effectiveness and efficiency between supply chain partners (Cox, 1999). The supply chain area of strategy research, therefore, highlights the evolutionary nature of relationship advantages.

Resource-Based View and Knowledge-Based View

As noted earlier, a primary trait of the evolution of the strategic management discipline is that economics-based theories have supplanted sociology-based theories in offering explanations as to why some firms outperform others in markets. At the forefront of these theories are the resource-based (RBV) and knowledge-based (KBV) views of the firm, with RBV rooted primarily in economics and KBV merging economics and sociological perspectives. Both RBV and KBV propose that performance differences across firms occur as firms are able to access, develop, and apply unique combinations of resources and capabilities that fit within the firm's strategic focus and environmental context (Barney, 1991).

Although power and politics are not emphasized within RBV and KBV applications, the theories provide a solid base for when and how firms develop different levels of skill and knowledge important to competitive advantage. Also, although power is not a necessary explanation in either theory, it is consistent with both to view power as being reflected in resources, know-how, and ultimately competitive advantage. RBV emphasizes the evolutionary nature of resource investments. Capabilities are built over time as firms develop unique bundles of resources that other firms do not have and cannot obtain. Since there are path dependencies in the evolution of resource investments and their underlying value may be causally ambiguous, the advantages are potentially sustainable.

KBV differs from traditional RBV theory in that KBV posits that a firm's ability to build competitive advantage over time rests in intangible resources and know-how. Knowledge and skills are embedded in organizational routines (Nelson & Winter, 1982). Further, firms are viewed as learning from past experience and adapt their routines to reflect this learning. Knowledge investments, like other resource investments, are evolutionary in nature where skills are developed and honed over time (Reus et al., 2009). Therefore, the RBV and KBV literature offers a theoretical base for skill differences across firms and why they affect performance. Although it has not been a topic in strategy research to date, it is reasonable to expect political skills and competencies to vary across organizations and to be embedded in routines developed over time that would enhance firm performance.

In sum, the strategic management literature highlights a number of factors that are important to power and politics in organizations that may serve as a base to extend the recent work on CPA. TMTs appear important in developing strategy and affecting outcomes. There also appears to be power in relationships that evolve over time. The exercise of power and political maneuvering play out in a competitive landscape. Furthermore political skill and competencies are likely to be embedded in organizational routines, to differ across firms, and to affect performance. These insights are now applied to the emerging CPA literature.

Applying Organizational Politics to Corporate Political Activity

Lux et al. (2011) observed that organizational politics perspectives perhaps provided the greatest potential for explaining why firms engage in CPA and how some firms outperform others in CPA. Interestingly, much of the early CPA scholarship would be readily recognized by strategy scholars studying power and politics. Similar to Mintzberg (1983) and Pfeffer (1981), both Epstein (1969) and Miles (1987) engaged in qualitative field studies of firm management and boards to understand why firms engage in CPA. However, subsequent CPA scholarship largely has been based on economic and political science theory evaluated with secondary data using quantitative methods.

In this section, it is suggested that an organizational politics perspective when combined with insights from the broader strategy literature can inform and develop CPA scholarship. This is done by applying organizational politics and strategic management perspectives to two of the core questions in CPA scholarship: Why do firms engage in CPA, and how does CPA affect performance? For the latter question, the focus is on how organization politics explains political competition among firms.

Why Do Firms Engage in CPA?

Traditionally, scholars have conceptualized the decision to engage in CPA as an investment decision (Mitchell, Hansen, & Jepsen, 1997; North, 1990). Firms engage in CPA when the perceived returns of investment in political activities are greater than perceived returns in other activities (e.g., research and development, manufacturing capacity, marketing). In this perspective, firms engage in CPA when influencing government entities is perceived to generate economic returns by encouraging government intervention on the behalf of individual or select groups of firms.

Government intervention is one of three means to sustain economic competitive advantage in neoclassical economic theory (Barney & Ouchi, 1986). However, it long has been suggested that the advantages obtained through political activities come at a social cost (Krueger, 1974; Posner, 1975; Tullock, 1967). The majority of CPA scholarship thus has addressed *why* firms engage in CPA question in hopes of identifying the factors that make CPA attractive for firms to mitigate those factors.

The majority of scholarship developed to explain why firms engage in CPA is based in economic and political science theory. However, Lux et al. (2011) found that this scholarship provided limited insight into why firms engage in CPA. Here, several means by which microlevel perspectives might inform firm decisions to engage in CPA are proposed. It is believed that the most fruitful research application of this perspective is examining how TMT and board composition and characteristics affect the decision to engage in CPA. These new causal antecedents to CPA are introduced beginning with stable individual characteristics, proceeding to acquired or developed attitudes and skills, and ending with how the TMT group politics may affect firms' decisions to engage in CPA.

TMT Characteristics

Organizational scholars long have observed that some individuals are more disposed to engage in politics than others. Ferris et al. (2007) asserted that an individual's propensity to engage (and succeed) in politics is composed of five main attributes: perceptiveness, control, affability, active influence, and developmental exercises. Here, it is described how the extent to which TMT members are predisposed to engage in organizational politics likely provides insight into the extent they will lead their firms to engage in CPA.

One limitation to this approach is assuming that TMT members will have fairly homogenous political attributes. While recognizing that some TMTs will be composed of members with more diverse political attributes, it is asserted that this approach is valid for two primary reasons. First, organizations tend to become more homogenous over time (Schneider, 1987). In organizations with individuals disposed toward engaging in political activity, these individuals are likely to form dominant coalitions that favor politics as a way of business (Lux et al., 2008). Second, in many firms decision making will be more concentrated in one founder or CEO than across several managers. When referring to TMTs in this chapter, it is acknowledged that many teams will be a team of one, particularly in entrepreneurial ventures. Because the interest here is in how individual characteristics affect the decision to engage in CPA, the more centralized the decision making is in a firm the more relevant are the assertions. To extend the applicability of the framework to larger, more established firms, after the political skill of top managers is addressed, however, the possibility of political skill being an organizational-level phenomenon embodied in organizational routines is then considered.

TMT Perceptiveness and CPA

Ferris et al. (2007) described perceptiveness as "the ability of individuals to monitor and regulate their own behavior" (p. 296), and they argued that highly perceptive individuals are likely to be high self-monitors. Self-monitors are highly perceptive of their social surroundings and seek to regulate their behavior to perceived social norms (Snyder, 1974). Highly perceptive individuals also are likely to be high in conscientiousness (Ferris et al.). Conscientious individuals possess a high need for achievement and a strong work ethic (Digman, 1990) and are likely to demonstrate the high attention to detail necessary for accurately perceiving surrounding social complexities (Ferris et al.; Pfeffer, 1992).

Perceptive executives perhaps are more likely than their less perceptive peers to engage their firms in CPA. Most individuals outside of government entities are rationally ignorant of government actions; that is, most of what the government does has little direct impact on them, so not investing effort into monitoring government action is the optimal strategy. Highly perceptive managers are predisposed to monitoring and comprehending social interactions and are thus more likely to follow politics and government activities both in general and as specifically related to their industry. Because highly perceptive TMTs are more likely to monitor and comprehend government and political activities, it is expected that they also will be quicker to accurately identify opportunities for CPA to economically benefit (or threaten) their firms and thus will be more likely to engage in CPA.

TMT Control and CPA

A key component in determining individuals' likelihood in engaging in an activity is their perceived control over the activity (Azjen, 1991). Individuals high in political control are likely to be high in both locus of control (Levenson, 1981) and self-efficacy. TMTs that possess high levels of perceived control are more likely to engage in CPA because they intrinsically believe they can affect outcomes in government and political arenas. TMTs with lower levels of control are less likely to engage in CPA because they are likely to perceive their efforts to influence government and political as ineffectual and thus a poor investment choice.

TMT Affability and CPA

Affability is "an outgoing, likeable, interpersonally pleasant orientation, and is represented by such constructs as extraversion, agreeableness, and positive affectivity" (Ferris et al., 2007, p. 298). Affable individuals are more likely to engage in organizational politics because they are predisposed toward social interaction and able to engage with a wider range of individuals. For these same reasons, it is believed that affable TMT members are more likely to engage in CPA.

Most CPAs are fundamentally social interactions. Of the 13 CPA tactics Hillman and Hitt (1999) identified, 6 are direct social interactions (i.e., lobbying, testifying as expert witness, personal service to politicians, grassroots mobilization of employees, public relations, and press conferences), and 3 tactics (i.e., contributions, honoraria for speaking, and paid travel) create opportunities for TMT members to interact with politicians and officials (i.e., fundraisers, hosting during speaking engagements, and accompanying on travel, respectively). Two other tactics (i.e., advocacy advertising and political education programs) also involve some degree of social interaction. Affable TMT members are more likely to want to engage in these socially based CPAs and also are more likely to be successful in their interactions with politicians, officials, employees, and the public.

Affable TMT members also are more likely to develop stronger social ties with politicians and officials than less affable individuals. Perceived similarity long has been recognized as a driver of relationship formation. Because most politicians are highly affable individuals (Cialdini, 1984), affable TMT members and politicians likely will perceive each other to be similar and thus more likely to develop relationships. Affable TMT members likely will want to engage in CPA more so than their less affable peers and are likely to be more successful in CPA.

TMT Active Influence and CPA

Similar to proactive personality (Bateman & Crant, 1993), active influence is the extent to which individuals are disposed toward taking action

(Ferris et al., 2007). Individuals high in proactive personality are more likely to perceive opportunities and seek to exploit those opportunities until they have accomplished their desired goals (Bateman & Crant, 1993). TMT members high in active influence are more likely to perceive opportunities or needs for CPA and see them through to successful execution of firm CPA. TMT members low in active influence are less likely to perceive CPA opportunities in the political and government arenas. Additionally, they will be less likely to see through any firm attempts at CPA.

TMT Learning Experiences and CPA

Individuals that rise to the highest levels of firm management are likely to have had many experiences and opportunities to develop their political skill. TMT members are thus more likely than the average individual to have developed a more advanced understanding of social interactions and politics. The learning experiences of most TMT members are believed to make them more successful in engaging in CPA because socially experienced TMT members will have a better understanding of what is appropriate and socially acceptable.

CPA is not without its downside for firms. Firm CPA is not always likely to align with the needs, ideology, and social agendas of all firm stakeholders. Misalignment between a firm's CPA and those of key stakeholders can damage firm revenues, relationships, and reputation. Target Corporation's CPA in the 2010 Minnesota Gubernatorial Election is illustrative. A board member made a contribution to a Republican gubernatorial candidate on behalf of Target, based on the candidate's tax policy. However, the candidate also had held negative social positions against gays and lesbians. Therefore, Target's contribution inflamed many gay and lesbian rights organizations and led to those groups to call for boycotts of Target stores. Because TMT members are likely more experienced in social interactions than most, this would be expected to occur infrequently for firms engaged in CPA (*WSJ*, 2010).

TMT Attitudes Toward CPA

Azjen and Fishbein (1977) asserted that an individual's attitude toward a behavior and social norms relating to that behavior were accurate predictors of an individual engaging in the behavior. In the limited field studies of CPA, attitude toward business involvement in politics was one of the largest predictors of CPA (Miles, 1987). The Perceptions of Organizational

Politics Scale (POPS; Ferris & Kacmar, 1992) provides a means for evaluating both attitudes and norms relating to CPA. Organizations with high POPS scores likely contain individuals with propolitical attitudes, and social norms conducive towards political behavior. Future scholarship should examine the extent POPS explains firm CPA.

Why Do Some Firms Outperform Others in CPA?

Firms engage in political competition with a range of social and economic actors. Firms and trade associations often have politically competed with trade unions and environmental groups, whereas the recent *net neutrality* policy battle was fought among firms with Internet companies led by Google on one side and telecommunications firms led by AT&T and Verizon on the other. Because policy outcomes can have serious implications for firm performance and survival, how some firms and not others succeed in political competition is an important research question for any student of economic competition (Lux et al., 2011).

The limited scholarship examining political competition among firms has applied economic and political science perspectives to explain how some and not other firms win policy battles (e.g., Hersch & McDougall, 2000). In resource-based theory (RBT), some firms outperform others by developing and using rare, valuable, inimitable, and nonsubstitutable resources and capabilities (Barney, 1991). Political resources and capabilities may provide some firms competitive advantage in political competition (Aharoni, 1993; Hillman & Keim, 2001).

Previous scholarship evaluated this hypothesis mainly by evaluating whether having a full-time Washington, D.C., office was positively related to engaging in CPA. But political success is due to far more than this. First, how the political skill of TMTs may provide insights into how some firms obtain competitive advantage in political competition is explored. Political skill (Ferris, Davidson, & Perrewé, 2005) is composed of four factors: social astuteness, interpersonal influence, networking ability, and apparent sincerity.

TMT Social Astuteness and CPA Performance

Socially astute individuals have the ability understand the social interactions in which they participate (Ferris, Davidson, & Perrewé, 2005).

Socially astute TMT members are likely to have several advantages in engaging in CPA. First, socially astute TMT members are more likely to perceive which politicians and government officials are likely to be sympathetic to their firm's policy needs. Politicians have a vested interest in appeasing as many constituents as possible and often communicate in a more nuanced manner that leads the audience to believe the politician is supportive of their viewpoint. Unless politicians are forced to vote or take other actions against the constituents' interests, the constituents will never know that the politicians do not support their positions.

More socially astute individuals will be able to accurately interpret more nuanced political communication and comprehend the political positions and resources that may constrain politician from otherwise supporting the constituent's interests. Thus, socially astute TMT members are likely to be more efficient in their CPA (e.g., knowing which politicians to influence and which to not), providing an advantage over less socially astute competitors.

Second, socially astute TMT members will be more likely to choose the best lobbyists to meet the firm's desired political outcomes. A great deal of lobbyists' success in obtaining desired policy comes from previously working for politicians in office. Lobbyists develop relationships with their former employers and with other politicians and key staffers over years of service. Socially astute TMT members likely will be able to better perceive which lobbyists can better serve their firm's interests by perceiving lobbyists' network of alliances and rivals and how these actors relate to the firm's desired policy outcomes. The ability to hire the proper lobbyists can provide a firm competitive advantage in policy competition over less socially astute competitors.

Third, more socially astute TMTs should be more likely to perceive when CPA may potentially offend firm stakeholders. Less socially astute TMTs may not be able to perceive how CPA directed at benefiting may offend customers, shareholders, and other key stakeholders. Social astuteness enables some TMTs to mitigate the downside risk of CPA as well as enhance CPA effectiveness.

TMT Interpersonal Influence and CPA Performance

Interpersonal influence involves is the ability to adopt and enact the proper influence style for each influence target (Ferris, Davidson, & Perrewé, 2005). Policy competition requires influencing a wide range of actors, from politicians and government officials to special interest groups and the general public. TMT members high in interpersonal influence are likely to be able to adopt and execute the right influence techniques for all of these varied parties. TMT members high in interpersonal influence are more likely to be able to convince politicians, officials, and other key stakeholders that their policy positions are more worthy of support than other competing policy outcomes.

TMT Networking Ability and CPA Performance

Individuals high in networking ability are able to develop large and diverse social networks (Ferris, Davidson, & Perrewé, 2005). Public policy rarely is made without broad consensus across many diverse social groups and actors. TMT members high in networking ability are more likely to develop the broad range of contacts necessary for developing consensus, coordinating action, and mitigating rival threats. TMT members with well-developed networks also are more likely to possess information asymmetries over less connected individuals, which can provide TMT members with unique insight into potential policy opportunities and weaknesses in rivals' political activities.

Large and diverse social networks also are more likely to enhance the TMT member's reputation. Individuals' reputations often are influenced by their social contacts; that is, the more important and powerful people in one's network, the more others' perceive the individual to also be powerful and influential. TMT members with important politicians and officials in their networks are likely to receive preferential treatment from their less connected peers.

TMT Apparent Sincerity and CPA Performance

Individuals with high apparent sincerity "appear to others as having high levels if integrity and as being authentic, sincere, and genuine. They are, or appear, to be honest and forthright" (Ferris et al., 2007, p. 292). TMT members with high apparent sincerity are likely to have several advantages in engaging in CPA. First, TMT efforts to promote policy positions beneficial to their firms will appear to be more prosocial than similar attempts by less socially skilled individuals. Firm policy position will appear to be more of a win–win to individuals on the receiving end of firm CPA.

Second, political and social attacks on the firm will not be as effective for firms with high apparent sincerity TMTs. TMTs with high apparent sincerity will be more effective at diffusing such attacks.

From TMT to Organization Political Competencies

Political skill can also be viewed as an organizational level phenomenon. Like other organizational skills, political skill can be viewed as embodied in routines (Nelson & Winter, 1982) and as a product of past knowledge investments and learning (Reus et al., 2009). That is, for example, companies hire staff and develop systems and routines to systematically gather information about and to reshape industry standards and norms to their firms' advantages. They also invest in and manage relationships with other firms, governmental agencies, and industry associations by building effective routines to do so.

Knowledge investments are shaped by the preferences of the TMT but are also evolutionary and shaped by institutional history, organizational culture, and industry context (Reus et al., 2009). Some firms are likely to be more politically skilled than others because of past experiences and learning that have been incorporated into routines to identify and exploit new opportunities. These skills may be akin to astuteness and network ties, and may influence effectiveness at the individual level. Therefore, to more fully understand the effectiveness of CPA, it may be useful to view political skill as a multilevel phenomenon, involving individual traits of leaders, which may be shared in teams and reflected in investments of supporting routines.

CONCLUSION

Our central message is the organizational politics literature offers a common language and perspective that can usefully inform entrepreneurship, strategy, and specifically, CPA research. However, the relationships among the three areas of research are likely to be reciprocal and nested. Organizational politics is all about influence. Entrepreneurship places the influence in a specific context, whereas strategic management emphasizes the top-management team and organizational routines that may play a role in intra- and interorganizational influence attempts. Therefore, advancements in any one of these research domains can potentially inform all three. Perhaps a better understanding of the multilevel nature of organizational influence and its boundaries will be found at the intersections of these typically disparate research domains.

REFERENCES

Aharoni, Y. (1993). From Adam Smith to Schumpeterian global firms. In A. Rugman & A. Verbeke (Eds.), *Research in global strategic management* (Vol. 4, pp. 231–261). Greenwich, CT: JAI Press.

Allgood, S., & Farrell, K. (2000). The effect of CEO tenure on the relationship between firm performance and turnover. *Journal of Financial Research, 23,* 373–390.

Allison, G.T. (1971). *Essence of decision: Explaining the Cuban missile crisis.* Boston: Little, Brown.

Azjen, I. (1991). The theory of planned behavior. *Organizational Behavior and Human Decision Making Processes, 50,* 179–211.

Azjen, I., & Fishbein, M. (1977). Attitude-behavior relations: A theoretical analysis and review of empirical research. *Psychological Bulletin, 84,* 888–918.

Barney, J.B. (1991). Firm resources and sustained competitive advantage. *Journal of Management, 17,* 99–120.

Barney J.B., & Arikan A.M. (2001). The resource-based view: Origins and implications. *Handbook of strategic management* (pp. 124–188). Oxford, UK: Blackwell.

Barney, J.B., & Ouchi, W.G. (1986). *Organizational economics.* San Francisco: Jossey-Bass Publishers.

Baron, R.A. (2007). Behavioral and cognitive factors in entrepreneurship: Entrepreneurs as the active element in new venture creation. *Strategic Entrepreneurship Journal, 1,* 167–182.

Baron, R.A. (2008). The role of affect in the entrepreneurial process. *Academy of Management Review, 33,* 328–340.

Baron, R.A., & Branscombe, N.R. (2011). *Social psychology* (13th ed.) Boston: Allyn & Bacon/Pearson.

Baron, R.A., Tang, J., & Hmieleski, K.D. (2011). The downside of being "up": Entrepreneurs' dispositional positive affect and firm performance. *Strategic Entrepreneurship Journal, 5,* 101–119.

Baron, R.A., & Markman, G.D. (2003). Beyond social capital: The role of entrepreneurs' social competence in their financial success. *Journal of Business Venturing, 18,* 41–60.

Baron, R.A., & Tang, J. (2009). Entrepreneurs' social competence and new venture performance: Evidence on potential mediators and cross-industry generality. *Journal of Management, 34,* 282–306.

Bateman, T.S., & Crant, J.M. (1993). The proactive component of organizational behavior: A measure and correlates. *Journal of Organizational Behavior, 14,* 103–118.

Burger, J.M. (1986). Increasing compliance by improving the deal: The that's not all technique. *Journal of Personality and Social Psychology, 51,* 277–283.

Cardon, M.S., Wincent, J., Sing, J., & Drnvosek, M. (2009). The nature and experience of entrepreneurial passion. *Academy of Management Review, 34,* 511–532.

Chanlat, J. (1997). Conflict and politics. In A. Sorge & M. Warner (Eds.), *Handbook of organizational behavior* (pp. 472–480). London: International Thomson.

Cialdini, R.B. (2008). *Influence: Science and practice* (5th ed.). Boston: Allyn & Bacon.

Cox, A. (1999). Power, value and supply chain management. *Supply Chain Management: An International Journal. 4*(4), 167–175.

Daily, C., & Johnson, J. (1997). Sources of CEO power and firm financial performance: A longitudinal assessment. *Journal of Management, 23,* 97–117.

Derfus, P.J., Maggitti, P.G., Grimm, C.M., & Smith, K.G. (2008). The red queen effect: Competitive action and firm performance. *Academy of Management Journal, 51*(1), 61–80.

Digman, J.M. (1990). Personality structure: Emergence of the five-factor model. *Annual Review of Psychology, 41,* 417–440.

Epstein, E.M. (1969). *The corporation in American politics.* Englewood Cliffs, NJ: Prentice-Hall.

Epstude, K., & Mussweiler, T. (2009). What you feel is how you compare: How comparisons influence the social induction of affect. *Emotion, 9,* 1–14.

Ferris, G.R., Davidson, S.L., & Perrewé, P.L. (2005). *Political skill at work: Impact on work effectiveness.* Mountain View, CA: Davies-Black Publishing.

Ferris, G.R., & Hochwarter, W.A. (2011). Organizational politics. In S. Zedeck (Ed.), *APA handbook of industrial and organizational psychology* (Vol. 3, pp. 435–459). Washington, DC: American Psychological Association.

Ferris, G.R., & Kacmar, M.K. (1992). Perceptions of organizational politics. *Journal of Management, 18,* 83–116.

Ferris, G.R., Russ, G.S., & Fandt, P.M. (1989). Politics in organizations. In R.A. Giacalone & P. Rosenfeld (Eds.), *Impression management in the organization* (pp. 143–170). Hillsdale, NJ: Lawrence Erlbaum.

Ferris, G.R., Treadway, D.C., Kolodinsky, R.W., Hochwarter, W.A., Kacmar, C.J., Douglas, C., et al. (2005). Development and validation of the political skill inventory. *Journal of Management, 31,* 126–152.

Ferris, G.R., Treadway, D.C., Perrewé, P.L., Brouer, R.L., Douglas, C., & Lux, S. (2007). Political skill in organizations. *Journal of Management, 33,* 290–320.

Gioia, D., & Longenecker, C. (1994). Delving into the dark side: The politics of executive appraisal. *Organizational Dynamics, 22,* 47–58.

Greenwood, R., Suddaby, R., & Hinings, C.R. (2002). Theorizing change: The role of professional associations in the transformation of institutional fields. *Academy of Management Journal, 45*(1), 58–80.

Grimm, C.M., & Smith, K.G. (1997). *Strategy as action: Industry rivalry and coordination.* Cincinnati: South-Western.

Guéguen, N. (2003). Fund-raising on the web: The effect of an electronic door-in-the-face technique in compliance to a request. *Cyberpsychology & Behavior, 2,* 189–193.

Haleblian, J., & Finkelstein, S. (1993). Top management team size, CEO dominance, and firm performance. *Academy of Management Journal, 36,* 844–859.

Herman, E.S. (1981). *Corporate control, corporate power.* Cambridge, UK: Cambridge University Press.

Hersch, P., & McDougall, G. (2000). Determinants of contributions to House incumbents: Own versus rival effects. *Public Choice, 104,* 329–343.

Hillman, A.J., & Hitt, M.A. (1999). Corporate political strategy formation: A model of approach, participation, and strategy models. *Academy of Management Review 24*, 825–842.

Hillman, A.J., & Keim, G.D. (2001). Shareholder value, stakeholder management and social issues: What's the bottom line? *Strategic Management Journal, 22*(2), 125–139.

Hillman, A.J., Keim, G.D., & Schuler, D. (2004). Corporate political activity: A review and research agenda. *Journal of Management, 30*, 837–858.

Hoffer, E. (1976). *The ordeal of change.* New York: Buccaneer Books.

Hofer, C.W., & Schendel, D. (1978). *Strategy formulation: Analytical concepts.* St. Paul, MN: West.

Kacmar, K.M., & Baron, R.A. (1999). Organizational politics: The state of the field, links to related processes, and an agenda for future research. In G.R. Ferris (Ed.), *Research in personnel and human resources management* (Vol. 17, pp. 1–39). Stamford, CT: JAI Press.

Kipnis, D., Schmidt, S.M., & Wilkinson, I. (1980). Intraorganizational influence tactics: Explorations in getting one's way. *Journal of Applied Psychology, 63*, 440–452.

Koenig, T., Gogel, R., & Sonquist, J. (1979). Models of the significance of interlocking corporate directorates. *American Journal of Economics and Sociology, 38*, 173–186.

Kosnik, R. (1987). Greenmail: A study of board performance in corporate governance. *Administrative Science Quarterly, 32*, 163–185.

Krueger, A.O. (1974). The political economy of the rent seeking society. *American Economic Review, 64*, 291–303.

Levenson, H. (1981). Differentiating among internality, powerful others, and chance. In H. Lefcourt (Ed.), *Research with the locus of control construct* (Vol. 1, pp. 15–63). New York: Academic Press.

Lux, S., Crook, T.R., & Woehr, D.J. (2011). Mixing business with politics: A meta-analysis of the antecedents and outcomes of corporate political activity. *Journal of Management, 37*, 223–247.

Lux, S., Ferris, G.R., Brouer, R.L., Laird, M.D., & Summers, J. (2008). A multi-level conceptualization of organizational politics. In C.L. Cooper & J. Barling (Eds.), *The SAGE handbook of organizational behavior* (pp. 353–371). Thousand Oaks, CA: Sage Publications.

Mace, M.L. (1971). *Directors: Myth and reality.* Boston: Harvard University Press.

MacMillan, I., & Jones, P. (1978). *Strategy formulation: Power and politics.* St. Paul: West.

Mayes, B.T., & Allen, R.W. (1977). Towards a definition of organizational politics. *Academy of Management Review, 2*, 672–678.

Miles, R.H. (1987). *Managing the corporate social environment.* Englewood Cliffs, NJ: Prentice-Hall.

Mintzberg, H. (1983). *Power in and around organizations.* Englewood Cliffs, NJ: Prentice-Hall.

Mintzberg, H. (1985). The organization as political arena. *Journal of Management Studies, 22*(2), 133–154.

Mitchell, N.J., Hansen, W.L., & Jepsen, E.M. (1997). The determinants of domestic and foreign corporate political activity. *Journal of Politics, 59*, 1096–1113.

Mizruchi, M. (1983). Who controls whom? An examination of the relation between management and boards of directors in large American corporations. *Academy of Management Review, 8*, 426–435.

Mizruchi, M. (1996). What do interlocks do? An analysis, critique, and assessment of research on interlocking directorates. *Annual Review of Sociology, 22*, 271–298.

Nahapiet, J., & Ghoshal, S. (1998). Social capital, intellectual capital, and the organizational advantage. *Academy of Management Review, 23*(2), 242–266.

Nelson, R., & Winter, S. (1982). *An evolutionary theory of economic change.* Cambridge, MA: Harvard University Press.

North, D. (1990). *Institutions, institutional change, and economic performance.* Oxford, UK: Cambridge University Press.

Nutt, P. (1986). Tactics of implementation. *Academy of Management Journal, 29,* 230–262.

Oliver, C., & Holzinger, I. (2008). The effectiveness of strategic political management: A dynamic capabilities framework. *Academy of Management Review, 33,* 496–520.

Pfeffer, J. (1981). *Power in organizations.* Boston: Pitman.

Pfeffer, J. (1992). Understanding power in organizations. *California Management Review, 34*(2), 29–50.

Porter (1980). *Competitive strategy: Techniques for analyzing industry and competitiors.* New York: Free Press.

Posner, R.A. (1975). The social cost of monopoly and regulation. *Journal of Political Economy, 83,* 807–827.

Pronin, E., Berger, J., & Molouki, S. (2007). Alone in a crowd of sheep: Asymmetric perceptions of conformity and their roots in an introspection illusion. *Journal of Personality and Social Psychology, 92,* 585–595.

Reus, T., Ranft, A., Lamont, B., & Adams, G. (2009). An interpretive systems view of knowledge investments. *Academy of Management Review, 34,* 382–400.

Riggio, R.E. (1986). Assessment of basic social skills. *Journal of Personality and Social Psychology, 51,* 649–660.

Rindova, V.P., Williamson, I.D., Petkova, A.P., & Sever, J.M. (2005). Being good or being known: An empirical examination of the dimensions, antecedents, and consequences of organizational reputation. *Academy of Management Journal, 48,* 1033–1048.

Schneider, B. (1987). The people make the place. *Personnel Psychology, 40,* 437–453.

Schreisheim, C.A., & Neider, L.L. (Eds.) (2006). *Power and influence in organizations: New empirical and theoretical perspectives.* Charlotte, NC: Information Age Publishing.

Shane, S., & Venkataraman, S. (2000). The promise of entrepreneurship as a field of research. *Academy of Management Review, 25,* 217–226.

Silvester, J. (2008). The good, the bad, and the ugly: Politics and politicians at work. In G. P. Hodgkinson & J. K. Ford (Eds.), *International review of industrial and organizational psychology* (Vol. 23, pp. 107–148). Chichester, UK: John Wiley & Sons.

Smith, K.G., Grimm, C.M., & Gannon, M.J. (1992). *Dynamics of competitive strategy.* Knobbier Park, CA: Sage Publications.

Snyder, M. (1974). Self-monitoring of expressive behavior. *Journal of Personality and Social Psychology, 30,* 526–537.

Staw, B.M. (1991). Dressing up like an organization: When psychological theories can explain organizational action. *Journal of Management, 17*(4): 805–819.

Tullock, G. (1967). The welfare cost of tarriffs, monopoly and theft. *Economic Inquiry, 5,* 224–232.

Vance, S.C. (1983). *Corporate leadership: Boards, directors, and strategy.* New York: McGraw-Hill.

Welch, J.A., & Nayak, P.R. (1992). Strategic sourcing: A progressive approach to the make-or-buy decision. *Academy of Management Executive, 6*(1), 23–31.

Williamson, O.E. (1964). *The economics of discretionary behavior: Managerial objectives in the theory of the firm.* Englewood Cliffs, NJ: Prentice-Hall.

Zahra, S.A., Neubaum, D.O., & El-Hagrassey, G.M. (2002). Competitive analysis and new venture performance: Understanding the impact of strategic uncertainty and venture origin. *Entrepreneurship Theory and Practice, 27,* 1–28.

Zahra, S.A., & Pearce, J.A. (1989). Boards of directors and corporate financial performance: A review and integrative model. *Journal of Management,* 15, 291–334.

14

The Cultural Psychology of Social Influence: Implications for Organizational Politics

Lisa M. Leslie
University of Minnesota

Michele J. Gelfand
University of Maryland

Organizational politics, defined as "social influence attempts directed at those who can provide rewards that will help promote or protect the self-interests of the actor" (Kacmar & Carlson, 1997, p. 657) is a reality of organizational life. Not surprisingly, a large research industry has developed on the existence, antecedents, and consequences of organizational politics (see Ferris, Adams, Kolodinsky, Hochwarter, & Ammeter, 2002; Ferris, Hochwarter, Douglas, Blass, Kolodinsky, & Treadway, 2002 for reviews). Like most organizational phenomena, organizational politics is context dependent. Specifically, the organizational context is a determinant of the degree of politics within organizations as well as a boundary condition for outcomes of organizational politics (e.g., Ferris, Adams, et al., 2002; Andrews, Kacmar, & Harris, 2009). As such, accounting for contextual contingencies is critical for fully understanding the nature and consequences of organizational politics.

In addition to organizational contexts, organizational politics likely are shaped by the broader national culture. It has been long argued that organizations are open systems and therefore are influenced by the societies in which they are embedded (Katz & Kahn, 1978). Moreover, societal culture has a powerful impact on a wide range of behaviors within organizations (see Gelfand, Erez, & Aycan, 2007 for a review), and organizational politics is likely to be of no exception. As such, a given political act, such as the use of gifts to persuade others, may be seen as normative and legitimate in one culture but unethical and problematic in another (cf. Steidlmeier, 1999).

Theory suggests that cultural differences are relevant for understanding organizational politics, yet organizational politics research largely has relied on Western samples and has yet to fully integrate culture into its theories and findings. Although cross-cultural research exists on certain aspects of organizational politics (i.e., influence tactics), others have been investigated with little attention to the cultural context (i.e., perceptions of politics and political behavior), and no comprehensive review of culture and organizational politics exists.

The goal of this chapter is to better integrate research streams on organizational politics and culture. To this end, an integrative model of how culture affects the construct space of organizational politics is presented. Then, research relevant to the model's propositions is reviewed, and key knowledge gaps and avenues for future research are highlighted. In reviewing and synthesizing the literature, the intended contributions are theoretical and practical in nature.

First, an effort is made to advance organizational politics theory and research, which has a predominantly Western focus, to be more global in scope, with the hope that further understanding cultural contingencies will help move toward more sophisticated theories of organizational politics and its correlates. Second, differences in the nature of organizational politics across country can cause major hurdles for expatriates navigating different political systems as well as for organizations engaged in multinational mergers. Thus, practical insights also are provided for individuals and organizations working across the intercultural divide.

AN INTEGRATIVE MODEL OF CULTURE AND ORGANIZATIONAL POLITICS

The proposed integrative model of culture and organizational politics is presented in Figure 14.1. Advancing a cross-cultural model of organizational politics first requires defining the model's two core constructs, specifically culture and organizational politics. The definition of culture has been debated among anthropologists and psychologists, and many definitions

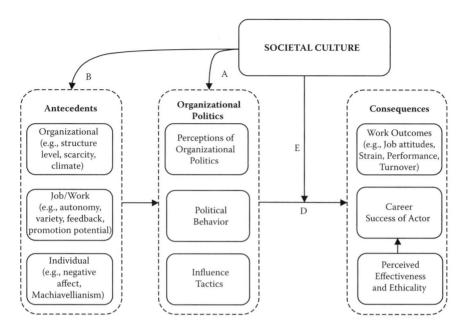

FIGURE 14.1

An integrative model of societal culture and organizational politics.

of culture exist. Geertz (1973), an anthropologist, and Kluckhohn (1954), a psychologist, both defined culture as a pattern of meaning that is transmitted through symbols. Skinner (1981), a behaviorist, argued that culture is a set of reinforcements. Hofstede (1980) asserted that culture consists of mental programs that guide individuals' responses, and Triandis (1972) distinguished between objective (e.g., housing, roads, tools) and subjective (e.g., attitudes, norms, values) culture.

These definitions share several important elements of culture—namely, that it is a pattern of values, norms, and assumptions that are shared by members of a given society. In this chapter, culture is conceptualized as a societal-level construct, yet it also is acknowledged that culture may exist at other levels. In describing culture in this chapter, Hofstede's (1980) cultural value dimensions (e.g., individualism-collectivism, power distance) have been the subject of much organizational research (see Taras, Piers, & Kirkman, 2010). Additional culture values (e.g., fatalism) that are relevant to organizational politics are discussed as well.

The proposed model encompasses three key organizational politics constructs, including political behavior, perceptions of organizational politics, and influence tactics. Political behavior is any act intended to influence others and advance one's self-interests, whereas perceptions of organizational politics reflect the belief that political behavior is prevalent in a given organization (cf. Ferris, Adams, et al., 2002). Alternatively, influence tactics are the specific behaviors individuals use to influence others, such as rational arguments or ingratiating oneself to others. Notably, several constructs that similarly focus on social influence have received attention in the organizational literature, including leadership and negotiation (see Gelfand & Brett, 2004; House, Hanges, Javidan, Dorfman, & Gupta, 2004 for reviews). However, these topics fall outside the scope of the present chapter and are therefore omitted from this review.

The proposed model of culture and organizational politics is based on two core assumptions. First, organizational politics is purported to be a pan-cultural phenomenon that is part and parcel of everyday organizational life around the globe. By definition, organizations create interdependencies among their members. In any interdependent social environment, there is a fundamental need for coordinated social action and mechanisms through which individuals can pursue the interests of the self and valued social groups, regardless of the cultural context (cf. Katz & Kahn, 1978). It follows that existence of organizational politics is likely universal.

In spite of the existence of organizational politics around the globe, the nature, prevalence, and consequences of organizational politics are likely to vary across cultures. Thus, the second core assumption is that cultural influences on organizational politics are multifinal, in that culture affects organizational politics through multiple pathways. The ways culture shapes organizational politics are represented by linkages A through E in Figure 14.1.

Linkage A suggests a direct effect of culture on the existence, nature, and prevalence of organizational politics, including political behavior, perceptions of organizational politics, and influence tactics. Linkage B suggests that culture has a direct effect on a number of organizational, job, and individual factors, and linkage C indicates that these organizational, job, and individual factors in turn predict the three organizational politics constructs of interest. Thus, taken together, linkages B and C suggest an indirect effect of culture on the nature and level of organizational politics. Linkage D represents the consequences of organizational politics, including work outcomes (e.g., job attitudes), career success, and success in influencing others. Finally, linkage E suggests that culture is a boundary condition for these outcomes, such that the magnitude of the relationship between organizational politics and their consequences varies with the cultural context.

In what follows, cultural influences on political behavior and perceptions of politics are discussed, followed by a discussion on influence tactics. Each section begins by reviewing support for the first assumption—that is, that organization politics is a pan-cultural phenomenon. Theory and research are then reviewed on the nature, prevalence, and consequences of organizational politics across cultures, and key knowledge gaps and avenues for future research are highlighted. Both etic studies, which assess if what is known about organizational politics in one culture generalizes to other cultures, as well as emic studies, which seek to understand the unique features of organizational politics in a particular cultural setting (Berry, 1969), are included in the review. The chapter concludes by discussing the importance of better understanding organizational politics in multicultural work settings and the practical implications of the proposed model.

POLITICAL BEHAVIOR AND PERCEPTIONS OF POLITICS

Political behavior is defined as acts aimed at influencing others and advancing self-interests, whereas perceptions of organizational politics are defined as the belief that political behavior is present in an organization. Political behavior and perceptions of organizational politics are distinct constructs that are reciprocally related. Specifically, high levels of perceptions of organizational politics increase the tendency to engage in political behavior, which in turn reinforces perceptions of organizational politics (cf. Ferris, Adams, et al., 2002; Ferris, Harrell-Cook, & Dulebohn, 2000). The interrelationship between political behavior and perceptions of organizational politics suggests that they have similar nomological networks. Therefore, the existence, nature, prevalence, and consequences of political behavior and perceptions of organizational politics across cultures are discussed in the same section. For the sake of parsimony, the term *political activity* is used to refer to political behavior and perceptions of organizational politics simultaneously.

Linkage A: Existence and Nature Across Cultures

Consistent with the notion that organizational politics is a pan-cultural phenomenon, evidence suggests that political behavior and perceptions of organizational politics are meaningful constructs across cultures. Treadway, Hochwarter, Kacmar, and Ferris (2005) developed a measure of political behavior in the United States (e.g., "I use my interpersonal skills to influence people at work"). At least one other study administered the measure in China and similarly found that political behavior is a reliable construct (Liu, Liu, & Wu, 2010).

Most research on perceptions of organizational politics has used the Perception of Organizational Politics Scale (POPS), which was developed and validated in the United States (e.g., "Favoritism, rather than merit, determines who gets good raises and promotions around here"; Kacmar & Carlson, 1997; Kacmar & Ferris, 1991). Scholars have administered the POPS in many cultures and found that perceptions of organizational politics emerges as a reliable construct in Britain, China, Finland, India, Israel, Kuwait, Malaysia, Nigeria, and Taiwan (see Table 14.1). Reliable and valid measures of perceptions of organizational politics also have been developed in other cultures, including Canada (Darr & Johns, 2004), Finland (Salimäki & Jämsén, 2010), France (Tziner, Latham, Price, & Haccoun, 1996), and Israel (Drory, 1993).

Political behavior and perceptions of organizational politics appear to be meaningful constructs across cultures, yet these constructs may not have the same meaning in different cultural contexts. Culture affects cognition, such that the same behavior is often interpreted differently (e.g., Markus & Kitayama, 1991), and the definition of political behavior may therefore vary across cultures. For example, research on the definition of political behavior across cultures suggests that informal influence attempts are viewed as more political than formal influence attempts in both Canada and Israel (Drory & Romm, 1988; Romm & Drory, 1988). At the same time, the same behaviors are viewed as less political in Israel than in Canada, perhaps because political acts are a normative part of life in Israel (Romm & Drory). These findings suggest that political behavior exists across cultures but that there are differences the in the tendency to perceive behavior as political.

Political activity also may differ in its goals across cultures. American definitions of political behavior and perceptions of organizational politics focus on efforts to advance self-interests (e.g., Kacmar & Carlson, 1997),

TABLE 14.1

Studies of Perceptions of Politics Conducted Outside the United States

Article	Country	Scale	M	SD	N	α
Vigoda (2001)	Britain	POPS	3.03/5	1.12	149	.94
Darr and Johns (2004)	Canada	Original scale	2.30/5	.78	626	.92
Liu et al. (2010)	China	POPS	3.46/5	1.00	283	.89
Salimäki and Jämsén (2010)	Finland	Original scale	3.51/5	.89	367	.79
Tziner et al. (1996, Sample 1)	France	Original scale	2.63/6	.88	51	.97
Tziner et al. (1996, Sample 2)	France	Original scale	2.35/6	.88	157	.98
Aryee et al. (2004, Study 2)	India	POPS	2.70/5	.58	211	.75
Aryee et al. (2004, Study 3)	India	POPS	2.75/5	.62	176	.80
Drory (1993)	Israel	Original scale	—	—	200	.78
Vigoda and Cohen (2002)	Israel	POPS	3.06/5	.60	303	.77
Vigoda (2000b)	Israel	POPS	3.06/5	.60	303	.77
Vigoda (2001)	Israel	POPS	2.94/5	.77	303	.79
Vigoda (2002, Study 1)	Israel	POPS	2.69/5	.78	155	.77
Vigoda (2002, Study 2)	Israel	POPS	2.90/5	.65	185	.78
Vigoda (2002, Study 3)	Israel	POPS	3.29/5	.64	201	.68
Vigoda-Gadot et al. (2003, Study 1)	Israel	POPS	3.25/5	.71	169	.78
Vigoda-Gadot et al. (2003, Study 2)	Israel	POPS	2.76/5	.58	224	.65
Vigoda-Gadot (2007)	Israel	POPS	2.56/5	.67	201	.83
Vigoda (2000a)	Israel	POPS	3.06/5	.60	303	.77
Muhammed (2007)	Kuwait	POPS	2.86/5	.83	206	.88
Poon (2003)	Malaysia	POPS	5.04/10	1.76	208	.90
Poon (2004)	Malaysia	POPS	2.74/5	.47	103	.74
Poon (2006)	Malaysia	POPS	2.73/5	.48	106	.74
Ladebo (2006)	Nigeria	POPS	2.64/5	.87	229	.79
Chen and Fang (2008)	Taiwan	POPS	—	—	290	.94
Huang et al. (2003)	Taiwan	POPS	3.05/5	.61	612	.87

which is consistent with the focus on individualism and the self in the United States (Markus & Kitayama, 1991). In collectivistic cultures, group memberships are highly salient, and work tends to be organized around groups (cf. Kashima & Callan, 1994; Markus & Kitayama, 1991). Thus, political activity may be defined as efforts to advance group interests in these settings, although this hypothesis has not been tested. In all, measures of political activity seem to tap relevant construct space across cultures but also may be *deficient* (i.e., exclude some political behaviors) or *contaminated* (i.e., include behaviors that are not relevant in some cultures).

Linkage A: Prevalence Across Cultures (Direct Effects)

In addition to variation in the nature of political activity across cultures, linkage A suggests that the degree of political activity varies across cultures. Cultural psychology theory and research suggest that cultural values influence the types of behaviors that are normative and accepted and that organizational behaviors and practices are more common when they are consistent with cultural norms (Erez & Earley, 1993). For example, evidence supports that organizational newcomers are more likely to seek feedback in highly assertive cultures than in less assertive cultures (Morrison, Chen, & Salgado, 2004) and that leaders are more likely to use participative leadership styles in low power distance cultures, where employee proactivity is valued, compared with high power distance cultures (House et al., 2004).

Several cultural dimensions are likely to lead to high base rates of political activity. In *fatalistic* cultures, individuals lack the ability to control their outcomes through formal mechanisms, which breeds ambiguity and uncertainty (e.g., Acevedo, 2005; Moaddel & Karabenick, 2008). Political activity is common in ambiguous contexts (Ferris & Judge, 1991; Ferris, Russ, & Fandt, 1989; Ferris et al., 2000), which suggests that fatalistic cultures will be characterized by high levels of political behavior and perceptions of organizational politics. Political activity also is likely to be prevalent in high *power distance* cultures, at least among those who lack power. In high power distance cultures, social hierarchies are fixed, and there are few formal mechanisms for advancement (cf. Hofstede, 1980). At the same time, power is greatly valued, and individuals with low power are likely to work outside the system to gain power.

In contrast, political activity is likely to be infrequent in *uncertainty avoidant* cultures, where individuals are risk averse (cf. Hofstede, 1980). Efforts to influence others by working outside the formal system are likely to be viewed as threatening, with the result that political behavior and perceptions of organizational politics will be low in high uncertainty avoidant cultures. Political activity also is likely to vary with *individualism-collectivism* and *universalism-particularism*. In individualistic cultures, equity and merit are valued, and there is a general expectation that hard work leads to advancement (cf. Hofstede, 1980). Therefore, attempts to advance by working around the system should be less frequent in individualistic than collectivistic cultures. Similarly, everyone is expected to follow the same rules in universalistic cultures, whereas rules vary with ascribed status and relationships in particularistic cultures (Smith, Dugan, & Trompenaars, 1996). Political activity should therefore be less prevalent in universalistic than particularistic cultures.

A variety of cultural dimensions are likely to affect base rates of political activity, yet surprisingly little research has investigated this possibility. Two studies compared the level of political activity across cultures. Romm and Drory (1988) found that political behavior is more prevalent in Israel than Canada, a difference that may reflect greater informality in Israeli culture. Alternatively, Vigoda (2001) compared perceptions of organizational politics in Israel and Britain but found no significant difference. Researchers also have reported the mean level of perceptions of organizational politics in a number of cultures other than the United States (see Table 14.1). Importantly, these samples vary on a number of contextual factors other than culture (e.g., industry, public versus private sector), and thus it is difficult to use these studies to draw inferences about mean differences in perceptions of organizational politics across cultures.

Linkages B + C: Prevalence Across Cultures (Indirect Effects)

In addition to direct effects, culture may exert indirect effects on the prevalence of political activity across cultures. Specifically, linkages B and C in Figure 14.1 suggest that culture affects organizational, job, and individual characteristics, which in turn impact political activity. This combined pathway implies that the antecedents of political activity are universal but that certain antecedents are more prevalent in some cultures than in others. First, evidence regarding the universality of antecedents of political activity is described, and then the dimensions of culture that may have an indirect effect on political activity base rates are examined.

Antecedents

A number of organizational-level factors predict political activity across cultures. Formal organizational structures create tight control and reduce ambiguity, which is likely to reduce political activity. Research supports that formalization and perceptions of organizational politics are indeed negatively correlated in the United States (Ferris, Adams, et al., 2002), India (Aryee, Chen, & Budhwar, 2004), and Kuwait (Muhammed, 2007). Alternatively, in organizations with centralized structures, power is concentrated at the top, which is likely to increase political activity, particularly at low levels in the organization. The correlation between centralization and perceptions of organizational politics is usually positive in the United States (Ferris, Adams, et al., 2002), and one study found a positive correlation in Kuwait (Muhammed).

Theory also suggests that political activity will be greater at higher organizational levels. Research conducted in the United States has found that hierarchical level is either positively related or unrelated to perceptions of organizational politics (Ferris, Adams, et al., 2002), but one study found that hierarchical level was negatively related to perceptions of organizational politics in Kuwait (Muhammed, 2007). Kuwait is high in power distance, and this finding could be explained by the previous proposition that power distance results in high levels of political activity among those who lack power. Finally, several studies have investigated trust climate (i.e., positive expectations regarding the motives of organizational members) as an antecedent to political activity and found that trust climate is negatively related to perceptions of organizational politics in Kuwait (Muhammed, 2007) and Malaysia (Poon, 2003).

In addition to organizational factors, job characteristics have been investigated as antecedents to political activity. For example, work role ambiguity and work role conflict are likely to create ambiguity and uncertainty and therefore increase political activity. Research indeed supports that these characteristics are positively correlated with perceptions of organizational politics in Kuwait (Muhammed, 2007), Malaysia (Poon, 2003), Taiwan (Huang, Chuang, & Lin, 2003), and Canada (Darr & Johns, 2004). Scarcity (e.g., few advancement opportunities) also is likely to increase political activity by increasing the need to take action to procure favorable outcomes for the self, and research supports a positive relationship between scarcity and perceptions of organizational politics in Malaysia (Poon, 2003), Taiwan (Huang et al.), and the United States (Ferris, Adams, et al. 2002).

In all, research supports that many antecedents of political activity are universal, with several caveats. First, research has focused on perceptions of organizational politics more than political behavior, which is not surprising given that perceptions of organizational politics have been proposed as an antecedent to political behavior (Ferris et al., 2000). Second, a number of job characteristics (e.g., feedback) and individual differences (e.g., Machiavellianism) that are antecedents to political activity have not been tested in multiple cultures (Ferris, Adams, et al., 2002). Third, additional antecedents that are common in other cultures but that exhibit low base rates in the United States may exist.

Indirect Effects

The antecedents of political activity may be universal, yet culture is likely to demonstrate an indirect effect on political activity through the antecedents discussed previously. For example, in *fatalistic* cultures, where there is little perceived control and high uncertainty, organizations are likely to have low trust climates. Trust climate is negatively associated with perceptions of organizational politics, which suggests that fatalism will lead to high levels of political activity indirectly through trust climate. Similarly, in high *power distance* cultures, where power is concentrated, organizations are likely characterized by centralized structures, few opportunities for advancement, and little employee participation, all of which increase political activity among employees who lack power (Ferris, Adams, et al., 2002). Thus, power distance also is likely to indirectly increase political activity among low-level employees.

In high *uncertainty avoidant* cultures, individuals seek to minimize risk, with the result that formal organizational structures are prevalent and work role ambiguity is rare. Thus, uncertainty avoidance should indirectly reduce political behavior through high formalization and low role ambiguity. *Individualism-collectivism* is correlated with affluence, such that individualistic cultures are more affluent than collectivistic cultures (Gelfand, Bhawuk, Nishii, & Bechtold, 2004). Scarcity (e.g., few resources or opportunities) increases political activity, which suggests that political activity will be lower in individualistic than collectivistic cultures due to greater affluence. In all, macrocultural context is likely to affect political activity not only directly, but also indirectly through more micro-organizational and job features, although these indirect effects have not been tested empirically.

Linkage E: Consequences Across Cultures

Linkage E suggests that culture moderates the consequences of political activity. Political behavior and perceptions of organizational politics share similar antecedents but have different consequences. In particular, political behavior has positive outcomes for the actor, while perceptions of organizational politics have negative outcomes for the perceiver. Therefore, culture is first discussed as a moderator of the consequences of political behavior, and then discussed as a moderator of the consequences of perceptions of organizational politics.

Political Behavior

Theory and research, primarily conducted within the United States, suggest that political behavior has positive career consequences. Performance appraisals, promotion decisions, and other aspects of human resource management are subjective, and efforts to influence others may therefore help individuals achieve career success (Ferris, Fedor, & King, 1994; Ferris & Judge, 1991). However, the relationship between political behavior and career success also is dependent on political skill, a construct developed in the United States that includes the four dimensions of networking ability, social astuteness, interpersonal influence, and apparent sincerity (Ferris et al., 2005). Specifically, individuals are most likely to benefit from political behavior if their political skill is high (Ferris et al., 1994, 2005; Semadar, Robins, & Ferris, 2006).

The positive impact of political behavior and skills on career success is likely to hold in other cultures. Consistent with research based on American samples, researchers in China have found that political skill has a positive effect on career development (Wei, Liu, Chen, & Wu, 2010) and that political behavior is positively associated with career potential ratings for employees high in political skill (Liu et al., 2010).*

At the same time, political behavior is more likely to be an effective means of achieving career success in some cultural contexts than in others. Research supports that management practices and behaviors are more effective when well aligned with cultural values and norms. For example, individuals from collectivistic cultures, who are socialized to cooperate with others, achieve higher levels of performance when working in groups than when working individually, whereas the reverse is true of individuals from individualistic cultures (Earley, 1993). Similarly, allowing group participation in goal setting has a stronger impact on performance in

---

* It remains unknown, however, if the political skill construct has the same meaning across cultures.

collectivistic cultures than in individualistic cultures (Erez & Earley, 1987). It follows that political behavior is more likely to lead to career success when engaging in political acts is considered normative within the cultural contexts.

It was previously argued that political behavior is likely to be normative and prevalent in *fatalistic* and high *power distance* cultures. Therefore, political behavior should be a highly effective means of achieving career success in these cultural contexts because political behavior is an accepted part of organizational life. Alternatively, it is proposed that political behavior is rare in *uncertainty avoidant, individualistic,* and *universalistic* cultures. Thus, political behavior is less likely to result in career success in these cultural contexts, given that pursuing self-interests through informal mechanisms is inconsistent with cultural values and norms. However, we are unaware of research that provides insight into these propositions.

Perceptions of Organizational Politics

Unlike political behavior, perceptions of organizational politics are associated with negative outcomes. High levels of perceptions of organizational politics signal a threatening work environment in which employees need to rely on informal behaviors to succeed and also breed uncertainty regarding whether hard work will lead to favorable outcomes (cf. Chang, Rosen, & Levy, 2009; Ferris et al., 1989). As a result, perceptions of organizational politics are associated with increased strain (e.g., stress, burnout, exhaustion), poor job attitudes (e.g., satisfaction, commitment), high turnover (intentions), and poor performance (e.g., objective, manager-rated, citizenship; Chang et al.). Many of the consequences of perceptions of organizational politics have been replicated in different cultures, including France, Israel, Malaysia, Nigeria, Taiwan, and the United States (Chang et al., 2003; Chen & Fang, 2008; Huang et al., 2003; Ladebo, 2006; Poon, 2003; Tziner et al., 1996), which suggests that perceptions of organizational politics have negative consequences across cultures.

Even if perceptions of organizational politics have similar consequences across cultures, culture is likely to moderate the magnitude of the relationship between perceptions of organizational politics and these consequences (see linkage E). For example, in cultural contexts where it is normative to get things done through informal mechanisms, high levels of perceptions of organizational politics are unlikely to cause severe distress. It was previously hypothesized that perceptions of organizational politics will be prevalent in *fatalistic* and high *power distance* cultures, which suggests that the negative consequences of perceptions of organizational politics will be mitigated in these cultural contexts. Alternatively, it is proposed that perceptions of organizational politics will be rare in high *uncertainty avoidant*, *individualistic*, and *universalistic* cultures which suggests that high levels of perceptions of organizational politics are likely to be particularly distressing in these settings.

Two meta-analyses have investigated whether culture moderates the consequences of perceptions of organizational politics. Chang and colleagues (2009) found that the negative effects of perceptions of organizational politics on job attitudes were stronger in the United States than in Israel, perhaps because the United States is more individualistic than Israel. However, the magnitude of the relationship between perceptions of organizational politics and stress, performance, and turnover did not vary across cultures. Miller, Rutherford, and Kolodinsky (2008) similarly found that the relationship between perceptions of organizational politics and commitment was stronger in the United States than outside the United States, although the magnitude of the relationship did not differ for satisfaction, stress, turnover, or performance. This study did not report the countries in the non-U.S. samples, and the findings are therefore difficult to interpret. Finally, one primary study also found that the relationship between perceptions of organizational politics and turnover and satisfaction was stronger in Britain than in Israel (Vigoda, 2001). In all, research supports that culture moderates perceptions of politics consequences, but provides little insight into the cultural values that drive these effects.

Summary and Future Research

Extant research on culture and political activity provides both insights and avenues for future research. Political behavior and perceptions of organizational politics appear to be pan-cultural phenomenon, but the nature of political activity likely varies with the cultural context. Limited evidence supports that the same behaviors are viewed as more political in some cultures than others (Romm & Drory, 1988), and it is likely that the political behavior construct may include group-serving behaviors instead of or in additional to self-serving behaviors in collectivistic cultures. At the same time, additional research is needed to understand which aspects of political behavior and perceptions of organizational politics are universal and which are culture-specific.

For example, perceptions of organizational politics are often treated as a unidimensional construct, but evidence from studies conducted in the United States supports that they can be broken down into a number of different dimensions, including perceptions of going along to get ahead, self-serving behaviors, coworker behaviors, clique behaviors, and politics in pay and promotions (Kacmar & Ferris, 1991). Although considered an indication of organizational politics in the United States, use of cliques and other social networks to promote one's interests may be seen as a normative part of life in collectivistic and relational cultures and thus not considered part of the perceptions of organizational politics construct. Comparative studies are unlikely to provide useful findings if the validity of the measures used is culture dependent. As such, research that uses confirmatory factor analysis and other techniques to assess the construct equivalence of measures of political behavior and perceptions of organizational politics across cultures is needed (cf. Gelfand, Leslie, & Shteynberg, 2007; Peng, Nisbett, & Wong, 1997).

The prevalence and consequences of political activity also are likely to vary with cultural value dimensions, including fatalism, power distance, uncertainty avoidance, individualism-collectivism, and universalism-particularism. Given the paucity of comparative studies of the level and consequences of political activity, research that assesses differences in political behavior and perceptions of organizational politics across cultures as well as efforts to unpack the specific dimensions of culture that explain any observed differences are needed.

Additional topics for future research include work on culture as a moderator of the relationship between the antecedents included in Figure 14.1 and political activity as well as efforts to identify culture-specific antecedents. Finally, although the focus of this chapter is social influence in organizations, the appropriateness of political behavior in other domains of life may vary across cultures. For example, it is normative to engage in political behavior in a wide range of life domains in the Middle East, including interactions with government offices, professors, and job interviewers, whereas political behavior is not acceptable in all of these domains in the United States (Cunningham & Sarayrah, 1993). Therefore, use of political behavior outside of organizations may be more effective in some cultural contexts than in others.

INFLUENCE TACTICS

In addition to research on political activity, much research exists on the tactics used to influence others. In this section, an overview of the tactics research has focused on to date is provided. Then, the existence and nature of different influence tactics across cultures are discussed, followed by a review of the prevalence and effectiveness of influence tactics across cultures. Finally, key findings and important avenues for future research are highlighted.

Influence Tactic Taxonomies

Several taxonomies of influence tactics exist (see Table 14.2 for a list and tactic definitions), yet the majority of organizational research has relied on the Profile of Organizational Influence Strategies (POIS), which was developed in the United States (Kipnis, Schmidt, & Wilkinson, 1980). The original taxonomy was composed of eight tactics:

1. Pressure: Use force
2. Ingratiation: Create a favorable impression
3. Reason: Use logic
4. Exchange: Offer something in return
5. Authority: Seek help from an authority
6. Coalitions: Mobilize others
7. Sanctions: Use rewards or punishments
8. Blocking: Prevent noncompliance

The first six tactics are tactics used in upward, downward, and peer influence attempts, whereas sanctions and blocking are limited to downward and peer attempts (Terpstra-Tong & Ralston, 2001). Since its initial development, several scholars have refined and expanded the POIS (Table 14.2). For example, Yukl and colleagues developed the Influence Behavior Questionnaire (IBQ), which contains five POIS tactics and six new tactics (Yukl, Seifert, & Chavez, 2008), and Ralston and colleagues developed the Strategies of Upward Influence (SUI) inventory, which includes two POIS

TABLE 14.2

Influence Tactic List and Definitions

Tactic	Inventory	Dimension	Definition
Original POIS tactics			
Pressure/Assertiveness	POIS, IBQ	AST	Use of force, demands, etc.
Authority/Upward appeal	POIS, SI	AST	Seek help from a higher authority
Coalitions	POIS, IBQ	AST	Mobilize others to gain support
Exchange/Bargaining/ Reciprocity	POIS, IBQ, SI	REL/RAT	Offer something in exchange
Ingratiation/Friendliness/ Liking	POIS, IBQ, SUI, SI	REL	Create a favorable impression/flatter
Reason/Rationality	POIS, IBQ, SUI	RAT	Use logical arguments and facts
Sanctions	POIS	—	Use rewards or punishments
Blocking	POIS	—	Prevent noncompliance
Additional tactics			
Apprising	IBQ	—	Indicate that compliance will help target
Collaboration	IBQ	RAT	Create a win–win solution
Consultation	IBQ	RAT	Seek target's input or participation
Inspiration	IBQ	RAT	Use appeal to values or ideals
Legitimating	IBQ	—	Establish legitimacy of request
Personal appeal	IBQ	REL	Frame request as a personal favor
Gift-giving	—	REL	Offer gifts to target
Informal	—	REL	Request in nonwork environment
Persistence	—	AST	Repeat pleading with target
Socializing	—	REL	Discuss irrelevant topic first
Written explanation	—	RAT	Use a written rational appeal
Good soldier	SUI	—	Get ahead through hard work
Image management	SUI	—	Present oneself in a positive manner
Personal network	SUI	—	Develop/use informal relationships
Information control	SUI	—	Control information others do not have
Strong-arm coercion	SUI	—	Use blackmail and other illegal tactics
Additional SI principles			
Commitment/consistency	SI	—	Note consistency with past behavior
Social proof	SI	—	Note consistency with peer behavior
Scarcity	SI	—	Highlight urgency/rarity

Notes: POIS, Profile of Organizational Influence Strategies. IBQ, Influence Behavior Questionnaire. SUI, Strategies of Upward Influence. SI, Social influence. AST, assertive (or hard). REL, relational (or soft). RAT, rational (or persuasive).

tactics and five new tactics (Ralston, Giacalone, & Terpstra, 1994; Ralston, Gustafson, Mainiero, & Umstot, 1993).*

Other researchers have also added tactics to the POIS (e.g., gift giving) without renaming the taxonomy (e.g., Fu & Yukl, 2000). Given the large number of tactics examined, scholars have grouped the POIS and related tactics into three higher-order categories: rational tactics (e.g., reason); relationship-based or soft tactics (e.g., gift giving); and assertiveness-based or hard tactics (e.g., pressure; Kipnis & Schmidt, 1985). Research supports that many, but not all, of the POIS tactics factor into these three categories (Table 14.3).†

Linkage A: Existence and Nature Across Cultures

Consistent with our proposition that organizational politics is a pan-cultural phenomenon, influence tactics are likely to exist universally across cultures. At the same time, some tactics may be culture specific. In what follows, both etic and emic studies that assess the universality of influence tactics are reviewed.

Etic Studies

Several studies have examined the existence of influence tactics across cultures by administering the POIS outside of the United States and examining the factor structure (Table 14.3). Four of the original eight POIS strategies (i.e., assertiveness, authority, reason, sanctions) consistently emerge in other cultures. Alternatively, coalitions, ingratiation, and exchange have failed to emerge in at least one culture. (To the best of our knowledge, the factor structure of blocking has not been investigated outside the United States).

---

* The SUI tactics have been grouped into three metacategories: organizationally beneficial tactics; self-indulgent tactics; and destructive tactics (Ralston et al., 2009). We discuss SUI tactics, not metacategories, to better compare the SUI with the POIS.

† In addition to research on influence tactics used in organizational settings, social influence has also been the topic of much research in social psychology. In particular, Cialdini (1993) identified six general principles of social influence. As shown in Table 14.2, three of Cialdini's tactics (i.e., authority, reciprocity, liking) have analogs in the list of POIS and related tactics, but the remaining principles (i.e., commitment, social proof, scarcity) do not. Consistent with the chapter's focus on *organizational* politics, we focus on the POIS and related tactics; however, we also integrate research on the social influence principles when appropriate.

TABLE 14.3

Factor Analysis Results for Influence Tactics Across Cultures

Study	Schmidt and Yeh (1992)				Yeh (1995)	Rao and Hashimoto (1996)	Rao et al. (1997)	Fu et al. (2004)	Leong et al. (2006)	
Country	England	Australia	Taiwan	Japan	3 countries	Japan	Japan	12 countries	China–United States	
Original POIS Tactics										
Pressure	Y*	Y*	Y*	Y*	Y*	Y*	Y*	AST	AST	N
Authority	Y*	Y*	Y	Y*	Y*	Y*	Y*	AST	AST	REL/AST
Coalitions	Y*	Y*	Y*	Y*	N	N	N	N	N	N
Exchange	Y*	Y*	Y*	Y*	Y*	N	Y*	REL	REL	REL/AST
Ingratiation	Y*	N	Y*	Y*	Y*	N	Y*	N	N	N
Reason	Y*	Y*	Y*	Y*	Y*	Y*	Y*	RAT	RAT	RAT
Sanctions	Y*	Y*	Y*	Y*	Y*	Y*	Y*	—	—	—
Additional Tactics										
Apprising	—	—	—	—	—	—	—	N	N	N
Collaboration	—	—	—	—	—	—	—	—	RAT	RAT
Consultation	—	—	—	—	—	—	—	RAT	RAT	RAT
Gift Giving	—	—	—	—	—	—	—	REL	REL	REL/AST
Informal	—	—	—	—	—	—	—	REL	REL	REL/AST
Inspiration	—	—	—	—	—	—	—	RAT	RAT	RAT
Persistence	—	—	—	—	—	—	—	AST	AST	N
Personal Appeal	—	—	—	—	—	—	—	REL	REL	REL/AST
Socializing	—	—	—	—	—	—	—	REL	REL	REL/AST
Written Explanation	—	—	—	—	—	—	—	N	N	RAT

Notes: Y, emerged as a meaningful factor. Y*, emerged as a meaningful factor but all items did not load as expected. N, did not emerge as a meaningful factor or load on a higher-order factor. AST, assertiveness factor. RAT, rational factor. REL, relational factor. Schmidt and Yeh (1992), Yeh (1995), Rao and Hashimoto (1996), and Rao et al. (1997) focused on downward influence only; Fu et al. (2004) and Leong et al. (2006) focused on downward, upward, and peer influence. Tactics not included here have not been subjected to factor analysis in cultures outside the United States.

Many of the POIS tactics emerge across cultures, yet studies conducted outside the United States have not replicated the factor structure of the POIS perfectly, in that all behaviors intended to assess a given tactic do not consistently load on the intended factor (Table 14.3). For example, Schmidt and Yeh (1992) found that a reason tactic emerged in each culture they studied but that it included pressure and ingratiation items in some cultures. Thus, the behaviors used to enact each influence tactic may vary across cultures. However, it is important to note that studies conducted in the United States also have failed to replicate the POIS factor structure perfectly (e.g., Hochwarter, Pearson, Ferris, Perrewé, & Ralston, 2000), and it is therefore unclear if variations in the POIS factor structure are a function of cultural differences.

Two studies have used a different approach by examining whether the POIS factors into the rational, relational, and assertive meta-categories in multicultural samples (Table 14.3). They found that the assertiveness category contains pressure, authority, and persistence (i.e., plead repeatedly); the relational category contains exchange, gift giving, informal appeal (i.e., request in a nonwork setting), personal appeal (i.e., frame as a personal favor), and socializing (i.e., discuss an irrelevant topic first); and the rational category contains reason, collaboration (i.e., create a win–win situation), consultation (i.e., seek target's input), and inspiration (i.e., appeal to values). Alternatively, coalitions, ingratiation, apprising (i.e., highlight that compliance will help target), and written explanation (i.e., written rational appeal) do not fit into any of the three metacategories.

Emic Studies

Etic studies are limited in that they may fail to capture culture-specific (i.e., emic) influence strategies. Therefore, several researchers have used an emic approach to investigate if additional influence strategies exist in other cultures. Rao, Hashimoto, and Rao (1997) supplemented their etic study of the POIS with an emic study in which they found evidence for nine tactics in Japan. Three of the tactics had direct analogs in the original POIS (i.e., ingratiation, pressure, reason), and an additional three tactics—personal development (i.e., apprising), open communication (i.e., consultation), and socializing—are included in the expanded list of POIS tactics.

Two unique tactics also emerged: firm authority (i.e., indicate that compliance will help the firm) and role model (i.e., set a good example). The firm authority tactic may reflect Japan's collectivistic culture, in which group identities (e.g., organization membership) are salient and meaningful (cf. Hofstede, 1980). Similarly, the role model tactic may reflect the preference for indirect and subtle communication styles that exist in collectivistic cultures (Hall, 1976). Finally, they found evidence for a coalitions tactic, even though this tactic did not emerge in their analysis of the POIS, suggesting that coalitions may be enacted differently across cultures.

Ralston and colleagues (1993) also conducted an emic study in that they developed the SUI in a sample of American and Hong Kong Chinese managers. The SUI contains two POIS tactics, ingratiation and reason, as well as several unique tactics, including good soldier (i.e., get ahead through hard work), image management (i.e., present oneself positively), personal network (i.e., use informal relationships), information control (i.e., control others' access to information), and strong-arm coercion (i.e., use blackmail and other illegal tactics).

The emergence of the personal networks tactic may reflect the importance of *guanxi*, defined as informal connections that imply favors and trust in Chinese culture (Chen & Chen, 2004). Similarly, information control, a behind-the-scenes tactic, may reflect the preference for indirect communication in Hong Kong and other collectivistic cultures (Hall, 1976). It is important to note, however, that the SUI focuses on upward influence attempts only, whereas the POIS focuses on upward, downward, and lateral attempts. Thus, some SUI strategies may be unique to upward influence attempts, not unique to a particular cultural context.

The emergence of unique tactics in some cultures raises the question of whether these tactics exist only in certain cultures or are simply more prevalent in some cultures than others. Smith, Huang, Harb, and Torres (in press) investigated this question by examining three indigenous influence tactics: (1) *guanxi*, defined as personal connections that create mutual long-term obligations in China; (2) *wasta*, a process through which individuals use connections to powerful others to achieve goals in Arab cultures; and (3) *jeitinho*, or the use of creative solutions to solve short-term problems in Brazil. They examined these tactics in Brazil, China, Lebanon, and the United Kingdom and found that each tactic existed in all cultures studied. They concluded that culture impacts influences tactics in terms of quantity more than quality. Thus, research supports that many influence tactics are universal, but, as is discussed next, the prevalence and effectiveness of different influence tactics is likely to vary across cultures.

Linkages A and E: Prevalence and Consequences Across Cultures

There are some similarities in the prevalence and consequences (i.e., effectiveness in influencing others, perceived ethicality) of influence tactics across cultures.* For example, reason is the most common and effective influence tactic in a wide variety of cultures (Fu & Yukl, 2000; Fu et al., 2004; Higgins et al., 2003; Kipnis, Schmidt, Swaffin-Smith, & Wilkinson, 1984; Rao et al., 1997; Schermerhorn & Bond, 1991; Xin & Tsui, 1996; Yeh, 1995; Yukl, Fu, & McDonald, 2003). At the same time, linkages A and E in Figure 14.1 suggest that culture is likely to influence the base rates and effectiveness of influence tactics. It was previously argued that political activity is more prevalent when political behavior is consistent with the broader culture. Similarly, a given influence tactic likely will be more common when the strategy converges with cultural values. With regard to consequences, organizational practices are also more effective when well aligned with what is culturally normative (Erez & Earley, 1993), which suggests that tactics will be more effective when aligned with the culture.

For the sake of parsimony, the discussion of influence tactic prevalence and consequences is organized around the influence tactic metacategories (i.e., rational, relational, assertive), but it is acknowledged that all strategies do not fit into these categories (Table 14.3). It is generally proposed that rational tactics will be more common and effective in individualistic than collectivistic cultures; relational tactics likely will be more common and effective in collectivistic than individualistic cultures; and prevalence and effectiveness of assertive tactics will vary with masculinity as well as power distance and the direction of influence. The discussion is limited to the direct effects of influence tactics (linkage A), but it is acknowledged

---

* Research conducted in the United States has linked influence tactics to a variety of consequences, including success in influencing others, job performance, and career advancement (see Ferris, Hochwarter et al., 2002; Higgins et al., 2003 for reviews). Yet the literature on consequences of influence tactics across cultures has focused on influence effectiveness and to a lesser extent perceived ethicality. We therefore focus our discussion of consequences on effectiveness and ethicality, under the assumption that effectiveness leads to other favorable career consequences (see Figure 14.1).

that culture also may exhibit indirect effects through organizational, job, and individual characteristics (linkages B + C).

Rational Tactics

Rational tactics (e.g., reason, consultation, inspiration) should be more common and effective in *individualistic* cultures, where task performance and outcomes are valued over relationships and process, than in *collectivistic* cultures. Scholars have compared base rates of rational tactics in collectivistic East Asian cultures and the U.S., which is an individualistic culture, but have found mixed results. One study found that reason was more common in the United States than in China (Schermerhorn & Bond, 1991); another study found that the prevalence of reason did not differ in the United States, Taiwan, and Japan (Yeh, 1995); and a third study found that reason was more common in China than in the United States, but only in upward influence attempts (Xin & Tsui, 1996). Thus, no strong conclusion exists regarding the prevalence of rational tactics across cultures.

Alternatively, rational tactics generally are more effective in Western cultures as compared to East Asian cultures. Evidence supports that reason, inspiration, and consultation are more effective in the United States and Switzerland than in China and Hong Kong (Fu & Yukl, 2000; Yukl et al., 2003) and that reason is similarly viewed as more ethical in the United States than in Hong Kong (Ralston et al., 1994, 1995). In addition, Leong, Bond, and Fu (2006) found that a composite rational tactics factor, including reason, collaboration, consultation, inspiration, and written appeals, was more effective in the United States than in China, Hong Kong, or Taiwan.

Similarly, Fu and colleagues (2004) investigated a composite rational tactics factor that included reason, inspiration, and consultation in a 12-country study. The effectiveness of rational tactics did not vary with country scores on individualism-collectivism; however, rational tactics were less effective in high uncertainty avoidant cultures, perhaps because the rigid structures present in high uncertainty avoidant cultures may reduce openness to rational arguments. In all, rational tactics appear to be more effective in Western cultures (individualistic, low uncertainty avoidance) than East Asian cultures (collectivistic, high uncertainty avoidance), and uncertainty avoidance may explain this difference.

Relational Tactics

Relational tactics should be more prevalent and effective in *collectivistic* than in *individualistic* cultures due to the focus on relationships and personal connections. Two original POIS tactics (i.e., exchange and ingratiation) are considered relational tactics. Although some have argued that exchange may be relational or rational (Farmer, Maslyn, Fedor, & Goodman, 1997; Terpstra-Tong & Ralston, 2001), this tactic consistently factors with other relational tactics (Table 14.3). Several studies have found that exchange is more common in collectivistic cultures, including China, Taiwan, and Japan, than in the United States (Xin & Tsui, 1996; Yeh, 1995). Yet one study also found that exchange was more common in the United States than in China (Schermerhorn & Bond, 1991), and research on the effectiveness of the exchange tactic suggests it is more effective in the United States than in China (Fu & Yukl, 2000). In all, research on the prevalence and effectiveness of exchange has produced mixed findings, perhaps because this tactic is enacted differently in different cultural contexts.

Some research suggests that ingratiation is more common in collectivistic cultures, including China and Taiwan, than in the United States (Xin & Tsui, 1996; Yeh, 1995). At the same time, one study found that ingratiation did not differ between the United States and Japan (Yeh, 1995), and another found that ingratiation was more common in the United States than in China, at least in upward influence attempts (Schermerhorn & Bond, 1991). Research on the effectiveness of ingratiation across cultures is similarly mixed; one study found that the effectiveness of ingratiation did not differ in the United States and China (Fu & Yukl, 2000), and several studies found that ingratiation is viewed as more ethical in the United States than in Hong Kong (Ralston et al., 1994, 1995). However, ingratiation does not consistently factor with other relational tactics across cultures, which could explain the mixed findings (Table 14.3).

A number of additional POIS tactics (e.g., gift giving, informal appeals, personal appeals, socializing) also have been classified as relational, both theoretically and empirically (Table 14.3). Researchers have not investigated the prevalence of these tactics, but evidence supports that they are more effective in collectivistic than individualistic cultures. For example, several studies found that gift giving, informal appeals, and personal appeals are more effective in China than in the United States (Fu & Yukl,

2000; Yukl et al., 2003). However, one study found that informal appeals were equally effective in the United States and Hong Kong (Yukl et al.). The SUI personal networks tactic also is a relational tactic. One study found that personal networks were viewed as more ethical in Hong Kong than in the United States (Ralston et al., 1995), but another found no difference (Ralston et al., 1994).

Finally, Fu and colleagues (2004) investigated a composite relational tactics factor, including gift giving, informal appeals, personal appeals, socializing, and exchange, and found that its effectiveness was positively correlated with country-level scores on both collectivism and uncertainty avoidance. Leong and colleagues (2006) similarly investigated a composite influence tactic factor (i.e., labeled contingent control) that contained many relational tactics (i.e., exchange, gifting, informal, personal appeal, socializing) and one assertive tactic (i.e., authority), but the composite's effectiveness did not differ in the United States and China.

Assertive Tactics

Assertive tactics (i.e., pressure, persistence, authority, coalitions) should be more common and effective in *masculine* cultures, where competition and aggression are valued, than in *feminine* cultures, where solidarity and concern for others are valued (Hofstede, 1980). The prevalence and effectiveness of assertive tactics also are likely to vary with *power distance* and the direction of influence. For downward influenced attempts, assertive tactics should be more common and effective in high than low power distance cultures, as they serve to reinforce and maintain the hierarchy.

Alternatively, for upward influence attempts, assertive tactics should be less common in high than low power distance cultures, as they may be viewed as a challenge to the existing hierarchy. Research on assertive tactics has focused on comparisons between the United States (i.e., low power distance, moderately masculine) and East Asian cultures (i.e., high power distance, moderately masculine) and therefore allows comparisons across low and high power distance cultures but not across masculine and feminine cultures.

For downward influence attempts, research supports that assertive tactics are more common in high than low power distance cultures. Specifically, authority and coalitions are more common in China (Xin & Tsui, 1996), and pressure and authority are more common in Japan and Taiwan (Yeh, 1995), compared with the United States. Alternatively, for upward influence attempts, authority and coalitions are more common in the United States than in China (Xin & Tsui, 1996). However, a few studies found that pressure is more or equally common in China compared with the United States (Schermerhorn & Bond, 1991; Xin & Tsui, 1996).

With regard to effectiveness and ethicality, findings seem to differ by the specific tactic of interest. One study found that the effectiveness of pressure did not differ in the United States and China, although this study collapsed the results across different influence directions (Fu & Yukl, 2000). Research on the related SUI tactic of strong-arm coercion suggests that it is viewed as most ethical in the United States and the Netherlands, followed by Germany and India, Hong Kong, and Mexico (Ralston et al., 1994, 1995; Ralston, Vollmer, Srinvasan, Nicholson, Tang, & Wan, 2001). Importantly, the SUI focuses on upward influence only, and this finding supports that assertive tactics are more effective in upward attempts when power distance is low.

Several studies have found that authority is more effective in China than in the United States and Switzerland, regardless of influence direction, although the effectiveness of this tactic did not differ in the United States and Hong Kong (Fu & Yukl, 2000; Yukl et al., 2003). Similarly, an advertising study found that authority was more effective in France (i.e., comparatively high power distance) than in the United States (Jung & Kellaris, 2006). Thus, authority may be more effective in high power distance cultures regardless of the influence direction.

Research on coalitions has produced mixed findings. One study of upward influence found that coalitions are more effective in the United States and Switzerland than in China and that coalitions were equally effective in the United States and Hong Kong (Yukl et al., 2003). Another study that collapsed the findings across influence direction found that coalitions were more effective in China than in the United States (Fu & Yukl, 2000). Although classified as an assertive tactic, coalitions may have a relational component, which could perhaps explain the Fu and Yukl (2000) finding. Moreover, the coalitions tactic may be enacted differently across cultures (Rao et al., 1997), which could explain the inconsistent findings.

Finally, Fu and colleagues (2004) investigated the effectiveness of a composite assertiveness factor that included persistence, pressure, and authority. They combined the results across influence direction and found that the assertiveness factor was positively related to country scores on collectivism, which is surprising given that indirectness and a lack of assertion is normative in collectivistic cultures. However, the study did not assess power distance, which is positively correlated with collectivism. Thus, power distance may be a third variable that explains this surprising finding (Fu et al., 2004).

Additional SUI Tactics

The prevalence and effectiveness of the SUI tactics that cannot be easily classified as rational, relational or assertive also are likely to vary across cultures. For example, the image management and good solider tactics are likely to be more common, effective, and ethical in individualistic cultures due to a greater emphasis on the self and meritocracy compared with collectivistic cultures. Ralston and colleagues (1993) indeed found that image management was more common in the United States than in Hong Kong. In addition, both the image management and good solider tactics are perceived as most ethical in the United States and the Netherlands, followed by Germany and India, then Hong Kong, and finally Mexico (Ralston et al., 1993, 1994, 1995, 2001).

Alternatively, information control should be more common and effective in collectivistic than individualistic cultures, given that information control is an indirect, behind-the-scenes tactic that can be used to maintain face. Evidence supports that the information control tactic is more common in Hong Kong than in the United States (Ralston et al., 1993), and is viewed as more ethical in the United States and the Netherlands than in India, Germany, Hong Kong, and Mexico (Ralston et al., 1993, 1994, 1995, 2001).

Additional Cialdini Tactics

Cialdini has identified several social influence principles that do not have analogues in the POIS, including commitment/consistency (i.e., note consistency with prior behavior), social proof (i.e., note consistency with prior behavior), social proof (i.e., note consistency with peer behavior), and scarcity (i.e., highlight urgency/rarity) also have been shown to vary across cultures. Several studies suggest that commitment/consistency is more effective in individualistic cultures (i.e., the United States), where the past actions and behaviors of the self are salient motivator. Alternatively, social proof is more effective in collectivistic cultures (i.e., China, Hong Kong, Poland), where the behavior of others is a salient motivator (Chen et al., 2006; Cialdini, Wosinska, Barrett, Butner, & Gornik-Durose, 1999; Zou, Tam, Morris, Lee,

Lau, & Chiu, 2009). In addition, at least one study investigated the scarcity tactic across cultures and found that it was more effective in the United States than in France (Jung & Kellaris, 2004). The authors attributed the effect to differences in indirect (France) versus direct (United States) communication, although the mechanism was not measured directly.

Summary and Future Research

Several conclusions can be drawn based on existing research on culture and influence tactics. First, a variety of different tactics seem to exist universally, although the behaviors used to enact different tactics may be culture specific. Second, the prevalence and effectiveness of influence tactics varies substantially across cultures. The prevalence of rational tactics does not seem to vary across cultures, although rational tactics generally are more effective in the West than in the East, perhaps due to differences in uncertainty avoidance. Alternatively, relational tactics are more prevalent and effective in the East than in the West, likely due to differences in both individualism-collectivism and uncertainty avoidance. Finally, use of assertive tactics are more common in the West than in the East for upward influence attempts but more common in the East than in the West for downward influence attempts. However, the effectiveness of assertive tactics seems to vary with the specific tactic investigated.

In spite of much research, a number of knowledge gaps exist within the literature on culture and influence tactics. First, more research on the different behavioral manifestations of specific influence tactics is needed. Many, if not all, of the POIS tactics could be enacted in either direct ways, which are likely to be common in individualistic cultures, or indirect ways, which are likely to be common in collectivistic cultures. For example, coalitions may be enacted by staging a direct intervention in individualistic cultures but by using an intermediary in collectivistic cultures. A deeper understanding of cultural differences in the ways strategies are enacted could help resolve some of the inconsistent findings for certain influence tactics. Second, most studies have focused on country comparisons, and particularly comparisons between East Asian and Western cultures, with some notable exceptions (e.g., Fu et al., 2004; Ralston et al., 2009). More research that seeks to unpack the cultural dimensions that explain differences in the prevalence and effectiveness of influence tactics would be useful.

With regard to consequences, research primarily has focused on perceived effectiveness. To the extent that there are differences in perceived versus actual effectiveness, the focus on perceived effectiveness could explain some of the surprising findings regarding the effectiveness of assertive tactics, for example. Research on the effectiveness of different tactics also brings the utility of the metacategories of rational, relational, and assertive tactics into question. For example, the effectiveness of assertive tactics in Eastern versus Western cultures was highly variable, even though a composite measure of assertive tactics was positively correlated with societal collectivism (Fu et al., 2004). Thus, although the metacategories provide a useful framework, they also may hide cultural differences among tactics within the same category.

Finally, future research should explore additional tactics that are likely to vary across cultures. In particular, emotional appeals may have different base rates and consequences in different cultural settings. Although generally omitted from research on influence tactics, negotiation research suggests that Arabs use emotional appeals more frequently compared with Americans and Russians (Leung & Wu, 1990). Research also suggests that anger displays are more normative in the West than in the East; as a result, use of anger in negotiation leads to larger concessions from Caucasian Americans than from Asians (Adam, Shirako, & Maddux, 2010). In addition to use of emotion, appeals to a higher spiritual authority are likely to be a common and effective influence tactic in Middle Eastern and other fatalistic cultures.

SOCIAL INFLUENCE IN MULTICULTURAL SETTINGS

Thus far, we have presented theory and research on how culture affects organizational politics and social influence in situations where the actor and target have the same cultural background. Politicking that crosses cultural boundaries, including influence attempts in multicultural teams and organizations, is also an important area of inquiry, given that the use of inappropriate tactics could lead to severe misunderstandings. A handful of studies have investigated influence tactics in multicultural work settings. For example, Rao and Schmidt (1995) found that Indian employees used influence tactics, including exchange, assertiveness, and coalitions, more frequently when interacting with Indian coworkers than with American coworkers, perhaps because they were more confident that these behaviors were appropriate when interacting with culturally similar others.

In contrast, however, Rao and Hashimoto (1996) found that Japanese managers in Canada used influence tactics, including reason, authority, sanctions, and reciprocity (i.e., a factor that combined ingratiation and exchange), more frequently with Canadian subordinates than with Japanese subordinates. Finally, Yeh (1995) found some evidence of assimilation, such that Taiwanese managers used tactics common in the United States with American coworkers but tactics common in Japan with Japanese coworkers.

Although useful, these studies have focused on the prevalence of different influence tactics rather than their effectiveness. When individuals attempt to influence culturally dissimilar others, cultural distance and cultural intelligence are likely to determine the success of influence attempts. With regard to cultural distance, even highly motivated expatriates have a difficult time adjusting to new work environments and achieving strong performance when the cultural difference between the home and host culture is great (Chen, Kirkman, Kim, Farh, & Tangirala, 2010), which suggests that political behaviors may be less effective when cultural distance is high.

In addition, research on negotiation suggests that cultural intelligence facilitates higher joint outcomes in cross-cultural negotiations (Imai & Gelfand, 2010). Thus, individuals who are culturally intelligent in general and also possess knowledge regarding which tactics are appropriate across cultures may be better able to reap the benefits of political behavior. Finally, organizational also may play a role in determining the success of influence attempts in multicultural settings. For example, although culture exhibits a large impact on individual behavior, strong situations create a shared reality that helps coordinate action (Adam et al., 2010; Gelfand & Realo, 1999). Thus, cultural differences in political behavior and the associated potential for cross-cultural misunderstandings may be mitigated by strong organizational cultures.

PRACTICAL IMPLICATIONS AND CONCLUSIONS

In this chapter, theory and research were presented on the existence, nature, prevalence, and consequences of organizational politics in different cultural settings. Understanding the cultural psychology of social influence not only is important for advancing theory but also has practical implications. In organizational settings, inability to successfully influence others may lead to poor performance and even early return for expatriate managers. Similarly, a lack of understanding regarding which influence tactics are normative, effective, and ethical may be a key cause of failed negotiations in the context of international mergers and acquisitions.

Also, it could be argued that the cultural contingencies of organizational politics have implications that extend beyond organizational boundaries. Indeed, a deeper understanding of the cultures in which political behavior is normative and expected, as well as the specific tactics that are effective, may lead to smoother diplomatic encounters and help facilitate more peaceful international relations around the globe.

The perspective adopted in this chapter suggests that understanding cultural influences on organizational politics is of great theoretical and practical importance due to large and persistent cultural differences. At the same time, some have pondered whether increasing globalization will result in homogeneous organizational practices and behavior as organizations in different parts of the world gravitate toward global best practices (cf. Pudelko & Harzing, 2008). Yet there is reason to doubt that organizational practices and behaviors will converge across time.

Although some superficial aspects of American culture have become popular around the globe (e.g., McDonald's, Coca-Cola), deeper cultural differences persist (cf. Huntington, 1996). Indeed, research on cultural values that was first pioneered by Hofstede (1980) and later replicated by the GLOBE research team (House et al., 2004) provides firm evidence that variability in cultural values is alive and well (Huntington). As such, it is necessary to continue to understand the implications of the cultural context for organizational politics as well as other aspects of organizational behavior.

ACKNOWLEDGMENTS

This research is based upon work supported in part by the U.S. Army Research Laboratory and the U.S. Army Research Office under grant number W911NF-08-1-0144. The authors are grateful to Si Ahn Mehng and Sam South for their assistance in preparing this chapter.

REFERENCES

Adam, H. Shirako, A., & Maddux, W. (2010). Cultural variation the interpersonal effects of anger in negotiation. *Psychological Science, 21,* 882–889.

Acevedo, G. (2005). Turning anomie on its head: Fatalism as Durkheim's concealed and multidimensional alienation theory. *Sociological Theory, 23,* 75–85.

Andrews, M.C., Kacmar, K.M., & Harris, K.J. (2009). Got political skill? The impact of justice on the importance of political skill for job performance. *Journal of Applied Psychology, 94,* 1427–1437.

Aryee, S., Chen, Z., & Budhwar, P. (2004). Exchange fairness and employee performance: An examination of the relationship between organizational politics and procedural justice. *Organizational Behavior and Human Decision Processes, 94,* 1–14.

Berry, J.W. (1969). On cross-cultural comparability. *International Journal of Psychology, 4,* 119–28.

Chang, C., Rosen, C.C., & Levy, P.E. (2009). The relationship between perceptions of organizational politics and employee attitudes, strain, and behavior: A meta-analytic examination. *Academy of Management Journal, 52,* 779–801.

Chen, X.P., & Chen, C.C. (2004). On the intricacies of the Chinese *guanxi*: A process model of *guanxi* development. *Asia Pacific Journal of Management, 21,* 305–324.

Chen, G., Kirkman, B.L., Kim, K., Farh, C.I.C., & Tangirala, S. (2010). When does cross-cultural motivation enhance expatriate effectiveness? A multilevel investigation of the moderating roles of subsidiary support and cultural intelligence. *Academy of Management Journal, 53,* 1110–1130.

Chen, Y., & Fang, W. (2008). The moderating effect of impression management on the organizational politics-performance relationship. *Journal of Business Ethics, 79,* 263–277.

Chen, S.X., Hui, N.H.H., Bond, M.H., Sit, A.Y.F., Wong, S., Chow, V.X.Y., et al. (2006). Reexamining personal, social, and cultural influences on compliance behavior in the United States, Poland, and Hong Kong. The *Journal of Social Psychology, 146,* 223–244.

Cialdini, R.B. (1993). *Influence: Science and practice.* New York: Harper.

Cialdini, R.B., Wosinska, W., Barrett, D.W., Butner, J., & Gorik-Durose, M. (1999). Compliance with a request in two cultures: The differential influence of social proof and commitment/consistency on collectivists and individualists. *Personality and Social Psychology Bulletin, 25,* 1242–1253.

Cunningham, R.B., & Sarayrah, Y.K. (1993). *Wasta: The hidden force in Middle Eastern society.* Westport, CT: Praeger

Darr, W., & Johns, G. (2004). Political decision-making climates: Theoretical processes and multi-level antecedents. *Human Relations, 57,* 169–200.

Drory, A. (1993). Perceived political climate and job attitudes. *Organization Studies, 14,* 59–71.

Drory, A., & Romm, T. (1988). Politics in organization and its perception within the organization. *Organization Studies, 9,* 165–179,

Earley, P.C. (1993). East meets west meets Mideast: Further explorations of collectivistic and individualistic work groups. *Academy of Management Journal, 36,* 319–348.

Erez, M., & Earley, P.C. (1987). Comparative analysis of goal-setting strategies across cultures. *Journal of Applied Psychology, 72,* 658–665.

Erez, M., & Earley, P.C. (1993). *Culture, self-identity, and work.* New York: Oxford University Press.

Farmer, S.M., Maslyn, J.M., Fedor, D.B., & Goodman, J.S. (1997). Putting upward influence strategies in context. *Journal of Organizational Behavior, 18,* 17–42.

Ferris, G.R., Adams, G., Kolodinsky, R.W., Hochwarter, W.A., & Ammeter, A.P. (2002). Perceptions of organizational politics: Theory and research directions. *Research in Multi-Level Issues, 1,* 179–254.

Ferris, G.R., Fedor, D.B., & King, T.R. (1994). A political conceptualization of managerial behavior. *Human Resource Management Review, 4,* 1–34.

Ferris, G.R., Harrell-Cook, G., & Dulebohn, J.H. (2000). Organizational politics: The nature of the relationship between politics perceptions and political behavior. *Research in the Sociology of Organizations, 17,* 89–130.

Ferris, G.R., Hochwarter, W.A., Douglas, C., Blass, F.R., Kolodinsky, R.W., & Treadway, D.C. (2002). Social influence processes in organizations and human resources systems. *Research in Personnel and Human Resource Management, 21,* 65–127.

Ferris, G.R., & Judge, T.A. (1991). Personnel/human resources management: A political influence perspective. *Journal of Management, 17,* 447–488.

Ferris, G.R., Russ, G.S., & Fandt, P.M. (1989). Politics in organizations. In R.A. Giacalone and P. Rosenfeld (Eds.), *Impression management in the organization* (pp.143–170). Hillsdale, NJ: Lawrence Erlbaum.

Ferris, G.R., Treadway, D.C., Kolodinsky, R.W., Hochwarter, W.A., Kacmar, C.J., Douglas, C., et al. (2005). Development and validation of the political skills inventory. *Journal of Management, 31,* 126–152.

Fu, P.P., & Yukl, G. (2000). Perceived effectiveness of influence tactics in the United States and China. *Leadership Quarterly, 11,* 251–66.

Fu, P.P., Kennedy, J., Tata, J., Yukl, G., Bond, M.H., Peng, T., et al. (2004). The impact of societal cultural values and individual social beliefs on the perceived effectiveness of managerial influence strategies: A meso approach, *Journal of International Business Studies, 35,* 284–305.

Geertz, C. (1973). *The interpretation of cultures.* New York: Basic Books.

Gefland, M.J., Bhawuk, D.P.S., Nishii, L.H., & Bechtold, D J. (2004). Individualism and collectivism. In R.J. House, P.J. Hanges, M. Javidan, P.W. Dorfman, & V. Gupta (Eds.), *Culture leadership, and organizations: The GLOBE study of 62 societies* (pp. 438–512). Thousand Oaks, CA: Sage Publications.

Gelfand, M.J., & Brett, J.M. (2004). *The handbook of negotiation and culture.* Stanford, CA: Stanford University Press.

Gelfand, M.J., Erez, M., & Aycan, Z. (2007). Cross-cultural organizational behavior. *Annual Review of Psychology, 58,* 479–514.

Gelfand, M.J., Leslie, L.M., & Shteynberg, G. (2007). Cross-cultural research methods and theory. In S. G. Rogelberg (Ed.), *The encyclopedia of industrial and organizational psychology* (pp.136–143). Thousand Oaks, CA: Sage Publications

Gelfand, M.J., & Realo, A. (1999). Individualism-collectivism and accountability in inter-group negotiations. *Journal of Applied Psychology, 84,* 721–736.

Hall, E.T. (1976). *Beyond culture.* New York: Anchor Press.

Higgins, C.A., Judge, T.A., & Ferris, G.R. (2003). Influence tactics and work outcomes: A meta-analysis. *Journal of Organizational Behavior, 24*(1), 89–106.

Hochwarter, W.A., Pearson, A.W., Ferris, G.R., Perrewé, P.L., & Ralston, D.A. (2000). A reexamination of Schriesheim and Hinkin's (1990) measure of upward influence. *Educational and Psychological Measurement, 60,* 755–771.

Hofstede, G. (1980). *Culture's consequences: Comparing values, behaviors, institutions, and organizations across nations.* Thousand Oaks, CA: Sage Publications.

House, R.J., Hanges, P.J., Javidan, M., Dorfman, P.W., & Gupta, V. (2004). *Culture, leadership, and organizations: The GLOBE study of 62 societies.* Thousand Oaks, CA: Sage Publications.

Huang, I., Chuang, C.J., & Lin, H. (2003). The role of burnout in the relationship between perceptions of organizational politics and turnover intentions. *Public Personnel Management, 32,* 519–531.

Huntington, S.P. (1996). *The clash of civilizations: Remaking of world order.* New York: Simon & Schuster.

Imai, L., & Gelfand, M. J. (2010). The culturally intelligent negotiator: The impact of cultural intelligence (CQ) on negotiation sequences and outcomes. *Organizational Behavior and Human Decision Processes, 112,* 83–98.

Jung, J.M., & Kellaris, J.J. (2006). Responsiveness to authority appeals among young French and American consumers. *Journal of Business Research, 59,* 735–744.

Kacmar, K.M., & Carlson, D.S. (1997). Further validation of the Perceptions of Politics Scale (POPS): A multisample approach. *Journal of Management, 23,* 627–658.

Kacmar, K.M., & Ferris, G.R. (1991). Perceptions of Organizational Politics Scale (POPS): Development and construct validation. *Educational and Psychological Measurement, 51,* 193–205.

Kashima, Y., & Callan, V. (1994). The Japanese work group. In H.C. Triandis, M.D. Dunnette, & L.M. Hough (Eds.), *Handbook of industrial/organizational psychology* (Vol. 4, 610–646). Palo Alto, CA: Consulting Psychologists Press.

Katz, D., & Kahn, R.L. (1978). *The social psychology of organizations* (2nd ed.). New York: Wiley.

Kluckhohn, C. (1954). Culture and behavior. In G. Lindzey (Ed.), *Handbook of social psychology* (Vol. 2, pp. 921–976). Cambridge, MA: Addison-Wesley.

Kipnis, D., & Schmidt, S.M. (1985). The language of persuasion. Hard, soft or rational: Our choice depends on power, expectations and what we hope to accomplish. *Psychology Today, 4,* 40–6.

Kipnis, D., Schmidt, S.M., & Wilkinson, I. (1980). Intraorganizational influence tactics: Explorations in getting one's way. *Journal of Applied Psychology, 65,* 440–452.

Kipnis, D., Schmidt, S.M., Swaffin-Smith, C., & Wilkinson, I. (1984). Patterns of managerial influence: Shotgun managers, tacticians and bystanders. *Organizational Dynamics, 12*(3), 58–67.

Ladebo, O. (2006). Perceptions of organizational politics: Examination of a situational antecedent and consequences among Nigeria's extension personnel. *Applied Psychology: An International Review, 55,* 255–281.

Leong, L.T.J., Bond, M.H., & Fu, P.P. (2006). Perceived effectiveness of influence strategies in the United States and three Chinese societies. *International Journal of Cross Cultural Management, 6,* 101–120.

Leung, K., & Wu, P.-G. (1990). Dispute processing: A cross-cultural analysis. In R.W. Brislin (Ed.), *Applied cross-cultural psychology* (pp. 209–231). Thousand Oaks, CA: Sage Publications.

Liu, Y., Liu, J., & Wu, L. (2010). Are you willing and able? Roles of motivation, power, and politics in career growth. *Journal of Management, 36,* 1432–1460.

Markus, H.R., & Kitayama, S. (1991). Culture and the self: Implications for cognition, emotion, and motivation. *Psychological Review, 98,* 224–253.

Miller, B.K., Rutherford, M.A., & Kolodinsky, R.W. (2008). Perceptions of organizational politics: A meta-analysis of outcomes. *Journal of Business and Psychology, 22,* 209–222.

Moaddel, M., & Karabenick, S.A. (2008). Religious fundamentalism among young Muslims in Egypt and Saudi Arabia. *Social Forces, 86,* 1675–1710.

Morrison, E.W., Chen, Y., & Salgado, S.R. (2004). Cultural differences in newcomer feedback seeking: A comparison of the United States and Hong Kong. *Applied Psychology, 53,* 1–22.

Muhammed, A.H. (2007). Antecedents of organizational politics perceptions in Kuwait business organizations. *Competitiveness Review: An International Business Journal, 17,* 234–247.

Peng, K., Nisbett, R., & Wong, N. (1997). Validity problems comparing values across cultures and possible solutions. *Psychological Methods, 2,* 329–344.

Poon, J. (2003). Situational antecedents and outcomes of organizational politics perceptions. *Journal of Managerial Psychology, 18,* 138–155.

Poon, J. (2004). Moderating effect of perceived control on perceptions of organizational politics outcomes. *International Journal of Organization Theory and Behavior, 7,* 22–40.

Poon, J. (2006). Trust-in-supervisor and helping coworkers: moderating effect of perceived politics. *Journal of Managerial Psychology, 21,* 518–532.

Pudelko, M., & Harzing, A. (2008). The golden triangle for MNCs: Standardization towards headquarters practices, standardization towards global best practices and localization. *Organizational Dynamics, 37,* 394–404.

Ralston, D.A., Giacalone, R.A., & Terpstra, R. (1994). Ethical perceptions of organizational politics: A comparative evaluation of American and Hong Kong Managers. *Journal of Business Ethics, 13,* 989–999.

Ralston, D.A., Gustafson, D.J., Mainiero, L., & Umstot, D. (1993). Strategies of upward influence: A cross-national comparison of Hong Kong and American managers. *Asia-Pacific Journal of Management, 10(2),* 157–175.

Ralston, D.A., Vollmer, G.R., Srinvasan, N., Nicholson, J. D., Tang, M., & Wan, P. (2001). Strategies of upward influence: A study of six cultures from Europe, Asia, and America. *Journal of Cross Cultural Psychology, 32,* 728–735.

Ralston, D.A., Gustafson, D.J., Mainiero, L., Umstot, D., Terpstra, R.H., Cunniff, M.K., et al. (1995). Do expatriates change their behavior to fit a foreign culture? A study of American expatriates' strategies of upward influence. *Management International Review, 35(1),* 109–122.

Ralston, D.A., Egri, C.P., de la Garza-Carranza, M.T., Ramburuth, P., Terpstra-Tong, J., Pekerti, A.A., et al. (2009). Ethical preferences for influencing superiors: A 41-Society study. *Journal of International Business Studies, 40,* 1022–1045.

Rao, A., & Hashimoto, K. (1996). Intercultural influence: A study of Japanese expatriate managers. *Journal of International Business Studies, 27(3),* 443–466.

Rao, A., Hashimoto, K., & Rao, A. (1997). Universal and culturally specific aspects of managerial influence: A study of Japanese managers. *Leadership Quarterly, 8,* 295–312.

Rao, A., & Schmidt, S.M. (1995). Influence strategies in intercultural interaction: The view from Asia. *Advances in International Comparative Management, 10,* 79–98.

Romm, T., & Drory, A. (1988). Political behavior in organizations: A cross-cultural comparison. *International Journal of Value Based Management, 1,* 97–113.

Salimäki, A., & Jämsén, S. (2010). Perceptions of politics and fairness in merit pay. *Journal of Managerial Psychology, 25,* 229–251.

Schmidt, S.M., & Yeh, R.H. (1992). The structure of leader influence: A cross national comparison. *Journal of Cross-Cultural Psychology, 23,* 251–262.

Schermerhorn, J.E., & Bond, M.H. (1991). Upward and downward influence tactics in managerial networks: A comparative study of Hong Kong Chinese and Americans. *Asia Pacific Journal of Management, 8,* 147–158.

Semadar, A., Robins, G., & Ferris, G.R. (2006). Comparing the validity of multiple social effectiveness constructs in the prediction of managerial job performance. *Journal of Organizational Behavior, 27,* 443–461.

Skinner, B.F. (1981). Selection by consequence. *Science, 213,* 351–367.

Smith, P.B., Dugan, S., & Trompenaars, F. (1996). National culture and the values of organizational employees: A dimensional analysis across 43 nations. *Journal of Cross-Cultural Psychology, 27,* 231–264.

Smith, P.B., Huang, H.J., Harb, C., & Torres, C. (in press). How distinctive are indigenous ways of achieving influence? A comparative study of *guanxi, wasta, jeitinho,* and "pulling string." *Journal of Cross-Cultural Psychology.*

Steidlmeier, P. (1999). Gift giving, bribery and corruption: Ethical management of business relationships in China. *Journal of Business Ethics, 20,* 121–132.

Taras, V., Piers, S., & Kirkman, B.L. (2010). Examining the impact of culture's consequences: A three-decade, multilevel, meta-analytic review of Hofstede's cultural value dimensions. *Journal of Applied Psychology, 95,* 405–439.

Terpstra-Tong, J., & Ralston, D.A. (2001). Moving toward a global understanding of upward influence strategies: An Asian perspective with directions for cross-cultural research. *Asian Pacific Journal of Management, 19,* 373–404.

Treadway, D.C., Hochwarter, W.A., Kacmar, C.J., & Ferris, G.R. (2005). Political will, political skill, and political behavior. *Journal of Organizational Behavior, 26,* 229–245.

Triandis, H.C. (1972). *The analysis of subjective culture.* New York: Wiley.

Tziner, A., Latham, G., Price, B., & Haccoun, R. (1996). Development and validation of a questionnaire for measuring perceived political considerations in performance appraisal. *Journal of Organizational Behavior, 17,* 179–190.

Vigoda, E. (2000a). Internal politics in public administration systems: An empirical examination of its relationship with job congruence, organizational citizenship behavior, and in-role performance. *Public Personnel Management, 29,* 185–210.

Vigoda, E. (2000b). Organizational politics, job attitudes, and work outcomes: Exploration and implications for the public sector. *Journal of Vocational Behavior, 57,* 326–347.

Vigoda, E. (2001). Reactions to organizational politics: A cross-cultural examination in Israel and Britain. *Human Relations, 54,* 1483–1518.

Vigoda, E. (2002). Stress-related aftermaths to workplace politics: The relationships among politics, job distress, and aggressive behavior in organizations. *Journal of Organizational Behavior, 23,* 571–591.

Vigoda-Gadot, E. (2007). Leadership style, organizational politics, and employees' performance. *Personnel Review, 36,* 661–683.

Vigoda, E., & Cohen, A. (2002). Influence tactics and perceptions of organizational politics: A longitudinal study. *Journal of Business Research, 55,* 311–324.

Vigoda-Gadot, E., Vinarski-Peretz, H., & Ben-Zion, E. (2003). Politics and image in the organizational landscape: An empirical examination among public sector employees. *Journal of Managerial Psychology, 18,* 764–787.

Wei, L.-Q., Liu, J., Chen, Y.-Y., & Wu, L.-Z. (2010). Political skill, supervisor-subordinate guanxi and career prospects in Chinese firms. *Journal of Management Studies, 47,* 437–454.

Xin, K., & Tsui, A.S. (1996). Different strokes for different folks: Influence tactics by Asian-American and Caucasian-American managers. *Leadership Quarterly, 7*(1), 109–132.

Yeh, R.S. (1995). Downward influence styles in cultural diversity settings. *International Journal of Human Resource Management, 6,* 627–641.

Yukl, G., Fu, P.P., & McDonald, R. (2003). Cross-cultural differences in perceived effectiveness of influence tactics for initiating or resisting change. *Applied Psychology: An International Review, 52,* 68–82.

Yukl, G., Seifert, C.F., & Chavez, C. (2008). Validation of the extended Influence Behavior Questionnaire. *Leadership Quarterly, 19,* 609–621.

Zou, X., Tam, K.-P., Morris, M.W., Lee, S.-l., Lau, I. Y-M., & Chiu, C.-Y. (2009). Culture as common sense: Perceived consensus versus personal beliefs as mechanisms of cultural influence. *Journal of Personality and Social Psychology, 97,* 579–597.

Section III

Individual Differences in Organizational Politics

15

The Intersection of Race and Politics: A Framework for Racialized Organizational Politics Perceptions

Atira C. Charles
Florida State University

Stella M. Nkomo
University of Pretoria

> A fully functional multiracial society cannot be achieved without a sense of history and open, honest dialogue.
>
> **—Dr. Cornel West**

In this chapter, an interdisciplinary framework is presented that allows for an open and honest dialogue about the intricacies and intersectionalities of race and politics in organizations while taking a sociohistorical journey through time to better understand why race holds the critical meaning and relevance in today's organizations and society as a whole.

Although all individuals, regardless of race, experience politics in organizations at a basic human level, this chapter suggests that another type of organizational politics carries with it a burden deeply rooted in sociohistorical, organizational, group, and intra-individual perspectives uniquely embedded within and intersected with each other. This type of organizational politics is referred to as racialized organizational politics perceptions (ROPP). ROPP are defined as the extent to which individuals believe their racial category or identity is influencing their social interactions and shared meanings within the organization as well as the opportunity to navigate the environment in a way that is favorable and of benefit to them and members of their racial category or identity.

In this chapter, the construct of race in society and in organizational studies initially is discussed. Next, ROPP as a construct are developed, and the theoretical paradigms that support the construct and the proposed framework are explained. The chapter concludes with a detailed description of the framework, including the multiple causal influences of ROPP, the individual outcomes of ROPP, and the mitigating resources that individuals can use to reduce the negative impact of ROPP on their work-related attitudes and behaviors.

RACE IN ORGANIZATIONS

Conceptualization of Race

Within the social scientific study of race, it was for a long time conceptualized as a biological construct, and there was belief in the idea of different races with innate distinctive characteristics (Winant, 2006). Race signified a permanent category of humans equivalent to species categorization—hence, the birth of the idea of different races (Banton, 1998). Over time, these distinctions deepened into a racial hierarchy with the White race designated as superior to non-White races (Banton; Fluehr-Lobban, 2006).

Today, scientists all agree that race is a social construction primarily recognized by physical appearance or phenotype. In a social constructionist view, race exists not for biological reasons but for social reasons (Proudford & Nkomo, 2006, p. 325). Race can be best understood as a social creation that divides and categorizes individuals by phenotypical markers, such as skin color, supposedly signifying underlying essential differences (Proudford & Nkomo). Markus (2008, p. 654) offered the following thorough definition:

> Race is a dynamic set of historically derived and institutionalized ideas and practices that (1) sorts people into ethnic groups according to perceived physical and behavioural characteristics; (2) associates differential value, power, and privilege with these characteristics and establishes a social status ranking among the different groups; and (3) emerges (as) when groups are perceived to pose a threat (political, economic or cultural) to each other's world view or way of life; and/or (b) to justify the denigration and exploitation (past, current, or future) of, and prejudice toward, other

groups. It is also important to point out that the meanings attached to race are dependent upon the social relations and historical context of a particular society or nation.

Relevance of Race in the Global Context

What has not changed over time is the fact that race continues to be used as a basis for discrimination and exclusion in many societies around the globe (Winant, 2006). It is hard to find a society where some group has not been classified as the *other* on the basis of race or ethnicity (Sidanius & Pratto, 1999). For example, in many parts of Europe, the term *race* is perceived to have less meaning, and the term *ethnicity* is preferred. Dutch citizens avoid references to skin color and to Whiteness because of the racial connotations. The inequalities that exist in Dutch society are discussed in terms of ethnicity, citizenship, and national identity (Essed & Trienekens, 2008). Issues of difference increasingly have drawn attention in Europe because of changing demographics. Increasing ethnic diversity has occurred largely due to immigration and demographic, economic, and labor market trends. This has resulted in the increased demand for skilled foreigners in, for example, the health-care sector and the revival or intensification of temporary, or *guest worker*, migration schemes (Castles, 2006; Ruhs, 2006).

According to the International Labor Organization (ILO), Europe constitutes the region with the largest volume of migrant workers (27.5 million, or 34%), followed by Asia with 22.1 million (ILO, 2004, p. 7). In many countries in Western Europe, the preservation of national culture often becomes a powerful barrier to ethnic pluralism and inclusiveness. Exclusion and restriction of immigrant populations from North Africa, Turkey, or Slavic countries is practiced under the guise of *differentialism* (Winant, 2002). There is a body of research that strongly suggests that immigrants continue to face substantial barriers to full participation in mainstream societies (Takaki, 2008). Similar immigration issues have arisen in Australia, and race continues to cause major divisions in South African society despite the end of apartheid and a new democratic dispensation (Booysen, 2007).

In many countries in Europe, the discourse of difference generally rejects the concept of race as inappropriate for their societies. This is understandable, but what research suggests is that there are other *isms* and prejudices (e.g., Islamophobia) that nonnative members or immigrant minorities in those societies experience (Alba, 2005; Pettigrew & Meertens, 1995; Rustenbach, 2010). For example, in a large probability sample in 15 Western European countries, James and colleagues found that self-reported racism explained considerable variance in attitudes toward immigration, with dominant group members perceiving threats from immigration (James, Brown, Brown, & Marks, 2001).

Relevance of Race in the U.S. Context

In the United States, race continues to have political, economic, and social significance and remains consequential in terms of everyday experience (Goldberg, 2009). Yet scholars continue to debate whether the concept of race has any analytical value. Some have gone so far as to call for the abandonment of the term because its very use evokes essentialist meanings of race as innate and fixed (Gilroy, 2001). Others have argued that, to the extent people believe race is real and act upon it, it is important to study and examine the concept and how it influences and shapes social reality and experiences of difference (Alexander & Alleyne, 2002). Closely related to this problem of denial is that too many everyday people around the world, including the United States, believe racial, ethnic, and cultural differences are essential, fixed, and immutable. The phrases *they are not like us* or *people who do not look like us* remain a profound means for discrimination and exclusion in many parts of the world.

What is clear is that the effects of race on different groups have taken a different form today, which social psychologists label *aversive racism* or *modern racism* (Dovidio & Gaertner, 2000). According to proponents, racial discrimination has not disappeared but is being replaced by less overt and direct forms (Dovidio & Gaertner). This change largely is due to the belief, particularly in U.S. society, that we are in a postrace era. Sociologist Eduardo Bonilla-Silva (2006) delineated four dominant types of modern postrace ideology: (1) only minimal, if any, racial disparities still exist; (2) the few that exist are caused by cultural deficiencies in certain groups and not by structural constraints that unfairly impinge on different groups; (3) patterns of exclusions race or culture simply reflect the natural tendency of people to prefer to associate with similar others; and (4) meritocracy assures equality if individuals are willing to work hard and take advantage of opportunities. Thus, in the United States in particular, despite arguments and research evidence that racism and prejudice still continue the belief is that racism is no longer a problem but has been dealt with successfully. The notions of *race fatigue*, as well as what Picca and Feagin in their book *Two-Faced Racism* labeled *backstage racism,* might even be pointed to.

Conceptualization of Race in Organizational Studies

The study of race in organizations has had an interesting trajectory (Nkomo, 1992; Proudford & Nkomo, 2006). Race always has been present in organizations, even if not always formally studied (Nkomo, 2009). The earliest organized labor in the United States was African slaves, indentured servants, Native Americans, and convicts (Cooke, 2003; Gutman, 1977). In Europe, as a result of earlier colonization, immigrants from Africa, the West Indies, and India became part of the workforce of many European countries.

Yet the formal study of race in organizations emerged in the 1970s, largely as a result of the passage of landmark civil rights legislation in the United States that specified antidiscrimination regulations for employment practices in organizations and institutions (i.e., 1964 Civil Rights Act, Title VII). Legislation also came into law in certain parts of Europe somewhat later. The passage of Title VII in the United States spurred scholars to begin to explicitly study race in organizations. The research centered on two questions: Does racial discrimination exist, and, if it does exist, how can it be addressed (Nkomo, 1992, 2009)?

These questions resulted in numerous studies documenting discrimination and prejudice in selection, performance evaluation, promotion and compensation, and prescriptions for prejudice and discrimination reduction. In the area of selection, much of this work was confined to surfacing differences in workplace outcomes for Blacks and Whites (e.g., Brown & Ford, 1977; Newman & Krzystofiak, 1979; Tepstra & Larsen, 1985), as well as differential validity in employment tests and how to overcome the problems (e.g., Hunter, Schmidt, & Hunter, 1979). Other scholars focused on bias and discrimination in performance ratings and evaluation (e.g., Dipboye, 1985; Greenhaus, Parasuraman & Wormley, 1990; Roth, Huffcutt, & Bobko, 2003), and still others examined compensation practices (e.g., Dreher & Cox, 2000).

These types of studies dominated research on race in organizations throughout the 1970s, 1980s, and early 1990s. However, what was studied and who was studied has changed over time. For example, in response to Brief's (1998) call for research that examines the context of discrimination and how discrimination affects targets, a small but significant body of research can be found along these lines (e.g., Bell & Nkomo, 2001; Dietch, Barsky, Butz, Chan, Brief, & Bradely, 2003; Rosette, Leonardelli & Phillips, 2008; Thomas & Gabarro, 1999).

Dietch et al. (2003) demonstrated evidence of everyday workplace discrimination against Blacks, which was negatively associated with various indicators of well-being. In a four-experiment study, Rosette et al. (2008) found being White was perceived to be an attribute of the business leader prototype, where participants assumed that business leaders, more than nonleaders, were White. Moreover, leader categorization could best account for differences in White and non-White leader evaluations. From that literature, it can be seen that race shapes psychological experience and that racial identity is an important predictor of attitudes, beliefs, motivation, and performance (e.g., Richeson & Shelton, 2007).

Race, along with class and gender, continues to be central to economic and social inequality in the world. As Acker (2006) argued, these dimensions of difference produce and reproduce inequalities in the daily activities of work and the organization of work. She used the term *inequality regimes* to capture the notion that all organizations have loosely interrelated processes, practices, actions, and meanings that create and perpetuate systematic disparities among members in power and control over goals, resources, and outcomes. Thus, as Nkomo (1992) observed 2 decades ago, race is a necessary and productive analytical category for theorizing about organizations.

Studies also emerged that began to examine the experiences of other population groups in organizations beyond African Americans. Several studies can be found on Hispanics and Asians in the workplace (e.g., Prasad, 2001). From a theoretical perspective, much of the extant research on race in organizations primarily has relied on social identity theory and other cognitive theories of prejudice and discrimination, like modern racism and stereotype threat (Proudford & Nkomo, 2006; Steele, Spencer, & Aronson, 2002).

Currently, much of the research on race has been subsumed under the work on diversity in organizations (Proudford & Nkomo, 2006). This burgeoning body of work has focused on diversity management paradigms, effects of diversity on organizational performance, diversity in work teams and groups, and diversity training interventions (Nkomo & Stewart, 2006; Zanoni,

Janssens, Benschop, & Nkomo, 2010). More recently, critical treatments of diversity management discourse can be found in the extant literature.

Relationship Between Race and Organizational Politics

It is important to point out that scholarly writing about the influence of race on organizational politics is virtually nonexistent. In one of the few studies identified, Brouer, Duke, Treadway, and Ferris (2009) found political skill to be a significant moderator of the effect of race in the leader–subordinate relationship. Specifically, high political skill ameliorated the effects of racial dissimilarity in the quality of supervisor–subordinate relationships. Their research underscores the centrality of the idea of racial similarity emanating from research suggesting that people tend to interact with similar others in social interactions (Blau, 1977). At a minimum, this strongly suggests that those engaged in organizational politics are most likely to engage and share political information with similar others.

Brouer et al.'s (2009) research provides an excellent segue into interrogating race and organizational politics given the undertheorization of the topic. Thus, in this section, extant knowledge of the effects of race in organizations is drawn on to extend its possible significance in organizational politics. To the extent that race is not inside people or something people have but is indeed a result of perceptions distributed and institutionalized in the social context and used by people to guide their own behavior and make sense of the behavior of others, then clearly one cannot fully conceptualize organizational politics without attention to race (Markus, 2008, p. 659).

One of the consistent findings of the research on race in organizations is its impact on access to organizational networks (Bell & Nkomo, 2001; Ibarra, 1995; Thomas & Gabarro, 1999). Obtaining access to power holders and political information is important in terms of organizational politics. Research suggests that the extent to which members of nondominant racial groups have a token presence rather than a substantial representation in an organization tends to shape their social interaction experiences and access to important organizational networks. Specifically, racial minorities tend to experience exclusion from informal networks.

Bell and Nkomo (2001) found that the Black women in their study reported less access to informal networks compared with White men and women. As a result, they reported being cut off from important organizational information and felt less accepted as full members of their organizations. Likewise, Mehra, Kilduff, and Brass (1998) reported that the marginalization of racial minorities in friendship networks resulted both from exclusionary pressures and from minority individuals' own preference for same-race friends.

In her seminal study of race and social circles in managerial networks, Ibarra (1995) found that minority managers had more racially heterogeneous but fewer intimate network relationships. More importantly, and consistent with Brouer et al.'s (2009) findings, Ibarra reported that high-potential minorities had more contacts outside their own groups, suggesting the importance of having diverse networks. To the extent that access to mentors and sponsorships is facilitated by participation in informal networks, then the lack of access to such networks can be a barrier to advancement and other career outcomes (Bell & Nkomo, 2001). Further, it may be more challenging for racial minorities to "read" the culture of organizations, especially in terms of what Schein (1990) referred to as the deeply embedded assumptions and theories-in-use without participation in informal networks. Being able to correctly interpret these aspects of the organization's culture is important to being politically savvy.

Research also suggests that successful racial minorities may compensate for not having access to information networks by employing substitutes for gaining needed information. The influence tactics used by the Black women Bell and Nkomo (2001) studied included creating formal ways of acquiring informal information about the organization, although one has to note that Aquino and Bommer's (2003) research suggests that Blacks are less likely to benefit from exhibiting prosocial behaviors in the workplace.

Interestingly, Thau, Aquino, and Bommer (2008) found racial differences in organization citizenship behaviors (OCB) in light of supervisor mistreatment. The authors concluded that Black employees are less likely to retaliate against supervisory mistreatment than White employees and continue to engage in citizenship behaviors despite being recipients of noncontingent punishment. Again, though, it is not clear that such behavior benefits Black employees. The authors speculated that one possible explanation for the response of Black employees is their relative powerlessness and need to convey an outward image of commitment and cooperativeness so as not to be perceived negatively by their supervisors.

Organizational politics injects a type of ambiguity into performance and reward standards (Vigoda, 2002). In a large meta-analysis study using U.S. samples, McKay and McDaniel (2006) found larger racioethnic effects for subjective measures of performance. Wilson (2010) found that although supervisors provided overwhelmingly positive feedback in rating various racial groups they systematically assigned lower numerical ratings to Black staff relative to White staff, which they did not explain in their narrative summaries. Also, she found that supervisors emphasized social factors (i.e., interpersonal and social skills) more in their evaluations of the Asians and Blacks in the sample than she did for Whites. When these findings are considered through the lens of organizational politics, two possible dynamics may be relevant.

First, in an effort to mitigate the effects of stereotypes of Blacks as incompetent, Black employees in organizations may turn a blind eye to playing politics and instead aim to consistently exceed objective performance standards. Several research studies have supported this contention. Studies focusing on the organizational experiences of racial minorities have reported that participants believed that they had to exceed objective performance standards to be viewed as competent (Bell & Nkomo, 2001). Second, this may be futile behavior on the part of racioethnic minorities if indeed subjective factors are more salient in evaluations of their performance than are objective requirements. This almost would argue for racial minorities to engage in political behavior to "impression manage" their personas (Hewlin, 2003).

RACIALIZED ORGANIZATIONAL POLITICS PERCEPTIONS

ROPP are presented as a construct that brings to light the intersectionality of race and politics. ROPP are defined as the extent to which individuals believe their racial category or identity is influencing their social interactions and shared meanings within the organization as well as the opportunity to navigate the environment in a way that is favorable and of benefit to them and members of their racial category or identity. For example, how individuals perceive the environment is based on a set of histories, belief systems, and schemas (Goldstein & Chance, 1980). It is suggested that this process becomes very different when the environment is analyzed through a racial lens. The process is different when race is involved because race is one of the most salient, visible, and stigma-associated demographic categories in the workplace. In addition to this, race carries a social history that is different from many other identities. Also, this process is exacerbated by the disproportionate distribution of racial categories in the corporate/business context (http://www.workforce2020.polk.net).

Due to the fact that all organizational members belong to a racial identity group, all social interactions are embedded in the intergroup relations of the various racial groups. It is for this reason that the process of politics can be complicated by the tensions or harmonies between various racial groupings. For example, the politics of promotions is a daily issue in most organizations because individuals have expectations, organizations have agendas, resources have limitations, and status hierarchies exist to be maintained.

However, this political process can become racialized and can impact one's ROPP when issues of tokenism, racial discrimination, status characteristic expectations, and similarity–attraction biases become part of the process. It is at this point that you may hear involved organizational members make statements such as "She got the promotion because she is Asian," "I didn't get the promotion because I am African American," "I knew she wouldn't get that promotion because she is Hispanic," and "Our next hire needs to be Native American to meet our diversity program objectives." All of these statements, whether "real" or not, are examples of racialized organizational politics perceptions.

Individuals of all racial categories have ROPP. Frequently, issues of racial identity and categorization are confined to the *minority perspective*. This perspective suggests that race is salient and more "meaningful" to those in stigmatized and disenfranchised racial groups. It is suggested that race-based perceptions, especially ROPP, are experienced and internalized by all racial groups because all individuals have membership in a racial identity group. The variation in ROPP becomes relevant when an individual is in one of two categories: (1) stigmatized group versus non-stigmatized group; and (2) numerical minority versus numerical majority. Traditionally, racial minorities often are categorized as the stigmatized group and the numerical minority (DiTomaso, Post, & Parks-Yancy, 2007). However, in the context of ROPP, it is important to state that the proposed model does not make this claim. In certain organizations, it may be White employees who carry the stigma and who are in the numerical minority category. Therefore, it is important to be inclusive in this theorization.

A variety of theoretical paradigms contribute to the racialization of organizational politics: (1) social identity theory; (2) similarity–attraction paradigm;

and (3) contact hypothesis. The identity-oriented theories are frameworks that explain how various factors are related to cross-identity interactions. Social identity theory (Tajfel & Turner, 1986) and self-categorization theory (Turner, Hogg, Oakes, Reicher, & Wetherell, 1987) are theoretical paradigms that explain how individuals conceptualize, value, and categorize their membership in various identity groups. The frameworks suggest that individuals hold individual and collective concepts of self that are based on their identity categorizations and identification levels.

Ellemers, Spears, and Doosje (2002) stated that "there is a substantial body of research reporting on phenomena that illustrate the powerful impact of people's social identities on their perceptions, emotions, and behavior" (p.163). This confirms the notion that, with regard to racial identity and group membership, the way individuals perceive the organization and its processes are affected by their perspectives and identification levels with their racial groups. Research has shown that racial identification influences factors such as identity threat. The similarity–attraction paradigm (Byrne, 1971) suggests that individuals have higher levels of trust, comfort, and liking when the individual is demographically similar to them. This suggests that there is a psychological tendency for individuals to favor and prefer individuals who are racially similar. When this tendency is accounted for in the workplace, many political processes can become racialized, such as in the contexts of promotions, raises, and performance evaluations.

The contact hypothesis (Allport, 1954) is a framework suggesting that when two groups interact overtime then more accurate social information is acquired, which in turn decreases the stereotypes and bias that lead to noninteraction. Allport also suggested four criteria for effective intergroup contact: (1) equal status within the contact situation; (2) intergroup cooperation; (3) common goals; and (4) support of authorities, law, or custom (Dovidio, Gaertner, & Kawakami, 2003). These criteria suggest that organizations have to take a lot of conscious action to create an environment that fosters positive cross-race interactions. Many organizations, which do not effectively manage diversity, will have more racialized political issues in the workplace.

The theoretical framework that this model uses as the guiding perspective is the embedded group theory (Alderfer, 1987). This theory outlines the socially shared meanings about histories, contexts, environments, organizations, and identities and how they all come together to influence

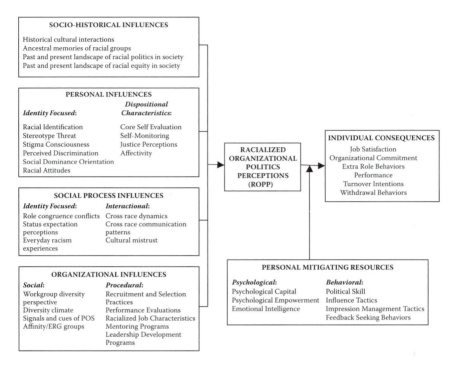

FIGURE 15.1
Theoretical framework of ROPP.

one's identity, which in turn influences one's emotions, attitudes, and behaviors. The socially shared meanings are products of intergroup relations, both sociologically and organizationally (Alderfer & Smith, 1982). Therefore, it is critical when trying to understand ROPP to detail all of the factors and influences that are intertwined and embedded within the larger societal, organizational, and individual contexts.

This chapter presents a model (Figure 15.1) of ROPP. In this model, a set of associated antecedents, outcomes, and moderating contingencies of ROPP are described. The model is aligned with the embedded group theory (Alderfer, 1987) in that the antecedents are categorized by multi-level categories spanning varying levels of proximity: sociohistorical influences; organizational influences; social process influences; and personal influences. This approach was taken because the discussion of race is embedded in an array of distal and proximal factors and influences.

The proposed model extends the work of Ferris, Adams, Kolodinsky, Hochwarter, and Ammeter (2002), who categorized the correlates of organizational politics perceptions as *influences*, and also offers and contributes race-relevant and identity-relevant factors to the organizational politics story. A set of personal mitigating resources also is proposed, which refer to resources that individuals can use to prevent ROPP from triggering and increasing the negative individual consequences.

SOCIOHISTORICAL INFLUENCES ON ROPP

The renowned sociologist W. E. B Du Bois (1903/1969, p. 54) identified race as one of the most significant problems in the twentieth century in this often cited quote: "The problem of the Twentieth Century is the problem of the color-line, the relation of the darker to the lighter races of men in Asia and Africa, America and the islands of the sea...." The race problem was one of the many exacerbated by the political, social, and industrial changes that took place in the early years of the twentieth century (Gutman, 1977; Nkomo, 2009; Takaki, 1979). Many different scholarly and nonscholary ideologies contributed to how societies came to understand and employ race.

As noted by many scholars, the so-called science of race met the politics of race over issues of slavery and colonization. For example, increasing colonization and subjugation of non-European people was justified by their racial inferiority. The practice of slavery in the Americas and other parts of the world was justified by the belief that Africans or Blacks were members of an inferior race (Loomba, 2005). In the United States, the conquest and removal of Native Americans from the lands they originally occupied was justified by race. In Europe, race was used by Adolf Hitler to propagate the idea of Aryan supremacy as justification for the genocide of Jewish people (Fluehr-Lobban, 2008). Thus, what became known as scientific racism rooted in a hierarchical racial classification system dominated understandings of race in society through the second half of the twentieth century.

Social Darwinism, embraced by the founders of sociology in the United States such as Herbert Spencer and William Graham Summer, was premised on the belief that non-White races did not evolve at the same rate as did the White race (McKee, 1993). These ideologies about race served as the underpinnings of racial segregation, racism, and discrimination that permeated U.S. society through the mid-twentieth century (Gossett, 1963). Even after the emancipation of slaves in the United States, ideas like eugenics and social Darwinism were used to exclude former slaves from basic rights like suffrage, equal education, and occupations.

Legal rulings like the infamous *Plessey vs. Ferguson* (1896) confirmed the legitimacy of the so called one-drop rule—that is, one drop of "Black" blood made a person Black and also enshrined the separate but equal doctrine of the legality of segregated facilities for Blacks and Whites. Racial discrimination and segregation remained a persistent feature of U.S. society until it was legally outlawed with the passage of the historic Civil Rights Act of 1964. The dark side of this was the brutality—often murder and lynching—toward Black men and women because of their race, especially in the South. Racial riots resulting in the death of Blacks and Whites were not uncommon during the early years of the twentieth century.

Yet, in understanding the contemporary political and social significance of race in the United States, it is important to also recognize how Whiteness enabled European immigrants, who often had been racially despised in their own nations (e.g., the Irish in the United Kingdom and the Jews in Eastern European), as well as poor indentured White servants to assimilate and benefit from being White (Ignatiev, 1996). This phenomenon has given birth to the *melting pot* description of U.S. society. Yet many scholars have pointed out that the legacy of slavery and the idea of White superiority have remained formidable obstacles to the attainment of equality for Black Americans.

Race still determines to a large degree who can melt or not melt into American society. Asian Americans are often touted as *model minorities*, and it has afforded them some semblance of assimilation, although they still experience degrees of exclusion and discrimination routed in stereotypes (Lin, Kwan, Cheung, & Fiske, 2005). Scholars of Whiteness point out how Whites continue to accrue overt and implicit benefits and privileges in U.S. society, although they may not always be cognizant of these privileges (Twine & Gallagher, 2008). The history of race and racism in the United States and the particular forms it has taken continue to reverberate in the current state of American race relations (Goldberg, 2009).

Race still matters and rears its significance politically, socially, and economically in the United States and other parts of the world, despite the current denial mantra that this country is experiencing a postrace era (Goldberg, 2009). The historic election of America's first Black president, Barack Obama, generated much talk about race (Feagin, 2010). Public discourse about his presidency paradoxically suggests evidence of a postrace

America as well as the continuing significance of aversive racism. Yet talking about or evoking race makes many Americans ambivalent about calling attention to racial differences, because it is at odds with long-standing democratic and liberal ideals like equality and equal opportunity for all (Markus, 2008; Mydral, 1994). All of the racial dynamics between various racial groupings offer support for how and why these occurrences would influence how individuals perceive race and, more specifically, the politics of race in organizations.

PERSONAL INFLUENCES ON ROPP

When making reference to the antecedents of ROPP, it is critical to acknowledge the attributes of the perceiver, which are referred to in the model as the personal influences on ROPP. When attempting to understand individuals' attitudes and subsequent behaviors, it is important to be aware of some of the individual factors that play a role. In this model, the personal influences are separated into two categories: (1) identity focused; and (2) dispositional characteristics.

Identity-Focused Personal Influences

The identity-focused factors are attitudes and perceptions held by individuals and based on membership in a specific racial identity group. Based on the fact that some individuals belong to identity groups that are stigmatized and that others belong to identity groups that are nonstigmatized and entitled (Nkomo, 1992), it is important to understand how these identity factors influence the ways people perceive the racialization of politics within organizations. In this section, the following identity-focused personal influences are discussed: racial identification, stereotype threat, stigma consciousness, perceived discrimination, racial attitudes, and social dominance orientation.

Racial identification reflects the level of attachment individuals have with their racial identity group. This attachment is based on affective, cognitive, and behavioral associations with the racial group (Phinney, 1992). The more individuals identify with their racial identity group, the more salient racialized organizational politics will be to them. Individuals who belong to and highly identify with the lower-status racial identity group in their work environment, such as African Americans and Hispanics, will be more likely to see the environment through a racialized lens. This salience will then bring to light and magnify their ROPP.

Racial identification is directly correlated with other personal influences, such as stereotype threat, stigma consciousness, and perceived discrimination. The logic is that individuals who identify more have a higher level of sensitivity to race-related issues, such as racialized organizational politics. For example, if a Black middle manager is the only person of his race at his organizational level and also highly identifies with his racial group, he will have a higher likelihood of seeing racialized politics as the reason for being passed over for a promotion.

Stereotype threat is defined as the perception individuals who belong to a stigmatized identity group have about confirming a negative stereotype that is attached to their identity group (Steele & Aronson, 1995). The stereotype threat framework suggests that when racial identity is made salient during an identity-relevant task anxiety levels increase and performance decreases. If consideration is given to navigating the political landscape of an organization as a dimension of performance, it is likely that individuals who have increased stereotype threat perceptions will perceive the organizational environment as more racialized (Aronson, Lustina, Good, Keough, Steele, & Brown, 1999, Davis, Aronson, & Salinas, 2006). This would especially be true if there are not many individuals of their racial group in the environment.

Stereotype threat also can influence status granted to racial identity groups, such as Whites. A stereotype attached to Whites is that of being racist (Roberson & Kulik, 2007). If White employees have stereotype threat perceptions of being seen as racist, they will be hypersensitive to how cross-race interactions and shared meanings play out in the organization. For example, if a White manager has a high level of stereotype threat related to being seen as racist, she may engage in overcompensating behaviors, such as inflation of performance evaluations of non-White employees or giving other subjective benefits to non-White employees and also is likely to perceive higher levels of ROPP.

Stigma consciousness also is a factor that is aligned with sensitivity to being judged and evaluated based on stigmas and stereotypes (Link & Phelan, 2001; Pinel, 1999). Individuals high on stigma consciousness have a hyperawareness to how they are being perceived and treated based on their stigmatized identity, which is race in this context (Brown & Pinel, 2003; McKown & Weinstein, 2003). If individuals are high on stigma consciousness, they will perceive higher levels of ROPP, whether it is Black or Hispanic employees who are conscious of being perceived as incompetent and unintelligent or White employees who are conscious of being perceived as racist. Similarly, perceived discrimination, which is the extent to which individuals perceive they are being discriminated against, also can influence the manner in which one perceives the racialization of the organization's political landscape. If individuals of low or high racial status perceive they are being discriminated against based on their racial group, they subsequently will perceive higher levels of ROPP.

Although personal influences that are connected to how individuals feel their racial identity is being perceived and treated have been discussed, it is also important to examine factors that explain individuals' general perspectives and orientations related to race, status, power, and social hierarchy. Racial attitude is defined as an individual's favorable or unfavorable attitude (implicit or explicit) and orientation toward other races. When individuals have favorable attitudes toward another race, the favorable attitude transfers to individuals within that racial group. For example, Buttner, Lowe, and Billings-Harris (2007) found that White leaders who had positive racial attitudes toward minorities made more positive attributions about their Black employees' experiences. Negative racial attitudes also influence racial discrimination (Ziegert & Hanges, 2005), which also would have an impact on ROPP.

Another attitudinal orientation that is relevant to the conversation is social dominance orientation (SDO), which is "the extent to which one desires that one's in-group dominate and be superior to outgroups" (Pratto, Sidanius, Stallworth, & Malle, 1994, p. 742). SDO is aligned with individuals' perception of how identity groups, in this case racial groups, should be socially ordered on a continuum of superiority–inferiority. For example, if White employees have a high level of SDO, they will perceive the advancement, promotion, or hiring of Black employees as actions that are inconsistent with their social hierarchical schemas. This would lead high SDO individuals to also have higher levels of ROPP. In this example, if resources and opportunities were given to Blacks, the high SDO individuals would perceive that these actions are hindering their ability and their race's (Whites) ability to benefit from and acquire resources, which is an example of a racialized organizational politics perception.

Dispositional Characteristic Personal Influences

The dispositional factors relevant to the ROPP model are individual differences that are aligned with how aware individuals are of themselves (core self-evaluation), their environment (self-monitoring), others (justice perceptions), and their emotions (affectivity). Individuals differences aligned with awareness are likely to influence the way individuals would perceive organizational politics in a racialized manner. Individuals that are high on the dispositional factors are more likely to internalize social cues and to make more confident and unbiased attributions and evaluations of the political environment.

Judge, Locke, and Durham (1997) established the construct of core self-evaluation (CSE), which is a multidimensional concept that captures four dispositional dimensions: self-esteem; generalized self-efficacy; locus of control; and emotional stability. These dimensions speak to how much individuals feel positive about themselves, feel confident about their abilities, feel as though they have control over things that occur, and have the ability to handle the demands of various stressors. If individuals high on CSE are less likely to attribute their experiences in the organization to their collective racial identity group and attribute more to themselves, this would lead to less of an identity bias and more accurate evaluations about their navigation through the political landscape.

Individuals high on self-monitoring "are thought to regulate their expressive self-presentation for the sake of desired public appearances, and thus be highly responsive to social and interpersonal cues of situationally appropriate performances" (Snyder & Gangestad, 1986, p. 125). Individuals who possess an increased ability to monitor social cues and to adapt their behaviors will more than likely to have a heightened awareness of racialized organizational politics than individuals who have a low ability to observe because high self-monitors are constantly scanning their environment. Therefore, such high self-monitors have more social cue "data points" to make their analysis, which could lead to a more accurate assessment of the organization's political environment.

Equity theory (Adams, 1965) suggests that individuals cognitively assess a ratio of inputs to outcomes, which is then compared with other individuals' input–outcome ratios. If the ratios are perceived as being unjust, then the individual has decreased perceptions of justice and fairness. Colquitt, Conlon, Wesson, Porter, and Ng (2001) discussed the various dimensions of justice perceptions in which individuals engage (i.e., interpersonal, informational, distributive, and procedural). These perceptions relate to the degree of fairness individuals perceive in the quality of interpersonal relationships, the fairness of how information is processed, and how resources are distributed. Individuals reflecting high levels of justice perceptions will be less likely to make an attribution of race to the organizational politics in the organization. A contingency factor that could influence this relationship is the perception of the diversity climate. If the diversity climate is positive and inclusive, there is a higher likelihood that even racialized organizational politics will be perceived as more just and fair, even if race is a factor.

Affectivity, which can be conceptualized at the trait and state level, is a construct that reflects persistent differences in emotionality and self-concept, either positively or negatively; Watson & Clark, 1984), and influences a host of attitudes and behaviors (Cropanzano, Weiss, Hale, & Reb, 2003). Typically, positive affectivity is directly correlated with positive and engaging attitudes and behaviors, whereas negative affectivity is directly correlated with negative and disengaging attitudes. Therefore, it is argued that individuals with positive affectivity will view the racialized organizational politics from a more positive and functional perspective, whereas those high in negative affectivity will view racialized organizational politics from a more negative and dysfunctional perspective. Even if one individual high in positive affectivity and one individual high in negative affectivity each perceives equal levels of ROPP, the tone in which they internalize and evaluate it can differ.

SOCIAL PROCESS INFLUENCES ON ROPP

As previously discussed, the theoretical perspective that supports this model is the embedded group theory (Alderfer, 1987), which suggests that the shared meanings about histories, environments, organizations, and identities all come together to influence one's identity, cross-identity interactions, attitudes, and behaviors. Although the sociohistorical and personal influences that impact one's racialized organizational politics perceptions have been discussed, it is important to explore the social interactions and processes that occur in the workplace that also can influence how individuals perceive the racialization of organizational politics in their work environment. In the following pages, two types of social processes are discussed: (1) identity focused; and (2) interactional.

Identity-Focused Social Process Influences

When exploring how individuals perceive their environments relative to their identities, it is essential to explore some of the social processes that occur within organizations. Three identity-focused social processes are discussed: (1) role congruence conflicts; (2) status expectations perceptions; and (3) everyday racism experiences. Role congruence conflicts occur as a result of individuals carrying schemas that support social roles and stratification. Much of the research in this area has focused on the identity group of gender. Eagly (1987) presented a model of social role theory of sex differences and similarities. In 2002, Eagly and Karau then extended this model into the context of leadership roles. They proposed that, based on social schemas, women are expected to be in certain roles and men are expected to be in certain roles. When a woman is in a role that is incongruent with individuals' expectations, she is likely to be perceived less favorably.

This framework can be extended into social schemas of racial roles. Based on the race-related sociohistorical context of the United States, there are expectations of certain races occupying certain roles. Specifically, Blacks primarily were either slaves or low-income, blue-collar workers, until the civil rights movement allowed access to the educational and professional opportunities. Therefore, if individuals have perceptions that Blacks should not be in certain roles of authority, status, or control, then their perceptions of the racialization of politics in the workplace will be influenced. Also, if a large proportion of individuals perceive racial role incongruence, this will impact the interpersonal and work-related interactions of cross-race interactions in that organization.

This logic also is associated with the theory of status characteristics and expectation states (Berger & Conner, 1969), which proposes that a number of members of a group are treated in an unequal manner based on the unequal expectations of performance that others hold of them (Driskell & Mullen, 1990). These status expectation differentials can be based on a variety of characteristics, such as gender, age, and educational background. "Status characteristics serve as cues to performance capability because they are culturally evaluated (e.g., it is considered preferable in our culture to be White, male, and professional) and carry performance connotations (e.g., Whites, males, and professionals are thought to do better at most tasks)" (Driskell & Mullen, p. 542). If organizations have a prevalence of this type of attitude and behavior, there will be increased levels of racialized organizational politics perceptions.

The everyday experiences of racism that exist within organizations represent a less complex but more toxic social process that can influence ROPP. Although racism often is discussed in the context of extreme cases, there has been recent work on *everyday racism,* which is "characterized by routine encounters with another's prejudice (negative affect and beliefs based upon racial group membership) and discriminatory behavior (differential treatment based upon racial group membership) that pervade people's daily social interactions" (Swim, Hyers, Cohen, Fitzgerald, & Bylsma, 2003, p. 40). This research focuses on the target's perceptions of what is experienced (Dietch et al., 2003). Examples of everyday racism include hostile glares, prejudiced verbal expressions, poor service, and awkward conversations based on race. When these types of encounters become a major part of the experience of being in certain organizations, target individuals will perceive increased racialized organizational politics perceptions.

Interactional Social Process Influences

When discussing social processes and interactions, the impact of within-race and cross-race dynamics and their influence on ROPP must be discussed. Social identity theory (Tajfel & Turner, 1986) suggests that individuals group and categorize themselves based on group membership. The similarity–attraction paradigm (Byrne, 1971) suggests that individuals like, trust, and feel more comfortable with people who are similar to them. These two aforementioned psychological tendencies provide for a context of difference and segregation. In the organizational context, it can be called *organizational tribalism,* which is when individuals, based on racial grouping, choose to engage, socialize, communicate, and fellowship only with racially similar individuals. If organizations suffer from this condition, the *us versus them* mentality will escalate individuals' perceptions of how race is impacting the organizational politics.

Combs and Griffith (2007) presented a model of interracial communication and interaction in organizations. They suggested that if individuals can increase their cross-race interpersonal efficacy, then a host of positive diversity outcomes will emerge, such as cooperation, respect, and less prejudice. However, to increase cross-race interpersonal efficacy, certain organizational conditions must be met, such as avoidance of intergroup competition and institutional and managerial support. Also, individual conditions that have to be addressed include equal status, voluntary contact, proximity to racially different others, and availability. This model presents a useful framework for understanding the conditions that influence effective and functional cross-race interpersonal communications, which is critical to minimizing racialized organizational politics.

Trust is defined as "a psychological state comprising the intention to accept vulnerability based upon expectations of the intentions or behavior of another" (Rousseau, Sitkin, Burt, & Camerer, 1998, p. 395), and it is critical to positive interpersonal and social interactions. For individuals to fully accept vulnerability, trust barriers must be minimized. Basically, trusting racially dissimilar others runs counter to human psychological tendencies. So the question then becomes how can trust be fostered between various racial groups? This question cannot be answered until the concept of cultural mistrust is explored.

Most of the research in the area of cultural mistrust is in the domains of health care and mental health-care research. This work explores the role of cultural mistrust in the relationship between patients and providers. This construct is a great interdisciplinary opportunity to explore the intersection of race and trust, given the positive social power of trust in organizations.

The logic is the same when there is a history of cultural mistrust (e.g., between Blacks and Whites, Hispanics and Whites, and Native Americans and Whites) and an *ancestral memory* is transferred down. For example, Black persons who have heard from grandparents and parents "not to trust White folks" is going to subconsciously internalize this level of cultural mistrust without realizing that the attribution of mistrust toward Whites (albeit a salient context for their grandparent or parent who lived in the Jim Crow era) may not be as intense in today's context. Therefore, this notion of mistrusting collective identity groups can interfere with the interpersonal "human-to-human" trust that is essential to effective and functional interactions in the workplace, such as self-disclosure and transparency (Poston, Craine, & Atkinson, 1991). If an organization is plagued with issues of general mistrust and cultural mistrust, the perceptions of racialized organizational politics will be intensified for members of all racial groups.

ORGANIZATIONAL INFLUENCES ON ROPP

Throughout this interdisciplinary model of embedded influences on ROPP, various levels of influence from individuals to groups have been discussed, and now the causal antecedents of ROPP are further explored by discussing two types of organizational influences: (1) social and (2) procedural. Most of the dialogue in this framework to this point has focused on the experiences of racial identity groups, but now we examine the contextual factors that are created, controlled, or communicated by the organization and its leadership.

Social Organizational Influences

When discussing the social context of an organization, especially when associated with identity and identity groups such as race, it is imperative that the structure, culture, and climate of support and inclusion are examined. When exploring how an environment influences identity groups, specifically race, the first step is to understand the structural composition by identity group, which is described as organizational demography (Pfeffer, 1983). There are various consequences to different demographic distributions (Carroll & Harrison, 1998). Tsui and Gutek's (1999) introduction of the importance of demographic distributions in organizations spurred researchers to study race as an important demographic variable in organizations and to use an intersectional framework recognizing simultaneous demographic variables and their effects on individuals, groups, and organizations (Riordan, 2000; Tsui, Egan, & Xin, 1995).

It is suggested here that the racial composition of an organization serves as a communication tool transmitting information about what is valued, who is valued, and the opportunities allowed for some and for all. It communicates the social stratification cues that can serve as an empowering tool for those in a well-represented racial group but as a source of threat for a person who belongs to a racial group that is underrepresented. If an organization is not aware of the representation of racial groups—at all levels of the organization—the perceptions of how racialized the environment and politics are will be magnified.

Another concept that gives more insight into the effects of demographic compositions on teams, groups, and organizations is the fault-line hypothesis. Lau and Murnighan (1998) posited that in most groups an "invisible" division line exists based on separating two or more subgroups that are homogenous, or based on a psychological or demographic attribute. The hypothesis suggests that these subgroup divisions can create division within the group, given a condition that makes the fault line salient. Typically, conflict or another type of issue brings the fault line to light. An event can occur in society, such as the election of Barack Obama as president of the United States, to make race salient. The day after the election, the fault line of race or political affiliation could emerge in an organization. It is critical for organizations to be aware of and manage the potential fault lines to decrease ROPP.

The climate and culture of support also influences individuals' ROPP. For example, the diversity perspective of a work group and the organization can serve as a proxy for the value and emphasis that the organization puts toward inclusionary multiculturalism. Ely and Thomas (2001) offered a fascinating framework conceptualizing various types of diversity perspectives that are characterized by a work group's rationale for diversifying, such as the value given to cultural identity, the connection between cultural diversity and work, and the indicators of progress.

The optimal perspective presented in the Ely and Thomas (2001) framework is the integration and learning perspective in which a work group or organization diversifies with the intent to enhance core work processes while valuing racial identity as a resource for learning, change, and renewal. In an environment like this, a person who is a member of the lower-status, stigmatized, or underrepresented group will perceive less racialization of organizational politics based on the cues sent from the team or organization.

Additionally, diversity climates impact not only individuals but also organizational processes. In Cox's (1994) interactional model of cultural diversity, he explicated the idea that diversity climate facilitates positive employee attitudes and achievement outcomes. This suggests that diversity climate can demonstrate a positive impact on how members of various racial groups feel about themselves and their contributions, which implies that the environment is not highly political in a racialized fashion.

Two other influences can signal support and mitigate the increase in racialized organizational politics perceptions: employee resource groups and perceived organizational support. Employee resource groups, also called affinity groups, are extrarole groups that meet often, are self-managing creators of their own missions and domains, and are organized by similar demographic associations such as race (Van Aken, Monetta, & Sink, 1994). These groups organize as a means of facilitating employee involvement while also allowing for individuals of various identity groups to build a community in an organization where they are numerical or status minorities. If organizations are committed to lending resources to these groups, it can communicate a message of "we value you."

Similarly, perceived organizational support is conceptualized as the exchanges between the organization and employees (Eisenberger, Huntington, Hutchison, & Sowa, 1986). Eisenberger et al (1986) proposed that "employees develop global beliefs concerning the extent to which the organization values their contributions and cares about their well-being" (p. 501). Therefore, if individuals perceive higher levels of perceived organizational support, they are likely to perceive less racialized organizational politics perceptions because they will develop more belief in the organization, which also makes them more committed to the organization.

Procedural Organizational Influences

Organizations are not inanimate entities that exist simply as aggregates of individuals. Organizations become decision-making, dynamic, and live entities when they come to the implementation of processes and procedures. The way organizations manage their processes, procedures, and systems also sends signals to employees about what the organizations stand for or represent. The first process that employees see and experience is the employee recruitment and selection process. Organizations must be aware of how they manage this process, because who gets recruited, interviewed, and hired sends a message to other employees and to outside stakeholders of the organization.

For example, if an organization doesn't recruit from historically Black colleges and universities or from predominately Hispanic institutions, it can send a message that it doesn't value racial diversity. Similarly, if an organization doesn't hire any of the African American and Hispanic employees they interview, other employees can start to question the organization's diversity intentions. Although recruitment and selection processes implicitly communicate organizational values, organizations also can use recruitment tools to indicate to internal and external stakeholders the importance of racial diversity to the organization at all position levels

(Avery, 2003). Actions that don't communicate the value of racial diversity or racial minorities in the workplace are positively associated with ROPP.

Performance evaluations also can be construed as a systematic message conveyer. Roberson, Galvin, and Charles (2007) discussed the issues related to how group identities (e.g., race) influence bias in performance evaluation and appraisal systems. The general consensus on the relationship between bias and evaluations is that individuals rate racially dissimilar persons more negatively, even after controlling for a number of factors. While theories such as the similarity–attraction paradigm can explain the psychological tendency, systematic and institutional biases may be present (e.g., having racialized jobs and a lack of diversity in the managerial ranks). When members of the underrepresented, low-status, or numerical minority racial groups begin to notice trends in biased evaluations, it increases their perceptions that the systems and processes are racialized, which in turn increases ROPP.

The last two procedural organizational influences that are discussed are programs both related to talent retention and development: mentoring programs and leadership development programs. These are programs that signal support, value, investment, and confidence in the abilities of employees. Although these programs are of benefit to all employees, research has shown that these programs serve as a specific resource for racial minorities in the workplace (Blake-Beard, Murrell, & Thomas, 2007). Given the barriers to success that racial minorities may encounter in organizations, these programs step in and give them the tools, relationships, and networks that can assist in their successful navigation through organizations. If organizations have effective mentoring and leadership development programs, they have the potential to decrease the perceptions of a racialized political environment.

PERSONAL MITIGATING RESOURCES FOR ROPP

In this framework, it is proposed that when individuals—both of racial minority and nonracial minority status—perceive high levels of ROPP, there will be an impact on a host of traditional organizational science attitudes and behaviors. Specifically, it is argued that ROPP are negatively associated with positive outcomes such as job satisfaction, organizational commitment, extrarole behaviors, and performance. On the other hand, ROPP are positively associated with outcomes, such as turnover intentions, withdrawal behaviors, and job stress.

These relationships clearly imply that racialized organizational politics perceptions are negative for individuals. The logic for the relationships is aligned with that of the stereotype threat framework. If individuals concern themselves with how their race and the race of others influences their organizational experiences, navigation, and social sensemaking, this focus will initiate stress and consume cognitive resources that could be directed toward positive work-related attitudes and behaviors. However, the realistic perspective is that race and politics intersect and that individuals have a sensory, emotional, and cognitive awareness of when "the elephant is in the room." If individuals have to acknowledge the elephant, it is best to discuss the types of psychological and behavioral resources that can mitigate the negative pathways that follow ROPP.

Psychological Mitigating Resources

Psychological safety is a resource that allows individuals to handle negative experiences and stressors. In a stressful situation, such as perceiving high levels of ROPP, individuals can tap into a set of resources that offer characteristics such as empowerment, awareness of self, positive cognition building, confidence, and awareness of others and the environment. Psychological capital (Psycap) and psychological empowerment (Spreitzer, 1995) both are multidimensional constructs that have been shown to motivate effort, satisfaction, and performance.

Psycap is defined as "one's positive appraisal of circumstances and probability for success based on motivated effort and performance" (Luthans, Avolio, Avey, & Norman, 2007, p. 550). With Psycap, individuals have the capacity to appraise the negative and potentially toxic context of racialized organizational politics in a positive light, through the use of self-efficacy, hope, optimism, and resilience. Similarly, psychological empowerment increases intrinsic task motivation through the cognitions of meaning, competence, self-determination, and impact. This would allow individuals to focus more on not letting their ROPP negatively affect their performance.

Emotional intelligence is another multidimensional construct that assists high ROPP individuals with engaging in acts such as extrarole behaviors and avoiding behaviors such as withdrawal. Through the use of self-awareness, self-regulation, self-motivation, social awareness, and empathy, individuals holding a negative view of the racialized political landscape of the work environment can mitigate the negative effects of ROPP.

Behavioral Mitigating Resources

All of the behaviors proposed as resources in this framework allow for individuals perceiving high levels of ROPP to relate more positively with others, to build more effective relationships, to manage their impressions, and to behaviorally cope with any stressors that stem from the racialized political environment. Through the use of political skill, individuals possess the ability to better comprehend the environment and other organizational members. Also, political skill can be used to influence others to maximize the achievement of one's personal and organizational goals (Ferris, Davidson, & Perrewé, 2005; Ferris, Treadway, et al., 2005).

Similarly, political skill combined with influence tactics can function as a strategy to execute and influence without being perceived as negative or manipulative, as reported by Treadway, Ferris, Duke, Adams, and Thatcher (2007). Impression management tactics also have an ability to override other characteristics or biases that influence how individuals are perceived you (Gilmore & Ferris, 1989). The ways individuals present themselves and their various identities can assist in navigation through the political landscape of organizations. "Once motivated, individuals must enact their personal and social identities in order to create their desired professional images" (Roberts, 2005, p. 693). In her model of professional image construction, Roberts also suggested that effective impression management tactics have many benefits, such as increases in well-being, task engagement, and high-quality relationships.

Another resource for handling the racialized political landscape of organizations is to engage in feedback-seeking behaviors. Feedback seeking is the act of deliberately and consciously seeking feedback from supervisors, peers, or the environment to gain accurate information that assists in both personal and professional goal attainment (Ashford & Cummings, 1983). The benefits that derive from feedback-seeking behaviors, such as higher performance and more positive evaluations (Ashford & Tsui 1991; Tsui, Ashford, St. Clair, & Xin, 1995), also can mitigate the potentially negative effects of ROPP.

CONCLUDING REMARKS

As previously detailed, ROPP are defined as the extent to which individuals believe their racial category or identity is influencing their social interactions and shared meanings within the organization as well as the opportunity to navigate the environment in a way that is favorable and of benefit to them and members of their racial category or identity. The framework presented in this chapter allows for an interdisciplinary approach to understanding how race and politics intersect in the organizational context. A host of causal influences were discussed, which are embedded in multiple levels of analysis and impact, from sociohistorical perspectives to personality characteristics. This chapter also delineates the difference between general perceptions of organizational politics and the nuanced implications of organizational politics when it becomes racialized.

Hopefully, scholars can use this framework as a springboard into a whole new world of racial dynamics in the workplace, the theories that reflect identity interactions, and the individual differences that may explain many of the racial differences and racial effects that are found in the literature. This chapter not only contributes to the nomological network of politics in organizations but also takes a deep look into why race is a central construct and extremely relevant to understanding the organizational landscape and the world as well. From a practical perspective, this chapter can be used by practitioners to understand how to manage the racial dynamics of the workplace from multiple levels and perspectives.

The proposed framework also can offer coaching to organizational members who do not understand how their identities, characteristics, personalities, and experiences may influence their perceptions of the workplace. Additionally, through the lens of the mitigating resources, individuals can develop and use the cognitive and behavioral resources that this framework presents. Finally, this chapter serves as one response to Nkomo's (1992) appeal, 2 decades ago, for research that develops a more informed understanding of the nature of race in organizations.

REFERENCES

Acker, J. (2006). Inequality regimes: Gender, class and race in organizations. *Gender and Society, 20*(4), 441–464.

Adams, J.S. (1965). Inequity in social exchange. In L. Berkowitz (Ed.), *Advances in experimental social psychology* (Vol. 2, pp. 267–299). New York: Academic Press.

Alba, R. (2005). Bright vs. blurred boundaries: Second generation assimilation and exclusion in France, Germany and the United States. *Ethnic and Racial Studies, 28,* 20–49.

Alderfer, C.P. (1987). An inter-group perspective on group dynamics. In J. Lorsch (Ed.), *Handbook of organizational behavior* (pp. 190–222). Englewood Cliffs, NJ: Prentice-Hall.

Alderfer, C.P., & Smith, K.K. (1982). Studying intergroup relations: Embedded in organizations. *Administrative Science Quarterly, 27,* 35–65.

Alexander, C., & Alleyne, B. (2002). Framing the difference: Racial and ethnic studies in twenty-first century Britain. *Ethnic and Racial Studies, 25(4),* 541–551.

Allport, G.W. (1954). *The nature of prejudice.* Cambridge, MA: Addison-Wesley.

Aquino, K., & Bommer, W.H. (2003). Preferential mistreatment: How victim status moderates the relationship between organizational citizenship behavior and workplace victimization. *Organizational Science, 14*(4), 374–385.

Aronson, J., Lustina, M. J., Good, C., Keough, K., Steele, C. M., & Brown, J. (1999). When White men can't do math: Necessary and sufficient factors in stereotype threat. *Journal of Experimental Social Psychology, 35,* 29–46.

Ashford, S.J., & Cummings, L.L. (1983). Feedback as an individual resource: Personal strategies of creating information. *Organizational Behavior and Human Performance, 32,* 370–398.

Ashford, S.J., & Cummings, L.L. (1985). Proactive feedback seeking: The instrumental use of the information environment. *Journal of Occupational Psychology, 58,* 67–79.

Ashford, S.J., & Tsui, A.S. (1991). Self-regulation for managerial effectiveness: The role of active feedback seeking. *Academy of Management Journal, 34,* 251–280.

Avery, D.R. (2003). Reactions to diversity in recruitment advertising: Are differences black and white? *Journal of Applied Psychology, 58,* 672–679.

Banton, M. (1998). *Racial theories.* Cambridge: Cambridge University Press.

Bell, E.L.J., & Nkomo, S. M. (2001). *Our separate ways: Black and White women and the struggle for professional identity.* Boston, MA: Harvard Business School Press.

Berger, J., & Conner, T.L. (1969). Performance expectations and behavior in small groups. *Acta Sociologica, 12*(4), 186–198.

Blake-Beard, S., Murrell, A.J., & Thomas, D.A. (2007). Unfinished business: The impact of race on understanding mentoring relationships. In B. Rose-Ragins & K. Kram (Eds.), *Handbook on mentoring* (pp. 223–247). Thousand Oaks, CA: Sage Publications.

Blau, P.M. (1977). *Inequality and Heterogeneity.* New York: Free Press.

Bonilla-Silva, E. (2006). *Racism without racist: Color-blind racism and the persistence of racial inequality in the United States.* Lanham, MD: Rowman and Littlefield.

Booysen, L. (2007). Societal power shifts and changing social identities in South Africa: Workplace implications. *Southern African Journal of Economic and Management Sciences 10*(1), 1–20.

Brief, A.P. (1998). *Attitudes in and around organizations.* Thousand Oaks, CA: Sage Publications.

Brief, A.P., Dietch, E.A., Cohen, R.R., Pugh, S.D., & Vaslow, J.B. (2000). Just doing business: Modern racism and obedience to authority as explanations for employment discrimination. *Organization Behavior and Human Decision Processes, 81,* 72–97.

Brouer, R.L., Duke, A., Treadway, D.C., & Ferris, G.R. (2009). The moderating effect of political skill on the demographic dissimilarity-leader-member exchange quality relationship. *Leadership Quarterly, 20,* 61–69.

Brown, H.A., & Ford, D.L. (1977). An exploratory analysis of discrimination in the employment of Black MBA graduates. *Journal of Applied Psychology, 62,* 50–56.

Brown, R.P., & Pinel, E.C. (2003). Stigma on my mind: Individual differences in the experience of stereotype threat. *Journal of Experimental Social Psychology, 39,* 626–633.

Buttner, E.H., Lowe, K.B., & Billings-Harris, L. (2007). Impact of leader racial attitude on ratings of causes and solutions for an employee of color shortage. *Journal of Business Ethics, 73,* 129–144.

Byrne, D. (1971). *The attraction paradigm.* New York: Academic Press.

Carroll, G.R., & Harrison, J.R. (1998). Organizational demography and culture: Insights from a formal model. *Administrative Science Quarterly 43,* 637–667.

Castles, S. (2006). Guestworkers in Europe: A resurrection? *International Migration Review, 40*(4), 741–766.

Colquitt, J.A., Conlon, D.E., Wesson, M.J., Porter, C., & Ng, K.Y. (2001). Justice at the Millenium: A meta-analytic review of 25 years of organizational justice research. *Journal of Applied Psychology, 86,* 425–445.

Combs, G., & Griffith, J. (2007). An examination of inter-racial contact: The influence of cross-race interpersonal efficacy and affect regulation. *Human Resource Development Review, 6,* 222–244.

Cooke, B. (2003). The denial of slavery in management studies. *Journal of Management Studies, 40*(1), 895–918.

Cox, T.H. (1994). A comment on the language of diversity. *Organization, 1*(1), 51–58.

Cropanzano, R., Weiss, H.M., Hale, J.M.S., & Reb, J. (2003). The structure of affect: Reconsidering the relationship between negative and positive affectivity. *Journal of Management, 29*(6), 831–857.

Davis III, C., Aronson, J., & Salinas, M. (2006). Shades of threat: Black racial identity as a moderator of stereotype threat. *Journal of Black Psychology, 32,* 399–417.

Dietch, E.A., Barsky, A., Butz, R.M., Chan, S., Brief, A.P., & Bradley, J.C. (2003). Subtle yet significant: The existence and impact of everyday racial discrimination in the workplace. *Human Relations, 56,* 1299–1324.

Dipboye, R.L. (1985). Some neglected variables in research on discrimination in appraisals. *Academy of Management Review, 10,* 116–127.

Dipboye, R.L., & Halverson, S.K. (2004). Subtle (and not so subtle) discrimination in organizations. In R.W. Griffin & A.M. O'Leary (Eds), *The dark side of organizational behavior* (pp. 131–158). San Francisco: Jossey-Bass.

DiTomaso, N., Post, C., & Parks-Yancy, R. (2007). Workforce diversity and inequality: Power, status, and numbers. *Annual Review of Sociology, 3,* 473–501.

Dovidio, J.F., & Gaertner, S.L. (2000). Aversive racism in selection decisions: 1989 and 1999. *Psychological Science, 11,* 315–319.

Dovidio, J.F., Gaertner, S.L., & Kawakami, K. (2003). The contact hypothesis: The past, the present, and the future. *Group Processes and Intergroup Relations, 6*(1), 5–21.

Dovidio, J.F., Gaertner, S.L., Kawakami, K., & Hodson, G. (2002). Why can't we just get along? Interpersonal biases and interracial distrust. *Cultural Diversity & Ethnic Minority Psychology, 8,* 88–102.

Dreher, G.F., & Cox, T.H. (2000). Labor market mobility and cash compensation: The moderating effects of race and gender. *Academy of Management Journal, 43,* 890–901.

Driskell, J.E., & Mullen, B. (1990). Status, expectations, and behavior: A meta-analytic review and test of the theory. *Personality and Social Psychology Bulletin, 16,* 541–553.

Du Bois, W.E.B. (1903/1969). *The souls of Black folk*. New York: Signet Classic.

Eagly, A.H. (1987). *Sex differences in social behavior: A social-role interpretation*. Hillsdale, NJ: Lawrence Erlbaum.

Eagly, A. H., & Karau, S. J. (2002). Role congruity theory of prejudice toward female leaders. *Psychological Review, 109,* 573–598.

Eisenberger, R., Huntington, R., Hutchison, S., & Sowa, D. (1986). Perceived organizational support. *Journal of Applied Psychology, 71,* 500–507.

Ellemers, N., Spears, R., & Doosje, B. (2002). Self and social identity. *Annual Review of Psychology, 53,* 161–186.

Ely, R.J., & Thomas, D.A. (2001). Cultural diversity at work: The moderating effects of work group perspectives on diversity. *Administrative Science Quarterly, 46,* 229–273.

Essed, P., & Trienekens, S. (2008). Who wants to feel White? Race, Dutch culture, and contested identities. *Ethnic and Racial Studies*, 31(1), 52–72.

Feagin, J.R. (2010). *The White racial frame: Centuries of racial framing and counter-framing*. New York: Routledge.

Ferris, G.R., Adams, G., Kolodinsky, R.W., Hochwarter, W.A., & Ammeter, A.P. (2002). Perceptions of organizational politics: Theory and research directions. In F. Yammarino & F. Dansereau (Eds.), *Research in multi-level issues, Volume 1: The many faces of multi-level issues* (pp. 179–254). Oxford, UK: JAI Press/Elsevier Science.

Ferris, G.R., Davidson, S.L., & Perrewé, P. L. (2005). *Political skill at work: Impact on work effectiveness*. Mountain View, CA: Davies-Black Publishing.

Ferris, G.R., Treadway, D.C., Kolodinsky, R.W., Hochwarter, W.A., Kacmar, C.J., Douglas, C., et al. (2005). Development and validation of the political skill inventory. *Journal of Management, 31,* 126–152.

Fluehr-Lobban, C. (2008). *Race and racism: An introduction*. Oxford: AltaMira Press.

Gilmore, D.C., & Ferris, G.R. (1989). The effects of applicant impression management tactics on interviewer judgments. *Journal of Management, 15,* 557–564.

Gilroy, P. (2001). *Against race: Imagining political culture beyond the color line*. Cambridge, MA: Harvard University Press.

Goldberg, D.T. (2009). *The threat of race: Reflections on racial neo-liberalism*. Malden, MA: Wiley-Blackwell.

Goldstein, A.G., & Chance, J.E. (1980). Memory for faces and schema theory. *Journal of Psychology, 105,* 47–59.

Gossett, T.F. (1963). *Race: The history of the idea in America*. Dallas, TX: Southern Methodist University Press.

Greenhaus, J., Parasuraman, S., & Wormley, W. (1990). Effects of race on organizational experiences, job performance evaluations and career outcomes. *Academy of Management Journal*, 33(1), 64–86.

Gutman, H. (1977). *Work, culture and society in industrializing America*. New York: Vintage.

Hewlin, P.F. (2003). And the award for the best actor goes to…: Facades of conformity in organizational settings. *Academy of Management Review, 28,* 633–642.

Hunter, J.E., Schmidt, F.L., & Hunter, R. (1979). Differential validity of employment tests by race: A comprehensive review and analysis. *Psychological Bulletin, 85,* 721–735.

Ibarra, H. (1995). Race, opportunity, and diversity of social circles in managerial networks. *Academy of Management Journal*, 38(3), 673–703.

Ignatiev, N. (1996). *How the Irish became White*. New York: Routledge.

ILO. (2004). Towards a fair deal for migrant workers in the global economy. Unpublished paper presented at the International Labor Conference, 92nd session. Geneva.

James, J.S., Brown, K.T., Brown, T.N., & Marks, B. (2001). Contemporary immigration policy orientations among dominant-group members in Western Europe. *Journal of Social Issues, 57*(3), 431–456.

Judge, T.A., Locke, E.A., & Durham, C.C. (1997). The dispositional causes of job satisfaction: A core evaluations approach. In B.B. Straw & L.L. Cummings (Eds.), *Research in organizational behavior* (vol. 19, pp. 189–239). Greenwich, CT: JAI Press.

Judge, T.A., Locke, E.A., Durham, C.C., & Kluger, A.N. (1998). Dispositional effects on job and life satisfaction: The role of core evaluations, *Journal of Applied Psychology, 83,* 17–34.

Lau, D.C., & Murnighan, J.K. (1998). Demographic diversity and fault lines: The compositional dynamics of organizational groups. *Academy of Management Review, 23*(2), 325–340

Lin, M.H., Kwan, V.S., Cheung, A., & Fiske, S.T. (2005). Stereotype content model explains prejudice for an envied outgroup: Scale of anti-Asian American stereotypes. *Personality and Social Psychology Bulletin, 31,* 34–47.

Link, B.G., & Phelan, J.C. (2001). Conceptualising stigma. *Annual Review of Sociology, 27,* 363–385.

Loomba, A. (2005). *Colonialism/postcolonialism.* London: Routledge.

Luthans, F., Avolio, B.J., Avey, J.B., & Norman, S.M. (2007). Positive psychological capital: Measurement and relationship with performance and satisfaction. *Personnel Psychology, 60,* 541–572.

Markus, H.R. (2008). Pride, prejudice and ambivalence: Toward a unified theory of race and ethnicity. *American Psychologist, 63,* 651–670.

Markus, H.R., & Moya, P. (2010). *Doing race: 21 essays for the 21st century.* New York: Norton.

McKay, P.F., & McDaniel, M.A. (2006). A reexamination of Black–White mean differences in work performance: More data, more moderators. *Journal of Applied Psychology, 91,* 538–554.

McKee, J.B. (1993). *Sociology and the race problem: The failure of perspective.* Urbana: University of Illinois Press.

McKown, C., & Weinstein, R. (2003). The development and consequences of stereotype consciousness in middle childhood. *Child Development, 74,* 498–515.

Mehra, A., Kilduff, M., & Brass, D.J. (1998). At the margins: A distinctiveness approach to the social identity and social networks of underrepresented groups. *Academy of Management Journal, 41*(4), 441–452.

Montagu, A. (1997). *Man's most dangerous myth: The fallacy of race.* Walnut Creek, CA: AltaMira Press.

Mydral, G. (1944). *An American dilemma.* New York: Harper & Row.

Newman, J.M., & Krzystofiak, F. (1979). Self-reports versus unobtrusive measures: Balancing method variance and ethical concerns in employment discrimination research. *Journal of Applied Psychology, 64,* 2–85.

Nkomo, S.M. (1992). The emperor has no clothes: Rewriting "race in organizations." *Academy of Management Review, 17*(3), 487–513.

Nkomo, S.M. (2009). The sociology of race: The contributions of W.E.B. DuBois. In P. Adler (Ed.), *Handbook of sociology and organization studies: Classical foundations* (pp. 375–398). London: Oxford Press.

Nkomo, S., & Stewart, M. (2006). Diverse identities in organizations. In S. Clegg, C. Hardy, T. Lawrence, & W. Nord (Eds.), *The Sage handbook of organizational studies* (pp. 520–540). London: Sage Publications.

Pettigrew T.F., & Meertens, R.W. (1995). Subtle and blatant prejudice in Western Europe. *European Journal of Social Psychology, 25,* 57–75.

Pfeffer, J. (1983). Organizational demography, In L.L. Cummings & B.M. Staw (Eds.), *Research in organizational behavior* (Vol. 5, pp. 299–357). Greenwich, CT: JAI Press.

Phinney, J.S. (1992). The multigroup ethnic identity measure: A new scale for use with diverse groups. *Journal of Adolescent Research, 7,* 156–176.

Picca, L., & Feagin, J. (2007). *Two faced racism.* New York: Routledge.

Pinel, E.C. (1999). Stigma consciousness: The psychological legacy of social stereotypes. *Journal of Personality and Social Psychology, 76,* 114–128.

Poston, W.C., Craine, M., & Atkinson, D.R. (1991). Counseling dissimilarity confrontation, client cultural mistrust, and willingness to self disclose. *Journal of Multicultural Counseling and Development, 19,* 65–73.

Prasad, A. (2001). Understanding workplace empowerment as inclusion: A historical investigation of the discourse of difference in the United States. *Journal of Applied Behavioral Science, 27,* 33–50.

Pratto, F., Sidanius, J., Stallworth, L.M., & Malle, B.F. (1994). Social dominance orientation: A personality variable predicting social and political attitudes. *Journal of Personality and Social Psychology, 67,* 741–763.

Proudford, K., & Nkomo, S.M. (2006). Race in organizations. In A.M. Konrad, P. Prasad, & J.K. Pringle (Eds.), *Handbook of workplace diversity* (pp. 323–345). London: Sage Publications.

Richeson, J.A., & Shelton, N. (2007). Negotiating interracial interactions: Costs, consequences, and possibilities. *Current Directions in Psychological Science, 16,* 316–320.

Riordan, C.M. (2000). Relational demography within groups: Past developments, contradictions, and new directions. In G.R. Ferris (Ed.), *Research in personnel and human resources management* (Vol. 19, pp. 131–174). New York: JAI Press.

Roberson, L., Galvin, B.M., & Charles, A.C. (2007). When group identities matter: Bias in performance appraisal. *Academy of Management Annals, 1,* 617–650.

Roberson, L., & Kulik, C.T. (2007). Stereotype threat at work. *Academy of Management Perspectives, 21,* 24–40.

Roberts, L.M. (2005). Changing faces: Professional image construction in diverse organizational settings. *Academy of Management Review, 30,* 685–711.

Rosette, A.S., Leonardelli, G., & Phillips, K.W. (2008). The White standard: Racial bias in leader categorization. *Journal of Applied Psychology, 93*(4), 758–777.

Roth, P.L., Huffcutt, A.I., & Bobko, P. (2003). Ethnic group difference in measures of job performance: A new meta-analysis. *Journal of Applied Psychology, 88*(4), 694–706.

Rousseau, D.M., Sitkin, S.B., Burt, R.S., & Camerer, C. (1998). Not so different after all: A cross-discipline view of trust. *Academy of Management Review 23,* 393–404.

Ruhs, M. (2006). The potential of temporary migration programmes in future international migration policy. *International Labour Review, 145*(1–2), 7-36.

Rustenbach, E. (2010). Sources of negative attitudes toward immigrants in Europe: A multilevel analysis. *International Migration Review, 44,* 53–77.

Schein E. (1990). Organizational culture. *American Psychologist, 45*(2), 109–119.

Sidanius, J., & Pratto, F. (1999). *Social dominance: An intergroup theory of social hierarchy and oppression.* New York: Cambridge University Press.

Snyder, M., & Gangestad, S. (1986). On the nature of self-monitoring: Matters of assessment, matters of validity. *Journal of Personality and Social Psychology, 51*, 125–139.

Spreitzer, G.M. (1995). Psychological empowerment in the workplace: Dimensions, measurement, and validation. *Academy of Management Journal, 38*, 1442–1465.

Steele, C.M., & Aronson, J. (1995). Stereotype threat and the intellectual test performance of African Americans. *Journal of Personality and Social Psychology, 69*, 797–811.

Steele, C.M., Spencer, S.J., & Aronson, J. (2002). Contending with group image: The psychology of stereotype and social identity threat. In M.P. Zanna (Ed.), *Advances in experimental social psychology* (Vol. 34, pp. 379–440). San Diego, CA: Academic Press.

Swim, J.K., Hyers, L.L., Cohen, L.L., Fitzgerald, D.C., & Bylsma, W.H. (2003). African American college students' experiences with everyday racism: Characteristics of and responses to these incidents. *Journal of Black Psychology, 29*(1), 38–67.

Tajfel, H., & Turner, J.C. (1986). The social identity theory of intergroup behavior. In S. Worchel & W.G. Austin (Eds.), *Psychology of intergroup relations* (pp. 2–24). Chicago: Nelson-Hall.

Takaki, R. (1979). *Iron cages: Race and culture in the 19th century.* New York: Alfred Knopf.

Takaki, R.T. (2008). *A different mirror: A history of multicultural America.* Boston–Toronto–London: Back Bay Books.

Tepstra, D., & Larsen, M. (1985). A note on job type and applicant race as determinants of hiring decisions. *Journal of Occupational Psychology, 53*(3), 117–119.

Thau, S., Aquino, K., & Bommer, W. (2008). How employee race moderates the relationship between non-contingent punishment and organizational citizenship behaviors: A test of the negative adaptation hypothesis. *Social Justice Research, 21*, 297–312.

Thomas, D.A., & Gabarro, J.J. (1999). *Breaking through: The making of minority executives in corporate America.* Boston: Harvard Business School Press.

Treadway, D.C., Ferris, G.R., Duke, A., Adams, G., & Thatcher, J. (2007). The moderating role of subordinate political skill on supervisors' impressions of subordinate ingratiation and ratings of interpersonal facilitation. *Journal of Applied Psychology, 92*, 848–855.

Tsui, A.S., Ashford, S.J., St. Clair, L., & Xin, C. (1995). Dealing with discrepant expectations: Response strategies and managerial effectiveness. *Academy of Management Journal, 38*, 1515–1540.

Tsui, A.S., Egan, T.D., & Xin, K.R. (1995). Diversity in organizations: Lessons from demography research. In M. Chemers, S. Oskamp, & M. Costanzo (Eds.), *Diversity in the workplace* (pp. 37–61). Thousand Oaks, CA: Sage Publications.

Tsui, A.S., & Gutek, B. (1999). *Demographic differences in organizations: Current research and future directions.* Lanham, MD: Lexington Books.

Turkel, S. (1992). *Race: How Blacks and Whites feel about the American obsession with race.* New York: New Press.

Turner, J.C., Hogg, M.A., Oakes, P.J., Reicher, S.D., & Wetherell, M. (1987). *Rediscovering the social group: A self-categorization theory.* Oxford, UK: Basil Blackwell.

Twine, F.W., & Gallagher, C. (2008). The future of Whiteness: A map of the third wave. *Ethnic and Racial Studies, 31*(1), 4–24.

Van Aken, E.M., Monetta, D.J., & Sink, D.S. (1994). Affinity groups: The missing link in employee involvement. *Organizational Dynamics, 22*, 28–53.

Vigoda, E. (2002). Stress-related aftermaths to workplace politics: The relationship among politics, job distress, burnout, and aggressive behavior in organizations. *Journal of Organizational Behavior, 23*, 571–591.

Watson, D., & Clark, L.A. (1984). Negative affectivity: The disposition to experience negative aversive emotional states. *Psychological Bulletin, 96*, 465–490.

Winant, H. (2002). *The world is a ghetto: Race and democracy since World War II.* Basic Books.

Winant, H. (2006). Race and racism: Towards a global future. *Ethnic and Racial Studies, 29*(5), 986–1003.

Wilson, K. (2010). An analysis of bias in supervisor narrative comments in performance appraisal. *Human Relations, 63*(12), 1903–1933.

Zanoni, P., Jansens, M., Benschop, Y., & Nkomo, S.M. (2010). Unpacking diversity, rasping inequality: Rethinking difference through critical perspectives. *Organization: The Critical Journal of Organization, Theory and Society, 17*(1), 9–29.

Ziegert, J.C., & Hanges, P.J. (2005). Employment discrimination: The role of implicit attitudes, motivation, and a climate for racial bias. *Journal of Applied Psychology, 90*(3), 553–562.

16

Political Skill in the Organizational Sciences

Gerald R. Ferris
Florida State University

Darren C. Treadway
State University of New York at Buffalo

Robyn L. Brouer
State University of New York at Buffalo

Timothy P. Munyon
West Virginia University

Three decades ago, the political skill construct was introduced to the organizational sciences literature by Pfeffer (1981), advocating a political perspective on organizations, which was shared in independent and parallel work conducted by Mintzberg (1983, 1985). However, theory and research on political skill lay dormant until recently, when Ferris and his colleagues developed a program of research designed to establish a more informed understanding of this important construct (Ferris et al., 1999; Ferris, Treadway, et al., 2005; Ferris, Treadway, Perrewé, Brouer, Douglas, & Lux, 2007). In the ensuing period of time, an active program of research has been conducted, demonstrating the roles political skill plays in organizations and its importance to the field. Therefore, it seems timely to review and assess the current status of the political skill construct to date.

HISTORY AND CONSTRUCT SPECIFICATION

Early Construct Introduction: 1980s

In the early 1980s, Pfeffer (1981) first introduced the term *political skill* to the scholarly literature, as part of his political perspective on organizations. His approach to power essentially was structural in nature (e.g., created by the departmentalization, division of labor), was perceived to be a resource, and was acquired, used, and developed through the use of tactics and strategies of organizational politics. Pfeffer conceived of political skill as an individual characteristic that could be employed to effectively demonstrate political behavior to acquire or develop structurally determined power.

However, although Pfeffer (1981) argued that political skill is needed to be successful in organizations, he suggested that "substantial additional work will need to be done in identifying political skill" (p. 356). Thus, one could reasonably construe Pfeffer's position on the dynamics of these three critical constructs as arguing that power reflects the exercise of influence, that politics represent tactics employed to develop or acquire power, and that political skill provides the savvy and skill set to effectively leverage resources and execute political behavior to be identified by others as being powerful. Indeed, Pfeffer (2010a, 2010b) more recently argued that political skill is one of the best vehicles to secure power in organizations.

Around the same time, Mintzberg (1983, 1985) was conducting parallel but independent research in the areas of power, politics, and political skill within his political perspective on organizations. The players, or what he referred to as *influencers*, were characterized by possessing some base of power in addition to the interest and willingness to expend energy in this arena (i.e., *political will*; see Treadway, Chapter 17 in this volume) and to direct one's efforts and activities of influence in politically skillful ways (i.e., political skill).

More specifically, Mintzberg (1983, p. 26) characterized this new construct as follows: "Political skill means the ability to use the bases of power effectively—to convince those to whom one has access, to use one's resources, information, and technical skills to their fullest in bargaining, to exercise formal power with a sensitivity to the feelings of others, to know where to concentrate one's energies, to sense what is possible, to organize the necessary alliances." He viewed political skill as an interpersonal style and savvy construct, which could include charm, attractiveness, and charisma, and he believed that it contributed to adeptness in negotiation, manipulation, and persuasion.

Thus, a base of formal power seemed to play a key role in this conceptualization of power and political skill. As noted recently by Perrewé, Zellars, Ferris, Rossi, Kacmar, and Ralston (2004, p. 142), "whereas Mintzberg tended to associate political skill explicitly with formal power, the political skill construct, as it is characterized today, fits better with the ideas of some scholars concerning the exercise of influence devoid of formal authority."

Initial Construct Measurement: 1990s

The development and introduction of the political skill construct appropriately is attributed to Pfeffer (1981) and Mintzberg (1983). However, because neither scholar actively pursued further construct specification or an empirical research program, the construct was left unattended for a couple of decades. Clearly influenced by the earlier work of Pfeffer and Mintzberg, Ferris et al. (1999) suggested that it is not enough to study the particular influence tactics or political behaviors that reflect the *what* of influence. We also need to critically examine the political skill of the influencer to understand the *how* of influence.

Among other issues, political skill allows influencers to effectively manage attributions of intentionality and to disguise self-serving opportunistic motives (Ferris, Bhawuk, Fedor, & Judge, 1995), which has historically been regarded as the ultimate objective of an influence attempt (e.g., Jones, 1990). Indeed, Ferris et al.'s (1999) initial work on political skill also was very much influenced by Jones, who suggested that we have been studying influence tactics and strategies for decades and have learned a lot about such forms of influence. However, he argued that we still know almost nothing about the style of delivery and execution of the influence attempt, which mostly explains its effectiveness.

Ferris et al. (1999) provided a preliminary report on the conceptualization and validation of the Political Skill Inventory (PSI). They conceived of political skill as a complex and multidimensional construct. However, because of the nature of this construct, its establishment, delineation, development, and validation are going to involve a long-term program of research. They argued that, much like Snyder's (1987) development of his Self-Monitoring Scale, this initial effort would be directed toward establishing the nature of the construct, creating a simple measure, and verifying its relationship to other organizational constructs. Consequently, they sought to identify a parsimonious, unidimensional measure of political skill that had acceptable psychometric properties and demonstrated its convergence with and distinctiveness from other measures at this stage of construct development.

Five studies (Ferris et al., 1999) were conducted that individually addressed key issues in the development of the PSI ranging from item generation, refinement, content homogeneity through instrument validation and the establishment of convergent and discriminant validation evidence. Furthermore, collectively these studies identified and supported the unidimensional six-item PSI as a scientifically sound, parsimonious measure of the political skill construct that possesses acceptable psychometric properties. They argued that whereas they viewed this as an early point in the evolution of the PSI they were sufficiently encouraged with the results from the item content homogeneity and scale reliability and validity tests to move on to subsequent phases of expansion and validation, which would focus more on the scale's dimensionality and criterion-related validity.

Expanded Construct Conceptualization, Scale Development, and Validation: 2000s

Subsequent to the initial political skill scale development and validation efforts of Ferris et al. (1999), continued research was initiated in this area to expand on that six-item measure and to seek the development of a more extensive, multidimensional measure of political skill, which would provide broader coverage of the construct domain. These initial 7 years of the new decade yielded considerable advancements in political skill in the form of a new, expanded scale development and validation piece (Ferris, Treadway, et al., 2005), a book on political skill (Ferris, Davidson, & Perrewé, 2005), and a comprehensive review and theoretical statement explaining the dynamics and operation of the construct (Ferris et al., 2007). This work also provided a specific definition of political skill as "the ability to effectively understand others at work, and to use such knowledge to influence others to act in ways that enhance one's personal and/or organizational objectives" (Ferris, Treadway, et al., 2005, p. 127).

In a three-study, seven-sample investigation, Ferris, Treadway, et al. (2005) sought to further develop and to examine the conceptualization and measurement of the political skill construct as well as to provide extended validation evidence for the new and expanded PSI. This research resulted in the development of the four-factor (i.e., social astuteness, interpersonal influence, networking ability, and apparent sincerity), 18-item PSI, which demonstrated consistency of the four-factor structure across studies and evidence of both construct and criterion-related validity for the new scale. As hypothesized, political skill was found to relate positively, but modestly, to self-monitoring, political savvy, and emotional intelligence, inversely related to trait anxiety, and not correlated with general mental ability (i.e., the zero correlation also was found between GMA and the Ferris et al., 1999 six-item scale). In two samples, the PSI also predicted performance ratings of managers.

Ferris et al. (2007) provided the first systematic conceptualization and theoretical statement concerning the political skill construct, which they characterized as "a comprehensive pattern of social competencies, with cognitive, affective, and behavioral manifestations, which have both direct effects on outcomes, as well as moderating effects on predictor–outcome relationships" (p. 291). Also, they provided greater specificity for the four dimensions of political skill and their potential dispositional and developmental antecedents. The political skill construct consists of four critical underlying dimensions: social astuteness, interpersonal influence, networking ability, and apparent sincerity.

Social Astuteness

Politically skilled individuals are keen observers of their social environment, understanding not only the intricacies of their surroundings but also the motivations of themselves and others acting within that setting. Socially astute individuals possess superior self-awareness and can correctly interpret the behavior of others. Pfeffer (1992) believed that an integral aspect to being able to obtain desired results for oneself was the ability to identify with others, which he referred to as being sensitive to others. Social astuteness captures this idea and therefore, as Pfeffer argued, is quite necessary for someone trying to influence others effectively.

Interpersonal Influence

The politically skilled are characterized by a capability to subtly influence those around them. They have an effective communication style that puts others at ease. This equips the politically skilled with the facility to act as chameleons, changing and adapting to the environment in ways that provoke desired responses from others. Pfeffer (1992) termed this *flexibility* and saw it as important to achieving one's goals.

Networking Ability

Politically skilled individuals are adept relationship builders, able to forge strong bonds for friendships, alliances, and coalitions. This allows the politically skilled to develop and maintain vast networks of individuals that can ultimately help them achieve their goals. Further, the politically skilled know how to leverage their networks by ensuring that they are connected to influential others and that they are in a position to receive and generate opportunities (Pfeffer, 1992). Moreover, the politically skilled are capable of effectively handling conflict and negotiations, which reinforces the strong bonds they are able to form with others.

Apparent Sincerity

Politically skilled individuals are seen by others as being honest and sincere in their words and actions. They are described as being authentic and genuine. Therefore, when a politically skilled individual is trying to influence someone, this influence attempt comes across as trustworthy and veritable. This is vital to the success of influence, allowing the politically skilled to mask any ulterior motives if they are present. Because the politically skilled are not seen as manipulative or coercive, their influence behavior is likely to be more successful (Jones, 1990).

REVIEW OF POLITICAL SKILL RESEARCH

Studies Using Unidimensional Six-item PSI

Recall that one impetus for the Ferris et al. (1999) initial scale development research on political skill was to develop a measurement tool in this area that would at least permit some early efforts to reliably and validly assess political skill, and assess its relationships with other organizational science constructs. Therefore, a few studies conducted in the early 2000s used the unidimensional six-item version of the PSI. Three studies were published by Ferris, Witt, Hochwarter, and colleagues, and although the term *social skill* is included in the title of all three of these studies, the construct being measured actually was an early effort to assess political skill (Ferris, Witt, & Hochwater, 2001; Hochwater, Witt, Treadway, & Ferris, 2006; Witt & Ferris, 2003).

Because Ferris and his colleagues were actively engaged in an ongoing effort to develop an expanded political skill scale, new items were being written, subjected to extensive item and factor analyses, and so forth at the time. Also, the Ferris, Treadway, et al. (2005) 18-item PSI had not yet been developed (but was in development), and the conventional research being drawn from in these studies tended to use the term *social skill*. Therefore, the term social skill was employed in these three studies, but the items were developed as part of an extensive political skill item pool, consisting of nearly 100 items at one time.

Seven items were developed in the Ferris et al. (2001) study to assess social and political skill, and those same items also were used to measure the same construct in Witt and Ferris's (2003) and Hochwarter et al.'s (2006) investigations. Ferris et al. (2001) examined the interaction of social/political skill × general mental ability (GMA) on job performance and salary and found significant interactions on both in support of the hypothesis. Specifically, increases in social/political skill predicted increases in task performance for individuals high in GMA but not for those low in GMA, Interestingly, for salary, increases in social and political skill predicted increases in salary for individuals high in GMA. However, for those low in GMA, increases in social and political skill predicted decreases in salary.

Witt and Ferris (2003) investigated the notion that the conscientiousness–job performance relationship was moderated by social and political skill. This four-study investigation yielded supportive results, demonstrating that for individuals high in social/political skill conscientiousness was positively related to performance but that for individuals low in social and political skill the conscientiousness–performance relationship essentially was nonexistent in Study 2 but was negative in the other three studies.

Hochwarter, Witt, Treadway, and Ferris (2006) investigated the social and political skill × perceived organizational support on supervisor-rated job performance in two samples. The hypothesis in this investigation was that social and political skill would be more strongly related to job performance for individuals who perceived low rather than high of organizational support. The regression results supported the hypothesis, demonstrating that the relevance of social/political skill to job performance may be contextually dependent.

Some published studies employed the Ferris et al. (1999) unidimensional six-item version of the PSI to measure political skill. First, Ahearn, Ferris, Hochwarter, Douglas, and Ammeter (2004) investigated the relationship between leader political skill and team performance in a state child welfare system. After controlling for average caseload, average age of children served, average number of team placements, team member experience, leader experience, and team empowerment, leader political skill was found to account for a significant proportion of variance in team performance (i.e., operationalized as the successful placement of children in legally final living arrangements, as defined by adoption, successor guardianship, or return to natural parents).

Following the conceptual arguments of Perrewé, Ferris, Frink, and Anthony (2000), Perrewé et al. (2004) examined the interaction of role conflict × political skill on psychological anxiety, somatic complaints, and physiological strain (i.e., heart rate, systolic and diastolic blood pressure). The argument here was that political skill essentially neutralizes the strain consequences resulting from workplace stressors. The results supported the moderating effects of political skill and thus the notion that political skill serves as an antidote to the dysfunctional consequences of stress.

Examining another environmental stressor, Brouer, Harris, and Kacmar (in press) argued that perceptions of organizational politics might not be harmful for all individuals. They suggested that both employees' self-rated political skill and their managers' political skill might serve as moderators of the relationships between politics perceptions and the work outcomes of job satisfaction, job performance, and manager-rated commitment. In a sample of matched dyadic pairs, mixed support was reported for the joint moderating effect of subordinate and supervisor political skill.

Ferris, Treadway, et al. (2007) proposed that political skill renders influence attempts more effective through proper situational selection, demonstration, and execution of particular influence behaviors. Harris, Kacmar, Zivnuska, and Shaw (2007) found that political skill increased the effectiveness of five different influence tactics (i.e., intimidation, exemplification, ingratiation, self-promotion, and supplication) on supervisor ratings of performance. For individuals low in political skill, the opposite results occurred, whereby increases in influence tactic use was associated with decreases in supervisor-rated performance.

Studies Using the 18-Item PSI

When developing a new measurement scale for a construct (i.e., when an initial scale for that construct already exists), it is critical to establish that the new measure demonstrates improved psychometric properties over previous measures. Three of the six items from the Ferris et al. (1999) scale were included in the new 18-item PSI, and the correlation of the two scales was reported to be $r = .78$ ($p < .001$; Ferris, Treadway, et al., 2005). The relationships of the six-item and the 18-item versions of the PSI with some other constructs were very similar. However, the six-item measure demonstrated little relationship with other key constructs and relatively poor predictability compared with the 18-item measure.

Political Skill Effects on Self: Strain-Reducing Consequences

As noted already, political skill has been argued to demonstrate neutralizing effects on workplace stressors. Such effects have been argued to occur through the self-evaluations that produce the calm self-confidence emanating from the greater perceived control and personal security politically skilled individuals experience, thus positioning them to perceive environmental stressors as less threatening and to serve as an antidote of sorts to the potentially negative consequences on strain reactions (Ferris et al., 2007; Perrewé et al., 2000).

Similar to Perrewé et al. (2004), Perrewé et al. (2005) investigated political skill's moderating role on the perceived role overload–strain relationship (i.e., strain was operationalized as behavioral anxiety, cognitive anxiety, job dissatisfaction, job tension, and somatic anxiety). The results demonstrated support for the hypothesis that political skill would diminish the negative effects of role overload on all forms of strain.

In examination of the notion that individuals high in negative affectivity (NA) are destined to experience strain disproportionately higher level than those low in NA, Zellars, Perrewé, Rossi, Tepper, and Ferris (2008) tested for the significance of the NA × political skill interaction on physiological strain. NA was found to be positively related to the physiological strain measure (i.e., facial muscle tension), and this relationship was weaker among individuals higher in political skill. Mediated-moderation analyses further suggested the means by which political skill moderated the NA–strain relationship was through perceived control and, in turn, job-related efficacy.

In another study of the moderating role of political skill on stressor–strain relationships, Harvey, Harris, Harris, and Wheeler (2007) investigated the interactive influence of perceived social stressors × political skill on job and career satisfaction. The results demonstrated, as hypothesized, that increases in social stressors were associated with decreases in job and career satisfaction for individuals low in political skill. For individuals high in political skill, however, those negative consequences were attenuated.

Characterizing perceived or felt accountability as a workplace stressor, Hochwarter, Ferris, Gavin, Perrewé, Hall, and Frink (2007) examined its effects along with political skill and job tension on job performance ratings. It was hypothesized that felt accountability would be associated with higher job performance ratings when coupled with high levels of political skill and that job tension would mediate these relationships. Using data collected at multiple times over a 1-year period, strong support was shown for the total effects model. This model showed that political skill moderated felt accountability–job performance ratings, felt accountability–job tension, and job tension–job performance ratings relationships. More careful inspection, however, indicated that political skill most strongly moderated the job tension–job performance ratings linkage.

Perceptions of organizational politics also can serve as a work environment stressor, and Brouer, Ferris, Hochwarter, Laird, and Gilmore (2006) investigated its effects on strain reactions for those high and low in political skill. For those high in political skill, politics perceptions should be associated with less negative attitudes and reactions. Operationalizing strain as depressive symptoms, this three-study investigation reported that increases in politics perceptions were associated with decreases in depressive symptoms for individuals high in political skill. Alternatively, increases in politics perceptions were associated with increases in depressive symptoms for those low in political skill. Convergent results were found across all three studies.

Conflict certainly can be stressful, and Meurs, Gallagher, and Perrewé (2010) studied the conflict–emotional burnout and performance relationships in two samples, with examining the differential moderating effects of self- versus other-rated political skill. They hypothesized that self-reported political skill moderated the relationship between supervisor–subordinate conflict and emotional burnout. However, supervisor-rated political skill was not expected to moderate this relationship. Additionally, they hypothesized that supervisor-rated political skill would moderate the relationship conflict–job performance relationship but that self-reported political skill was not expected to moderate this relationship. Both self- and supervisor-rated political skill were found to diminish the negative effects of conflict on burnout, but only supervisor-rated political skill was found to reduce the negative effects of conflict on job performance.

The similarity between supervisors and subordinates long has been suggested to contribute to the development of high quality leader–member exchange (LMX) relationships, and that dissimilarity can produce potential tension and stress in dyadic relationships. Thus, Brouer, Duke, Treadway, and Ferris (2009) considered the influence of subordinates' political skill on the relationship between supervisor–subordinate racial similarity–dissimilarity LMX relationships. The results supported the prediction that political skill would moderator this relationship, thus reducing the potentially negative effects of racial dissimilarity in supervisor-subordinate dyads on LMX relationship quality.

A potentially new workplace stressor is entitlement behavior, and Hochwarter, Summers, Thompson, Perrewé, and Ferris (2010), in a three-sample investigation hypothesized that perceived entitlement behavior by others would predict increased job tension for those low in political skill. Perceived entitlement behavior by others was predicted to demonstrate little relationship with job tension for individuals high in political skill. The results provided support for the hypothesis in all three samples, whereby political skill was found to moderate the perceived entitlement behavior by others–job tension relationship.

Although job-limiting pain is an increasingly relevant topic in organizations, research has failed to examine the stress-inducing properties of pain and its effects on important work attitudes and behavior. Ferris, Rogers, Blass, and Hochwarter (2009) investigated the interactive relationship between job-limiting pain and political skill on job satisfaction (i.e., Studies 1 and 2) and organizational citizenship behavior (i.e., Study 2). Political skill neutralized the strain reactions of job-limiting pain as a stressor, whereby satisfaction and citizenship scores declined as pain increased for those with low levels of political skill. However, for individuals high in political skill, increases in job-limiting pain exhibited little effect on satisfaction and citizenship.

There is one three-study direct effect investigation, where Kolodinsky, Hochwarter, and Ferris (2004) argued for and found nonlinear effects on self attitudes. Because political skill is argued to operate differently for interpersonal outcomes than for intrapersonal effects (i.e., effects on self), Kolodinsky et al. examined the form and magnitude of the relationship between political skill and the self-reactions of job satisfaction and job tension. The results from the three separate studies supported the hypothesized relationships, in which moderate levels of political skill were associated with higher levels of job satisfaction and lower levels of job tension, and higher and lower levels of political skill were negatively related to these outcomes.

Political Skill Direct Effects on Others: Performance

Political skill presumably increases the impressions and evaluations others form of individuals, which lead to other evaluations regarding job performance ratings, assessments of reputation, career progress and success, and other work outcomes. A number of studies have now been conducted using the 18-item PSI to test the validity of these theoretical notions, examining a number of work outcome variables, with most studies focusing on job performance consequences.

Ferris, Treadway et al. (2005) investigated political skill's prediction of job performance ratings by supervisors beyond control variables (i.e., age, supervisor tenure, organization tenure, self-monitoring, exchange tactics, upward appeal, and coalition tactics). The addition of the political skill composite score, beyond the controls entered, in the second block of variables contributed significant incremental variance beyond the control variables as predicted. They also examined the individual dimensions of political skill in the prediction of job performance ratings and found that social astuteness was the most explanatory dimension of political skill.

Semadar, Robins, and Ferris (2006) examined the prediction of managerial performance from political skill when political skill was placed in predictive competition with self-monitoring, emotional intelligence, and leadership self-efficacy. Political skill was found to be both the strongest predictor of managerial performance and a key factor that differentiated between top performers and others. Although emotional intelligence also was found to be a significant predictor of managerial performance, it failed to account for significant variance in job performance beyond political skill. Furthermore, neither self-monitoring nor leadership self-efficacy emerged as significant predictors of managerial performance.

Drawing from the conceptualization of political skill, Liu, Ferris, Zinko, Perrewé, Weitz, and Xu (2007) conducted a four-study investigation testing the personality–political skill–reputation–job performance linkage sequence proposed by Ferris et al. (2007). Collectively, the four studies provided strong support for the predictive role of personality categories on political skill as well as the mediation of reputation in the political skill–job performance relationships.

Political skill was hypothesized to differentially predict several aspects of job performance by Jawahar, Meurs, Ferris, and Hochwarter (2008). They demonstrated that self-efficacy more strongly predicted task performance than contextual performance and that political skill more strongly predicted contextual than task performance. Also, political skill was a better predictor of contextual performance than self-efficacy, and self-efficacy was a stronger predictor of task performance than political skill.

Most of the validation studies of the PSI provided evidence in support of the four-factor structure. However, the existing research in this area had used self-report of only political skill, and furthermore none had investigated the notion that there might be a single, higher-order factor solution through second-order factor analysis, which could account for the relationships among the first-order primary factors. In a two-study investigation, Ferris et al. (2008) tested construct validity in study 1, combining self- and other-reports of political skill in a confirmatory factor analysis.

In the second study, they used longitudinal data to constructively replicate study 1 results and to test hypotheses regarding the antecedents and consequences of political skill. Study 1 results confirmed both a four-factor and a single higher-order factor solution of the political skill construct, and study 2 constructively replicated those factorial validity results and provided support for hypotheses concerning antecedents and consequences of political skill.

In an interesting qualitative investigation of plant managers from several organizations, Smith, Plowman, Duchon, and Quinn (2009) found that these managers were able to influence subordinates in ways that contributed positively to organizational outcomes through the managers' political skill. Effective, politically skilled plant managers were self-motivated, humble, and affable; they tended to create accountability in others, lead by example, and develop trust; and they focused on managerial processes such as goal setting, influencing and learning from below, and empowering their subordinates. Thus, they concluded that plant manager effectiveness was a combination of political skill and the use of unobtrusive and systemic power.

Political skill consistently has demonstrated the capacity to predict job performance. Yet, due to a nearly exclusive reliance on self-report measurement of political skill and as a function of the distrust of self-ratings of constructs in the organizational sciences, Blickle, Ferris, et al. (in press) argued there was a need to investigate how multiple alternative sources of political skill and job performance measures relate.

In three studies, employing a multisource, triadic data collection methodology and using both cross sectional and longitudinal designs, this investigation reported strong support across all three studies for the hypotheses that employee political skill, measured from the perspective of employees' assessor A, will positively predict job performance rated by assessor B and vice versa and that employee political skill measured by assessor B will predict job performance ratings measured by assessor A.

Although political skill has been found to predict job performance in several studies, it had not been included in competitive prediction situations against general mental ability and personality characteristics. Therefore, Blickle, Kramer, et al. (2011) conducted two studies to examine the job performance predictive effectiveness of political skill's relative predictability of job performance when investigated in conjunction with general mental ability and personality characteristics. The results demonstrated that political skill accounted for a significant proportion of job performance variance beyond GMA and personality variables cross sectionally and predicatively on multiple dimensions of job performance.

In an experimental field study, Blickle and Schnitzler (2010) investigated the construct and criterion-related validity of the PSI when used under conditions of personnel selection. The instructions asked job incumbents to complete a set of measures (i.e., the PSI, a social desirability scale, and a Big Five personality inventory) as if they took part in a personnel selection procedure for a personally very attractive position (i.e., the experimental group). Job incumbents simply were asked to answer all measures honestly in the control group. As hypothesized, the PSI correlated positively with extraversion, conscientiousness, and income and negatively with neuroticism but did not correlate with social desirability under both conditions.

Political Skill Effects on Others: Career Issues

Five additional studies investigated political skill's predictability of promotability ratings (Gentry, Gilmore, Porter, & Leslie, in press), occupational choice (Kaplan, 2008), and career success (Blickle, Oerder, & Summers, 2010; Blickle, Schneider, Liu, & Ferris, in press; Wei, Liu, Chen, & Wu, 2010; Zinko, Ferris, Humphrey, Meyer, & Aime, in press). Gentry et al. attempted to address limitations in prior research by examining the relationship between political skill and promotability and whether such relationship varied as a function of which rater source was evaluating promotability. Managers with higher political skill received higher promotability ratings from three different coworker perspectives, and the magnitude of the relationship varied for bosses and peers. Additionally, it was found that peer ratings of leader behavior mediated the relationship between political skill and ratings of promotability.

Kaplan (2008) investigated the extent to which political skill would be related to career decisions and occupational choices. He found that political skill tends to influence the pursuit of jobs that fall within the enterprising and social occupational types. Blickle, Schneider, et al. (in press) investigated theoretical arguments suggesting that career success is predicted by political skill and that this relationship operates through (i.e., is mediated by) employees' reputation at work. The hypotheses were tested in a predictive study, covering a 1-year timeframe, in which two waves of data were collected. The results demonstrated that political skill at time 1 predicted hierarchical position, income, and career satisfaction at time 2 and that reputation mediated the relationships between political skill and hierarchical position and career satisfaction.

Finally, Blickle, Oerder, et al. (2010) examined the political skill of German works councillors and its predictability of their career success. As elected representatives of employees in German organizations, works councillors bargain and negotiate for the interests of employees with management. This study measured these works councillors' political skill and found that it significantly predicted their career success (i.e., where career success was assessed based on success in elections), after controlling for sex, age, and union membership.

Blickle, Schneider, et al. (in press) argued, consistent with theory and research, that individuals' political skill would predict their career success and that this relationship is mediated by individuals' reputation in the workplace. In a study that collected two waves of data from 135 career employees, covering a 1-year time frame, political skill at time 1 predicted hierarchical position, income, and career satisfaction at time 2. Furthermore, it was found that reputation mediated the relationships between political skill and hierarchical position and career satisfaction.

Wei et al. (2010) investigated the role of political skill in the supervisor–subordinate relationship dynamics contributing to career prospects, using multiple data sources in Chinese firms. A total of 343 employees, their 343 direct supervisors, and 662 peers completed surveys to test a model suggesting that subordinates use their political skill to influence their *guanxi* with their supervisors, which in turn contributes to greater career prospects and development. Supervisor–subordinate *guanxi* was found to mediate the relationship between subordinate political skill and supervisor-rated career prospects of their subordinates. Finally, Zinko et al. (in press) supported these results by showing that personal reputation mediated the relationships between political skill and career success.

Political Skill Direct Effects on Others: Leader Political Skill and Outcomes

Several studies have investigated the relationship between leader political skill and leader or follower effectiveness measures. Douglas and Ammeter (2004) examined both the dimensionality of leader political skill as well as its relationship with leader effectiveness ratings. Instead of the four underlying factors proposed and found in some initial research, they found a two-dimensional structure (i.e., networking ability and interpersonal influence) best fit the data. Furthermore, they reported that after the entry of several control variables (i.e., leader education, gender, self-efficacy, and self-monitoring), the networking ability dimension of leader political skill explained significant incremental variance explained in leader performance ratings, and both networking ability and interpersonal influence accounted for a significant proportion of variance explained in work unit performance.

Brouer, Douglas, Treadway, and Ferris (2011) conducted a two-study investigation, testing a model suggesting that leader political skill relates to both leader and follower effectiveness through leader–follower relationship quality. The results provided support for the hypotheses, finding that leader political skill related to leader effectiveness through leader–follower relationship quality in study 1 and that leader–follower relationship quality mediates both the relationship between leader political skill and follower performance and the leader political skill–follower organization citizenship behaviors (OCB) relationship in study 2, thus constructively replicating and extending the results from study 1.

Treadway et al. (2004) used structural equation modeling to test a conceptual model of leader political skill and employee reactions. The results support the notion that politically skilled leaders affect the organizational experience of their employees by cultivating perceptions of organizational support. More specifically, leader political skill was found to lead to employee perceived organizational support, which predicted trust, cynicism, and job satisfaction and then affected organizational commitment.

Political Skill Interactive Effects on Others: Influence Tactics

Political skill also exerts effects on outcomes interactively with other constructs. Most notably, and proposed theoretically by Ferris et al. (2007), political skill is supposed to make influence tactics more effective, thus moderating the relationship between influence tactics and work outcomes. Thus, in addition to selecting influence tactics and strategies that are situationally appropriate, politically skilled individuals tend to deliver and execute influence attempts in a manner that contributes to their effectiveness.

Treadway, Ferris, Duke, Adams, and Thatcher (2007) proposed that political skill affects the style of execution of influence attempts to explain the moderating effect of employee political skill on the relationships between self- and supervisor-reported ingratiation. Also, supervisor reports of subordinate ingratiation were hypothesized to be negatively related to supervisor ratings of subordinate interpersonal facilitation. The results provided evidence that when subordinates demonstrated ingratiation behavior it was more likely to be perceived and interpreted by supervisors as a manipulative influence attempt if they were low in political skill. Politically skilled subordinates were less likely to have their ingratiation behavior perceived as such (i.e., as manipulative and self-serving).

Harris et al. (2007) found that political skill interacted with several different influence tactics as they affected evaluations of subordinate job performance by their supervisors. More specifically, they reported that subordinates high in political skill, who used high levels of any of intimidation, exemplification, ingratiation, self-promotion, and supplication, tended to achieve more favorable supervisor performance ratings than those subordinates lower in political skill.

Kolodinsky, Treadway, and Ferris (2007) investigated the roles of political skill and the influence tactic, rationality, with respect to their interactive effects on supervisor perceptions and evaluations. As hypothesized, political skill was found to moderate the positive relationship between rationality and two supervisory perceptions known to affect supervisor ratings of job performance, notably supervisor liking of subordinates and perceived similarity to subordinates. That is, for both outcomes (i.e., perceived similarity and liking), increases in the use of rationality were associated with increases in the outcome for individuals high in political skill. However, the results were just the opposite for individuals low in political skill (i.e., increases in rationality were associated with decreases in the outcomes).

Political Skill Interactive Effects on Others: Personality

Political skill also has been suggested to interact with personality and values to affect other-rated work outcomes. Specifically, Hogan's (e.g., Hogan, 1983; Hogan & Shelton, 1998) socioanalytic theory of work behavior has argued that distal influences like personality traits need more proximal influences like social/political skill to energize or ignite them into action, so they can demonstrate effects on work outcomes. Several studies have been conducted in this area.

Socioanalytic theory argues that ratings of job performance are predicted by basic social motives and are moderated by social competency, and the motive to get along with others and the motive to get ahead are the two motives. In a two-study investigation, Blickle, Frohlich, et al. (2011) examined these motives as work values and their interactions with political skill on supervisors' job performance and promotability assessments. The results provided strong and consistent support for the hypotheses, demonstrating that a significant positive interaction of the work value of getting ahead and political skill on supervisors' assessments of job performance.

Specifically, for employees high on political skill, higher levels of getting along are associated with higher levels of job performance ratings and cooperation. For employees low on political skill, lower levels of getting along are associated with lower levels of job performance ratings and cooperation. Also, there was a significant positive interaction of the work value of getting ahead and political skill on supervisors' assessments of employees' promotability. Specifically, for employees high on political skill, higher levels of getting ahead were associated with higher promotability ratings. For employees low on political skill, higher levels of getting ahead are associated with lower promotability ratings.

Blickle et al. (2008) investigated whether motives to get along and to get ahead (i.e., testing socioanalytic theory, and operationalizing the motives using the agreeableness and conscientiousness personality constructs from the Five-Factor Model) produced greater job performance when interactively combined with political skill. The results reported a significant agreeableness–political skill interaction, in support of the hypothesis. Furthermore, after applying corrections for unreliability and restriction in range for conscientiousness, its interaction with political skill also significantly predicted job performance.

In another test of socioanalytic theory and using a sample automobile salespersons, Blickle, Wendel, and Ferris (2010) tested whether the motive to get ahead, as operationalized by the personality traits of extraversion and openness to experience, is associated with higher performance when interactively combined with social effectiveness competencies, as operationalized by political skill. The results supported the hypothesized extraversion × political skill interaction such that, for politically skilled individuals, increases in extraversion were associated with increased sales performance. However, for those low on political skill, increases in extraversion were associated with lower levels of automobile sales performance. Unfortunately, the openness to experience × political skill interaction did not achieve statistical significance.

Political Skill Interactive Effects on Others: Contextual Factors

Ferris, Perrewé, and Douglas (2002) appealed for research that would examine the boundaries of political skill's predictive effectiveness, thus searching for moderators of the political skill-performance or effectiveness outcomes. Several studies have now been reported in this area using different contextual moderators of the political skill–job performance relationship, with one study investigating organizational politics perceptions as a contextual moderator (Kapoutsis, Papalexandris, Nikolopoulos, Hochwarter, & Ferris, 2011), one examining justice as a moderator (Andrews, Kacmar, & Harris, 2009), and one studying occupational classification as a feature of the context that constrains the political skill–job performance relationship (Blickle et al., 2009).

Much prior research has reported negative consequences resulting from perceptions of organizational politics. The Kapoutsis et al. (2011) two-study, cross-national investigation was designed to examine the political skill × organizational politics perceptions as a moderator of the political skill–job performance relationship. Supportive of the hypothesis, increases in political skill were associated with increases in job performance for individuals who perceived low politics. However, for individuals who perceived politics to be high, political skill demonstrated no relationship with job performance. Therefore, the results of this investigation and of Brouer et al. (in press) mentioned previously in the six-item political skill measure section, confirm the importance of considering political features of the external environment when conducting substantive research.

The Andrews et al. (2009) study investigated the moderating effects of procedural and distributive justice on the relationships political skill demonstrated with task performance and organizational citizenship behavior. Employing a strong versus weak situations perspective (i.e., where low justice conditions were characterized as weak situations and high justice conditions as strong situations), political skill was positively related to performance when both procedural and distributive justice were low. Under both high procedural and distributive justice conditions, political skill was negatively related to performance. In conditions of low distributive justice, political skill was positively related to citizenship behavior, whereas political skill exhibited minimal effect on citizenship behavior under conditions of high distributive justice.

Finally, Blickle et al. (2009) attempted to determine whether political skill is equally effective in its prediction of job performance for different job demands or occupational categories. Using self-report sources of employee performance along with three target individuals' ratings of job demands and self-report of political skill after several weeks, the results supported the hypothesis that Holland's (1976) enterprising occupational category moderated the relationship between political skill and job performance, demonstrating stronger predictability under high enterprising job demands. Additionally, the social and conventional occupational categories did not significantly moderate the political skill–job performance relationships.

Political Skill Interactive Effects on Others: Resources

Finally, politically skilled individuals are argued to be able to more effectively use, present, and leverage resources at their disposal, thus contributing to positive outcomes. Some recent research has demonstrated that politically skilled individuals present their performance information in influential ways that increases other perceptions of the individuals' power (Treadway, Breland, Williams, Cho, Yang, & Ferris, in press) and reputation (Laird, Zboja, Martinez, & Ferris, 2011).

Also, another study by Treadway, Adams, Hanes, Magnusen, Perrewé, & Ferris, 2011) showed that politically skilled college football recruiters can leverage key aspects of organizational reputation in ways that result in greater recruitment effectiveness (i.e., number and quality of high school recruits signed). Finally, Breland, Treadway, Duke, and Adams (2007) showed that politically skill interacted with leader–member exchange quality to affect career success.

DIRECTIONS FOR FUTURE RESEARCH

Testing Political Skill's Intermediate Linkages

More research is needed to empirically substantiate the theoretical arguments regarding the intermediate linkages between political skill and outcomes. Ferris et al. (2007) argued that politically skilled individuals inspire trust, confidence, and support in others, and Smith et al. (2009) found that politically skilled managers possessed a configuration of personal characteristics that included self-motivation, a sense of humility, and affability, which they used to create accountability in others, lead by example, and develop trust in their followers.

Political skill also theoretically influences the management of interpersonal conflict (Pfeffer, 1992). However, only Meurs and colleagues (2010) examined the ramifications of political skill as an enabler of conflict management, notably in a supervisor–subordinate context. More research is needed to study the effects of political skill on interpersonal conflict in other contexts, for example, within teams and with customers. The ability to manage conflict may also mediate the relationship between political skill and other outcomes, for example, team cohesion and customer satisfaction.

Similarly, the political skill–distance relationship also merits further empirical study. Distance generally refers to the perceived degree of similarity or dissimilarity between two actors (i.e., individuals, groups/teams, or organizations; Napier & Ferris, 1993). Generally, distance is assumed to have a negative effect on interpersonal interactions (Antonakis & Atwater, 2002). Nevertheless, it is possible that politically skilled individuals are able to manage perceptions of distance by appealing to similarities between actors, positively influencing subsequent interactions (e.g., Ferris, Liden et al., 2009).

Reversing causality, it is also possible that distance mitigates the positive effects of political skill in a relational context. The social influence literature is largely premised on the assumption that individuals engage in frequent social exchanges that enable knowledge (and influence) transfer. However, high levels of distance, be it physical, psychological, or both, would likely impede this transfer of information. Thus, in lieu of direct contact with an individual, personal reputation (e.g., Zinko, Ferris, Blass, & Laird, 2007) may enable the extension of social influence through others. Further conceptual and empirical work is needed to elucidate the links among political skill, social influence, and personal reputation, particularly as intermediary influences on performance outcomes.

Unfortunately, only Treadway et al. (2004) has empirically searched for such intermediate linkages on others, demonstrating that perceived organizational support, trust, cynicism, and job satisfaction mediated the relationships between leader political skill and follower organizational commitment. We encourage more work in this area and also to systematically examine how political skill affects one's own self, both psychologically and physically.

Further research also is needed to explore the situational context of political skill. A primary assumption made by scholars is that politically skilled employees adapt to situations (e.g., Ferris, Treadway et al., 2005). However, this assumption offers an incomplete picture of political skill and situations. In particular, we would expect that politically skilled individuals also select into and craft (e.g., Wrzesniewski & Dutton, 2001) elements of work to suit individual goals, acting and shaping the environment through the effective use of influence. Thus, rather than acting as passive recipients to situations, politically skill may play a large role in shaping the enacted (Weick, 1969), or social, environment of work. This proposition has critical implications for organizations regarding the use of politically skilled employees, and theoretical and empirical research is needed to explore the processes by which politically skilled employees shape the work environment.

The incorporation of job and work design may also prove useful in exploring situational antecedents and outcomes of political skill. For example, the distinctions among task, knowledge, and social work features found in the job and work design literature (e.g., Humphrey, Nahrgang, & Morgeson, 2007) may help distinguish among the work tasks and roles in which political skill results in the greatest positive effects for the organization. This knowledge is particularly important as organizations seek to effectively deploy politically skilled employees to create value.

Dimensions of Political Skill

Research in the future desperately needs to examine the individual dimensions of political skill (i.e., social astuteness, interpersonal influence, networking ability, and apparent sincerity) and how they might represent differential relationships on work outcomes. Very little research to date has investigated the separate dimensions of political skill, and much of the research conducted has looked at the antecedents of the individual dimensions. When outcomes are studied, they have been examined almost exclusively as objective career success indicators.

Ferris, Blickle et al. (2008) attempted to confirm the construct and criterion-related validity of the PSI. Therefore, they examined the separate dimensions of political skill. In doing so, their results indicated a four-factor structure with a single-factor higher order structure. Further, they found that each dimension of political skill was predicted by a different set of antecedents. Mentoring, extraversion, and self-efficacy were antecedents of social astuteness; networking ability was predicted by extraversion and mentoring; self-efficacy, self-monitoring, and extraversion were antecedents of interpersonal influence; and apparent sincerity was predicted by self-efficacy and mentoring.

In examining career-related outcomes, networking ability, social astuteness, and interpersonal influence predicted career satisfaction. Networking ability was the only predictor of income, and networking ability, social astuteness, and apparent sincerity were related to hierarchical position. Additionally, Blickle, Momm et al. (2009) supported the notion that emotional reasoning skills increase social astuteness, interpersonal influence, and apparent sincerity and that social astuteness, interpersonal influence, and apparent sincerity mediate the relationship between emotional reasoning skills and job performance above personality and cognitive ability.

Some research have explored the relationship between networking ability and mentoring (e.g., Blass, Brouer, Perrewé, & Ferris, 2007). Blass et al. reported that understanding the political environment would mediate the relationship between mentoring and networking ability, suggesting that understanding the politics in the environment stimulates the drive to develop and use social networks. However, these effects were found only for Caucasians and men.

In studying the outcomes of the various dimensions of political skill, Ferris, Treadway, et al. (2005) reported that social astuteness was the only political skill dimension to significantly predict job performance ratings by supervisors. Douglas and Ammeter (2004) found that the networking ability dimension of leader political skill significantly predicted leader performance ratings, and both networking ability and interpersonal influence significantly predicted work unit performance. Finally, Thompson (2005) found that proactive personality was associated with the networking ability dimension of the PSI and furthermore that networking ability mediated the relationship between proactive personality and performance.

Networking ability is expected to be important for leader effectiveness. Scholars have found leader effectiveness to be associated with facilitation and coordination of others, particularly when such behaviors are utilized as part of broader efforts aimed at positioning, networking, coalition building, and social capital creation (e.g., Brass, 2001; House, 1995). All of these activities tend to be facilitated by political skill. Well-positioned and networked leaders are better able to maximize resource attainment for their units, which builds greater appreciation and support from their teams (House). Also, alliances, coalitions, and networking ability have been argued to be related to the success of entrepreneurs (e.g., Baron & Markman, 2000).

Therefore, although there has been some work on the antecedents and objective career outcomes of the separate dimensions of political skill, much of it focused on networking ability, more research is necessary. It may be that different dimensions of political skill play varying roles in meditational relationships. For instance, in the influence tactic choice, tactic effectiveness, and job outcome relationship, it may be that social astuteness and networking ability aid in tactic choice because both can provide the politically skilled individual with information regarding the influence target and the situational appropriateness of various influence tactics.

On the other hand, interpersonal influence and apparent sincerity might play a greater role in the tactic choice–effectiveness relationship, enabling individuals to adjust their behavior to employ the tactic with subtly and genuineness. Newer methods of moderated mediation, such as those developed by Preacher, Rucker, and Hayes (2007) and Edwards and Lambert (2007) will enable researchers to test more complicated models of moderated mediation and thus further inform exactly how political skill operates.

The Proliferation of Social Effectiveness Constructs: Establishing the Boundaries

Although political skill has been empirically differentiated from a number of somewhat similar constructs (e.g., self-monitoring, self-efficacy, emotional intelligence), because it is still a relatively new construct in the field it bears the burden of establishing its uniqueness and distinction from other constructs. It is fair to state that the past decade has witnessed increased research attention and interest in the nature of social effectiveness competencies. As noted by Ferris et al. (2002, p. 49), "Indeed, one could legitimately argue that we have witnessed a proliferation of constructs that all address aspects of effectiveness in social interactions at work. This renewed interest, in conjunction with changing conditions in work organizations, suggests that we need to develop a more informed understanding of social effectiveness, how these various social effectiveness constructs are similar and different, and how and why they are associated with performance and effectiveness in jobs, careers, and organizations."

Five years later, in their discussion of the political skill construct, Ferris et al. (2007) reissued this appeal to sort out and delineate the construct domain space of political skill and other social effectiveness constructs because little empirical work had been published to date (for a couple of exceptions, see Hall & Bernieri, 2001; Levy, Collins, & Nail, 1998). Interestingly, a recent study has attempted to address this issue by conducting an inductive exploration of the social effectiveness domain (Heggestad

& Morrison, 2008). Their exploratory factor analysis of a number of scales yielded four factors identified as social potency, social appropriateness, social emotional expression, and social reputation.

In a broader characterization of this social effectiveness area, Cherniss (2010, p. 184) recently made reference to this category of social constructs as "emotional and social competences (ESC)," which he defined as "those emotional abilities, social skills, personality traits, motivations, interests, goals, values, attachment styles, and life narratives that can contribute to (or detract from) effective performance across a variety of positions." He views ESC as a large set of attributes of individuals, not a single attribute or characteristic. Cherniss would certainly include political skill as an ESC construct.

Similarly, we suggest research on the apparently related constructs of charisma, celebrity leaders, and political skill. Without a doubt, charisma is the leadership quality that we read most about and associate with leadership effectiveness. Generally, charisma can be characterized as charm, inspirational appeal, or *savoir-faire* that draws or inspires individuals to follow a course of action or vision (e.g., Gardner & Avolio, 1998; Greer, 2005; Khurana, 2002). However, Ferris et al. (2007) suggested that charisma and political skill seemed to be quite similar constructs. Mintzberg (1983) suggested that political skill is related to leadership characteristics such as charm and attractiveness or what Kipnis (1974, p. 88) referred to as *personal resources*. Mintzberg also made reference to charisma here in his discussion of political skill—suggesting that charisma was that "mystical quality that attracts followers to an individual" (p. 26).

If we also add in the recent interest and research attention devoted to *celebrity leaders* (e.g., Hayward, Rindova, & Pollack, 2004; Treadway, Adams, Ranft, & Ferris, 2009; Wade, Porac, Pollack, & Graffin, 2006), then we can strongly urge future research into the construct domain distinctiveness and/or similarity among these three constructs.

Leadership and Political Skill

The foregoing discussion of concepts like charisma and celebrity leadership relates to a growing interest in research on leadership and political skill. The role of political skill in leadership and follower effectiveness is a logical one, given the requisite skill sets, and scholars recently have discussed the importance of this role (e.g., Ferris, Davidson, et al., 2005; Ferris et al., 2007; Greenstein, 2004).

In response to appeals for a political theory of leadership (e.g., House & Aditya, 1997), Ammeter, Douglas, Gardner, Hochwarter, and Ferris (2002) proposed a political conceptualization of leadership that included political will and skill as key attributes of leaders. Because organizational politics in this model was defined as the constructive management of shared meaning, the conceptualization presented leaders not in a negative (e.g., personally self-interested, manipulative) but rather as a consensus and constituency builder, thus contributing to effectiveness.

Leaders high in political skill realize their effectiveness through their ability to read and understand situations and people and then to act on such knowledge by situationally adapting, adjusting, and calibrating their behavior to convey the desired images deploy and leverage social capital to further reinforce such images, all the time conveying an air of sincerity and authenticity (Douglas, Ferris, & Perrewé, 2005). As such, political skill appears to be quite similar in nature to charisma (Mintzberg, 1983), because charismatic leaders can effectively read others' interests, motivations, and emotions and can easily adapt and adjust to different situations (Greer, 2005).

Political skilled leaders use their increased capacity to orchestrate, coordinate, and facilitate group or team member interaction in productive ways, thus building unit effectiveness (Ahearn et al., 2004; Ferris et al., 2007). Suggesting that a particularly well-developed type of social/political skill is required of effective leaders, Kotter (1985) argued that such skills are critical for coordinated action in pursuit of important goal accomplishment through both inspiration and mobilization of followers.

Coordination and facilitation both with and through others is associated with leader effectiveness, especially when employed as part of a larger coalition building, positioning, networking, and social capital creation portfolio (e.g., Brass, 2001; House, 1995), all of which are facilitated by political skill. Well-positioned and networked leaders are better able to maximize resource attainment for their units, which builds greater appreciation and support from their teams (House, 1995).

As noted in the review given under the section with studies that used the initial Ferris et al. (1999) six-item measure, two early studies were conducted on leadership and political skill. Douglas and Ammeter (2004) reported that leader political skill was a significant predictor of leader effectiveness ratings. Ahearn et al. (2004) found that leader political skill predicted team performance in a state child welfare system. There have been several more recent studies on the political skill of leaders and the resulting effects on both leader and follower attitudes, behavior, and effectiveness. Furthermore, Treadway et al. (2004) found effects of leader political skill on employee reactions of trust and support.

Treadway, Breland, Williams, Yang, and Williams (in press) provided meaningful conceptual extensions of relational leadership theory, framing political behavior and political skill as elements of relational control, and examining their roles in light of both leaders' and followers' relational self perceptions. This integrative social influence-relational control perspective also examines the role of dyadic distance and affect in the formation of high-quality work relationships.

DeRue, Nahrgang, Wellman, and Humphrey (2011) positioned political skill as one of the interpersonal leader traits they believed to serve as an antecedent of leadership effectiveness through its impact on leader behaviors. Following this, Brouer et al. (2011) found effects of leader political skill on leader and follower effectiveness through LMX. Finally, some research has suggested that political skill serves as a key antecedent of leader reputation (Ammeter et al., 2002; Blass & Ferris, 2007; Hall, Blass, Ferris, & Massengale, 2004), which could mediate the relationship between leader political skill and leader effectiveness.

Related to the importance of future research on leader political skill, scholars should pursue research like Jo Silvester's work, which has investigated political skill and political performance of politicians, focusing initially on British politicians (see Silvester, 2008 for review). These initial results are fascinating and beg the question of whether such predictive results could be found in other countries and cultures. It might be interesting to compare the results of Silvester's research and future work on political skill of politicians with Greenstein's (2004) evaluation of U.S. presidents on the important qualities of public communication, organizational capacity, political skill, vision, cognitive style, and emotional intelligence.

Greenstein (2004) characterized political skill as the use of power to develop support for policies and to establish a reputation among others in the political arena for understanding and being able to work the political system to one's advantage. Lyndon Johnson was noted as the master of political skill, and he worked very hard at developing his craft.

Ronald Reagan, Theodore Roosevelt, and Bill Clinton also were noted for their well-developed political skill.

In addition, researchers could explore the relationship between political skill and leadership emergence. Perceptions of leadership emergence has been explained on the basis of implicit leadership theories; that is, people tend to believe that certain traits characterize leaders in various situations, and when individuals display those traits they are most likely to emerge as leaders (e.g., Lord, Foti, & De Vader, 1984; Smith & Foti, 1998). Additionally, it is important that these traits be perceived by followers, allowing them to notice and understand the leadership behavior (Smith & Foti). Numerous traits have been found to be related to leadership emergence, such as intelligence, dominance, and ambition (e.g., Hogan, Raskin, & Fazzini, 1990; Lord et al., 1984). Others have found that likeability and sociability are also related to leadership emergence (e.g., Hogan et al., 1990; Morrow & Stern, 1990). More recently, Foti and Hauenstein (2007) found that high intelligence, dominance, general self-efficacy, and self-monitoring were associated with leadership emergence.

Politically skilled individuals, therefore, may be more likely to emerge as informal leaders. The ability of the politically skilled to understand the environment and others acting in that environment, in addition to the ease in which they influence people, will likely make them an important and central node in their informal work group and thus seen as a prototypical or ideal leader. Additionally, politically skilled individuals, because of their understanding of the environment and those acting in it (i.e., their social astuteness), will be able to engage in behaviors that the followers notice and recognize as leadership behaviors. Future researchers should investigate the impact of political skill on leadership emergence and implicit leadership.

Political Skill, Work Relationships, and Social Networks

Political skill should play a key role in interpersonal interactions that take place through formal human resources practices, such as performance evaluation. Pfeffer (2009, p. 68) argued that political skill "...helps individuals put a gloss on their performance that ensures a higher rating," and recent research has shown political skill to be a strong and consistent predictor of job performance ratings (e.g., for a review, see Ferris, Munyon, Basik, & Buckley, 2008). Also, a meta-analytic review of the relevant literature (cf. Ng, Eby, Sorensen, & Feldman, 2005) shows that political savvy and social capital (i.e., quantity or quality of accumulated contacts) constitute potent predictors of career success.

Additionally, the nature and underlying dimensions of both formal and informal work relationships have received increased attention recently, and it appears that political skill could play an important role here as well, whether the relationships be between two persons, two groups or units, or two organizations (e.g., Ferris, Liden, Munyon, Summers, Basik, & Buckley, 2009; Munyon, Perryman, Morgante, & Ferris, 2011). For example, trust, support, and commitment are widely regarded as important components of effective social relationships of all types, including those at work. Political skill has been argued and found empirically by Treadway et al. (2004) to favorably increase these reactions and thus presumably to help build higher-quality work relationships. More research should be done in this area.

It has been suggested that the social astuteness and authenticity of the politically skilled should lead to the development of richer and more expansive social networks. Recent work by Treadway, Breland, Williams, Yang, and Shaughnessy (2011) indicates that this is indeed the case. Specifically, this research investigated the interactive effect of employee narcissism and political skill on positioning in performance, advice, and influence networks in the workplace. While the interaction was not significant for influence networks, political skill did demonstrate a significant main effect. In contrast, neither political skill nor narcissism exhibited a main effect on advice networks or performance networks, but the interaction suggested that narcissists are more motivated to engage in these networks and when coupled with high levels of political skill, these employees were more strongly positioned within these networks.

Thus, it appears that politically skilled individuals are more likely to engage their skill in networking activities only when motivated to do so. Adding to this idea, Treadway, Breland, Adams, Duke, and Williams (2010) found that politically skilled employees were more likely to engage in career networking behavior when their future time perspective was long and more likely to engage in community networking behavior when their organizational future time perspective was short. This suggests that politically skilled employees are more likely to use their ability to network with others across various domains of their life, not just in the workplace.

In a unique use of social network methodology, Treadway and his colleagues (Treadway, Shaughnessy, et al., 2010) measured the extent to which individuals were involved in bullying networks in organizations. Using the social information processing of social competence (Dodge, 1986), this research hypothesized that politically skilled bullies were more capable of selecting vulnerable targets and coercing them into engaging in behavior that supports the bully's agenda. Furthermore, they argued that politically skilled bullies would be less likely to have their behavior detected by powerful others and, as such, be less likely to be sanctioned for their behavior. Their results supported these arguments, and although the results are not a traditional measurement of social networks they do provide preliminary evidence that politically skilled employees are more capable of leveraging their advantageous positioning in social networks.

PRACTICAL IMPLICATIONS

For relatively new constructs in the field, it is premature to make specific comments regarding implications for practice until the construct has been subjected to rigorous empirical validation and demonstrated sound results. The research interest in political skill in the short time since it was introduced has resulted in a solid base of findings. Furthermore, there has emerged considerable interest in the applied literature in concepts including political skill, political savvy, and political intelligence (e.g., Ciampa, 2005; DeLuca, 1999; Reardon, 2005).

Thus, there appears to be a ready acceptance of a political perspective on organizations and the requisite skills knowledge, skills, and abilities it takes to be successful and survive in organizations today. Indeed, Ciampa (2005) attested to the critical importance of political skill, when he argued that without it individuals—particularly those in leadership positions—likely would fail. He reported that 40% of new CEOs fail within their first 18 months on the job. He suggested that because top executives tend not to receive much systematic feedback, they must be politically skilled and be able to develop a keen understanding of the organization's political environment.

Selecting for Political Skill

In the personnel selection literature, there has been a call to expand beyond the traditional use of cognitive abilities alone to select job candidates

(Guion, 1998; Wagner, 1997). For instance, Guion called for a broader array of individual traits to be considered in selection, including social skills, which allows harmonious working relationships to form in work groups, teams, and organizations. Additionally, more recent models of job performance have formulated distal and proximal influences believed to affect performance that go beyond general cognitive ability (e.g., Campbell, 1990; McCloy, Campbell, & Cudeck, 1994; Zaccaro, Kemp, & Bader, 2004).

These models recognize personality and general mental abilities as being distal antecedents of job performance, whereas social effectiveness is more proximal. Political skill is one such social effectiveness construct that has demonstrated impressive validity and reliability in its relationship with job performance and can be considered a more proximal measure of job performance to be used in conjunction with other selection assessments such as general mental ability and personality.

As mentioned in the previous review, much work has been done to validate the PSI, and in the process political skill has been found to be positively related to job performance in numerous studies (e.g., Blickle, Kramer, et al., 2011; Blickle, Ferris, et al., in press; Ferris, Witt, & Hochwarter, 2001; Ferris, Treadway et al., 2005; Jawahar et al., 2008; Semadar et al., 2006). Further, Blickle, Kramer, and their colleagues examined the impact of political skill on job performance while controlling for general mental ability and personality. Across three studies, their results provide support for the notion that political skill accounted for a significant increase in overall job performance ratings above personality and general mental ability.

In addition to predicting job performance, political skill may be beneficial in job candidates for other reasons, specifically for allowing adaptability and flexibility in the workplace and acting as a buffer against strain reactions to stressors. Politically skilled individuals are able to read and adapt to their environment (Ferris et al., 2007). This ability is seen as vastly important in today's turbulent work environment. For instance, Guion (1998) argued that individuals might be hired based on one set of criteria and then quickly transferred to another job that may have nothing to do with the hiring criteria.

However, if part of the personnel selection test included political skill, employers could be assured that the politically skilled individuals they hired would adapt to new job duties and demands. In support of this notion, Momm, Blickle, and Liu (2010) found that politically skilled individuals were better able to use feedback and training given during emotional cue learning to improve their performance on emotion recognition. These results give credence to the idea that the politically skill would be better able to use feedback and training to their advantage to adapt to new environments.

It may be argued that the competencies associated with political skill, such as adaptability and influence, are more suited for managerial positions. However, as noted by Blickle and Schnitzler (2010) and as reviewed previously, political skill has also been found to mitigate the negative effects stress. Therefore, it is suggested that the PSI be added to the selection criteria for ordinary, nonmanagerial employees as well.

In their development of the PSI, Ferris, Treadway, et al. (2005) took the first steps of eliminating response bias due to social desirability by removing times in the test construction process that correlated with social desirability. Therefore, a recent experimental field study was undertaken to assess the construct and criterion-related validity of the PSI when used under conditions of personnel selection, specifically in concern of social desirability. Two groups of working individuals filled out the PSI, a measure of the Big Five personality factors, and a measure of social desirability. In one group, the participants were told that they should fill out the materials as if they were being used for personnel selection decisions at job that they very much desired (i.e., faking condition).

The second group was told to fill out the materials honestly (i.e., honesty condition). As expected, the personnel selection group did show socially desirable response bias on the social desirability, conscientiousness, and neuroticism scales. However, the mean difference on the PSI scale between the faking and honest conditions was marginal and not significant, suggesting that the PSI may not be affected by socially desirable responding. Additionally, the PSI was not significantly correlated with social desirability.

To further test the construct validity, the authors examined the relationships between political sill and extraversion, conscientiousness, and neuroticism in both the faking and honesty conditions. Although extraversion, conscientiousness, and neuroticism were affected by social desirability, their relationships with political skill were not significantly different between the faking and honesty condition, suggesting that political skill had equal relationships of construct validity in both conditions.

Therefore, taken together, the PSI has shown to be related to numerous important work outcomes, such as job performance and adaptability. Additionally, the PSI does not seem to be impacted by the response bias of social desirability and even though the Big Five is impacted by social desirability, their relationships with the PSI remained the same regardless. It is suggested, then, that practitioners begin to use the PSI as an additional component of their personnel selection testing or battery. Doing so will ensure that the workers hired have the necessary competencies to adapt to the ever changing workplace, can positively handle workplace stressors, and will do their job.

Training and Development of Political Skill

Although political skill is thought to be partly innate, it is also considered malleable, suggesting it can be trained, developed, and shaped by the environment. In line with the micro-skills approach, which suggests that more specific interpersonal skills are more trainable (Hayes, 2002), it is recommended that political skill be broken down into its four dimensions, social astuteness, interpersonal influence, networking ability, and apparent sincerity for training purposes.

Although research on the development of political skill is in its infancy, some work has shown that networking ability can be increased by mentoring. Specifically, Blass and his colleagues (2007) found that mentoring could increase political understanding of the workplace and that this understanding increased a person's networking ability. That is to say, individuals who are mentored get an understanding of the political landscape of their organization. They learn from their mentors, who is important, whose support is needed, and how to go about gaining that support. This knowledge then directly increases the protégés' ability to network. Therefore, one of the crucial ways organizations can foster political skill, and more specifically networking ability, is to provide individuals with seasoned, politically skilled mentors.

Far less research has been devoted to the development of the other dimensions of political skill, but it has been suggested that mentoring can also increase social astuteness, interpersonal influence, and apparent sincerity. Politically skilled mentors not only provide protégés with valuable network information but also can be a source of valuable knowledge of how to use influence, language, facial expressions, and gestures (Ferris et al., 2007). Not only can the protégés learn by observation, but effective mentors would also take time to explain social interactions to enhance their protégés' understanding.

Beyond mentoring, training for social astuteness, apparent sincerity, and interpersonal influence could involve aspects of active empathetic listening. To improve your ability to understand others and thus influence them, you must listen to them (Ferris, Davidson et al., 2005). Additionally, one way to appear sincere is to careful listen to others (Ferris, Davidson et al.). Active empathetic listening can be defined as the process of receiving verbal and nonverbal messages, processing those messages cognitively while trying to understand their underlying meaning by putting oneself in the position of the sender (Comer & Drollinger, 1999). Training active empathetic listening could be done by showing people the types of cues they may expect in the workplace and how best to respond to them (Comer & Drollinger). This type of training could also involve role-play and scenarios, allowing the trainee to put into practice the concepts learned by studying common cues.

CONCLUSION

Politics in organizations has become accepted as a practical reality and also an area of active scientific inquiry in the organizational sciences. Because of the realization that the political perspective in organizations is an important one, it is incumbent upon scholars to develop a comprehensive understanding of the behaviors, attitudes, and effectiveness of individuals working in political environments. Pfeffer (1981) introduced the political skill construct to the field and argued that a priority for future research should be to develop a better understanding of its nature and consequences. Indeed, Pfeffer envisioned an optimal fit between individuals' political skill and their preference for political environments.

Furthermore, in independent, parallel research conducted at about the same time, Mintzberg (1983, 1985) characterized organizations as political arenas, and he suggested that for survival and effectiveness in such contexts required political will and political skill. This chapter was an attempt to trace the historical roots of the political skill, characterize its development as a scientific construct, and critically review empirical research conducted to date. Finally, the reader is left with suggestions for needed future research as well as how political skill might have implications for management practice.

REFERENCES

Ahearn, K.K., Ferris, G.R., Hochwarter, W.A., Douglas, C., & Ammeter, A.P. (2004). Leader political skill and team performance. *Journal of Management, 30,* 309–327.

Ammeter, A.P., Douglas, C., Gardner, W.L., Hochwarter, W.A., & Ferris, G.R. (2002). Toward a political theory of leadership. *Leadership Quarterly, 13,* 751–796.

Andrews, M., Kacmar, K., & Harris, K. (2009). Got political skill? The impact of justice on the importance of political skill for job performance. *Journal of Applied Psychology, 94,* 1427–1437.

Antonakis, J., & Atwater, L. (2002). Leader distance: A review and a proposed theory. *Leadership Quarterly, 13,* 396–402.

Baron, R.A., & Markman, G.D. (2000). Beyond social capital: The role of social skills in entrepreneurs' success. *Academy of Management Executive, 14,* 1–15.

Blass, F.R., Brouer, R.L., Perrewé, P.L., & Ferris, G.R. (2007). Politics understanding and networking ability as a function of mentoring: The role of gender and race. *Journal of Leadership & Organizational Studies, 14,* 93–105.

Blass, F.R., & Ferris, G.R. (2007). Leader reputation: The roles of mentoring, political skill, contextual learning, and adaptation. *Human Resource Management, 46,* 5–19.

Blickle, G., Ferris, G.R., Munyon, T.P., Momm, T., Zettler, I., Schneider, P.B. et al. (in press). A multi-source, multi-study investigation of job performance prediction by political skill. *Applied Psychology: An International Review.*

Blickle, G., Frohlich, J., Ehlert, S., Pirner, K., Dietl, E., Hanes, T.J. et al. (2011). Socioanalytic theory and work behavior: Roles of work values and political skill in job performance and promotability assessment. *Journal of Vocational Behavior, 78,* 136–148.

Blickle, G., Kramer, J., Schneider, P.B., Meurs, J.A., Ferris, G.R., Mierke, J. et al. (2011). Role of political skill in job performance prediction beyond general mental ability and personality in cross-sectional and predictive studies. *Journal of Applied Social Psychology, 41,* 239–265.

Blickle, G., Kramer, J., Zettler, I., Momm, T., Summers, J.K., Munyon, T.P. et al. (2009). Job demands as a moderator of the political skill–job performance relationship. *Career Development International, 14,* 333–350.

Blickle, G., Meurs, J.A., Schneider, P.B., Kramer, J., Zettler, I., Maschler, J., Noethen, D. et al. (2008). Personality, political skill, and job performance. *Journal of Vocational Behavior, 72,* 377–387.

Blickle, G., Momm, T.S., Kramer, J., Meerke, J., Liu, Y., & Ferris, G.R. (2009). Construct and criterion-related validation of a measure of emotional reasoning skills: A two-study investigation. *International Journal of Selection and Assessment, 17,* 101–118.

Blickle, G., Oerder, K., & Summers, J.K. (2010). The impact of political skill on career success of employees' representatives. *Journal of Vocational Behavior, 77,* 383–390.

Blickle, G., Schneider, P.B., Liu, Y., & Ferris, G.R. (in press). A predictive investigation of reputation as mediator of the political skill–career success relationships. *Journal of Applied Social Psychology.*

Blickle, G., & Schnitzler, A. (2010). Is the political skill inventory fit for personnel selection? An experimental field study. *International Journal of Selection and Assessment, 18,* 155–165.

Blickle, G., Wendel, S., & Ferris, G.R. (2010). Political skill as moderator of personality–job performance relationships in socioanalytic theory: Test of the getting ahead motive in automobile sales. *Journal of Vocational Behavior, 76,* 326–335.

Brass, D.J. (2001). Social capital and organizational leadership. In S.J. Zaccaro & R.J. Klimoski (Eds.), *The nature of organizational leadership* (pp.132–152). San Francisco: Jossey-Bass.

Breland, J., Treadway, D., Duke, A., & Adams, G. (2007). The interactive effect of leader–member exchange and political skill on subjective career success. *Journal of Leadership and Organizational Studies, 13*, 1–14.

Brouer, R.L., Douglas, C., Treadway, D.C., & Ferris, G.R. (2011). Leader political skill, relationship quality, and leader effectiveness: A two-study model test and constructive replication. Manuscript under review.

Brouer, R.L., Duke, A., Treadway, D.C., & Ferris, G.R. (2009). Moderating effect of political skill on the demographic dissimilarity—leader-member exchange quality relationship. *Leadership Quarterly, 20*, 61–69.

Brouer, R.L. Ferris, G.R., Hochwarter, W.A., Laird, M.D., & Gilmore, D.C. (2006). The strain-related reactions to perceptions of organizational politics as a workplace stressor: Political skill as a neutralizer. In E. Vigoda-Gadot & A. Drory (Eds.), *Handbook of organizational politics* (pp. 187–206). Northampton, MA: Edward Elgar Publishing, Inc.

Brouer, R.L., Harris, K.J., & Kacmar, M.K. (in press). The moderating effects of political skill on the perceived politics–outcomes relationships. *Journal of Organizational Behavior.*

Campbell, J.P. (1990). Modeling the performance prediction problem in industrial and organizational psychology. In M.D. Dunnette & L.M. Hough (Eds.), *Handbook of industrial and organizational psychology* (2nd ed., Vol. 1, pp. 687–732). Palo Alto, CA: Consulting Psychologists Press.

Cherniss, C. (2010). Emotional intelligence: New insights and further clarifications. *Industrial and Organizational Psychology, 3*, 183–191.

Ciampa, D. (2005, January). Almost ready: How leaders move. *Harvard Business Review,* 46–53.

Comer, L.B., & Drollinger, T. (1999). Active empathetic listening and selling success: A conceptual framework. *Journal of Personal Selling and Sales Management, 19*, 15–29.

DeLuca, J.R. (1999). *Political savvy: Systematic approaches to leadership behind the scenes.* Berwyn, PA: Evergreen Business Group.

Dodge, K.A. (1986). A social information processing model of social competence in children. In M. Perlmutter (Ed.), *The Minnesota symposia in child psychology* (Vol. 18, pp. 77–125). Hillsdale, NJ: Erlbaum.

DuBrin, A.J. (2009). *Political behavior in organizations.* Thousand Oaks, CA: Sage Publications.

DeRue, D.S., Nahrgang, J.D., Wellman, N., & Humphrey, S.E. (2011). Trait and behavioral theories of leadership: An integration and meta-analytic test of their relative validity. *Personnel Psychology, 64*, 7–52.

Douglas, C., & Ammeter, A.P. (2004). An examination of leader political skill and its effect on ratings of leader effectiveness. *Leadership Quarterly, 15*, 537–550.

Douglas, C., Ferris, G.R., & Perrewé (2005). Leader political skill and authentic leadership. In W.L. Gardner, B.J. Avolio, & F.O. Walumbwa (Eds.), *Authentic leadership theory and practice: Origins, effects, and development* (Vol. 3, pp. 139–154 of the *Monographs in Leadership Management* series, J.G. Hunt, Sr. Ed.). Oxford, UK: Elsevier Science.

Edwards, J.R., & Lambert, L.S. (2007). Methods for integrating moderation and mediation: A general analytical framework using moderated path analysis. *Psychological Methods, 12*, 1–22.

Ferris, G.R., Berkson, H.M., Kaplan, D.M., Gilmore, D.C., Buckley, M.R., Hochwarter, W.A. et al. (1999). *Development and initial validation of the political skill inventory.* Paper presented at the Academy of Management, 59th Annual National Meeting, Chicago.

Ferris, G.R., Bhawuk, D.P.S., Fedor, D.B., & Judge, T.A. (1995). Organizational politics and citizenship: Attributions of intentionality and construct definition. In M.J. Martinko (Ed.), *Advances in attribution theory: An organizational perspective* (pp. 231–252). Delray Beach, FL: St. Lucie Press.

Ferris, G.R., Blickle, G., Schneider, P.B., Kramer, J., Zettler, I., Solga, J. et al. (2008). Political skill construct and criterion-related validation: A two-study investigation. *Journal of Managerial Psychology, 23,* 744–771.

Ferris, G.R., Davidson, S.L., & Perrewé, P.L. (2005). *Political skill at work: Impact on work effectiveness.* Mountain View, CA: Davies-Black Publishing.

Ferris, G.R., Liden, R.C., Munyon, T.P., Summers, J.K., Basik, K., & Buckley, M.R. (2009). Relationships at work: Toward a multidimensional conceptualization of dyadic work relationships. *Journal of Management, 35,* 1379–1403.

Ferris, G.R., Munyon, T.P., Basik, K.J., & Buckley, M.R. (2008). The performance evaluation context: Social, emotional, cognitive, political, and relationship components. *Human Resource Management Review, 18,* 146–163.

Ferris, G.R., Perrewé, P.L., & Douglas, C. (2002). Social effectiveness in organizations: Construct validity and research directions. *Journal of Leadership & Organizational Studies, 9,* 49–63.

Ferris, G.R., Rogers, L.M., Blass, F.R., & Hochwarter, W.A. (2009). The interaction of job-limiting pain and political skill on job satisfaction and organizational citizenship behavior. *Journal of Managerial Psychology, 24,* 584–608.

Ferris, G.R., Treadway, D.C., Kolodinsky, R.W., Hochwarter, W.A., Kacmar, C.J., Douglas, C. et al. (2005). Development and validation of the political skill inventory. *Journal of Management, 31,* 126–152.

Ferris, G.R., Treadway, D.C., Perrewé, P.L., Brouer, R.L., Douglas, C., & Lux, S. (2007). Political skill in organizations. *Journal of Management, 33,* 290–320.

Ferris, G.R., Witt, L.A., & Hochwarter, W.A. (2001). Interaction of social skill and general mental ability on job performance and salary. *Journal of Applied Psychology, 86,* 1075–1082.

Foti, R.J., & Hauenstein, N.M.A. (2007). Pattern and variable approaches in leadership emergence and effectiveness. *Journal of Applied Psychology. 92,* 347–355.

Gardner, W.L., & Avolio, B.J. (1998). The charismatic relationship: A dramaturgical perspective. *Academy of Management Review, 23,* 32–58.

Gentry, W.A., Gilmore, D.C., Porter, M.L.S., & Leslie, J.B. (in press). Political skill as an indicator of promotability among multiple rater sources. *Journal of Organizational Behavior.*

Greenstein, F.I. (2004). *The presidential difference: Leadership style from FDR to George W. Bush.* Princeton, NJ: Princeton University Press.

Greer, M. (2005). The science of savoir faire. *Monitor on Psychology, 36,* 28–30.

Guion, R.M. (1998). Some virtues of dissatisfaction in the science and practice of personnel selection. *Human Resource Management Review, 8,* 351–365.

Hall, J.A., & Bernieri, F.J. (2001). *Interpersonal sensitivity: Theory and measurement.* Mahwah, NJ: Lawrence Erlbaum.

Hall, A.T., Blass, F.R., Ferris, G.R., & Massengale, R. (2004). Leader reputation and accountability: Implications for dysfunctional leader behavior. *Leadership Quarterly, 15,* 515–536.

Harris, K.J., Kacmar, K.M., Zivnuska, S., & Shaw, J.D. (2007). The impact of political skill on impression management effectiveness. *Journal of Applied Psychology, 92,* 278–285.

Hayes, J. (2002). *Interpersonal skills at work.* London: Routledge, Taylor & Francis Group.

Harvey, P., Harris, R.B., Harris, K.J., & Wheeler, A.R. (2007). Attenuating the effects of social stress: The impact of political skill. *Journal of Occupational Health Psychology, 12,* 105–115.

Hayward, M.L.A, Rindova, V.P., & Pollack, T.G. (2004). Believing one's own press: The causes and consequences of CEO celebrity. *Strategic Management Journal, 25,* 637–653.

Heggestad, E.D., & Morrison, M.J. (2008). An inductive exploration of the social effectiveness construct space. *Journal of Personality, 76,* 839–873.

Hochwarter, W.A., Ferris, G.R., Gavin, M.B., Perrewé, P.L., Hall, A.T., & Frink, D.D. (2007). Political skill as neutralizer of felt accountability – job tension effects on job performance ratings: A longitudinal investigation. *Organizational Behavior and Human Decision Processes, 102,* 226–239.

Hochwarter, W.A., Summers, J.K., Thompson, K.W., Perrewé, P.L., & Ferris, G.R. (2010). Strain reactions to perceived entitlement behavior by others as a contextual stressor: Moderating role of political skill in three samples. *Journal of Occupational Health Psychology, 15*(4), 388–398.

Hochwarter, W.A., Witt, L.A., Treadway, D.C., & Ferris, G.R. (2006). The interaction of social skill and organizational support on job performance. *Journal of Applied Psychology, 91,* 482–489.

Hogan, R. (1983). A socioanalytic theory of personality. In M.M. Page (Ed.), *1982 Nebraska symposium on motivation.* (pp. 55–89). Lincoln: University of Nebraska Press.

Hogan, R., Raskin, R., & Fazzini, D. (1990). The dark side of charisma. In K. Clark & M. Clark (Eds.), *Measures of leadership* (pp. 343–354). West Orange, NJ: Leadership Library of America.

Hogan, R., & Shelton, D. (1998). A socioanalytic perspective on job performance. *Human Performance, 11,* 129–144.

Holland, J.L. (1976). Vocational preferences. In M.D. Dunnette (Ed.), *Handbook of industrial and organizational psychology* (pp. 521–570). Chicago: Rand McNally.

House, R.J. (1995). Leadership in the twenty-first century. In A. Howard (Ed.), *The changing nature of work* (pp. 411–450). San Francisco: Jossey-Bass.

House, R.J., & Aditya, R.N. (1997). The social scientific study of leadership: Quo vadis? *Journal of Management, 23,* 409–473.

Humphrey, S.E., Nahrgang, J.D., & Morgeson, F.P. (2007). Integrating motivational, social, and contextual work design features: A meta-analytic summary and theoretical extension of the work design literature. *Journal of Applied Psychology, 92*(5), 1332–1356.

Jawahar, I.M., Meurs, J.A., Ferris, G.R., & Hochwarter, W.A. (2008). Self-efficacy and political skill as comparative predictors of task and contextual performance: A two-study constructive replication. *Human Performance, 21,* 138–157.

Jones, E.E. (1990). *Interpersonal perception.* New York: W.H. Freeman.

Kaplan, D.M. (2008). Political choices: The role of political skill in occupational choice. *Career Development International, 13,* 46–55.

Kapoutsis, I., Papalexandris, A., Nikolopoulos, A., Hochwarter, W.A., & Ferris, G.R. (2011). Politics perceptions as moderator of the political skill–job performance relationship: A two-study, cross-national, constructive replication. *Journal of Vocational Behavior, 78,* 123–135.

Khurana, R. (2002). *Searching for a corporate savior: The irrational quest for charismatic CEOs*. Princeton, NJ: Princeton University Press.

Kipnis, D. (1974). The powerholders. In J.T. Tedeschi (Ed.), *Perspectives on social power* (pp. 82–122). Chicago, IL: Aldine.

Kolodinsky, R.W., Hochwarter, W.A., & Ferris, G.R. (2004). Nonlinearity in the relationship between political skill and work outcomes: Convergent evidence from three studies. *Journal of Vocational Behavior, 65*, 294–308.

Kolodinsky, R.W., Treadway, D.C., & Ferris, G.R. (2007). Political skill and influence effectiveness: Testing portions of an expanded Ferris and Judge (1991) model. *Human Relations, 60*, 1747–1777.

Kotter, J.P. (1985). *Power and influence: Beyond formal authority*. New York: Free Press.

Laird, M.D., Zboja, J., Martinez, A.D., & Ferris, G.R. (2011). The interaction of performance and political skill on personal reputation: An adaptive self-regulation approach. Manuscript under review.

Levy, D.A., Collins, B.E., & Nail, P.R. (1998). A new model of interpersonal influence characteristics. *Journal of Social Behavior and Personality, 13*, 715–733.

Liu, Y., Ferris, G.R., Zinko, R., Perrewé, P.L., Weitz, B., & Xu, J. (2007). Dispositional antecedents and outcomes of political skill in organizations: A four-study investigation with convergence. *Journal of Vocational Behavior, 71*, 146–165.

Lord, R.G., Foti, R.J., & De Vader, C.L. (1984). A test of leadership categorization theory: Internal structure, information processing, and leadership perceptions. *Organizational Behavior and Human Performance, 34*, 343–378.

McCloy, R.A., Campbell, J.P., & Cudeck, R. (1994). A confirmatory test of a model of performance determinants. *Journal of Applied Psychology, 79*, 493–505.

Meurs, J.A., Gallagher, V.C., & Perrewé, P.L. (2010). The role of political skill in the stressor-outcome relationship: Differential predictions for self and other reports of political skill. *Journal of Vocational Behavior, 76*, 520–533.

Mintzberg, H. (1983). *Power in and around organizations*. Englewood Cliffs, NJ: Prentice-Hall.

Mintzberg, H. (1985). The organization as political arena. *Journal of Management Studies, 22*, 133–154.

Momm, T., Blickle, G., & Liu, Y. (2010). Political skill and emotional cue learning. *Personality and Individual Differences, 49*, 396–401.

Morrow. I.J., & Stern, M. (1990). Stars. adversaries, producers and phantoms at work: A new leadership typology. In K. Clark & M. Clark (Eds.), *Measures of leadership* (pp. 419–440). West Orange, NJ: Leadership Library of America.

Munyon, T.P., Perryman, A.A., Morgante, J.P., & Ferris, G.R. (2011). Firm relationships: The dynamics of effective organization alliances. *Organizational Dynamics, 40*, 96–103.

Napier, B.J., & Ferris, G.R. (1993). Distance in organizations. *Human Resource Management Review, 3*, 321–357.

Ng, T.W.H., Eby, L.T., Sorensen, K.L., & Feldman, D.C. (2005). Predictors of objective and subjective career success: A meta-analysis. *Personnel Psychology, 58*, 367–408.

Perrewé, P.L., Ferris, G.R., Frink, D.D., & Anthony, W.P. (2000). Political skill: An antidote for workplace stressors. *Academy of Management Executive, 14*, 115–123.

Perrewé, P.L., Zellars, K.L., Ferris, G.R., Rossi, A.M., Kacmar, C.J., & Ralston, D.A. (2004). Neutralizing job stressors: Political skill as an antidote to the dysfunctional consequences of role conflict stressors. *Academy of Management Journal, 47*, 141–152.

Perrewé, P.L., Zellars, K.L., Rossi, A.M., Ferris, G.R., Kacmar, C.J., Liu, Y. et al. (2005). Political skill: An antidote in the role overload–strain relationship. *Journal of Occupational Health Psychology, 10,* 239–250.

Pfeffer, J. (1981). *Power in organizations.* Boston: Pitman.

Pfeffer, J. (1992). *Managing with power.* Boston: Harvard University Press.

Pfeffer, J. (2009). Low grades for performance reviews. *Business Week,* August 3, p. 68.

Pfeffer, J. (2010a). *Power: Why some people have it and others don't.* New York: HarperCollins Publishers.

Pfeffer, J. (2010b, July–August). Power play. *Harvard Business Review,* 84–92.

Preacher, K.J., Rucker, D.D., & Hayes, A.F. (2007). Addressing moderated mediation hypotheses: Theory, methods, and prescriptions. *Multivariate Behavioral Research, 42,* 185–227.

Reardon, K.K. (2005). *It's all politics: Winning in a world where hard work and talent aren't enough.* New York: Doubleday.

Semadar, A., Robins, G., & Ferris, G.R. (2006). Comparing the validity of multiple social effectiveness constructs in the prediction of managerial job performance. *Journal of Organizational Behavior, 27,* 443–461.

Silvester, J. (2008). The good, the bad, and the ugly: Politics and politicians at work. In G.P. Hodgkinson & J.K. Ford (Eds.), *International review of industrial and organizational psychology* (Vol. 23, pp. 107–148). Chichester, UK: John Wiley & Sons.

Smith, J.A., & Foti, R.J. (1998). A pattern approach to the study of leader emergence. *Leadership Quarterly, 9,* 147–160.

Smith, A.D., Plowman, D., Duchon, D., & Quinn, A. (2009). A qualitative study of high-reputation plant managers: Political skill and successful outcomes. *Journal of Operations Management, 27,* 428–443.

Snyder, M. (1987). *Public appearances, private realities: The psychology of self-monitoring.* New York: W.H. Freeman.

Thompson, J.A. (2005). Proactive personality and job performance: A social capital perspective. *Journal of Applied Psychology, 90,* 1011–1017.

Treadway, D.C. (2012). Political will. In G.R. Ferris & D.C. Treadway (Eds.), *Politics in organizations: Theory and research considerations* (pp. 529–554). New York: Routledge/Taylor & Francis.

Treadway, D.C., Adams, G., Hanes, T.J., Perrewé, P.L., Magnusen, M.J., & Ferris, G.R. (2011). Roles of recruiter political skill and performance resource leveraging on recruitment effectiveness: The case of NCAA football recruiting. Manuscript under review.

Treadway, D.C., Adams, G.L., Ranft, A.L., & Ferris, G.R. (2009). A meso-level conceptualization of CEO celebrity effectiveness. *Leadership Quarterly, 20,* 554–570.

Treadway, D.C., Breland, J.W., Adams, G.L., Duke, A.B., & Williams, L.A. (2010). The interactive effects of political skill and future time perspective on career and community networking behavior. *Social Networks, 32,* 138–147.

Treadway, D.C., Breland, J.W., Williams, L.M., Cho, J., Yang, J., & Ferris, G.R. (in press). Social influence and interpersonal power in organizations: Roles of performance and political skill in two studies. *Journal of Management.*

Treadway, D.C., Breland, J.W., Williams, L.V., Yang, J., & Shaughnessy, B.A. (2011). *Interactive effects of narcissism and political skill on network positioning.* Paper presented at the Annual Meeting of the Society for Industrial and Organizational Psychology, Chicago.

Treadway, D.C., Breland, J.W., Williams, L.A., Yang, J., & Williams, L. (in press). Political skill, relational control, and the relational self in the process of relational leadership. In M. Uhl-Bien & S.M. Ospina (Eds.), *Advancing relational leadership theory: A conversation among perspectives* (Leadership Horizons Series). Charlotte, NC: Information Age Publishing

Treadway, D.C., Ferris, G.R., Douglas, C., Hochwarter, W.A., Kacmar, C.J., Ammeter, A.P. et al. (2004). Leader political skill and employee reactions. *Leadership Quarterly, 15,* 493–51.

Treadway, D.C., Ferris, G.R., Duke, A.B., Adams, G., & Thatcher, J.B. (2007). The moderating role of subordinate political skill on supervisors' impressions of subordinate ingratiation and ratings of interpersonal facilitation. *Journal of Applied Psychology, 92,* 848–855.

Treadway, D.C., Shaughnessy, B.A., Breland, J.W., Yang, J., Reeves, M., & Roberts, M. (2011). When bullying pays off. Paper presented at the Annual Meeting of the Society for Industrial and Organizational Psychology. Chicago.

Wade, J.B., Porac, J.F., Pollock, T.G., & Graffin, S.D. (2006). The burden of celebrity: The impact of CEO certification contests on CEO pay and performance. *Academy of Management Journal, 49,* 643–660.

Wagner, R.K. (1997). Intelligence, training, and employment. *American Psychologist, 52,* 1059–1069.

Weick, K.E. (1969). *The psychology of organizing.* Reading, MA: Addison-Wesley.

Wei, L-Q., Liu, J., Chen, Y-Y., & Wu, L-Z. (2010). Political skill, supervisor-subordinate *guanxi* and career prospects in Chinese firms. *Journal of Management Studies, 47,*437–54.

Witt, L.A., & Ferris, G.R. (2003). Social skill as moderator of the conscientiousness–performance relationship: Convergent evidence across four studies. *Journal of Applied Psychology, 88,* 809–820.

Wrzesniewski, A., & Dutton, J.E. (2001). Crafting a job: Revisioning employees as active crafters of their own work. *Academy of Management Review, 26,* 179–201.

Zaccaro, S.J., Kemp, C., & Bader, P. (2004). Leader traits and attributes. In J. Antonakis, A.T. Cianciolo, & R.J. Sternberg (Eds.), *The nature of leadership* (pp. 101–124). Thousand Oaks, CA: Sage Publications.

Zellars, K.L., Perrewé, P.L., Rossi, A.M., Tepper, B.J., & Ferris, G.R. (2008). Moderating effects of political skill, perceived control, and self-efficacy on the relationship between negative affectivity and physiological strain. *Journal of Organizational Behavior, 29,* 549–571.

Zinko, R., Ferris, G.R., Blass, F.R., & Laird, M.D. (2007). Toward a theory of reputation in organizations. In J.J. Martocchio (Ed.), *Research in personnel and human resources management* (Vol. 26, pp.169–209). Oxford, UK: JAI Press/Elsevier Science Ltd.

Zinko, R., Ferris, G.R., Humphrey, S.E., Meyer, C.J., & Aime, F. (in press). Personal reputation in organizations: Two-study constructive replication and extension of antecedents and consequences. *Journal of Occupational and Organizational Psychology.*

17

Political Will in Organizations

Darren C. Treadway
State University of New York at Buffalo

> They realized that to be in power, you didn't need guns or money or even numbers. You just needed the will to do what the other guy wouldn't.
>
> —**Verbal Quint,** *The Usual Suspects*

Climate change, famine in Africa, the ongoing war in Afghanistan: What do these things have in common? The failure to effectively address each has been, at least partially, attributed to a lack of political will. While it cannot be denied that these events are more globally significant when compared with the treatments of organizational politics familiar in the organizational sciences, it cannot be denied that the ability to change these events is a contest of wills—that is, the will of those who desire change pitted against the will of those protecting the status quo. Ultimately, this battle will be won decision by decision and initiative by initiative and represents the cumulative impact of countless individual acts designed to influence others and affect change. Inherent in each of these acts is personal risk ranging from potential losses of social capital to the loss of life. Thus, what sets leaders in these situations apart from others is their motivation to accept this risk and to move their initiatives forward.

It is the contention of this chapter that when individuals strategically invest themselves in ways that risk their social capital in efforts to influence others and attain personal objectives, this constitutes political behavior. The magnitude of the goal or objective is immaterial, but instead the intent of the efforts must be self-serving in nature to be referred to as *political behavior*. Thus, for example, the initiation of large-scale social change and efforts to obtain a larger pay raise and simply to be well liked satisfy these imposed conditions because they are focused on the advancements of the actors' specific agenda by engaging in influence for personal gain. Accordingly, a broad view of political behavior is taken here that includes perspectives on self-presentation, impression management, influence tactics, voice behavior, and political behavior. In casting such a wide net, the intention is to understand the full spectrum of motivations that might generate political behavior in organizations.

Although it has been frequently discussed in the business and popular press as well as in academic circles, political will is an ambiguous concept, with poorly defined parameters. Toward clarifying and refining this concept, there are several goals of the present chapter. First, this chapter provides a comprehensive review of the motivational forces addressed in the organizational and political science literatures as they relate to the enactment of individual political behavior in organizations. Second, from this review, a definition of political will is proposed and justified. Third, from the components of this definition, a multidimensional perspective of political will is developed, and previous literature is discussed. Finally, future research directions are discussed for this interesting but previously underdeveloped construct.

TOWARD A DEFINITION OF POLITICAL WILL

Political will is a widely used but poorly understood term. Most often used in the popular press, it has come to be viewed as a catchall for anything from a risk of political capital by a particular governmental leader to a more amorphous connotation of the broad spectrum of individuals, groups, and systems that are needed to impact and sustain social and/or policy change. Hammergren (1998) appropriately characterized the utility of this ambiguity stating that political will is "the slipperiest concept in the policy lexicon" (p. 12)" and recognizing its essentialness to any successful policy initiative by suggesting that it "is never defined except by its absence" (p. 12).

This chapter is not alone in seeking a more precise definition of the political will construct. Indeed, recent efforts within political science have offered important insights into both the magnitude and specification of the construct, a few of which seem particularly relevant in developing a definition for the organizational sciences. Kpundeh (1998, p. 92) defined political will as "the demonstrated credible intent of political actors (e.g., elected or appointed leaders, civil society watchdogs, stakeholder groups, etc.) to attack perceived causes or effects of corruption at a systemic level." From this definition, it can be seen that political will manifests itself within behaviors and thus is characterized by actions and not intentions.

Expanding upon the definition of political will as it relates to governance, Brinkerhoff (2000, p. 241) suggested that it is:

> A phenomenon that includes (a) individual actors along with their aspirations, motivations, and capacities (b) organizations within which individuals function and on whose behalf individuals often act (c) socio-economic and governance systems, which frame both constraints and incentives for individuals and organizations, and (d) the policies, programmes, and activities that actors and organizations are involved with at various stages.

He further articulated that political will could be identified by five characteristics: (1) whether the focus of the agenda is driven by the reformer or if it is imposed on the reformer; (2) the degree to which the reformer analyzes the situation in a manner that communicates analytic rigor; (3) the "willingness and ability of the reformer to mobilize support" (p. 242) for the initiative; (4) the degree to which sanctions and rewards are applied by the reformer; and (5) the level of resources that are applied to ongoing support of the initiative. This more expansive definition shows the interdependent nature of individual action, group behavior, and systems in the goal attainment process.

Most recently, Post, Raile, and Raile (2010) offered a comprehensive evaluation of the political will concept. In comparing the previous definitions of political will, they surmised that three common categories emerged. The first of these categories had to do with the distribution of preferences with regard to the policy or initiative. Second, they felt these definitions each focused on the authority, capacity, and legitimacy of the decision makers. A third category dealt with the commitment to preferences held by the decision makers. From these categories, they articulated that "plainly speaking, political will is the extent of committed support among key decision-makers for a particular policy solution to a particular problem" (p. 659).

Post et al. (2010) further suggested that fundamental questions exist in the development of a political will definition. One, in particular, is whether the *will* is attached to a single outcome or if it is continuous? Furthermore, it is important to determine if political will is an individual-level or group-level construct. Whereas Post et al. suggested that because their concern is the social collective and public policy, *political* must represent a group-level construct. Therefore, they concluded that individuals' personal motivation represents political will only in instances where they have complete authoritarian control.

The advances in the political science field to provide definitional clarity are rendered more notable in that no similar attempt has been made in the organizational sciences despite dozens of articles that have dealt directly with individuals' motivation to engage in political or influence behavior. Mintzberg (1983) is perhaps the first to use the term political will, and although he did not provide a formal definition he suggested that it represented individuals' "capacity to expend energy" toward a particular objective.

Expanding on Mintzberg's (1983) discussions, Treadway, Hochwarter, Kacmar, and Ferris (2005) described political will as "actor's willingness to expend energy in pursuit of political goals, and it is viewed as an essential precursor to engaging in political behavior" (p. 231). Although these views advance understanding of political will in organizations, they do not take into account the level of specification suggested by Post et al. (2010). As such, they do not articulate a framework upon which a body of knowledge can be created in the organizational sciences.

The orientation of the present chapter differs from Post et al.'s (2010) perspective on political will in two important ways. Although it must be acknowledged that political will can function as a group-level construct, and certainly individuals' will is easier to facilitate goal attainment if they have dictatorial-type control, these conclusions are based on the assumption that political will operates in a vacuum and, by itself, affects change. Absent from their conclusions is the acceptance that it is from individual influences that group action is developed. Thus, this chapter differs in assuming that political will can ensure only that individuals will engage in behaviors designed to motivate influential others to engage in change-related behaviors but does not guarantee group action or success. Furthermore, it is acknowledged that personal political will is most effective, and thus most likely to succeed, when coupled with elevated levels of personal political skill.

This chapter thus integrates views of the political and organizational sciences to examine the most critical aspect of politics in and around organizations—that is, an individual's motivation to influence others. The centrality of the individual clearly is seen in the Treadway et al. (2005)

description of political will but also is apparent in the more ecological definitions provided in political science. While these definitions focus primarily on aggregate levels of analysis that cumulatively affect policy decisions, they acknowledge the role of individual participants' motivations and abilities—or more broadly discussed as aspirations—when they are part of an ongoing initiative.

In consideration of these previous treatments, political will is defined here as the motivation to engage in strategic, goal-directed behavior that advances the personal agenda and objectives of the actor that inherently involves the risk of relational or reputational capital. Implied in this definition are three central tenets: strategy, self-serving, and risk. Because behavior is viewed as strategic, this definition of political will excludes the concept of automaticity of behavior.

While acknowledging that not all behaviors are thoroughly processed, it is believed that each individual behavior is part of an ongoing influence effort designed to increase the likelihood that actors achieve their objectives. Also, it is suggested that these objectives ultimately emanate from personal goals regardless of whether they benefit the collective, and as such these behaviors must be considered, by their very nature, as self-serving. Finally, the competition for resources and recognition in organizations produces an environment in which each political behavior carries with it inherent personal risk.

A MULTIDIMENSIONAL CONCEPTUALIZATION OF POLITICAL WILL

Research on motivation and political behavior has not been slowed by the lack of a concise definition of political will. Over the last 20 years, dozens of studies in the organizational sciences have examined aspects of motivation and its impact on the use of political behavior, impression management, self-presentation, and influence tactics. Before proceeding, it is useful to acknowledge previous frameworks of motivation and political behavior. These frameworks both outline the general content areas of work on political will and allude to the multilevel and multidimensional nature of political will.

One of the most widely recognized frameworks addressing motivation is Leary and Kowalski's (1990) two-component model of impression management. Similar to Mintzberg's (1983) framing of political will and political skill, the Leary and Kowalski framework suggests that influence behavior is the product of the two processes of impression motivation and impression construction. In relation to motivation, the authors suggested that the level of goal relevance of the behavior, the value of desired goals, and the discrepancy between the image the actor wishes to project and their current image increase the motivation to engage in impression management behavior. Thus, these three factors are seen as driving individuals' basic motivations of obtaining social or material outcomes, maintaining their self-esteem, or developing their identity.

This chapter also suggests that political will is a multidimensional construct. Similar notions were advanced by Barbuto, Fritz, and Marx (2002), who used the Multidimensional Motivation Sources Inventory (Barbuto & Scholl, 1998) to investigate a leader's motivation to engage in impression management behavior. This scale assesses five bases of motivation. Intrinsic process motivation accounts for instances in which the work is motivating in and of itself. Instrumental motivation is the degree to which employees perceive that their work-related behaviors will lead to instrumental or tangible outcomes.

Self-concept external motivation assesses if the employees are motivated to act in a manner that is consistent with others' expectations and to seek feedback from external sources that aligns with their own self-concept. In contrast, employees with high self-concept internal motivation have personal standards or goals that represent their ideal self and are motivated to engage in behaviors that align with this ideal. Finally, employees' goal internalization motivation is the degree to which they are motivated to engage in behaviors that are aligned with their personal values.

Barbuto and his colleagues (2002) found that leaders high in intrinsic process motivation more likely would use personal appeals, legitimating, rational persuasion, exchange, ingratiation, inspirational appeals, and coalitions to influence their subordinates. Their correlation analysis established that instrumental motivation was related only to exchange tactics, and self-concept external needs were related to personal appeals and exchange tactics. Self-concept internal needs were negatively related to legitimating and rational persuasion tactics. Goal internalization, need for power, need for affiliation, and need for achievement were not related to any of the influence tactics. Though the conclusions drawn from this study are limited due to the use of correlation analysis, this study benefited from using a wide range of tactics and motivations and from multisource data rating the leaders' influence behavior. As such, it represents an important contribution to the understanding of influence behavior and motivation.

Although the research discussed undoubtedly has moved the discipline forward, it has taken a limited view of political behavior phenomena, investigating only impression management behavior. As previously discussed, this chapter takes a more inclusive view of political behavior and assumes that the fine line among impression management, self-presentation, influence tactics, and political behavior, which usually is defined by the attributions of the target or bystanders (Ferris, Bhawuk, Fedor, & Judge, 1995) is unnecessarily limiting to the development of the organizational politics literature.

It is the contention advanced here that while these previous conceptualizations certainly are notable, little attempt has been made to look across the wide spectrum of studies on motivation in impression management, influence tactics, and political behavior, to offer a framework that can both make sense of the foundations of this work, and also to serve to better understand the contexts in which these motivations may be most relevant. In the following space, the previous literature is reviewed in a manner that illustrates the interrelatedness of these studies while simultaneously postulating differences that will explicate the complexity that these competing human drives create in assessing the risk of and the benefits for engaging in political behavior. This review of the literature yields five dimensions of motivation that are presented as a multidimensional framework of political will: instrumental, relational, concern for the self, concern for others, and risk.

Whereas these dimensions are expected to be conceptually and empirically related, the modest nature of such relationships suggests that not only are they unique but also that they should be simultaneously considered in comprehensive models of political behavior. Toward understanding how these categories may be integrated to predict behavior, it is suggested that the first four dimensions roughly can be distinguished on two axes (i.e., the target of concern and the basis of the outcome). The target of concern reflects the competing drives of concern for self versus concern for others, and the basis of the outcome can be distinguished as either relational or instrumental.

It is proposed that in any situation all individuals will experience these competing motivations and that individuals' behavior can be predicted by

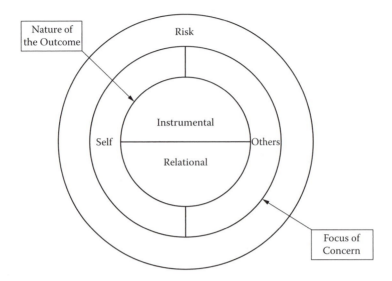

FIGURE 17.1
Interrelations of the dimensions of political will.

understanding the relative salience and importance of these rival drives. These motivations are depicted in the two inner rings of Figure 17.1. This part of the diagram can be seen as much like a padlock where the relative importance of each dimension is "dialed in" for any particular decision or outcome. The fifth dimension, risk, is seen as a buffer that impacts the likelihood and type of political behavior enacted.

Dimension 1: Instrumental

Perhaps one of the most distinguishing tenets of the organizational politics literature is that individuals are self-interested and that their behaviors and actions are driven solely by the need to satisfy their own desires and objectives. More expansively, Schlenker (1980) proposed the widely accepted view that one of the most fundamental aspects of human existence is that individuals are motivated to gain pleasure and avoid aversive outcomes. Congruently, Cobb's (1984) episodic model of power suggested that the psychological orientation of individuals is important to their use of power. Specifically, he argued that individuals would be more likely to use their power when they found the use of such power as intrinsically or instrumentally rewarding. Thus, any consideration of the motivations that influence individuals to engage in political behavior initially must consider the basic needs of such individuals as they relate to obtaining both instrumentally and intrinsic aspects of need satisfaction.

Perhaps the most obvious of these basic need states is presented in McClelland's (1961) discussion of power motivation and need for achievement. McClelland suggested that individuals with a high need for power are driven to exert influence and control over others. Those with high need achievement can be seen as having a need to master their environments, to overcome obstacles, and to surpass others (Murray, 1938). Given these characteristics, it should not be surprising that these constructs often have been investigated in relation to the implementation of political behaviors.

In an early investigation of need for power and political behavior, Browning and Jacob (1964) used the Thematic Apperception Test (TAT) to assess whether the motivations of career politicians were different from those in the general population. The assumption was that those engaged in politicking as a career would be more motivated by power than those who were not. However, this research found that politicians did not differ from nonpoliticians in relation to their power motivation. The authors further hypothesized that those politicians would be less concerned with establishing warm relationships with others. Thus, they asserted that politicians would have lower levels of affiliation motivation. However, their research found that businessmen-politicians were more likely driven by the need for affiliation than businessmen who were nonpoliticians. However, the differences in these scores were not statistically significant.

Treadway and his colleagues (2005) were the first to categorize disparate motivations under the rubric of political will and operationalized need for achievement and intrinsic motivation as indicators of this construct. Building off competitive nature of those high in need for achievement, they found that need for achievement was positively related to self-reported political behavior. Similarly, Leary and Kowalski (1990) found that individuals high in need for achievement engaged in self-presentation behaviors designed to project an impression of competence.

This assertion of individuals' competence through the use of political behavior also was seen in Treadway et al.'s (2005) framing of intrinsic motivation as a type of political will. These researchers used self-determination theory as a basis for proposing the impact of intrinsic motivation on political behavior. This theory asserts that the pursuit of intrinsic goals positively impacts individuals' needs for competence and relatedness (Deci & Ryan, 1985). They suggested that because the demonstration of individuals' competence is intrinsically rewarding, those high in intrinsic motivation will engage in political behavior to assure that their competence is recognized. They found that intrinsic motivation was related to higher levels of political behavior.

Expanding the domain of instrumental antecedents, Vredenburgh and Bender (1998) proposed a conceptual model of the abuse of power in organizations and suggested that employees' abuse of power could be predicted by attributes such as high need for power, low self-esteem, low concern for others, low ethical sensitivity, risk-taking propensity, and high emotionality. Furthermore, they articulated activating conditions (e.g., uncertainty, pressure to perform, risk consideration, and norms) as affecting the ultimate type of power abuse in which employees might engage. This model is of interest to the present discussion and conceptualization because not only does it suggest that need for power is one of the most important factors in power abuse but because it also articulates that individuals are driven by a multitude of individual characteristics to engage in the use and abuse of power.

In a study of ingratiatory behaviors and dispositional motivations, illustrating the complexity of the often conflicting motivations, Kacmar, Carlson, and Bratton (2004) found that employees' use of favor-rendering and other-enhancing ingratiatory behaviors was negatively related to need for power and self-esteem but positively related to job involvement. However, need for power, self-esteem, and shyness all were positively predictive of self-promotion behavior.

More directly linked to the notion of instrumental rewards, Becker and Martin (1995) assessed why employees may try to look bad at work rather than projecting an image of competence. The assumption of these authors was that individuals often choose to look bad to obtain conditions that most align with their personal goals. This research found that the use of self-deprecation, limitation broadcasting, and irrational and aggressive acts was related to avoiding unpleasant tasks or trying to obtain valued outcomes.

Thus, the instrumental dimension of political will reflects traditional notions of political behavior in organizations in that it explicitly acknowledges that employees often act in their own self-interest. Although dominant in the literature, this view rings hollow as a sole determinant for engaging in political activity. One only need look to the reality of historic social change efforts to see that self-serving behavior could not, in and of itself, explain the political activity and leadership provided by

Martin Luther King Jr., Susan B. Anthony, or Nelson Mandela. While the outcomes of their actions had the potential to benefit them in both the short- and long-term, they took on great personal risk, and the results of their actions primarily were focused on the collective rather than themselves. Therefore, additional considerations must be developed to capture the totality of political motivations.

Dimension 2: Relational

In contrast to the clearly economic and practical nature of the instrumental dimension of political will, it is important to recognize that relationships are far more than simply conduits through which individuals may achieve their personal goals. Relationships carry with them meaning, through creating internal definitions of self and signaling character and reputation to others. It is suggested here that the relational dimension of political will encompasses constructs that reflect the content within and around the relationships employees form with their supervisors, coworkers, company, or network as precursors to political behavior.

From an individual need basis, the need to belong may be a strong, but largely untested, driver of political behavior. Baumeister and Leary (1995) discussed the belongingness hypothesis that "human beings have a pervasive drive to form and maintain at least a minimum quantity of lasting, positive and significant interpersonal relationships" (p. 497). Although this behavior has not been studied directly with regard to political behavior, it serves as a general basis for understanding the powerful force that human attachment plays in everyday life. Indeed, this need to belong may be at the very core of existence and survival as human beings (Leary & Cox, 2008).

If the belonging hypothesis is accepted, then the most fundamental relationship unit to fulfill this innate need may be the dyad. Within dyadic relations, several aspects may affect the choice and frequency of political behavior. For example, DeReuver (2006) showed that the power dynamics between two participants can affect the type of interactions they experience. Subjects were more likely to engage in submissive behaviors when their hierarchical superior acted with dominance, and they were more likely to act reciprocally to subordinates that engaged in submissive behaviors.

This reciprocality found in DeReuver's (2006) work reflects the path-dependent and temporal nature of relational development expressed by Treadway, Breland, Williams, Williams, and Yang (in press) in their discussion of relational leadership. They proposed that within leader–follower dyads, the relationship (i.e., as a separate entity) was a core source of personal meaning for the participants. Specifically, the actors engaged in influence (i.e., as relational control mechanisms) to achieve the desired self-concept effect on the target, who engaged in reciprocal relational control behavior based on the desired self-image and the importance of the relationship. This model demonstrates how the strong desire to have enduring and relatively pleasant interactions (Baumeister & Leary, 1995) ultimately directs individuals' behavior and makes it more likely that these interactions become part of how individuals' self-concepts are defined.

Van Knippenberg, van Knippenberg, Blaauw, and Vermunt (1999) moved beyond the relational dyad and suggested that situational motivators may exist in the use of influence tactics. Specifically, when individuals felt they were treated unfairly, they were more likely to engage in aggressive influence tactics. In contrast, when individuals liked the target, they were less likely to engage in such tactics. However, if individuals felt dependent on others, they were less likely to engage in influence tactics.

A more expansive treatment of context, and its impact on political behavior, was offered by Kahn, Wolfe, Quinn, Snoek, and Rosenthal (1964), who assessed how individuals' position in the formal or informal structure affected their use of political behavior. These researchers found that individuals who were more advantageously positioned in the hierarchy had more discretion to use an array of influence tactics than less advantageously positioned individuals. Similarly, Thibodeaux and Lowe (1996) framed individuals' positioning within a mentoring relationship as a source of social power.

In an intriguing study, Vecchio and Sussmann (1991) demonstrated that the use of influence tactics may be driven by socially conditioned perceptions of the roles that managers are supposed to play. This role-play-based study used MBA students and placed them in the roles of a maintenance foreman, plant superintendent, or vice president of marketing. Each role was described as having supervisory capacity congruent with the particular role. They found that the higher up individuals were positioned in the organization, the greater they made use of upward appeals as influence tactics. They also found that middle managers (i.e., superintendents) were more likely to use coalitions than were either lower- or higher-level employees. Furthermore, they found that high Machiavellianism was related to increased levels of the blocking tactic. Therefore, they concluded that organizational level was related to the use of only a few tactics.

A final area in which relational aspects of individuals' lives may affect their use of political behavior is research that viewed employees' work-related values and their use of influence attempts. Blickle (2000) proposed that work-related values operate as higher order goals in that they drive individuals' behavior to obtain those things that reflect these goals but also function as constraints on influence behavior because they provide the employees' sense of what is morally or ethically acceptable. More broadly, the concept that cultural values may impact the degree to which certain behaviors are deemed acceptable is echoed in work by Fu and Yukl (2000), which found that the effectiveness of influence behaviors was dependent on the culture in which they operated. Specifically, they found that rationality was more effective in the United States but that coalitions were more effective in China.

Chapter 14 in this volume recognizes the pervasive influence of culture on the meaning of politics in organizations. The integrative model of societal culture and organizational politics presented there suggests that culture impacts the manner in which organizations and work is structured, an employees' choice of political behavior, their perception of politics, and the outcomes that individuals may experience as a result of politics in and around their organization. Interestingly, the capacity to address political environments appears to be universal (Lvina, Johns, Treadway, Blickle, & Ferris, under review). That is, several studies have provided evidence that political skill is a construct that not only has a similar factor structure across cultures but also similarly impacts individuals' effectiveness in organizations. Collectively, these studies indicate that although the game may change as a result of culture players can still play.

Dimension 3: Concern for the Self

The self is one of the most fundamental concepts in the social sciences. Thus, it is not surprising that a great deal of the work on impression management, influence, self-presentation, and politics has tried to unpack the many aspects and layers of individuals' construction of self. Accordingly, Pfeffer and Fong (2005) defined self-enhancement as "the desire or observed reality of seeing oneself and by extension one's actions, traits, and attitudes in the most positive light" (p. 374). These authors positioned self-enhancement as the driving force for the acquisition of power and influence across the career span.

While critically important to individuals' healthy functioning, the complex nature of the self has led to a lack of understanding of the self—so much so that Baumeister (1987) posited that the self has become a "problem." Although this chapter does not articulate the self as a problem per se, we agree with Baumeister's assertion that individuals actively create their identities and seek to better understand their self as it relates to both their capacity and the environment in which they operate. As such, the dimension of concern for self is not bound solely by the selfish notions of instrumental gain that traditionally have permeated scholarly definitions of political behavior but focuses more on how the pursuit and attainment of such outcomes serves to integrate into individuals' definitions of self.

Self-esteem is defined as individuals' overall evaluation about their competencies (Rosenberg, 1965) and has been used as a loose proxy for individuals' sense of well-being or confidence. This aspect of the self is by far the most widely researched. For example, Baumeister, Tice, and Hutton (1989) found that those with high self-esteem typically used self-enhancement behavior and those with low self-esteem engaged in self-protection behavior. Graham and Van Dyne (2006) found that self-esteem positively related to civic virtue-influence, which are influence behaviors that represent attempts to enhance the effectiveness of the organization. These authors argued that because those high in self-esteem are more likely to voice their opinion and be assertive, this type of behavior was more likely.

Other research in this area has indicated that the impact of self-esteem on political behavior may be a product of the degree of threat individuals perceive from the environment. Schlenker, Weigold, & Hallam (1990) reported that when those high in self-esteem encountered pressure to make a good impression, high self-esteem individuals were more assertive in the face of critical feedback. Rhodewalt (1990) indicated that those higher in self-esteem were more likely to self-handicap, and Self (1990) concluded that self-handicapping is more likely when an important aspect of the self is threatened.

The idea that the context affects the activation of the self as a driving force behind political behavior is further enhanced by research that considers the relational nature of the self. De Cremer, Snyder, and Dewitte (2001) argued that low trusters will contribute more to maintain their self-image in high accountability conditions. Specifically, they suggested that when trust is low, high self-monitors will be more likely to adjust behavior and thus to cooperate more in high accountability conditions. Such ideas were echoed by Farrell and Petersen (1982), who suggested trust as one of four dimensions that may be useful in predicting political behavior in organizations.

Farrell and Petersen (1982) suggested that when employees situated lower on the hierarchical ladder did not trust those at higher levels, they were more likely to engage in political behavior as a remedy for improving their work environment. Building from Hirschman's (1970) model of exit, voice, and loyalty, these authors also suggested that when employees perceived they had several alternatives in the labor market they were likely to engage in internal political behavior.

Given that the leader–subordinate dyad is likely to be the most important relationship employees have within organizations, it is not surprising that some scholars have attempted to distinguish the impact that leader–member relations demonstrate on the self. Sosik, Avolio, and Jung (2002) evaluated the role of a leaders' self-image on their use of self-presentation behavior. They found that leaders' desire for a charismatic identity positively impacted their use of self-monitoring, which in turn was positively related to self-serving impression management and negatively related to prosocial impression management behavior.

The importance of social abilities, such as self-monitoring, also has been studied by Turnley and Bolino (2001). Although not investigating leadership dyads, they found in a sample of students that high self-monitors were more capable of using of ingratiation, self-promotion, and exemplification to improve their classmates' views of them being likeable and competent. The correlations within this analysis demonstrated that self-monitors also were more likely to engage in self-promotion and exemplification behaviors.

Treadway et al. (in press) both integrated the potential of the self to act as a motivator of, and social skill to determine the quality of, political behavior. In general, their model presented the use of influence tactics by the members of a leadership dyad as an exercise in maintaining and cultivating self-concept in oneself and others. These authors suggested that self-concept drives individuals' choice of political behavior. Ultimately, the effective navigation of this developmental cycle is dependent on the political skill of each participant and tends to result in increased affect and trust within the dyad.

Dimension 4: Concern for Others

Less traditionally viewed as political behaviors are those that are designed to improve the conditions of others rather than the conditions of the self. This view may be perceived as similar to McClelland's (1961) view of socialized power motivation (i.e., the motivation to obtain power for the benefit of others). In the organizational sciences literature, much can be taken from research on organizational citizenship behavior. For example, Graham and Van Dyne (2006) proposed a decidedly different perspective on the role of politics in organizations. Although not entirely disavowing the self-serving framing of the definition of political will presented here, they suggested that exercising influence can be a form of civic virtue, and as such it promotes positive results for the causes individuals hope to achieve or promote. This framing moved beyond Bolino's (1999) suggestion that individuals simply may be acting like good citizens and implies that individuals may engage in behaviors for the common good that also are beneficial to their own goals and motivations.

"Speaking up," or "openly stating one's views or opinions about workplace matters, including the actions or ideas of others, suggested or needed changes and alternative approaches or different lines of reasoning for addressing job-related issues" (Premeaux & Bedeian, 2003, p. 1538), represents forms of behavior designed to influence others in the workplace, especially those with formal authority. As specified in this definition, these voice behaviors are motivated by situations in which Premeaux and Bedeian (2003) found that the relationship between self-monitoring and speaking up was moderated by individuals' locus of control, self-esteem, and trust in supervisor.

Fuller, Barnett, Hester, Relyea, and Frey (2007) positioned the broader construct of employee voice as an impression management behavior. Specifically, they evaluated whether self-monitoring and past performance would interact to predict the likelihood that employees would engage in voice behavior. The results of this study indicated that, indeed, voice behaviors were more likely when the employees were both higher self-monitors and had elevated past performance. Their theory development articulated both the motivational and skill-related aspects of the self-monitoring construct, and thus from these results it could be suggested that those with a greater concern for others in relation to political will are more likely to engage in employee voice.

Dimension 5: Personal Risk

The definition of political will presented in this chapter recognizes personal risk as critical to understanding the nature of the construct. Thus, it is envisioned that personal risk does not impact those internal and external triggers that motivate employees to view a particular type of political behavior as acceptable in a given situation but instead acts as an environmental regulator of sorts for political behavior. That is, individuals' assessments of risk may restrict both the range and likelihood of political behavior in which they might engage. Thus, while previously positioning the focus of concern and nature of outcome axes as the driver of political behavior, personal risk acts as a regulatory buffer that inhibits the expression of political behavior (Figure 17.1).

The importance of risk is evident in work by Morrison and Bies (1991), who positioned feedback seeking as partially motivated by impression management concerns. These authors indicated that employees would be more likely to look for feedback when they felt the costs of doing so would be less likely to damage their public image or to be viewed favorably by others in the work environment. Furthermore, to the degree that whistle-blowing can be viewed as political behavior, some work implies that risk is an important factor in individuals' decisions to speak up. Indeed, employees are more likely to speak up in organizational climates that have less threatening parameters (Miceli & Near, 1985).

Similarly, such risk is reflected in counterstereotypical impression management research. Rudman (1998) argued that because society tends to view it as most appropriate for women to present themselves in a manner that reflects modesty, their use of self-promotion behavior can be detrimental to their success. More recently, Shaughnessy, Treadway, Breland, Williams, and Brouer (in press) used this line of reasoning to suggest that women and men would be socially sanctioned for engaging in counter-stereotypical behavior. However, they added to this proposition by indicating that employees' political skill could help to overcome these sanctions. Their results indicated that although individuals were not sanctioned for engaging in counterstereotypical behavior their political skill improved only the implementation of gender-normed political behavior (i.e., ingratiation for women and assertiveness for men).

Certainly, although various conditions of the environment may render engaging in political behavior as more risky than not, it must be recognized that some individuals ultimately are more comfortable with risk and thus have a higher propensity to engage in riskier behaviors. This capacity was reflected in the findings reported by Howell and Higgins (1990) indicating that leaders of change efforts were more likely to engage in influence behavior due, in part, to their increased risk-taking propensity.

FUTURE RESEARCH CONSIDERATIONS

The objective of this chapter was to refine the concept of political will in the organizational sciences and to offer a conceptualization that can serve as the basis for future research. The chapter took a broad view of political behavior in reviewing the literature on motivational processes in impression management, influence tactics, and self-presentation and reviewed the literature to date on the role of motivation. This review offers several clear extensions for future research.

Perhaps the most obvious extension of the current work is the development of a scale to reflect the five dimensions of the construct discussed. This chapter makes it clear that previous research has used scattered constructs to reflect motivations that drive political activity. Rather than continue to simply lump previously developed constructs into research on political activity, future research should develop a scale that reflects the specific nature of political behavior and ignores broader considerations for which other scales were developed. Certainly, this scale development process would need to demonstrate the distinction of this construct from the other motivational ideas contained herein (Figure 17.2).

Complicating the scale development process will be the difficulty involved in choosing which behaviors to predict. The present chapter took a broad perspective in defining what constitutes political behavior and what does not. However, as any researcher in this area knows, this perspective is not widely shared, and although the case may be made that the differences between these behavioral constructs are not significant enough to warrant their mutually exclusive analysis other researchers might rightfully disagree.

Thus, for this concept to move forward, better measurement of the concept of political behavior is warranted, or at least a better and more conclusive statement needs to be made about the relationship between the

Dimension	Related Construct
Nature of Outcome — Instrumental	Need for Power Need for Achievement Intrinsic Motivation
Nature of Outcome — Relational	Need for Belonging Dyadic Power Differences Values Hierarchical Positioning Relational Meaning Fairness Perceptions Role Perceptions Machiavellianism
Focus of Concern — Concern for Self	Self-Enhancement Self-Esteem Self-Monitoring Threat to Self Self-Image
Focus of Concern — Concern for Others	Socialized Power Motivation Civic Virtue Locus of Control
Risk — Personal Risk	Feedback-Seeking Propensity Organizational Climate Social Norms Risk-Taking Propensity

FIGURE 17.2

Political will dimensions and related constructs.

conceptualization and measurement of impression management and influence tactics. Indeed, few measures of political behavior exist, and they do not seem to capture the multidimensional nature of the behavior that is most often discussed. In lieu of this new scale development, studies should use both impression management and influence tactic scales, as using either alone would fail to capture the uniqueness of the political will dimensions.

Ultimately, the development of a political will scale should benefit the understanding of organizational politics and political behavior in several ways. One such way is through the development of boundary conditions for the utility of political will. Most individuals inherently believe that things can be accomplished if one just tries a little harder or finds the right level of support from others. Thus, every failed initiative or social change usually is viewed as simply a matter of a lack of will. Implied, but not well understood, in this framework is the constant pressure of relatively immovable institutions and social pressures.

Browning and Jacob (1964) spoke of this underdeveloped understanding: "The common assumption, reflected in many political biographies and in popular writing, is that the quest for power propels many into politics and is a most likely explanation for much of the politician's activity" (p. 75). They went on to suggest that the highly politically motivated were perhaps too "rigid and compulsive" to be effective and thus likely were marginalized in organizations. Therefore, future research would benefit from understanding the when and how behind the use of political behavior by members or leaders of disadvantaged individuals and groups. In these situations, it may be the case that leaders emerge and fall simply on the basis of their own will.

Given the inevitable risk associated with political behavior and leadership, it would be useful to understand not only from what basis individuals are motivated but also to what degree. This becomes even more critical when one considers the dimensions not as a continuum but rather as elements of which individuals' motivation is partially composed and constantly shifting from instance to instance. Thus, individuals who are motivated primarily by instrumental issues also will have relational considerations that vary across various contexts and ultimately change the frequency and type of behavior in which they engage. Similarly, whereas individuals generally may be less concerned with others, the instance of sexual harassment may evoke strong motivations to change that situation and may assist victims in alleviating the abuse and obtaining justice.

Obviously, this contingency notion of political will suggests that future research must consider the salience of each dimension within a given context. The goal of such research would be to identify the particular *cocktail of motivations* that elicits effective action under various conditions and under which conditions particular motivations are dominant. To this point, Mintzberg (1983) argued "that influencers pick and choose their issues, concentrating efforts on the ones most important to them, and, of course, those they think they can win" (p. 25). This statement, although acknowledging the issue of motivational salience, also demonstrates the importance of accurately perceiving one's environment and thus highlights the issue of political skill.

The latest and perhaps most promising development in the area of organizational politics has been the development of the PSI (Ferris et al., 2005) and the subsequent research that has sprung from this scale development work. Despite results that support the underlying theory of political skill (Ferris, Treadway, Brouer, Perrewé, Douglas, & Lux, 2007; see Chapter 16 in this volume for an extensive review), little of this work has evaluated whether individuals' use of political skill is dependent on their motivation to engage this resource. Mintzberg (1983) hinted at this dynamic when discussing his political perspective on organizations and the key notions of political skill and political will.

Positioning political activity as behavior that, at the very least, encompassed the expenditure of personal energy and social capital, Mintzberg (1983) understood that individuals could not martyr themselves to every cause but must choose wisely what those critical causes might be. He argued that "the requirement that energy be expended to achieve outcomes, and the fact that those with the important bases of power have only so much personal energy to expend, means that power gets distributed more widely than our discussion of the bases of power would suggest" (p. 25).

The political skill–political will framework has been used to advance few, if any, discussions of the topic in the literature (e.g., Treadway et al., 2005; Treadway, Breland, Adams, & Duke, 2010), and each of these studies has taken the view that political will helps an individual achieve functional outcomes. Absent from these discussions is any consideration of the possibility that employees' motivations are not just dysfunctional for the organization, but truly dysfunctional in general. Thus, the study of abusive personality types, narcissism, and destructive leadership would seem to represent worthwhile areas of exploration. Such efforts would significantly advance understanding of political skill in that previous research has focused on the positive effects of political skill on performance, leadership, and stress-related outcomes, thus providing the impression that political skill is solely a positive trait. Though this is an appealing notion, and certainly accurate in some circumstances, undoubtedly there exist politically skilled individuals with very bad intentions.

Two recent papers offer some support for the integration of political skill and less positive motivational bases. Treadway, Breland, Williams, Yang, and Shaughnessy (2011) hypothesized and found that narcissists were driven by their desire for feedback and control to be better positioned in advice networks when they possessed political skill. However, narcissism did not exhibit a main effect on positioning within influence networks (i.e., only political skill predicted this positioning). A second study by Treadway et al. (2011) found that bullies were more likely to be effective performers when they possessed higher levels of political skill. Indeed, politically skilled bullies' ability to leverage their bullying behavior prevented them from realizing the decrease in performance ratings that their less politically skilled bullying colleagues incurred.

The model presented in this chapter suffers from several errors of ambition and/or parsimony. Perhaps most unfulfilling is the model's inability, in its current form, to predict specific political behaviors. Much of this deficiency rests within an inability to clearly make sense of previous findings, due to the variability in actions that may all reflect political behavior. Moving forward, the outer, predictive ring depicted in Figure 17.1 will benefit from a more critical analysis of the behavioral elements of political behavior.

CONCLUSION

The present chapter sought to accomplish four overarching objectives. First, a comprehensive review of the motivational forces addressed in the organizational and political science literatures was provided, as it related to the enactment of individual political behavior in organizations (Figure 17.2). Second, from this review, a definition of political will was established. Third, the literature was discussed in a way that developed a multi-dimensional perspective of political will. It was proposed that an inclusive construct of political will would be composed of five dimensions (i.e., instrumental, relational, concern for self, concern for others, and risk). It was further suggested that the instrumental and relational dimensions work independently but usually as inversely related along a continuum that reflects the nature of the outcome. Similarly, the focus on self or others also is important in determining the type and frequency of political behavior. Finally, the risk dimension operates as a buffer of the internal motivation to engage in political behavior.

The critical review of the relevant literature in the present chapter promoted several conclusions regarding the nature of political will as a scientific construct. Previous research within the domain of political behavior has treated the concept of motivation loosely and the construct of political will looser still. Perhaps as a product of this loose treatment, no unified frame-work of motivation exists in relation to political behavior, self-presentation, or impression management. Moving forward, the proposed conceptualization may assist in unifying these behaviors by clearly identifying the overlap and distinction that is produced from a more fundamental application of motivation to understanding political behavior.

Indeed, if organizations can be characterized as political arenas, as Mintzberg (1983) suggested nearly 3 decades ago, and thus require political will and political skill in order to survive and be effective, then it is incumbent upon organizational scholars to develop a more informed understanding of these two fundamental constructs. Progress has begun with regard to the political skill construct, although much more research is needed. The hope is that the present chapter will serve to stimulate further scientific inquiry into the nature of political will and its role in the organizational sciences.

REFERENCES

Barbuto, J.E., Fritz, S.M., & Marx, D. (2002). A field examination of two measures of work motivation as predictors of leaders' influence tactics. *Journal of Social Psychology, 142*, 601–616.

Barbuto, J.E., & Scholl (1998). Motivation sources inventory: Development and validation of new scales to measure an integrative taxonomy of motivation. *Psychological Reports, 82*, 1087–1098.

Baumeister, R.F. (1987).How the self became a problem: A psychological review of historical research. *Journal of Personality and Social Psychology, 52*, 163–176.

Baumeister, R.F., & Leary, M.R. (1995). The need to belong: Desire for interpersonal attachments as a fundamental human motivation. *Psychological Bulletin, 117*, 497–529.

Baumeister, R.F., Tice, D.M., & Hutton, D.G. (1989). Self-presentational motivation and personality differences in self-esteem. *Journal of Personality, 57*, 547–579.

Becker, T.E., & Martin, S.L. (1995). Trying to look bad at work: Methods and motives for managing poor impression in organizations. *Academy of Management Journal, 38*, 174–199.

Blickle, G. (2000). Do work values predict the use of interorganizatioanl influence strategies? *Journal of Applied Social Psychology, 30*, 196–205.

Bolino, M.C. (1999). Citizenship and impression management: Good soldiers or good actors? *Academy of Management Review, 24*, 82–98.

Bolino, M.C., Kacmar, M., Turnley, W.H., & Gilstrap, J.B. (2008). A multi-level review of impression management motives and behaviors. *Journal of Management, 34*, 1080–1109.

Brinkerhoff, D.W. (2000). Assessing political will for anti-corruption efforts: An analytic framework. *Public Administration and Development, 20*, 239–252.

Browning, R.P., & Jacob, H. (1964). Power motivation and the political personality. *Public Opinion Quarterly, 28*, 75–90.

Cobb, A.T. (1984). An episodic model of power: Toward an integration of theory and research. *Academy of Management Review, 9*, 482–493.

De Cremer, D., Snyder, M., & Dewitte, S. (2001). "The less I trust, the less I contribute (or not)": The effects of trust, accountability, and self-monitoring in social dilemmas. *European Journal of Social Psychology, 31*, 93–107.

Deci, E., & Ryan, R. (1985). *Intrinsic motivation and self-determination in human behavior.* New York: Plenum Press.

DeReuver, R. (2006). The influence of organizational power on conflict dynamics. *Personnel Review, 35*, 589–603.

Farrell, D., & Petersen, J.C. (1982). Patterns of political behavior in organizations. *Academy of Management Review, 7*, 403–412.

Ferris, G.R., Bhawuk, D.P.S., Fedor, D.F., & Judge, T.A. (1995). Organizational politics and citizenship: Attributions of intentionality and construct definition. In M.J. Martinko (Ed.), *Advances in attribution theory: An organizational perspective* (pp. 231–252). Delray Beach, FL: St. Lucie Press.

Ferris, G.R., Treadway, D.C., Brouer, R., Perrewé, P.L, Douglas, C., & Lux, S. (2007). Political skill in organizations. *Journal of Management, 33*, 290–320.

Ferris, G.R., Treadway, D.C., Kolodinsky, R.W., Hochwarter, W.A., Kacmar, C.J., Douglas, C., et al. (2005). Development and validation of the political skill inventory. *Journal of Management, 31*, 126–152.

Fu, P.P., & Yukl, G. (2000). Perceived effectiveness of influence tactics in the United States and China. *Leadership Quarterly, 11*, 251–266.

Fuller, J.B., Barnett, T., Hester, K., Relyea, C., & Frey, L. (2007). An exploratory examination of voice behavior from an impression management perspective. *Journal of Managerial Issues, 19*, 134–151.

Graham, J.W., & Van Dyne, L. (2006). Gathering information and exercising influence: Two forms of civic virtue organizational citizenship behavior. *Employee Responsibilities and Rights Journal, 18*, 89–109.

Hammergren, L. (1998). *Political will, constituency building, and public support in rule of law programs.* Center for Democracy Governance, Bureau for Global Programs, Field Support and Research, U.S. Agency for International Development, PN-ACD-023.

Hirschman, A.O. (1970). *Exit, voice, and loyalty: Responses to decline in firms, organizations, and states.* Boston: Harvard University Press.

Howell, J.M., & Higgins, C.A. (1990). Champions of technological innovation. *Administrative Science Quarterly, 35*, 317–341.

Kacmar, K.M., Carlson, D.S., & Bratton, V.K. (2004). Situational and dispositional factors as antecedents of ingratiatory behaviors in organizational settings. *Journal of Vocational Behavior, 65*, 309–331.

Kahn, R.L., Wolfe, D.M., Quinn, R.P., Snoek, J.D., & Rosenthal, R.A. (1964). *Organizational stress: Studies in role conflict and ambiguity.* New York: Wiley.

Kpundeh, S.J. (1998). Political will in fighting corruption. In S. Kpundeh & I. Hors (Eds.), *Corruption and integrity improvement initiatives in developing countries* (pp. 91–110). United Nations Development Programme.

Leary, M.R., & Cox, C.B. (2008). Belongingness motivation: A mainspring of social action. In J.Y. Shah & W.L. Gardner (Eds.), *Handbook of motivation science* (pp. 27–40). New York: Guilford Press.

Leary, M.R., Downs, D., Leary, M.R., & Kowalski, R.M. (1990). Impression management: A literature review and two-component model. *Psychological Bulletin, 107*, 34–47.

Leary, M.R., & Kowalski, R.M. (1990). Impression management: A literature review and two-component model. *Psychological Bulletin*, 107, 34–47.

Lvina, E., Johns, G., Treadway, D.C., Blickle, G., & Ferris, G.R. (2011). International political skill: Construct and measure validation across five cultures. *International Journal of Cross-Cultural Management.*

McClelland, D.C. (1961). *The achieving society.* Princeton, NJ: Van Nostrand.

Miceli, M.P., & Near, J.P. (1985). Characteristics of organizational climate and perceived wrongdoing associated with whistle-blowing decisions. *Personnel Psychology, 38*, 525–544.

Mintzberg, H. (1983). *Power in and around organizations.* Englewood Cliffs, NJ: Prentice-Hall.

Morrison, E.W., & Bies, R.J. (1991). Impression management in the feedback seeking process: A literature review and research agenda. *Academy of Management Review, 16*, 522–541.

Murray, H.A. (1938). *Explorations in personality.* New York: Oxford University Press.

Pfeffer, J., & Fong, C.T. (2005). Building organization theory from first principles: The self-enhancement motive and understanding power and influence. *Organization Science, 16*, 372–288.

Post, L.A., Raile, A.N.W., & Raile, E.D. (2010). Defining political will. *Politics and Policy, 38*, 653–676.

Premeaux, S.F., & Bedeian, A.G. (2003). Breaking the silence: The moderating effects of self-monitoring in predicting speaking up in the workplace. *Journal of Management Studies, 40*, 1537–1562.

Rhodewalt, F. (1990). Self-handicappers: Individual differences in the preference for anticipatory self-protective acts. In R. Higgins, C.R. Snyder, & S. Berglas, (Eds.), *Self-handicapping: The paradox that isn't.* New York: Plenum Press.

Rosenberg, M. (1965). *Society and the adolescent self-image.* Princeton, NJ: Princeton University Press.

Rudman, L.A. (1998). Self-promotion as a risk factor for women: The costs and benefits of counterstereotypical impression management. *Journal of Personality and Social Psychology, 74*, 629–645.

Schlenker, B. (1980). *Impression management.* Monterey, CA: Brooks/Cole.

Schlenker, B.R., Weigold, M.F., & Hallam, J.R. (1990). Self-serving attributions in social contexts: Effects of self-esteem and social pressure. *Journal of Personality and Social Psychology*, 58, 855–863.

Self, E.A. (1990). Situational influences on self-handicapping. In R.L. Higgins (Ed.), *Self-handicapping: The paradox that isn't* (pp. 37–68). New York: Plenum Press.

Shaughnessy, B.A., Treadway, D.C., Breland, J.W., Williams, L.V., & Brouer, R.L. (in press). Influence and promotability: Importance of female political skill. *Journal of Managerial Psychology.*

Sosik, J.J., Avolio, B.J., & Jung, D.I. (2002). Beneath the mask: Examining the relationship of self-presentation attributes and impression management to charismatic leadership. *Leadership Quarterly, 13*, 217–242.

Thibodeaux, H.F., & Lowe, R.H. (1996). Convergence of leader-member exchange and mentoring: An investigation of social influence patterns. *Journal of Social Behavior and Personality, 11*, 97–115.

Treadway, D.C., Breland, J.W., Williams, L.A., Williams, L., & Yang, J. (in press). Political skill, relational control, and the relational self in the process of relational leadership. In M. Uhl-Bien & S.M. Ospina (Eds.), *Advancing relational leadership theory: A conversation among perspectives* (Leadership Horizons Series). Charlotte, NC: Information Age Publishing.

Treadway, D.C., Hochwarter, W.A., Kacmar, C.J., & Ferris, G.R. (2005). Political will, political skill, and political behavior. *Journal of Organizational Behavior, 26,* 229–245.

Treadway, D.C., Breland, J.W., Adams, G.L., & Duke, A.B. (2010). The interactive effects of political skill and future time perspective on career and community networking behavior. *Social Networks,* 138–147.

Treadway, D.C., Breland, J.W., Williams, L.V., Yang, J., & Shaughnessy, B.A. (2011). *Interactive effects of narcissism and political skill on network positioning.* Paper presented at the Annual Meeting of the Society for Industrial and Organizational Psychology, Chicago.

Treadway, D.C., Shaughnessy, B.A., Breland, J.W., Yang, J., Reeves, M., & Roberts, M. (2011). *When bullying pays off.* Paper presented at the annual meeting of the Society for Industrial and Organizational Psychology, Chicago.

Turnley, W.H., & Bolino, M.C. (2001). Achieving desired images while avoiding undesired images: Exploring the role of self-monitoring in impression management. *Journal of Applied Psychology, 86,* 351–360.

van Knippenberg, B., van Knippenberg, D., Blaauw, E., & Vermunt, R. (1999). Relational considerations in the use of influence tactics. *Journal of Applied Social Psychology, 29*(4), 806–819.

Vecchio, R., & Sussman, M. (1991). Choice of influence tactics: Individual and organizational determinants. *Journal of Organizational Behavior, 12,* 73–80.

Vredenbergh, D., & Bender, Y. (1998). The hierarchical abuse of power in work organizations. *Journal of Business Ethics, 17,* 1337–1347.

18

Personality and Reactions to Organizational Politics

L. A. Witt
University of Houston

Paul E. Spector
University of South Florida

A growing body of literature has shown that organizational politics can demonstrate detrimental effects on both people and organizations. Following the publication of Ferris, Russ, and Fandt's (1989) model of organizational politics, scholars have noted that individual differences not only act as antecedents of politics perceptions but also affect reactions to those perceptions (e.g., O'Connor & Morrison, 2001; Rosen, Chang, & Levy, 2006). Organizational politics can demonstrate effects on employees in two ways. First, politics is a form of stressor that can lead to strains in employees (Miller, Rutherford, & Kolodinsky, 2008; Vigoda, 2002). Hence, it might be considered an interpersonal conflict stressor (Siu, Spector, Cooper, & Lu, 2005).

Second, it has been argued that organizational politics will lead to reduced job performance (Chang, Rosen, & Levy, 2009), although the direct relationship between politics and performance is equivocal (Miller et al., 2008) and is likely due to individual differences (e.g., Treadway, Ferris, Hochwarter, Perrewé, Witt, & Goodman, 2005 found a relationship only for older workers). Thus, it is important to ascertain how individual differences generally, and personality in particular, play roles in both perceptions of, and reactions to, politics. Unfortunately, there has been little work conducted linking personality to perceived politics, so our discussion is largely speculative.

THE NATURE OF ORGANIZATIONAL POLITICS

As reflected in other chapters in this volume, a considerable literature has highlighted the impact of perceived organizational politics, a facet of an organization's overall climate, reflecting the extent to which organization members promote self-interest without regard to, or even at the expense of, organizational goals or other people (Ferris et al., 1989; Mintzberg, 1983). In many ways, perceived organizational politics is the mirror image of the construct of perceived organizational support (Nye & Witt, 1993), a facet of an organization's overall climate, reflecting the extent to which organization members care about each other and share information and other resources (Eisenberger, Huntington, Hutchison, & Sowa, 1986). Consistent with Lewin's (1936) notion that individuals respond to their perceptions of reality, not to reality itself, organizational politics researchers have focused on *perceptions* of organizational politics (e.g., Ferris & Kacmar, 1992; Gandz & Murray, 1980; Miller et al., 2008).

Scholars have identified three dimensions of perceptions of organizational politics: (1) general political behavior; (2) going along to get ahead; and (3) pay and promotion policies (Kacmar & Carlson, 1997; Kacmar & Ferris, 1991). General political behavior stems from situations in which resources are scarce, there is an absence of clear rules and regulations, and considerable ambiguity concerning one's job or the organization's priorities. The idea is that in such environments workers default to self-serving behavior. In contrast, going along to get ahead reflects a conflict between two or more parties, which is an impetus to either retaliate or blend in. Finally, by not clearly linking employee performance with personnel decisions, poorly designed pay and promotion policies actually might encourage political behavior beyond pure task performance (Kacmar & Carlson, 1997; Kacmar & Ferris, 1991).

Scholars have described organizational politics as both functional (e.g., Buchanan & Badham, 1999) and dysfunctional (e.g., Gandz & Murray, 1980). However, the more common view is that it is dysfunctional. Indeed, reporting the results of their meta-analysis, Miller et al. (2008) concluded that perceptions of organizational politics are related to a number of negative organizational outcomes, including high levels of job dissatisfaction, job stress, and turnover intentions as well as low levels of organizational commitment. Although robustly related to work attitudes, Cropanzano, Howes, Grandey, and Toth (1997) observed that perceptions of organizational politics have been less consistently related to job behaviors. Perhaps explaining some of the lack of success linking perceived politics with behaviors are studies indicating that perceptions of organizational politics interact with individual variables in the prediction of important work outcomes (e.g., Hochwarter, Perrewé, Ferris, & Guercio, 1999; Kacmar, Bozeman, Carlson, & Anthony, 1999).

Scholars primarily have offered motivation-based explanations of how perceptions of organizational politics influence worker behavior. Some of the work has focused on social exchange theory (e.g., Hall, Hochwarter, Ferris, & Bowen, 2004; Vigoda, 2000), whereby, for example, unfavorable situations (i.e., high levels of politics) lead workers to retaliate with negative behavior, such as counterproductive work behavior (CWB) targeted toward individuals (e.g., Colbert, Mount, Harter, Witt, & Barrick, 2004). The social exchange approach to linking both politics and support with work-related outcomes has yielded a considerable literature (e.g., Wayne, Coyle-Shapiro, Eisenberger, Liden, Rousseau, & Shore, 2009). However, social exchange theory may be limited in its capacity to fully explain how perceptions of organizational politics affect behavior directed toward individual employees, such as CWB.

Social exchange relationships involve reciprocal exchanges between employees and other parties (i.e., the employing organization and individual customers, vendors, coworkers, supervisors, and managers; Blau, 1964). As noted by Chang et al. (2009), "perceptions of organizational politics represent evaluations of social aspects of organizational settings (i.e., witnessing members politicking and receiving rewards)" (p. 795). Thus, perceptions of high levels of politics may not represent something the organization or any particular organization member is doing to the employee but instead reflect "how things are done around here." With no clear exchange partner, social exchange theory is insufficient to explain how organizational politics affects behavior targeted toward individuals.

Researchers also have applied stress theories to understand the impact of organizational politics (e.g., Vigoda, 2002). From this perspective, politics is a job stressor (i.e., a condition at work that elicits a negative emotional response; Spector, 1998), and dysfunctional outcomes typically linked to high levels of organizational politics are seen as behavioral responses that help employees cope with the stressor or the concomitant negative emotions. As pointed out by David, Witt, and Penney (2011), this approach does not predict the specific manner in which employees will respond to stressors (e.g., whether employees will engage in person- or organization-focused CWB). Hence, stress theories also are insufficient to explain how organizational politics affects worker behavior.

Consistent with Chang et al.'s (2009) argument that perceptions of organizational politics is an assessment of social nuances of the organizational context, it is suggested that perceptions of organizational politics provide cues that communicate behavioral norms that are expected (Cialdini & Trost, 1998; Ehrhart & Naumann, 2004). Therefore, social learning theories are used to provide a third possible mechanism with which to explain how perceptions of organizational politics affect worker behavior. Social cognitive and social information processing theories explain how individuals make sense of themselves and their environment. The idea is that individuals observe and model others' behavior and simultaneously link these acts with information about environmental incentives (Bandura, 1971). These contextual cues make it possible for individuals to interpret events, to understand norms, and to make decisions accordingly (Crick & Dodge, 1994). Hence, contextual cues lead to the development of socially constructed realities, which indicate what behaviors are acceptable, appropriate, expected, and therefore required for survival.

As personal assessments of social aspects of organizations, how might perceptions of organizational politics influence behavior at work? Bandura (1991) identified two categories of motivational processes—namely, achievement-striving behavior and social and moral behavior. Self-efficacy (i.e., perceived capability) is a critical element of the former but not the latter. Whereas many aspects of organizational climate are linked with achievement-striving behavior (e.g., climate for service), perceptions of organizational politics is unusual in that it may influence both achievement-striving and social and moral behavior. For example, CWB clearly falls into the category of social and moral behavior.

Social cues affect social and moral behavior in three ways (Bandura, 1986). First, they establish the standards for social and moral conduct. Second, they establish the support in the social collective for adherence to those standards. Third, they permit selective activation and disengagement of moral self-regulation. In other words, contextual cues may override personal standards of moral conduct. This "enables otherwise considerate people to perform self-serving activities that have detrimental social effects" (Bandura, 1991, p. 280). As these processes indicate how cues shape behavioral responses, it is suggested that social cognitive theory is a viable approach for explaining the links between organizational politics and performance-related work behavior.

ORGANIZATIONAL POLITICS AND PERFORMANCE

For more than 50 years, scholars have articulated the importance of examining interactions between ability and motivation as determinants of key work outcomes (e.g., Gagne & Fleishman, 1959; Pinder, 1984; Vroom, 1964). Most point to Maier (1955) as having formalized the notion that job performance is an interactive function of motivation and ability with the formula $P = f(M \times A)$. That is, greater ability has greater effect at higher levels of motivation. In other words, capable individuals who make little effort because they are unmotivated perform poorly. Similarly, if individuals are incapable of performing, they will perform poorly (e.g., make mistakes or cause accidents) even if they are highly motivated. Studies testing the interaction hypothesis have yielded mixed results (e.g., Sackett, Gruys, & Ellingson, 1998; Wright, Kacmar, McMahan, & Deleeuw, 1995).

Hollenbeck, Brief, Whitener, and Pauli (1988) reported that personality traits used as motivation proxies interacted with general mental ability in some samples to predict job performance but not in others. They concluded that external constraints should be added as a third variable in the equation (i.e., $P = f[M \times A \times C]$). Similarly, Hirschfeld, Lawson, and Mossholder (2004) made the distinction between general trait motivation and context-specific motivation in their tests of interactive hypotheses. They found that whereas general trait motivation combined additively with ability, context-specific motivation combined interactively.

Combining the logic of these two studies, and consistent with the person–situation interaction literature (e.g., Endler & Magnusson, 1976; Lewin, 1936; Pervin, 1989; Schneider, 1983), David and Witt (2010) posited that one of the reasons that researchers have found inconsistent results in testing the $P = f(M \times A)$ is the failure to take into consideration a key determinant of behavior, namely, the context. They then revised Hollenbeck et al.'s (1988) expansion of the formula, suggesting that the third element, C, refer to the *context* rather than *constraints* per se. David and Witt argued that because some environmental factors might be neutral rather than negative (i.e., presence of constraints), *context* rather than *constraints* might better represent the situational component of the formula.

In this chapter, the focus is on organizational politics as an important contextual variable and how it might relate to personality, which is done largely by applying the $P = f(M \times A \times C)$ formula to explain how constellations of personality traits likely affect how workers respond to organizational politics. Specifically, the influences of politics and personality are discussed on the following five performance–relevant work behaviors: task performance, team player behavior, adaptive performance, counterproductive work behavior (CWB), and withdrawal behavior.

First, three theoretical approaches are described that explain the effects of organizational politics on individual-level behavior. Second, these theoretical approaches are applied to describe how perceptions of organizational politics influence our five criterion behaviors of interest. Third, interactions among dimensions of the five-factor model (FFM; Digman, 1990) with perceptions of organizational politics are discussed:

- Conscientiousness × emotional stability × perceptions of organizational politics
- Agreeableness × emotional stability × perceptions of organizational politics
- Openness to experience × emotional stability × perceptions of organizational politics

THE CONTEXT: HOW DOES ORGANIZATIONAL POLITICS INFLUENCE WORKER BEHAVIOR?

Following Campbell, Gasser, and Oswald (1996), we argue that it is necessary to differentiate specific facets of performance and to link them with the relevant personality traits. Furthermore, it is necessary to differentiate performance outcomes from performance behaviors. Clearly, organizational constituents care more about business outcomes (e.g., sales made) than behaviors (e.g., conversations with customers). However, because workers have more control over their behavior (Campbell, McCloy, Oppler, & Sager, 1993) than performance outcomes (e.g., a worker may make an effective sales pitch but is unlikely to make the sale if the products were not delivered to the store), organizational scientists typically operational-ize performance in terms of performance behaviors. For the same reason, the focus here is on five behaviors: task performance, team player behav-ior, adaptive performance, CWB, and withdrawal behavior. In doing so, different combinations of traits are positioned to interact with organiza-tional politics to influence worker behavior.

Task Performance

Following Campbell (1990), Borman, Motowidlo, and their colleagues firmly established the distinction between task performance and contextual per-formance as distinct dimensions of job performance across types of jobs (e.g., Borman & Motowidlo, 1993; Borman & Motowidlo, 1997a, 1997b; Motowidlo & Van Scotter, 1994; Van Scotter, Motowidlo, & Cross, 2000). Task performance refers to behaviors involving the set of core substantive tasks and duties central to a job. Hence, task performance behaviors are unique to each job. Relationships of task performance to perceptions of orga-nizational politics have been equivocal, with some studies finding significant relationships (e.g., Witt, 1998) and some not (Treadway et al., 2005).

Miller et al.'s (2008) meta-analysis found a nonsignificant –.10 mean correlation between the two variables. Treadway et al. (2005) found in three samples that the performance and politics relationship was moderated by age, such that there was a negative relationship for older but not younger employees. Their explanation is that the effects of politics are cumulative over time, as it tends to wear down employees by consuming resources. Thus, the relationship of organizational politics is likely to be dynamic.

Team Player Behavior

In contrast to task performance, contextual performance behaviors are not explicitly or formally prescribed by a specific job. Rather, they are inher-ent in all jobs and support the social fabric of the organization. Borman and Motowidlo (1993) described contextual performance in terms of help-ing, cooperating, following rules, volunteering, and so forth, which are behaviors resembling organizational citizenship behaviors (Organ, 1988, 1997). Later, Van Scotter and Motowidlo (1996) purported that contex-tual performance consists of two dimensions, namely, job dedication and interpersonal facilitation. According to Van Scotter and Motowidlo, job dedication refers to "self-disciplined behaviors such as following rules, working hard, and taking the initiative to solve a problem at work," and interpersonal facilitation refers to "interpersonally oriented behaviors that contribute to organizational goal accomplishment" (p. 526).

David and Witt (2010) described team player behavior as a combination reflecting both job dedication and interpersonal facilitation. Following considerable discussion of team players in both the empirical literature (e.g., Parker, 1996) and the popular press (e.g., Brookman, 2007; White, 2004, 2007), they suggested that the contemporary use of the term *team player* refers to employees who cooperate with the social, tactical, and strategic zeitgeist of the work group. In other words, they argued that team players put aside personal ambitions, proactively cooperate with others, and adhere to informal norms designed to maintain order and accomplish common goals. Such behaviors are the antithesis of political behavior in that they are not self-serving.

David and Witt (2010) emphasized that supervisors and managers, like team players, are concerned with influencing a group to meet a common goal; however, they do so external to the work group. In contrast, team players may hold any rank in the organization and often perform the tasks themselves rather than directing others to do so. Workers manifesting high levels of team player behavior often are the members of the work team who are willing to make sacrifices and are unlikely to attribute blame to others. Moreover, they exert the effort and "right attitude" necessary for the team to be successful. It is argued herein that high levels of organizational politics are likely to reduce levels of team player behavior.

Adaptive Performance

Griffin, Neal, and Parker (2007) pointed out that the interdependence and uncertainty of work systems require new and expanded models of job performance. Emphasizing that dealing with workplace change is an important element of performance, they identified three facets of work behavior: proficiency, proactivity, and adaptivity. They viewed proficiency as task performance, proactivity as "self-directed action to anticipate or initiate change in the work system or work roles" (p. 329), and adaptivity as adjustment to "changes in a work system or work roles" (p. 329).

Further differentiating between proactivity and adaptivity, Griffin, Parker, and Mason (2010, p. 175) described proactivity as self-initiated change to "alter the external environment so that it fits with individual needs" (i.e., primary control; Rothbaum, Weisz, & Snyder, 1982) and adaptivity as "accepting the change and adapting oneself to it" (i.e., secondary control; Rothbaum et al., 1982). Clearly, there are times when organizations need each of these approaches, with proactivity being valuable for innovation and problem solving and adaptivity as being necessary for individuals to perform day-to-day functions at work.

Adaptive performance involves efforts to enhance one's skill set in response to a changing environment as well as to cooperate with workplace changes, such as the implementation of new policies (Griffin & Hesketh, 2003; Johnson, 2001; Ployhart & Bliese, 2006; Pulakos, Arad, Donovan, & Plamondon, 2000). Furthermore, adaptive performance is strategically relevant to the organization compared with adaptive behavior that is intended to promote the career of the individual without concern for the benefit to the organization. Krischer and Witt (2010) emphasized that adaptive performance encompasses a set of behaviors, not ability or intent. Moreover, they emphasized that organizations need workers to successfully deal with the ambiguity and anxiety that change yields and also to be capable to develop and apply new skills. The next section explains how high levels of organizational politics are likely to reduce levels of adaptive performance.

Counterproductive Work Behavior

CWB is a form of performance that consists of acts that run counter to the legitimate interests of an organization (Sackett & DeVore, 2002). CWB can be targeted toward organizations (e.g., wasting time, theft, performing work incorrectly, and withholding effort), or it can be targeted toward individuals (e.g., spreading false rumors, insulting, ignoring, and making fun of others). High levels of organizational politics are likely to promote CWB, and it has been found that perceptions of organizational politics are associated with high levels of interpersonal CWB (Vigoda, 2002). Furthermore, political behavior at times might involve acts of CWB, such as spreading false rumors to undermine a rival's reputation with management.

Withdrawal Behavior

Although some scholars include withdrawal as a form of CWB (e.g., Spector, Fox, Penney, Bruursema, Goh, & Kessler, 2006 treated withdrawal as a CWB dimension), it is treated here as a separate dimension of performance that consists of behavior that results in absence from work in the forms of tardiness, absenteeism, or turnover that stems from a voluntary decision to be absent. In other words, involuntary absence (i.e., induced by management decision or health-related issues) is not considered here. Moreover, for purposes of understanding the link between organizational politics and withdrawal behavior, dysfunctional and not functional withdrawal behavior (Dalton, Krackhardt, & Porter, 1981) is being considered. The literature has shown that perceptions of organizational politics are positively related to turnover intentions (Miller et al., 2008) and actual turnover (Witt, 1999).

THEORETICAL EXPLANATIONS FOR THE EFFECTS OF PERCEIVED ORGANIZATIONAL POLITICS

Three possible explanations are offered for how perceptions of organizational politics affect task performance, team player behavior, adaptive performance, counterproductive work behavior, and withdrawal behavior. First, and consistent with social exchange theory, the less-than-clear links between performance and valued personnel outcomes (e.g., merit raises and promotion) associated with high levels of organizational politics adversely affect motivation and lead employees to withhold work effort and cooperation, which leads to lower team player behavior and adaptive performance. Such unclear links also may lead workers to focus on self-promotion rather than task activities, leading to lower core task performance. They likely also lead to increased CWB, absenteeism, and tardiness, and they act as a "shock" (Lee & Mitchell, 1994; Mobley, 1977) that reduces the desire to remain a member of the organization (i.e., turnover).

Second, organizational politics serve as an interpersonal or social stressor that leads to increased negative emotions and other strains (Kacmar et al., 1999; Miller et al., 2008; Siu et al., 2005; Vigoda, 2002). The negative emotions associated with perceiving high levels of politics can have detrimental effects on performance directly. For example, high levels of emotions can serve as a distraction that can reduce an individual's capacity (i.e., ability in the $M \times A \times C$ model) to complete job tasks. Research has shown that individuals reporting high levels of work strains showed attentional and cognitive deficits on cognitive tasks (van der Linden, Keijsers, Eling, & van Schaijk, 2005), and cognitive deficits have been linked to workplace performance errors (Wadsworth, Moss, Simpson, & Smith, 2003).

Furthermore, perceptions of organizational politics have been shown to relate to job attitudes, including job satisfaction, organizational commitment, and turnover intentions (Miller et al., 2008). Such attitudes are likely to be associated with the motivation component of the performance model. In addition, interpersonal conflicts among employees have been linked to perceptions of organizational politics (Siu et al., 2005), and conflict has been shown to relate to CWB, particularly directed at other individuals (Spector et al., 2006). Finally, exposure to stressful job conditions has been linked to withdrawal behaviors (Spector et al.). Not surprisingly, individuals experiencing stressful job conditions are likely to avoid work to escape them.

Third, and consistent with social cognitive theory, perceptions of low levels of politics likely indicate that the norms for (1) mutual accountability is strong, such that the goals and efforts of workers are aligned and interdependent; and (2) interpersonal treatment is one of respect for common interests and mutual support. As situational cues identify what is appropriate, expected, and required for success (Bandura, 1977; Miller & Dollard, 1941; Salancik & Pfeffer, 1978), workers perceiving these norms are likely to recognize that hard work, cooperation, and positive interpersonal conduct are valued and expected. Furthermore, the paths to success and failure are likely to be relatively clear.

In contrast, perceptions of high levels of politics are likely to indicate that self-interested behavior leads to rewards, and there are few norms for being loyal to the organization and treating others with respect. Accordingly, workers in highly political organizations may follow suit by exploiting others in the organization (Kacmar & Carlson, 1997; Miller et al., 2008). Hence, they are likely to have a high tolerance for self-interest as a method of getting ahead and have a corresponding belief that political behavior is normatively appropriate. Consequently, those experiencing high levels of perceptions of organizational politics are likely to withdraw from the organization when it is convenient to do so. Similarly, they are likely to conclude that withholding effort on activities that may not enhance career progression (i.e., low task and adaptive performance) is not inappropriate and is likely to go unpunished.

In such environments, workers may be motivated to let go of personal standards through the psychological processes of displacement or diffusion of responsibility and may disregard or even distort the consequences of their actions. The cognitive restructuring of moral conduct "not only eliminates self-deterrents but engages in self-approval in the service of deleterious conduct" (Bandura, 1991, p. 280). Hence, workers who lower their task effort withhold organization-relevant adaptive behaviors. For example, they may exert effort to build competencies that enhance their own career mobility, even at the expense of ignoring competencies that are of benefit to the organization. This focus on their own career building can lead to reduced effort on required performance, to being absent from work to engage in self-serving activities (e.g., learning new skills), and eventually to turnover when career-enhancing opportunities present themselves.

Whereas the social cognitive theory explanations of the links of organizational politics with task performance, adaptive performance, and withdrawal behavior are relatively straightforward, the explanation for how high levels of politics affect team player behavior and CWB are not. High levels of organizational politics yield an environment in which high visibility in touting unpopular positions can be dangerous. Because team player behavior was defined in terms of cooperation with the social, tactical, and strategic zeitgeist of the workgroup, it seems logical that high levels of organizational politics give birth to many pseudo-team players. Indeed, behaving consistent with the political winds is inherent in lay definitions of *team player*. However, behaviors associated with low levels of team player behavior include openly complaining, expressing little interest in considering others' points of view, putting their own interests first, and calling attention to the errors of others.

Whereas the risks inherent in a political environment are suspected to induce some workers to "pretend" to be team players, it is argued that situational cues indicating that self-interested behavior is the norm actually will reduce true team player behavior. Indeed, high levels of organizational politics signal to workers that it is "every person for himself"; that is, all individuals are exclusively looking after their own interests, which inherently is at odds with team player behavior. Similarly, it was mentioned that high levels of team player behavior include adherence to informal norms designed to maintain order and accomplish common goals. In a highly political environment, this is hard to accomplish because the informal norms designed to maintain order and accomplish common goals are likely to be weak or nonexistent.

David et al. (2011) argued that contextual cues rarely signal that organization-targeted CWB is a path to success because they threaten both work unit performance and individual job security. Acting in self-interest is one thing, but explicit sabotage directed toward the organization is another. Hence, social cognitive theory is inappropriate for explaining a link between politics and organization-targeted CWB. In contrast, it is argued that social cognitive theory is appropriate for explaining the link between politics and person-targeted CWB; that is, highly political environments sometimes indicate that person-targeted CWB may lead to resource acquisition and career success (e.g., Ferris et al., 1989).

THEORETICAL EXPLANATIONS OF PERSONALITY EFFECTS

The Five Factor Model (FFM; Digman & Takemoto-Chock, 1981; Fiske, 1949; Goldberg, 1992; John & Srivastava, 1999; Norman, 1963) is a useful framework for classifying personality traits into a manageable set of underlying dimensions. Although there has been some variability among researchers, the dimensions typically have been labeled extraversion, agreeableness, conscientiousness, emotional stability, and openness to experience.

Despite the relative popularity of the FFM in organizational research, meta-analytic studies have revealed that correlations of the five dimensions with performance typically vary from weak to moderate and that moderators may affect the personality–performance relationships (e.g., Barrick & Mount, 1991; Berry, Ones, & Sackett, 2007; Hurtz & Donovan, 2000; Salgado, 2002; Tett, Jackson, & Rothstein, 1991). In part, this might be because studies merely relating personality to performance fail to recognize the complexities involved, as personality might be relevant to all of the components of the $M \times A \times C$ model. Also, it is important to match the individual personality variable to the specific aspect of performance rather than assuming a given variable will be related to all aspects of performance in all circumstances.

FFM Dimensions Defined

Agreeableness refers to such traits as tolerance, helpfulness, selflessness, cooperativeness, generosity, courtesy, and sympathy (Digman, 1990) as well as congeniality, amiability, and friendliness (Costa, McCrae, & Dye, 1991). High-agreeableness individuals tend to maintain social affiliations, deal with conflict cooperatively or collaboratively, and strive for common understanding (Digman, 1990). Low-agreeableness individuals tend to act defiantly and even go out of their way to be uncooperative. Moreover, they care little about others' feelings and thoughts and can be low in empathy. Agreeableness has been shown to relate negatively to CWB, particularly directed toward other people (Berry et al., 2007).

McCrae and John (1992) applied such adjectives as organized, planful, reliable, thorough, responsible, and efficient to describe conscientiousness. As noted by John and Srivastava (1999, p. 121), "conscientiousness describes socially prescribed impulse control that facilitates task- and goal-directed behavior, such as thinking before acting, delaying gratification, following norms and rules, and planning, organizing and prioritizing tasks." Similarly, Goldberg (1993a) observed that conscientiousness is associated with such traits as thoroughness and dependability versus negligence and carelessness.

Considering these descriptions, it is not surprising that scholars testing the interaction hypothesis have operationalized motivation in terms of conscientiousness. Some researchers have argued that with the exception of cognitive ability, conscientiousness is the strongest personality predictor of job performance (e.g., Behling, 1998; Dunn, Mount, Barrick, & Ones, 1995). Also, it relates negatively to CWB, especially directed toward organizations (Berry et al., 2007).

Emotional stability is the extent to which individuals vary in their tendency to experience negative emotions across time and situations. It contrasts such traits as nervousness and moodiness with stability and imperturbability (Goldberg, 1993b). Other labels for this dimension have included emotional control (Fiske, 1949), adjustment (Hogan & Hogan, 1992), and neuroticism (inflected; Costa & McCrae, 1992). Individuals low in emotional stability tend to have irrational perfectionistic beliefs, low self-esteem, and pessimistic attitudes; they tend to be worrying, tense, anxious, touchy, unstable, and self-pitying (McCrae & John, 1992). Such individuals see themselves as victims, experience less satisfaction and more strain, doubt their abilities, and require considerable emotional support from others. In contrast, persons high in emotional stability tend to be relatively calm across most situations and are less likely to experience distress.

Openness to experience reflects "a broad range of intellectual, creative, and artistic inclinations, preferences, and skills found foremost in highly original and creative individuals" (John & Srivastava, 1999, p. 114). It refers to such traits as imagination and creativity versus imperceptiveness and shallowness (Goldberg, 1993b) and "describes the breadth, depth, originality, and complexity of an individual's mental and experiential life" (John & Srivastava, p. 121). Openness to experience is distinct from cognitive ability, although they are not uncorrelated (Holland, Dollinger, Holland, & MacDonald, 1995). Individuals high in openness to experience are predisposed to work independently (Judge, Higgins, Thoresen, & Barrick, 1999; Saucier, 2000), think out of the box (Judge et al.), and embrace change (Wanberg & Banas, 2000). In contrast, persons low in openness to experience prefer routine and tradition and maintain cognitive inflexibility (i.e., they are stubborn).

Extraversion is characterized by such traits as assertiveness, activity, and sociability and reflects an "energetic approach to the social and material world" (John & Srivastava, 1999, p. 121). McCrae and Costa (1999) noted that high-extraversion individuals typically have numerous friendships and enterprising vocational interests. Whereas they seek out interpersonal interaction, persons low in extraversion typically need "quiet time" to "reenergize their batteries." It is not proposed that extraversion will be related to performance or perceptions of organizational politics, and it will not be dealt with further.

How Personality Influences Performance

The predominant approach to addressing how personality influences performance has relied on a motivational explanation and has focused on the cognitive processes underlying goal-setting and defined motivation in terms of the arousal, direction, intensity, and persistence of goal-directed actions. Barrick and his colleagues (e.g., Barrick, Mitchell, & Stewart, 2003; Barrick & Mount, 2005; Barrick, Stewart, & Piotrowski, 2002) described three motivational mechanisms that influence workplace behavior. One is communion striving, which refers to goals involving favorable interpersonal relationships. Another is status striving, which refers to "goals directed toward obtaining power and dominance within a status hierarchy" (Barrick et al., p. 66). The third motivational mechanism is accomplishment striving, which refers to goals related to performance-related achievement. Empirical work has shown that personality traits influence the type of environments to which workers are attracted (Barrick, Mount, & Gupta, 2003; Judge & Cable, 1997), such that personality affects whether an individual seeks an environment to fulfill their goals for communion, status, or accomplishment.

Barrick and Mount (2005) argued that personality can affect motivation by influencing either the direction or the intensity of the behavior. Considerable work has focused on the link between personality and the intensity of work behavior, and nearly all of it has focused on conscientiousness (e.g., Gellatly, 1996). Schmidt and Hunter (1998) even cited conscientiousness as the most important trait-based motivation variable in organizational science. Scholars have employed conscientiousness as a proxy for motivation, noting that high-conscientiousness workers tend to be more proactive (Barrick, Mount, & Strauss, 1993) and persevere longer and more effectively engage in self-discipline (Colquitt & Simmering, 1998) than low-conscientiousness workers.

Barrick et al. (2003) posited that the other FFM dimensions also may affect job performance through their effect on one or more proximal motivational variables. Agreeableness is associated with communion striving (i.e., high-agreeableness individuals tend to strive for communion). Because openness to experience is not related to many work outcomes and is the least understood of the FFM dimensions, Barrick et al. (2003) did not link it with motivation. However, Barrick et al. (2003) did link emotional stability with accomplishment striving. Consistent with Malouff, Schutte, Bauer, and Mantelli's (1990) finding that individuals high in instability, hopelessness, and depression (i.e., low emotional stability) are unlikely to be goal oriented, they argued that low-emotional stability persons are relatively unconcerned with completing tasks.

We advocate an alternative perspective here. Rather than viewing emotional stability solely in motivational terms, it is seen also as influencing capability (i.e., or "ability" in the $M \times A \times C$ model). Individuals low in emotional stability will tend to experience negative emotions that can interfere with their ability to perform tasks. As noted earlier in the chapter, such emotional experiences can affect attention and cognitive functioning adversely (van der Linden et al., 2005), which will reduce an individual's capacity to perform many tasks, at least during the time that the negative emotion is aroused.

APPLYING THE $P = F(M \times A \times C)$ FORMULA

In reporting the results of their meta-analysis, Miller at al. (2008) concluded that there is no clear evidence of a relationship between perceptions of organizational politics and job performance and that "moderators are likely to impact this relationship" (p. 215). It is suggested that personality might well moderate the effects of perceptions of organizational politics on performance-related behavior. Furthermore, it is argued that different personality variables likely are relevant to specific dimensions of performance. Conscientiousness is most strongly related to task performance, CWB, and withdrawal. Openness to experience is most strongly related to adaptive performance. Agreeableness is most strongly related to team player behavior and CWB. It is argued that all of these proposed connections are due primarily to the influence of personality on motivation—that is, a functional dispositional motivation. Emotional stability, which influences capability, is most relevant to CWB and withdrawal as well as to task performance and adaptive performance.

Although some of these links between personality and performance might be direct, in many cases it is the interaction of personality and perceptions of organizational politics that is more important. In predicting each of the criterion behaviors, ability (i.e., or more accurately stated, capability) is operationalized in terms of emotional stability. How does emotional stability affect the impact of dispositional motivation (i.e., agreeableness, conscientiousness, or openness to experience) on the negative relationship between organizational politics and favorable workplace behavior? To begin with, individuals low in emotional stability are more sensitive to adverse job conditions, including perceptions of organizational politics, and they tend to experience negative emotions in response.

As noted earlier, such emotional states can interfere with engaging in positive workplace behaviors, such as performance. It should be kept in mind that under conditions of low perceptions of organizational politics and other adverse conditions, such individuals will not likely experience high levels of emotion. Thus, it is mainly the combination of personality and perceptions of organizational politics that reduces performance-related behavior. In general, emotionally stable workers are expected to behave favorably if they possess a functional dispositional motivation, perceive the situation to be favorable (i.e., low levels of organizational politics), or both.

The high levels of emotional stability permit either the favorable work climate or functional dispositional motivation (or both) to provide the motivation to behave favorably. That is, because these workers are not focused on experiencing and coping with their negative emotions, they are emotionally capable of responding favorably to positive motivational influences. Emotionally stable workers who both possess a functional dispositional motivation and perceive a favorable work climate are likely to behave at the highest levels of functionality (i.e., high levels of task performance, team player behavior, adaptability, and low levels of CWB and withdrawal). It is argued that in the absence of one but not both motivational forces, the presence of one compensates for the absence of the other. Thus, these workers will behave functionally.

Emotionally stable workers in unfavorable situations (i.e., high levels of organizational politics) are certainly capable of adopting a dysfunctional motivation and behaving dysfunctionally. However, they are less sensitive to perceptions of organizational politics and thus are less likely to experience adverse emotional responses. Therefore, they are less likely than individuals low in emotional stability to adopt a dysfunctional motivation. When they adopt such a motivation, perhaps because their political environment provides cues indicating that norms for interpersonal mistreatment are expected, likely to go unpunished, and sometimes necessary to enhance career mobility, they are likely to withhold positive performance while engaging in CWB and withdrawal. Moreover, they are likely to do so more calmly and with less angst than their low-emotional stability counterparts, at least until reaching a much higher threshold for provoking strong negative emotion.

The interpersonal circumplex now is used to discuss how perceptions of organizational politics and emotional stability interact with the specific traits that have been identified as representing dispositional motivation (i.e., agreeableness, conscientiousness, and openness to experience) in the prediction of the criterion behaviors of interest. The interpersonal circumplex (Leary, 1957) is an alternative to the principal components analysis approach to personality. Traits on the two-dimensional circumplex appear on a circle around the bipolar, orthogonal coordinates of extraversion and agreeableness (e.g., Lorr & Youniss, 1974; Wiggins, 1982). In contrast, on the three-dimensional circumplex, traits appear around extraversion, agreeableness, or emotional stability (Saucier, 1992), or extraversion, agreeableness, and conscientiousness (Peabody & Goldberg, 1989).

An advantage of the circumplex approach is that it provides "much more opportunity for identifying clusters of traits that are semantically cohesive" (Hofstee, de Raad, & Goldberg, 1992, p. 146). Accordingly, it provides detailed personality descriptions (Becker, 1999). However, a disadvantage is that facet scores add no additional variance beyond what is explained by the major factors (see Hofstee, Ten-Berge, & Hendriks, 1998). Another disadvantage is that they are missing at least two of the five general personality factors (Hofstee et al., 1992). As a consequence, organizational scientists have seen little utility in applying circumplex models.

Recognizing these limitations, Hofstee et al. (1992) and Johnson and Ostendorf (1993) offered an integration of the FFM and circumplex models: the Abridged Big Five Dimensional Circumplex (AB5C). It consists of 10 two-dimensional circumplexes including all possible pairs of the FFM factors as coordinates. It presents the facets in terms of their two highest factor loadings; that is, each trait is characterized by its loadings on a subset of two of the five factors at a time. The AB5C is distinct from the traditional personality assessment that has relied solely on the FFM, which essentially has yielded a loss of precision in measurement and a corresponding error in prediction. In contrast, the application of the AB5C allows the examination of interactions among the FFM dimensions and, thus, assessment of the extent to which any particular personality dimension affects the relationship between any other personality dimension and behavior.

As noted by Hogan, Hogan, and Roberts (1996), the joint impact of multiple traits should be explored if our goal is to more fully explain behavior. As argued by Penney, David, and Witt (in press), there are at least two reasons for investigating the joint impact of at least two traits. First, items designed to assess specific traits may have meaningful secondary loadings on other traits (Hofstee et al., 1992; Johnson & Ostendorf, 1993). In other words, the FFM may not be as orthogonal as once thought (Ones, Viswesvaran, & Dilchert, 2005). Second, despite studies showing the validity of the AB5C, and calls for research examining trait interactions (Barrick & Mount, 2005; Hogan et al., 1996; John & Srivastava, 1999), only a handful of studies have investigated the interaction of FFM factors in predicting performance–relevant work outcomes (e.g., Judge & Erez, 2007; Witt, 2002). In these studies, the interaction between two factors explained incremental variance in performance beyond the main and additive effects of individual factors.

In the following sections, each possible combination of the dispositional motivation variables and emotional stability is discussed at low and high levels of organizational politics. In so doing, the empirically derived adjectives associated with the AB5C are listed to describe the personality characteristics reflecting the combinations of the dispositional motivation variables and emotional stability.

Conscientiousness by Emotional Stability

Four studies were found that examined a conscientiousness × emotional stability interaction to predict workplace behavior (King, George, & Hebl, 2005; Perry, Lorinkova, & Witt, 2010; Witt, 2001; Witt & Jones, 2003). In general, conscientiousness was positively related to favorable outcomes among emotionally stable workers and negatively related (or unrelated) to favorable outcomes among emotionally unstable workers. Thus, low levels of emotional stability seemed to counteract the tendency of the highly conscientious to be productive. The following sections discuss the possible combinations of conscientiousness and emotional stability.

Low Conscientiousness, Low Emotional Stability

Adjectives associated with individuals low in both conscientiousness and emotional stability include weak-willed, unstable, quitting, careless, impractical, wasteful, absent-minded, forgetful, scatterbrained, erratic, inconsistent, impulsive, unstable, self-indulgent, hypocritical, gossipy, moody, and jealous (Hofstee et al., 1992; Johnson & Ostendorf, 1993). Because of their low levels of motivation (i.e., low conscientiousness), these workers are unlikely to either exert much focused effort on work tasks. Given their emotional reactivity, high levels of perceptions of organizational politics would reduce their capabilities, thus further reducing their effectiveness.

Low Conscientiousness, High Emotional Stability

The adjective associated with individuals low in conscientiousness and high in emotional stability is informal (Hofstee et al., 1992). It is argued that among these workers, their low motivation is likely to lead to low levels of task performance, team player behavior, and adaptive performance regardless of perceptions of organizational politics. At high levels of organizational politics, these workers likely exert minimal levels of effort toward tasks and take opportunities to withdraw.

High Conscientiousness, Low Emotional Stability

The adjective associated with individuals high in conscientiousness and low in emotional stability is particular (Hofstee et al., 1992). Because of their low emotional stability, these workers are incapable of effectively leveraging their high levels of motivation (i.e., high conscientiousness) when they are experiencing adverse situations, such as perceptions of organizational politics. As a consequence, under high levels of perceptions of organizational politics, their task performance is likely to suffer and withdrawal behavior is likely to increase.

High Conscientiousness, High Emotional Stability

Adjectives associated with individuals high in both conscientiousness and emotional stability include practical, persevering, self-disciplined, stable, well read, rational, objective, steady, consistent, logical, decisive, poised, concise, thorough, economical, systematic, precise, and efficient (Hofstee et al., 1992; Johnson & Ostendorf, 1993). Accordingly, these individuals are likely to be highly motivated to achieve and to be capable of focusing on the task across most situations.

In terms of the three theories, relative to other workers, these workers are likely to want to achieve (i.e., high task performance and refraining from withdrawal behavior) despite an unclear effort–reward link (i.e., social exchange theory), to be unaffected by stressors (i.e., stress theories), and to somewhat ignore workplace cues (i.e., social cognitive theory) that point to the appropriateness of dysfunctional behavior. However, it is expected that low levels of organizational politics have some moderate influence by creating additional motivation to further activate the high levels of conscientiousness. Consequently, these workers are likely to work harder and withdraw less in low- than high-political climates.

Agreeableness by Emotional Stability

Social exchange, stress, and social cognitive theories provide slightly different explanations for how high levels of organizational politics yield high levels of person-targeted CWB. That is, high levels of organizational politics give rise to the desire to retaliate (i.e., social exchange theory), act as a stressor that create negative emotions requiring an emotional or instrumental coping response (i.e., stress theories), or provide cues that interpersonal mistreatment is acceptable and likely to go unpunished. The focus here is on social cognitive theory. As mentioned earlier, Bandura (1991) listed achievement-striving behavior and social and moral behavior as two categories of motivational processes.

In a high-politics situation, in which interpersonal mistreatment is acceptable, workers might engage in person-targeted CWB as an instrumental means of achieving goals, therefore fulfilling achievement-striving needs. We believe that agreeableness and emotional stability are particularly relevant for explaining responses to organizational politics in terms of social and moral behavior. In line with Bandura's (1991) arguments, it is suggested that high levels of organizational politics (1) establish standards that promote, if not permit, social and moral conduct, (2) indicate that most others do not consider such behavior inappropriate, and (3) drive selective activation and disengagement of moral self-regulation (i.e., override personal standards of moral conduct), a process that is affected by agreeableness and emotional stability.

Previously, it was posited that although the social cognitive theory explanations of the links of organizational politics with task performance, adaptive performance, and withdrawal behavior are relatively straightforward, the explanation for how high levels of politics affect team player behavior and CWB are not. It is argued here that the application of the AB5C suggests that there may be slightly different ways agreeableness and emotional stability affect how workers respond to high levels of organizational politics in terms of team player behavior and person-targeted CWB.

Low Agreeableness, Low Emotional Stability

Adjectives associated with individuals low in both agreeableness and emotional stability include critical, negativistic, stubborn, uncooperative, inflexible, vengeful, irritable, envious, moody, distrustful, suspicious, selfish, high-strung, excitable, impatient, temperamental, quarrelsome, crabby, cranky, grumpy, and defensive (Hofstee et al., 1992; Johnson & Ostendorf, 1993). Because of their low levels of motivation to engage in cooperative behavior (i.e., low agreeableness) and low capability to do so (i.e., low emotional stability), these workers are unlikely to express team player behavior, regardless of the level of organizational politics. Moreover, these excitable, impatient, and temperamental workers are likely to engage in CWB across most situations, especially when high levels of perceptions of organizational politics provoke them.

Low Agreeableness, High Emotional Stability

Adjectives associated with individuals low in agreeableness and high in emotional stability include unemotional, insensitive, unaffectionate, passionless, and masculine (Hofstee et al., 1992). At high levels of organizational politics, these workers are likely to engage in very low levels of team player behavior and high levels of CWB. Contextual cues that signal utility in person-targeted CWB are likely to activate these personality characteristics, leading the workers to calmly and impassionedly manifest CWB. Although by nature these workers are uncooperative, low levels of organizational politics position them to express at least moderate levels of team player behavior. Similarly, capable of recognizing the risk of CWB, they are likely to manifest somewhat lower levels of CWB in low-politics situations.

High Agreeableness, Low Emotional Stability

Adjectives associated with individuals high in agreeableness and low in emotional stability include gullible, lenient, sentimental, affectionate, sensitive, soft, passionate, romantic, feminine, and emotional (Hofstee et al., 1992; Johnson & Ostendorf, 1993). Although their basic tendency is to be team players, high levels of perceptions of organizational politics will induce negative emotion that will interfere with their performance. However, given their sensitive, gullible, and emotional characteristics, they are likely to engage in moderate levels of CWB to defend threatened compatriots (or retaliate against those who have attacked them) in high-politics situations because cues indicate that doing so is appropriate.

High Agreeableness, High Emotional Stability

Adjectives associated with individuals high in both agreeableness and emotional stability include patient, relaxed, undemanding, uncritical, optimistic, conceitless, down-to-earth, unpretentious, trustful, pleasant, tolerant, peaceful, generous, easygoing, fair, charitable, flexible, cooperative, forgiving, good-natured, steady, poised, composed, even-tempered, and unselfish (Hofstee et al., 1992; Johnson & Ostendorf, 1993). Therefore, these individuals are likely to be highly motivated to cooperate and to be capable of doing so across most situations.

However, low levels of organizational politics likely have some moderate influence by creating additional motivation to further activate the high levels of agreeableness. Consequently, these workers are likely to make greater efforts to be team-players in low- than high-political climates. Furthermore, this personality profile likely acts as a self-regulatory governor against dysfunctional interpersonal behavior, even in dysfunctional situations, thus resulting in low levels of CWB and withdrawal.

Openness to Experience by Emotional Stability

Because adaptive performance is about change and adaptation to it, openness to experience is likely to be the appropriate proxy for motivation. There do not appear to have been any previous studies examining an openness to experience × emotional stability experience interaction, but speculation concerning the anticipated outcomes of such research are provided in the following sections.

Low Openness to Experience, Low Emotional Stability

Adjectives associated with individuals low in both openness to experience and emotional stability are inartistic and contemptuous (Hofstee et al., 1992; Johnson & Ostendorf, 1993). Neither interested in making change (i.e., low openness to experience) nor capable of dealing with adverse conditions (i.e., low emotional stability), these workers are unlikely to engage in adaptive performance behaviors, even when perceptions of organizational politics is low. The contextual cues largely are irrelevant to them.

Low Openness to Experience, High Emotional Stability

Adjectives associated with individuals low in openness to experience and high in emotional stability include imperturbable, unreflective, unsophisticated, imperceptive, and provincial (Hofstee et al., 1992). Such individuals are not particularly interested in making change and are likely to exhibit low levels of adaptive performance. Because they are high in emotional stability, the effects of perceptions of organizational politics will be attenuated because they will not induce an emotional response. However, in a low-politics environment, cues may signal that adaptive performance is expected and rewarded, and thus it might tend to induce a moderate level of adaptive performance. In a high-politics environment, cues may signal the opposite and thus slightly reduce this aspect of performance.

High Openness to Experience, Low Emotional Stability

The adjective associated with persons high in openness to experience and low in emotional stability is underdeveloped (Hofstee et al., 1992). However, generally, it is anticipated that these highly angst-ridden workers are particularly sensitive to perceptions of organizational politics. When perceptions of organizational politics are low, their motivation to engage in new activities would result in high levels of adaptive performance. When perceptions of organizational politics are high, it would result in emotionality that interferes with adaptive performance.

High Openness to Experience, High Emotional Stability

Adjectives associated with individuals high in both openness to experience and emotional stability include versatile, intellectual, inventive, innovative, ingenious, and aesthetic (Hofstee et al., 1992; Johnson & Ostendorf, 1993). Hence, these individuals are likely to be highly motivated to adapt and to be capable of doing so creatively across most situations. Again, it is expected that low levels of organizational politics provide additional motivation to further activate the high levels of openness to experience. Consequently, these workers are likely to engage in the highest levels of adaptive performance.

CONCLUSION

As suggested in this chapter, the effects of perceptions of organizational politics on people's performance are complex, as perceptions of organizational politics interact with personality in its effects that can vary depending on the specific dimension of performance. From an FFM perspective, specific personality dimensions can be linked to particular aspects of performance, with conscientiousness being most relevant to task performance, CWB, and withdrawal, agreeableness being most relevant to team player behavior and CWB, openness to experience being most relevant to adaptive performance, and emotional stability being relevant to all five of our performance dimensions.

In general, the first three personality dimensions are associated with the motivation to engage in the various forms of performance behavior. For example, those high in openness to experience seek out new experiences and would be motivated to innovate and try new things at work in response to challenges that require adaptation. In contrast, those low in agreeableness have little motivation to cooperate with others, so they likely engage in low levels of team player behavior. Emotional stability has to do more with capability, as those low on this dimension have a low threshold for emotional arousal, thus they might experience frequent negative emotions that interfere with positive performance behaviors. Furthermore, the experience of negative emotions is likely to motivate CWB and withdrawal.

Relationships of personality with performance generally have been rather small and in some cases disappointing. This is likely because personality does not work in a vacuum but is relevant to only part of the $P = f[M \times A \times C]$ model. What is important is how people with varying personality characteristics, particularly in combination with one another, react to situations, with perceptions of organizational politics being an important situational or contextual variable. High levels of perceptions of organizational politics induce high levels of negative emotion, particularly among those low in emotional stability. Such working environments also signal information about acceptable norms. To the extent these norms are consistent with an individual's personality, they will enhance their tendencies to either engage or avoid engaging in both productive and counterproductive behavior. Thus, high perceptions of organizational politics, for example, likely will encourage low-agreeableness behavior in those inclined to be low in agreeableness.

Comparatively little research has explored configurations of personality variables. Interactions between emotional stability and other FFM dimensions were discussed, speculating that certain combinations might interact with perceptions of organizational politics. As noted earlier, low levels of emotional stability might well counteract the tendencies of high conscientious individuals to perform at high levels. This might well explain at least in part why the conscientiousness–performance relationship has been disappointing in past research. Additional research might explore the extent to which the interaction between these two personality variables relates to performance and other behaviors.

Consideration of three-way interactions among two personality dimensions and an environmental variable like perceptions of organizational politics might prove to be particularly enlightening and might well account for more performance variance than individual personality variables in isolation or combined with others additively. In other words, performance-related behavior can best be understood by considering complex interactions. Thus, it might not be the case that low emotional stability counteracts conscientiousness in all situations, but instead it might work this way only when individuals are exposed to high levels of stressful job conditions like politics.

Also, it is worth going beyond the FFM in exploring personality relationships with various aspects of performance. The FFM dimensions tend to be rather broad, encompassing sets of distinct traits. It is possible that within some dimensions the component traits relate differentially to performance. One example of this is Hastings and O'Neill (2009), who showed such within-dimension variability among individual traits in predicting CWB. Other researchers have extended the FFM to include additional dimensions that are likely relevant to various aspects of job performance. For example, Marcus, Lee, and Ashton (2007) applied the HEXACO model of personality to the prediction of CWB. This model includes an additional dimension of honesty–humility that in their study predicted CWB more strongly than any of the FFM dimensions.

The literature suggests that organizational politics can have a detrimental effect on organizations and their members. Those effects can be particularly significant for individuals whose personalities render them vulnerable. As suggested, those effects can be complex and can vary across different performance-related behaviors. It is recommended that future researchers look more closely at how individual differences interact with perceptions of organizational politics in determining its effects, not only on performance but also on people's attitudes, cognitions, emotions, and well-being.

REFERENCES

Bandura, A. (1971). *Social learning theory.* Morristown, NJ: General Learning Press.

Bandura, A. (1977). Self-efficacy: Toward a unifying theory of behavioral change. *Psychological Review, 84,* 191–215.

Bandura, A. (1986). *Social foundations for thought and action: A social cognitive theory.* Englewood Cliffs, NJ: Prentice-Hall.

Bandura, A. (1991). Social cognitive theory of self-regulation. *Organizational Behavior and Human Decision Processes, 50,* 248–287.

Barrick, M.R., & Mount, M.K. (1991). The Big Five personality dimensions and job performance: A meta-analysis. *Personnel Psychology, 44,* 1–26

Barrick, M.R., & Mount, M.K. (2005). Yes, personality matters: Moving on to more important matters. *Human Performance, 18,* 359–372.

Barrick, M.R., Mitchell, T.R., & Stewart, G.L. (2003). Situational and motivational influences on trait–behavior relationships. In M.R. Barrick & A.M. Ryan (Eds.), *Personality and work: Reconsidering the role of personality in organizations* (pp. 60–82). San Francisco: Jossey-Bass.

Barrick, M.R., Mount, M.K., & Strauss, J.P. (1993). Conscientiousness and performance of sales representatives: Test of mediating effects of goal setting. *Journal of Applied Psychology, 78,* 715–722.

Barrick, M.R., Stewart, G.L., & Piotrowski, M. (2002). Personality and job performance: Test of the mediating effects of motivation among sales representatives. *Journal of Applied Psychology, 87,* 43–51.

Barrick, M.R., Mount, M.K., & Gupta, R. (2003). Meta-analysis of the relationship between the five-factor model of personality and Holland's occupational types. *Personnel Psychology, 56,* 45–74.

Becker, P. (1999). Beyond the Big Five. *Personality and Individual Differences, 26,* 511–530.

Behling, O. (1998). Employee selection: Will intelligence and conscientiousness do the job? *Academy of Management Executive, 12,* 77–86.

Berry, C.M., Ones, D.S., & Sackett, P.R. (2007). Interpersonal deviance, organizational deviance, and their common correlates: A review and meta-analysis. *Journal of Applied Psychology, 92,* 410–424.

Blau, P.M. (1964). *Exchange and power in social life.* New York: Wiley.

Borman, W.C., & Motowidlo, S.J. (1993). Expanding the criterion domain to include elements of contextual performance. In N. Schmitt & W.C. Borman (Eds.), *Personnel selection* (pp. 71–98). San Francisco: Jossey-Bass.

Borman, W.C., & Motowidlo, S.J. (1997a). Introduction: Organizational citizenship behavior and contextual performance. *Human Performance, 10,* 67–69.

Borman, W.C., & Motowidlo, S.J. (1997b). Task performance and contextual performance: The meaning for personnel selection research. *Human Performance, 10,* 99–109.

Brookman, F. (2007). Team player. *Stores, 89,* 82.

Buchanan, D., & Badham, R. (1999). Politics and organizational change: The lived experience. *Human Relations, 52,* 609–629.

Campbell, J.P. (1990). Modeling the performance prediction problem in industrial and organizational psychology. In M.D. Dunnette & L.M. Hough (Eds.), *Handbook of industrial and organizational psychology* (2nd ed., Vol. 1, pp. 687–732). Palo Alto, CA: Consulting Psychologists Press.

Campbell J.P., Gasser M.B., & Oswald F.L. (1996). The substantive nature of performance variability. In K.R. Murphy (Ed.), *Individual differences and behavior in organizations* (pp. 258–299). San Francisco: Jossey-Bass.

Campbell, J.P., McCloy, R.A., Oppler, S.H., & Sager, C.E. (1993). A theory of performance. In N. Schmitt & W. C. Borman (Eds.), *Personnel selection in organizations* (pp. 35–70). San Francisco: Jossey-Bass.

Chang, C.H., Rosen, C.C., & Levy, P.E. (2009). The relationship between perceptions of organizational politics and employee attitudes, strain, and behavior: A meta-analytic examination. *Academy of Management Journal, 52,* 779–801.

Cialdini, R., & Trost, M. (1998). Social influence: Social norms, conformity and compliance. *The handbook of social psychology* (4th ed., Vols. 1 & 2, pp. 151–192). New York: McGraw-Hill.

Colbert, A.E., Mount, M.K., Harter, J.K., Witt, L.A., & Barrick, M.R. (2004). Interactive effects of personality and perceptions of work situation on workplace deviance. *Journal of Applied Psychology, 89,* 599–609.

Colquitt, J., & Simmering, M. (1998). Conscientiousness, goal orientation, and motivation to learn during the learning process: A longitudinal study. *Journal of Applied Psychology, 83,* 654–665.

Costa Jr., P.T., & McCrae, R.R. (1992). *NEO-PI-R professional manual.* Odessa, FL: Psychological Assessment Resources.

Costa Jr., P.T., McCrae, R.R., & Dye, D.A. (1991). Facet scales for agreeableness and conscientiousness: A revision of the NEO personality inventory. *Personality and Individual Differences, 12,* 887–898.

Crick, N.R., & Dodge, K.A. (1994). A review and reformulation of social-information processing mechanisms in children's development. *Psychological Bulletin, 115,* 74–101.

Cropanzano, R., Howes, J., Grandey, A., & Toth, P. (1997). The relationship of organizational politics and support to work behaviors, attitudes, and stress. *Journal of Organizational Behavior, 18,* 159–180.

Dalton, D.R., Krackhardt, D.M., & Porter, L.W. (1981). Functional turnover: An empirical assessment. *Journal of Applied Psychology, 66,* 716–721.

David, E.M., Witt, L.A., & Penney, L.M. (2011). *Self-regulation in dysfunctional situations: Beware the socially unskilled.* Working Paper, University of Houston.

David, E., & Witt, L.A. (2010, August). *P = f(M × A × C): A three-way interaction predicting team-player behavior.* Paper presented at the annual conference of the Academy of Management, Montreal.

Digman, J.M. (1990). Personality structure: Emergence of the five-factor model. *Annual Review of Psychology, 41,* 417–440.

Digman, J.M., & Takemoto-Chock, N.K. (1981). Factors in the natural language of personality: Re-analysis, comparison, and interpretation of six major studies. *Multivariate Behavioral Research, 16,* 148–170.

Dunn, W.S., Mount, M.K., Barrick, M.R., & Ones, D.S. (1995). Relative importance of personality and general mental ability in managers' judgments of applicant qualifications. *Journal of Applied Psychology, 80,* 500–510.

Ehrhart, M., & Naumann, S. (2004). Organizational citizenship behavior in work groups: A group norms approach. *Journal of Applied Psychology, 89,* 960–974.

Eisenberger, R., Huntington, R., Hutchison, S., & Sowa, D. (1986). Perceived organizational support. *Journal of Applied Psychology, 71,* 500–507.

Endler, N.S., & Magnusson, D. (1976). Toward an interaction psychology of personality. *Psychological Bulletin, 83*, 956–974.

Ferris, G.R., & Kacmar, K.M. (1992). Perceptions of organizational politics. *Journal of Management, 18*, 93–116.

Ferris, G.R., Russ, G.S., & Fandt, P.M. (1989). Politics in organizations. In R.A. Giacalone & P. Rosenfeld (Eds.), *Impression management in the organization* (pp. 143–170). Hillsdale, NJ: Lawrence Erlbaum.

Fiske, D.W. (1949). Consistency in the factorial structures of personality ratings from different sources. *Journal of Abnormal and Social Psychology, 44*, 329–344.

Gagne, R.M., & Fleishman, E.A. (1959). *Psychology and human performance.* New York: Holt.

Gandz, J., & Murray, V. (1980). The experience of workplace politics. *Academy of Management Journal, 23*, 237–251.

Gellatly, I. (1996). Conscientiousness and task performance: Test of a cognitive process model. *Journal of Applied Psychology, 81*, 474–482.

Goldberg, L.R. (1992). The development of markers for the Big Five factor structure. *Psychological Assessment, 4*, 26–42.

Goldberg, L.R. (1993a). The structure of phenotypic personality traits. *American Psychologist, 48*, 26–34.

Goldberg, L.R. (1993b). The structure of personality traits: Vertical and horizontal aspects. In D.C. Funder, R.D. Parke, C. Tomlinson-Keasey, & K. Widamin (Eds.), *Studying lives through time: Personality and development* (pp. 169–188), Washington, DC: American Psychological Association.

Griffin, B., & Hesketh, B. (2003). Adaptable behaviours for successful work and career adjustment. *Australian Journal of Psychology, 55*, 65–73.

Griffin, M.A., Neal, A., & Parker, S.K. (2007). A new model of work role performance and positive behavior in uncertain and interdependent contexts. *Academy of Management Journal, 50*, 327–347.

Griffin, M.A., Parker, S.K., & Mason, C.M. (2010). Leader vision and the development of adaptive and proactive performance: A longitudinal study. *Journal of Applied Psychology, 95*, 174–182.

Hall, A.T., Hochwarter, W.A., Ferris, G.R., & Bowen, M.G. (2004). The dark side of politics in organizations. In R.W. Griffin & A.M. O'Leary-Kelly (Eds.), *The dark side of organizational behavior* (pp. 237–261). San Francisco: Jossey-Bass.

Hastings, S.E., & O'Neill, T.A. (2009). Predicting workplace deviance using broad versus narrow personality variables. *Personality and Individual Differences, 47*, 289–293.

Hirschfeld, R., Lawson, L., & Mossholder, K. (2004). Moderators of the relationship between cognitive ability and performance: General versus context-specific achievement motivation. *Journal of Applied Social Psychology, 34*, 2389–2409.

Hochwarter, W.A., Perrewé, P.L., Ferris, G.R., & Guercio, R. (1999). Commitment as an antidote to the tension and turnover consequences of organizational politics. *Journal of Vocational Behavior, 55*, 277–297.

Hofstee, W.K.B., de Raad, B., & Goldberg, L.R. (1992). Integration of the Big Five and circumplex approaches to trait structure. *Journal of Personality and Social Psychology, 65*, 563–576.

Hofstee, W.K.B., Ten-Berge, J.M.F., & Hendriks, A.A.J. (1998). How to score questionnaires. *Personality and Individual Differences, 25*, 897–909.

Hogan, R.T., & Hogan, J. (1992). *Hogan personality inventory manual.* Tulsa, OK: Hogan Assessment Systems.

Hogan, R., Hogan, J., & Roberts, B.W. (1996). Personality measurement and employment decisions: Questions and answers. *American Psychologist, 51*, 469–477.

Holland, D.C., Dollinger, S.J., Holland, C.J., & MacDonald, D.A. (1995). The relationship between psychometric intelligence and the five-factor model of personality in a rehabilitation sample. *Journal of Clinical Psychology, 51*, 79–88.

Hollenbeck, J.R., Brief, A.P., Whitener, E.M., & Pauli, K.E. (1988). An empirical note on the interaction of personality and aptitude in personnel selection. *Journal of Management, 14*, 441–451.

Hurtz, G.M., & Donovan, J.J. (2000). Personality and job performance: The Big Five revisited. *Journal of Applied Psychology, 85*, 869–879.

John, O.P., & Srivastava, S. (1999). The Big Five trait taxonomy: History, measurement, and theoretical perspectives. In L.A. Pervin & O.P. John (Eds.), *Handbook of personality: Theory and research* (pp. 102–138). New York: Guilford.

Johnson, J.A., & Ostendorf, F. (1993). Clarification of the five-factor model with the abridged big five dimensional circumplex. *Journal of Personality and Social Psychology, 65*, 563–576.

Johnson, J.W. (2001). The relative importance of task and contextual performance dimensions to supervisor judgments of overall performance. *Journal of Applied Psychology, 86*, 984–996.

Judge, T.A., & Cable, D.M. (1997). Applicant personality, organizational culture, and organization attraction. *Personnel Psychology, 50*, 359–394.

Judge, T.A., & Erez, A. (2007). Interaction and intersection: The constellation of emotional stability and extraversion in predicting performance. *Personnel Psychology, 60*, 573–596.

Judge, T.A., Higgins, C.A., Thoresen, C.J., & Barrick, M.R. (1999). The big five personality traits, general mental ability, and career success across the life span. *Personnel Psychology, 52*, 621–652.

Kacmar, K.M., & Carlson, D. (1997). Further validation of the Perception of Politics Scale (POPs): A multiple sample investigation. *Journal of Management, 23*, 627–658.

Kacmar, K.M., & Ferris, G.R. (1991). Perceptions of Organizational Politics Scale (POPS): Development and construct validation. *Educational and Psychological Measurement, 51*, 193–205.

Kacmar, K., Bozeman, D., Carlson, D., & Anthony, W. (1999). An examination of the perceptions of organizational politics model: Replication and extension. *Human Relations, 52*, 383–416.

King, E.B., George, J.M., & Hebl, M.R. (2005). Linking personality to helping behaviors at work: An interactional perspective. *Journal of Personality, 72*, 585–607.

Krischer, M., & Witt, L. A. (2010, April). *Achieving adaptive performance in the workplace: The compensatory effects of general mental ability and adaptive leadership.* Paper presented at the conference of the Society for Industrial and Organizational Psychology, Atlanta.

Leary, T. (1957). *Interpersonal diagnosis of personality.* New York: Ronald Press.

Lee, T.W., & Mitchell, T.R. (1994). An alternative approach: The unfolding model of voluntary employee turnover. *Academy of Management Review, 19*, 51–89.

Lewin, K. (1936). *Principles of topological psychology.* New York: McGraw-Hill.

Lorr, M., & Youniss, R.P. (1974). An inventory of interpersonal style. *Journal of Personality Assessment, 37*, 165–173.

Maier, N.R.F. (1955). *Psychology in industry* (2nd ed.). Boston: Houghton-Mifflin.

Malouff, J., Schutte, N., Bauer, M., & Mantelli, D. (1990). Development and evaluation of a measure of the tendency to be goal oriented. *Personality and Individual Differences, 11*, 1191–1200.

Marcus, B., Lee, K., & Ashton, M.C. (2007). Personality dimensions explaining relationships between integrity tests and counterproductive behavior: Big five, or one in addition? *Personnel Psychology, 60*, 1–34.

McCrae, R.R., & John, O.P. (1992). An introduction to the five-factor model and its applications. *Journal of Personality, 60*, 175–216.

Miller, B., Rutherford, M., & Kolodinsky, R. (2008). Perceptions of organizational politics: A meta-analysis of outcomes. *Journal of Business and Psychology, 22*, 209–222.

Miller, N.E., & Dollard, J. (1941). *Social learning and imitation.* New Haven, CT: Yale University Press.

Mintzberg, H. (1983). *Power in an around organizations.* Englewood Cliffs, NJ: Prentice-Hall.

Mobley, W.H. (1977). Intermediate linkages in the relationship between job satisfaction and employee turnover. *Journal of Applied Psychology, 62*, 237–240.

Motowidlo, S.J., & Van Scotter, J.R. (1994). Evidence that task performance should be distinguished from contextual performance. *Journal of Applied Psychology, 79*, 71–83.

Norman, W.T. (1963). Toward an adequate taxonomy of personality attributes: Replicated factor structure in peer nomination personality ratings. *Journal of Abnormal and Social Psychology, 66*, 574–583.

Nye, L.G., & Witt, L.A. (1993). Dimensionality and construct validity of the perceptions of organizational politics scale (POPS). *Educational and Psychological Measurement, 53*, 821–829.

O'Connor, W., & Morrison, T. (2001). A comparison of situational and dispositional predictors of perceptions of organizational politics. *Journal of Psychology: Interdisciplinary and Applied, 135*, 301–312.

Ones, D.S., Viswesvaran, C., & Dilchert, S. (2005). Personality at work: Raising awareness and correcting misconceptions. *Human Performance, 18*, 389–404.

Organ, D.W. (1988). *Organizational citizenship behaviors: The good soldier syndrome.* Lexington, MA: Lexington.

Organ, D.W. (1997). Organizational citizenship behavior: It's construct clean-up time. *Human Performance, 10*, 85–97.

Parker, G. (1996). *Team players and teamwork: The new competitive business strategy.* San Francisco, CA: Jossey-Bass.

Peabody, D., & Goldberg, L.R. (1989). Some determinants of factor structures from personality-trait descriptors. *Journal of Personality and Social Psychology, 57*, 552–567.

Penney, L.M., David, E.M., & Witt, L.A. (in press). A review of personality and performance: Identifying boundaries, contingencies, and future research directions. *Human Resources Management Review.*

Perry, S.J., Lorinkova, S., & Witt, L.A. (2010, April). Emotional stability and conscientiousness as moderators of the virtuality–performance relationship. In S.J. Perry & L.A. Witt (Chairs), *Predicting virtual team effectiveness: Focusing on the micro-level.* Paper presented at the annual conference of the Society for Industrial and Organizational Psychology, Atlanta.

Pervin, L. (1989). Persons, situations, interactions: The history of a controversy and a discussion of theoretical models. *Academy of Management Review, 3*, 350–360.

Pinder, C.C. (1984). *Work motivation.* Glenview, IL: Scott Foresman.

Ployhart, R.E., & Bliese, P.D. (2006). Individual adaptability (I-ADAPT) theory: Conceptualizing the antecedents, consequences, and measurement of individual differences in adaptability. *Advances in Human Performance and Cognitive Engineering Research, 6,* 3–39.

Pulakos, E.D., Arad, S., Donovan, M., & Plamondon, K.E. (2000). Adaptability in the workplace: Development of a taxonomy of adaptive performance. *Journal of Applied Psychology, 85,* 612–624.

Rosen, C., Chang, C., & Levy, P. (2006). Personality and politics perceptions: A new conceptualization and illustration using OCBs. In E. Vigoda-Gadot & A. Drory (Eds.), *Handbook of organizational politics* (pp. 29–52). Cheltenham: Edward Elgar.

Rothbaum, F., Weisz, J.R., & Snyder, S.S. (1982). Changing the world and changing the self: A two-process model of perceived control. *Journal of Personality and Social Psychology, 42,* 5–37.

Sackett, P.R., & DeVore, C.J. (2001). Counterproductive behaviors at work. In. N. Anderson, D.S. Ones, H.K. Sinangil, & C. Viswesvaran (Eds.), *Handbook of industrial, work and organizational psychology* (Vol. 1, pp. 145–164). Thousand Oaks, CA: Sage Publications.

Sackett, P.R., Guys, M.L., & Ellingson, J.E. (1998). Ability-personality interactions when predicting job performance. *Journal of Applied Psychology, 83,* 545–556.

Salancik, G.R., & Pfeffer, J. (1978). A social information processing approach to job attitudes and task design. *Administrative Science Quarterly, 23,* 224–253.

Salgado, J.F. (2002). The Big Five personality dimensions and counterproductive behavior. *International Journal of Selection and Assessment, 10,* 117–125.

Saucier, G. (1992). Openness versus intellect: Much ado about nothing? *European Journal of Personality, 6,* 381–386.

Saucier, G. (2000). Isms and the structure of social attitudes. *Journal of Personality and Social Psychology, 78,* 366–385.

Schmidt, F.L., & Hunter, J.E. (1998). The validity and utility of selection methods in personnel psychology: Practical and theoretical implications of 85 years of research findings. *Psychological Bulletin, 124,* 262–274.

Schneider, B. (1983). Interactional psychology and organizational behavior. In L.L. Cummings & B.M. Staw (Eds.), *Research in organizational behavior* (Vol. 5, pp. 1–31). Greenwich, CT: JAI Press.

Siu, O.-L., Spector, P.E., Cooper, C.L., & Lu, C.-Q. (2005). Work stress, self-efficacy, Chinese work values, and work well-being in Hong Kong and Beijing. *International Journal of Stress Management, 12,* 274–288.

Spector, P.E. (1998). A control theory of the job stress process. In C.L. Cooper (Ed.), *Theories of organizational stress* (pp. 153–169). New York: Oxford University Press.

Spector, P.E., Fox, S., Penney, L.M., Bruursema, K., Goh, A., & Kessler, S. (2006). The dimensionality of counterproductivity: Are all counterproductive behaviors created equal? *Journal of Vocational Behavior, 68,* 446–460.

Tett, R.P., Jackson, D.N., & Rothstein, M. (1991). Personality measures as predictors of job performance: A meta-analytic review. *Personnel Psychology, 44,* 703–742.

Treadway, D.C., Ferris, G.R., Hochwarter, W.A., Perrewe, P.L., Witt, L.A., & Goodman, J.M. (2005). The role of age in the perceptions of politics–job performance relationship: A three-study constructive replication. *Journal of Applied Psychology, 90,* 872–881.

van der Linden, D., Keijsers, G.P., Eling, P., & van Schaijk, R. (2005). Work stress and attentional difficulties: An initial study on burnout and cognitive failures. *Work & Stress, 19,* 23–36.

Van Scotter, J.R., & Motowidlo, S.J. (1996). Interpersonal facilitation and job dedication as separate facets of contextual performance. *Journal of Applied Psychology, 81*, 525–531.

Van Scotter, J.R., Motowidlo, S.J., & Cross, T.G. (2000). Effects of task performance and contextual performance on systemic rewards. *Journal of Applied Psychology, 85*, 526–535.

Vigoda, E. (2000). Organizational politics, job attitudes, and work outcomes: Exploration and implications for the public sector. *Journal of Vocational Behavior, 57*, 326–347.

Vigoda, E. (2002). Stress-related aftermaths to workplace politics: the relationships among politics, job distress, and aggressive behavior in organizations. *Journal of Organizational Behavior, 23*, 571–591.

Vroom, V.H. (1964). *Work and motivation.* New York: Wiley.

Wadsworth, E.J., Moss, S.C., Simpson, S.A., & Smith, A.P. (2003). Preliminary investigation of the association between psychotropic medication use and accidents, minor injuries and cognitive failures. *Human Psychopharmacology: Clinical and Experimental, 18*, 535–540.

Wanberg, C.R., & Banas, J.T. (2000). Predictors and outcomes of openness to changes in a reorganizing workplace. *Journal of Applied Psychology, 85*, 132–142.

Wayne, S., Coyle-Shapiro, J., Eisenberger, R., Liden, R., Rousseau, D., & Shore, L. (2009). Social influences. In H.J. Klein, T.E. Becker, & J.P. Meyer (Eds.), *Commitment in organizations: Accumulated wisdom and new directions* (pp. 253–284). New York: Routledge/Taylor & Francis Group.

White, E. (2004). On the job: Master the culture at a new employer. *Wall Street Journal*, December 24, p. 3.

White, E. (2007). How a company made everyone a team player. *Wall Street Journal*, August 13, p. B1.

Wiggins, J. (1982). Circumplex models of interpersonal behavior in clinical psychology. In P.C. Kendall & J.N. Butcher (Eds.), *Handbook of research methods in clinical psychology* (pp. 183–221). New York: Wiley.

Witt, L.A. (1998). Enhancing organizational goal congruence: A solution to organizational politics. *Journal of Applied Psychology, 83*, 666–674.

Witt, L.A. (1999, August). *I am outta here: Organizational politics vs. personality predicting turnover.* Paper presented at the annual conference of the Academy of Management, Chicago.

Witt, L.A. (2001, November). *Emotional stability and conscientiousness as interactive predictors of job performance.* Unpublished paper presented at the annual meeting of the Southern Management Association, New Orleans.

Witt, L.A. (2002). The interactive effects of extraversion and conscientiousness on job performance. *Journal of Management, 28*, 835–851.

Witt, L.A., & Jones, J.W. (2003, April). *Very particular people quit first.* Unpublished paper presented at the meeting of the Society for Industrial and Organizational Psychology, Orlando.

Wright, P.M., Kacmar, K.M., McMahan, G.C., & Deleeuw, K. (1995). $P = f(M \times A)$: Cognitive ability as a moderator of the relationship between personality and job performance. *Journal of Management, 21*, 1129–1139.

Index

A

Abusive supervision, 191–212
  aggression, 193
  amygdala dysfunction, 193
  belief in just world, 201
  career prospects, 200, 502
  cognitive processes, underlying
    strategic abuse, 202–203
  damaging reputation of envied
    subordinate, 200
  envy, 200
  homeomorphic reciprocity, 201
  impressions, managing, 199–200
  impulsive abuse, 194, 206, 209
  injustices, redressing, 201
  insults, 191
  manifestations of, 192–193
  moral disengagement, 203–206, 209, 261
    agent's responsibility, 205
    conduct reconstrual, 205
    effects of agent's behavior, 206
    hot *vs.* cold attributions, 208
    interpersonal influence tactic, 207
  neurobiological research, 192–193
  orbital frontal cortex, 193
  organizational support for, 207–208
  pecking order, 199
  political activity, 194–196
  profanity, 191
  *Profile of Organizational Influence
    Strategies,* 207
  strategic abuse, 203–206
  strategic objectives, 196–201
  subordinates, controlling, 197–199
  target of injurious behavior, 206
  threat, 191
  underlying strategic abuse, 202–203
  workplace deviance, 197
  yelling, 193
Academy of Management Journal,
  Administrative Science
  Quarterly, 15

*Academy of Management Journal,
  Administrative Science
  Quarterly,* 15
Accomplishment, 44, 261, 279, 311, 367,
  513, 562, 570
Accuracy, 35, 109, 141, 182, 303, 311, 333
Achievement-striving behavior, 558, 576
Acrimony, 35
Action, behavior, distinguishing between,
  74
Actions not officially sanctioned, 85
Actors within political process, positions
  of, 86
Ad hoc teams, 309–310
Adaptability, 35, 50, 238, 338, 388–389,
  518–519, 572
Adaptive mechanism, politics as, 36–39
  ambiguous environments, 39
  attentional effectiveness, 37
  belief sharing, 39
  building consensus, 39
  ego nurturing, 36
  external disruption, 37
  interlocked behavior, 38
  internal disruptions, 37
  knowledge gaps, 37, 412, 415, 438
  self-determination, 36, 477, 537
  self-regulation, 36–37, 576
  self-regulation success, 37
  sensemaking, 38–39, 331–332, 477
  sensemaking acts, 38–39
  social engagement, 38
  transformation, 38
Adaptive performance, 560–566, 571, 574,
  576, 578–580
Adjustment, 41, 238, 562, 568
Administration of justice, 259
Administrative man, 70
Adrenaline, 239
Affiliation, 35
Agent, 39, 84, 88, 194–195, 266
Agentic bias, 264–267, 270–271